AF380645

Physics Galaxy

JEE ADVANCED
Chapter-Wise PYQ Analysis

Physics

Ashish Arora
Mentor & Founder

PHYSICS GALAXY

World's largest encyclopedia of online video courses for High School Students preparing for
** JEE Main * JEE Advanced * NEET * NSEJS * NSEP/INPhO/IPhO/IAO*

G K Publications (P) Ltd

Title   : Physics Galaxy : JEE Advanced - Chapter-Wise PYQ Analysis

Language   : English

Author's Name : Ashish Arora

Copyright ©   : 2023 Ashish Arora

No part of this book may be reproduced in a retrieval system or transmitted, in any form or by any means, electronics, mechanical, photocopying, recording, scanning and or without the written permission of the Author/Publisher.

Typeset & Published by :

Career Launcher Infrastructure (P) Ltd.

A-45, Mohan Cooperative Industrial Area, Near Mohan Estate Metro Station, New Delhi - 110044

Marketed by :

G.K. Publications (P) Ltd.

Plot No. 9A, Sector-27A, Mathura Road, Faridabad, Haryana-121003

ISBN   : **978-93-56813-47-2**

Printer's Details : Printed in India, New Delhi.

For product information :

Visit ***www.gkpublications.com*** or email to ***gkp@gkpublications.com***

Dedicated

to

My Parents, Son, Daughter

and

My beloved wife

In his teaching career since 1992 Ashish Arora personally mentored more than 10000 IITians and students who reached global heights in various career and profession chosen. It is his helping attitude toward students with which all his students remember him in life for his contribution in their success and keep connections with him live. Below is the list of some of the successful students in International Olympiad personally taught by him.

NAVNEET LOIWAL	*International GOLD Medal in IPhO-2000 at LONDON,* Also secured **AIR-4** in **IIT JEE 2000**
	PROUD FOR INDIA : Navneet Loiwal was the first Indian Student who won first International GOLD Medal for our country in International Physics Olympiad.
DUNGRA RAM CHOUDHARY	**AIR-1** in **IIT JEE 2002**
HARSHIT CHOPRA	*National Gold Medal in INPhO-2002* and got **AIR-2** in **IIT JEE-2002**
KUNTAL LOYA	A Girl Student got position **AIR-8** in **IIT JEE 2002**
LUV KUMAR	*National Gold Medal in INPhO-2003* and got **AIR-3** in **IIT JEE-2003**
RAJHANS SAMDANI	*National Gold Medal in INPhO-2003* and got **AIR-5** in **IIT JEE-2003**
SHANTANU BHARDWAJ	*International SILVER Medal in IPhO-2002 at INDONESIA*
SHALEEN HARLALKA	*International GOLD Medal in IPhO-2003 at CHINA* and got **AIR-46** in **IIT JEE-2003**
TARUN GUPTA	*National GOLD Medal in INPhO-2005*
APEKSHA KHANDELWAL	*National GOLD Medal in INPhO-2005*
ABHINAV SINHA	*Hon'ble Mension Award in APhO-2006 at KAZAKHSTAN*
RAMAN SHARMA	*International GOLD Medal in IPhO-2007 at IRAN* and got **AIR-20** in **IIT JEE-2007**
PRATYUSH PANDEY	*International SILVER Medal in IPhO-2007 at IRAN* and got **AIR-85** in **IIT JEE-2007**
GARVIT JUNIWAL	*International GOLD Medal in IPhO-2008 at VIETNAM* and got **AIR-10** in **IIT JEE-2008**
ANKIT PARASHAR	*National GOLD Medal in INPhO-2008*
HEMANT NOVAL	*National GOLD Medal in INPhO-2008* and got **AIR-25** in **IIT JEE-2008**
ABHISHEK MITRUKA	*National GOLD Medal in INPhO-2009*
SARTHAK KALANI	*National GOLD Medal in INPhO-2009*
ASTHA AGARWAL	*International SILVER Medal in IJSO-2009 at AZERBAIJAN*
RAHUL GURNANI	*International SILVER Medal in IJSO-2009 at AZERBAIJAN*
AYUSH SINGHAL	*International SILVER Medal in IJSO-2009 at AZERBAIJAN*
MEHUL KUMAR	*International SILVER Medal in IPhO-2010 at CROATIA* and got **AIR-19** in **IIT JEE-2010**
ABHIROOP BHATNAGAR	*National GOLD Medal in INPhO-2010*
AYUSH SHARMA	*International Double GOLD Medal in IJSO-2010 at NIGERIA*
AASTHA AGRAWAL	*Hon'ble Mension Award in APhO-2011 at ISRAEL* and got **AIR-93** in **IIT JEE 2011**
ABHISHEK BANSAL	*National GOLD Medal in INPhO-2011*
SAMYAK DAGA	*National GOLD Medal in INPhO-2011*
SHREY GOYAL	*National GOLD Medal in INPhO-2012* and secured **AIR-24** in **IIT JEE 2012**
RAHUL GURNANI	*National GOLD Medal in INPhO-2012*
JASPREET SINGH JHEETA	*National GOLD Medal in INPhO-2012*
DIVYANSHU MUND	*National GOLD Medal in INPhO-2012*
SHESHANSH AGARWAL	*International SILVER Medal in IAO-2012 at KOREA*
SWATI GUPTA	*International SILVER Medal in IJSO-2012 at IRAN*
PRATYUSH RAJPUT	*International SILVER Medal in IJSO-2012 at IRAN*
SHESHANSH AGARWAL	*International BRONZE Medal in IOAA-2013 at GREECE*
SHESHANSH AGARWAL	*International GOLD Medal in IOAA-2014 at ROMANIA*
SHESHANSH AGARWAL	*International SILVER Medal in IPhO-2015 at INDIA* and secured **AIR-58** in **JEE(Advanced)-2015**
VIDUSHI VARSHNEY	*International SILVER Medal in IJSO-2015 at SOUTH KOREA*
AMAN BANSAL	**AIR-1** in **JEE Advanced 2016**
KUNAL GOYAL	**AIR-3** in **JEE Advanced 2016**
GOURAV DIDWANIA	**AIR-9** in **JEE Advanced 2016**
DIVYANSH GARG	*International SILVER Medal in IPhO-2016 at SWITZERLAND*
NALIN KHANDELWAL	**AIR-1** in **NEET 2019**

ABOUT THE AUTHOR

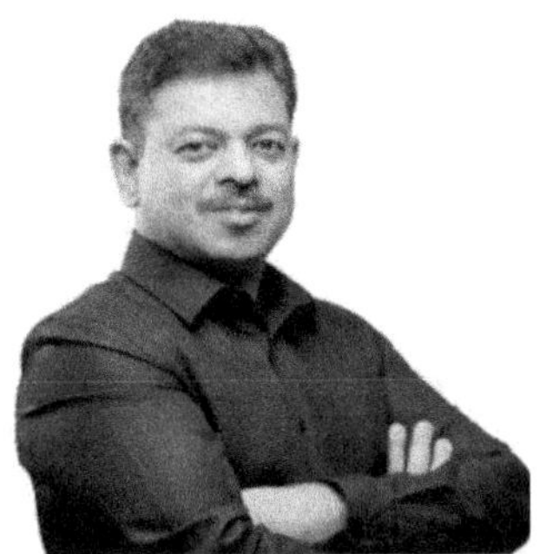

The complexities of Physics have given nightmares to many, but the homegrown genius of Jaipur- Ashish Arora has helped millions of students to live their dreams by decoding it.

Newton Law of Gravitation and Faraday's Magnetic induction force apply perfectly well with this unassuming genius. A Pied Piper of students, his webportal https://www.physicsgalaxy.com, The world's largest encyclopedia of video lectures on high school Physics possesses strong gravitational pull and magnetic attraction for students who want to make it big in life.

Ashish Arora, gifted with rare ability to train masterminds, has mentored over 10,000 IITians and Medicos in his past over three decades of teaching sojourn including lots of students made it to Top 100 in IIT-JEE/JEE(Advance) including multiple times AIR-1 and many in Top-10. Apart from that, he has also groomed hundreds of students for cracking International Physics Olympiad. No wonder his student Navneet Loiwal brought laurel to the country by becoming the first Indian to win a Gold medal at the 2000 - International Physics Olympiad in London (UK).

His special ability to simplify the toughest of the Physics theorems and applications rates him as one among the best Physics teachers in the world. With this, Arora simply defies the logic that perfection comes with age. Even at 18 when he started teaching Physics while pursuing engineering, he was as engaging as he is now. Experience, besides graying his hair, has just widened his horizon.

Now after encountering all tribes of students - some brilliant and some not-so-intelligent - this celebrated teacher has embarked upon a noble mission to make the entire galaxy of Physics inform of his webportal PHYSICSGALAXY.COM to serve and help global students in the subject. Today students from 183 countries are connected with this webportal. On any topic of physics students can post their queries in INTERACT tab of the webportal on which many global experts with Ashish Arora reply to several queries posted online by students.

Dedicated to global students of middle and high school level, his website *www.physicsgalaxy.com* also has teaching sessions dubbed in American accent and subtitles in 87 languages. For students in India preparing for JEE & NEET, his online courses will be available soon on PHYSICSGALAXY.COM.

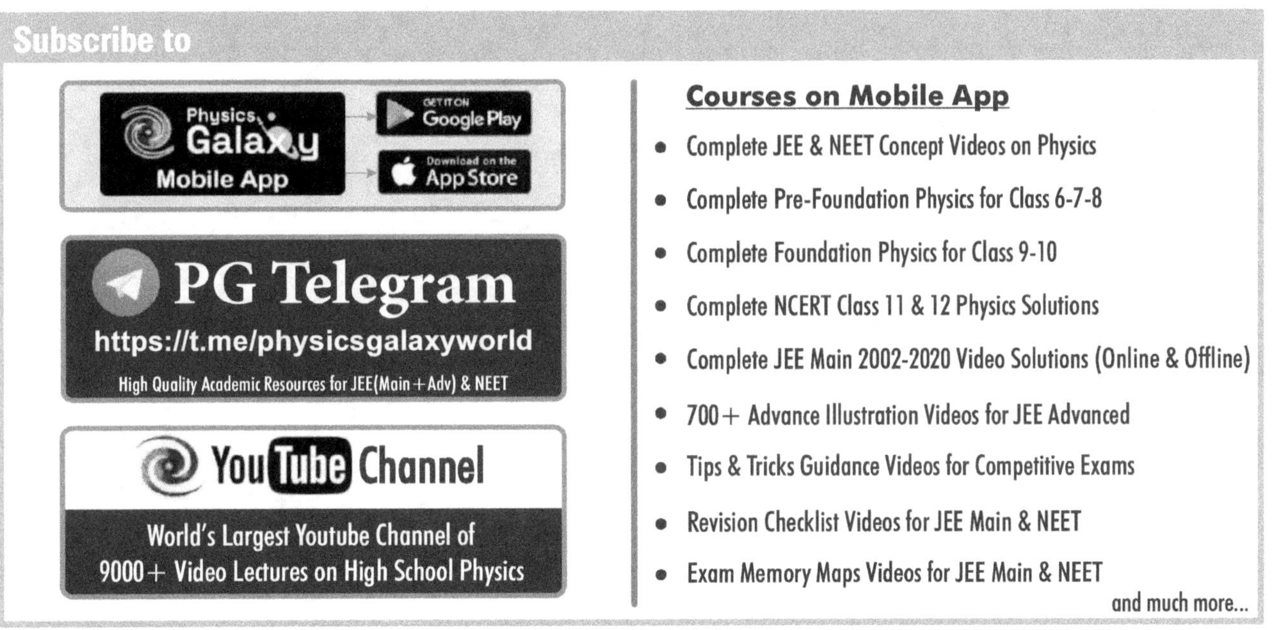

FOREWORD

I am extremely happy to share my views about this book written by Er. Ashish Arora. He has contributed immensely to the teaching-learning of Physics though many innovative ways. His approach has always been student centric and this contribution is yet another example of the same.

As the title states "Physics Galaxy JEE Advanced Solution" the book provides comprehensive detailed solutions to every problem of JEE Advanced and covers the necessary components by offering solution to all questions asked in old JEE Advanced (all Online & Offline since 2007) with detailed explanations. All questions are categorized into 23 topics based on applications of questions at the level of IITJEE, however in this book all questions are included with comprehensive solutions and most of the questions have video solutions available on YouTube channel of Physics Galaxy as 'speed solutions'. This is to indicate and promote understanding of the methods or reasons for specific/particular solutions. All solutions of the questions are based on the conceptual analysis covered in the popular Physics Galaxy book series (5 volumes) so that aspirants following the book series will be able to relate and recall all the explanations already done.

I am sure the book promotes the concept of deeper learning in the domain of Physics. My best wishes to the many aspirants who will certainly find this book a very valuable tool to enhance thorough understanding of the subject and the book will also promote and enhance learning experience on concept applications at the level of JEE Advanced.

August, 2023

Prof. Sandeep Sancheti
Ph. D. (U.K.), B.Tech. FIETE, FIE (I), SMIEEE

Vice-Chancellor (Provost) Marwadi University, Rajkot
Member Executive Council, Association of Commonwealth Universities, London
Former President, AIU, New Delhi
Former Vice-Chancellor, SRMIST, Chennai
Former President, Manipal University, Jaipur
Former-Director NIT Surathkal, NIT New Delhi, NIT Trichy,
NIT Calicut, SPA Delhi; Former-Mentor Director NIT Goa,
NIT Sikkim, NIT Puducherry
Former-Member JEE Apex Board (JAB), MHRD, GoI
Former-Chairman, Central Counselling Board (CCB), AIEEE, MHRD, GoI
Former-Chairman, Direct Admission of Students Abroad (DASA), MHRD, GoI

PREFACE

For the aspiration of becoming an engineer, that too from prestigious IITs preparing for JEE Advanced, Physics is the most important subject, unlike to other subjects it requires logical reasoning and high imagination in brain. Without improving the level of physics applications at high level it is very difficult to achieve this goal in the present age of competitions. To score better, one does not require hard working at least in physics. It just requires a simple understanding and approach to think a physical situation. Actually physics is the surrounding of our everyday life. If you wish to make the higher applications of physics strong, you should try to understand core concepts of physics in practical approach rather than theoretical.

This book *"Comprehensive & Detailed Solutions of JEE ADVANCED Physics PYQs"* is designed with an entirely different and friendly approach to develop the higher applications of physics concepts at psychological level. The book covers detailed solutions to all the questions previously asked in JEE Advanced all online and offline papers from 2007 to 2022. From the analysis the questions asked in these papers of JEE Advanced, it is clearly seen that all these papers are designed in similar way with innovative problems of real life physics. More than 60% questions every year in IITJEE or JEE Advanced are based on concepts related to practical approach.

All the questions of these papers are divided in 23 topics for chapter level understanding of questions asked in JEE Advanced. In my classroom teaching also I found that topic level understanding of JEE Advanced PYQ solutions in a comprehensive approach of exam helps students a lot in concept visualization from the point of view of giving final shape to their preparation as well as for the purpose of last moment revision of all topics.

For most of the question asked in old JEE Advanced papers, video solutions are made available for students on YouTube channel of Physics Galaxy as well as these video solutions can be accessed through Physics Galaxy mobile app available on iOS and Android play store. While following the book if students face any doubt in understanding the solution of the specific question then they can follow 'Concept Video Series' or 'Revision Checklist Series' available on Physics Galaxy youtube channel to build their physics understanding at fundamental level.

I don't have words for my best friend my wife Anuja for always being together with me to complete this book in the unique style and format along with the whole series of Physics Galaxy books.

I would like to pay my gratitude to Sh. Dayashankar Prajapati in assisting me to complete the task in Design Labs of PHYSICS GALAXY and presenting the book in totally new format.

At last but the most important persons of my life, my mother & father who have devoted their valuable time of life on me to make me able enough to finally build the series of Physics Galaxy books in such a format and a simple language. Even after their departure from life they are with me full time as a constant source of energy and inspiration to work on student fraternity.

In this first edition of book I have tried my best to make this book error free but owing to the nature of work, inadvertently, there is possibility of errors left untouched. I shall be grateful to the readers, if they point out me regarding errors and oblige me by giving their valuable and constructive suggestions via emails for further improvement of the book.

Date : August, 2023

Ashish Arora

PHYSICSGALAXY.COM
e-mail: ashisharora@physicsgalaxy.com

CONTENTS

1 UNITS & DIMENSIONS

MCQ with Single Options Correct

1. Young's modulus of elasticity Y is expressed in terms of three derived quantities, namely, the gravitational constant G, Planck's constant h and the speed of light c, as $Y = C^\alpha h^\beta G^\gamma$. Which of the following is the correct option ?

[JEE Adv 2023, P-2]

(A) $\alpha = 7, \beta = -1, \gamma = -2$ (B) $\alpha = -7, \beta = -1, \gamma = -2$

(C) $\alpha = 7, \beta = -1, \gamma = 2$ (D) $\alpha = -7, \beta = 1, \gamma = -2$

MCQ with One or More than One Options Correct

2. Planck's constant h, speed of light c and gravitational constant G are used to form a unit of length L and a unit of mass M. Then the correct option(s) is(are)

[JEE Adv 2015, P-1]

(A) $M \propto \sqrt{c}$ (B) $M \propto \sqrt{G}$

(C) $L \propto \sqrt{h}$ (D) $L \propto \sqrt{G}$

3. In terms of potential difference V, electric current I, permittivity ε_0, permeability μ_0 and speed of light c, the dimensionally correct equation(s) is(are) : **[JEE Adv 2015, P-2]**

(A) $\mu_0 I^2 = \varepsilon_0 V^2$ (B) $\varepsilon_0 I = \mu_0 V$

(C) $I = \varepsilon_0 cV$ (D) $\mu_0 cI = \varepsilon_0 V$

4. A length-scale (l) depends on the permittivity (ε) of a dielectric material, Boltzmann constant (k_B), the absolute temperature (T), the number per unit volume (n) of certain charged particles, and the charge (q) carried by each of the particles. Which of the following expression(s) for l is (are) dimensionally correct ? **[JEE Adv 2016, P-1]**

(A) $l = \sqrt{\left(\dfrac{nq^2}{\varepsilon k_B T}\right)}$ (B) $l = \sqrt{\left(\dfrac{\varepsilon k_B T}{nq^2}\right)}$

(C) $l = \sqrt{\left(\dfrac{q^2}{\varepsilon n^{2/3} k_B T}\right)}$ (D) $l = \sqrt{\left(\dfrac{q^2}{\varepsilon n^{1/3} k_B T}\right)}$

5. Let us consider a system of units in which mass and angular momentum are dimensionless. If length has dimension of L, which of the following statement (s) is/are correct ?

[JEE Adv 2019, P-1]

(A) The dimension of force is L^{-3}

(B) The dimension of energy is L^{-2}

(C) The dimension of power is L^{-5}

(D) The dimension of linear momentum is L^{-1}

6. Sometimes it is convenient to construct a system of units so that all quantities can be expressed in terms of only one physical quantity. In one such system, dimensions of different quantities are given in terms of a quantity X as follows: [position] = $[X^\alpha]$; [speed] = $[X^\beta]$; [acceleration] = $[X^p]$; [linear momentum] = $[X^q]$; [force] = $[X^r]$. Then : **[JEE Adv 2020, P-1]**

(A) $\alpha + p = 2\beta$ (B) $p + q - r = \beta$

(C) $p - q + r = \alpha$ (D) $p + q + r = \beta$

7. A physical quantity $\vec{S}$ is defined as $\vec{S} = (\vec{E} \times \vec{B})/\mu_0$ where $\vec{E}$ is electric field, $\vec{B}$ is magnetic field and μ_0 is the permeability of free space. The dimensions of $\vec{S}$ are the same as the dimensions of which of the following quantity(ies)?

[JEE Adv 2021, P-2]

(A) $\dfrac{\text{Energy}}{\text{Charge} \times \text{Current}}$ (B) $\dfrac{\text{Force}}{\text{Length} \times \text{Time}}$

(C) $\dfrac{\text{Energy}}{\text{Volume}}$ (D) $\dfrac{\text{Power}}{\text{Area}}$

Matrix Match MCQ

8. Some physical quantities are given in **Column-I** and some possible SI units in which these quantities may be expressed are given in **Column-II**. Match the physical quantities in **Column-I** with the units in **Column-II** and indicate your answer by darkening appropriate bubbles in the 4 × 4 matrix given in the ORS : **[JEE Adv 2007, P-1]**

Column-I

(A) $GM_e M_s$; $G \to$ universal gravitational constant, $M_e \to$ mass of the earth, $M_s \to$ mass of the Sun

(B) $\dfrac{3RT}{M}$; $R \to$ universal gas constant, $T \to$ absolute temperature, $M \to$ molar mass

(C) $\dfrac{F^2}{q^2 B^2}$; $F \to$ force, $q \to$ charge, $B \to$ magnetic field

(D) $\dfrac{GM_e}{R_e}$, $G \to$ universal gravitational constant, $M_e \to$ mass of the earth, $R_e \to$ radius of the earth

Column-I

(p) (volt) (coulomb) (metre)

(q) (kilogram) (metre)^3 (second)$^{-2}$

(r) (metre)^2 (second)$^{-2}$

(s) (farad) (volt)^2 (kg)$^{-1}$

Comprehension based MCQ

Paragraph-1 (Q. No. 9-10)

In electromagnetic theory, the electric and magnetic phenomena are related to each other. Therefore, the dimensions of electric and magnetic quantities must also be related to each other. In the questions below, $[E]$ and $[B]$ stand for dimensions of electric and magnetic fields respectively, while $[\epsilon_0]$ and $[\mu_0]$ stand for dimensions of the permittivity and permeability of free space respectively. $[L]$ and $[T]$ are dimensions of length and time respectively. All the quantities are given in SI units.

[JEE Adv 2018, P-1]

9. The relation between $[E]$ and $[B]$ is :
(A) $[E] = [B][L][T]$ (B) $[E] = [B][L]^{-1}[T]$
(C) $[E] = [B][L][T]^{-1}$ (D) $[E] = [B][L]^{-1}[T]^{-1}$

10. The relation between $[\epsilon_0]$ and $[\mu_0]$ is :
(A) $[\mu_0] = [\epsilon_0][L]^2[T]^{-2}$ (B) $[\mu_0] = [\epsilon_0][L]^{-2}[T]^2$
(C) $[\mu_0] = [\epsilon_0]^{-1}[L]^2[T]^{-2}$ (D) $[\mu_0] = [\epsilon_0]^{-1}[L]^{-2}[T]^2$

Integer Answer based Questions

11. To find the distance d over which a signal can be seen clearly in foggy conditions, a railways engineer uses dimensional analysis and assume that the distance depends on the mass density ρ of the fog, intensity (power/area) S of the light from the signal and its frequency f. The engineer finds that d is proportional to $S^{1/n}$. The value of n is ? **[JEE Adv 2014, P-1]**

12. A steel wire of diameter 0.5 mm and Young's modulus 2×10^{11} Nm^{-2} carries a load of mass M. The length of the wire with the load is 1.0 m. A vernier scale with 10 divisions is attached to the end of this wire. Next to the steel wire is a reference wire to which a main scale, of least count 1.0 mm, is attached. The 10 divisions of the vernier scale correspond to 9 divisions of the main scale. Initially, the zero of vernier scale coincides with the zero of main scale. If the load on the steel wire is increased by 1.2 kg, the vernier scale division which coincides with a main scale division is _______ Take $g = 10$ ms^{-2} and $\pi = 3.2$. **[JEE Adv 2018, P-2]**

13. In a particular system of units, a physical quantity can be expressed in terms of the electric charge e, electron mass m_e, Plank's constant h, and Coulomb's constant $k = \dfrac{1}{4\pi\,\epsilon_0}$, where ϵ_0 is the permittivity of vacuum. In terms of these physical constants, the dimension of the magnetic field is $[B] = [e]^\alpha\,[m_e]^\beta\,[h]^\gamma\,[k]^\delta$. The value of $\alpha + \beta + \gamma + \delta$ is _______.

[JEE Adv 2022, P-2]

∗   ∗   ∗   ∗   ∗

MCQ with Single Option Correct

1. Two particles of mass m each are tied at the ends of a light string of length $2a$. The whole system is kept on a frictionless horizontal surface with the string held tight so that each mass is at a distance 'a' from the center P (as shown in the figure). Now, the mid-point of the string is pulled vertically upwards with a small but constant force F. As a result, the particles move towards each other on the surface. The magnitude of acceleration, when the separation between them becomes $2x$, is :

[JEE Adv 2007, P-1]

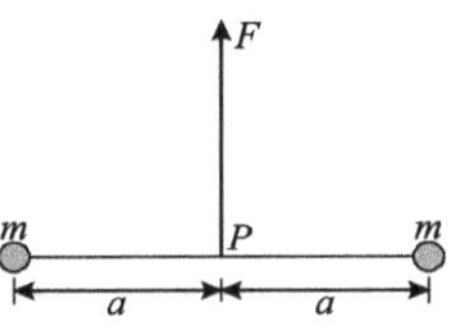

(A) $\dfrac{F}{2m}\dfrac{a}{\sqrt{a^2-x^2}}$

(B) $\dfrac{F}{2m}\dfrac{x}{\sqrt{a^2-x^2}}$

(C) $\dfrac{F}{2m}\dfrac{x}{a}$

(D) $\dfrac{F}{2m}\dfrac{\sqrt{a^2-x^2}}{x}$

2. A particle moves in the X-Y plane under the influence of a force such that its linear momentum is $\vec{P}(t) = A[\hat{i}\cos(kt) - \hat{j}\sin(kt)]$, where A and k are constants. The angle between the force and the momentum is :

[JEE Adv 2007, P-2]

(A) $0°$ (B) $30°$

(C) $45°$ (D) $90°$

3. A block of base $10\text{ cm} \times 10\text{ cm}$ and height 15 cm is kept on an inclined plane. The coefficient of friction between them is $\sqrt{3}$. The inclination θ of this inclined plane from the horizontal plane is gradually increased from $0°$. Then :

[JEE Adv 2009, P-1]

(A) At $\theta = 30°$, the block will start sliding down the plane

(B) The block will remain at rest on the plane up to certain θ and then it will topple

(C) At $\theta = 60°$, then block will start sliding down the plane and continue to do so at higher angles

(D) at $\theta = 60°$, the block will start sliding down the plane and on further increasing θ, it will topple at certain θ

4. A piece of wire is bent in the shape of a parabola $y = kx^2$ (y-axis vertical) with a bead of mass m on it. The bead can slide on the wire without friction. It stays at the lowest point of the parabola when the wire is at rest. The wire is now accelerated parallel to the x-axis with a constant acceleration a. The distance of the new equilibrium position of the bead, where the bead can stay at rest with respect to the wire, from the y-axis is :

[JEE Adv 2009, P-2]

(A) $\dfrac{a}{gk}$ (B) $\dfrac{a}{2gk}$

(C) $\dfrac{2a}{gk}$ (D) $\dfrac{a}{4gk}$

5. A block of mass m is on an inclined plane of angle θ. The coefficient of friction between the block and the plane is μ and $\tan\theta > \mu$. The block is held stationary by applying a force P parallel to the plane. The direction of force pointing up the plane is taken to be positive. As P is varied from $P_1 = mg(\sin\theta - \mu\cos\theta)$ to $P_2 = mg(\sin\theta + \mu\cos\theta)$, the frictional force f versus P graph will look like :

[JEE Adv 2010, P-1]

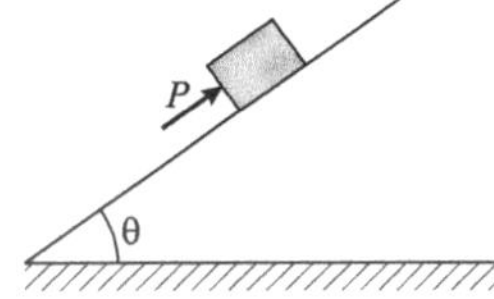

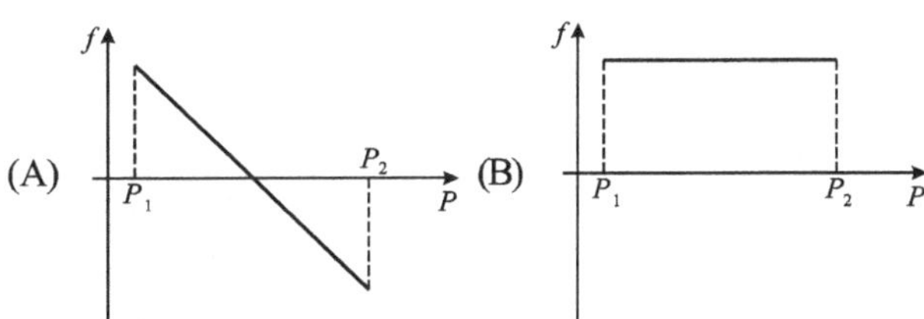

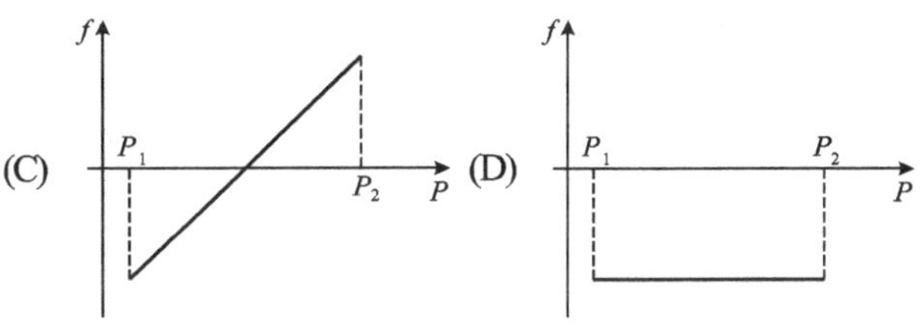

6. A small block is connected to one of a massless spring of unstretched length 4.9 m. The other end of the spring (see the figure) is fixed. The system lies on a horizontal frictionless surface. The block is stretched by 0.2 m and released from rest at $t = 0$. It then executes simple harmonic motion with angular frequency $\omega = \pi/3$ rad/s. Simultaneously at $t = 0$, a small pebble is projected with speed v from point P at an angle of 45° as shown in the figure. Point P is at a horizontal distance of 10 m from O. If the pebble hits the block at $t = 1$s, the value of v is (take $g = 10$ m/s^2) : **[JEE Adv 2012, P-1]**

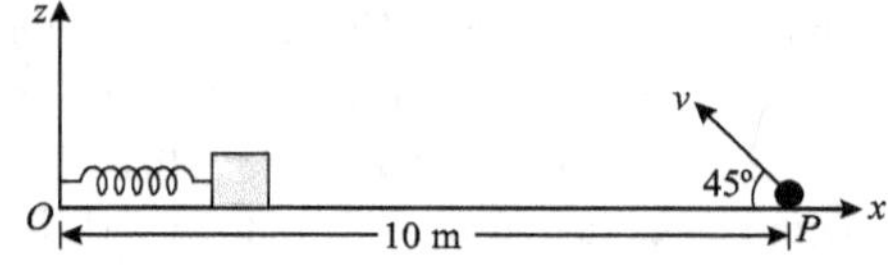

(A) $\sqrt{50}$ m/s (B) $\sqrt{51}$ m/s

(C) $\sqrt{52}$ m/s (D) $\sqrt{53}$ m/s

7. A wire, which passes through the hole in a small bead, is bent in the form of quarter of a circle. The wire is fixed vertically on ground as shown in the figure. The bead is released from near the top of the wire and it slides along the wire without friction. As the bead moves from A to B, the force it applies on the wire is : **[JEE Adv 2014, P-2]**

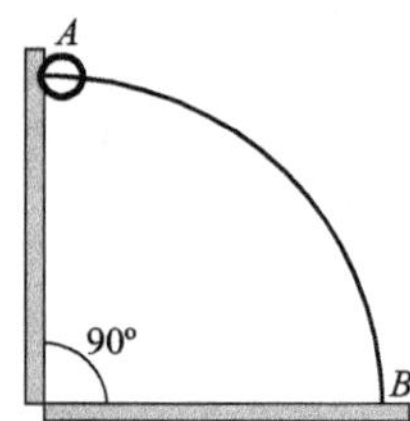

(A) Always radially outwards
(B) Always radially inwards
(C) Radially outwards initially and radially inwards later
(D) Radially inwards initially and radially outwards later

8. A uniform wooden stick of mass 1.6 kg and length l rests in an inclined manner on a smooth, vertical wall of height h ($< l$) such that a small portion of the stick extends beyond the wall. The reaction force of the wall on the stick is perpendicular to the stick. The stick makes an angle of 30° with the wall and the bottom of the stick is on a rough floor. The reaction of the wall on the stick is equal in magnitude to the reaction of the floor on the stick. The ratio h/l and the frictional force f at the bottom of the stick are : **[JEE Adv 2016, P-1]**

(A) $\dfrac{h}{l} = \dfrac{\sqrt{3}}{16}, f = \dfrac{16\sqrt{3}}{3}$ N (B) $\dfrac{h}{l} = \dfrac{3}{16}, f = \dfrac{16\sqrt{3}}{3}$ N

(C) $\dfrac{h}{l} = \dfrac{3\sqrt{3}}{16}, f = \dfrac{8\sqrt{3}}{3}$ N (D) $\dfrac{h}{l} = \dfrac{3\sqrt{3}}{16}, f = \dfrac{16\sqrt{3}}{3}$ N

9. Three vectors $\vec{P}$, $\vec{Q}$ and $\vec{R}$ are shown in the figure. Let S be any point on the vector $\vec{R}$. The distance between the points P and S is $b\,|\vec{R}|$. The general relation among vector $\vec{P}$, $\vec{Q}$ and $\vec{S}$ is : **[JEE Adv 2017, P-2]**

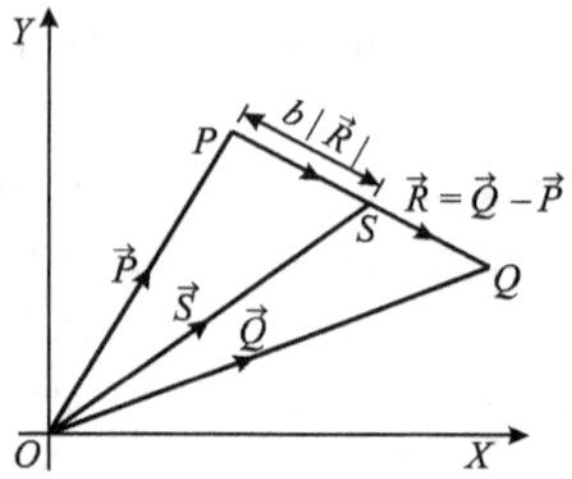

(A) $\vec{S} = (1 - b)\vec{P} + b^2\vec{Q}$ (B) $\vec{S} = (1 - b)\vec{P} + b\vec{Q}$

(C) $\vec{S} = (1 - b)\vec{P} + b\vec{Q}$ (D) $\vec{S} = (1 - b)\vec{P} + b\vec{Q}$

10. A particle of mass m is moving in the xy-plane such that its velocity at a point (x, y) is given as $\vec{v} = \alpha(y\,\hat{x} + 2x\hat{y})$, where α is a non-zero constant. What is the force $\vec{F}$ acting on the particle? **[JEE Adv 2023, P-2]**

(A) $\vec{F} = 2m\alpha^2(x\hat{x} + y\hat{y})$ (B) $\vec{F} = m\alpha^2(y\hat{x} + 2x\hat{y})$

(C) $\vec{F} = 2m\alpha^2(y\hat{x} + x\hat{y})$ (D) $\vec{F} = m\alpha^2(x\hat{x} + 2y\hat{y})$

MCQ with One or More than One Options Correct

11. If the resultant of all external forces acting on a system of particles is zero, then from an inertial frame, one can surely say that : **[JEE Adv 2009, P-1]**
(A) Linear momentum of the system does not change in time
(B) Kinetic energy of the system does not change in time
(C) Angular momentum of the system does not change in time
(D) Potential energy of the system does not change in time

12. A small block of mass of 0.1 kg lies on a fixed inclined plane PQ which makes an angle θ with the horizontal. A horizontal force of 1 N acts on the block through its centre of mass as shown in the figure. The block remains stationary if (take $g = 10$ m/s^2) : **[JEE Adv 2012, P-1]**

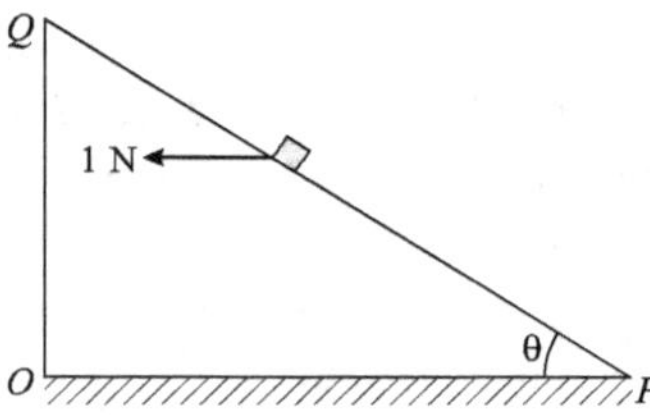

(A) $\theta = 45°$

(B) $\theta > 45°$ and a frictional force acts on the block towards P
(C) $\theta > 45°$ and a frictional force acts on the block towards Q
(D) $\theta < 45°$ and a frictional force acts on the block towards Q

13. In the figure, a ladder of mass m is shown leaning against a wall. It is in static equilibrium making an angle θ with the horizontal floor. The coefficient of friction between the wall and the ladder is μ_1 and that between the floor and the ladder is μ_2. The normal reaction of the wall on the ladder is N_1 and that of the floor is N_2. If the ladder is about to slip, then :

[JEE Adv 2014, P-1]

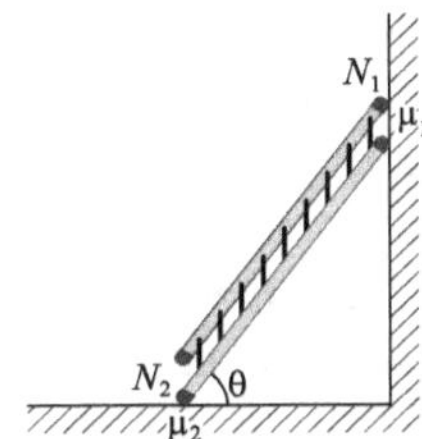

(A) $\mu_1 = 0$ $\mu_2 \neq 0$ and $N_2 \tan\theta = \dfrac{mg}{2}$

(B) $\mu_1 \neq 0$ $\mu_2 = 0$ and $N_1 \tan\theta = \dfrac{mg}{2}$

(C) $\mu_1 \neq 0$ $\mu_2 \neq 0$ and $N_2 = \dfrac{mg}{1+\mu_1\mu_2}$

(D) $\mu_1 = 0$ $\mu_2 \neq 0$ and $N_1 \tan\theta = \dfrac{mg}{2}$

14. Starting at time $t = 0$ from the origin with speed 1 ms^{-1}, a particle follows a two-dimensional trajectory in the x-y plane so that its coordinates are related by the equation $y = x^2/2$. The x and y components of its acceleration are denoted by a_x and a_y, respectively. Then : **[JEE Adv 2020, P-2]**

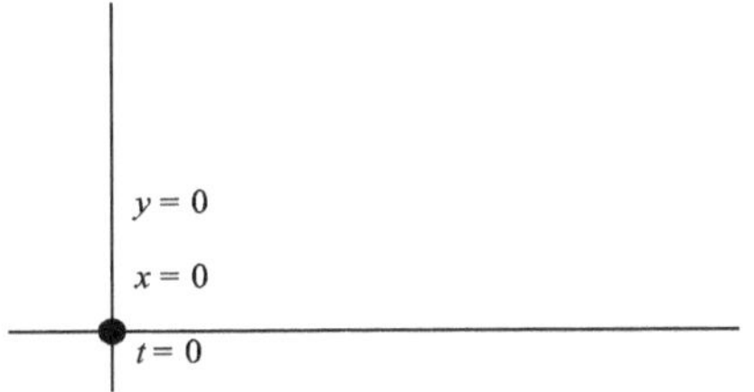

(A) $a_x = 1$ ms^{-2} implies that when the particle is at the origin, $a_y = 1$ ms^{-2}
(B) $a_x = 0$ implies $a_y = 1$ ms^{-2} at all times
(C) at $t = 0$, the particle's velocity points in the x-direction
(D) $a_x = 0$ implies that at $t = 1$ s, the angle between the particle's velocity and the x-axis is 45°

15. A slide with a frictionless curved surface, which becomes horizontal at its lower end, is fixed on the terrace of a building of height $3h$ from the ground, as shown in the figure.

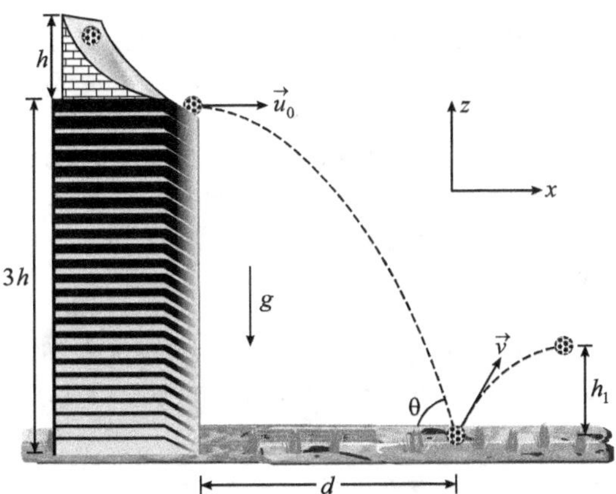

A spherical ball of mass m is released on the slide from rest at a height h from the top of the terrace. The ball leaves the slide with a velocity $\vec{u}_0 = u_0 \hat{x}$ and falls on the ground at a distance d from the building making an angle θ with the horizontal. It bounces off with a velocity $\vec{v}$ and reaches a maximum height h_1. The acceleration due to gravity is g and the coefficient of restitution of the ground is $1/\sqrt{3}$. Which of the following statement(s) is (are) correct? **[JEE Adv 2023, P-1]**

(A) $\vec{u}_0 = \sqrt{2gh}\,\hat{x}$ (B) $\vec{v} = \sqrt{2gh}(\hat{x} - \hat{z})$

(C) $\theta = 60°$ (D) $d / h_1 = 2\sqrt{3}$

Assertion Reason based on MCQ

16. STATEMENT-1   **[JEE Adv 2007, P-1]**
A block of mass m starts moving on a rough horizontal surface with a velocity v. It stops due to friction between the block and the surface after moving through a certain distance. The surface is now tilted to an angle of 30° with the horizontal and the same block is made to go up on the surface with the same initial velocity v. The decrease in the mechanical energy in the second situation is smaller than that in the first situation :

because

STATEMENT-2
The coefficient of friction between the block and the surface decreases with the increase in the angle of inclination :
(A) Statement-1 is True, Statement-2 is True; Statement-2 is a correct explanation for Statement-1
(B) Statement-1 is True, Statement-2 is True; Statement-2 is **NOT** a correct explanation for Statement-1
(C) Statement-1 is True, Statement-2 is False
(D) Statement-1 is False, Statement-2 is True

17. STATEMENT-1   **[JEE Adv 2007, P-2]**
A cloth covers a table. Some dishes are kept on it. The cloth can be pulled out without dislodging the dishes from the table.

because

STATEMENT-2

For every action there is an equal and opposite reaction.

(A) Statement-1 is True, Statement-2 is True; Statement-2 is a correct explanation for Statement-1

(B) Statement-1 is True, Statement-2 is True; Statement-2 is **NOT** a correct explanation for Statement-1

(C) Statement-1 is True, Statement-2 is False

(D) Statement-1 is False, Statement-2 is True

---

18. STATEMENT-1   **[JEE Adv 2008, P-2]**

It is easier to pull a heavy object than to push it on a level ground.

because

STATEMENT-2

The magnitude of frictional force depends on the nature of the two surfaces in contact :

(A) Statement-1 is True, Statement-2 is True; Statement-2 is a correct explanation for Statement-1

(B) Statement-1 is True, Statement-2 is True; Statement-2 is **NOT** a correct explanation for Statement-1

(C) Statement-1 is True, Statement-2 is False

(D) Statement-1 is False, Statement-2 is True

---

19. STATEMENT-1   **[JEE Adv 2008, P-2]**

For an observer looking out through the window of a moving train, the nearby objects appear to move in the opposite direction to the train, while the distant objects appear to be stationary.

because

STATEMENT-2

If the observer and the object are moving at velocities $\vec{V}_1$ and $\vec{V}_2$ respectively with reference to a laboratory frame, the velocity of the object with respect to the observer is $\vec{V}_2 - \vec{V}_1$:

(A) Statement-1 is True, Statement-2 is True, Statement-2 is a correct explanation for Statement-1

(B) Statement-1 is True, Statement-2 is True; Statement-2 is NOT a correct explanation for Statement-1

(C) Statement-1 is True, Statement-2 is False

(D) Statement-1 is False, Statement-2 is True

Matrix Match MCQ

20. Column-II shows five systems in which two objects are labelled as X and Y. Also in each case a point P is shown. **Column-I** gives some statements about X and/or Y. Match these statements to the appropriate system(s) from **Column-II** :

[JEE Adv 2009, P-1]

Column-I

(A) The force exerted by X on Y has a magnitude Mg.

(B) The gravitational potential energy of X is continuously increasing.

(C) Mechanical energy of the system $X + Y$ is continuously decreasing.

(D) The torque of the weight of Y about point P is zero.

Column-II

(p) Block Y of mass M left on a fixed inclined plane X, slides on it with a constant velocity.

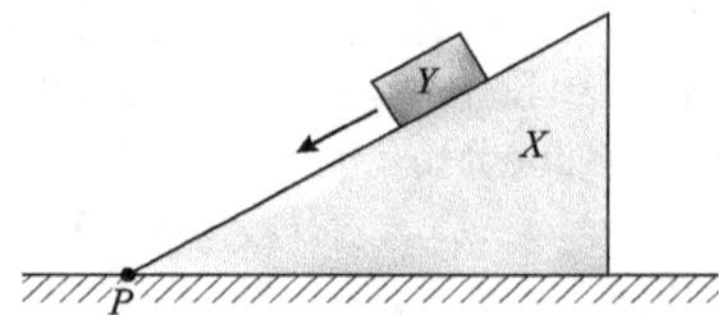

(q) Two ring magnets Y and Z, each of mass M, are kept in frictionless vertical plastic stand so that they repel each other. Y rests on the base X and Z hangs in air in equilibrium. P is the topmost point of the stand on the common axis of the two rings. The whole system is in a lift that is going up with a constant velocity.

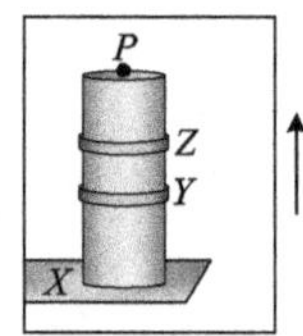

(r) A pulley Y of mass m_0 is fixed to a table through a clamp X. A block of mass M hangs from a string that goes over the pulley and is fixed at point P of the table. The whole system is kept in a lift that is going down with a constant velocity.

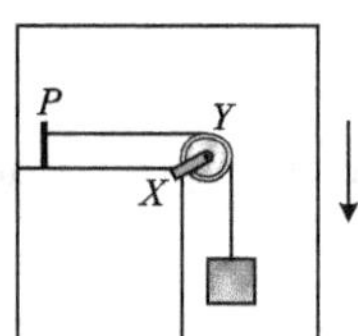

(s) A sphere Y of mass M is put in a nonviscous liquid X kept in a container at rest. The sphere is released and it moves down in the liquid.

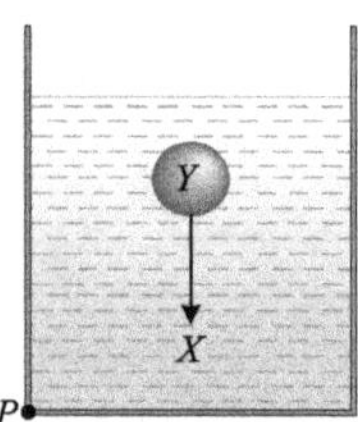

(t) A sphere Y of mass M is falling with its terminal velocity in a viscous liquid X kept in a container.

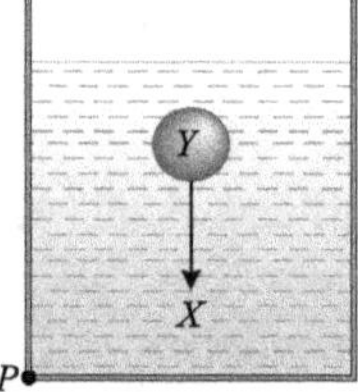

21. A block of mass $m_1 = 1$ kg another mass $m_2 = 2$ kg, are placed together (see figure) on an inclined plane with angle of inclination θ. Various values of θ are given in **Column-I**. The coefficient of friction between the block m_1 and the plane is always zero. The coefficient of static and dynamic friction between the block m_2 and the plane are equal to $\mu = 0.3$. In **Column-II** expressions for the friction on block m_2 are given. Match the correct expression of the friction in **Column-II** with the angle given in **Column-I**, and choose the correct option. The acceleration due to gravity is denoted by g.

[Useful information : $\tan(5.5°) \approx 0.1$; $\tan(11.5°) \approx 0.2$; $\tan(16.5°) \approx 0.3$] **[JEE Adv 2014, P-2]**

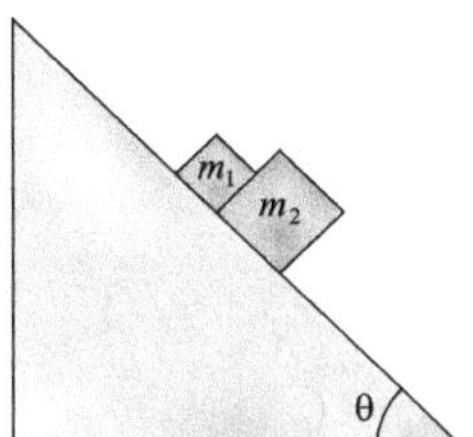

Column-I	Column-II
(P) $\theta = 5°$	(1) $m_2 g \sin\theta$
(Q) $\theta = 10°$	(2) $(m_1 + m_2)g \sin\theta$
(R) $\theta = 15°$	(3) $\mu m_2 g \cos\theta$
(S) $\theta = 20°$	(4) $\mu(m_1 + m_2)g \cos\theta$

Code:
(A) $P \to 1, Q \to 1, R \to 1, S \to 3$
(B) $P \to 2, Q \to 2, R \to 2, S \to 3$
(C) $P \to 2, Q \to 2, R \to 2, S \to 4$
(D) $P \to 2, Q \to 2, R \to 3, S \to 3$

Comprehension based MCQ

Paragraph-1 (Q. No. 22-23)

A projectile is thrown from a point O on the ground at an angle $45°$ from the vertical and with a speed $5\sqrt{2}$ m/s. The projectile at the highest point of its trajectory splits into two equal parts. One part falls vertically down to the ground, 0.5 s after the splitting. The other part, t seconds after the splitting, falls to the ground at a distance x meters from the point O. The acceleration due to gravity $g = 10$ m/s^2.   **[JEE Adv 2021, P-1]**

22. The value of t is __________.

23. The value of x is __________.

Integer Answer based Questions

24. A block is moving on an inclined plane making an angle $45°$ with the horizontal and the coefficient of friction is μ. The force required to just push it up the inclined plane is 3 times the force required to just prevent it from sliding down. If we define $N = 10\,\mu$, then N is ?   **[JEE Adv 2011, P-1]**

25. A train is moving along a straight line with a constant acceleration α. A boy standing in the train throws a ball forward with a speed of 10 m/s, at an angle of $60°$ to the horizontal. The boy has to move forward by 1.15 m inside the train to catch the ball back at the initial height. The acceleration of the train, in m/s^2, is ?   **[JEE Adv 2011, P-2]**

26. A rocket is moving in a gravity free space with a constant acceleration of 2 ms^{-2} along $+x$ direction (see figure). The length of a chamber inside the rocket is 4 m. A ball is thrown from the left end of the chamber in $+x$ direction with a speed of 0.3 ms^{-1} relative to the rocket. As the same time, another ball is thrown in $-x$ direction with a speed of 0.2 ms^{-1} from its right end relative to the rocket. The time in seconds when the two balls hit each other is ?   **[JEE Adv 2014, P-1]**

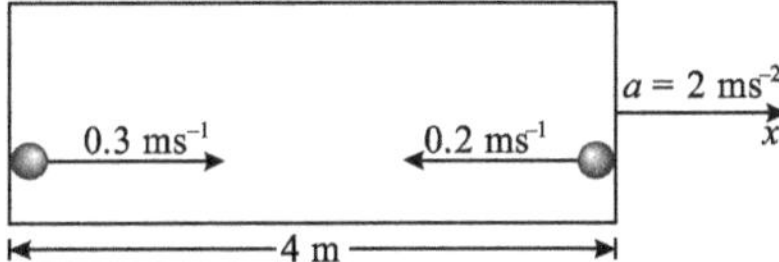

27. Airplanes A and B are flying with constant velocity in the same vertical plane at angles $30°$ and $60°$ with respect to the horizontal as shown in figure. The speed of A is $100\sqrt{3}$ ms^{-1}. At time $t = 0$ s, an observer in A finds B at a distance of 500 m. This observer sees B moving with a constant velocity perpendicular to the line of motion of A. If at $t = t_0$, A just escapes being hit by B, t_0 in seconds is ?   **[JEE Adv 2014, P-1]**

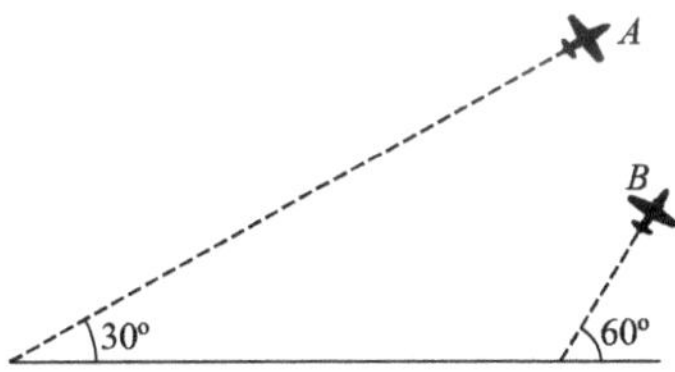

28. A ball is projected from the ground at an angle of $45°$ with the horizontal surface. It reaches a maximum height of 120 m and returns to the ground. Upon hitting the ground for the first time, it loses half of its kinetic energy. Immediately after the bounce, the velocity of the ball makes an angle of $30°$ with the horizontal surface. The maximum height it reaches after the bounce, in metres, is _______ .   **[JEE Adv 2018, P-2]**

29. A ball is thrown from ground at an angle θ with horizontal and with an initial speed u_0. For the resulting projectile motion, the magnitude of average velocity of the ball up to the point when it hits the ground for the first time is v_1. After hitting the ground, ball rebounds at the same angle θ but with a reduced speed of u_0/α. Its motion continues for a long time as shown in figure. If the magnitude of average velocity of the ball for entire duration of motion is $0.8v_1$, the value of α is______ .

[JEE Adv 2019, P-2]

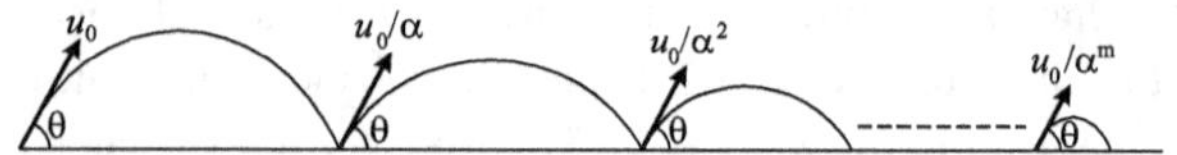

30. A projectile is fired from horizontal ground with speed v and projection angle θ. When the acceleration due to gravity is g, the range of the projectile is d. If at the highest point in its trajectory, the projectile enters a different region where the effective acceleration due to gravity is $g' = \dfrac{g}{0.81}$, then the new range is $d' = nd$. The value of n is ______.

[JEE Adv 2022, P-1]

31. A person of height 1.6 m is walking away from a lamp post of height 4 m along a straight path on the flat ground. The lamp post and the person are always perpendicular to the ground. If the speed of the person is 60 cm s^{-1}, the speed of the tip of the person's shadow on the ground with respect to the person is ______ cm s^{-1}.

[JEE Adv 2023, P-1]

* * * * *

WORK ENERGY POWER & CIRCULAR MOTION

MCQ with Single Option Correct

1. A bob of mass M is suspended by a massless string of length L. The horizontal velocity V at position A is just sufficient to make it reach the point B. The angle θ at which the speed of the bob is half of that at A, satisfies :   **[JEE Adv 2008, P-2]**

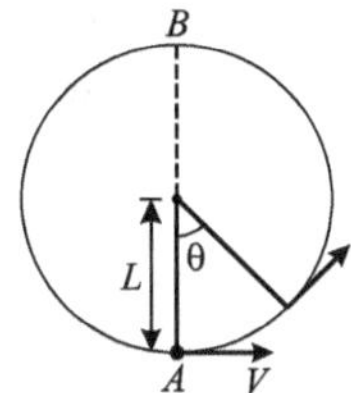

(A) $\theta = \dfrac{\pi}{4}$

(B) $\dfrac{\pi}{4} < \theta < \dfrac{\pi}{2}$

(C) $\dfrac{\pi}{2} < \theta < \dfrac{3\pi}{4}$

(D) $\dfrac{3\pi}{4} < \theta < \pi$

2. A block (B) is attached to two unstretched springs $S1$ and $S2$ with spring constants k and $4k$, respectively (see figure-I). The other ends are attached to identical supports $M1$ and $M2$ not attached to the walls. The springs and supports have negligible mass. There is no friction anywhere. The block B is displaced towards wall 1 by a small distance x (figure-II) and released. The block returns and moves a maximum distance y towards wall 2. Displacements x and y are measured with respect to the equilibrium position of the block B. The ratio y/x is :

[JEE Adv 2008, P-2]

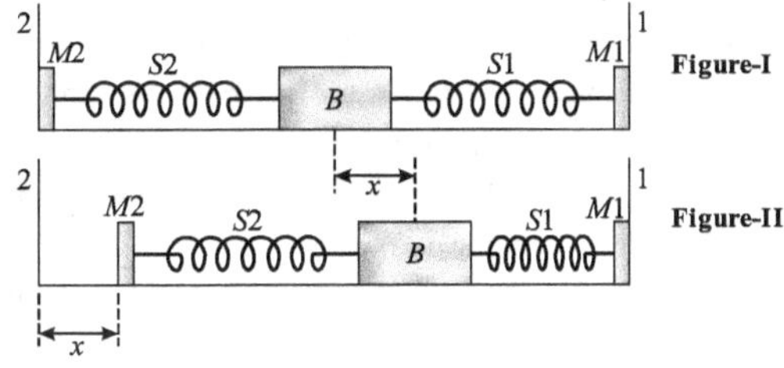

(A) 4

(B) 2

(C) $\dfrac{1}{2}$

(D) $\dfrac{1}{4}$

3. A block of mass 2 kg is free to move along the x-axis. It is at rest and from $t = 0$ onwards it is subjected to a time-dependent force $F(t)$ in the x direction. The force $F(t)$ varies with t as shown in the figure. The kinetic energy of the block after 4.5 seconds is :   **[JEE Adv 2010, P-2]**

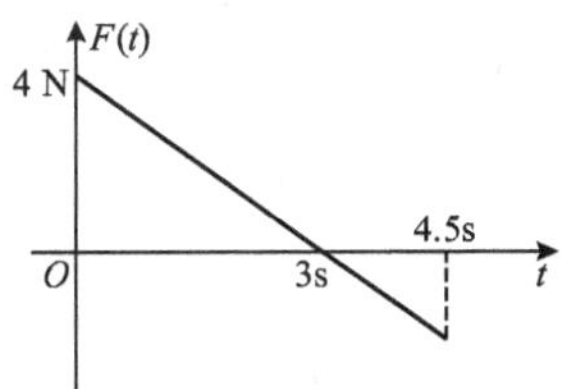

(A) 4.50 J

(B) 7.50 J

(C) 5.06 J

(D) 14.06 J

4. A ball of mass $m = 0.5$ kg is attached to the end of a string having length $L = 0.5$ m. The ball is rotated on a horizontal circular path about vertical axis. The maximum tension that the string can bear is 324 N. The maximum possible value of angular velocity of ball (in radian/s) is :   **[JEE Adv 2011, P-1]**

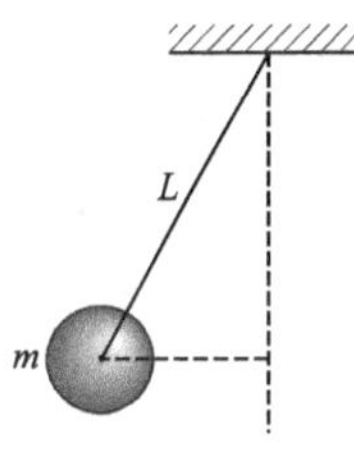

(A) 9

(B) 18

(C) 27

(D) 36

5. Two identical discs of same radius R are rotating about their axes in opposite directions with the same constant angular speed ω. The discs are in the same horizontal plane. At time $t = 0$, the points P and Q are facing each other as shown in the figure. The relative speed between the two points P and Q is v_r. In one time period (T) of rotation of the discs, v_r as a function of time is best represented by :   **[JEE Adv 2012, P-2]**

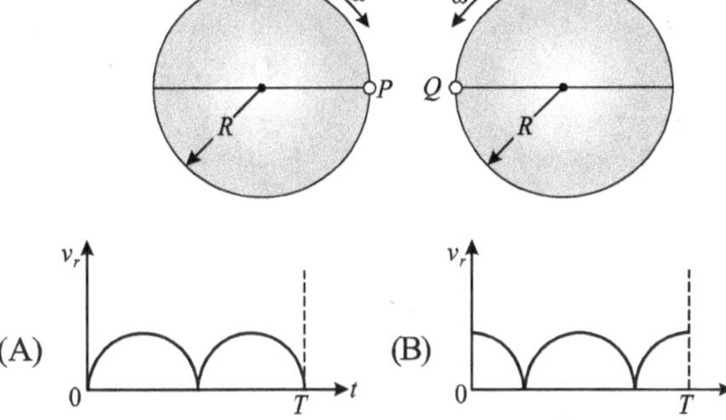

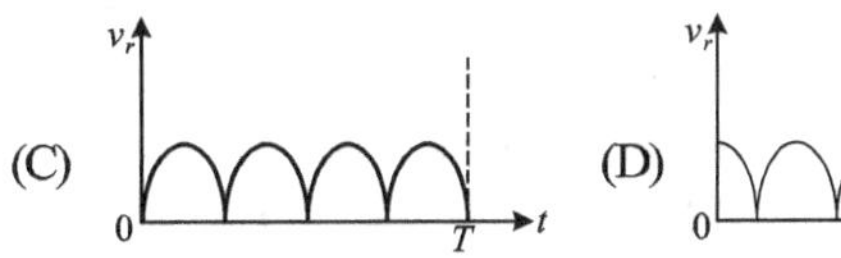

6. The work done on a particle of mass m by a force,

$$K\left[\frac{x}{(x^2+y^2)^{3/2}}\,\hat{i} + \frac{y}{(x^2+y^2)^{3/2}}\,\hat{j}\right]$$ (K being a constant of

appropriate dimensions), when the particle is taken from the point $(a, 0)$ to point $(0, a)$ along a circular path of radius a about the origin in the x-y plane is :　　　**[JEE Adv 2013, P-1]**

(A) $\dfrac{2K\pi}{a}$　　　　　　(B) $\dfrac{K\pi}{a}$

(C) $\dfrac{K\pi}{2a}$　　　　　　(D) 0

7. A tennis ball is dropped on a horizontal smooth surface. It bounces back to its original position after hitting the surface. The force on the ball during the collision is proportional to the length of compression of the ball. Which one of the following sketches describes the variation of its kinetic energy K with time t most appropriately ? The figures are only illustrative and not to the scale :　　**[JEE Adv 2014, P-2]**

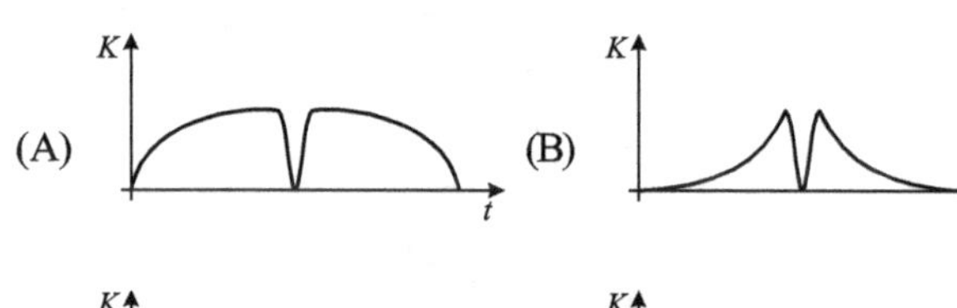

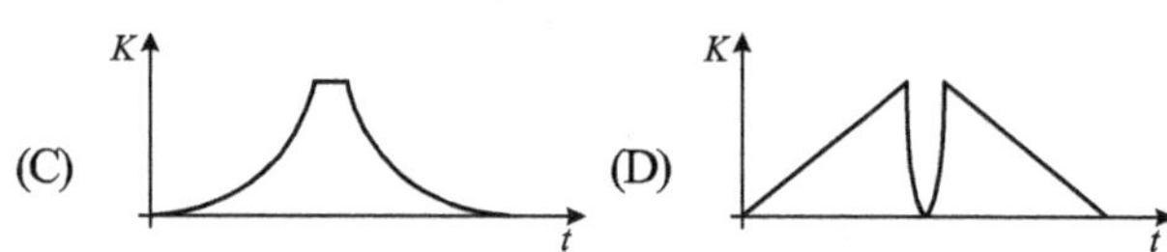

MCQ with One or More than One Options Correct

8. The potential energy of a particle of mass m at a distance r from a fixed point O is given by $V(r) = kr^2/2$, where k is a positive constant of appropriate dimensions. This particle is moving in a circular orbit of radius R about the point O. If v is the speed of the particle and L is the magnitude of its angular momentum about O, which of the following statements is (are) true ?　　**[JEE Adv 2018, P-1]**

(A) $v = \sqrt{\dfrac{k}{2m}}\,R$　　　　(B) $v = \sqrt{\dfrac{k}{m}}\,R$

(C) $L = \sqrt{mk}\,R^2$　　　　(D) $L = \sqrt{\dfrac{mk}{2}}\,R^2$

9. A particle of mass m is initially at rest at the origin. It is subjected to a force and starts moving along the x-axis. Its kinetic energy K changes with time as $dK/dt = \gamma t$, where γ is a positive constant of appropriate dimensions. Which of the following statements is (are) true ?　　**[JEE Adv 2018, P-2]**

(A) The force applied on the particle is constant
(B) The speed of the particle is proportional to time
(C) The distance of the particle from the origin increases linearly with time
(D) The force is conservative

10. A student skates up a ramp that makes an angle 30° with the horizontal. He/she starts (as shown in the figure) at the bottom of the ramp with speed v_0 and wants to turn around over a semicircular path xyz of radius R during which he/she reaches a maximum height h (at point y) from the ground as shown in the figure. Assume that the energy loss is negligible and the force required for this turn at the highest point is provided by his/her weight only. Then (g is the acceleration due to gravity) :　　**[JEE Adv 2020, P-2]**

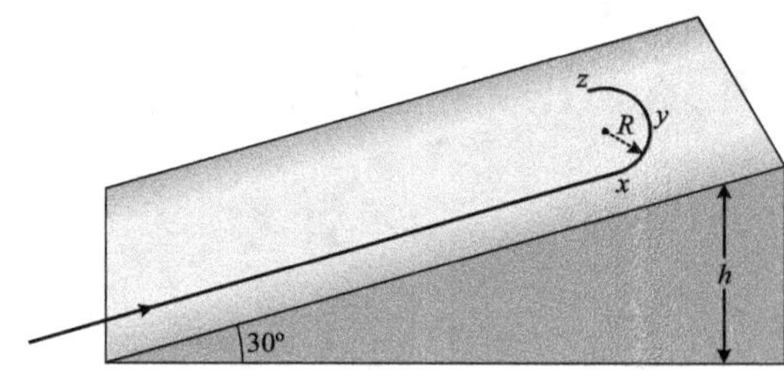

(A) $v_0^2 - 2gh = \dfrac{1}{2}gR$

(B) $v_0^2 - 2gh = \dfrac{\sqrt{3}}{2}gR$

(C) The centripetal force required at points x and z is zero
(D) The centripetal force required is maximum at points x and z

Matrix Match MCQ

11. Column-I gives a list of possible set of parameters measured in some experiments. The variations of the parameters in the form of graphs are shown in **Column-II**. Match the set of parameters given in **Column-I** with the graphs given in **Column-II**. Indicate your answer by darkening the appropriate bubbles of the 4 × 4 matrix given in the ORS :　　**[JEE Adv 2008, P-2]**

Column-I

(A) Potential energy of a simple pendulum (y-axis) as a function of displacement (x-axis)
(B) Displacement (y-axis) as a function of time (x-axis) for a one dimensional motion when the body is moving along the positive x-direction
(C) Range of a projectile (y-axis) as a function of its velocity (x-axis) when projected at a fixed angle
(D) The square of the time period (y-axis) of a simple pendulum as a function of its length (x-axis)

Column-II

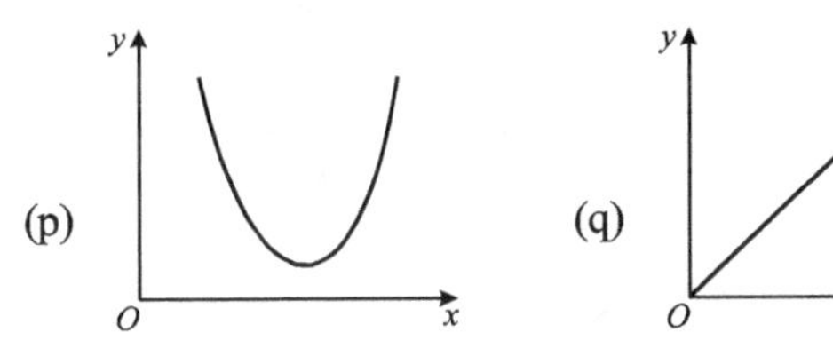

(p)   (q)

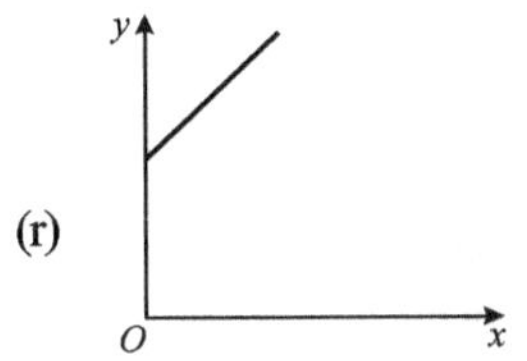   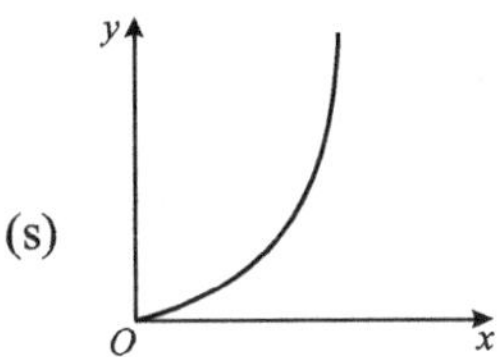

(r)   (s)

12. A particle of unit mass is moving along the x-axis under the influence of a force and its total energy is conserved. Four possible forms of the potential energy of the particle are given in **column-I** (a and U_0 are constants). Match the potential energies in **Column-I** to the corresponding statement(s) in **Column-II**.   **[JEE Adv 2015, P-1]**

Column-I

(A) $U_1(x) = \dfrac{U_0}{2}\left[1 - \left(\dfrac{x}{a}\right)^2\right]^2$

(B) $U_2(x) = \dfrac{U_0}{2}\left(\dfrac{x}{a}\right)^2$

(C) $U_3(x) = \dfrac{U_0}{2}\left(\dfrac{x}{a}\right)^2 \exp\left[-\left(\dfrac{x}{a}\right)^2\right]$

(D) $U_4(x) = \dfrac{U_0}{2}\left[\dfrac{x}{a} - \dfrac{1}{3}\left(\dfrac{x}{a}\right)^3\right]$

Column-II

(p) The force acting on the particle is zero at $x = a$
(q) The force acting on the particle is zero at $x = 0$
(r) The force acting on the particle is zero at $x = -a$
(s) The particle experiences an attractive force towards $x = 0$ in the region $|x| < a$

(t) The particle with total energy $\dfrac{U_0}{4}$ can oscillate about the point $x = -a$

13. In the **Column-I** below, four different paths of a particle are given as functions of time. In these functions, α and β are positive constants of appropriate dimensions and $\alpha \ne B$. In each case, the force acting on the particle is either zero or conservative. In **Column-II**, five physical quantities of the particle are mentioned; $\vec{p}$ is the linear momentum $\vec{L}$ is the angular momentum about the origin, K is the kinetic energy, U is the potential energy and E is the total energy. Match each path in **Column-I** with those quantities in **Column-II**, which are conserved for that path.   **[JEE Adv 2018, P-2]**

	Column-I		**Column-II**
P.	$\vec{r}\,(t) = \alpha t\,\hat{i} + \beta t\,\hat{j}$	**1.**	$\vec{p}$
Q.	$\vec{r}\,(t) = \alpha\cos\omega t\,\hat{i} + \beta\sin\omega t\,\hat{j}$	**2.**	$\vec{L}$
R.	$\vec{r}\,(t) = \alpha(\cos\omega t\,\hat{i} + \sin\omega t\,\hat{j})$	**3.**	K
S.	$\vec{r}\,(t) = \alpha t\,\hat{i} + \dfrac{\beta}{2}t^2\,\hat{j}$	**4.**	U
		5.	E

(A) P → 1, 2, 3, 4, 5; Q → 2, 5; R → 2, 3, 4, 5; S → 5
(B) P → 1, 2, 3, 4, 5; Q → 3, 5; R → 2, 3, 4, 5; S → 2, 5
(C) P → 2, 3, 4; Q → 5; R → 1, 2, 4; S → 2, 5
(D) P → 1, 2, 3, 5; Q → 2, 5; R → 2, 3, 4, 5; S → 2, 5

Comprehension based MCQ

Paragraph-1 (Q. No. 14-15)

A small block of mass 1 kg is released from rest at the top of a rough track. The track is a circular arc of radius 40 m. The block slides along the track without toppling and a frictional force acts on it in the direction opposite to the instantaneous velocity. The work done in overcoming the friction up to the point Q, as shown in the figure below, is 150 J. (Take the acceleration due to gravity, $g = 10$ ms^{-2}).   **[JEE Adv 2013, P-2]**

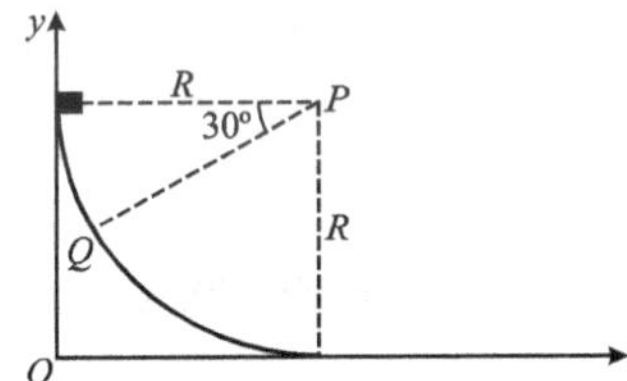

14. The speed of the block when it reaches the point Q is :
(A) 5 ms^{-1} (B) 10 ms^{-1}

(C) $10\sqrt{3}$ms^{-1} (D) 20 ms^{-1}

15. The magnitude of the normal reaction that acts on the block at the point Q is :
(A) 7.5 N   (B) 8.6 N
(C) 11.5 N   (D) 22.5 N

Paragraph-2 (Q. No. 16-17)

A pendulum consists of a bob of mass $m = 0.1$ kg and a massless inextensible string of length $L = 1.0$ m. It is suspended from a fixed point at height $H = 0.9$ m above a frictionless horizontal floor. Initially, the bob of the pendulum is lying on the floor at rest vertically below the point of suspension. A horizontal impulse $P = 0.2$ kg-m/s is imparted to the bob at some instant. After the bob slides for some distance, the string becomes taut and the bob lifts off the floor. The magnitude of the angular momentum of the pendulum about the point of suspension just before the bob lifts off is J kg-m^2/s. The kinetic energy of the pendulum just after the lift-off is K Joules. **[JEE Adv 2021, P-2]**

16. The value of J is _______.

17. The value of K is _______.

Integer Answer based Questions

18. A light inextensible string that goes over a smooth fixed pulley as shown in the figure connects two blocks of masses 0.36 kg and 0.72 kg. Taking $g = 10$ m/s^2, find the work done (**in joules**) by the string on the block of mass 0.36 kg during the first second after the system is released from rest.

[JEE Adv 2009, P-2]

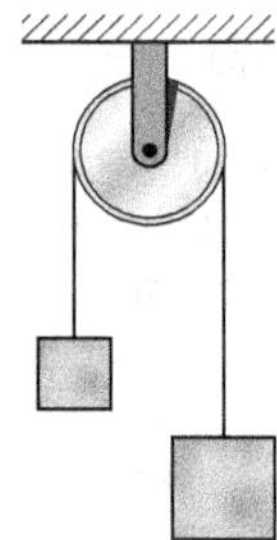

19. A block of mass 0.18 kg is attached to a spring of force-constant 2 N/m. The coefficient of friction between the block and the floor is 0.1. Initially the block is at rest and the spring is unstretched. An impulse is given to the block as shown in the figure. The block slides a distance of 0.06 m and comes to rest for the first time. The initial velocity of the block in m/s is $V = N/10$. Then N is ? **[JEE Adv 2011, P-2]**

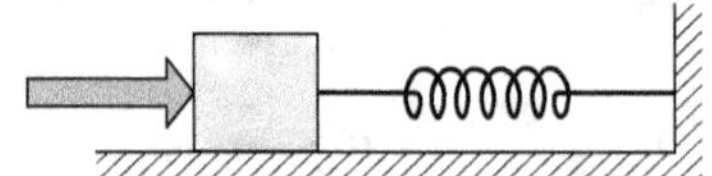

20. A particle of mass 0.2 kg is moving in one dimension under a force that delivers a constant power 0.5 W to the particle. If the initial speed (in ms^{-1}) of the particle is zero, the speed (in ms^{-1}) after 5 s is ? **[JEE Adv 2013, P-1]**

21. Consider an elliptically shaped rail PQ in the vertical plane with $OP = 3$ m and $OQ = 4$ m. A block of mass 1 kg is pulled along the rail from P to Q with a force of 18 N, which is always parallel to line PQ (see the figure given). Assuming no frictional losses, the kinetic energy of the block when it reaches Q is ($n \times 10$) Joules. The value of n is (take acceleration due to gravity = 10 ms^{-2}) **[JEE Adv 2014, P-1]**

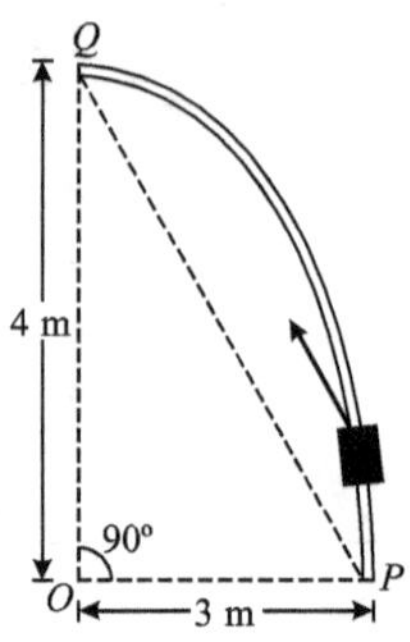

22. Two vectors $\vec{A}$ and $\vec{B}$ are defined as $\vec{A} = a\,\hat{i}$ and $\vec{B} = a(\cos\omega t\,\hat{i} + \sin\omega t\,\hat{j})$, where a is a constant and $\omega = \pi/6$ rad s^{-1}. If $|\vec{A} + \vec{B}| = \sqrt{3}\,|\vec{A} - \vec{B}|$ at time $t = \tau$ for the first time, the value of τ, in seconds, is _______. **[JEE Adv 2018, P-1]**

23. A particle is moved along a path AB-BC-CD-DE-EF-FA, as shown in figure, in presence of a force $\vec{F} = (\alpha y\,\hat{i} + 2\alpha x\,\hat{j})$ N, where x and y are in meter and $\alpha = -1$ N/m^{-1}. The work done on the particle by this force $\vec{F}$ will be _______ Joule. **[JEE Adv 2018, P-2]**

24. A particle of mass 1 kg is subjected to a force which depends on the position as $\vec{F} = -k(x\,\hat{i} + y\,\hat{j})$ kg ms^{-2} with $k = 1$ kg s^{-2}. At time $t = 0$, the particle's position $\vec{r} = \left(\dfrac{1}{2}\hat{i} + \sqrt{2}\hat{j}\right)$ m and its velocity $\vec{v} = \left(-\sqrt{2}\hat{i} + \sqrt{2}\hat{j} + \dfrac{2}{\pi}\hat{k}\right)$ ms^{-1}. Let v_x and v_y denote the x and the y components of the particle's velocity, respectively. Ignore gravity. When $z = 0.5$ m, the value of $(xv_y - yv_x)$ is _______ m^2 s^{-1}. **[JEE Adv 2022, P-2]**

* * * * *

SYSTEM OF PARTICLES AND ROTATIONAL MOTION

MCQ with Single Option Correct

1. A small object of uniform density rolls up a curved surface with an initial velocity v. It reaches up to a maximum height of $\dfrac{3v^3}{4g}$ with respect to the initial position. The object is :

[JEE Adv 2007, P-2]

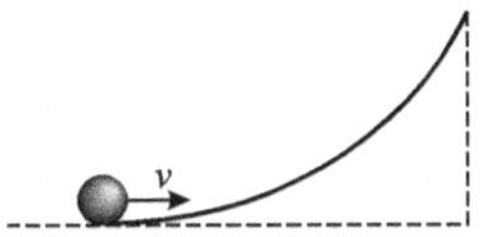

(A) Ring   (B) Solid sphere
(C) Hollow sphere   (D) Disc

2. Look at the drawing given in the figure which has been drawn with ink of uniform line thickness. The mass of ink used to draw each of the two inner circles, and each of the two line segments is m. The mass of the ink used to draw the outer circle is $6m$. The coordinates of the centres of the different parts are: outer circle $(0, 0)$, left inner circle $(-a, a)$, right inner circle (a, a), vertical line $(0, 0)$ and horizontal line $(0, -a)$. The y-coordinate of the centre of mass of the ink in this drawing is :

[JEE Adv 2009, P-1]

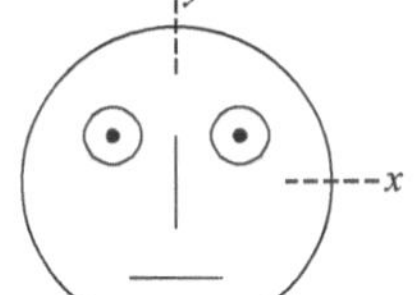

(A) $\dfrac{a}{10}$ (B) $\dfrac{a}{8}$

(C) $\dfrac{a}{12}$ (D) $\dfrac{a}{3}$

3. Two small particles of equal masses start moving in opposite directions from a point A in a horizontal circular orbit. Their tangential velocities are v and $2v$, respectively, as shown in the figure. Between collisions, the particles move with constant speeds. After making how many elastic collisions, other than that at A, these two particles will again reach the point A ?

[JEE Adv 2009, P-1]

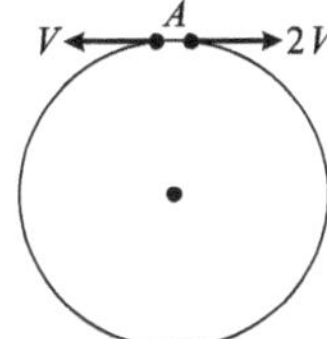

(A) 4   (B) 3
(C) 2   (D) 1

4. A uniform rod of length L and mass M is pivoted at the centre. Its two ends are attached to two springs of equal constants k. The springs are fixed to rigid supports as shown in the figure, and the rod is free to oscillate in the horizontal plane. The rod is gently pushed through a small angle θ in one direction and released. The frequency of oscillation is :

[JEE Adv 2009, P-2]

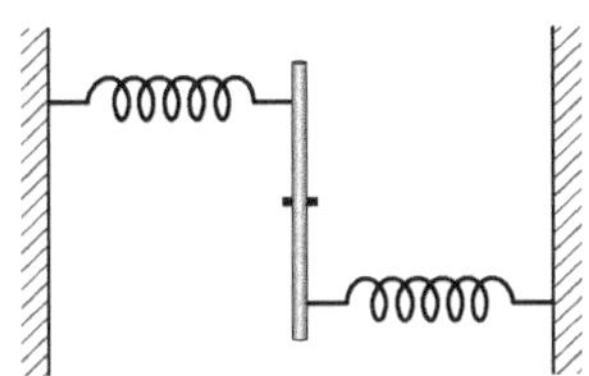

(A) $\dfrac{1}{2\pi}\sqrt{\dfrac{2k}{M}}$ (B) $\dfrac{1}{2\pi}\sqrt{\dfrac{k}{M}}$

(C) $\dfrac{1}{2\pi}\sqrt{\dfrac{6k}{M}}$ (D) $\dfrac{1}{2\pi}\sqrt{\dfrac{24k}{M}}$

5. A ball of mass 0.2 kg rests on a vertical post of height 5 m. A bullet of mass 0.01 kg, traveling with a velocity V m/s in a horizontal direction, hits the center of the ball. After the collision, the ball and bullet travel independently. The ball hits the ground at a distance of 20 m and bullet at a distance of 100 m from the foot of the post. The initial velocity V of the bullet is :

[JEE Adv 2011, P-2]

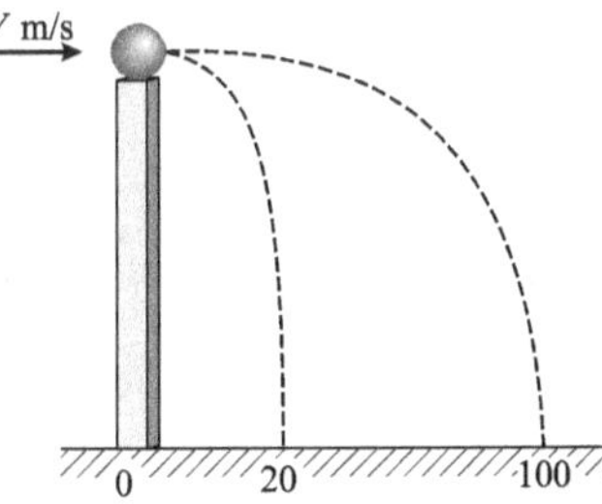

(A) 250 m/s   (B) $250\sqrt{2}$ m/s
(C) 400 m/s   (D) 500 m/s

6. A thin uniform rod, pivoted at O, is rotating in the horizontal plane with constant angular speed ω, as shown in the figure. At time $t = 0$, a small insect starts from O and moves with constant speed v with respect to the rod towards the other end. It reaches the end of the rod at $t = T$ and stops. The angular speed of the system remains ω throughout. The magnitude of the torque $(|\vec{\tau}|)$ on the system about O, as a function of time is best represented by which plot :

[JEE Adv 2012, P-1]

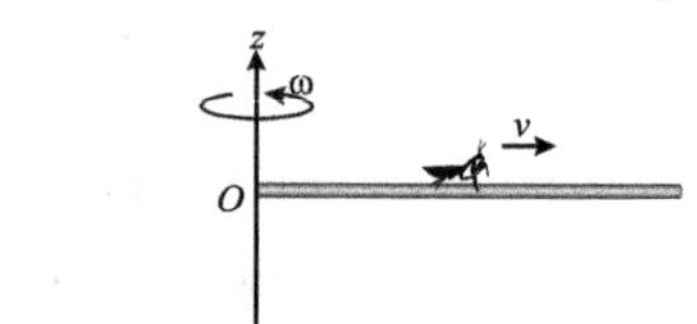

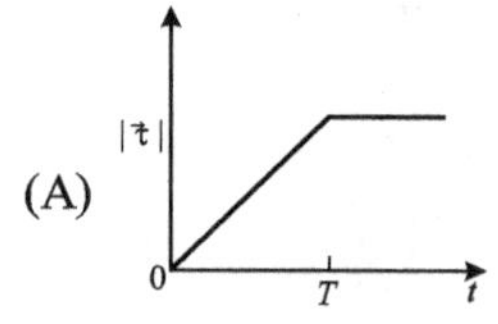

(A)

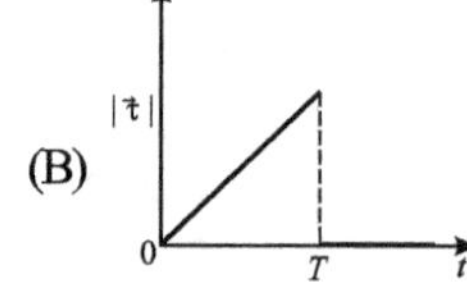

(B)

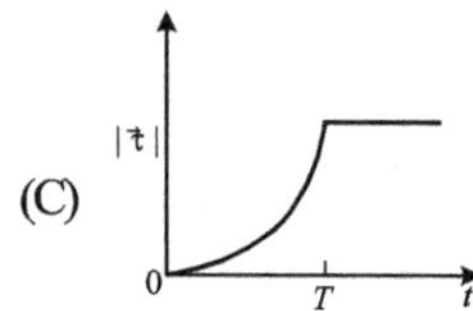

(C)

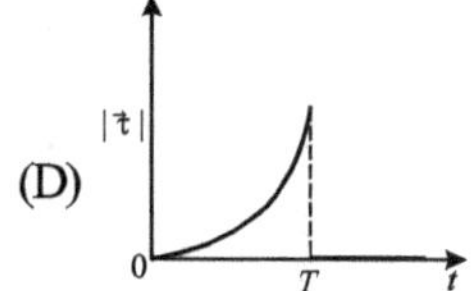

(D)

7. A small mass m is attached to a massless string whose other end is fixed at P as shown in the figure. The mass is undergoing circular motion in the x-y plane with centre at O and constant angular speed ω. If the angular momentum of the system, calculated about O and P are denoted by $\vec{L}_0$ and $\overrightarrow{L_P}$ respectively, then :

[JEE Adv 2012, P-1]

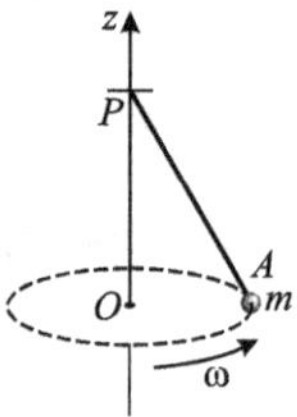

(A) $\overrightarrow{L_0}$ and $\overrightarrow{L_P}$ do not vary with time

(B) $\overrightarrow{L_0}$ varies with time while $\overrightarrow{L_P}$ remains constant

(C) $\overrightarrow{L_0}$ remains constant while $\overrightarrow{L_P}$ varies with time

(D) $\overrightarrow{L_0}$ and $\overrightarrow{L_P}$ both vary with time

8. Consider a disc rotating in the horizontal plane with a constant angular speed ω about its centre O. The disc has a shaded region on one side of the diameter and an unshaded region on the other side as shown in the figure. When the disc is in the orientation as shown, two pebbles P and Q are simultaneously projected at an angle towards R. The velocity of projection is in the y-z plane and is same for both pebbles with respect to the disc. Assume that (i) they land back on the disc before the disc has completed 1/8 rotation, (ii) their range is less than half the disc radius, and (iii) ω remains constant

throughout. Then :

[JEE Adv 2012, P-2]

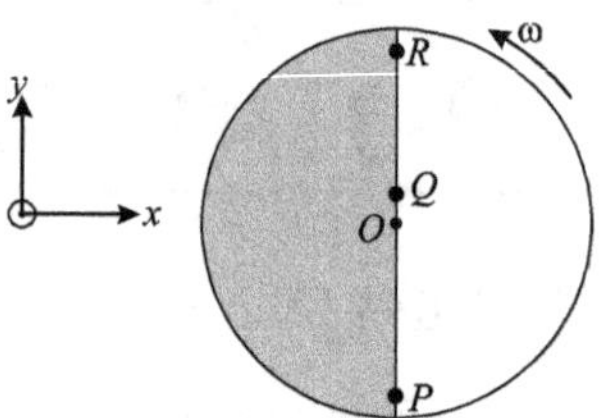

(A) P lands in the shaded region and Q in the unshaded region

(B) P lands in the unshaded region and Q in the shaded region

(C) Both P and Q land in the unshaded region

(D) Both P and Q land in the shaded region

9. A particle of mass m is projected from the ground with an initial speed u_0 at an angle α with the horizontal. At the highest point of its trajectory, it makes a completely inelastic collision with another identical particle, which was thrown vertically upward from the ground with the same initial speed u_0. The angle that the composite system makes with the horizontal immediately after the collision is :

[JEE Adv 2013, P-1]

(A) $\dfrac{\pi}{4}$

(B) $\dfrac{\pi}{4} + \alpha$

(C) $\dfrac{\pi}{4} - \alpha$

(D) $\dfrac{\pi}{2}$

10. Consider regular polygons with number of sides $n = 3, 4, 5$ …… as shown in the figure. The centre of mass of all the polygons is at height h from the ground. They roll on a horizontal surface about the leading vertex without slipping and sliding as depicted. The maximum increase in height of the locus of the center of mass for each polygon is Δ. Then Δ depends on n and h as :

[JEE Adv 2017, P-2]

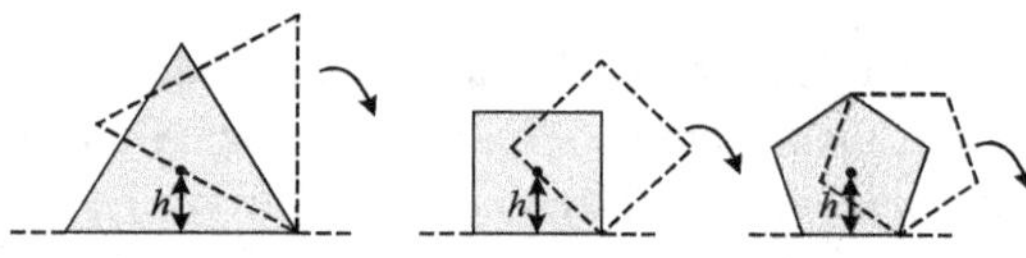

(A) $\Delta = h \sin^2\left(\dfrac{\pi}{n}\right)$

(B) $\Delta = h \sin\left(\dfrac{2\pi}{n}\right)$

(C) $\Delta = h\left(\dfrac{1}{\cos\left(\dfrac{\pi}{n}\right)} - 1\right)$

(D) $\Delta = h \tan^2\left(\dfrac{\pi}{2n}\right)$

11. A football of radius R is kept on a hole of radius r ($r < R$) made on a plank kept horizontally. One end of the plank is now lifted so that it gets tilted making an angle θ from the horizontal as shown in the figure below. The maximum value of θ so that the football does not start rolling down the plank satisfies (figure is schematic and not drawn to scale) :

[JEE Adv 2020, P-1]

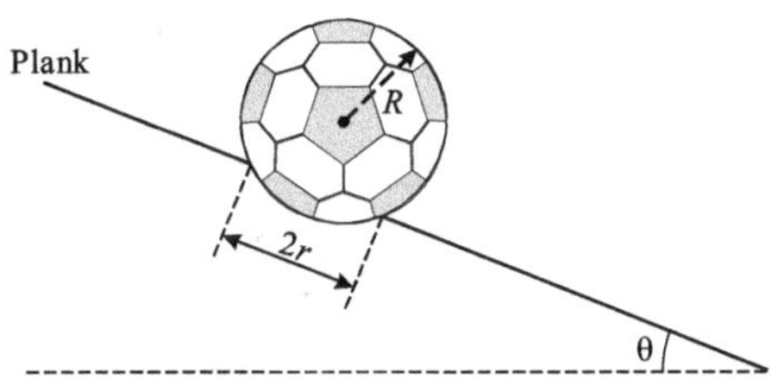

(A) $\sin \theta = \dfrac{r}{R}$ (B) $\tan \theta = \dfrac{r}{R}$

(C) $\sin \theta = \dfrac{r}{2R}$ (D) $\cos \theta = \dfrac{r}{2R}$

12. A small roller of diameter 20 cm has an axle of diameter 10 cm (see figure below on the left). It is on a horizontal floor and a meter scale is positioned horizontally on its axle with one edge of the scale on top of the axle (see figure on the right). The scale is now pushed slowly on the axle so that it moves without slipping on the axle, and the roller starts rolling without slipping. After the roller has moved 50 cm, the position of the scale will look like (figures are schematic and not drawn to scale) **[JEE Adv 2020, P-1]**

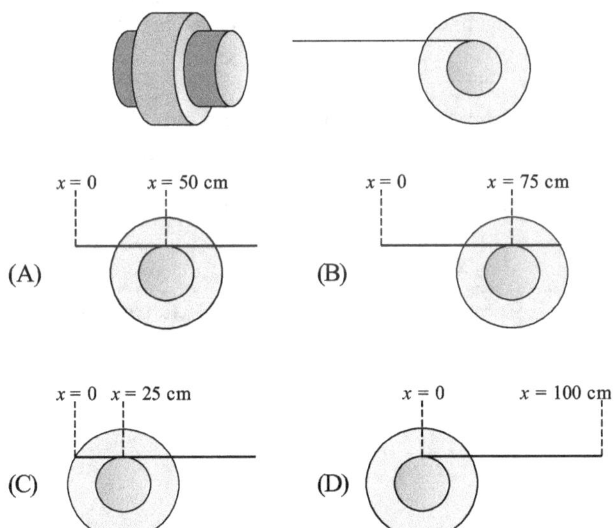

13. A flat surface of a thin uniform disk A of radius R is glued to a horizontal table. Another thin uniform disk B of mass M and with the same radius R rolls without slipping on the circumference of A, as shown in the figure. A flat surface of B also lies on the plane of the table. The center of mass of B has fixed angular speed ω about the vertical axis passing through the center of A. The angular momentum of B is $nM\omega R^2$ with respect to the center of A. Which of the following is the value of n ?

[JEE Adv 2022, P-2]

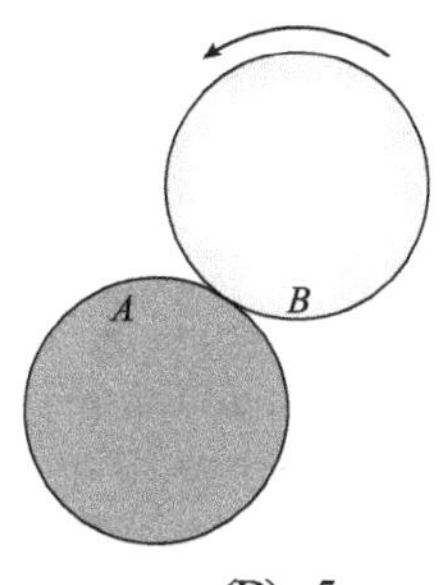

(A) 2   (B) 5

(C) $\dfrac{7}{2}$ (D) $\dfrac{9}{2}$

14. A bar of mass $M = 1.00$ kg and length $L = 0.20$ m is lying on a horizontal frictionless surface. One end of the bar is pivoted at a point about which it is free to rotate. A small mass $m = 0.10$ kg is moving on the same horizontal surface with 5.00 ms^{-1} speed on a path perpendicular to the bar. It hits the bar at a distance $L/2$ from the pivoted end and returns back on the same path with speed v. After this elastic collision, the bar rotates with an angular velocity ω. Which of the following statement is correct?

[JEE Adv 2023, P-1]

(A) $\omega = 6.98$ rad s^{-1} and $v = 4.30$ m s^{-1}
(B) $\omega = 3.75$ rad s^{-1} and $v = 4.30$ m s^{-1}
(C) $\omega = 3.75$ rad s^{-1} and $v = 10.0$ m s^{-1}
(D) $\omega = 6.80$ rad s^{-1} and $v = 4.10$ m s^{-1}

MCQ with One or More than One Options Correct

15. Two balls, having linear momenta $\vec{p}_1 = p\,\hat{i}$ and $\vec{p}_2 = -p\,\hat{i}$, undergo a collision in free space. There is no external force acting on the balls. Let $\vec{p}_1'$ and $\vec{p}_2'$ be their final momenta. The following option(s) is (are) **NOT ALLOWED** for any non-zero value of $p, a_1, a_2, b_1, b_2, c_1$ and c_2 :   **[JEE Adv 2008, P-1]**

(A) $\vec{p}_1' = a_1\,\hat{i} + b_1\,\hat{j} + c_1\,\hat{k}$; $\vec{p}_2' = a_2\,\hat{i} + b_2\,\hat{j}$
(B) $\vec{p}_1' = c_1\,\hat{k}$; $\vec{p}_2' = c_2\,\hat{k}$
(C) $\vec{p}_1' = a_1\,\hat{i} + b_1\,\hat{j} + c_1\,\hat{k}$; $\vec{p}_2' = a_2\,\hat{i} + b_2\,\hat{j} - c_1\,\hat{k}$
(D) $\vec{p}_1' = a_1\,\hat{i} + b_1\,\hat{j}$ $\vec{p}_2' = a_2\,\hat{i} + b_1\,\hat{j}$

16. A sphere is rolling without slipping on a fixed horizontal plane surface. In the figure, A is the point of contact, B is the centre of the sphere and C is its topmost point. Then :

[JEE Adv 2009, P-2]

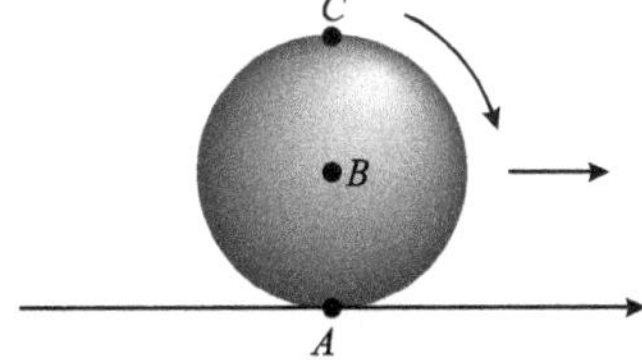

(A) $\vec{V}_C - \vec{V}_A = 2(\vec{V}_B - \vec{V}_C)$ (B) $\vec{V}_C - \vec{V}_B = \vec{V}_B - \vec{V}_A$

(C) $\left|\vec{V}_C - \vec{V}_A\right| = 2\left|\vec{V}_B - \vec{V}_C\right|$ (D) $\left|\vec{V}_C - \vec{V}_A\right| = 4\left|\vec{V}_B\right|$

17. A Point mass of 1 kg collides elastically with a stationary point mass of 5 kg. After their collision, the 1 kg mass reverses its direction and moves with a speed of 2 ms^{-1}. Which of the following statement(s) is (are) correct for the system of these two masses ?   **[JEE Adv 2010, P-1]**
(A) Total momentum of the system is 3 kg ms^{-1}
(B) Momentum of 5 kg mass after collision is 4 kg ms^{-1}
(C) Kinetic energy of the centre of mass is 0.75 J
(D) Total kinetic energy of the system is 4 J

18. A thin ring of mass 2 kg and radius 0.5 m is rolling without slipping on a horizontal plane with velocity 1 m/s. A small ball of mass 0.1 kg, moving with velocity 20 m/s in the opposite direction, hits the ring at a height of 0.75 m and goes vertically up with velocity 10 m/s. Immediately after the collision :

[JEE Adv 2011, P-2]

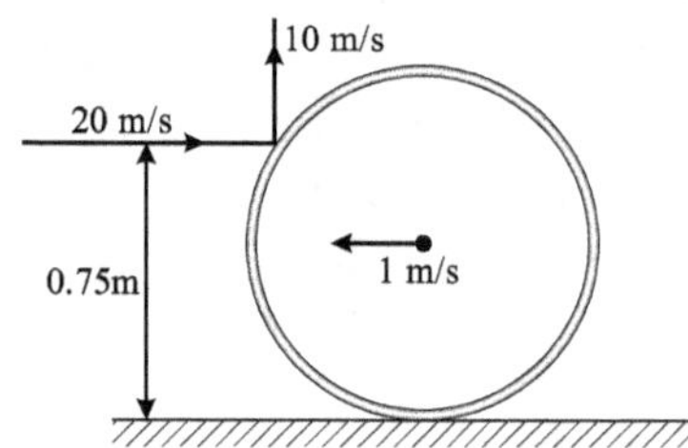

(A) The ring has pure rotation about its stationary *CM*
(B) The ring comes to a complete stop
(C) Friction between the ring and the ground is to the left
(D) There is no friction between the ring and the ground

19. Two solid cylinders P and Q of same mass and same radius start rolling down a fixed inclined plane from the same height at the same time. Cylinder P has most of its mass concentrated near its surface, while Q has most of its mass concentrated near the axis. Which statement(s) is (are) correct :

[JEE Adv 2012, P-2]
(A) Both cylinders P and Q reach the ground at the same time
(B) Cylinder P has larger linear acceleration than cylinder Q
(C) Both cylinders reach the ground with same translational kinetic energy
(D) Cylinder Q reaches the ground with larger angular speed

20. The figure shows a system consisting of (i) a ring of outer radius 3R rolling clockwise without slipping on a horizontal surface ω and (ii) and inner disc of radius 2R rotating anti-clockwise with angular speed ω/2. The ring and disc are separated by frictionless ball bearings. The system is in the x-z plane. The point P on the inner disc is at a distance R from the origin, where OP makes an angle of 30° with the horizontal. Then with respect to the horizontal surface :

[JEE Adv 2012, P-2]

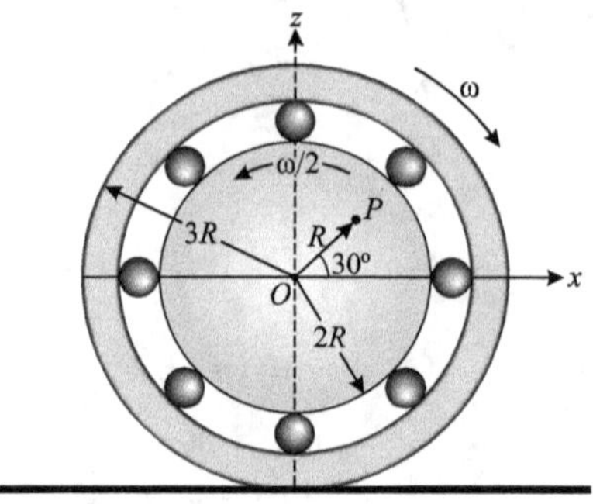

(A) The point O has a linear velocity $3R\omega\,\hat{i}$

(B) The point P has a linear velocity $\dfrac{11}{4}R\omega\hat{i} + \dfrac{\sqrt{3}}{4}R\omega\hat{k}$

(C) The point P has a linear velocity $\dfrac{13}{4}R\omega\hat{i} - \dfrac{\sqrt{3}}{4}R\omega\hat{k}$

(D) The point P has a linear velocity $\left(3 - \dfrac{\sqrt{3}}{4}\right)R\omega\hat{i} + \dfrac{1}{4}R\omega\hat{k}$

21. A ring of mass M and radius R is rotating with angular speed ω about a fixed vertical axis passing through its centre O with two point masses each of mass $\dfrac{M}{8}$ at rest at O. These masses can move radially outwards along two massless rods fixed on the ring as shown in the figure. At some instant the angular speed of the system is $\dfrac{8}{9}$ ω and one of the masses is at a distance of $\dfrac{3}{5}R$ from O. At this instant the distance of the other mass from O is :   **[JEE Adv 2015, P-1]**

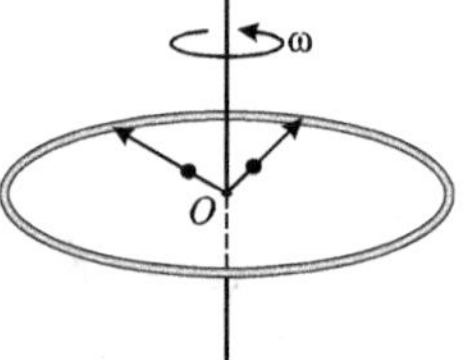

(A) $\dfrac{2}{3}R$ (B) $\dfrac{1}{3}R$

(C) $\dfrac{3}{5}R$ (D) $\dfrac{4}{5}R$

22. The position vector $\vec{r}$ of a particle of mass m is given by the following equation $\vec{r}(t) = \alpha t^3\hat{i} + \beta t^2\hat{j}$, where $\alpha = 10/3$ ms^{-3}, $\beta = 5$ ms^{-2} and $m = 0.1$ kg. At $t = 1$ s, which of the following statement (s) is (are) true about the particle ?

[JEE Adv 2016, P-1]

(A) The velocity $\vec{v}$ is given by $\vec{v} = (10\,\hat{i} + 10\,\hat{j})\,\text{ms}^{-1}$

(B) The angular momentum $\vec{L}$ with respect to the origin is given by $\vec{L} = -5\,(5/3)\,\hat{k}\,\text{N ms}$

(C) The force $\vec{F}$ is given by $\vec{F} = (\hat{i} + 2\,\hat{j})\,\text{N}$

(D) The torque $\vec{\tau}$ with respect to the origin is given by $\vec{\tau} = -(20/3)\,\hat{k}\,\text{Nm}$

23. Two thin circular discs of mass m and $4\,m$, having radii of a and $2a$, respectively, are rigidly fixed by a massless, rigid rod of length $l = \sqrt{24}\,a$ through their centers. This assembly is laid on a firm and flat surface, and set rolling without slipping on the surface so that the angular speed about the axis of the rod is ω. The angular momentum of the entire assembly about the point 'O' is $\vec{L}$ (see the figure). Which of the following statement(s) is (are) true ? **[JEE Adv 2016, P-2]**

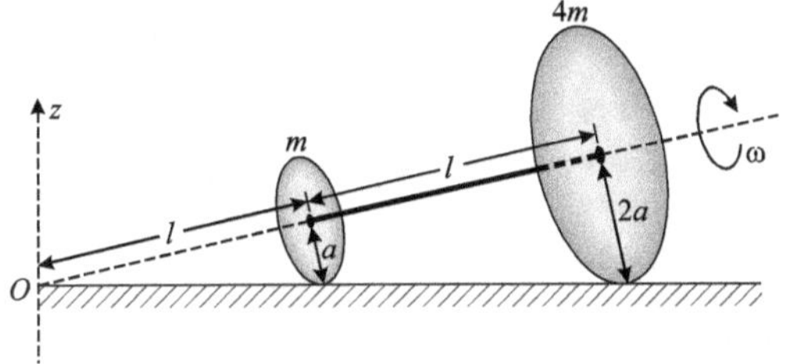

(A) The magnitude of angular momentum of the assembly about its center of mass is $17\,ma^2\omega/2$

(B) The magnitude of the z-component of $\vec{L}$ is $55\,ma^2\omega$

(C) The magnitude of angular momentum of center of mass of the assembly about the point O is $81\,ma^2\omega$

(D) The center of mass of the assembly rotates about the z-axis with an angular speed of $\omega/5$

24. A block of mass M has a circular cut with a frictionless surface as shown. The block rests on the horizontal frictionless surface of a fixed table. Initially the right edge of the block is at $x = 0$, in a co-ordinate system fixed to the table. A point mass m is released from rest at the topmost point of the path as shown and it slides down. When the mass loses contact with the block, its position is x and the velocity is v. At that instant, which of the following options is/are correct : **[JEE Adv 2017, P-1]**

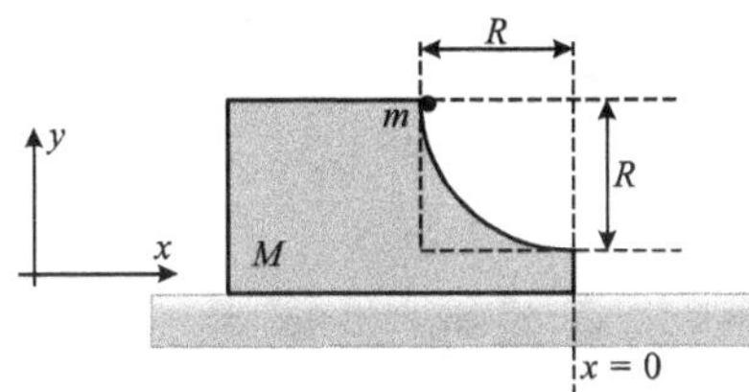

(A) The x component of displacement of the center of mass of the block M is $-\dfrac{mr}{M+m}$

(B) The position of the point mass is $x = -\sqrt{2}\,\dfrac{mR}{M+m}$

(C) The velocity of the point mass m is $v = \sqrt{\dfrac{2gR}{1+\dfrac{m}{M}}}$

(D) The velocity of the block M is $V = -\dfrac{m}{M}\sqrt{2gR}$

25. A flat plate is moving normal to its plane through a gas under the action of a constant force F. The gas is kept at a very low pressure. The speed of the plate v is much less than the average speed u of the gas molecules. Which of the following options is/are true : **[JEE Adv 2017, P-1]**

(A) The resistive force experienced by the plate is proportional to v

(B) The pressure difference between the leading and trailing faces of the plate is proportional to uv

(C) The plate will continue to move with constant non-zero acceleration, at all times

(D) At a later time the external force F balances the resistive force

26. A rigid uniform bar AB of length L is slipping from its vertical position on a frictionless floor (as shown in the figure). At some instant of time, the angle made by the bar with the vertical is θ. Which of the following statements about its motion is/are correct : **[JEE Adv 2017, P-2]**

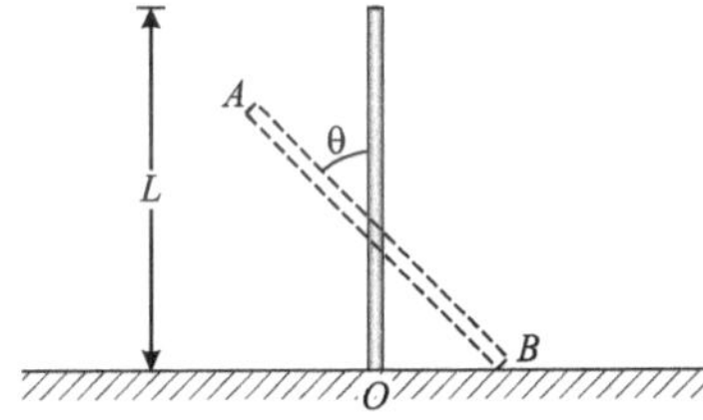

(A) When the bar makes an angle θ with the vertical, the displacement of its midpoint from the initial position is proportional to $(1 - \cos\theta)$

(B) The midpoint of the bar will fall vertically downward

(C) Instantaneous torque about the point in contact with the floor is proportional to $\sin\theta$

(D) The trajectory of the point A is a parabola

27. A wheel of radius R and mass M is placed at the bottom of a fixed step of height R as shown in the figure. A constant force is continuously applied on the surface of the wheel so that it just climbs the step without slipping. Consider the torque τ about an axis normal to the plane of the paper passing through the point Q. Which of the following options is/are correct : **[JEE Adv 2017, P-2]**

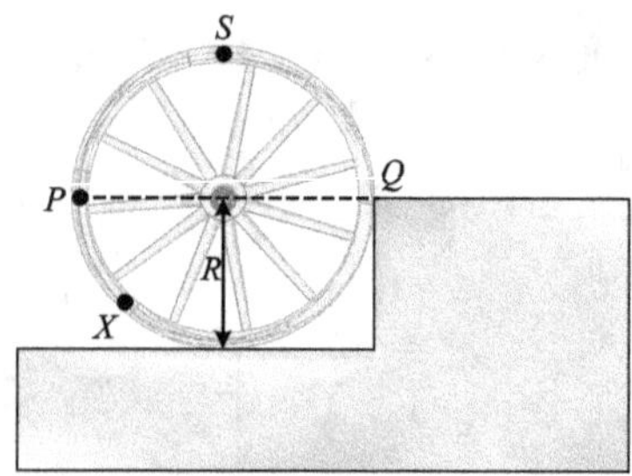

(A) If the force is applied normal to the circumference at point X then τ is constant

(B) If the force is applied tangentially at point S then $\tau \neq 0$ but the wheel never climbs the step

(C) If the force is applied normal to the circumference at point P then τ is zero

(D) If the force is applied at point P tangentially then τ decreases continuously as the wheel climbs

28. Consider a body of mass 1.0 kg at rest at the origin at time $t = 0$. A force $\overline{F} = (\alpha t\,\hat{i} + \beta\,\hat{j})$ is applied on the body, where $\alpha = 1.0\,\mathrm{Ns^{-1}}$ and $\beta = 1.0\,\mathrm{N}$. The torque acting on the body about the origin at time $t = 1.0$ s is $\overline{\tau}$. Which of the following statements is (are) true ? **[JEE Adv 2018, P-1]**

(A) $|\overline{\tau}| = \dfrac{1}{3}\,\mathrm{Nm}$

(B) The torque $\overline{\tau}$ is in the direction of the unit vector $+\hat{k}$

(C) The velocity of the body at $t = 1$ s is $\vec{v} = \dfrac{1}{2}(\hat{i} + 2\,\hat{j})\,\mathrm{ms^{-1}}$

(D) The magnitude of displacement of the body at $t = 1$ s is $\dfrac{1}{6}\,\mathrm{m}$

29. A thin and uniform rod of mass M and length L is held vertical on a floor with large friction. The rod is released from rest so that it falls by rotating about its contact-point with the floor without slipping. Which of the following statement(s) is/are correct, when the rod makes an angle 60° with vertical ? [g is the acceleration due to gravity] **[JEE Adv 2019, P-2]**

(A) The radial acceleration of the center of mass will be $\dfrac{3g}{4}$

(B) The angular acceleration of the rod will be $\dfrac{2g}{L}$

(C) The angular speed of the rod will be $\sqrt{\dfrac{3g}{2L}}$

(D) The normal reaction force from the floor on the rod will be $\dfrac{Mg}{16}$

30. A rod of mass m and length L, pivoted at one of its ends, is hanging vertically. A bullet of the same mass moving at speed v strikes the rod horizontally at a distance x from its pivoted end and gets embedded in it. The combined system now rotates with angular speed ω about the pivot. The maximum angular speed ω_M is achieved for $x = x_M$. Then

[JEE Adv 2020, P-2]

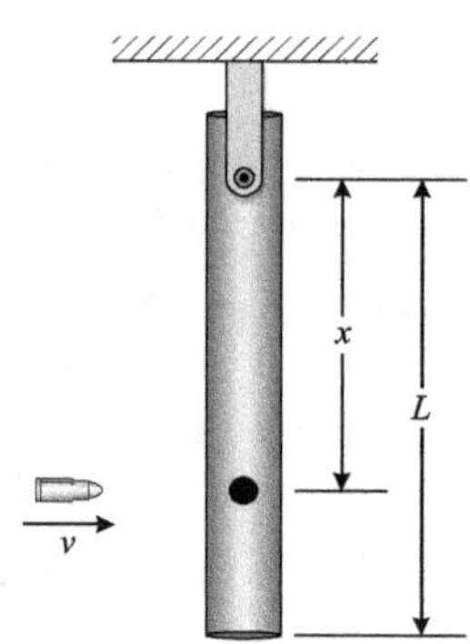

(A) $\omega = \dfrac{3vx}{L^2 + 3x^2}$ (B) $\omega = \dfrac{12vx}{L^2 + 12x^2}$

(C) $x_M = \dfrac{L}{\sqrt{3}}$ (D) $\omega_M = \dfrac{v}{2L}\sqrt{3}$

31. A horizontal force F is applied at the center of mass of a cylindrical object of mass m and radius R, perpendicular to its axis as shown in the figure. The coefficient of friction between the object and the ground is μ. The center of mass of the object has an acceleration a. The acceleration due to gravity is g. Given that the object rolls without slipping, which of the following statement(s) is (are) correct? **[JEE Adv 2021, P-1]**

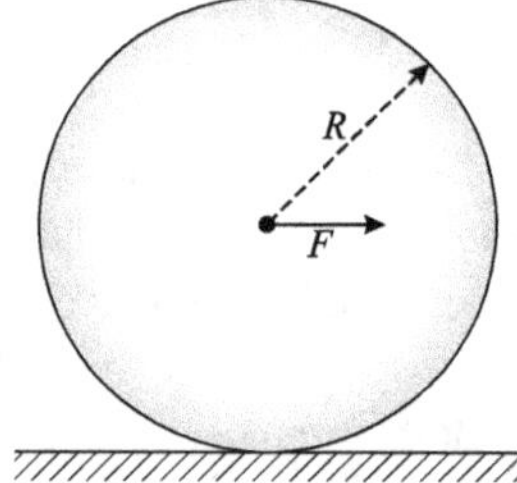

(A) For the same F, the value of a does not depend on whether the cylinder is solid or hollow

(B) For a solid cylinder, the maximum possible value of a is $2\,\mu g$

(C) The magnitude of the frictional force on the object due to the ground is always μmg

(D) For a thin-walled hollow cylinder, $a = \dfrac{F}{2m}$

32. A particle of mass $M = 0.2$ kg is initially at rest in the xy-plane at a point $(x = -l, y = -h)$, where $l = 10$ m and $h = 1$ m. The particle is accelerated at time $t = 0$ with a constant acceleration $a = 10$ m/s² along the positive x-direction. Its angular momentum and torque with respect to the origin, in SI units, are represented by $\vec{L}$ and $\vec{\tau}$, respectively. $\hat{i}$, $\hat{j}$ and $\hat{k}$ are unit vectors along the positive x, y and z-directions, respectively. If $\hat{k} = \hat{i} \times \hat{j}$ then which of the following statement(s) is (are) correct ?

[JEE Adv 2021, P-1]

(A) The particle arrives at the point $(x = l, y = -h)$ at time $t = 2$ s

(B) $\vec{\tau} = 2\hat{k}$ when the particle passes through the point $(x = l, y = -h)$

(C) $\vec{L} = 4\hat{k}$ when the particle passes through the point $(x = l, y = -h)$

(D) $\vec{\tau} = \hat{k}$ when the particle passes through the point $(x = 0, y = -h)$

33. One end of a horizontal uniform beam of weight W and length L is hinged on a vertical wall at point O and its other end is supported by a light inextensible rope. The other end of the rope is fixed at point Q, at a height L above the hinge at point O. A block of weight αW is attached at the point P of the beam, as shown in the figure (not to scale). The rope can sustain a maximum tension of $(2\sqrt{2})\,W$. Which of the following statement(s) is(are) correct?

[JEE Adv 2021, P-2]

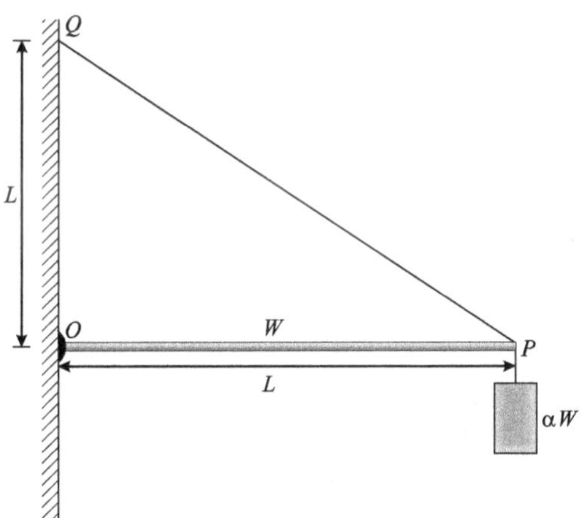

(A) The vertical component of reaction force at O does **not** depend on α

(B) The horizontal component of reaction force at O is equal to W for $\alpha = 0.5$

(C) The tension in the rope is $2W$ for $\alpha = 0.5$

(D) The rope breaks if $\alpha > 1.5$

34. An annular disk of mass M, inner radius a and outer radius b is placed on a horizontal surface with coefficient of friction μ, as shown in the figure. At some time, an impulse $\hat{j}_0 \hat{x}$ is applied at a height h, above the center of the disk. If $h = h_m$ then the disk

rolls without slipping along the x-axis. Which of the following statement(s) is(are) correct?

[JEE Adv 2023, P-2]

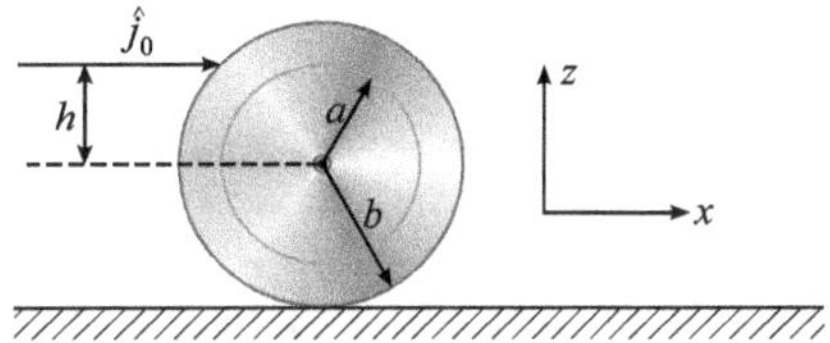

(A) For $\mu \neq 0$ and $a \to 0$, $h_m = b/2$

(B) For $\mu \neq 0$ and $a \to b$, $h_m = b$

(C) For $h = h_m$, the initial angular velocity does not depend on the inner radius a

(D) For $\mu = 0$ and $h = 0$, the wheel always slides without rolling

Assertion Reason based on MCQ

35. STATEMENT-1   **[JEE Adv 2007, P-1]**

In a elastic collision between two bodies, the relative speed of the bodies after collision is equal to the relative speed before the collision.

because

STATEMENT-2

In an elastic collision, the linear momentum of the system is conserved :

(A) Statement-1 is True, Statement-2 is True; Statement-2 is a correct explanation for Statement-1

(B) Statement-1 is True, Statement-2 is True; Statement-2 is **NOT** a correct explanation for Statement-1

(C) Statement-1 is True, Statement-2 is False

(D) Statement-1 is False, Statement-2 is True

36. STATEMENT-1   **[JEE Adv 2007, P-2]**

If there is no external torque on a body about its center of mass, then the velocity of the center of mass remains constant.

because

STATEMENT-2

The linear momentum of an isolated system remains constant.

(A) Statement-1 is True, Statement-2 is True; Statement-2 is a correct explanation for Statement-1

(B) Statement-1 is True, Statement-2 is True; Statement-2 is **NOT** a correct explanation for Statement-1

(C) Statement-1 is True, Statement-2 is False

(D) Statement-1 is False, Statement-2 is True

37. STATEMENT-1   **[JEE Adv 2008, P-1]**

Two cylinders, one hollow (metal) and the other solid (wood) with the same mass and identical dimensions are simultaneously allowed to roll without slipping down an inclined plane from the same height. The hollow cylinder will reach the bottom of the inclined plane first.

because

STATEMENT-2

By the principle of conservation of energy, the total kinetic energies of both the cylinders are identical when they reach the bottom of the incline.

(A) Statement-1 is True, Statement-2 is True; Statement-2 is a correct explanation for Statement-1

(B) Statement-1 is True, Statement-2 is True, Statement-2 is **NOT** a correct explanation for Statement-2

(C) Statement-1 is True, Statement-2 is False

(D) Statement-1 is False, Statement-2 is True

Comprehension based MCQ

Paragraph-1 (Q. No. 38-40)

Two discs A and B are mounted coaxially on a vertical axle. The discs have moments of inertia I and $2I$ respectively about the common axis. Disc A is imparted an initial angular velocity 2ω using the entire potential energy of a spring compressed by a distance x_1. Disc B is imparted an angular velocity ω by a spring having the same spring constant and compressed by a distance x_2. Both the discs rotate in the clockwise direction.

[JEE Adv 2007, P-1]

38. The ratio x_1/x_2 is :

(A) 2

(B) $\dfrac{1}{2}$

(C) $\sqrt{2}$

(D) $\dfrac{1}{\sqrt{2}}$

39. When disc B is brought in contact with disc A, they acquire a common angular velocity in time t. The average frictional torque on one disc by the other during this period is :

(A) $\dfrac{2I\omega}{3t}$

(B) $\dfrac{9I\omega}{2t}$

(C) $\dfrac{9I\omega}{4t}$

(D) $\dfrac{3I\omega}{2t}$

40. The loss of kinetic energy during the above process is :

(A) $\dfrac{I\omega^2}{2}$

(B) $\dfrac{I\omega^2}{3}$

(C) $\dfrac{I\omega^2}{4}$

(D) $\dfrac{I\omega^2}{6}$

Paragraph-2 (Q. No. 41-43)

A small block of mass M moves on a frictionless surface of an inclined plane, as shown in figure. The angle of the incline suddenly changes from 60° to 30° at point B. The block is initially at rest at A. Assume that collisions between the block and the incline are totally inelastic ($g = 10$ m/s^2) : **[JEE Adv 2008, P-1]**

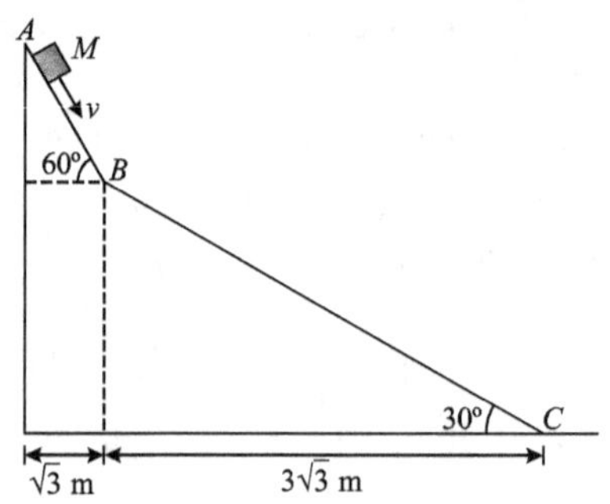

41. The speed of the block at point B immediately after it strikes the second incline is :

(A) $\sqrt{60}$ m/s

(B) $\sqrt{45}$ m/s

(C) $\sqrt{30}$ m/s

(D) $\sqrt{15}$ m/s

42. The speed of the block at point C, immediately before it leaves the second incline is :

(A) $\sqrt{120}$ m/s

(B) $\sqrt{105}$ m/s

(C) $\sqrt{90}$ m/s

(D) $\sqrt{75}$ m/s

43. If collision between the block and the incline is completely elastic, then the vertical (upward) component of the velocity of the block at point B, immediately after it strikes the second incline is :

(A) $\sqrt{30}$ m/s

(B) $\sqrt{15}$ m/s

(C) 0

(D) $-\sqrt{15}$ m/s

Paragraph-3 (Q. No. 44-46)

A uniform thin cylindrical disk of mass M and radius R is attached to two identical massless springs of spring constant k which are fixed to the wall as shown in the figure. The springs are attached to the axle of the disk symmetrically on either side at a distance d from its centre. The axle is massless and both the springs and the axle are in a horizontal plane. The unstretched length of each spring is L. The disk is initially at its equilibrium position with its centre of mass (CM) at a distance L from the wall. The disk rolls without slipping with velocity $\vec{V}_0 = V_0\hat{i}$. The coefficient of friction is μ : **[JEE Adv 2008, P-2]**

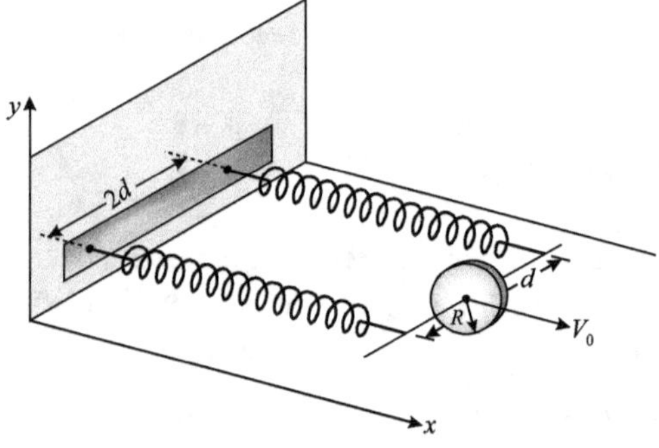

44. The net external force acting on the disk when its centre of mass is at displacement x with respect to its equilibrium position is :

(A) $-kx$

(B) $-2kx$

(C) $-\dfrac{2kx}{3}$

(D) $-\dfrac{4kx}{3}$

45. The centre of mass of the disk undergoes simple harmonic motion with angular frequency ω equal to :

(A) $\sqrt{\dfrac{k}{M}}$

(B) $\sqrt{\dfrac{2k}{M}}$

(C) $\sqrt{\dfrac{2k}{3M}}$

(D) $\sqrt{\dfrac{4k}{3M}}$

46. The maximum value of V_0 for which the disk will roll without slipping is :

(A) $\mu g\sqrt{\dfrac{M}{k}}$

(B) $\mu g\sqrt{\dfrac{M}{2k}}$

(C) $\mu g\sqrt{\dfrac{3M}{k}}$

(D) $\mu g\sqrt{\dfrac{5M}{2k}}$

Paragraph-4 (Q. No. 47-48)

The general motion of a rigid body can be considered to be a combination of (i) a motion of its centre of mass about an axis, and (ii) its motion about an instantaneous axis passing through the centre of mass. These axes need not be stationary. Consider, for example, a thin uniform disc welded (rigidly fixed) horizontally at its rim to a massless stick, as shown in the figure. When the disc-stick system is rotated about the origin on a horizontal frictionless plane with angular speed ω, the motion at any instant can be taken as a combination of (i) a rotation of the centre of mass of the disc about the z-axis, and (ii) a rotation of the disc through an instantaneous vertical axis passing through its centre of mass (as is seen from the changed orientation of points P and Q). Both these motions have the same angular speed ω in this case.

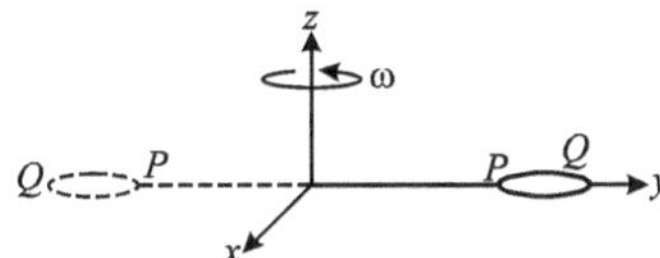

Now consider two similar systems as shown in the figure: Case (a) the disc with its face vertical and parallel to x-z plane; Case (b) the disc with its face making an angle of 45° with x-y plane and its horizontal diameter parallel to x-axis. In both the cases, the disc is welded at point P, and the systems are rotated with constant angular speed ω about the z-axis.

[JEE Adv 2012, P-2]

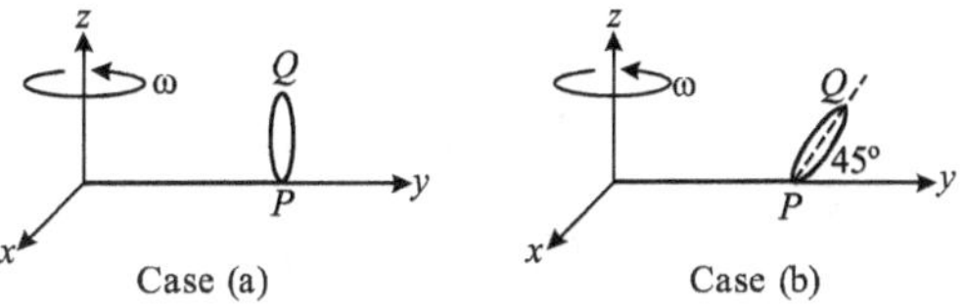

47. Which of the following statements about the instantaneous axis (passing through the centre of mass) is correct :

(A) It is vertical for both the cases (a) and (b)

(B) It is vertical for case (a); and is at 45° to the x-z plane and lies in the plane of the disc for case (b)

(C) It is horizontal for case (a); and is at 45° to the x-z plane and is normal to the plane of the disc for case (b)

(D) It is vertical for case (a); and is at 45° to the x-z plane and is normal to the plane of the disc for case (b)

48. Which of the following statements regarding the angular speed about the instantaneous axis (passing through the centre of mass) is correct :

(A) It is $\sqrt{2}\,\omega$ for the cases

(B) It is ω for case (a); and $\dfrac{\omega}{\sqrt{2}}$ for case (b)

(C) It is ω for case (a); and $\sqrt{2}\,\omega$ for case (b)

(D) It is ω for both the cases

Paragraph-5 (Q. No. 49-50)

A frame of reference that is accelerated with respect to an inertial frame of reference is called a non-inertial frame of reference. A coordinate system fixed on a circular disc rotating about a fixed axis with a constant angular velocity ω is an example of a non-inertial frame of reference. The relationship between the force $\vec{F}_{rot}$ experienced by a particle of mass m moving on the rotating disc and the force $\vec{F}_{in}$ experienced by the particle in an inertial frame of reference is

$$\vec{F}_{rot} = \vec{F}_{in} + 2\,m\,(\vec{v}_{rot} \times \vec{\omega}) + m\,(\vec{\omega} \times \vec{r}) \times \vec{\omega}$$

where $\vec{v}_{rot}$ is the velocity of the particle in the rotating frame of reference and $\vec{r}$ is the position vector of the particle with respect to the centre of the disc.

Now consider a smooth slot along a diameter of a disc of radius R rotating counter-clockwise with a constant angular speed ω about its vertical axis through its center. We assign a coordinate system with the origin at the center of the disc, the x-axis along the slot, the y-axis perpendicular to the slot and the z-axis along the rotation axis ($\vec{\omega} = \omega\,\hat{k}$). A small block of mass m is gently placed in the slot at $\vec{r} = (R/2)\,\hat{i}$ at $t = 0$ and is constrained to move only along the slot. **[JEE Adv 2016, P-2]**

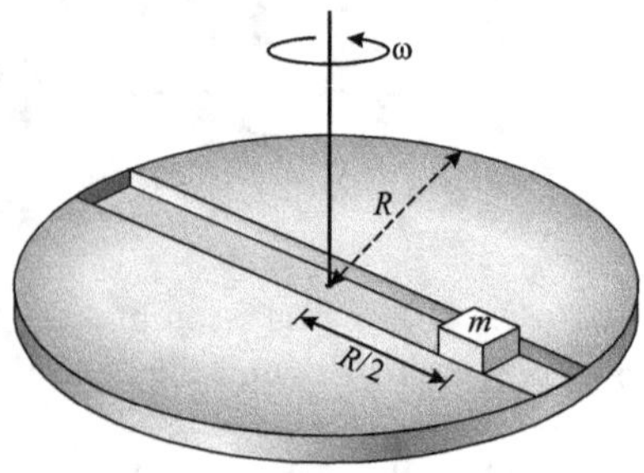

49. The distance r of the block at time t is :

(A) $\dfrac{R}{4}(e^{2\omega t} + e^{-2\omega t})$

(B) $\dfrac{R}{2}\cos 2\,\omega t$

(C) $\dfrac{R}{2}\cos\,\omega t$

(D) $\dfrac{R}{4}(e^{\omega t} + e^{-\omega t})$

50. The net reaction of the disc on the block is :

(A) $-m\omega^2 R\cos\omega t\,\hat{j} - mg\,\hat{j}$

(B) $m\omega^2 R\sin\omega t\,\hat{j} - mg\,\hat{k}$

(C) $\dfrac{1}{2}m\omega^2 R\,(e^{\omega t} - e^{-\omega t})\,\hat{j} + mg\,\hat{k}$

(D) $\dfrac{1}{2}m\omega^2 R\,(e^{2\omega t} - e^{-2\omega t})\,\hat{j} + mg\,\hat{k}$

Paragraph-6 (Q. No. 51-52)

One twirls a circular ring (of mass M and radius R) near the tip of one's finger as shown in Figure-1. In the process the finger never loses contact with the inner rim of the ring. The finger traces out the surface of a cone, shown by the dotted line. The radius of the path traced out by the point where the ring and the finger is in contact is r. The finger rotates with an angular velocity ω_0. The rotating ring rolls without slipping on the outside of a smaller circle described by the point where the ring and the finger is in contact (Figure-2). The coefficient of friction between the ring and the finger is μ and the acceleration due to gravity is g. **[JEE Adv 2017, P-2]**

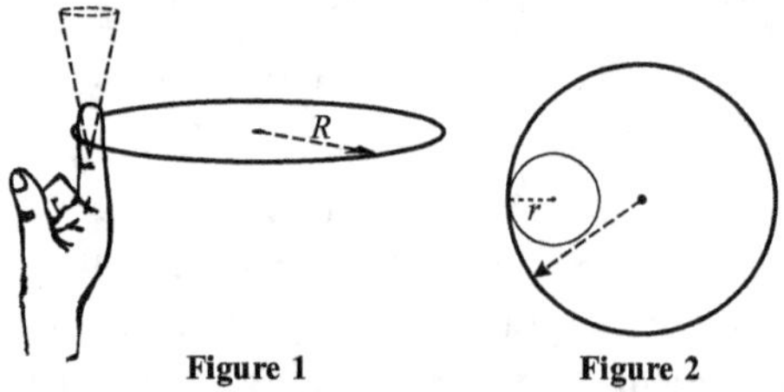

Figure 1   Figure 2

51. The total kinetic energy of the ring is :
(A) $M\omega_0^2 R^2$

(B) $M\omega_0^2(R-r)^2$

(C) $\dfrac{1}{2}M\omega_0^2(R-r)^2$

(D) $\dfrac{3}{2}M\omega_0^2(R-r)^2$

52. The minimum value of ω_0 below which the ring will drop down is :

(A) $\sqrt{\dfrac{3g}{2\mu(R-r)}}$

(B) $\sqrt{\dfrac{g}{\mu(R-r)}}$

(C) $\sqrt{\dfrac{2g}{\mu(R-r)}}$

(D) $\sqrt{\dfrac{g}{2\mu(R-r)}}$

Integer Answer based Questions

53. Three objects A, B and C are kept in a straight line on a frictionless horizontal surface. These have masses m, $2m$ and m respectively. The object A moves towards B with a speed 9 m/s and makes an elastic collision with it. Thereafter, B makes completely inelastic collision with C. All motions occur on the same straight line. Find the final speed (in m/s) of the object C : **[JEE Adv 2009, P-2]**

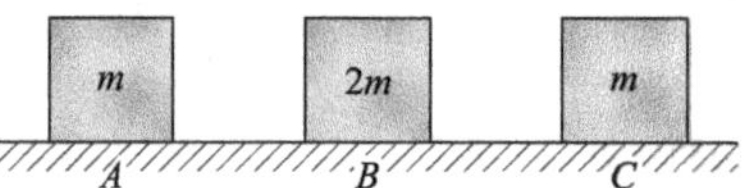

54. A boy is pushing a ring of mass 2 kg and radius 0.5 m with a stick as shown in the figure. The stick applies a force of 2 N on the ring and rolls it without slipping with an acceleration of 0.3 m/s^2. The coefficient of friction between the ground and the ring is large enough that rolling always occurs and the coefficient of friction between the stick and the ring is $(P/10)$. The value of P is ? **[JEE Adv 2011, P-1]**

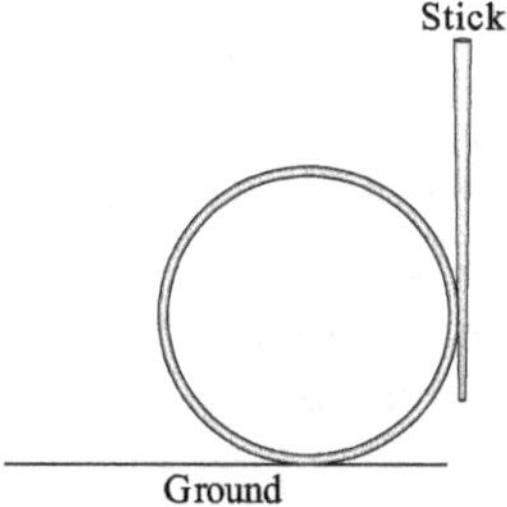

55. Four solid spheres each of diameter $\sqrt{5}$ cm mass 0.5 kg are placed with their centers at the corners of a square of side 4 cm. The moment of inertia of the system about the diagonal of the square is $N \times 10^{-4}$ kg-m^2, then N is ? **[JEE Adv 2011, P-1]**

56. A lamina is made by removing a small disc of diameter $2R$ from a bigger disc of uniform mass density and radius $2R$, as shown in the figure. The moment of inertia of this lamina about axes passing through O and P is I_0 and I_p, respectively. Both these axes are perpendicular to the plane of the lamina. The ratio I_P/I_0 to the nearest integer is : **[JEE Adv 2012, P-1]**

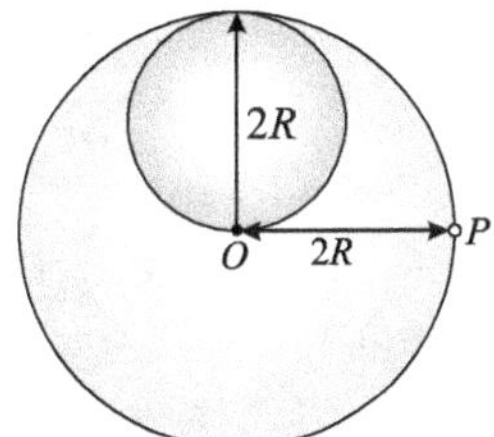

57. A bob of mass m, suspended by a string of length l_1, is given a minimum velocity required to complete a full circle in the vertical plane. At the highest point, it collides elastically with another bob of mass m suspended by a string of length l_2, which is initially at rest. Both the strings are massless and inextensible. If the second bob, after collision acquires the minimum speed required to complete a full circle in the vertical plane, the ratio l_1/l_2 is ? **[JEE Adv 2013, P-1]**

58. A uniform circular disc of mass 50 kg and radius 0.4 m is rotating with an angular velocity of 10 rad s^{-1} about its own axis, which is vertical. Two uniform circular rings, each of mass 6.25 kg and radius 0.2 m, are gently placed symmetrically on the disc in such a manner that they are touching each other along the axis of the disc and are horizontal. Assume that the friction is large enough such that the ring are at rest relative to the disc and the system rotates about the origin axis. The new angular velocity (in rad s^{-1}) of the system is ?

[JEE Adv 2013, P-1]

59. A horizontal circular platform of radius 0.5 m and mass 0.45 kg is free to rotate about its axis. Two massless spring toy-guns, each carrying a steel ball of mass 0.05 kg are attached to the platform at a distance 0.25 m from the centre on its either sides along its diameter (see figure). Each gun simultaneously fires the balls horizontally and perpendicular to the diameter in opposite directions. After leaving the platform, the balls have horizontal speed of 9 ms^{-1} with respect to the ground. The rotational speed of the platform in rads^{-1} after the balls leave the platform is : **[JEE Adv 2014, P-1]**

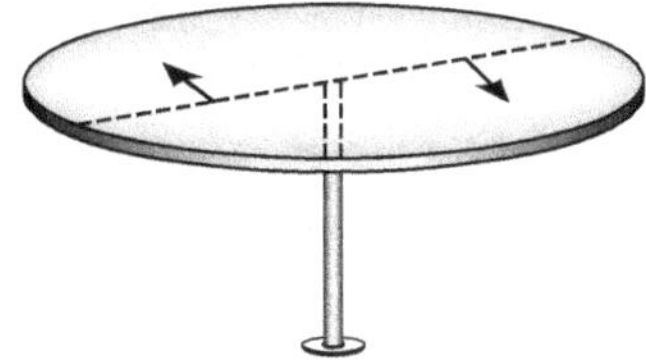

60. A uniform circular disc of mass 1.5 kg and radius 0.5 m is initially at rest on a horizontal frictionless surface. Three forces of equal magnitude $F = 0.5$ N are applied simultaneously along the three sides of an equilateral triangle XYZ with its vertices on

the perimeter of the disc (see figure). One second after applying the forces, the angular speed of the disc in rads^{-1} is ?

[JEE Adv 2014, P-1]

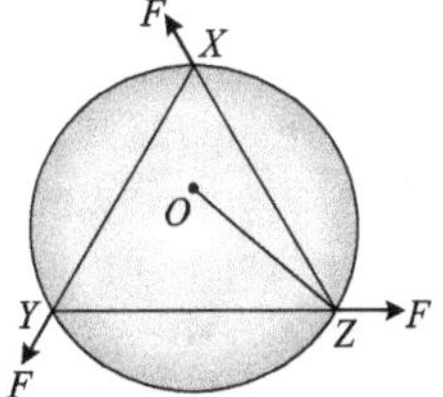

61. Two identical uniform discs roll without slipping on two different surfaces AB and CD (see figure) starting at A and C with linear speeds v_1 and v_2, respectively and always remain in contact with the surfaces. If they reach B and D with the same linear speed and $v_1 = 3$ m/s, then v_2 in m/s is ($g = 10$ m/s^2)

[JEE Adv 2015, P-1]

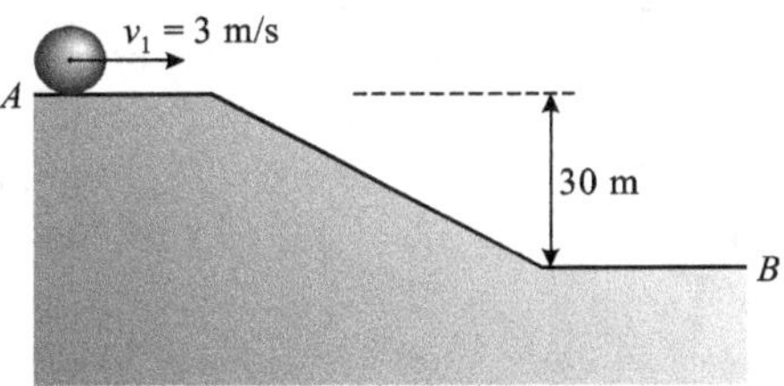

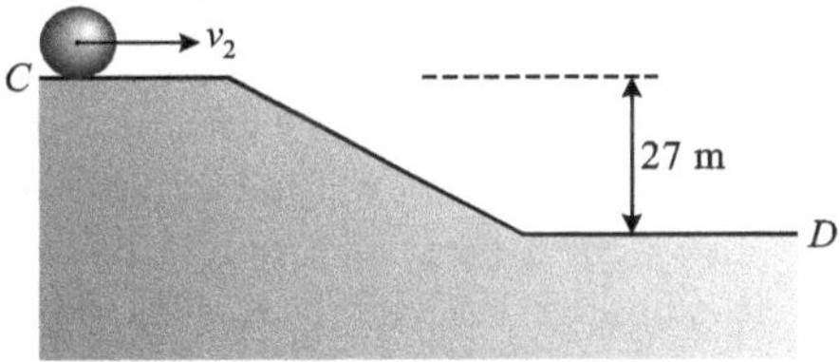

62. The densities of two solid spheres A and B of the same radii R vary with radial distance r as $\rho_A(r) = k\left(\dfrac{r}{R}\right)$ and $\rho_B(r) = k\left(\dfrac{r}{R}\right)^5$, respectively, where k is a constant. The moments of inertia of the individual spheres about axes passing through their centres are I_A and I_B, respectively. If $\dfrac{I_B}{I_A} = \dfrac{n}{10}$, the value of n is ? **[JEE Adv 2015, P-2]**

63. A ring and a disc are initially at rest, side by side, at the top of an inclined plane which makes an angle 60° with the horizontal. They start to roll without slipping at the same instant of time along the shortest path. If the time difference between their reaching the ground is $(2 - \sqrt{3})/\sqrt{10}$ s, then the height of the top of the inclined plane, in meters, is _______ . Take $g = 10$ ms^{-2}.

[JEE Adv 2018, P-1]

64. A spring-block system is resting on a frictionless floor as shown in the figure. The spring constant is 2.0 Nm^{-1} and the mass of the block is 2.0 kg. Ignore the mass of the spring. Initially the spring is in an unstretched condition. Another block of mass 1.0 kg moving with a speed of 2.0 ms^{-1} collides elastically with the first block. The collision is such that the 2.0 kg block does not hit the wall. The distance in metres, between the two blocks when the spring returns to its unstretched position for the first time after the collision is______. **[JEE Adv 2018, P-1]**

65. Put a uniform meter scale horizontally on your extended index fingers with the left one at 0.00 cm and the right one at 90.00 cm. When you attempt to move both the fingers slowly towards the center, initially only the left finger slips with respect to the scale and the right finger does not. After some distance, the left finger stops and the right one starts slipping. Then the right finger stops at a distance x_R from the center (50.00 cm) of the scale and the left one starts slipping again. This happens because of the difference in the frictional forces on the two fingers. If the coefficients of static and dynamic friction between the fingers and the scale are 0.40 and 0.32, respectively, the value of x_R (in cm) is ______. **[JEE Adv 2020, P-1]**

66. A thin rod of mass M and length a is free to rotate in horizontal plane about a fixed vertical axis passing through point O. A thin circular disc of mass M and of radius $a/4$ is pivoted on this rod with its center at a distance $a/4$ from the free end so that it can rotate freely about its vertical axis, as shown in the figure. Assume that both the rod and the disc have uniform density and they remain horizontal during the motion. An outside stationary observer finds the rod rotating with an angular velocity Ω and the disc rotating about its vertical axis with angular velocity 4Ω. The total angular momentum of the system about the point O is $\left(\dfrac{Ma^2\Omega}{48}\right) n$. The value of n is ______.

[JEE Adv 2021, P-1]

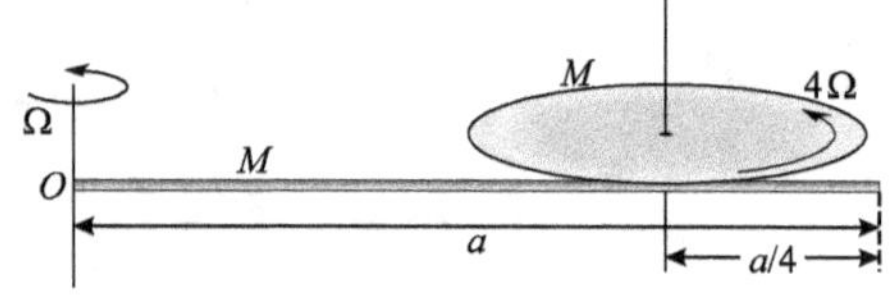

67. At time $t = 0$, a disk of radius 1 m starts to roll without slipping on a horizontal plane with an angular acceleration of $\alpha = \dfrac{2}{3}$ rad s^{-2}. A small stone is stuck to the disk. At $t = 0$, it is at the contact point of the disk and the plane. Later, at time $t = \sqrt{\pi}s$, the stone detaches itself and flies off tangentially from the disk. The maximum height (in m) reached by the stone measured from the plane is $\dfrac{1}{2} + \dfrac{x}{10}$. The value of x is ______.

[Take $g = 10$ ms^{-2}]   **[JEE Adv 2022, P-1]**

68. A solid sphere of mass 1 kg and radius 1 m rolls without slipping on a fixed inclined plane with an angle of inclination $\theta = 30°$ from the horizontal. Two forces of magnitude 1 N each, parallel to the incline, act on the sphere, both at distance $r = 0.5$ m from the center of the sphere, as shown in the figure. The acceleration of the sphere down the plane is ______ ms^{-2}. (Take $g = 10$ ms^{-2})   **[JEE Adv 2022, P-1]**

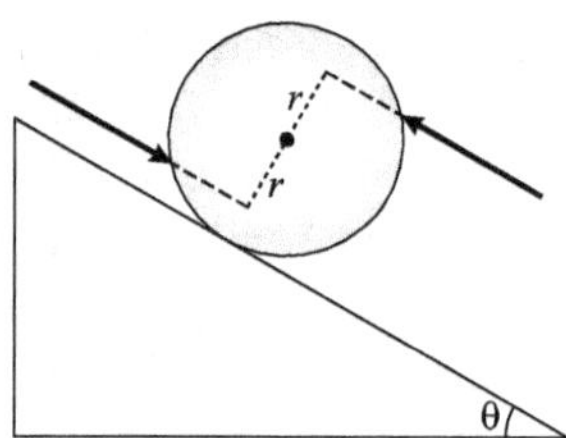

69. A thin circular coin of mass 5 gm and radius 4/3 cm is initially in a horizontal xy-plane. The coin is tossed vertically up (+z direction) by applying an impulse of $\sqrt{\dfrac{\pi}{2}} \times 10^{-2}$ N-s at a distance 2/3 cm from its center. The coin spins about its diameter and moves along the +z direction. By the time the coin reaches back to its initial position, it completes n rotations. The value of n is______.   **[JEE Adv 2023, P-2]**
[Given: The acceleration due to gravity $g = 10$ m s^{-2}]

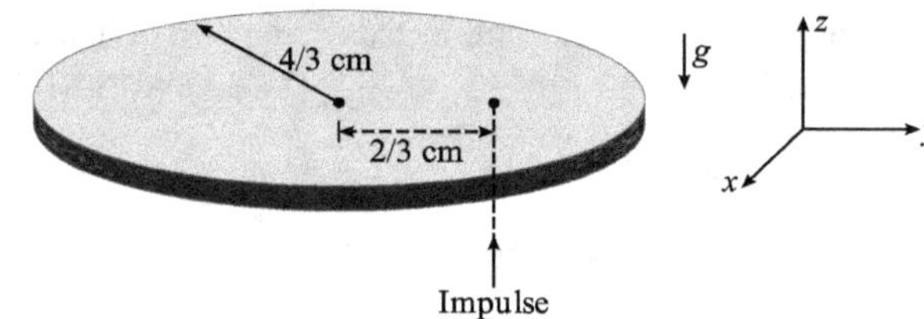

* * * * *

GRAVITATION

MCQ with Single Option Correct

1. A spherically symmetric gravitational system of particles

has a mass density $\rho = \begin{cases} \rho_0 & \text{for} \quad r \le R \\ 0 & \text{for} \quad r > R \end{cases}$ where ρ_0 is a

constant. A test mass can undergo circular motion under the influence of the gravitational field of particles. Its speed V as a function of distance r ($0 < r < \infty$) from the centre of the system is represented by : **[JEE Adv 2008, P-1]**

(A) 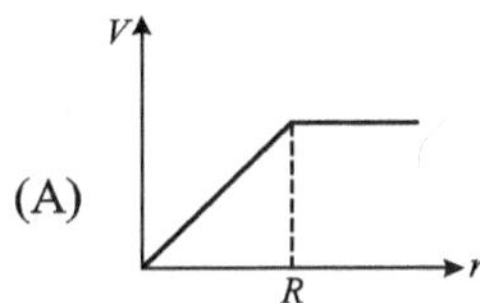

(B) 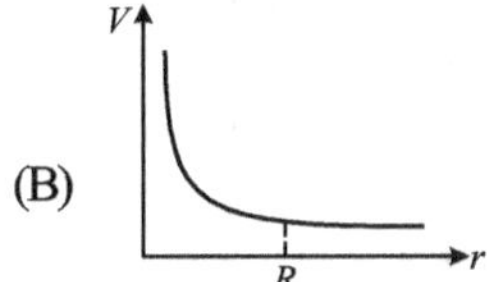

(C) 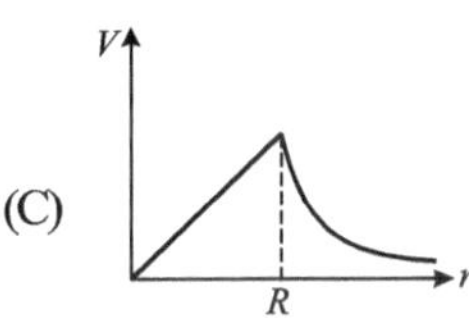

(D) 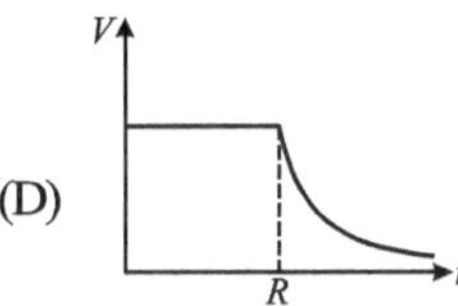

2. A thin uniform annular disc (sec figure) of mass M has outer radius $4R$ and inner radius $3R$. The work required to take a unit mass from point P on its axis to infinity is :

[JEE Adv 2010, P-1]

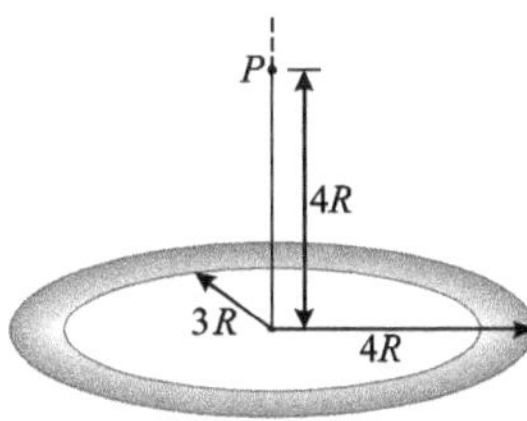

(A) $\dfrac{2GM}{7R}(4\sqrt{2}-5)$

(B) $-\dfrac{2GM}{7R}(4\sqrt{2}-5)$

(C) $\dfrac{GM}{4R}$

(D) $\dfrac{2GM}{5R}(\sqrt{2}-1)$

3. A satellite is moving with a constant speed V in a circular orbit about the earth. An object of mass m is ejected from the satellite such that it just escapes from the gravitational pull of the earth. At the time of its ejection, the kinetic energy of the object is : **[JEE Adv 2011, P-2]**

(A) $\dfrac{1}{2}mV^2$

(B) mV^2

(C) $\dfrac{3}{2}mV^2$

(D) $2mV^2$

4. A planet of radius $R = 1/10 \times$ (radius of Earth) has the same mass density as Earth. Scientists dig a well of depth $R/5$ on it and lower a wire of the same length and of linear mass density 10^{-3} kgm^{-1} into it. If the wire is not touching anywhere, the force applied at the top of the wire by a person holding it in place is (take the radius of Earth $= 6 \times 10^6$ m and the acceleration due to gravity on Earth is 10 ms^{-2}) : **[JEE Adv 2014, P-2]**

(A) 96 N

(B) 108 N

(C) 120 N

(D) 150 N

5. A rocket is launched normal to the surface of the Earth, away from the Sun, along the line joining the Sun and the Earth. The Sun is 3×10^5 times heavier than the Earth and is at a distance 2.5×10^4 times larger than the radius of the Earth. The escape velocity from Earth's gravitational field is $v_e = 11.2$ km s^{-1}. The minimum initial velocity (v_s) required for the rocket to be able to leave the Sun-Earth system is closest to : (Ignore the rotation and revolution of the Earth and the presence of any other planet) **[JEE Adv 2017, P-2]**

(A) $v_s = 22$ km s^{-1}

(B) $v_s = 72$ km s^{-1}

(C) $v_s = 42$ km s^{-1}

(D) $v_s = 62$ km s^{-1}

6. Consider an expanding sphere of instantaneous radius R whose total mass remains constant. The expansion is such that the instantaneous density ρ remains uniform throughout the volume. The rate of fractional change in density $\left(\dfrac{1}{\rho}\dfrac{d\rho}{dt}\right)$ is constant. The velocity v of any point on the surface of the expanding sphere is proportional to : **[JEE Adv 2017, P-2]**

(A) R^3

(B) $\dfrac{1}{R}$

(C) R

(D) $R^{2/3}$

7. Consider a spherical gaseous cloud of mass density $\rho(r)$ in free space where r is the radial distance from its center. The gaseous cloud is made of particles of equal mass m moving in circular orbits about the common center with the same kinetic energy K. The force acting on the particles is their mutual gravitational force. If $\rho(r)$ is constant in time, the particle

number density $n(r) = \rho(r)/m$ is :   **[JEE Adv 2019, P-1s]**
[G is universal gravitational constant]

(A) $\dfrac{K}{\pi r^2 m^2 G}$ (B) $\dfrac{K}{6\pi r^2 m^2 G}$

(C) $\dfrac{3K}{\pi r^2 m^2 G}$ (D) $\dfrac{K}{2\pi r^2 m^2 G}$

8. Two satellites P and Q are moving in different circular orbits around the Earth (radius R). The heights of P and Q from the Earth surface are h_P and h_Q, respectively, where $h_P = R/3$. The accelerations of P and Q due to Earth's gravity are g_P and g_Q, respectively. If $g_P/g_Q = 36/25$, what is the value of h_Q?

    [JEE Adv 2023, P-1]

(A) $3R/5$ (B) $R/6$
(C) $6R/5$ (D) $5R/6$

MCQ with One or More than One Options Correct

9. Two spherical planets P and Q have the same uniform density ρ, masses M_P and M_Q, and surface areas A and $4A$, respectively. A spherical planet R also has uniform density ρ and its mass is $(M_P + M_Q)$. The escape velocities from the planets P, Q and R, are V_P, V_Q and V_R, respectively. Then :

    [JEE Adv 2012, P-2]

(A) $V_Q > V_R > V_P$ (B) $V_R > V_Q > V_P$
(C) $V_R / V_P = 3$ (D) $V_P / V_Q = 1/2$

10. Two bodies, each of mass M, are kept fixed with a separation $2L$. A particle of mass m is projected from the midpoint of the line joining their centres, perpendicular to the line. The gravitational constant is G. The correct statement(s) is (are) :   **[JEE Adv 2013, P-2]**

(A) The minimum initial velocity of the mass m to escape the gravitational field of the two bodies is $4\sqrt{\dfrac{GM}{L}}$

(B) The minimum initial velocity of the mass m to escape the gravitational field of the two bodies is $2\sqrt{\dfrac{GM}{L}}$

(C) The minimum initial velocity of the mass m to escape the gravitational field of the two bodies is $\sqrt{\dfrac{GM}{L}}$

(D) The energy of the mass m remains constant

Assertion Reason based on MCQ

11. STATEMENT-1   **[JEE Adv 2008, P-1]**
An astronaut in an orbiting space station above the Earth experiences weightlessness.

because

STATEMENT-2
An object moving around the Earth under the influence of Earth's gravitational force is in a state of 'free-fall',
(A) Statement-1 is True, Statement-2 is True; Statement-2 is a correct explanation for Statement-1
(B) Statement-1 is True, Statement-2 is True, Statement-2 is **NOT** a correct explanation for Statement-2
(C) Statement-1 is True, Statement-2 is False
(D) Statement-1 is False, Statement-2 is True

Matrix Match MCQ

12. A planet of mass M, has two natural satellites with masses m_1 and m_2. The radii of their circular orbits are R_1 and R_2 respectively. Ignore the gravitational force between the satellites. Define v_1, L_1, K_1 and T_1 to be, respectively, the orbital speed, angular momentum, kinetic energy and time period of revolution of satellite 1; and v_2, L_2, K_2 and T_2 to be the corresponding quantities of satellite 2. Given $m_1/m_2 = 2$ and $R_1/R_2 = 1/4$, match the ratios in **Column-I** to the numbers in **Column-II**.   **[JEE Adv 2018, P-2]**

Column-I	Column-II
P. $\dfrac{v_1}{v_2}$	**1.** $\dfrac{1}{8}$
Q. $\dfrac{L_1}{L_2}$	**2.** 1
R. $\dfrac{K_1}{K_2}$	**3.** 2
S. $\dfrac{T_1}{T_2}$	**4.** 8

(A) $P \to 4 ; Q \to 2 ; R \to 1 ; S \to 3$
(B) $P \to 3 ; Q \to 2 ; R \to 4 ; S \to 1$
(C) $P \to 2 ; Q \to 3 ; R \to 1 ; S \to 4$
(D) $P \to 2 ; Q \to 3 ; R \to 4 ; S \to 1$

Integer Answer based Questions

13. A binary star consists of two stars A (mass $2.2\,M_S$) and B (mass $11\,M_S$), where M_S is the mass of the sun. They are separated by distance d and are rotating about their centre of mass, which is stationary. The ratio of the total angular momentum to that of star B about the centre of mass is ?

    [JEE Adv 2010, P-1]

14. Gravitational acceleration on the surface of a planet is $\dfrac{\sqrt{6}}{11} g$, where g is the gravitational acceleration on the surface of the earth. The average mass density of the planet is 2/3 times that of the earth. If the escape speed on the surface of the earth is taken to be 11 kms^{-1}, the escape speed on the surface of the planet in kms^{-1} will be ?   **[JEE Adv 2010, P-1]**

15. A bullet is fired vertically upwards with velocity v from the surface of a spherical planet. When it reaches its maximum height, its acceleration due to the planet's gravity is $1/4^{th}$ of its value at the surface of the planet. If the escape velocity from the planet is $v_{esc} = v\sqrt{N}$, then the value of N is (ignore energy loss due to atmosphere) : **[JEE Adv 2015, P-1]**

16. A large spherical mass M is fixed at one position and two identical point masses m are kept on a line passing through the centre of M (see figure). The point masses are connected by a rigid massless rod of length l and this assembly is free to move along the line connecting them. All three masses interact only through their mutual gravitational interaction. When the point mass nearer to M is at a distance $r = 3l$ from M, the tension in the rod is zero for $m = k\left(\dfrac{M}{288}\right)$. The value of k is :

[JEE Adv 2015, P-2]

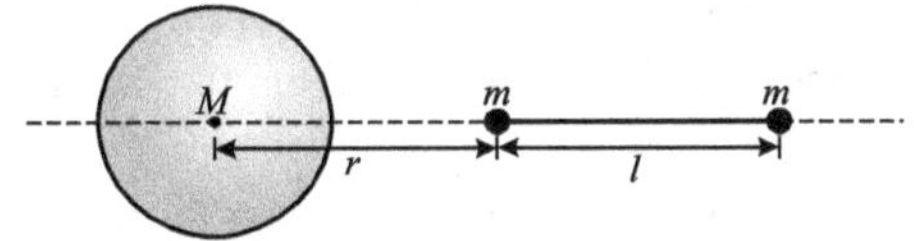

17. The distance between two stars of masses $3M_S$ and $6M_S$ is $9R$. Here R is the mean distance between the centers of the Earth and the Sun, and M_S is the mass of the Sun. The two stars orbit around their common center of mass in circular orbits with period nT, where T is the period of Earth's revolution around the Sun. The value of n is ______. **[JEE Adv 2021, P-2]**

18. Two spherical stars A and B have densities ρ_A and ρ_B, respectively. A and B have the same radius, and their masses M_A and M_B are related by $M_B = 2M_A$. Due to an interaction process, star A loses some of its mass, so that its radius is halved, while its spherical shape is retained, and its density remains ρ_A. The entire mass lost by A is deposited as a thick spherical shell on B with the density of the shell being ρ_A. If v_A and v_B are the escape velocities from A and B after the interaction process, the ratio $\dfrac{v_B}{v_A} = \sqrt{\dfrac{10n}{15^{1/3}}}$. The value of n is ______.

[JEE Adv 2022, P-1]

* * * * *

MCQ with Single Option Correct

1. One end of a horizontal thick copper wire of length $2L$ and radius $2R$ is welded to an end of another horizontal thin copper wire of length L and radius R. When the arrangement is stretched by applying forces at two ends, the ratio of the elongation in the thin wire to that in the thick wire is : **[JEE Adv 2013, P-1]**
(A) 0.25   (B) 0.50
(C) 2.00   (D) 4.00

MCQ with One or More than One Options Correct

2. In plotting stress versus strain curves for two materials P and Q, a student by mistake puts strain on the y-axis and stress on the x-axis as shown in the figure. Then the correct statement(s) is(are) **[JEE Adv 2015, P-2]**

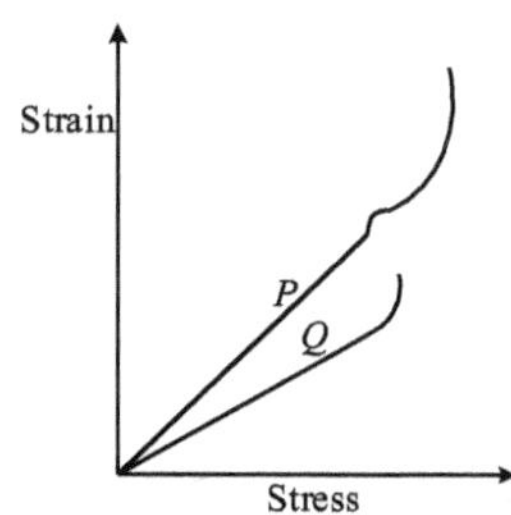

(A) P has more tensile strength than Q
(B) P is more ductile than Q
(C) P is more brittle than Q
(D) The Young's modulus of P is more than that of Q

Integer Answer based Questions

3. A 0.1 kg mass is suspended from a wire of negligible mass. The length of the wire is 1 m and its cross-sectional area is 4.9×10^{-7} m^2. If the mass is pulled a little in the vertically downward direction and released, it performs simple harmonic motion of angular frequency 140 rad s^{-1}. If the Young's modulus of the material of the wire is $n \times 10^9$ Nm^{-2}, the value of n is ?
[JEE Adv 2010, P-1]

4. Steel wire of length L at 40°C is suspended from the ceiling and then a mass m is hung from its free end. The wire is cooled down from 40°C to 30°C to regain its original length L. The coefficient of linear thermal expansion of the steel is 10^{-5}/°C, Young's modulus of steel is 10^{11} N/m^2 and radius of the wire is 1 mm. Assume that $L >>$ diameter of the wire. Then the value of m in kg is nearly ? **[JEE Adv 2011, P-1]**

5. A block of weight 100 N is suspended by copper and steel wires of same cross sectional area 0.5 cm^2 and, length $\sqrt{3}$m and 1 m, respectively. Their other ends are fixed on a ceiling as shown in figure. The angles subtended by copper and steel wires with ceiling are 30° and 60°, respectively. If elongation in copper wire is (Δl_C) and elongation in steel wire is (Δl_S), then the ratio $\dfrac{\Delta l_C}{\Delta l_S}$ is _______ ? **[JEE Adv 2019, P-1]**
[Young's modulus for copper and steel are 1×10^{11} N/m^2 and 2×10^{11} N/m^2 respectively]

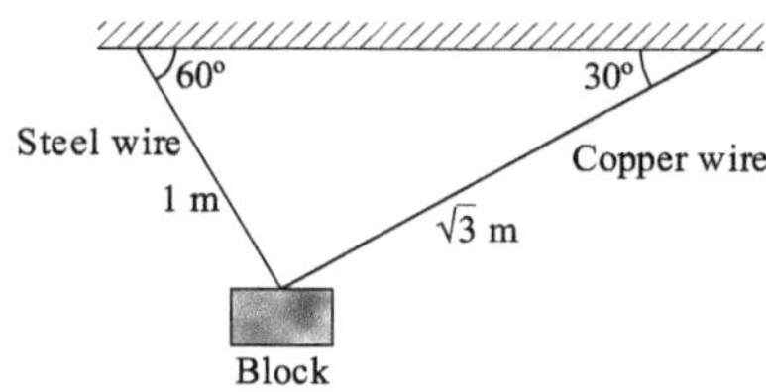

6. A cubical solid aluminium (bulk modulus $= -V\dfrac{dP}{dV} = 70$ (GPa) block has an edge length of 1 m on the surface of the earth. It is kept on the floor of a 5 km deep ocean. Taking the average density of water and the acceleration due to gravity to be 10^3 kg m^{-3} and 10 ms^{-2}, respectively, the change in the edge length of the block in mm is_______. **[JEE Adv 2020, P-2]**

*   *   *   *   *

MECHANICAL PROPERTIES OF FLUIDS

MCQ with Single Option Correct

1. Water is up to a height h in a beaker of radius R as shown in the figure. The density of water is ρ, the surface tension of water is T and the atmospheric pressure is P_0. Consider a vertical section $ABCD$ of the water column through a diameter of the beaker. The force on water on one side of this section by water on the other side of this section has magnitude :

[JEE Adv 2007, P-2]

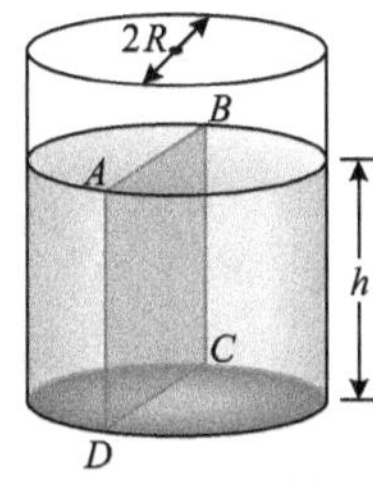

(A) $|2P_0Rh + \pi R^2\rho gh - 2RT|$ (B) $|2P_0Rh + R\rho gh^2 - 2RT|$
(C) $|P_0\pi R^2 + R\rho gh^2 - 2RT|$ (D) $|P_0\pi R^2 + R\rho gh^2 + 2RT|$

2. A glass tube of uniform internal radius (r) has a valve separating the two identical ends. Initially, the valve is in a tightly closed position. End 1 has a hemispherical soap bubble of radius r. End 2 has sub-hemispherical soap bubble as shown in figure. Just after opening the value :   **[JEE Adv 2008, P-2]**

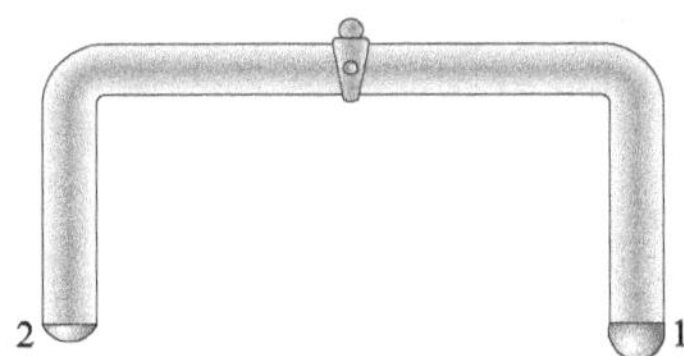

(A) Air from end 1 flows towards end 2. No change in the volume of the soap bubbles
(B) Air from end 1 flows towards end 2. Volume of the soap bubble at end 1 decreases
(C) No change occurs
(D) Air from end 2 flows towards end 1. Volume of the soap bubble at end 1 increases

3. A thin uniform cylindrical shell, closed at both ends, is partially filled with water. It is floating vertically in water in half-submerged state. If ρ_c is the relative density of the material of the shell with respect to water, then the correct statement is that the shell is :   **[JEE Adv 2012, P-2]**

(A) More than half-filled if ρ_c is less than 0.5
(B) More than half-filled if ρ_c is less than 1.0
(C) Half-filled if ρ_c is more than 0.5
(D) Less than half-filled if ρ_c is less than 0.5

4. A glass capillary tube is of the shape of a truncated cone with an apex angle α so that its two ends have cross sections of different radii. When dipped in water vertically, water rises in it to a height h, where the radius of its cross section is b. If the surface tension of water is S, its density is ρ, and its contact angle with glass is θ, the value of h will be (g is the acceleration due to gravity) :   **[JEE Adv 2014, P-2]**

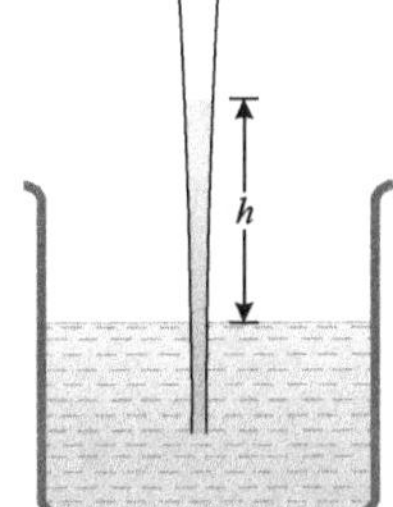

(A) $\dfrac{2S}{b\rho g}\cos(\theta-\alpha)$ (B) $\dfrac{2S}{b\rho g}\cos(\theta+\alpha)$

(C) $\dfrac{2S}{b\rho g}\cos(\theta-\alpha/2)$ (D) $\dfrac{2S}{b\rho g}\cos(\theta+\alpha/2)$

5. An open-ended U-tube of uniform cross-sectional area contains water (density 10^3 kg m^{-3}). Initially the water level stands at 0.29 m from the bottom in each arm. Kerosene oil (a water-immiscible liquid) of density 800 kg m^{-3} is added to the left arm until its length is 0.1 m, as shown in the schematic figure below. The ratio $\left(\dfrac{h_1}{h_2}\right)$ of the heights of the liquid in the two arms is :   **[JEE Adv 2020, P-1]**

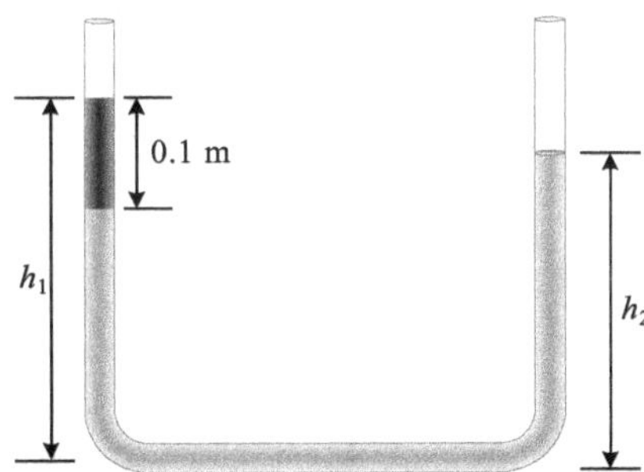

(A) $\dfrac{15}{14}$

(B) $\dfrac{35}{33}$

(C) $\dfrac{7}{6}$

(D) $\dfrac{5}{4}$

MCQ with One or More than One Options Correct

6. Two solid sphere A and B of equal volumes but of different densities d_A and d_B are connected by a string. They are fully immersed in a fluid of density d_F. They get arranged into an equilibrium state as shown in the figure with a tension in the string. The arrangement is possible only if :

[JEE Adv 2011, P-2]

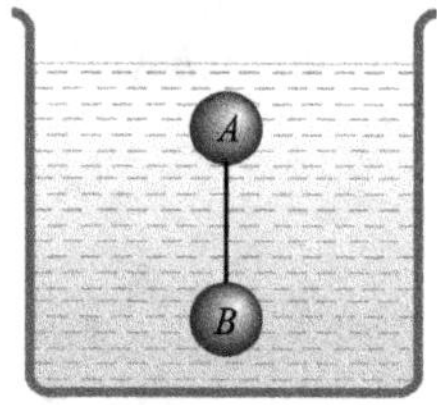

(A) $d_A < d_F$

(B) $d_B > d_F$

(C) $d_A > d_F$

(D) $d_A + d_B = 2\, d_F$

7. A solid sphere of radius R and density ρ is attached to one end of a mass-less spring of force constant k. The other end of the spring is connected to another solid sphere of radius R and density 3ρ. The complete arrangement is placed in a liquid of density 2ρ and is allowed to reach equilibrium. The correct statement(s) is are : **[JEE Adv 2013, P-1]**

(A) The net elongation of the spring is $\dfrac{4\pi R^3 \rho g}{3k}$

(B) The net elongation of the spring is $\dfrac{8\pi R^3 \rho g}{3k}$

(C) The light sphere is partially submerged

(D) The light sphere is completely submerged

8. A spherical body of radius R consists of a fluid of constant density and is in equilibrium under its own gravity. If $P(r)$ is the pressure at $r (r < R)$, then the correct option(s) is(are) :

[JEE Adv 2015, P-2]

(A) $P(r=0)=0$

(B) $\dfrac{P(r=3R/4)}{P(r=2R/3)} = \dfrac{63}{80}$

(C) $\dfrac{P(r=3R/5)}{P(r=2R/5)} = \dfrac{16}{21}$

(D) $\dfrac{P(r=R/2)}{P(r=R/3)} = \dfrac{20}{27}$

9. Two spheres P and Q of equal radii have densities ρ_1 and ρ_2, respectively. The spheres are connected by a massless string and placed in liquids L_1 and L_2 of densities σ_1 and σ_2 and viscosities η_1 and η_2, respectively. They float in equilibrium with the sphere P in L_1 and sphere Q in L_2 and the string being taut (see figure). If sphere P alone in L_2 has terminal velocity $\vec{V}_P$ and Q alone in L_1 has terminal velocity $\vec{V}_Q$, then :

[JEE Adv 2015, P-2]

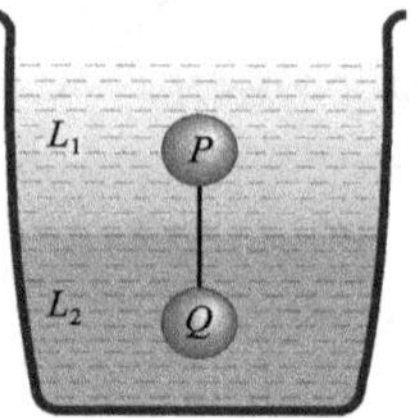

(A) $\dfrac{|\vec{V}_P|}{|\vec{V}_Q|} = \dfrac{\eta_1}{\eta_2}$

(B) $\dfrac{|\vec{V}_P|}{|\vec{V}_Q|} = \dfrac{\eta_2}{\eta_1}$

(C) $\vec{V}_P \cdot \vec{V}_Q > 0$

(D) $\vec{V}_P \cdot \vec{V}_Q < 0$

10. A uniform capillary tube of inner radius r is dipped vertically into a beaker filled with water. The water rises to a height h in the capillary tube above the water surface in the beaker. The surface tension of water is σ. The angle of contact between water and the wall of the capillary tube is θ. Ignore the mass of water in the meniscus. Which of the following statements is (are) true? **[JEE Adv 2018, P-1]**

(A) For a given material of the capillary tube, h decreases with increase in r

(B) For a given material of the capillary tube, h is independent of σ

(C) If this experiment is performed in a lift going up with a constant acceleration, then h decreases

(D) h is proportional to contact angle θ

11. Consider a thin square plate floating on a viscous liquid in a large tank. The height h of the liquid in the tank is much less than the width of the tank. The floating plate is pulled horizontally with a constant velocity u_0. Which of the following statements is (are) true ? **[JEE Adv 2018, P-2]**

(A) The resistive force of liquid on the plate is inversely proportional to h

(B) The resistive force of liquid on the plate is independent of the area of the plate

(C) The tangential (shear) stress on the floor of the tank increases with u_0

(D) The tangential (shear) stress on the plate varies linearly with the viscosity η of the liquid

12. A cylindrical capillary tube of 0.2 mm radius is made by joining two capillaries T1 and T2 of different materials having water contact angles of 0° and 60°, respectively. The capillary

tube is dipped vertically in water in two different configurations, case I and II as shown in figure. Which of the following option(s) is(are) correct ?
(Surface tension of water = 0.075 N/m, density of water = 1000 kg/m^3, take g = 10 m/s^2)   **[JEE Adv 2019, P-1]**

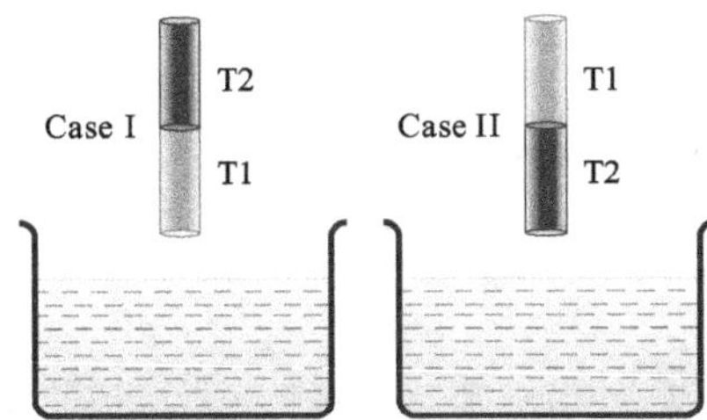

(A) The correction in the height of water column raised in the tube, due to weight of water contained in the meniscus, will be different for both cases.
(B) For case I, if the capillary joint is 5 cm above the water surface, the height of water column raised in the tube will be more than 8.75 cm. (Neglect the weight of the water in the meniscus)
(C) For case I, if the joint is kept at 8 cm above the water surface, the height of water column in the tube will be 7.5 cm. (Neglect the weight of the water in the meniscus)
(D) For case II, if the capillary joint is 5 cm above the water surface, the height of water column raised in the tube will be 3.75 cm. (Neglect the weight of the water in the meniscus)

13. A cylindrical tube, with its base as shown in the figure, is filled with water. It is moving down with a constant acceleration a along a fixed inclined plane with angle $\theta = 45°$. P_1 and P_2 are pressures at points 1 and 2, respectively, located at the base of the tube. Let $\beta = (P_1 - P_2)/(\rho g d)$, where ρ is density of water, d is the inner diameter of the tube and g is the acceleration due to gravity. Which of the following statement(s) is(are) correct?
                                     [JEE Adv 2021, P-1]

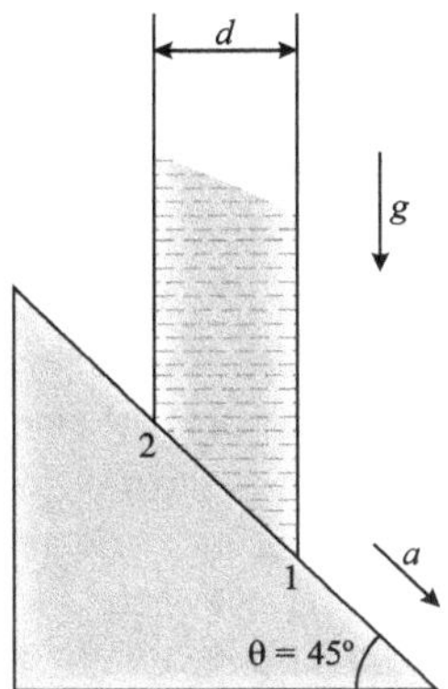

(A) $\beta = 0$ when $a = g/\sqrt{2}$ (B) $\beta > 0$ when $a = g/\sqrt{2}$
(C) $\beta = \dfrac{\sqrt{2}-1}{\sqrt{2}}$ when $a = g/2$ (D) $\beta = \dfrac{1}{\sqrt{2}}$ when $a = g/2$

14. A bubble has surface tension S. The ideal gas inside the bubble has ratio of specific heats $\gamma = \dfrac{5}{3}$. The bubble is exposed to the atmosphere and it always retains its spherical shape. When the atmospheric pressure is P_{a1}, the radius of the bubble is found to be r_1 and the temperature of the enclosed gas is T_1. When the atmospheric pressure is P_{a2}, the radius of the bubble and the temperature of the enclosed gas are r_2 and T_2, respectively. Which of the following statement(s) is (are) correct ?   **[JEE Adv 2022, P-2]**
(A) If the surface of the bubble is a perfect heat insulator then

$$\left(\frac{r_1}{r_2}\right)^5 = \frac{P_{a2} + \dfrac{2S}{r_2}}{P_{a1} + \dfrac{2S}{r_1}}$$

(B) If the surface of the bubble is a perfect heat insulator, then the total internal energy of the bubble including its surface energy does not change with the external atmospheric pressure.
(C) If the surface of the bubble is a perfect heat conductor and the change in atmospheric temperature is negligible, then

$$\left(\frac{r_1}{r_2}\right)^3 = \frac{P_{a2} + \dfrac{4S}{r_2}}{P_{a1} + \dfrac{4S}{r_1}}$$

(D) If the surface of the bubble is a perfect heat insulator, then

$$\left(\frac{T_2}{T_1}\right)^{5/2} = \frac{P_{a2} + \dfrac{4S}{r_2}}{P_{a1} + \dfrac{4S}{r_1}}$$

Assertion Reason based on MCQ

15. STATEMENT-1   **[JEE Adv 2008, P-1]**
The stream of water flowing at high speed from a garden hose pipe tends to spread like a fountain when held vertically up, but tends to narrow down when held vertically down.

because

STATEMENT-2
In any steady flow of an incompressible fluid, the volume flow rate of the fluid remains constant.
(A) Statement-1 is True, Statement-2 is True; Statement-2 is a correct explanation for Statement-1
(B) Statement-1 is True, Statement-2 is True, Statement-2 is **NOT** a correct explanation for Statement-2
(C) Statement-1 is True, Statement-2 is False
(D) Statement-1 is False, Statement-2 is True

Matrix Match MCQ

16. A person in a lift is holding a water jar, which has a small hole at the lower end of its side. When the lift is at rest, the water jet coming out of the hole hits the floor of the lift at a distance of 1.2 m from the person. In the following, state of the lift's motion is given in **Column-I** and the distance where the water jet hits the floor of the lift is given in **Column-II**. Match the statements from **Column-I** with those in **Column-II** and select the correct answer using the code given below the list.

[JEE Adv 2014, P-2]

Column-I		Column-II	
(P)	Lift is accelerating vertically up.	(1)	$d = 1.2$ m
(Q)	Lift is accelerating vertically down with an acceleration less than the gravitational acceleration.	(2)	$d > 1.2$ m
(R)	Lift is moving vertically up with constant speed.	(3)	$d < 1.2$ m
(S)	Lift is falling freely.	(4)	No water leaks out of the jar.

Code :

(A) $P \rightarrow 2, Q \rightarrow 3, R \rightarrow 2, S \rightarrow 4$

(B) $P \rightarrow 2, Q \rightarrow 3, R \rightarrow 1, S \rightarrow 4$

(C) $P \rightarrow 1, Q \rightarrow 1, R \rightarrow 1, S \rightarrow 4$

(D) $P \rightarrow 2, Q \rightarrow 3, R \rightarrow 1, S \rightarrow 1$

Comprehension based MCQ

Paragraph-1 (Q. No. 17-19)

A fixed thermally conducting cylinder has a radius R and height L_0. The cylinder is open at its bottom and has a small hole at its top. A piston of mass M is held at a distance L from the top surface, as shown in the figure. The atmospheric pressure is P_0.

[JEE Adv 2007, P-1]

17. The piston is now pulled out slowly and held at a distance $2L$ from the top. The pressure in cylinder between its top and the piston will then be :

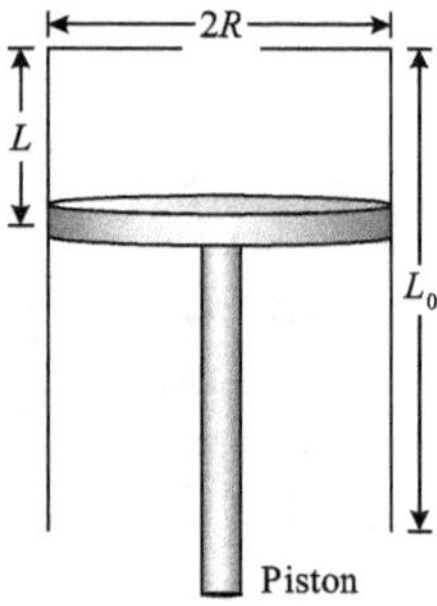

(A) P_0

(B) $\dfrac{P_0}{2} + \dfrac{Mg}{\pi R^2}$

(C) $\dfrac{P_0}{2}$

(D) $\dfrac{P_0}{2} - \dfrac{Mg}{\pi R^2}$

18. While the piston is at a distance $2L$ from the top, the hole at the top is sealed. The piston is then released, to a position where it can stay in equilibrium. In this condition, then distance of the piston from the top is :

(A) $\left(\dfrac{2P_0 \pi R^2}{\pi R^2 P_0 + Mg}\right)(2L)$

(B) $\left(\dfrac{P_0 \pi R^2 - Mg}{\pi R^2 P_0}\right)(2L)$

(C) $\left(\dfrac{P_0 \pi R^2 + Mg}{\pi R^2 P_0}\right)(2L)$

(D) $\left(\dfrac{P_0 \pi R^2}{\pi R^2 P_0 - Mg}\right)(2L)$

19. The piston is taken completely out of the cylinder. The hole at the top is sealed. A water tank is brought below the cylinder and put in a position so that the water surface in the tank is at the same level as the top of the cylinder as shown in the figure. The density of the water is ρ. In equilibrium, the height H of the water column in the cylinder satisfies :

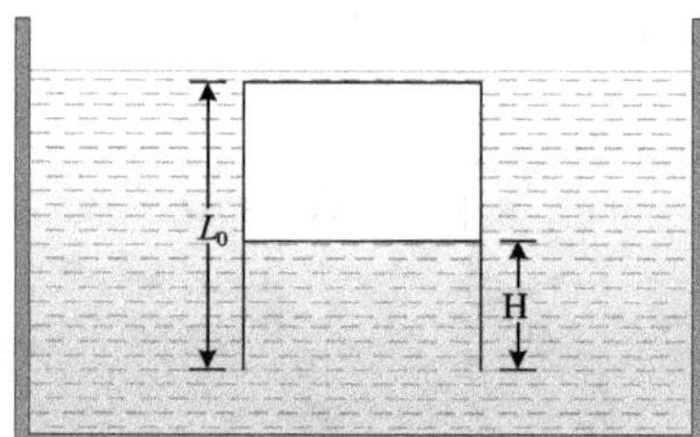

(A) $\rho g(L_0 - H)^2 + P_0(L_0 - H) + L_0 P_0 = 0$

(B) $\rho g(L_0 - H)^2 - P_0(L_0 - H) - L_0 P_0 = 0$

(C) $\rho g(L_0 - H)^2 + P_0(L_0 - H) - L_0 P_0 = 0$

(D) $\rho g(L_0 - H)^2 - P_0(L_0 - H) + L_0 P_0 = 0$

Paragraph-2 (Q. No. 20-22)

When liquid medicine of density ρ is to be put in the eye, it is done with the help of a dropper. As the bulb on the top of the dropper is pressed, a drop forms at the opening of the dropper. We wish to estimate the size of the drop. We first assume that the drop formed at the opening is spherical because that requires a minimum increase in its surface energy. To determine the size, we calculate the net vertical force due to the surface tension T when the radius of the drop is R. When this force becomes smaller than the weight of the drop, the drop gets detached from the dropper.

[JEE Adv 2010, P-2]

20. If the radius of the opening of the dropper is r, the vertical force due to the surface tension on the drop of radius R (assuming $r \ll R$) is :

(A) $2\pi r T$

(B) $2\pi R T$

(C) $\dfrac{2\pi r^2 T}{R}$

(D) $\dfrac{2\pi R^2 T}{r}$

21. If $r = 5 \times 10^{-4}$ m, $\rho = 10^3$ kgm^{-3} $g = 10$ ms^{-2}, $T = 0.11$ Nm^{-1}, then radius of the drop when it detaches from the dropper is approximately :

(A) 1.4×10^{-3} m

(B) 3.3×10^{-3} m

(C) 2.0×10^{-3} m

(D) 4.1×10^{-3} m

22. After the drop detaches, its surface energy is :

(A) 1.4×10^{-6} J

(B) 2.7×10^{-6} J

(C) 5.4×10^{-6} J

(D) 8.1×10^{-6} J

Paragraph-3 (Q. No. 23-24)

A spray gun is shown in the figure where a piston pushes air out of a nozzle. A thin tube of uniform cross section is connected to the nozzle. The other end of the tube is in a small liquid container. As the piston pushes air through the nozzle, the liquid from the container rises into the nozzle and is sprayed out. For the spray gun shown, the radii of the piston and the nozzle are 20 mm and 1 mm respectively. The upper end of the container is open to the atmosphere. **[JEE Adv 2014, P-2]**

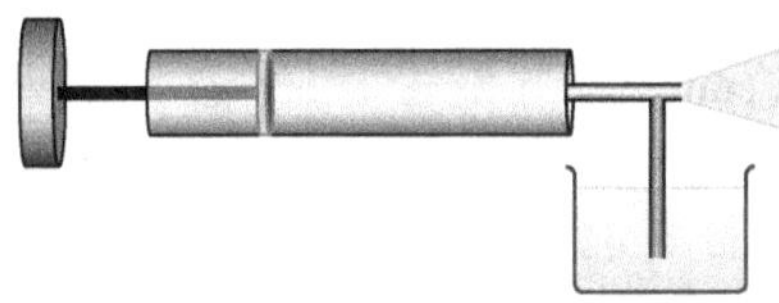

23. If the piston is pushed at a speed of 5 mms^{-1}, the air comes out of the nozzle with a speed of :

(A) 0.1 ms^{-1}

(B) 1 ms^{-1}

(C) 2 ms^{-1}

(D) 8 ms^{-1}

24. If the density of air is ρ_a and that of the liquid ρ_l, then for a given piston speed, the rate (volume per unit time) at which the liquid is sprayed will be proportional to :

(A) $\sqrt{\dfrac{\rho_a}{\rho_l}}$

(B) $\sqrt{\rho_a \rho_l}$

(C) $\sqrt{\dfrac{\rho_l}{\rho_a}}$

(D) ρ_l

Paragraph-4 (Q. No. 25-26)

A soft plastic bottle, filled with water of density 1 gm/cc, carries an inverted glass test-tube with some air (ideal gas) trapped as shown in the figure. The test-tube has a mass of 5 gm, and it is made of a thick glass of density 2.5 gm/cc. Initially the bottle is sealed at atmospheric pressure $p_0 = 10^5$ Pa so that the volume of the trapped air is $v_0 = 3.3$ cc. When the bottle is squeezed from outside at constant temperature, the pressure inside rises and the volume of the trapped air reduces. It is found that the test tube begins to sink at pressure $p_0 + \Delta p$ without changing its orientation. At this pressure, the volume of the trapped air is $v_0 - \Delta v$.

Let $\Delta v = X\,cc$ and $\Delta p = Y \times 10^3$ Pa. **[JEE Adv 2021, P-2]**

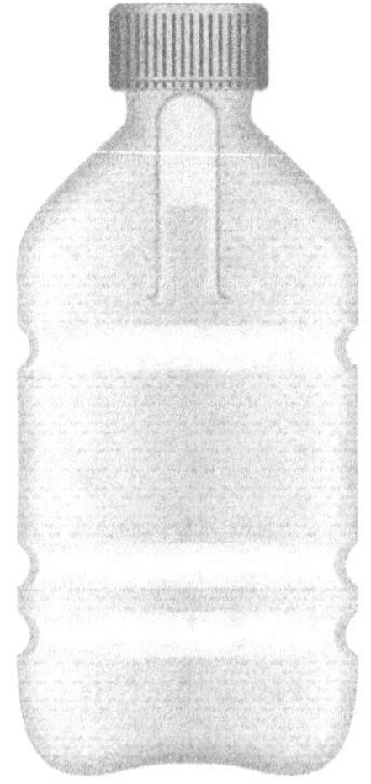

25. The value of X is _______.

26. The value of Y is _______.

Integer Answer based Questions

27. A cylindrical vessel of height 500 mm has on orifice (small hole) at its bottom. The orifice is initially closed and water is filled in it up to height H. Now the top is completely sealed with a cap and the orifice at the bottom is opened. Some water comes out from the orifice and the water level in the vessel becomes steady with height of water column being 200 mm. Find the fall in height (in mm) of water level due to opening of the orifice. [Take atmospheric pressure = 1.0×10^5 N/m^2, density of water = 1000 kg/m^3 and $g = 10$ m/s^2. Neglect any effect of surface tension.] **[JEE Adv 2009, P-2]**

28. Two soap bubbles A and B are kept in a closed chamber where the air is maintained at pressure 8 N/m^2. The radii of bubbles A and B are 2 cm and 4 cm, respectively. Surface tension of the soap water used to make bubbles is 0.04 N/m. Find the ratio n_B/n_A, where n_A and n_B are the number of moles of air in bubbles A and B, respectively. [Neglect the effect of gravity.] **[JEE Adv 2009, P-2]**

29. Consider two solid spheres P and Q each of density 8 gm cm^{-3} and diameters 1 cm and 0.5 cm, respectively. Sphere P is dropped into a liquid of density 0.8 gm cm^{-3} and viscosity $\eta = 3$

poiseulles. Sphere Q is dropped into a liquid of density 1.6 gm cm^{-3} and viscosity $\eta = 2$ poiseulles. The ratio of the terminal velocities of P and Q is ? **[JEE Adv 2016, P-1]**

30. A drop of liquid of radius $R = 10^{-2}$ m having surface tension $S = \dfrac{0.1}{4\pi}$ Nm^{-1} divides itself into K identical drops. In this process the total change in the surface energy $\Delta U = 10^{-3}$ J. If $K = 10^{\alpha}$ then the value of α is ? **[JEE Adv 2017, P-1]**

31. A solid horizontal surface is covered with a thin layer of oil. A rectangular block of mass $m = 0.4$ kg is at rest on this surface. An impulse of 1.0 N s is applied to the block at time to $t = 0$ so that it starts moving along the x-axis with a velocity $v(t) = v_0 e^{-t/\tau}$, where v_0 is a constant and $\tau = 4$ s. The displacement of the block, in metres, at $t = \tau$ is _______ Take $e^{-1} = 0.37$? **[JEE Adv 2018, P-2]**

32. When water is filled carefully in a glass, one can fill it to a height h above the rim of the glass due to the surface tension of water. To calculate h just before water starts flowing, model the shape of the water above the rim as a disc of thickness h having semicircular edges, as shown schematically in the figure. When the pressure of water at the bottom of this disc exceeds what can be withstood due to the surface tension, the water surface breaks near the rim and water starts flowing from there. If the density of water, its surface tension and the acceleration due to gravity are 10^3 kg m^{-3}, 0.07 Nm^{-1} and 10 ms^{-2}, respectively, the value of h (in mm) is _______.

[JEE Adv 2020, P-1]

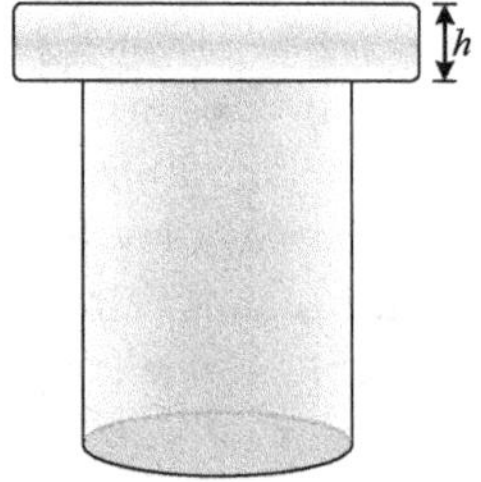

33. A train with cross-sectional area S_t is moving with speed v_t inside a long tunnel of cross-sectional area S_0 $(S_0 = 4S_t)$. Assume that almost all the air (density σ) in front of the train flows back between its sides and the walls of the tunnel. Also, the air flow with respect to the train is steady and laminar. Take the ambient pressure and that inside the train to be p_0. If the pressure in the region between the sides of the train and the tunnel walls is p, then $p_0 - p = \dfrac{7}{2N} \rho v_t^2$. The value of N is _______.

[JEE Adv 2020, P-2]

34. A hot air balloon is carrying some passengers, and a few sandbags of mass 1 kg each so that its total mass is 480 kg. Its effective volume giving the balloon its buoyancy is V. The balloon is floating at an equilibrium height of 100 m. When N number of sandbags are thrown out, the balloon rises to a new equilibrium height close to 150 m with its volume V remaining unchanged. If the variation of the density of air with height h from the ground is $\rho(h) = \rho_0 e^{h/h_0}$, where $\rho_0 = 1.25$ kg m^{-3} and $h_0 = 6000$ m, the value of N is _______.

[JEE Adv 2020, P-2]

35. A spherical bubble inside water has radius R. Take the pressure inside the bubble and the water pressure to be P_0. The bubble now gets compressed radially in an adiabatic manner so that its radius becomes $(R - a)$. For $a \ll R$ the magnitude of the work done in the process is given by $(4\pi P_0 Ra^2) X$, where X is a constant and $\gamma = C_p/C_v = 41/30$. The value of X is _______. **[JEE Adv 2020, P-2]**

36. An incompressible liquid is kept in a container having a weightless piston with a hole. A capillary tube of inner radius 0.1 mm is dipped vertically into the liquid through the airtight piston hole, as shown in the figure. The air in the container is isothermally compressed from its original volume to $\dfrac{100}{101} V_0$ with the movable piston. Considering air as an ideal gas, the height (h) of the liquid column in the capillary above the liquid level in cm is _______.

[Given: Surface tension of the liquid is 0.075 N m^{-1}, atmospheric pressure is 10^5 N m^{-2}, acceleration due to gravity (g) is 10 m s^{-2}, density of the liquid is 10^3 kg m^{-3} and contact angle of capillary surface with the liquid is zero] **[JEE Adv 2023, P-2]**

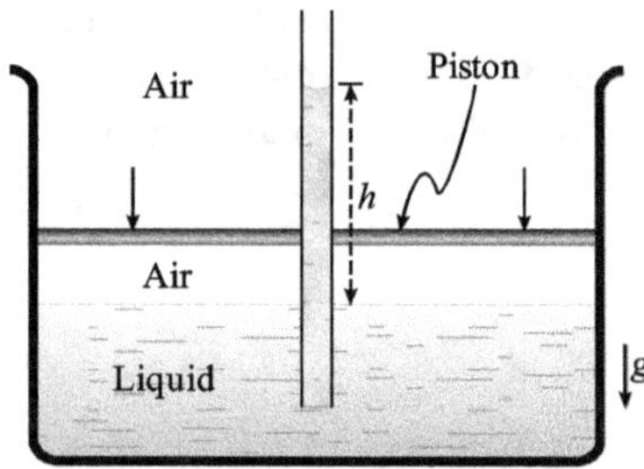

* * * * *

CHAPTER 8 — THERMAL PROPERTIES OF MATTER

MCQ with Single Option Correct

1. Three very large plates of same area are kept parallel and close to each other. They are considered as ideal black surfaces and have very high thermal conductivity. The first and third plates are maintained at temperatures $2T$ and $3T$ respectively. The temperature of the middle (i.e. second) plate under steady state condition is : **[JEE Adv 2012, P-1]**

(A) $\left(\dfrac{65}{2}\right)^{1/4} T$

(B) $\left(\dfrac{97}{4}\right)^{1/4} T$

(C) $\left(\dfrac{97}{2}\right)^{1/4} T$

(D) $(97)^{1/4} T$

2. Two rectangular blocks, having identical dimensions, can be arranged either in configuration I or in configuration II as shown in the figure. One of the blocks has thermal conductivity κ and the other 2κ. The temperature difference between the ends along the x-axis is the same in both the configuration. It takes $9s$ to transport a certain amount of heat from the hot end to the configuration I. The time to transport the same amount of heat in the configuration II is : **[JEE Adv 2013, P-1]**

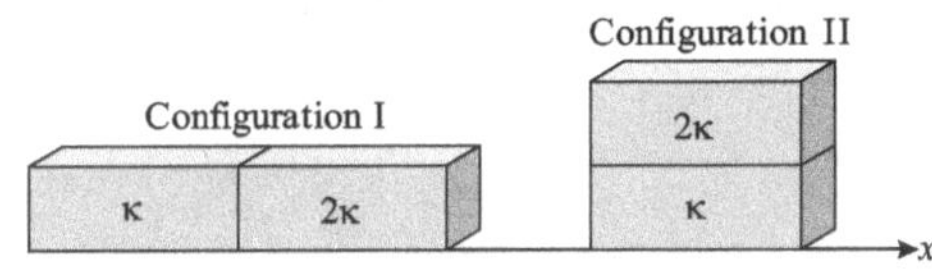

(A) 2.0 s

(B) 3.0 s

(C) 4.5 s

(D) 6.0 s

3. Parallel rays of light of intensity $I = 912$ Wm^{-2} are incident on a spherical black body kept in surroundings of temperature 300 K. Take Stefan-Boltzmann constant $\sigma = 5.7 \times 10^{-8}$ Wm^{-2}K^{-4} and assume that the energy exchange with the surrounding is only through radiation. The final steady state temperature of the black body is close to : **[JEE Adv 2014, P-2]**

(A) 330 K

(B) 660 K

(C) 990 K

(D) 1550 K

4. A water cooler of storage capacity 120 liters can cool water at a constant rate of P watts. In a closed circulation system (as shown schematically in the figure), the water from the cooler is used to cool an external device that generates constantly 3 kW of heat (thermal load). The temperature of water fed into the device cannot exceed 30°C and the entire stored 120 liters of water is initially cooled to 10°C. The entire system is thermally insulated. The minimum value of P (in watts) for which the device can be operated for 3 hours is : **[JEE Adv 2016, P-1]**

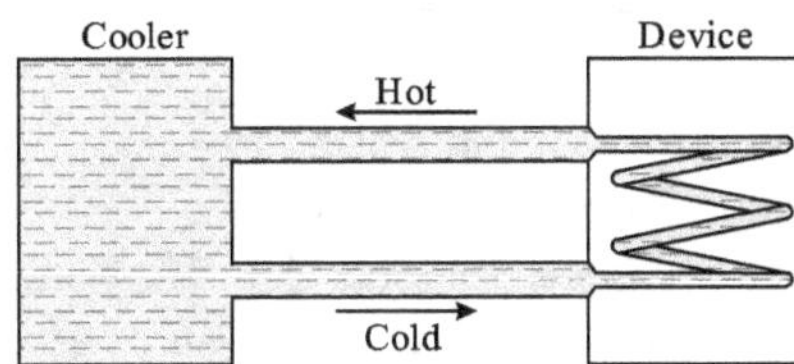

(Specific heat of water is 4.2 kJ kg^{-1} K^{-1} and the density of water is 1000 kg m^{-3})

(A) 1600

(B) 2067

(C) 2533

(D) 3933

5. The ends Q and R of two thin wires, PQ and RS, are soldered (joined) together. Initially each of the wires has a length of 1 m at 10°C. Now the end P is maintained at 10°C, while the end S is heated and maintained at 400°C. The system is thermally insulated from its surroundings. If the thermal conductivity of wire PQ is twice that of the wire RS and the coefficient of linear thermal expansion of PQ is 1.2×10^{-5} K^{-1}, the change in length of the wire PQ is : **[JEE Adv 2016, P-2]**

(A) 0.78 mm

(B) 0.90 mm

(C) 1.56 mm

(D) 2.34 mm

6. A current carrying wire heats a metal rod. The wire provides a constant power (P) to the rod. The metal rod is enclosed in an insulated container. It is observed that the temperature (T) in the metal rod changes with time (t) as :

$$T(t) = T_0 \left(1 + \beta t^{1/4}\right)$$

where β is a constant with appropriate dimension while T_0 is a constant with dimension of temperature. The heat capacity of the metal is : **[JEE Adv 2019, P-1]**

(A) $\dfrac{4P(T(t) - T_0)^3}{\beta^4 T_0^4}$

(B) $\dfrac{4P(T(t) - T_0)}{\beta^4 T_0^2}$

(C) $\dfrac{4P(T(t) - T_0)^4}{\beta^4 T_0^5}$

(D) $\dfrac{4P(T(t) - T_0)^2}{\beta^4 T_0^3}$

MCQ with One or More than One Options Correct

7. A composite block is made of slabs A, B, C, D and E of different thermal conductivities (given in terms of constant K) and sizes (given in terms of length, L) as shown in the figure. All slabs are of same width. Heat 'Q' flows only from left to right through the blocks. Then in steady state :

[JEE Adv 2011, P-1]

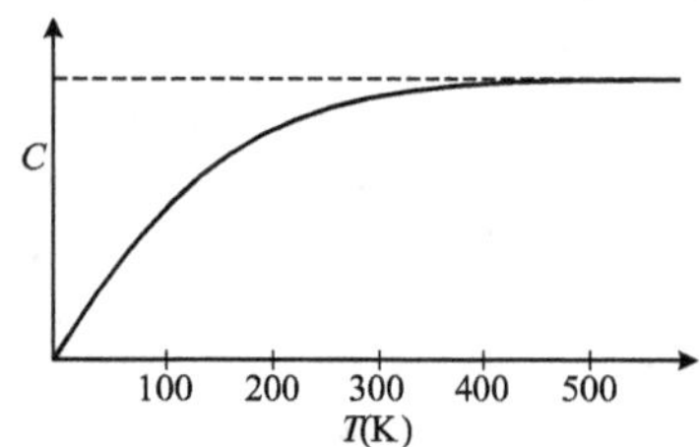

(A) Heat flow through A and E slabs are same

(B) Heat flow through slab E is maximum

(C) Temperature difference across slab E is smallest

(D) Heat flow through C = heat flow B + heat flow through D

8. The figure below shows the variation of specific heat capacity (C) of a solid as a function of temperature (T). The temperature is increased continuously from 0 to 500 K at a constant rate. Ignoring any volume change, the following statement(s) is (are) correct to a reasonable approximation :

[JEE Adv 2013, P-2]

(A) The rate at which heat is absorbed in the range 0-100 K varies linearly with temperature T

(B) Heat absorbed in increasing the temperature from 0-100 K is less than the heat required for increasing the temperature from 400-500 K

(C) There is no change in the rate of heat absorption in the range 400-500 K

(D) The rate of heat absorption increases in the range 200-300 K

9. A human body has a surface area of approximately 1 m^2. The normal body temperature is 10 K above the surrounding room temperature T_0. Take the room temperature to be $T_0 = 300$ K. For $T_0 = 300$ K, the value of $\sigma T_0^4 = 460$ Wm^{-2} (where σ is the Stefan-Boltzmann constant). Which of the following options is/are correct : [JEE Adv 2017, P-1]

(A) The amount of energy radiated by the body in 1 second is close to 60 Joules.

(B) If the surrounding temperature reduces by a small amount $\Delta T_0 \ll T_0$, then to maintain the same body temperature the same (living) human being needs to radiate $\Delta W = 4\sigma T_0^3 \Delta T_0$ more energy per unit time

(C) Reducing the exposed surface area of the body (e.g. by curling up) allows humans to maintain the same body temperature while reducing the energy lost by radiation.

(D) If the body temperature rises significantly then the peak in the spectrum of electromagnetic radiation emitted by the body would shift to longer wavelengths

10. The filament of a light bulb has surface area 64 mm^2. The filament can be considered as a black body at temperature 2500 K emitting radiation like a point source when viewed from far. At night the light bulb is observed from a distance of 100 m. Assume the pupil of the eyes of the observer to be circular with radius 3 mm. Then

(Take Stefan-Boltzmann constant = 5.67×10^{-8} Wm^{-2} K^{-4}, Wien's displacement constant =2.90×10^{-3} m-K, Planck's constant = 6.63×10^{-34} Js, speed of light in vacuum = 3.00×10^8 ms^{-1}) [JEE Adv 2020, P-1]

(A) Power radiated by the filament is in the range 642 W to 645 W

(B) Radiated power entering into one eye of the observer is in the range 3.15×10^{-8} W to 3.25×10^{-8} W

(C) The wavelength corresponding to the maximum intensity of light is 1160 nm

(D) Taking the average wavelength of emitted radiation to be 1740 nm, the total number of photons entering per second into one eye of the observer is in the range 2.75×10^{11} to 2.85×10^{11}

Matrix Match MCQ

11. Match **Coloum-I** with **Coloum-II** and select the correct answer using the codes given below the lists :

[JEE Adv 2013, P-2]

Coloum-I	Coloum-II
(P) Boltzmann constant	(1) $[ML^2T^{-1}]$
(Q) Coefficient of viscosity	(2) $[ML^{-1}T^{-1}]$
(R) Planck constant	(3) $[MLT^{-3}K^{-1}]$
(S) Thermal conductivity	(4) $[ML^2T^{-2}K^{-1}]$

Codes :

	P	Q	R	S
(A)	3	1	2	4
(B)	3	2	1	4
(C)	4	2	1	3
(D)	4	1	2	3

12. Match the temperature of a black body given in List-I with an appropriate statement in List-II, and choose the correct option.

[Given: Wien's constant as 2.9×10^{-3} m-K and $\dfrac{hc}{e}$ = 1.24×10^{-6} V-m] [JEE Adv 2023, P-1]

List-I	List-II
(P) 2000 K	(1) The radiation at peak wavelength can lead

to emission of photoelectrons from a metal of work function 4 eV.

(Q) 3000 K   (2) The radiation at peak wavelength is visible to human eye.

(R) 5000 K   (3) The radiation at peak emission wavelength will result in the widest central maximum of a single slit diffraction.

(S) 10000 K   (4) The power emitted per unit area is 1/16 of that emitted by a blackbody at temperature 6000 K.

   (5) The radiation at peak emission wavelength can be used to image human bones.

(A) $(P) \to (3), (Q) \to (5), (R) \to (2), (S) \to (3)$

(B) $(P) \to (3), (Q) \to (2), (R) \to (4), (S) \to (1)$

(C) $(P) \to (3), (Q) \to (4), (R) \to (2), (S) \to (1)$

(D) $(P) \to (1), (Q) \to (2), (R) \to (5), (S) \to (3)$

Integer Answer based Questions

13. A metal rod AB of length $10x$ has its one end A in ice at 0°C and the end B in water at 100°C. If a point P on the rod is maintained at 400°C, then it is found that equal amounts of water and ice evaporate and melt per unit time. The latent heat of evaporation of water is 540 cal/g and latent heat of melting of ice is 80 cal/g. If the point P is at a distance of λx from the ice end A, find the value of λ. **[JEE Adv 2009, P-2]**

14. Two spherical bodies A (radius 6 cm) and B (radius 18 cm) are at temperatures T_1 and T_2, respectively. The maximum intensity in the emission spectrum of A is at 500 nm and in that of B is at 1500 nm. Considering them to be black bodies, what will be the ratio of the rate of total energy radiated by A to that of B ? **[JEE Adv 2010, P-1]**

15. A piece of ice (heat capacity $= 2100$ J kg^{-1} °C^{-1} and latent heat $= 3.36 \times 10^5$ J kg^{-1}) of mass m grams is at -5°C at atmospheric pressure. It is given 420 J of heat so that the ice starts melting. Finally when the ice-water mixture is in equilibrium, it is found that 1 gm of ice has melted. Assuming there is no other heat exchange in the process, the value of m is ? **[JEE Adv 2010, P-1]**

16. Two spherical stars A and B emit blackbody radiation. The radius of A is 400 times that of B and A emits 10^4 times the power emitted from B. The ratio $\left(\dfrac{\lambda_A}{\lambda_B}\right)$ of their wavelengths λ_A and λ_B at which has peaks occur in their respective radiation curves is ? **[JEE Adv 2015, P-1]**

17. A metal is heated in a furnace where a sensor is kept above the metal surface to read the power radiated (P) by the metal. The sensor has a scale that displays $\log_2(P/P_0)$, where P_0 is a constant. When the metal surface is at a temperature of 487°C, the sensor shows a value 1. Assume that the emissivity of the metallic surface remains constant. What is the value displayed by the sensor when the temperature of the metal surface is raised to 2767°C ? **[JEE Adv 2016, P-1]**

18. Two conducting cylinders of equal length but different radii are connected in series between two heat baths kept at temperatures $T_1 = 300$ K and $T_2 = 100$ K, as shown in the figure. The radius of the bigger cylinder is twice that of the smaller one and the thermal conductivities of the materials of the smaller and the larger cylinders are K_1 and K_2 respectively. If the temperature at the junction of the two cylinders in the steady state is 200 K, then $K_1/K_2 = $ ______. **[JEE Adv 2018, P-1]**

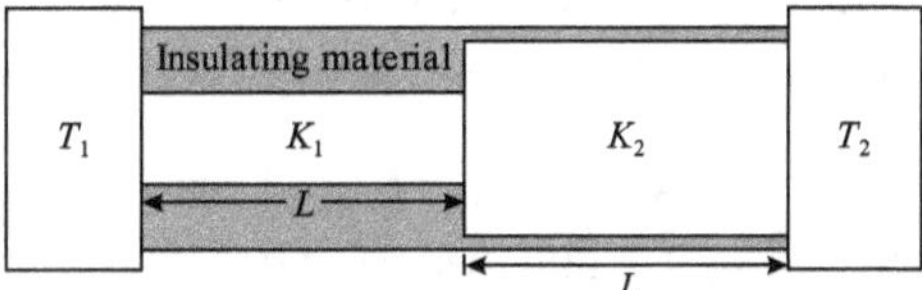

19. A liquid at 30°C is poured very slowly into a Calorimeter that is at temperature of 110°C. The boiling temperature of the liquid is 80°C. It is found that the first 5 gm of the liquid completely evaporates. After pouring another 80 gm of the liquid the equilibrium temperature is found to be 50°C. The ratio of the Latent heat of the liquid to its specific heat will be ______ °C. [Neglect the heat exchange with surrounding] **[JEE Adv 2019, P-1]**

20. A container with 1 kg of water in it is kept in sunlight, which causes the water to get warmer than the surroundings. The average energy per unit time per unit area received due to the sunlight is 700 Wm^{-2} and it is absorbed by the water over an effective area of 0.05 m^2. Assuming that the heat loss from the water to the surroundings is governed by Newton's law of cooling, the difference (in °C) in the temperature of water and the surroundings after a long time will be ______. (Ignore effect of the container, and take constant for Newton's law of cooling = 0.001 s^{-1}, Heat capacity of water = 4200 J kg^{-1} K^{-1}) **[JEE Adv 2020, P-2]**

*　*　*　*　*

CHAPTER 9

THERMODYNAMICS & KINETIC THEORY OF GASES

1. An ideal gas is expanding such that $PT^2 =$ constant. The coefficient of volume expansion of the gas is :

[JEE Adv 2008, P-1]

(A) $\dfrac{1}{T}$

(B) $\dfrac{2}{T}$

(C) $\dfrac{3}{T}$

(D) $\dfrac{4}{T}$

2. A real gas behaves like an ideal gas if its :

[JEE Adv 2010, P-1]

(A) Pressure and temperature are both high
(B) Pressure and temperature are both low
(C) Pressure is high and temperature is low
(D) Pressure is low and temperature is high

3. 5.6 litre of helium gas at STP is adiabatically compressed to 0.7 liter. Taking the initial temperature to be T_1, the work done in the process is : [JEE Adv 2011, P-1]

(A) $\dfrac{9}{8}RT_1$

(B) $\dfrac{3}{2}RT_1$

(C) $\dfrac{15}{8}RT_1$

(D) $\dfrac{9}{2}RT_1$

4. A mixture of 2 moles of helium gas (atomic mass = 4 amu) and 1 mole of argon gas (atomic mass = 40 amu) is kept at 300 K in a container. The ratio of the rms speeds $\left(\dfrac{v_{rms}\,(\text{helium})}{v_{rms}\,(\text{argon})}\right)$ is:

[JEE Adv 2012, P-1]

(A) 0.32
(B) 0.45
(C) 2.24
(D) 3.16

5. Two moles of ideal helium gas are in a rubber balloon at 30°C. The balloon is fully expandable and can be assumed to require no energy in its expansion. The temperature of the gas in the balloon is slowly changed to 35°C. The amount of heat required in raising the temperature is nearly :
(take $R = 8.31$ J/mol. K) [JEE Adv 2012, P-2]

(A) 62 J
(B) 104 J
(C) 124 J
(D) 208 J

6. Two non-reactive monoatomic ideal gases have their atomic masses in the ratio 2 : 3. The ratio of their partial pressures, when enclosed in a vessel kept at a constant temperature, is 4 : 3. The ratio of their densities is :

[JEE Adv 2013, P-1]

(A) 1 : 4
(B) 1 : 2
(C) 6 : 9
(D) 8 : 9

7. A student is performing an experiment using a resonance column and a tuning fork of frequency 244 s^{-1}. He is told that the air in the tube has been replaced by another gas (assume that the column remains filled with the gas). If the minimum height at which resonance occurs is (0.350 ± 0.005) m, the gas in the tube is : **[JEE Adv 2014, P-1]**
(**Useful information :** $\sqrt{167RT} = 640$ J$^{1/2}$ mole$^{1/2}$; $\sqrt{140RT} = 590$ J$^{1/2}$ mole$^{1/2}$. The molar masses M in grams are given in the options. Take the values of $\sqrt{\dfrac{10}{M}}$ for each gas as given there)

(A) Neon $(M = 20,\ \sqrt{\dfrac{10}{20}} = \dfrac{7}{10})$

(B) Nitrogen $(M = 28,\ \sqrt{\dfrac{10}{28}} = \dfrac{3}{5})$

(C) Oxygen $(M = 32,\ \sqrt{\dfrac{10}{32}} = \dfrac{9}{16})$

(D) Argon $(M = 36,\ \sqrt{\dfrac{10}{36}} = \dfrac{17}{32})$

8. A gas is enclosed in a cylinder with a movable frictionless piston. Its initial thermodynamic state at pressure $Pi = 10^5$ Pa and volume $V_i = 10^{-3}$ m^3 changes to a final state at $P_f = (1/32) \times 10^5$ Pa and $V_f = 8 \times 10^{-3}$ m^2 in an adiabatic quasi-static process, such that $P^3V^5 =$ constant. Consider another thermodynamic process that brings the system from the same initial state to the same final state in two steps: an isobaric expansion at P_i followed by an isochoric (isovolumetric) process at volume V_f. The amount of heat supplied to the system in the two-step process is approximately : **[JEE Adv 2016, P-2]**
(A) 112 J
(B) 294 J
(C) 588 J
(D) 813 J

9. An ideal gas undergoes a four step cycle as shown in the P-V diagram below. During this cycle, heat is absorbed by the gas in : **[JEE Adv 2021, P-1]**

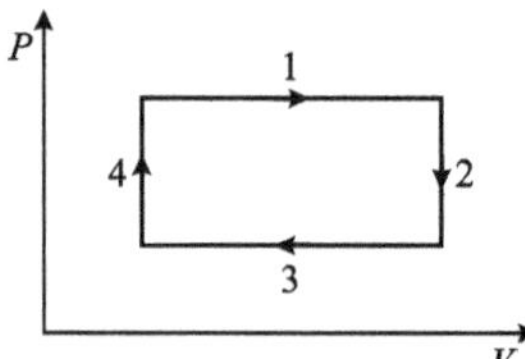

(A) steps 1 and 2   (B) steps 1 and 3
(C) steps 1 and 4   (D) steps 2 and 4

10. One mole of an ideal gas expands adiabatically from an initial state (T_A, V_0) to final state $(T_f, 5V_0)$. Another mole of the same gas expands isothermally from a different initial state (T_B, V_0) to the same final state $(T_f, 5V_0)$. The ratio of the specific heats at constant pressure and constant volume of this ideal gas is γ. What is the ratio T_A/T_B?   **[JEE Adv 2023, P-1]**

(A) $5^{\gamma-1}$ (B) $5^{1-\gamma}$
(C) 5^{γ} (D) $5^{1+\gamma}$

11. An ideal gas is in thermodynamic equilibrium. The number of degrees of freedom of a molecule of the gas is n. The internal energy of one mole of the gas is U_n and the speed of sound in the gas is v_n. At a fixed temperature and pressure, which of the following is the correct option?   **[JEE Adv 2023, P-2]**

(A) $v_3 < v_6$ and $U_3 > U_6$ (B) $v_5 > v_3$ and $U_3 > U_5$
(C) $v_5 > v_7$ and $U_5 < U_7$ (D) $v_6 < v_7$ and $U_6 < U_7$

MCQ with One or More than One Options Correct

12. C_V and C_P denote the molar specific heat capacities of a gas at constant volume and constant pressure, respectively. Then :   **[JEE Adv 2009, P-1]**

(A) $C_P - C_V$ is larger for a diatomic ideal gas than for a monoatomic ideal gas
(B) $C_P + C_V$ is larger for a diatomic ideal gas than for a monoatomic ideal gas
(C) C_P/C_V is larger for a diatomic ideal gas than for a monoatomic ideal gas
(D) $C_P \cdot C_V$ is larger for a diatomic ideal gas than for a monoatomic ideal gas

13. The figure shows the P-V plot of an ideal gas taken through a cycle $ABCDA$. The part ABC is a semi-circle and CDA is half of an ellipse. Then, :   **[JEE Adv 2009, P-2]**

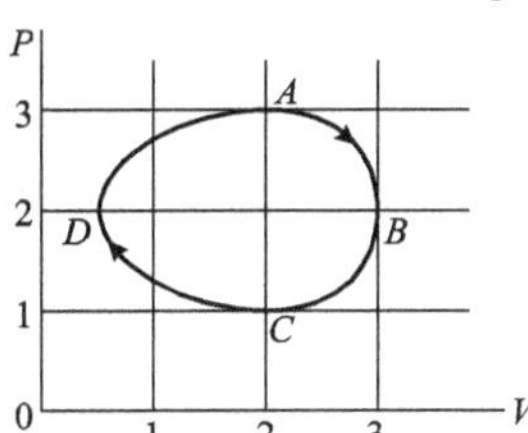

(A) The process during the path $A \to B$ is isothermal
(B) Heat flows out of the gas during the path $B \to C \to D$
(C) Work done during the path $A \to B \to C$ is zero
(D) Positive work is done by the gas in the cycle $ABCDA$

14. One mole of an ideal gas in initial state A undergoes a cyclic process $ABCA$, as shown in the figure. Its pressure at A is P_0. Choose the correct option(s) from the following :   **[JEE Adv 2010, P-1]**

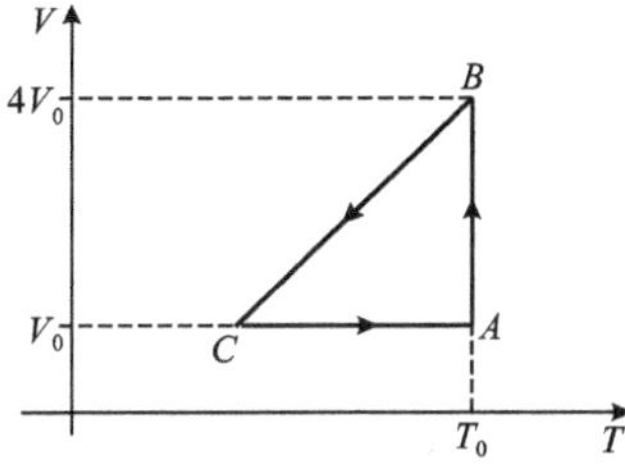

(A) Internal energies at A and B are the same
(B) Work done by the gas in process AB is $P_0V_0 \ln 4$
(C) Pressure at C is $\dfrac{P_0}{4}$
(D) Temperature at C is $\dfrac{T_0}{4}$

15. A container of fixed volume has a mixture of one mole of hydrogen and one mole of helium in equilibrium at temperature T. Assuming the gases are ideal, the correct statement(s) is (are) :   **[JEE Adv 2015, P-1]**

(A) The average energy per mole of the gas mixture is $2RT$
(B) The ratio of speed of sound in the gas mixture to that in helium gas is $\sqrt{6/5}$.
(C) The ratio of the rms speed of helium atoms to that of hydrogen molecules is $1/2$.
(D) The ratio of the rms speed of helium atoms to that of hydrogen molecules is $1/\sqrt{2}$.

16. An ideal monoatomic gas is confined in a horizontal cylinder by a spring loaded piston (as shown in the figure). Initially the gas is at temperature T_1, pressure P_1 and volume V_1 and the spring is in its relaxed state. The gas is then heated very slowly to temperature T_2, pressure P_2 and volume V_2. During this process the piston moves out by a distance x. Ignoring the friction between the piston and the cylinder, the correct statement(s) is(are) :   **[JEE Adv 2015, P-2]**

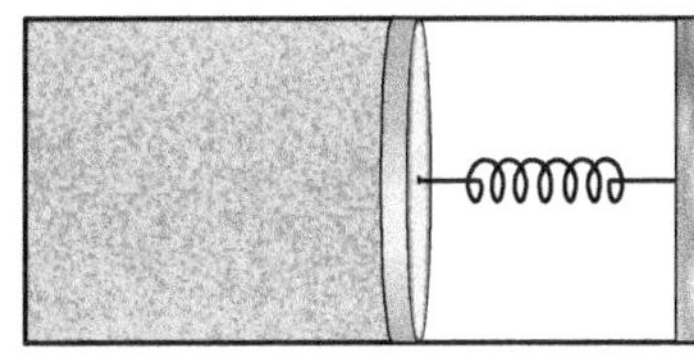

(A) If $V_2 = 2V_1$ and $T_2 = 3T_1$, then the energy stored in the spring is $\dfrac{1}{4}P_1V_1$
(B) If $V_2 = 2V_1$ and $T_2 = 3T_1$, then the change in internal energy is $3P_1V_1$
(C) If $V_2 = 3V_1$ and $T_2 = 4T_1$, then the work done by the gas is $\dfrac{7}{3}P_1V_1$
(D) If $V_2 = 3V_1$ and $T_2 = 4T_1$, then the heat supplied to the gas is $\dfrac{17}{6}P_1V_1$

17. One mole of a monatomic ideal gas undergoes a cyclic process as shown in the figure (where V is the volume and T is the temperature). Which of the statements below is (are) true ?

[JEE Adv 2018, P-1]

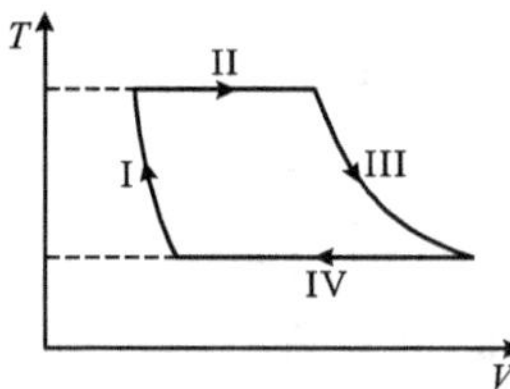

(A) Process I is an isochoric process
(B) In process II, gas absorbs heat
(C) In process IV, gas releases heat
(D) Processes I and II are not isobaric

18. One mole of a monoatomic ideal gas goes through a thermodynamic cycle, as shown in the volume versus temperature (V–T) diagram. The correct statement(s) is/are :
[R is the gas constant]   **[JEE Adv 2019, P-1]**

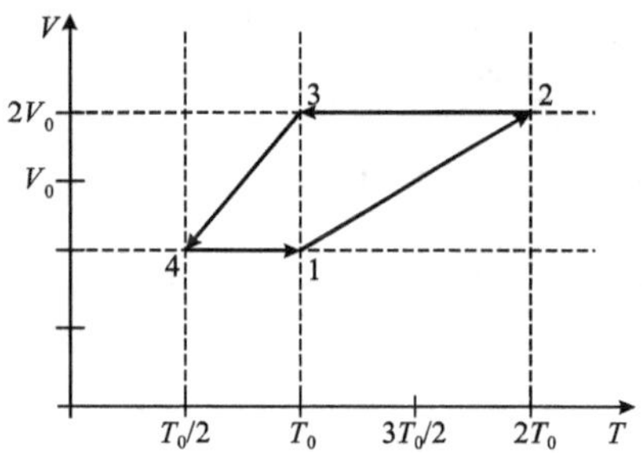

(A) Work done in this thermodynamic cycle $(1 \rightarrow 2 \rightarrow 3 \rightarrow 4 \rightarrow 1)$

is $|W| = \dfrac{1}{2} RT_0$

(B) The ratio of heat transfer during processes $1 \rightarrow 2$ and

$2 \rightarrow 3$ is $\left|\dfrac{Q_{1 \rightarrow 2}}{Q_{2 \rightarrow 3}}\right| = \dfrac{5}{3}$

(C) The above thermodynamic cycle exhibits only isochoric and adiabatic processes
(D) The ratio of heat transfer during processes $1 \rightarrow 2$ and

$3 \rightarrow 4$ is $\left|\dfrac{Q_{1 \rightarrow 2}}{Q_{3 \rightarrow 4}}\right| = \dfrac{1}{2}$

19. A mixture of ideal gas containing 5 moles of monatomic gas and 1 mole of rigid diatomic gas is initially at pressure P_0, volume V_0 and temperature T_0. If the gas mixture is adiabatically compressed to a volume $V_0/4$, then the correct statement(s) is/are, (Give $2^{1.2} = 2.3$; $2^{3.2} = 9.2$; R is gas constant) :

[JEE Adv 2019, P-2]

(A) The final pressure of the gas mixture after compression is in between $9P_0$ and $10P_0$
(B) The average kinetic energy of the gas mixture after compression is in between $18RT_0$ and $19RT_0$

(C) The work $|W|$ done during the process is $13RT_0$
(D) Adiabatic constant of the gas mixture is 1.6

20. A small particle of mass m moving inside a heavy, hollow and straight tube along the tube axis undergoes elastic collision at two ends. The tube has no friction and it is closed at one end by a flat surface while the other end is fitted with a heavy movable flat piston as shown in figure. When the distance of the piston from closed end is $L = L_0$ the particle speed is $v = v_0$. The piston is moved inward at a very low speed V such that

$V << \dfrac{dL}{L} v_0$, where dL is the infinitesimal displacement of the piston. Which of the following statement(s) is/are correct ?

[JEE Adv 2019, P-2]

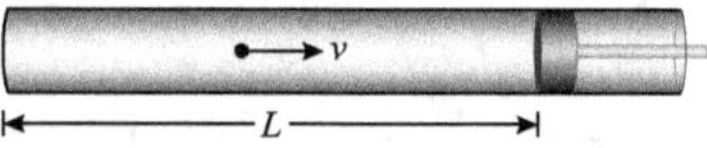

(A) The rate at which the particle strikes the piston is v/L
(B) After each collision with the piston, the particle speed increases by $2V$
(C) The particle's kinetic energy increases by a factor of 4

when the piston is moved inward from L_0 to $\dfrac{1}{2}L_0$

(D) If the piston moves inward by dL, the particle speed

increases by $2v\dfrac{dL}{L}$

21. As shown schematically in the figure, two vessels contain water solutions (at temperature T) of potassium permanganate ($KMnO_4$) of different concentrations n_1 and n_2 ($n_1 > n_2$) molecules per unit volume with $\Delta n = (n_1 - n_2) << n_1$. When they are connected by a tube of small length l and cross-sectional area S, $KMnO_4$ starts to diffuse from the left to the right vessel through the tube. Consider the collection of molecules to behave as dilute ideal gases and the difference in their partial pressure in the two vessels causing the diffusion. The speed v of the molecules is limited by the viscous force $-\beta v$ on each molecule, where β is a constant. Neglecting all terms of the order $(\Delta n)^2$, which of the following is/are correct? (k_B is the Boltzmann constant) :   **[JEE Adv 2020, P-1]**

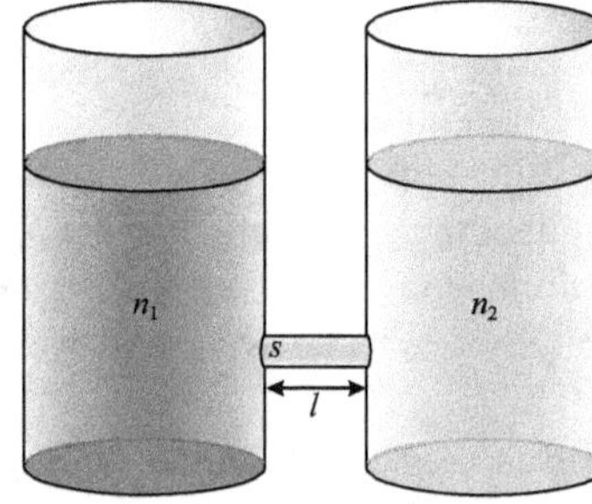

(A) The force causing the molecules to move across the tube is $\Delta n k_B T S$

(B) Force balance implies $n_1 \beta v l = \Delta n k_B T$

(C) Total number of molecules going across the tube per sec is $\left(\dfrac{\Delta n}{l}\right)\left(\dfrac{k_B T}{\beta}\right) S$

(D) Rate of molecules getting transferred through the tube does not change with time

22. An ideal gas of density $\rho = 0.2$ kg m^{-3} enters a chimney of height h at the rate of $\alpha = 0.8$ kg s^{-1} from its lower end, and escapes through the upper end as shown in the figure. The cross-sectional area of the lower end is $A_1 = 0.1$ m^2 and the upper end is $A_2 = 0.4$ m^2. The pressure and the temperature of the gas at the lower end are 600 Pa and 300 K, respectively, while its temperature at the upper end is 150 K. The chimney is heat insulated so that the gas undergoes adiabatic expansion. Take $g = 10$ ms^{-2} and the ratio of specific heats of the gas $\gamma = 2$. Ignore atmospheric pressure.

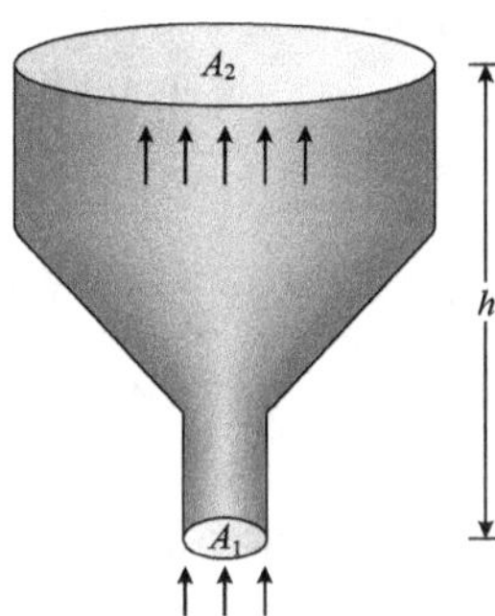

Which of the following statement(s) is(are) correct ?

[JEE Adv 2022, P-1]

(A) The pressure of the gas at the upper end of the chimney is 300 Pa

(B) The velocity of the gas at the lower end of the chimney is 40 ms^{-1} and at the upper end is 20 ms^{-1}

(C) The height of the chimney is 590 m

(D) The density of the gas at the upper end is 0.05 kg m^{-3}

23. In the given P-V diagram, a monoatomic gas $\left(\gamma = \dfrac{5}{3}\right)$ is first compressed adiabatically from state A to state B. Then it expands isothermally from state B to state C.

$\left[\text{Given}: \left(\dfrac{1}{3}\right)^{0.6} = 0.5, \ln 2 = 0.7\right]$

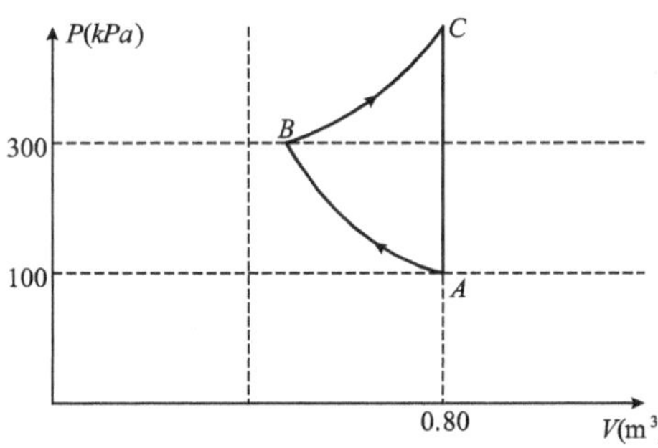

Which of the following statement(s) is(are) correct ?

[JEE Adv 2022, P-2]

(A) The magnitude of the total work done in the process $A \rightarrow B \rightarrow C$ is 144 kJ

(B) The magnitude of the total work done in the process $B \rightarrow C$ is 84 kJ

(C) The magnitude of the total work done in the process $A \rightarrow B$ is 60 kJ

(D) The magnitude of the total work done in the process $C \rightarrow A$ is zero

Assertion Reason based on MCQ

24. STATEMENT-1　　　　　**[JEE Adv 2007, P-2]**
The total translational kinetic energy of all the molecules of a given mass of an ideal gas is 1.5 times the product of its pressure and its volume.

because

STATEMENT-2
The molecules of a gas collide with each other and the velocities of the molecules change due to the collision.

(A) Statement-1 is True, Statement-2 is True; Statement-2 is a correct explanation for Statement-1

(B) Statement-1 is True, Statement-2 is True; Statement-2 is **NOT** a correct explanation for Statement-1

(C) Statement-1 is True, Statement-2 is False

(D) Statement-1 is False, Statement-2 is True

Matrix Match MCQ

25. Column-I contains a list of processes involving expansion of an ideal gas. Match this with **Column-II** describing the thermodynamic change during this process. Indicate your answer by darkening the appropriate bubbles of the 4 × 4 matrix given in the ORS :　　　**[JEE Adv 2008, P-2]**

Column-I

(A) An insulated container has two chambers separated by a value. Chamber I contains an ideal gas and the Chamber II has vacuum. The valve is opened.

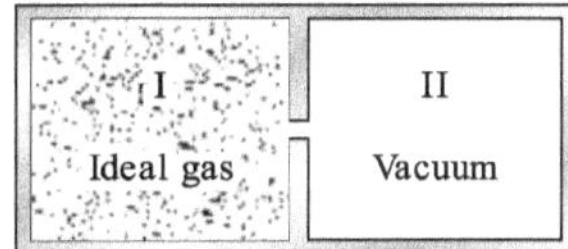

(B) An ideal monoatomic gas expands to twice its original volume such that its pressure $P \propto \dfrac{1}{V^2}$, where V is the volume of the gas.

(C) An ideal monoatomic gas expands to twice its original volume such that its pressure $P \propto \dfrac{1}{V^{4/3}}$, where V is its volume

(D) An ideal monoatomic gas expands such that its pressure P

and volume V follows the behaviour shown in the graph.

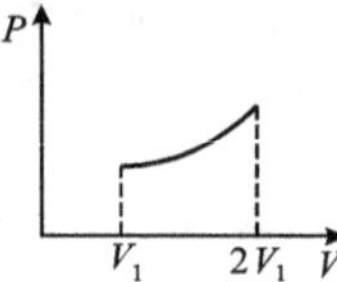

Column-II

(p) The temperature of the gas decreases
(q) The temperature of the gas increases or remains constant
(r) The gas loses heat
(s) The gas gains heat

26. One mole of a monatomic ideal gas is taken through a cycle $ABCDA$ as shown in the P-V diagram. **Column-II** gives the characteristics involved in the cycle. Match them with each of the processes given in **Column-I**.   [JEE Adv 2011, P-2]

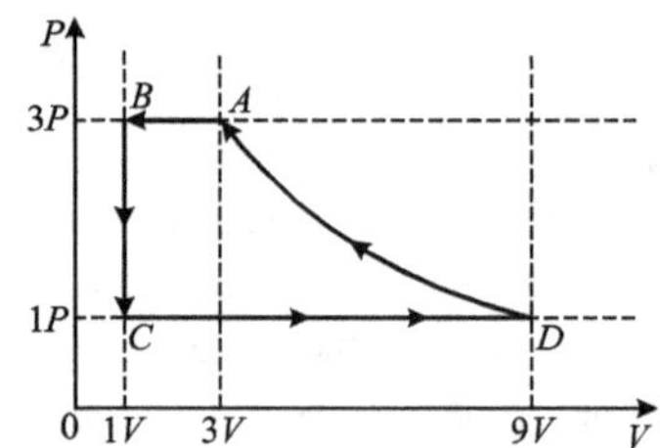

Column-I	**Column-II**
(A) Process $A \to B$	(p) Internal energy decreases
(B) Process $B \to C$	(q) Internal energy increases
(C) Process $C \to D$	(r) Heat is lost
(D) Process $D \to A$	(s) Heat is gained
	(t) Work is done on the gas

27. One mole of a monatomic ideal gas is taken along two cyclic processes $E \to F \to G \to E$ and $E \to F \to H \to E$ as shown in the PV diagram. The processes involved are purely isochoric, isobaric, isothermal or adiabatic :

[JEE Adv 2013, P-2]

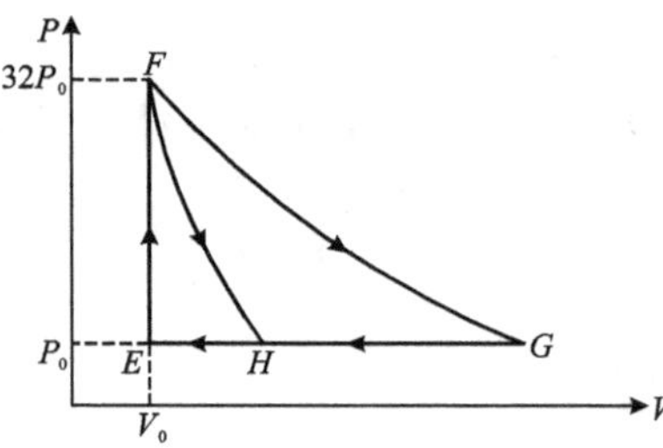

Match the paths is **Coloum-I** with magnitudes of the work done in **Coloum-II** and select the correct answer using the codes given below the lists :

Coloum-I	**Coloum-II**
(P) $G \to E$	(1) $160\,P_0 V_0 \ln 2$
(Q) $G \to H$	(2) $36\,P_0 V_0$
(R) $F \to H$	(3) $24\,P_0 V_0$
(S) $F \to G$	(4) $31\,P_0 V_0$

Codes :

	P	Q	R	S
(A)	4	3	2	1
(B)	4	3	1	2
(C)	3	1	2	4
(D)	1	3	2	4

Answer Q.28, Q.29 and Q.30 by appropriately matching the information given in the three columns of the following table.

An ideal gas is undergoing a cyclic thermodynamic process in different ways as shown in the corresponding P-V diagrams in column-3 of the table. Consider only the path from state 1 to state 2. W denotes the corresponding work done on the system. The equations and plots in the table have standard notations as used in thermodynamic processes. Here γ is the ratio of heat capacities at constant pressure and constant volume. The number of moles in the gas is n.   [JEE Adv 2017, P-1]

Column-I	**Column-II**	**Column-III**
(I) $W_{1\to2}=\dfrac{1}{\gamma-1}(P_2V_2-P_1V_1)$	(i) Isothermal	(P) 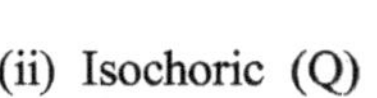
(II) $W_{1\to2}=PV_2-PV_1$	(ii) Isochoric	(Q) 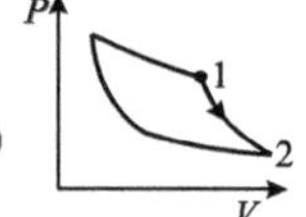
(III) $W_{1\to2}=0$	(iii) Isobaric	(R) 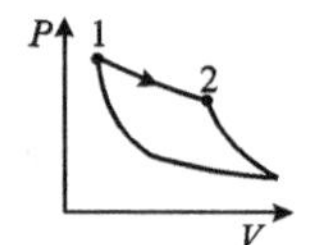
(IV) $W_{1\to2}=-nRT\ln\left(\dfrac{V_2}{V_1}\right)$	(iv) Adiabatic	(S)

28. Which of the following options is the only correct representation of a process in which $\Delta U = \Delta Q - P\Delta V$:
(A) (II) (iv) (R)   (B) (II) (iii) (P)
(C) (II) (iii) (S)   (D) (III) (iii) (P)

29. Which one of the following options is the correct combination?
(A) (III) (ii) (S)   (B) (II) (iv) (R)
(C) (II) (iv) (R)   (D) (IV) (ii) (S)

30. Which one of the following options correctly represents a thermodynamic process that is used as a correction in the determination of the speed of sound in an ideal gas?
(A) (III) (iv) (R)   (B) (I) (ii) (Q)
(C) (IV) (ii) (R)   (D) (I) (iv) (Q)

31. One mole of a monatomic ideal gas undergoes four thermodynamic processes as shown schematically in the *PV*-diagram below. Among these four processes, one is isobaric, one is isochoric, one is isothermal and one is adiabatic. Match the processes mentioned in **Column-I** with the corresponding statements in **Column-II**. **[JEE Adv 2018, P-2]**

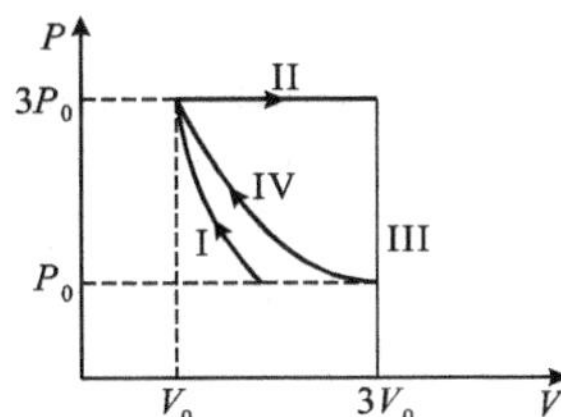

Column-I

P. In process I

Q. In process II

R. In process III

S. In process IV

Column-II

1. Work done by the gas is zero

2. Temperature of the gas remains unchanged

3. No heat is exchanged between the gas and its surroundings

4. Work done by the gas is $6P_0V_0$

(A) $P \to 4 ; Q \to 3 ; R \to 1 ; S \to 2$
(B) $P \to 1 ; Q \to 3 ; R \to 2 ; S \to 4$
(C) $P \to 3 ; Q \to 4 ; R \to 1 ; S \to 2$
(D) $P \to 3 ; Q \to 4 ; R \to 2 ; S \to 1$

Answer the following by appropriately matching the Columns based on the information given in the paragraph.

In a thermodynamics process on an ideal monatomic gas, the infinitesimal heat absorbed by the gas is given by $T\Delta X$, where T is temperature of the system and ΔX is the infinitesimal change in a thermodynamic quantity X of the system. For a mole of monatomic ideal gas $X = \frac{3}{2}R \, ln\left(\frac{T}{T_A}\right) + R \, ln\left(\frac{V}{V_A}\right)$.

Here, R is gas constant, V is volume of gas, T_A and V_A are constants.

The **Column-I** below gives some quantities involved in a process and **Column-II** gives some possible values of these quantities. **[JEE Adv 2019, P-2]**

Column-I

(I) Work done by the system in process $1 \to 2 \to 3$

(II) Change in internal energy in process $1 \to 2 \to 3$

(III) Heat absorbed by the system in process $1 \to 2 \to 3$

(IV) Heat absorbed by the system in process $1 \to 2$

Column-II

(P) $\frac{1}{3}RT_0 \ln 2$

(Q) $\frac{1}{3}RT_0$

(R) RT_0

(S) $\frac{4}{3}RT_0$

(T) $\frac{1}{3}RT_0(3 + \ln 2)$

(U) $\frac{5}{6}RT_0$

32. If the process carried out on one mole of monatomic ideal gas is as shown in figure in the *PV*-diagram with $P_0V_0 = \frac{1}{3}RT_0$, the correct match is,

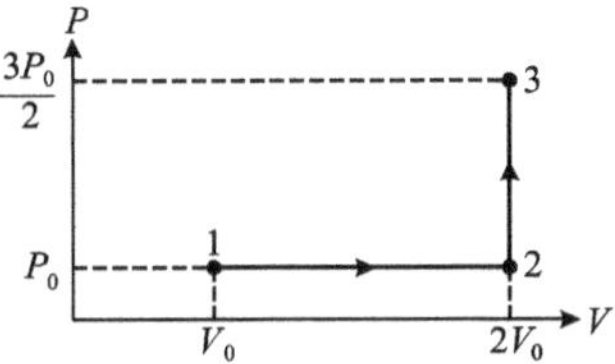

(A) $I \to Q, II \to R, III \to P, IV \to U$
(B) $I \to S, II \to R, III \to Q, IV \to T$
(C) $I \to Q, II \to R, III \to S, IV \to U$
(D) $I \to Q, II \to S, III \to R, IV \to U$

33. List-I describes thermodynamic processes in four different systems. List-II gives the magnitudes (either exactly or as a close approximation) of possible changes in the internal energy of the system due to the process. **[JEE Adv 2022, P-1]**

List-I	List-II
(I) 10^{-3} kg of water at 100°C is converted to steam at the same temperature, at a pressure of 10^5 Pa. The volume of the system changes from 10^{-6} m^3 to 10^{-3} m^3 in the process. Latent heat of water = 2250 kJ/kg	(P) 2 kJ
(II) 0.2 moles of a rigid diatomic ideal gas with volume V at temperature 500 K undergoes an isobaric expansion to volume $3V$. Assume $R = 8.0$ J mol^{-1} K^{-1}	(Q) 7 kJ
(III) One mole of a monatomic ideal gas is compressed adiabatically from volume $V = \frac{1}{3}$ m^3 and pressure 2 kPa to volume $\frac{V}{8}$	(R) 4 kJ
(IV) Three moles of a diatomic ideal gas whose molecules can vibrate, is given 9 kJ of heat and undergoes isobaric expansion	(S) 5 kJ
	(T) 3 kJ

Which one of the following options is correct ?

(A) $I \to T, II \to R, III \to S, IV \to Q$

(B) $I \to S, II \to P, III \to T, IV \to P$

(C) $I \to P, II \to R, III \to T, IV \to Q$

(D) $I \to Q, II \to R, III \to S, IV \to T$

Comprehension based MCQ

Paragraph-1 (Q. No. 34-36)

A small spherical monoatomic ideal gas bubble ($\gamma = 5/3$) is trapped inside a liquid of density ρ_l (see figure). Assume that the bubble does not exchange any heat with the liquid. The bubble contains n moles of gas. The temperature of the gas when the bubble is at the bottom is T_0, the height of the liquid is H and the atmospheric pressure is P_0 (Neglect surface tension) :

[JEE Adv 2008, P-1]

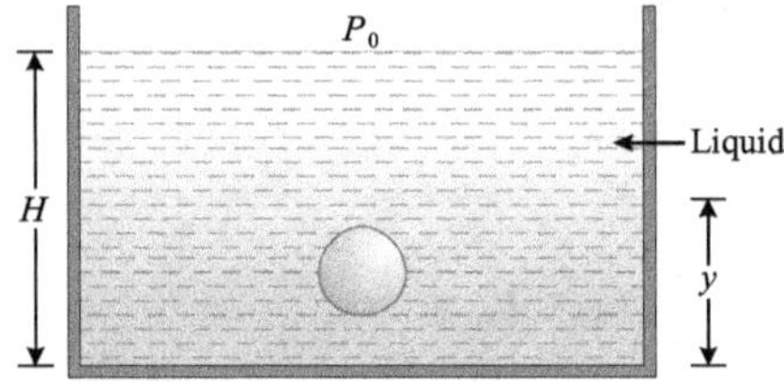

34. As the bubble moves upwards, besides the buoyancy force the following forces are acting on it :

(A) Only the force of gravity

(B) The force due to gravity and the force due to the pressure of the liquid

(C) The force due to gravity, the force due to the pressure of the liquid and the force due to viscosity of the liquid

(D) The force due to gravity and the force due to viscosity of the liquid

35. When the gas bubble is at a height y from the bottom, its temperature is :

(A) $T_0 \left(\dfrac{P_0 + \rho_l g H}{P_0 + \rho_l g y} \right)^{2/5}$

(B) $T_0 \left(\dfrac{P_0 + \rho_l g (H - y)}{P_0 + \rho_l g H} \right)^{2/5}$

(C) $T_0 \left(\dfrac{P_0 + \rho_l g H}{P_0 + \rho_l g y} \right)^{3/5}$

(D) $T_0 \left(\dfrac{P_0 + \rho_l g (H - y)}{P_0 + \rho_l g H} \right)^{3/5}$

36. The buoyancy force acting on the gas bubble is (Assume R is the universal gas constant) :

(A) $\rho_l n R T_0 \dfrac{(P_0 + \rho_l g H)^{2/5}}{(P_0 + \rho_l g y)^{7/5}}$

(B) $\dfrac{\rho_l \pi R g T_0}{(P_0 + \rho_l g H)^{2/5} [P_0 + \rho_l g (H - y)]^{3/5}}$

(C) $\rho_l n R g T_0 \dfrac{(P_0 + \rho_l g H)^{3/5}}{(P_0 + \rho_l g y)^{8/5}}$

(D) $\dfrac{\rho_l n R g T_0}{(P_0 + \rho_l g H)^{3/5} [P_0 + \rho_l g (H - y)]^{2/5}}$

Paragraph-2 (Q. No. 37-38)

In the figure a container is shown to have a movable (without friction) piston on top. The container and the piston are all made of perfectly insulating material allowing no heat transfer between outside and inside the container. The container is divided into two compartments by a rigid partition made of a thermally conducting material that allows slow transfer of heat. The lower compartment of the container is filled with 2 moles of an ideal monatomic gas at 700 K and the upper compartment is filled with 2 moles of an ideal diatomic gas at 400 K. The heat capacities per mole of an ideal monatomic gas are $C_V = 3/2R$, $C_P = 5/2R$, and those for an ideal diatomic gas are $C_V = 5/2R$, $C_P = 7/2R$.   **[JEE Adv 2014, P-2]**

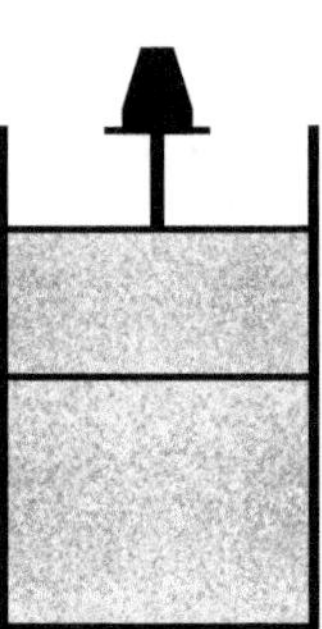

37. Consider the partition to be rigidly fixed so that it does not move. When equilibrium is achieved, the final temperature of the gasses will be :

(A) 550 K   (B) 525 K

(C) 513 K   (D) 490 K

38. Now consider the partition to be free to move without friction so that the pressure of gases in both compartments is the same. Then total work done by the gases till the time they achieve equilibrium will be :

(A) 250 R (B) 200 R

(C) 100 R (D) $-100\,R$

Paragraph-3 (Q. No. 39-40)

A thermally insulating cylinder has a thermally insulating and frictionless movable partition in the middle, as shown in the figure below. On each side of the partition, there is one mole of an ideal gas, with specific heat at constant volume, $C_V = 2R$. Here, R is the gas constant. Initially, each side has a volume V_0 and temperature T_0. The left side has an electric heater, which is turned on at very low power to transfer heat Q to the gas on the left side. As a result the partition moves slowly towards the right reducing the right side volume to $V_0/2$. Consequently, the gas temperatures on the left and the right sides become T_L and

T_R, respectively. Ignore the changes in the temperatures of the cylinder, heater and the partition.   **[JEE Adv 2021, P-2]**

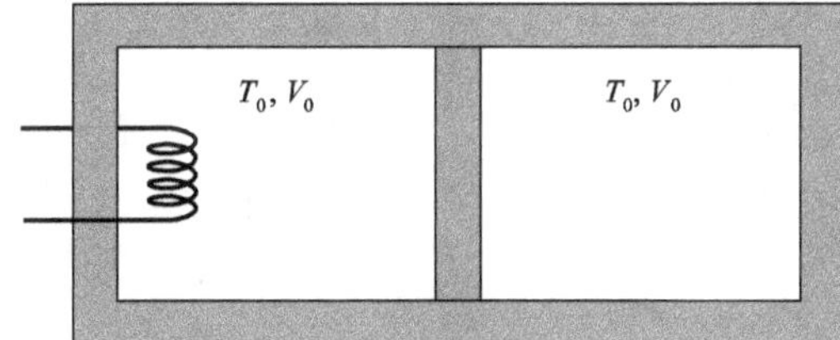

39. The value of $\dfrac{T_R}{T_0}$ is :

(A) $\sqrt{2}$ (B) $\sqrt{3}$

(C) 2 (D) 3

40. The value of $\dfrac{Q}{RT_0}$ is :

(A) $4(2\sqrt{2}+1)$ (B) $4(2\sqrt{2}-1)$

(C) $(5\sqrt{2}+1)$ (D) $(5\sqrt{2}-1)$

Paragraph-1 (Q. No.41–42)

A cylindrical furnace has height (H) and diameter (D) both 1 m. It is maintained at temperature 360 K. The air gets heated inside the furnace at constant pressure P_a and its temperature becomes $T = 360$ K. The hot air with density ρ rises up a vertical chimney of diameter $d = 0.1$ m and height $h = 9$ m above the furnace and exits the chimney (see the figure). As a result, atmospheric air of density $\rho_a = 1.2$ kg m^{-3}, pressure P_a and temperature $T_a = 300$ K enters the furnace. Assume air as an ideal gas, neglect the variations in ρ and T inside the chimney and the furnace. Also ignore the viscous effects.
[Given: The acceleration due to gravity $g = 10$ m s^{-2} and $\pi = 3.14$]
    [JEE Adv 2023, P-2]

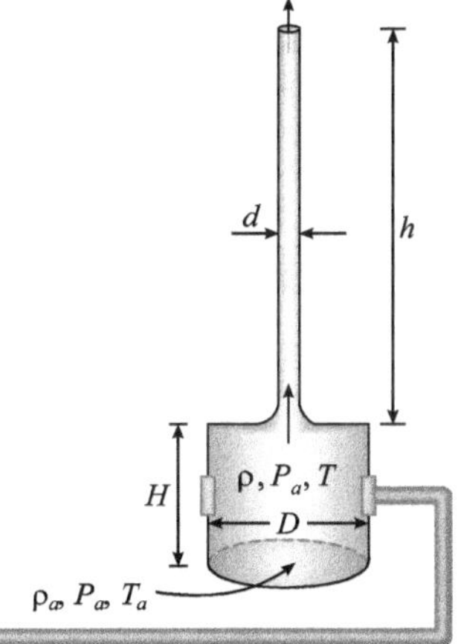

41. Considering the air flow to be streamline, the steady mass flow rate of air exiting the chimney is________ gm s^{-1}.

42. When the chimney is closed using a cap at the top, a pressure difference ΔP develops between the top and the bottom surfaces of the cap. If the changes in the temperature and density of the hot air, due to the stoppage of air flow, are negligible then the value of ΔP is________ N m^{-2}.

Integer Answer based Questions

43. A diatomic ideal gas is compressed adiabatically to $\dfrac{1}{32}$ of its initial volume. In the initial temperature of the gas is T_i (in Kelvin) and the final temperature is aT_i, the value of a is ?
    [JEE Adv 2010, P-2]

44. A thermodynamic system is taken from an initial state i with internal energy $U_i = 100$ J to the final state f along two different paths iaf and ibf, as schematically shown in the figure. The work done by the system along the paths af, ib and bf are $W_{af} = 200$ J, $W_{ib} = 50$ J and $W_{bf} = 100$ J respectively. The heat supplied to the system along the path iaf, ib and bf are Q_{iaf}, Q_{ib} and Q_{bf} respectively. If the internal energy of the system in the state b is $U_b = 200$ J and $Q_{iaf} = 500$ J, the ratio Q_{bf}/Q_{ib} is :
    [JEE Adv 2014, P-1]

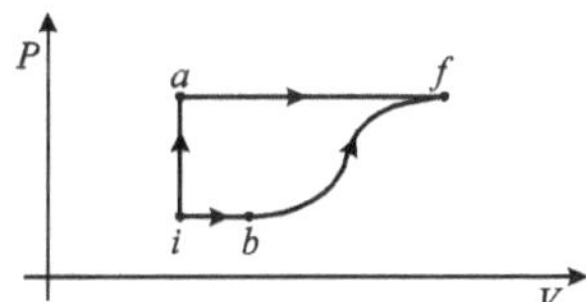

45. One mole of a monatomic ideal gas undergoes an adiabatic expansion in which its volume becomes eight times its initial value. If the initial temperature of the gas is 100 K and the universal gas constant $R = 8.0$ J mol^{-1} K^{-1}, the decrease in its internal energy, in Joule, is________.   **[JEE Adv 2018, P-2]**

46. Consider one mole of helium gas enclosed in a container at initial pressure P_1 and volume V_1. It expands isothermally to volume $4V_1$. After this, the gas expands adiabatically and its volume becomes $32V_1$. The work done by the gas during isothermal and adiabatic expansion processes are W_{iso} and W_{adia}, respectively. If the ratio $\sqrt{\dfrac{W_{iso}}{W_{adia}}} = f\ln 2$, then f is________.

    [JEE Adv 2020, P-1]

47. A thermally isolated cylindrical closed vessel of height 8 m is kept vertically. It is divided into two equal parts by a diathermic (perfect thermal conductor) frictionless partition of mass 8.3 kg. Thus the partition is held initially at a distance of

4 m from the top, as shown in the schematic figure below. Each of the two parts of the vessel contains 0.1 mole of an ideal gas at temperature 300 K. The partition is now released and moves without any gas leaking from one part of the vessel to the other. When equilibrium is reached, the distance of the partition from the top (in m) will be _______ . (Take the acceleration due to gravity $=10$ ms^{-2} and the universal gas constant $= 8.3$ J mol^{-1} K^{-1}). **[JEE Adv 2020, P-2]**

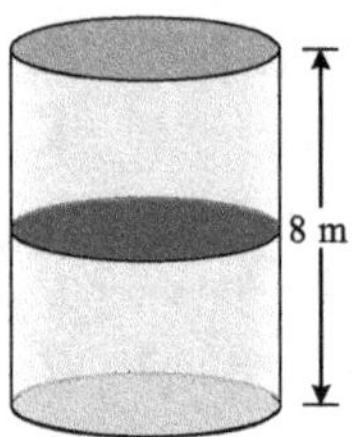

48. A closed container contains a homogeneous mixture of two moles of an ideal monatomic gas ($\gamma = 5/3$) and one mole of an ideal diatomic gas ($\gamma = 7/5$). Here, γ is the ratio of the specific heats at constant pressure and constant volume of an ideal gas. The gas mixture does a work of 66 joule when heated at constant pressure. The change in its internal energy is _______ joule. **[JEE Adv 2023, P-1]**

49. One mole of an ideal gas undergoes two different cyclic processes I and II, as shown in the P-V diagrams below. In cycle I, processes a, b, c and d are isobaric, isothermal, isobaric and isochoric, respectively. In cycle-II, processes a', b', c' and d' are isothermal, isochoric, isobaric and isochoric, respectively. The total work done during cycle-I is W_I and that during cycle II is W_{II}. The ratio W_I/W_{II} is _______ . **[JEE Adv 2023, P-2]**

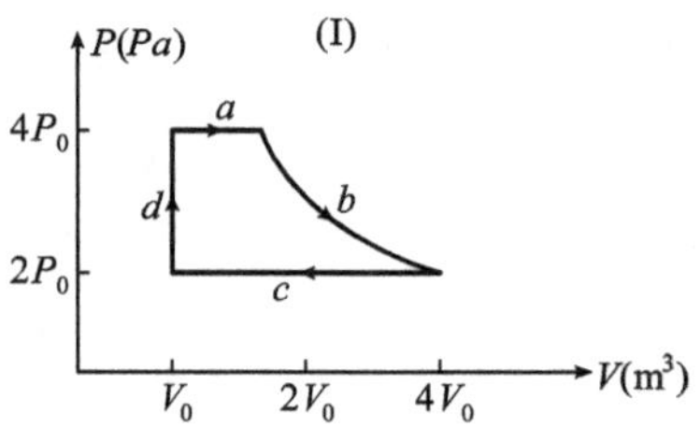

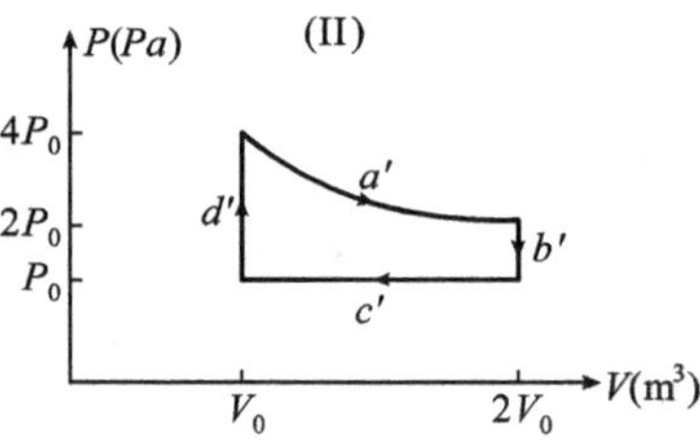

* * * * *

MCQ with Single Option Correct

1. The x-t graph of a particle undergoing simple harmonic motion is shown below. The acceleration of the particle at $t = 4/3$ s is : **[JEE Adv 2009, P-1]**

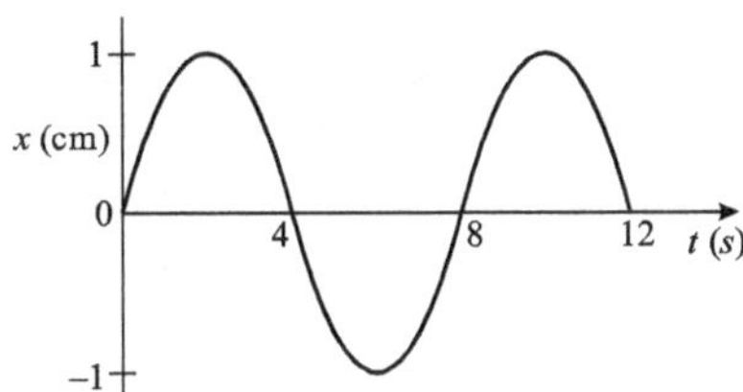

(A) $\dfrac{\sqrt{3}}{32} \pi^2$ cm/s^2

(B) $\dfrac{-\pi^2}{32}$ cm/s^2

(C) $\dfrac{\pi^2}{32}$ cm/s^2

(D) $-\dfrac{\sqrt{3}}{32} \pi^2$ cm/s^2

2. The mass M shown in the figure oscillates in simple harmonic motion with amplitude A. The amplitude of the point P is : **[JEE Adv 2009, P-2]**

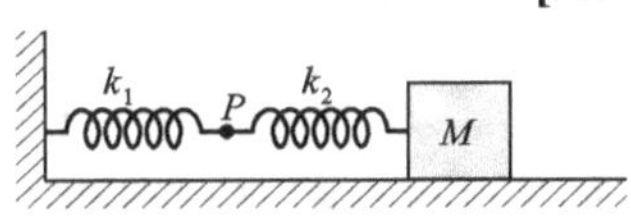

(A) $\dfrac{k_1 A}{k_2}$

(B) $\dfrac{k_2 A}{k_1}$

(C) $\dfrac{k_1 A}{k_1 + k_2}$

(D) $\dfrac{k_2 A}{k_1 + k_2}$

3. A wooden block performs SHM on a frictionless surface with frequency, ν_0. The block carries a charge $+Q$ on its surface.

If now a uniform electric field $\vec{E}$ is switched-on as shown, then the SHM of the block will be : **[JEE Adv 2011, P-2]**

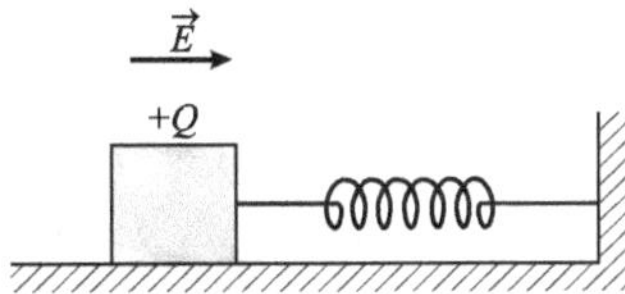

(A) of the same frequency and with shifted mean position
(B) of the same frequency and with the same mean position
(C) of charged frequency and with shifted mean position
(D) of charged frequency and with the same mean position

MCQ with One or More than One Options Correct

4. A metal rod of length L and mass m is pivoted at one end. A thin disk of mass M and radius R ($< L$) is attached at its center to the free end of the rod. Consider two ways the disc is attached: (case A) The disc is not free to rotate about its center and (case B) the disc is free to be rotated about its center. The rod-disc system performs SHM in vertical plane after being released from the same displaced position. Which of the following statements is (are) true : **[JEE Adv 2011, P-1]**

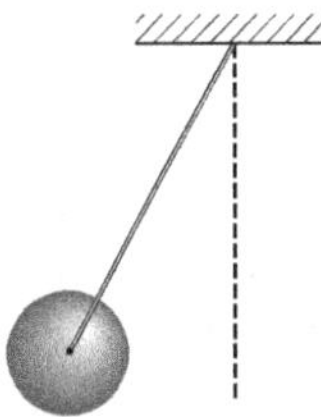

(A) Restoring torque in case A = Restoring torque in case B
(B) Restoring torque in case A < Restoring torque in case B
(C) Angular frequency for case A > Angular frequency for case B
(D) Angular frequency for case A < Angular frequency for case B

5. A particle of mass m is attached to one of a massless spring of force constant k, lying on a frictionless horizontal plane. The other end of the spring is fixed. The particle starts moving horizontally from its equilibrium position at time $t = 0$ with an initial velocity u_0. When the speed of the particle is $0.5\,u_0$, it collides elastically with a rigid wall. After this collision : **[JEE Adv 2013, P-2]**

(A) The speed of the particle when it returns to its equilibrium position is u_0
(B) The time at which the particle passes through the equilibrium position for the first time is $t = \pi\sqrt{\dfrac{m}{k}}$
(C) The time at which the maximum compression of the spring occurs is $t = \dfrac{4\pi}{3}\sqrt{\dfrac{m}{k}}$
(D) The time at which the particle passes through the equilibrium position for the second time is $t = \dfrac{5\pi}{3}\sqrt{\dfrac{m}{k}}$

6. Two independent harmonic oscillators of equal mass are oscillating about the origin with angular frequencies ω_1 and ω_2 and have total energies E_1 and E_2, respectively. The variations of their momenta p with positions x are shown in the figures. If $\dfrac{a}{b} = n^2$ and $\dfrac{a}{R} = n$, then the correct equation(s) is (are) : **[JEE Adv 2015, P-1]**

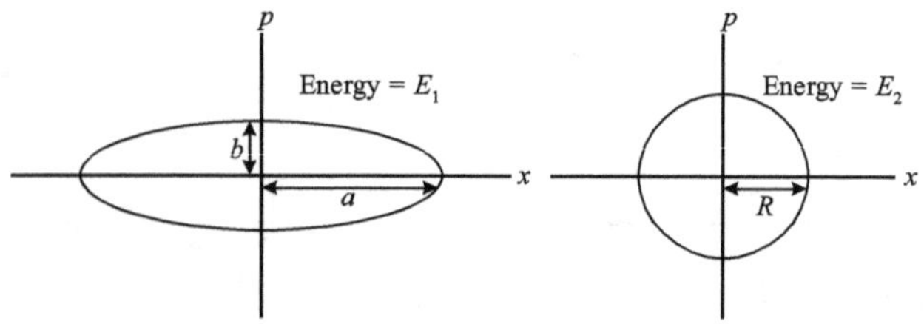

(A) $E_1\omega_1 = E_2\omega_2$

(B) $\dfrac{\omega_2}{\omega_1} = n^2$

(C) $\omega_1\omega_2 = n^2$

(D) $\dfrac{E_1}{\omega_1} = \dfrac{E_2}{E_2}$

7. A block with mass M is connected by a massless spring with stiffness constant k to a rigid wall and moves without friction on a horizontal surface. The block oscillates with small amplitude A about an equilibrium position x_0. Consider two cases : (i) when the block is at x_0; and (ii) when the block is at $x = x_0 + A$. In both the cases, a particle with mass m ($< M$) is softly placed on the block after which they stick to each other. Which of the following statements(s) is (are) true about the motion after the mass m is placed on the mass M?

[JEE Adv 2016, P-2]

(A) The amplitude of oscillation in the first case changes by a factor of $\sqrt{\dfrac{M}{m+M}}$, whereas in the second case it remains unchanged

(B) The final time period of oscillation in both the cases is same

(C) The total energy decreases in both the cases

(D) The instantaneous speed at x_0 of the combined masses decreases in both the cases

8. A block of mass $2M$ is attached to a massless spring with spring-constant k. This block is connected to two other blocks of masses M and $2M$ using two massless pulleys and strings. The accelerations of the blocks are a_1, a_2 and a_3 as shown in figure. The system is released from rest with the spring in its unstretched state. The maximum extension of the spring is x_0. Which of the following option(s) is/are correct ?

[g is the acceleration due to gravity. Neglect friction]

[JEE Adv 2019, P-2]

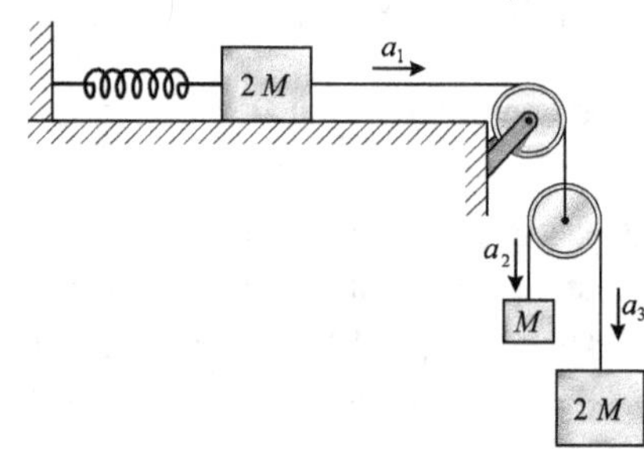

(A) $x_0 = \dfrac{4Mg}{k}$

(B) When spring achieves an extension of $\dfrac{x_0}{2}$ for the first time, the speed of the block connected to the spring is $3g\sqrt{\dfrac{M}{5k}}$

(C) $a_2 - a_1 = a_1 - a_3$

(D) At an extension of $\dfrac{x_0}{4}$ of the spring, the magnitude of acceleration of the block connected to the spring is $\dfrac{3g}{10}$

Matrix Match MCQ

9. **Column-I** describes some situations in which a small object moves. **Column-II** describes some characteristics of these motion. Match the situations in **Column-I** with the characteristics in **Column-II** and indicate your answer by darkening appropriate bubbles in the 4×4 matrix given in the ORS : **[JEE Adv 2007, P-2]**

Column-I

(A) The object moves on the x-axis under a conservative force in such a way that its "speed" and "position" satisfy $v = c_1\sqrt{c_2 - x^2}$, where c_1 and c_2 are positive constants.

(B) The object moves on the x-axis in such a way that its velocity and its displacement from the origin satisfy $v = -kx$, where k is a positive constant.

(C) The object is attached to one end of a massless spring of a given spring constant. The other end of the spring is attached to the ceiling of an elevator. Initially everything is at rest. The elevator starts going upwards with a constant acceleration a. The motion of the object is observed from the elevator during the period it maintains this acceleration.

(D) The object is projected from the earth's surface vertically upwards with a speed $2\sqrt{GM_e / R_e}$, where, M_e is the mass of the earth and R_e is the radius of the earth. Neglect forces from objects other than the earth.

Column-II

(P) The object executes a simple harmonic motion

(Q) The object does not change its direction

(R) The kinetic energy of the object keeps on decreasing

(S) The object can change its direction only once

10. List-I describes four systems, each with two particles A and B in relative motion as shown in figures. List-II gives possible magnitudes of their relative velocities (in ms^{-1}) at time $t = \dfrac{\pi}{3}$ s. **[JEE Adv 2022, P-1]**

List-I	List-II
(I) A and B are moving on a horizontal circle of radius 1 m with uniform angular speed $\omega = 1$ rad s^{-1}. The initial angular positions of A and B at time $t = 0$ are $\theta = 0$ and $\theta = \pi/2$, respectively	(P) $\dfrac{\sqrt{3}+1}{2}$

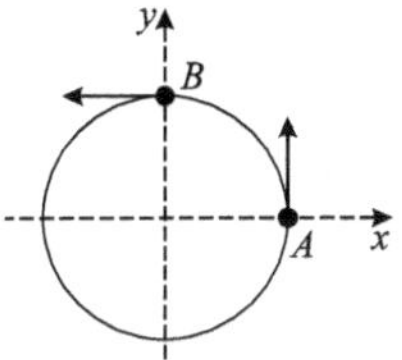

(II) Projectiles A and B are fired (in the same vertical plane) at $t = 0$ and $t = 0.1$ s respectively, with the same speed $v = \dfrac{5\pi}{\sqrt{2}}$ ms^{-1} and at 45° from the horizontal plane. The initial separation between A and B is large enough so that they do not collide. $(g = 10$ ms$^{-2})$

(Q) $\dfrac{(\sqrt{3}-1)}{\sqrt{2}}$

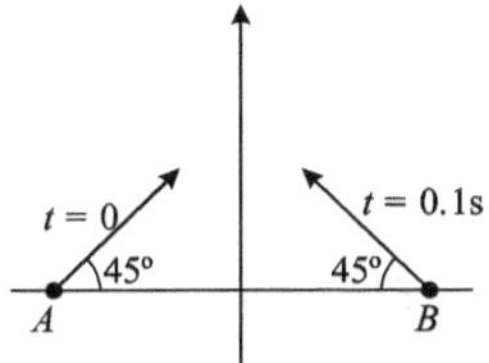

(III) Two harmonic oscillators A and B moving in the x direction according to $x_A = x_0 \sin \dfrac{t}{t_0}$ and $x_B = x_0 \sin\left(\dfrac{t}{t_0} + \dfrac{\pi}{2}\right)$ respectively, starting from $t = 0$. Take $x_0 = 1$ m, $t_0 = 1$ s

(R) $\sqrt{10}$

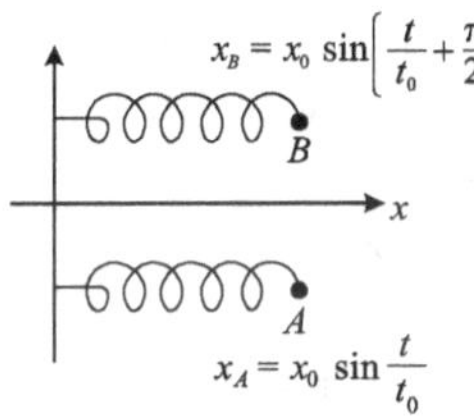

(IV) Particle A is rotating in a horizontal circular path of radius 1 m on the xy plane, with constant angular speed $\omega = 1$ rad s^{-1}. Particle B is moving up at a constant speed 3 m s^{-1} in the vertical direction as shown in the figure. (Ignore gravity).

(S) $\sqrt{2}$

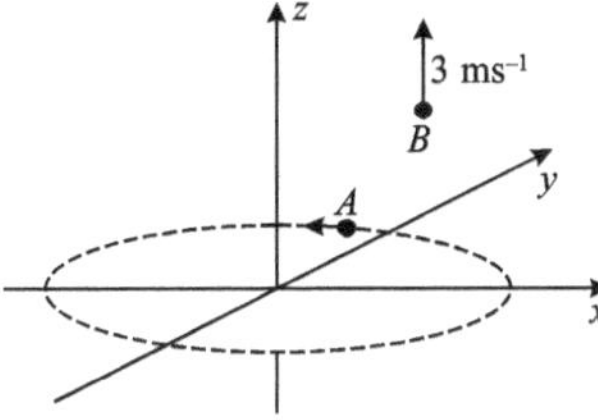

(T) $\sqrt{25\pi^2 + 1}$

Which one of the following options is correct?
(A) I $\to$ R, II $\to$ T, III $\to$ P, IV $\to$ S
(B) I $\to$ S, II $\to$ P, III $\to$ Q, IV $\to$ R
(C) I $\to$ S, II $\to$ T, III $\to$ P, IV $\to$ R

(D) I $\to$ T, II $\to$ P, III $\to$ R, IV $\to$ S

Comprehension based MCQ

Paragraph-1 (Q. No. 11 to 13)

When a particle of mass m moves on the x-axis in a potential of the form $V(x) = kx^2$, it performs simple harmonic motion. The corresponding time period is proportional to $\sqrt{\dfrac{m}{k}}$, as can be seen easily using dimensional analysis. However, the motion of a particle can be periodic even when its potential energy increases on both sides of $x = 0$ in a way different from kx^2 and its total energy is such that the particle does not escape to infinity. Consider a particle of mass m moving on the x-axis. Its potential energy is $V(x) = \alpha x^4$ $(\alpha > 0)$ for $|x|$ near the origin and becomes a constant equal to V_0 for $|x| \ge X_0$ (see figure) :

[JEE Adv 2010, P-1]

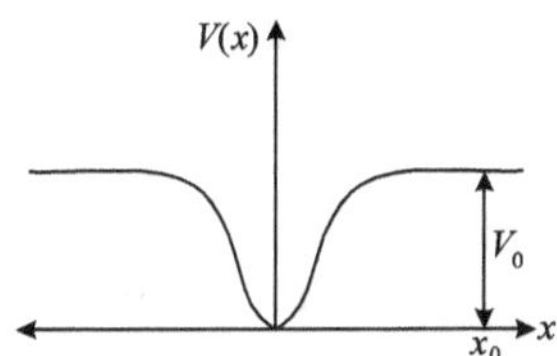

11. If the total energy of the particle is E, it will perform periodic motion only if :
(A) $E < 0$ (B) $E > 0$
(C) $V_0 > E > 0$ (D) $E > V_0$

12. For periodic motion of small amplitude A, the time period T of this particle is proportional to :
(A) $A\sqrt{\dfrac{m}{\alpha}}$ (B) $\dfrac{1}{A}\sqrt{\dfrac{m}{\alpha}}$
(C) $A\sqrt{\dfrac{\alpha}{m}}$ (D) $\dfrac{1}{A}\sqrt{\dfrac{\alpha}{m}}$

13. The acceleration of this particle for $|x| > X_0$ is :
(A) Proportional to $\dfrac{V_0}{mX_0}$ (B) Proportional to V_0
(C) Proportional to $\sqrt{\dfrac{V_0}{mX_0}}$ (D) Zero

Paragraph-2 (Q. No. 14 to 16)

Phase space diagrams are useful tools in analyzing all kinds of dynamical problems. They are especially useful in studying the changes in motion as initial position and momentum are changed. Here we consider some simple dynamical system in one-dimension. For such systems, phase space is a plane in which position is plotted along horizontal axis and momentum is plotted along vertical axis. The phase space diagram is $x(t)$

vs. $p(t)$ curve in this plane. The arrow on the curve indicates the time flow. For example, the phase space diagram for a particle moving with constant velocity is a straight line as shown in the figure. We use the sign convention in which position or momentum upwards (or to right) is positive and downwards (or to left) is negative : **[JEE Adv 2011, P-1]**

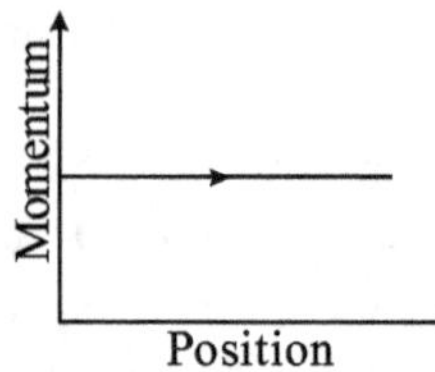

14. The phase space diagram for a ball thrown vertically up from ground is :

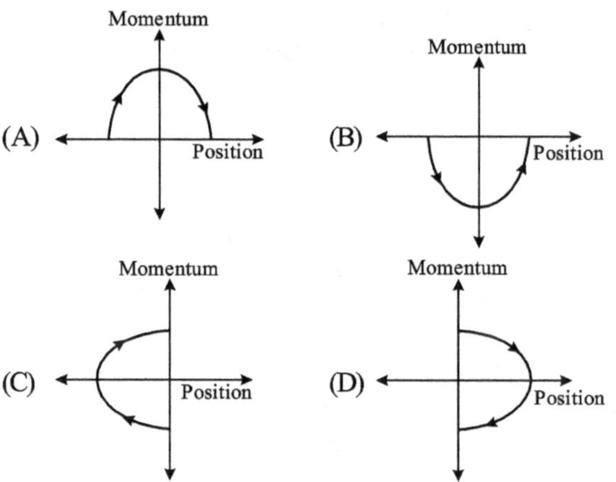

15. The phase space diagram for simple harmonic motion is a circle centered at the origin. In the figure, the two circles represent the same oscillator but for different initial conditions, and E_1 and E_2 are the total mechanical energies respectively. Then :

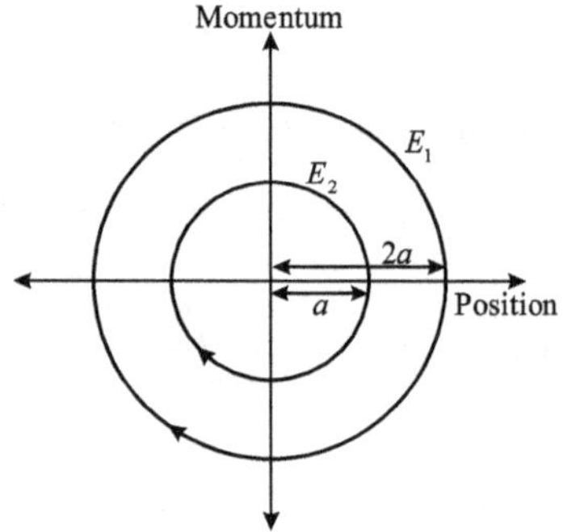

(A) $E_1 = \sqrt{2}E_2$ (B) $E_1 = 2E_2$

(C) $E_1 = 4E_2$ (D) $E_1 = 16E_2$

16. Consider the spring-mass system, with the mass submerged in water, as shown in the figure. The phase space diagram for one cycle of this system is :

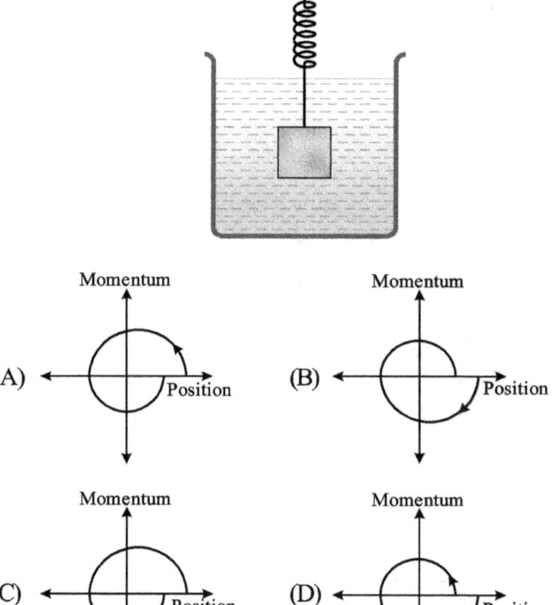

Integer Answer based Questions

17. On a frictionless horizontal plane, a bob of mass $m = 0.1$ kg is attached to a spring with natural length $l_0 = 0.1$ m. The spring constant is $k_1 = 0.009$ Nm^{-1} when the length of the spring $l > l_0$ and is $k_2 = 0.016$ Nm^{-1} when $l < l_0$. Initially the bob is released from $l = 0.15$ m. Assume that Hooke's law remains valid throughout the motion. If the time period of the full oscillation is $T = (n\,\pi)$ s, then the integer closest to n is _______.

[JEE Adv 2022, P-2]

18. Two point-like objects of masses 20 gm and 30 gm are fixed at the two ends of a rigid massless rod of length 10 cm. This system is suspended vertically from a rigid ceiling using a thin wire attached to its center of mass, as shown in the figure. The resulting torsional pendulum undergoes small oscillations. The torsional constant of the wire is 1.2×10^{-8} N m rad^{-1}. The angular frequency of the oscillations in $n \times 10^{-3}$ rad s^{-1}. The value of n is _______. **[JEE Adv 2023, P-1]**

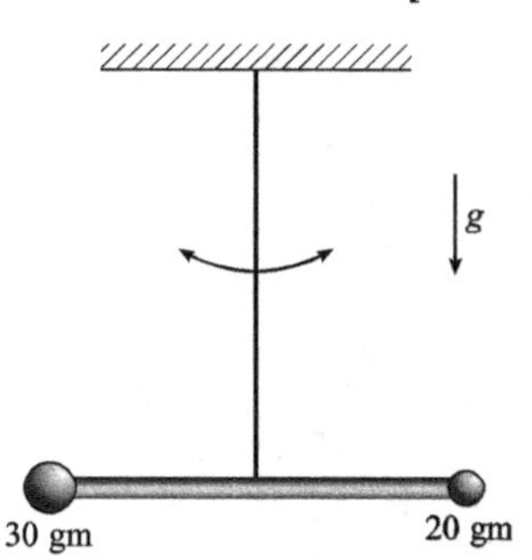

$*$ $*$ $*$ $*$ $*$

MCQ with Single Option Correct

1. In the experiment to determine the speed of sound using a resonance column : **[JEE Adv 2007, P-2]**
(A) Prongs of the tuning fork are kept in a vertical plane
(B) Prongs of the tuning fork are kept in a horizontal plane
(C) In one of the two resonances observed, the length of the resonating air column is close to the wavelength of sound in air
(D) In one of the two resonances observed, the length of the resonating air column is close to half of the wavelength of sound in air

2. A vibrating string of certain length l under a tension T resonates with a mode corresponding to the first overtone (third harmonic) of an air column of length 75 cm inside a tube closed at one end. The string also generates 4 beats per second when excited along with a tuning fork of frequency n. Now when the tension of the string is slightly increased the number of beats reduces to 2 per second. Assuming the velocity of sound in air to be 340 m/s, the frequency n of the tuning fork in Hz is : **[JEE Adv 2008, P-2]**
(A) 344 (B) 336
(C) 117.3 (D) 109.3

3. A transverse sinusoidal wave moves along a string in the positive x-direction at a speed of 10 cm/s. The wavelength of the wave is 0.5 m and its amplitude is 10 cm. At a particular time t, the snapshot of the wave is shown in figure. The velocity of point P when its displacement is 5 cm is : **[JEE Adv 2008, P-2]**

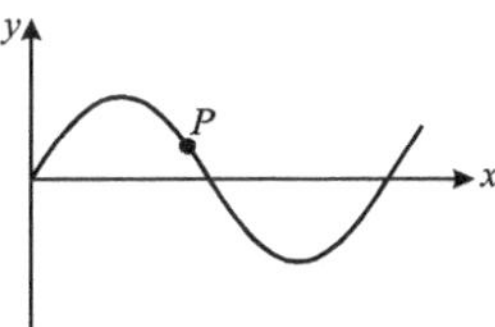

(A) $\dfrac{\sqrt{3}\pi}{50}\,\hat{j}$ m/s (B) $-\dfrac{\sqrt{3}\pi}{50}\,\hat{j}$ m/s

(C) $\dfrac{\sqrt{3}\pi}{50}\,\hat{i}$ m/s (D) $-\dfrac{\sqrt{3}\pi}{50}\,\hat{i}$ m/s

4. A hollow pipe of length 0.8 m is closed at one end. At its open end a 0.5 m long uniform string is vibrating in its second harmonic and it resonate with the fundamental frequency of the pipe. If the tension in the wire is 50 N and the speed of sound is 320 ms^{-1}, then mass of the string is : **[JEE Adv 2010, P-2]**
(A) 5 grams (B) 10 grams
(C) 20 grams (D) 40 grams

5. A police car with a siren of frequency 8 kHz is moving with uniform velocity 36 km/hr towards a tall building which reflects the sound waves. The speed of sound in air is 320 m/s. The frequency of the siren heard by the car driver is : **[JEE Adv 2011, P-1]**
(A) 8.50 kHz (B) 8.25 kHz
(C) 7.75 kHz (D) 7.50 kHz

6. A student is performing the experiment of Resonance Column. The diameter of the column tube is 4 cm. The frequency of the tuning fork is 512 Hz. The air temperature is 38°C in which the speed of sound is 336 m/s. The zero of the meter scale coincides with the top end of the Resonance Column tube. When the first resonance occurs, the reading of the water level in the column is : **[JEE Adv 2012, P-2]**
(A) 14.0 cm (B) 15.2 cm
(C) 16.4 cm (D) 17.6 cm

MCQ with One or More than One Options Correct

7. A student performed the experiment to measure the speed of sound in air using resonance air-column method. Two resonances in the air-column were obtained by lowering the water level. The resonance with the shorter air-column is the first resonance and that with longer air-column is the second resonance. Then, : **[JEE Adv 2009, P-2]**
(A) The intensity of the sound heard at the first resonance was more than that at the second resonance
(B) The prongs of the tuning fork were kept in a horizontal plane above the resonance tube
(C) The amplitude of vibration of the ends of the prongs is typically around 1 cm
(D) The length of the air-column at the first resonance was somewhat shorter than 1/4th of the wavelength of sound in air

8. A person blows into open-end of a long pipe. As a result, a high-pressure pulse of air travels down the pipe. When this pulse reaches the other end of the pipe : **[JEE Adv 2012, P-1]**
(A) A high-pressure pulse starts traveling up the pipe, if the other end of the pipe is open
(B) A low-pressure pulse starts traveling up the pipe, if the other end of the pipe is open

(C) A low-pressure pulse starts traveling up the pipe, if the other end of the pipe is closed

(D) A high-pressure pulse starts traveling up the pipe, if the other end of the pipe is closed

9. A horizontal stretched string, fixed at two ends, is vibrating in its fifth harmonic according to the equation, $y(x, t) = (0.01\text{ m}) \sin [(62.8\text{ m}^{-1})\, x] \cos[(628\text{ s}^{-1})\, t]$. Assuming $\pi = 3.14$, the correct statement(s) is (are) : **[JEE Adv 2013, P-1]**

(A) The number of nodes is 5

(B) The length of the string is 0.25 m

(C) The maximum displacement of the midpoint of the string, from its equilibrium position is 0.01 m

(D) The fundamental frequency is 100 Hz

10. Two vehicles, each moving with speed u on the same horizontal straight road, are approaching each other. Wind blows along the road with velocity w. One of these vehicles blows a whistle of frequency f_1. An observer in the other vehicle hears the frequency of the whistle to be f_2. The speed of sound in still air is V. The correct statement(s) is are :

[JEE Adv 2013, P-2]

(A) If the wind blows from the observer to the source, $f_2 > f_1$

(B) If the wind blows from the source to the observer, $f_2 > f_1$

(C) If the wind blows from observer to the source, $f_2 < f_1$

(D) If the wind blows from the source to the observer $f_2 < f_1$

11. One end of a taut string of length 3 m along the x-axis is fixed at $x = 0$. The speed of the waves in the string is 100 ms^{-1}. The other end of the string is vibrating in the y direction so that stationary waves are set up in the string. The possible waveform(s) of these stationary waves is (are) :

[JEE Adv 2014, P-1]

(A) $y(t) = A\sin\dfrac{\pi x}{6}\cos\dfrac{50\pi t}{3}$ (B) $y(t) = A\sin\dfrac{\pi x}{3}\cos\dfrac{100\pi t}{3}$

(C) $y(t) = A\sin\dfrac{5\pi x}{6}\cos\dfrac{250\pi t}{3}$ (D) $y(t) = A\sin\dfrac{5\pi x}{2}\cos 250\pi t$

12. Two loudspeakers M and N are located 20 m apart and emit sound at frequencies 118 Hz and 121 Hz, respectively. A car is initially at a point P, 1800 m away from the midpoint Q of the line MN and moves towards Q constantly at 60 km/hr along the perpendicular Bisector of MN. It crosses Q and eventually reaches a point R, 1800 m away from Q. Let $v(t)$ represent the beat frequency measured by a person sitting in the car at time t. Let v_P, v_Q and v_R be the beat frequencies measured at locations P, Q and R, respectively. The speed of sound in air is 330 ms^{-1}. Which of the following statement(s) is(are) true regarding the sound heard by the person ?   **[JEE Adv 2016, P-1]**

(A) The plot below represents schematically the variation of beat frequency with time

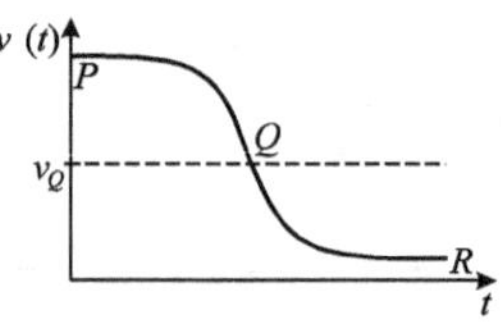

(B) The plot below represents schematically the variation of beat frequency with time

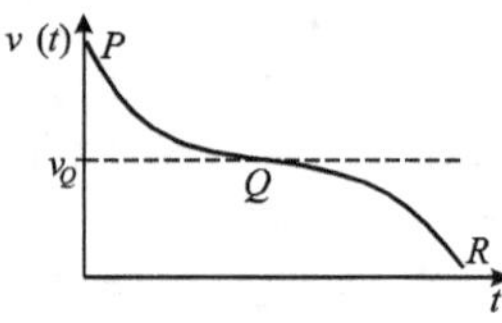

(C) The rate of change in beat frequency is maximum when the car passes through Q

(D) $v_P + v_R = 2v_Q$

13. A block M hangs vertically at the bottom end of a uniform rope of constant mass per unit length. The top end of the rope is attached to a fixed rigid support at O. A transverse wave pulse (Pulse 1) of wavelength λ_0 is produced at point O on the rope. The pulse takes time T_{OA} to reach point a. If the wave pulse of wavelength λ_0 is produced at point A (Pulse 2) without disturbing the position of M it takes time T_{AO} to reach point O. Which of the following options is/are correct :

[JEE Adv 2017, P-1]

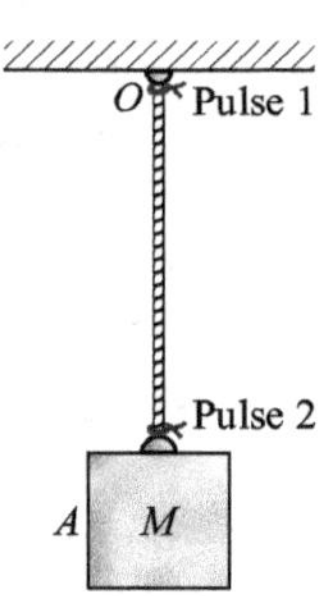

(A) The time $T_{AO} = T_{OA}$

(B) The velocities of the two pulses (Pulse 1 and Pulse 2) are the same at the midpoint of rope.

(C) The wavelength of Pulse 1 becomes longer when it reaches point A.

(D) The velocity of any pulse along the rope is independent of its frequency and wavelength.

14. In an experiment to measure the speed of sound by a resonating air column, a tuning fork of frequency 500 Hz is used. The length of the air column is varied by changing the level of water in the resonance tube. Two successive resonances are heard at air columns of length 50.7 cm and 83.9 cm. Which of the following statements is (are) true ? **[JEE Adv 2018, P-2]**

(A) The speed of sound determined from this experiment is $332\ \text{ms}^{-1}$

(B) The end correction in this experiment is 0.9 cm

(C) The wavelength of the sound wave is 66.4 cm

(D) The resonance at 50.7 cm corresponds to the fundamental harmonic

15. A source, approaching with speed u towards the open end of a stationary pipe of length L, is emitting a sound of frequency f_s. The farther end of the pipe is closed. The speed of sound in air is v and f_0 is the fundamental frequency of the pipe. For which of the following combination(s) of u and f_s, will the sound reaching the pipe lead to a resonance ? **[JEE Adv 2021, P-2]**

(A) $u = 0.8v$ and $f_s = f_0$ (B) $u = 0.8v$ and $f_s = 2f_0$

(C) $u = 0.8v$ and $f_s = 0.5f_0$ (D) $u = 0.5v$ and $f_s = 1.5f_0$

Matrix Match MCQ

16. **Column-I** show four system, each of the same length L, for producing standing waves. The lowest possible natural frequency of a system is called its fundamental frequency, whose wavelength is denoted as λ_f. Match each system with statements given in **Column-II** describing the nature and wavelength of the standing waves. **[JEE Adv 2011, P-2]**

Column-I	**Column-II**
(A) Pipe closed at one end	(p) Longitudinal waves

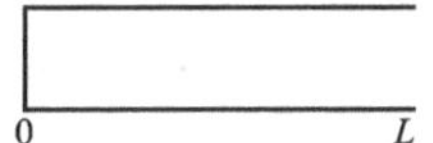

| (B) Pipe open at both ends | (q) Transverse waves |

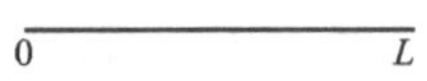

| (C) Stretched wire clamped at both ends | (r) $\lambda_f = L$ |

| (D) Stretched wire clamped at both ends and at mid-point | (s) $\lambda_f = 2L$ |

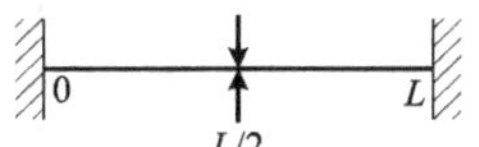

| | (t) $\lambda_f = 4L$ |

17. Answer the following by appropriately matching the Column based on the information given in the paragraph.

A musical instrument is made using four different metal strings, 1, 2, 3 and 4 with mass per unit length μ, 2μ, 3μ and 4μ respectively. The instrument is played by vibrating the strings by varying the free length in between the range L_0 and $2L_0$. It is found that in string-1 (μ) at free length L_0 and tension T_0 the fundamental mode frequency is f_0.

Column-I gives the above four strings while **Column-II** lists the magnitude of some quantity. **[JEE Adv 2019, P-2]**

Column-I	**Column-II**
(I) String-1 (μ)	(P) 1
(II) String-2 (2μ)	(Q) 1/2
(III) String-3 (3μ)	(R) $1/\sqrt{2}$
(IV) String-4 (4μ)	(S) $1/\sqrt{3}$
	(T) 3/16
	(U) 1/16

The length of the string 1, 2, 3 and 4 are kept fixed at L_0, $\dfrac{3L_0}{2}$, $\dfrac{5L_0}{4}$ and $\dfrac{7L_0}{4}$, respectively. Strings 1, 2, 3 and 4 are vibrated at their 1st, 3rd, 5th and 14th harmonics, respectively such that all the strings have same frequency. The correct match for the tension in the four strings in the units of T_0 will be.

(A) I → P, II → Q, III → T, IV → U

(B) I → T, II → Q, III → R, IV → U

(C) I → P, II → Q, III → R, IV → T

(D) I → P, II → R, III → T, IV → U

Comprehension based MCQ

Paragraph-1 (Q. No. 18-20)

Two trains A and B are moving with speeds 20 m/s and 30 m/s respectively in the same direction on the same straight track, with B ahead of A. The engines are at the front ends. The engine of train A blows a long whistle.

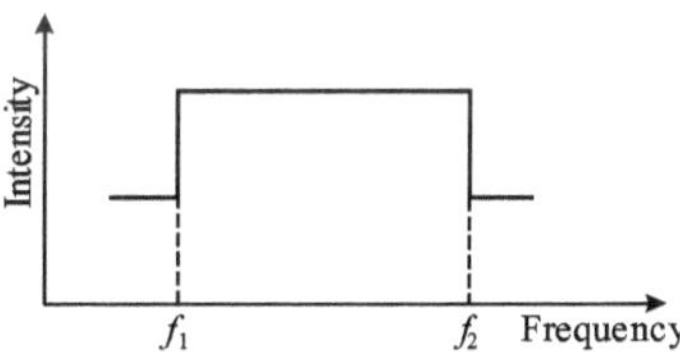

Assume that the sound of the whistle is composed of components varying in frequency from $f_1 = 800\ \text{Hz}$ to $f_2 = 1120\ \text{Hz}$, as shown in the figure. The spread in the frequency (highest frequency − lowest frequency) is thus 320 Hz. The speed of sound in still air is 340 m/s. **[JEE Adv 2007, P-2]**

18. The speed of sound of the whistle is :

(A) 340 m/s for passengers in A and 310 m/s for passengers is B

(B) 360 m/s for passengers is A and 310 m/s for passengers in B

(C) 310 m/s for passengers in A and 360 m/s for passengers in B

(D) 340 m/s for passengers in both the trains

19. The distribution of the sound intensity of the whistle as observed by the passengers in train A is best represented by :

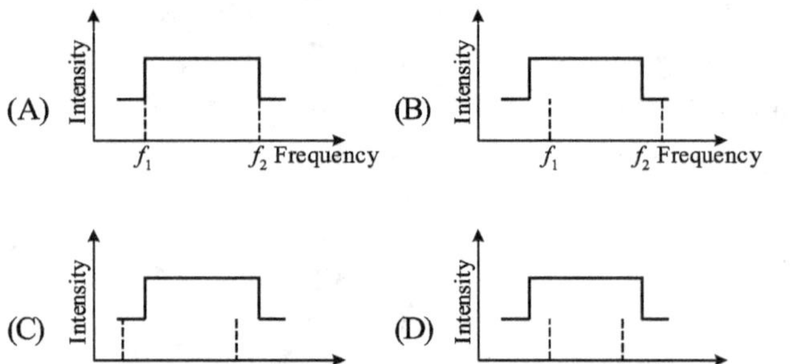

20. The spread of frequency as observed by the passengers in train B is :
(A) 310 Hz
(B) 330 Hz
(C) 350 Hz
(D) 290 Hz

Paragraph-1 (Q. No. 21-22)

S_1 and S_2 are two identical sound sources of frequency 656 Hz. The source S_1 is located at O and S_2 moves anti-clockwise with a uniform speed $4\sqrt{2}$ m s^{-1} on a circular path around O, as shown in the figure. There are three points P, Q and R on this path such that P and R are diametrically opposite while Q is equidistant from them. A sound detector is placed at point P. The source S_1 can move along direction OP.
[Given: The speed of sound in air is 324 m s^{-1}]

[JEE Adv 2023, P-2]

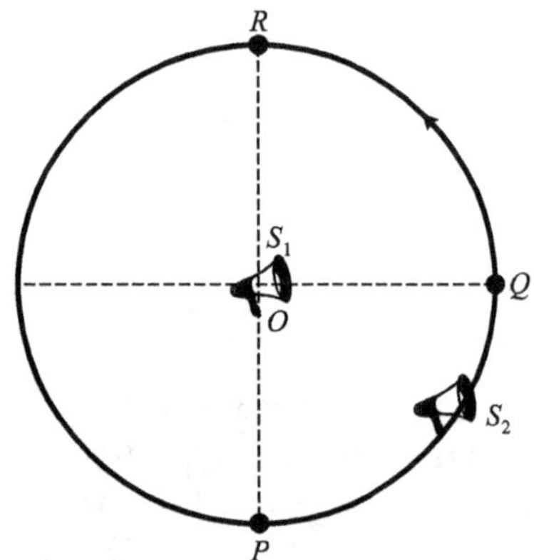

21. When only S_2 is emitting sound and it is at Q, the frequency of sound measured by the detector in Hz is______.

22. Consider both sources emitting sound. When S_2 is at R and S_1 approaches the detector with a speed 4 m s^{-1}, the beat frequency measured by the detector is______Hz.

Integer Answer based Questions

23. A 20 cm long string having a mass of 1.0 g, is fixed at both the ends. The tension in the string is 0.5 N. The string is set into vibration using an external vibrator of frequency 100 Hz. Find the separation (in cm) between the successive nodes on the string.   **[JEE Adv 2009, P-2]**

24. A stationary source is emitting sound at a fixed frequency f_0, which is reflected by two cars approaching the source. The difference between the frequencies of sound reflected from the cars is 1.2% of f_0. What is the difference in the speeds of the cars (in km per hour) to the nearest integer ? The cars are moving at constant speeds much smaller than the speed of sound which is 330 ms^{-1} ?   **[JEE Adv 2010, P-1]**

25. When two progressive waves $y_1 = 4 \sin(2x - 6t)$ and $y_2 = 3 \sin\left(2x - 6t - \dfrac{\pi}{2}\right)$ are superimposed, the amplitude of the resultant wave is ?   **[JEE Adv 2010, P-1]**

26. Four harmonic waves of equal frequencies and equal intensities I_0 have phase angles 0, $\pi/3$, $2\pi/3$ and π. When they are superposed, the intensity of the resulting wave is nI_0. The value of n is ?   **[JEE Adv 2015, P-2]**

27. A stationary source emits sound of frequency $f_0 = 492$ Hz. The sound is reflected by a large car approaching the source with a speed of 2 ms^{-1}. The reflected signal is received by the source and superposed with the original. What will be the beat frequency of the resulting signal in Hz ? (Given that the speed of sound in are is 330 ms^{-1} and the car reflects the sound at the frequency it has received) ?   **[JEE Adv 2017, P-1]**

28. Two men are walking along a horizontal straight line in the same direction. The man in front walks at a speed 1.0 ms^{-1} and the man behind walks at a speed 2.0 ms^{-1}. A third man is standing at a height 12 m above the same horizontal line such that all three men are in a vertical plane. The two walking men are blowing identical whistles which emit a sound of frequency 1430 Hz. The speed of sound in air is 330 ms^{-1}. At the instant, when the moving men are 10 m apart, the stationary man is equidistant from them. The frequency of beats in Hz, heard by the stationary man at this instant, is ______.

[JEE Adv 2018, P-1]

29. A train S1, moving with a uniform velocity of 108 km/h, approaches another train S2 standing on a platform. An observer O moves with a uniform velocity of 36 km/h towards S2, as shown in figure. Both the trains are blowing whistles of same frequency 120 Hz. When O is 600 m away from S2 and distance between S1 and S2 is 800 m, the number of beats heard by O is ______ . [Speed of the sound = 330 m/s]

[JEE Adv 2019, P-1]

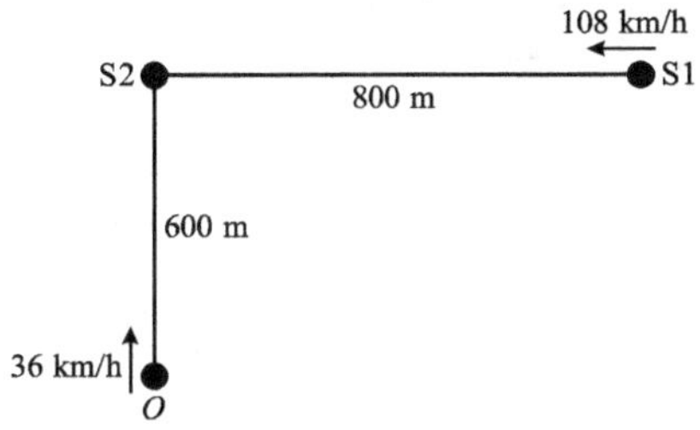

30. A stationary tuning fork is in resonance with an air column in a pipe. If the tuning fork is moved with a speed of 2 ms^{-1} in front of the open end of the pipe and parallel to it, the length of the pipe should be changed for the resonance to occur with the moving tuning fork. If the speed of sound in air is 320 ms^{-1}, the smallest value of the percentage change required in the length of the pipe is _______.   **[JEE Adv 2020, P-1]**

31. A string of length 1 m and mass 2×10^{-5} kg is under tension T. When the string vibrates, two successive harmonics are found to occur at frequencies 750 Hz and 1000 Hz. The value of tension T is______ Newton.   **[JEE Adv 2023, P-2]**

*   *   *   *   *

12 ELECTRIC CHARGES, FIELD & POTENTIAL

MCQ with Single Option Correct

1. Consider a neutral conducting sphere. A positive point charge is placed outside the sphere. The net charge on the sphere is then : **[JEE Adv 2007, P-1]**
(A) Negative and distributed uniformly over the surface of the sphere
(B) Negative and appears only at the point on the sphere closest to the point charge
(C) Negative and distributed non-uniformly over the entire surface of the sphere
(D) Zero

2. A long, hollow conducting cylinder is kept coaxially inside another long, hollow conducting cylinder of larger radius. Both the cylinders are initially electrically neutral :
[JEE Adv 2007, P-1]
(A) A potential difference appears between the two cylinders when a charge density is given to the inner cylinder
(B) A potential difference appears between the two cylinders when a charge density is given to the outer cylinder
(C) No potential difference appears between the two cylinders when a uniform line charge is kept along the axis of the cylinders
(D) No potential difference appears between the two cylinders when same charge density is given to both the cylinders

3. A spherical portion has been removed from a solid sphere having a charge distributed uniformly in its volume as shown in the figure. The electric field inside the emptied space is :
[JEE Adv 2007, P-2]

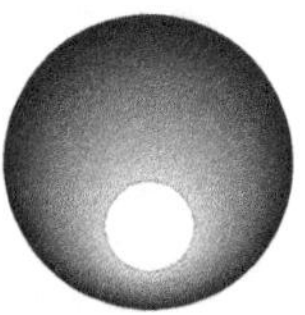

(A) Zero everywhere   (B) Non-zero and uniform
(C) Non-uniform   (D) Zero only at its center

4. Positive and negative point charges of equal magnitude are kept at $\left(0, 0, \dfrac{a}{2}\right)$ and $\left(0, 0, \dfrac{-a}{2}\right)$, respectively. The work done by the electric field when another positive point charge is moved from $(-a, 0, 0)$ to $(0, a, 0)$ is : **[JEE Adv 2007, P-2]**
(A) Positive
(B) Negative
(C) Zero

(D) Depends on the path connecting the initial and final positions

5. Consider a system of three charges $\dfrac{q}{3}, \dfrac{q}{3}$ and $-\dfrac{2q}{3}$ placed at points A, B and C, respectively, as shown in the figure. Take O to be the centre of circle of radius R and $CAB = 60°$:
[JEE Adv 2008, P-2]

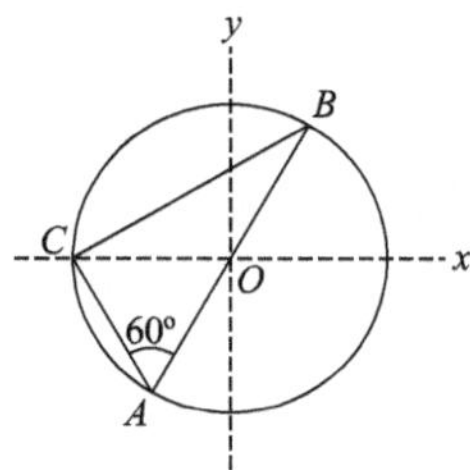

(A) The electric field at point O is $\dfrac{q}{8\pi\varepsilon_0 R^2}$ directed along the negative x-axis
(B) The potential energy of the system is zero
(C) The magnitude of the force between the charges at C and B is $\dfrac{q^2}{54\pi\varepsilon_0 R^2}$

(D) The potential at point O is $\dfrac{q}{12\pi\varepsilon_0 R}$

6. Three concentric metallic spherical shells of radii R, $2R$, $3R$, are given charges Q_1, Q_2, Q_3, respectively. It is found that the surface charge densities on the outer surfaces of the shells are equal. Then, the ratio of the charges given to the shells, $Q_1 : Q_2 : Q_3$, is : **[JEE Adv 2009, P-1]**
(A) $1 : 2 : 3$ (B) $1 : 3 : 5$
(C) $1 : 4 : 9$ (D) $1 : 8 : 18$

7. A disk of radius of $a/4$ having a uniformly distributed charge $6C$ is placed in the x-y plane with its centre at $(-a/2, 0, 0)$. A rod of length a carrying a uniformly distributed charge $8C$ is placed on the x-axis from $x = a/4$ to $x = 5a/4$. Two point charges $-7C$ and $3C$ are placed at $(a/4, -a/4, 0)$ and $(-3a/4, 3a/4, 0)$, respectively. Consider a cubical surface formed by six surfaces $x = \pm a/2$, $y = \pm a/2$, $z = \pm a/2$. The electric flux through this cubical surface is : **[JEE Adv 2009, P-1]**

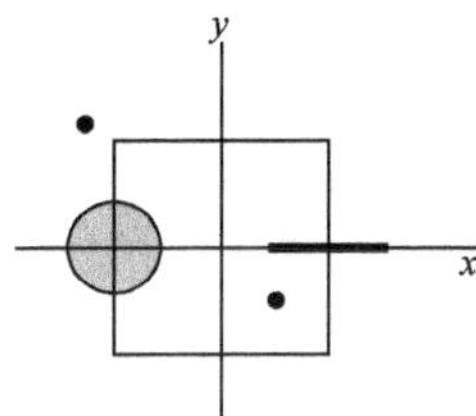

(A) $\dfrac{-2C}{\varepsilon_0}$

(B) $\dfrac{2C}{\varepsilon_0}$

(C) $\dfrac{10C}{\varepsilon_0}$

(D) $\dfrac{12C}{\varepsilon_0}$

8. A tiny spherical oil drop carrying a net charge q is balanced in still air with a vertical uniform electric field of strength $\dfrac{81\pi}{7} \times 10^5$ Vm^{-1}. When the field is switched off, the drop is observed to fall with terminal velocity 2×10^{-3} m s^{-1}. Given $g = 9.8$ m s^{-2}, viscosity of the air $= 1.8 = 10^{-5}$ Ns m^{-2} and the density of oil $= 900$ kg m^{-3}, the magnitude of q is :

[JEE Adv 2010, P-2]

(A) 1.6×10^{-19} C

(B) 3.2×10^{-19} C

(C) 4.8×10^{-19} C

(D) 8.0×10^{-19} C

9. A uniformly charged thin spherical shell of radius R carries uniform surface charge density of σ per unit area. It is made of two hemispherical shells, held together by pressing them with force F (see figure). F is proportional to : **[JEE Adv 2010, P-2]**

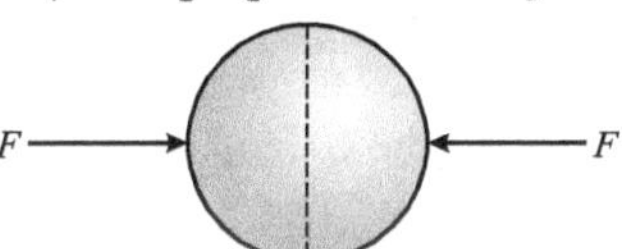

(A) $\dfrac{1}{\varepsilon_0} \sigma^2 R^2$

(B) $\dfrac{1}{\varepsilon_0} \sigma^2 R$

(C) $\dfrac{1}{\varepsilon_0} \dfrac{\sigma^2}{R}$

(D) $\dfrac{1}{\varepsilon_0} \dfrac{\sigma^2}{R^2}$

10. Consider an electric field $\vec{E} = E_0\hat{x}$, where E_0 is a constant. The flux through the shaded area (as shown in the figure) due to this field is : **[JEE Adv 2011, P-1]**

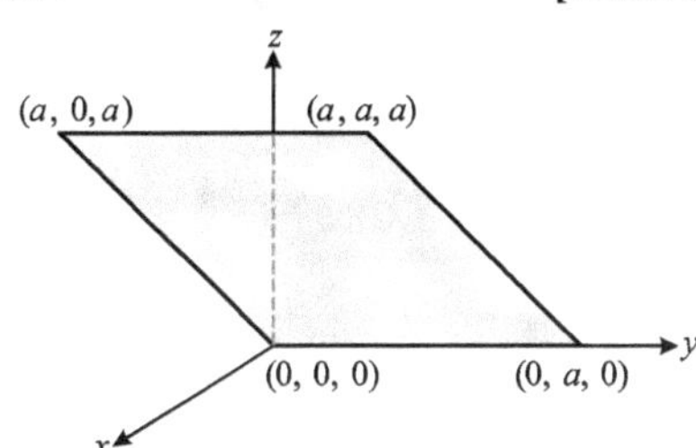

(A) $2E_0 a^2$

(B) $\sqrt{2}E_0 a^2$

(C) $E_0 a^2$

(D) $\dfrac{E_0 a^2}{\sqrt{2}}$

11. Two large vertical and parallel metal plates having a separation of 1 cm are connected to a DC voltage source of potential difference X. A proton is released at rest midway between the two plates. It is found to move at 45° to the vertical Just after release. Then X is nearly : **[JEE Adv 2012, P-1]**

(A) 1×10^{-5} V

(B) 1×10^{-7} V

(C) 1×10^{-9} V

(D) 1×10^{-10} V

12. Consider a thin spherical shell of radius R with its centre at the origin, carrying uniform positive surface charge density. The variation of the magnitude of the electric field $|\vec{E}(r)|$ and the electric potential $V(r)$ with the distance r from the centre, is best represented by which graph : **[JEE Adv 2012, P-1]**

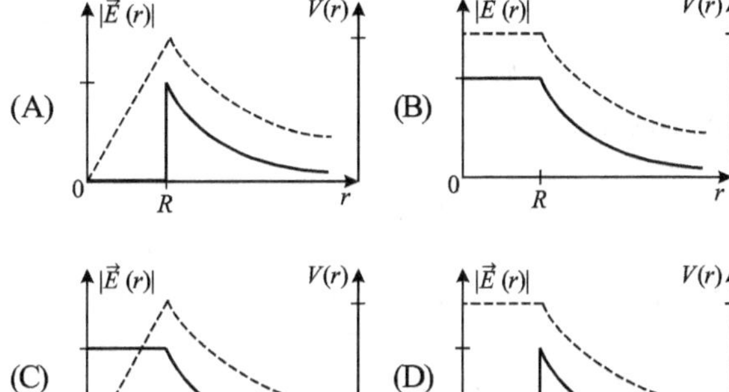

13. Let $E_1(r)$, $E_2(r)$ and $E_3(r)$ be the respective electric fields at a distance r from a point charge Q, an infinitely long wire with constant linear charge density λ, and an infinite plane with uniform surface charge density σ. If $E_1(r_0) = E_2(r_0) = E_3(r_0)$ at a given distance r_0, then : **[JEE Adv 2014, P-1]**

(A) $Q = 4\sigma\pi r_0^2$

(B) $r_0 = \dfrac{\lambda}{2\pi\sigma}$

(C) $E_1(r_0/2) = 2E_2(r_0/2)$

(D) $E_2(r_0/2) = 4E_3(r_0/2)$

14. Charges Q, $2Q$ and $4Q$ are uniformly distributed in three dielectric solid spheres 1, 2 and 3 of radii $R/2$, R and $2R$ respectively, as shown in figure. If magnitudes of the electric fields at point P at a distance R from the centre of spheres 1, 2 and 3 are E_1, E_2 and E_3 respectively, then : **[JEE Adv 2014, P-2]**

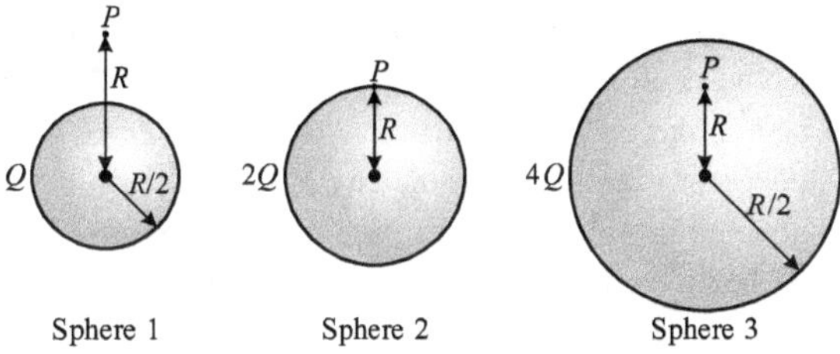

(A) $E_1 > E_2 > E_3$

(B) $E_3 > E_1 > E_2$

(C) $E_2 > E_1 > E_3$

(D) $E_3 > E_2 > E_1$

15. A thin spherical insulating shell of radius R carries a uniformly distributed charge such that the potential at its surface is V_0. A hole with a small area $\alpha 4\pi R^2$ ($\alpha \ll 1$) is made on the shell without affecting the rest of the shell. Which one of the following statements is correct : **[JEE Adv 2019, P-1]**

(A) The ratio of the potential at the center of the shell to that of the point at $\frac{1}{2}R$ from center towards the hole will be $\frac{1-\alpha}{1-2\alpha}$

(B) The magnitude of electric field at the center of the shell is reduced by $\frac{\alpha V_0}{2R}$

(C) The magnitude of electric field at a point, located on a line passing through the hole and shell's center on a distance $2R$ from the center of the spherical shell will be reduced by $\frac{\alpha V_0}{2R}$

(D) The potential at the center of the shell is reduced by $2\alpha V_0$

16. An electric dipole is formed by two charges $+q$ and $-q$ located in xy-plane at $(0, 2)$ mm and $(0, -2)$ mm, respectively, as shown in the figure. The electric potential at point $P(100, 100)$ mm due to the dipole is V_0. The charges $+q$ and $-q$ are then moved to the points $(-1, 2)$ mm and $(1, -2)$ mm, respectively. What is the value of electric potential at P due to the new dipole? **[JEE Adv 2023, P-2]**

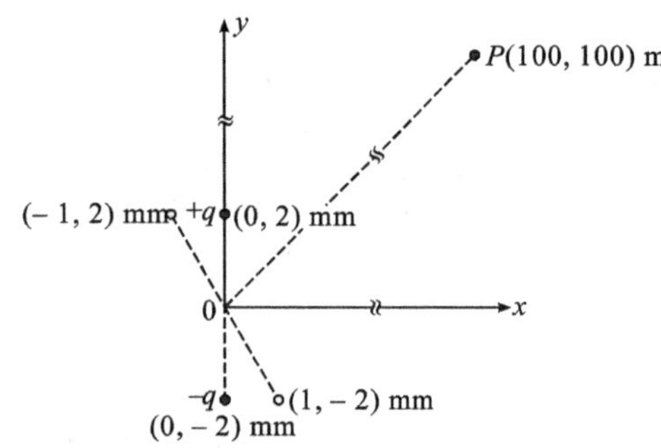

(A) $V_0/4$ (B) $V_0/2$

(C) $V_0/\sqrt{2}$ (D) $3V_0/4$

MCQ with One or More than One Options Correct

17. Under the influence of the Electric field of charge $+Q$, a charge $-q$ is moving around it in an elliptical orbit. Find out the correct statement(s) : **[JEE Adv 2009, P-2]**

(A) The angular momentum of the charge $-q$ is constant

(B) The linear momentum of the charge $-q$ is constant

(C) The angular velocity of the charge $-q$ is constant

(D) The linear speed of the charge $-q$ is constant

18. A few electric field lines for a system of two charges Q_1 and Q_2 fixed at two different points on the x-axis are shown in the figure. These lines suggest that : **[JEE Adv 2010, P-1]**

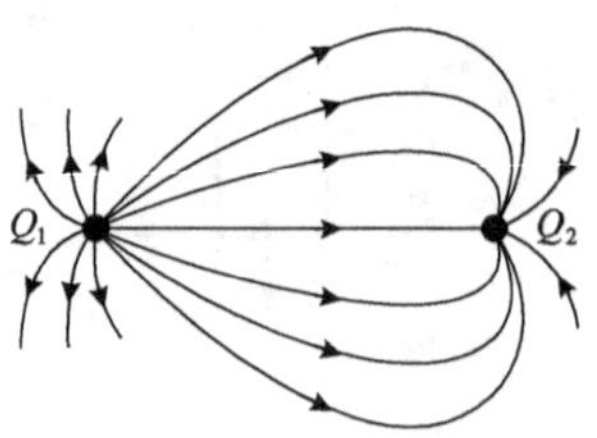

(A) $|Q_1| > |Q_2|$ (B) $|Q_1| < |Q_2|$

(C) At a finite distance to the left of Q_1 the electric field is zero

(D) At a finite distance to the right of Q_2 the electric field is zero

19. A spherical metal shell A of radius R_A and a solid metal sphere B of radius R_B $(< R_A)$ are kept far apart and each of these is given charge $+Q$. Now they are connected by a thin metal wire. Then : **[JEE Adv 2011, P-1]**

(A) $E_A^{\text{inside}} = 0$ (B) $Q_A > Q_B$

(C) $\dfrac{\sigma_A}{\sigma_B} = \dfrac{R_B}{R_A}$ (D) $E_A^{\text{on surface}} > E_B^{\text{on surface}}$

20. Which of the following statement(s) is/are correct : **[JEE Adv 2011, P-2]**

(A) If the electric field due to a point charge varies as $r^{-2.5}$ instead of r^{-2}, then the Gauss law will still be valid.

(B) The Gauss law can be used to calculate the field distribution around an electric dipole.

(C) If the electric field between two point charges is zero somewhere, then the sign of the two charges is the same.

(D) The work done by the external force in moving a unit positive charge from point A at potential V_A to point B at potential V_B is $(V_B - V_A)$.

21. A cubical region of side a has its centre at the origin. It encloses three fixed point charges, $-q$ at $(0, -a/4, 0)$, $+3q$ at $(0, 0, 0)$ and $-q$ at $(0, +a/4, 0)$. Choose the correct option : **[JEE Adv 2012, P-1]**

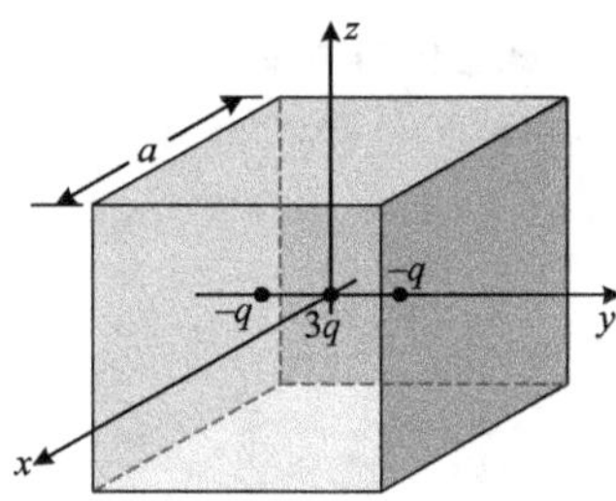

(A) The net electric flux crossing the plane $x = +a/2$ is equal to the net electric flux crossing the plane $x = -a/2$

(B) The net electric flux crossing the plane $y = +a/2$ is more than the net electric flux crossing the plane $y = -a/2$

(C) The net electric flux crossing the entire region is q/ε_0

(D) The net electric flux crossing the plane $z = +a/2$ is equal to the net electric flux crossing the plane $x = +a/2$

22. Six point charges are kept at the vertices of a regular hexagon of side L and centre O, as shown in the figure. Given that $K = \dfrac{1}{4\pi\varepsilon_0}\dfrac{q}{L^2}$, which of the following statement(s) is (are) correct :   **[JEE Adv 2012, P-2]**

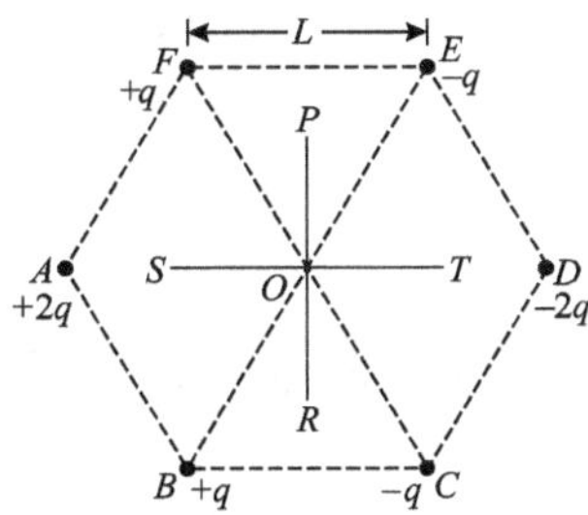

(A) The electric field at O is $6K$ along OD
(B) The potential at O is zero
(C) The potential at all points on the line PR is same
(D) The potential at all points on the line ST is same

23. Two non-conducting solid spheres of radii R and $2R$, having uniform volume charge densities ρ_1 and ρ_2 respectively, touch each other. The net electric field at a distance $2R$ from the centre of the smaller sphere, along the line joining the centres of the sphere, is zero. The ratio ρ_1/ρ_2 can be :   **[JEE Adv 2013, P-1]**

(A) -4

(B) $-\dfrac{32}{25}$

(C) $\dfrac{32}{25}$

(D) 4

24. Two non-conducting spheres of radii R_1 and R_2 and carrying uniform volume charge densities $+\rho$ and $-\rho$, respectively, are placed such that they partially overlap, as shown in the figure. At all point in the overlapping region :   **[JEE Adv 2013, P-2]**

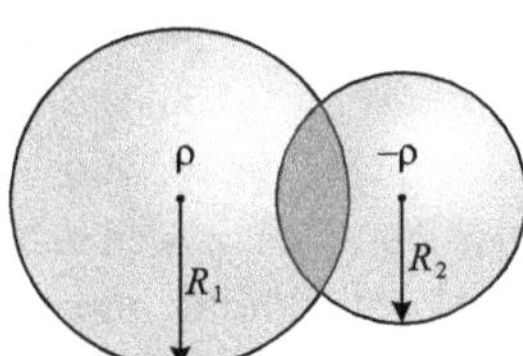

(A) The electrostatic field is zero
(B) The electrostatic potential is constant
(C) The electrostatic field is constant in magnitude
(D) The electrostatic field has same direction

25. The figures below depict two situations in which two infinitely long static line charges of constant positive line charge density λ are kept parallel to each other. In their resulting electric field, point charges q and $-q$ are kept in equilibrium between them. The point charges are confined to move in the x-direction only. If they are given a small displacement about their equilibrium positions, then the correct statement(s) is(are) :   **[JEE Adv 2015, P-1]**

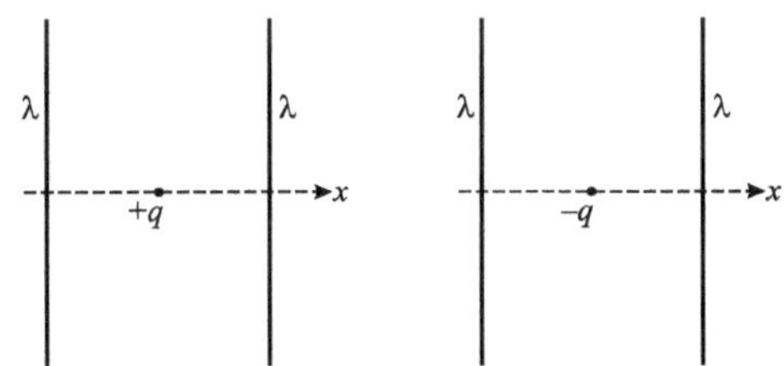

(A) Both charges execute simple harmonic motion.
(B) Both charges will continue moving in the direction of their displacement.
(C) Charge $+q$ executes simple harmonic motion while charge $-q$ continues moving in the direction of its displacement.
(D) Charge $-q$ executes simple harmonic motion while charge $+q$ continues moving in the direction of its displacement.

26. Consider a uniform spherical charge distribution of radius R_1 centred at the origin O. In this distribution, a spherical cavity of radius R_2, centred at P with distance $OP = a = R_1 - R_2$ (see figure) is made. If the electric field inside the cavity at position $\vec{r}$ is $\vec{E}(\vec{r})$, then the correct statement(s) is(are) :   **[JEE Adv 2015, P-2]**

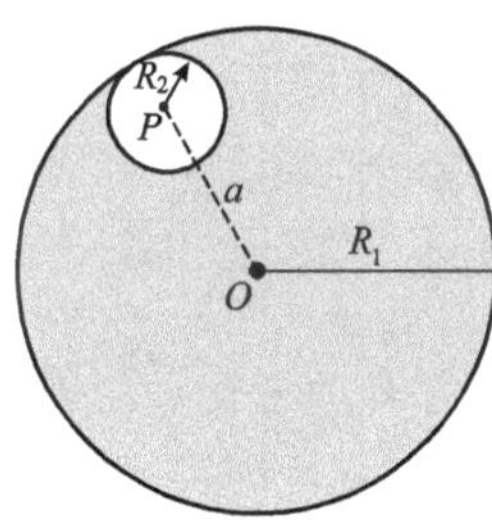

(A) $\vec{E}$ is uniform, its magnitude is independent of R_2 but its direction depends on $\vec{r}$

(B) $\vec{E}$ is uniform, its magnitude depends on R_2 and its direction depends on $\vec{r}$

(C) $\vec{E}$ is uniform, its magnitude is independent of a but its direction depends on $\vec{r}$

(D) $\vec{E}$ is uniform and both its magnitude and direction depend on $\vec{a}$

27. A point charge $+Q$ is placed just outside an imaginary hemispherical surface of radius R as shown in the figure. Which of the following statement is/are correct : **[JEE Adv 2017, P-2]**

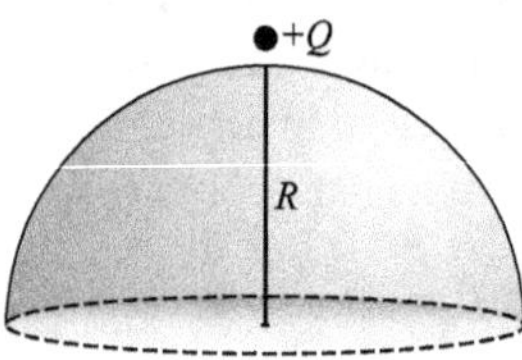

(A) The circumference of the flat surface is an equipotential

(B) The electric flux passing through the curved surface of the hemisphere is $-\dfrac{Q}{2\varepsilon_0}\left(1-\dfrac{1}{\sqrt{2}}\right)$

(C) Total flux through the curved and the flat surfaces is $\dfrac{Q}{\varepsilon_0}$

(D) The component of the electric field normal to the flat surface is constant over the surface

28. An infinitely long thin non-conducting wire is parallel to the z-axis and carries a uniform line charge density λ. It pierces a thin non-conducting spherical shell of radius R in such a way that the arc PQ subtends an angle $120°$ at the centre O of the spherical shell, as shown in the figure. The permittivity of free space is ε_0. Which of the following statements is (are) true ?

[JEE Adv 2018, P-2]

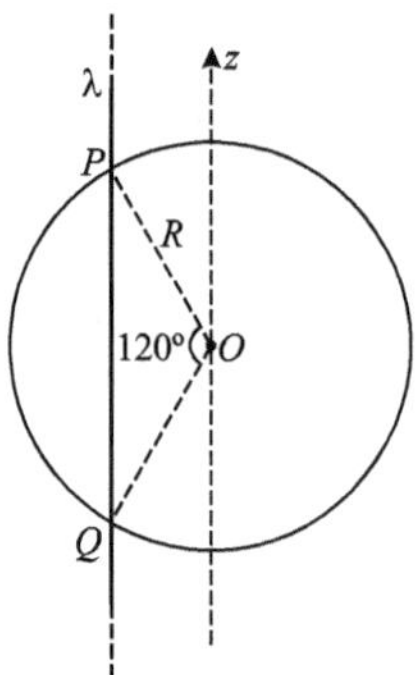

(A) The electric flux through the shell is $\sqrt{3}R\lambda/\varepsilon_0$

(B) The z-component of the electric field is zero at all the points on the surface of the shell

(C) The electric flux through the shell is $\sqrt{2}\,R\lambda/\varepsilon_0$

(D) The electric field is normal to the surface of the shell at all points

29. A charged shell of radius R carries a total charge Q. Given Φ as the flux of electric field through a closed cylindrical surface of height h, radius r and with its center same as that of the shell. Here, center of the cylinder is a point on the axis of the cylinder which is equidistant from its top and bottom surfaces. Which of the following option(s) is/are correct ? [ε_0 is the permittivity of free space] :

[JEE Adv 2019, P-1]

(A) If $h > 2R$ and $r > R$ then $\Phi = \dfrac{Q}{\in_0}$

(B) If $h < \dfrac{8R}{5}$ and $r = \dfrac{3R}{5}$ then $\Phi = 0$

(C) If $h > 2R$ and $r = \dfrac{4R}{5}$ then $\Phi = \dfrac{Q}{5\in_0}$

(D) If $h > 2R$ and $r = \dfrac{3R}{5}$ then $\Phi = \dfrac{Q}{5\in_0}$

30. An electric dipole with dipole moment $\dfrac{p_0}{\sqrt{2}}(\hat{i}+\hat{j})$ is held fixed at the origin O in the presence of a uniform electric field of magnitude E_0. If the potential is constant on a circle of radius R centered at the origin as shown in figure, then the correct statement(s) is/are : (ε_0 is permittivity of free space, $R >>$ dipole size)

[JEE Adv 2019, P-2]

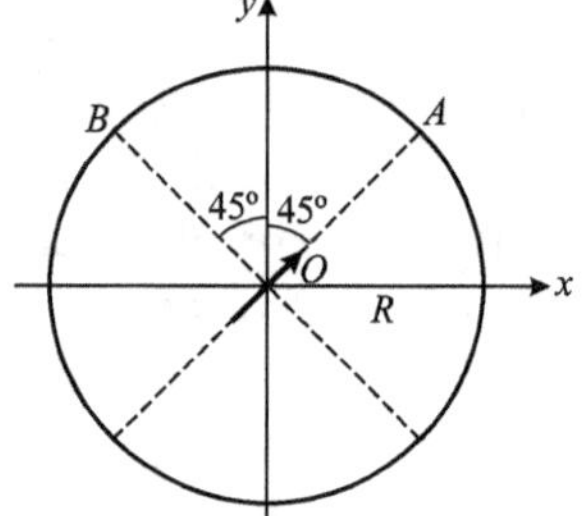

(A) $R = \left(\dfrac{p_0}{4\pi\varepsilon_0 E_0}\right)^{1/3}$

(B) The magnitude of total electric field on any two points of the circle will be same

(C) Total electric field at point A is $\vec{E}_A = \sqrt{2}E_0(\hat{i}+\hat{j})$

(D) Total electric field at point B is $\vec{E}_B = 0$

31. A uniform electric field, $\vec{E} = -400\sqrt{3}\hat{y}$ NC^{-1} is applied in a region. A charged particle of mass m carrying positive charge q is projected in this region with an initial speed of $2\sqrt{10}\times10^6$ ms^{-1}. This particle is aimed to hit a target T, which is 5 m away from its entry point into the field as shown schematically in the figure. Take $q/m = 10^{10}$ Ckg^{-1}. Then :

[JEE Adv 2020, P-1]

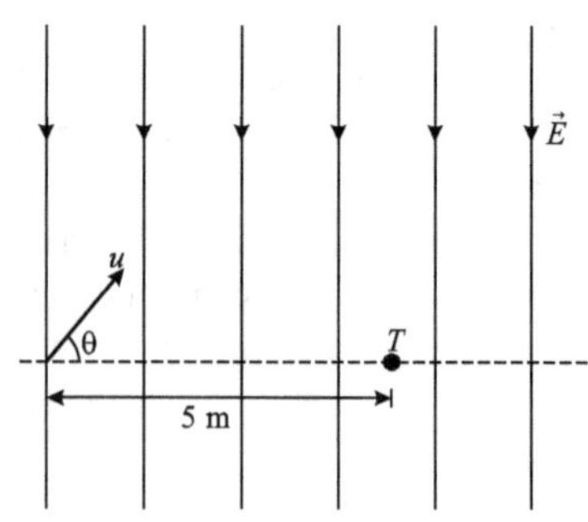

(A) The particle will hit T if projected at an angle 45° from the horizontal

(B) The particle will hit T if projected either at an angle 30° or 60° from the horizontal

(C) Time taken by the particle to hit T could be $\sqrt{\dfrac{5}{6}}$ μs as well as $\sqrt{\dfrac{5}{2}}$ μs

(D) Time taken by the particle to hit T is $\sqrt{\dfrac{5}{3}}$ μs

32. Shown in the figure is a semicircular metallic strip that has thickness t and resistivity ρ. Its inner radius is R_1 and outer radius is R_2. If a voltage V_0 is applied between its two ends, a current I flows in it. In addition, it is observed that a transverse voltage ΔV develops between its inner and outer surfaces due to purely kinetic effects of moving electrons (ignore any role of the magnetic field due to the current). Then (figure is schematic and not drawn to scale) :   **[JEE Adv 2020, P-1]**

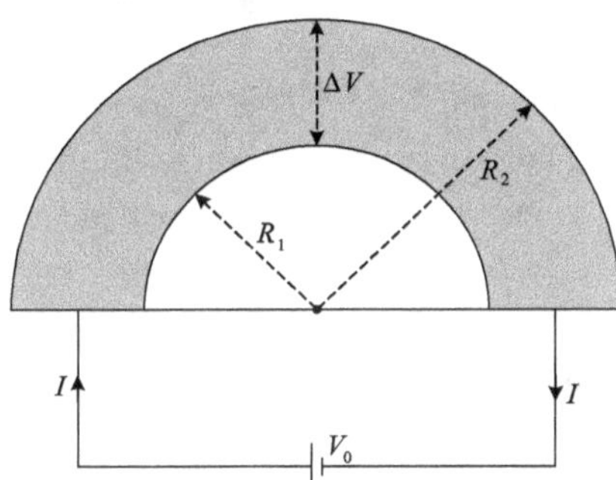

(A) $I = \dfrac{V_0 t}{\pi \rho} \ln\left(\dfrac{R_2}{R_1}\right)$

(B) The outer surface is at a higher voltage than the inner surface

(C) The outer surface is at a lower voltage than the inner surface

(D) $\Delta V \propto I^2$

33. Two identical non-conducting solid spheres of same mass and charge are suspended in air from a common point by two non-conducting, massless strings of same length. At equilibrium, the angle between the strings is α. The spheres are now immersed in a dielectric liquid of density 800 kg m^{-3} and dielectric constant 21. If the angle between the strings remains the same after the immersion, then :

[JEE Adv 2020, P-2]

(A) Electric force between the spheres remains unchanged

(B) Electric force between the spheres reduces

(C) Mass density of the sphere is 840 kg m^{-3}

(D) The tension in the strings holding the spheres remains unchanged

34. Six charges are placed around a regular hexagon of side length a as shown in the figure. Five of them have charge q, and the remaining one has charge x. The perpendicular from each charge to the nearest hexagon side passes through the center O of the hexagon and is bisected by the side.

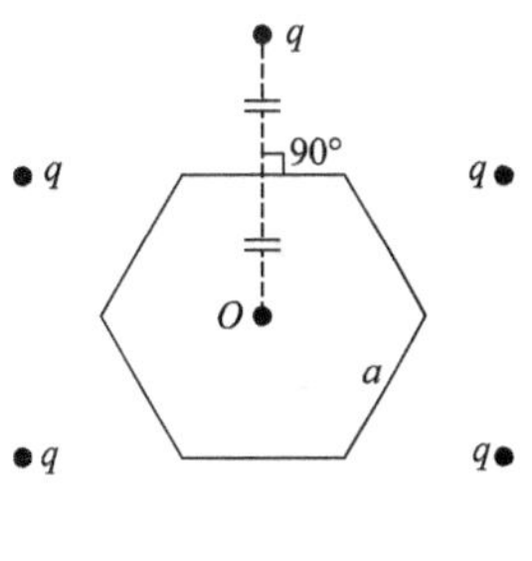

Which of the following statement(s) is(are) correct in SI units ?

[JEE Adv 2022, P-1]

(A) When $x = q$, the magnitude of the electric field at O is zero

(B) When $x = -q$, the magnitude of the electric field at O is $\dfrac{q}{6\pi\varepsilon_0 a^2}$

(C) When $x = 2q$, the potential at O is $\dfrac{7q}{4\sqrt{3}\pi\varepsilon_0 a}$

(D) When $x = -3q$, the potential at O is $-\dfrac{3q}{4\sqrt{3}\pi\varepsilon_0 a}$

35. In the figure, the inner (shaded) region A represents a sphere of radius $r_A = 1$, within which the electrostatic charge density varies with the radial distance r from the center as $\rho_A = kr$, where k is positive. In the spherical shell B of outer radius r_B, the electrostatic charge density varies as $\rho_B = \dfrac{2k}{r}$. Assume that dimensions are taken care of. All physical quantities are in their SI units.

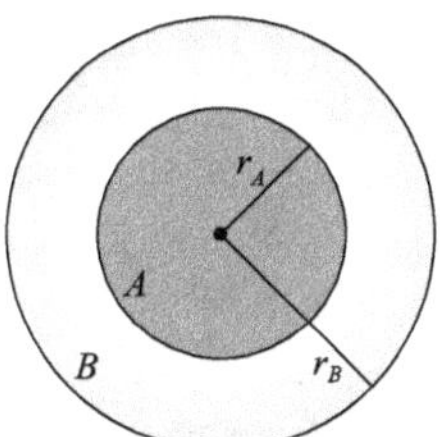

Which of the following statement(s) is(are) correct ?

[JEE Adv 2022, P-2]

(A) If $r_B = \sqrt{\dfrac{3}{2}}$, then the electric field is zero everywhere outside B

(B) If $r_B = \dfrac{3}{2}$, then the electric potential just outside B is $\dfrac{k}{\varepsilon_0}$

(C) If $r_B = 2$, then the total charge of the configuration is $15\pi k$

(D) If $r_B = \dfrac{5}{2}$, then the magnitude of the electric field just outside

B is $\dfrac{13\pi k}{\in_0}$

36. A disk of radius R with uniform positive charge density σ is placed on the xy plane with its center at the origin. The Coulomb potential along the z-axis is

$$V(z) = \frac{\sigma}{2\in_0}\left(\sqrt{R^2 + z^2} - z\right)$$

A particle of positive charge q is placed initially at rest at a point on the z-axis with $z = z_0$ and $z_0 > 0$. In addition to the Coulomb force, the particle experiences a vertical force $\vec{F} = -c\,\hat{k}$ with $c > 0$. Let $\beta = \dfrac{2c\in_0}{q\sigma}$. Which of the following statement(s) is(are) correct ?   **[JEE Adv 2022, P-2]**

(A) For $\beta = \dfrac{1}{4}$ and $z_0 = \dfrac{25}{7}R$, the particle reaches the origin

(B) For $\beta = \dfrac{1}{4}$ and $z_0 = \dfrac{3}{7}R$, the particle reaches the origin

(C) For $\beta = \dfrac{1}{4}$ and $z_0 = \dfrac{R}{\sqrt{3}}$, the particle returns back to $z = z_0$

(D) For $\beta > 1$ and $z_0 > 0$, the particle always reaches the origin

Assertion Reason based on MCQ

37. STATEMENT-1   **[JEE Adv 2008, P-2]**
For practical purposes, the earth is used as a reference at zero potential in electrical circuits.

because

STATEMENT-2
The electrical potential of a sphere of radius R with charge Q uniformly distributed on the surface is given by $\dfrac{Q}{4\pi\varepsilon_0 R}$:

(A) Statement-1 is True, Statement-2 is True; Statement-2 is a correct explanation for Statement-1
(B) Statement-1 is True, Statement-2 is True; Statement-2 is NOT a correct explanation for Statement-1
(C) Statement-1 is True, Statement-2 is False
(D) Statement-1 is False, Statement-2 is True

Matrix Match MCQ

38. Column-I gives certain situations in which a straight metallic wire of resistance R is used and **Column-II** gives some resulting effects. Match the statements in **Column-I** with the statements in **Column-II** and indicate your answer by darkening appropriate bubbles in the 4×4 matrix given in the ORS :

                           [JEE Adv 2007, P-1]

Column-I	Column-II
(A) A charged capacitor is connected to the ends of the wire	(p) A constant current flows through the wire
(B) The wire is moved perpendicular to its length with a constant velocity in a uniform magnetic field perpendicular to the plane of motion	(q) Thermal energy is generated in the wire
(C) The wire is placed in a constant electric field that has a direction along the length of the wire	(r) A constant potential difference develops between the ends of the wire
(D) A battery of constant emf is connected to the ends of the wire	(s) Charges of constant magnitude appear at the ends of the wire

39. Six point charges, each of the same magnitude q, are arranged in different manners as shown in **Column-II**. In each case, a point M and line PQ passing through M are shown. Let E be the electric field and V be the electric potential at M (potential at infinity is zero) due to the given charge distribution when it is at rest. Now, the whole system is set into rotation with a constant angular velocity about the line PQ. Let B be the magnetic field at M and μ be the magnetic moment of the system in this condition. Assume each rotating charge to be equivalent to a steady current :   **[JEE Adv 2009, P-1]**

Column-I	Column-II
(A) $E = 0$	(p) Charges are at the corners of a regular hexagon. M is at the centre of the hexagon. PQ is perpendicular to the plane of the hexagon.
(B) $V \neq 0$	(q) Charges are on a line perpendicular to PQ at equal intervals. M is the midpoint between the two innermost charges.

(C) $B = 0$ (r) Charges are placed on two coplanar insulating rings at equal intervals. M is the common centre of the rings. PQ is perpendicular to the plane of the rings.

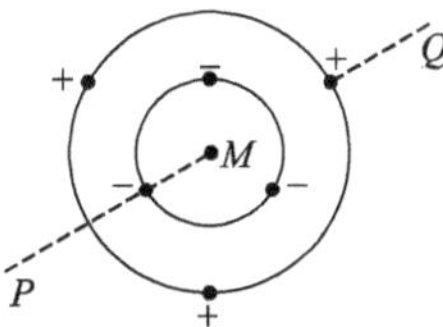

(D) $\mu \neq 0$ (s) Charges are placed at the corners of a rectangle of sides a and 2a and at the mid-points of the longer sides. M is at the centre of the rectangle. PQ is parallel to the longer sides.

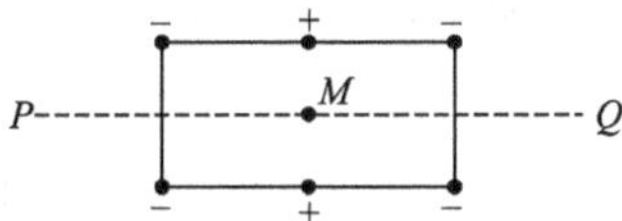

(t) Charges are placed on two coplanar, identical insulating rings at equal intervals. M is the mid-point between the centres of the rings. PQ is perpendicular to the line joining the centres and coplanar to the rings.

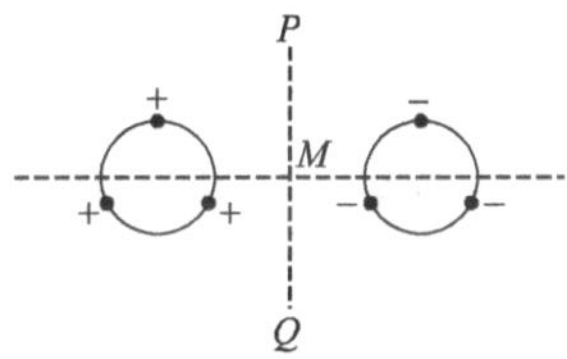

40. Four charges Q_1, Q_2, Q_3 and Q_4 of same magnitude are fixed along the x-axis at $x = -2a, -a, +a$ and $+2a$, respectively. A positive charge q is placed on the positive y-axis at a distance $b > 0$. Four options of the signs of these charges are given in **Column-I**. The direction of the forces on the charge q is given in **Column-II**. Match **Column-I** with **Column-II** and select the correct answer using the code given below the lists :

[JEE Adv 2014, P-2]

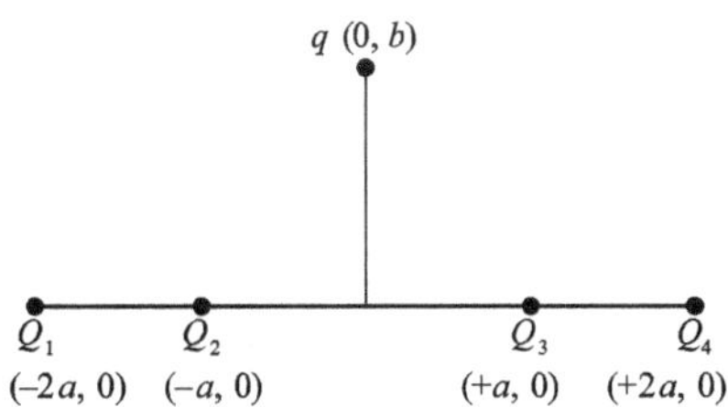

Column-I	Column-II
(P) $Q_1, Q_2, Q_3 Q_4$ all positive	(1) $+x$
(Q) Q_1, Q_2 positive; Q_3, Q_4 negative	(2) $-x$
(R) Q_1, Q_4 positive; Q_2, Q_3 negative	(3) $+y$
(S) Q_1, Q_3 positive; Q_2, Q_4 negative	(4) $-y$

Code :
(A) $P \to 3, Q \to 1, R \to 4, S \to 2$
(B) $P \to 4, Q \to 2, R \to 3, S \to 1$
(C) $P \to 3, Q \to 1, R \to 2, S \to 4$
(D) $P \to 4, Q \to 2, R \to 1, S \to 3$

41. The electric field E is measured at a point $P(0, 0, d)$ generated due to various charge distributions and the dependence of E on d is found to be different for different charge distributions. **Column-I** contains different relations between E and d. **Column-II** describes different electric charge distributions, along with their locations. Match the functions in **Column-I** with the related charge distributions in **Column-II**:

[JEE Adv 2018, P-2]

Column-I	Column-II
P. E is independent of d	1. A point charge Q at the origin
Q. $E \propto 1/d$	2. A small dipole with point charges Q at $(0, 0, l)$ and $-Q$ at $(0, 0, -l)$ Take $2l \ll d$
R. $E \propto 1/d^2$	3. An infinite line charge coincident with the x-axis, with uniform linear charge density λ.
S. $E \propto 1/d^3$	4. Two infinite wires carrying uniform linear charge density parallel to the x-axis. The one along $(y = 0, z = l)$ has a charge density $+\lambda$ and the one along $(y = 0, z = -l)$ has a charge density $-\lambda$. Take $2l \ll d$
	5. Infinite plane charge coincident with the xy-plane with uniform surface charge density

(A) $P \to 5; Q \to 3, 4; R \to 1; S \to 2$
(B) $P \to 5; Q \to 3,; R \to 1,4; S \to 2$
(C) $P \to 5; Q \to 3,; R \to 1,2; S \to 4$
(D) $P \to 4; Q \to 2, 3; R \to 1; S \to 5$

Comprehension based MCQ

Paragraph-1 (Q. No. 42-44)

The nuclear charge (Ze) is non-uniformly distributed within a nucleus of radius R. The charge density $\rho(r)$ [charge per unit volume] is dependent only on the radial distance r from the centre of the nucleus as shown in figure. The electric field is only along the radial direction : **[JEE Adv 2008, P-2]**

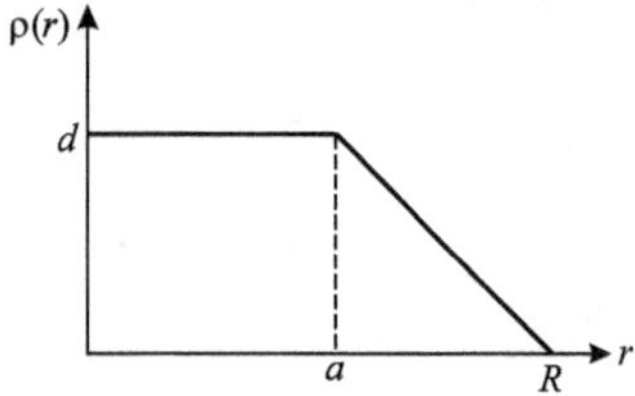

42. The electric field at $r = R$ is :
(A) Independent of a
(B) Directly proportional to a
(C) Directly proportional to a^2
(D) Inversely proportional to a

43. For $a = 0$, the value of d (maximum value of ρ as shown in the figure) is :

(A) $\dfrac{3Ze}{4\pi R^3}$ (B) $\dfrac{3Ze}{\pi R^3}$

(C) $\dfrac{4Ze}{3\pi R^3}$ (D) $\dfrac{Ze}{3\pi R^3}$

44. The electric field within the nucleus is generally observed to be linearly dependent on r. This implies :

(A) $a = 0$ (B) $a = \dfrac{R}{2}$

(C) $a = R$ (D) $a = \dfrac{2R}{3}$

Paragraph-2 (Q. No. 45-46)

A dense collection of equal number of electrons and positive ions is called neutral plasma. Certain solids containing fixed positive ions surrounded by free electrons can be treated as neutral plasma. Let N be the number density of free electrons, each of mass m. When the electrons are subjected to an electric field, they are displaced relatively away from the heavy positive ions. If the electric field becomes zero, the electrons begin to oscillate about the positive ions with a natural angular frequency ω_p, which is called the plasma frequency. To sustain the oscillations, a time varying electric field needs to be applied that has an angular frequency ω, where a part of the energy is absorbed and a part of it is reflected. As ω approaches ω_p, all the free electrons are set to resonance together and all the energy is reflected. This is the explanation of high reflectivity of metals. **[JEE Adv 2011, P-1]**

45. Taking the electronic charge as e and the permittivity as ε_0, use dimensional analysis to determine the correct expression for ω_p :

(A) $\sqrt{\dfrac{Ne}{m\varepsilon_0}}$ (B) $\sqrt{\dfrac{m\varepsilon_0}{Ne}}$

(C) $\sqrt{\dfrac{Ne^2}{m\varepsilon_0}}$ (D) $\sqrt{\dfrac{m\varepsilon_0}{Ne^2}}$

46. Estimate the wavelength at which plasma reflection will occur for a metal having the density of electrons $N = 4 \times 10^{27}$ m^{-3}. Take $\varepsilon_0 = 10^{-11}$ and $m = 10^{-30}$, where these quantities are in proper SI units :
(A) 800 nm   (B) 600 nm
(C) 300 nm   (D) 200 nm

Paragraph-3 (Q. No. 47-48)

Two point charges $-Q$ and $+Q/\sqrt{3}$ are placed in the xy-plane at the origin $(0, 0)$ and a point $(2, 0)$, respectively, as shown in the figure. This results in an equipotential circle of radius R and potential $V = 0$ in the xy-plane with its center at $(b, 0)$. All lengths are measured in meters. **[JEE Adv 2021, P-1]**

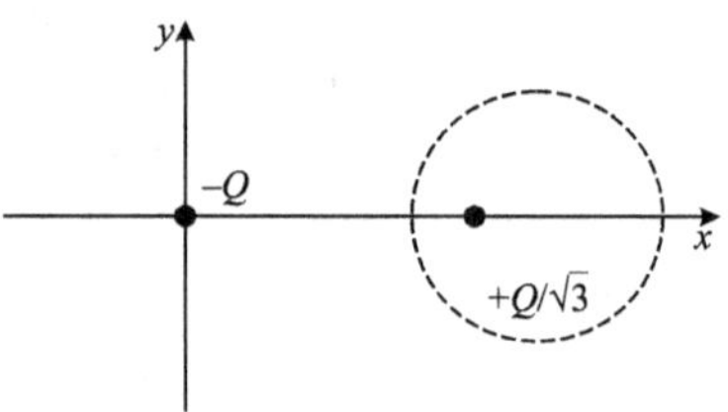

47. The value of R is __________ meter.

48. The value of b is __________ meter.

Integer Answer based Questions

49. A solid sphere of radius R has a charge Q distributed in its volume with a charge density $\rho = kr^\alpha$, where k and α are constants and r is the distance from its centre. If the electric field at $r = \dfrac{R}{2}$ is $\dfrac{1}{8}$ times that at $r = R$, find the value of α.

[JEE Adv 2009, P-2]

50. Four point charges, each of $+q$, are rigidly fixed at the four corners of a square planar soap film of side a. The surface tension of the soap film is γ. The system of charges and planar film are in equilibrium, and $a = k\left[\dfrac{q^2}{\gamma}\right]^{1/N}$, where k is a constant.

Then N is ? **[JEE Adv 2011, P-1]**

51. An infinitely long solid cylinder of radius R has a uniform volume charge density ρ. It has a spherical cavity of radius $R/2$ with its centre on the axis of the cylinder, as shown in the figure. The magnitude of the electric field at the point P, which is at a distance $2R$ from the axis of the cylinder, is given by the expression $\dfrac{23\rho R}{16k\varepsilon_0}$. The value of k is :   **[JEE Adv 2012, P-1]**

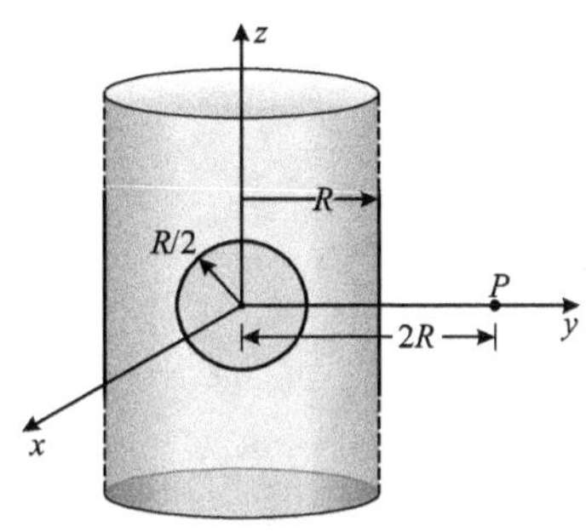

52. An infinitely long uniform line charge distribution of charge per unit length λ lies parallel to the y-axis in the y-z plane at $z = \dfrac{\sqrt{3}}{2}\,a$ (see figure). If the magnitude of the flux of the electric field through the rectangular surface $ABCD$ lying in the x-y plane with its centre at the origin is $\dfrac{\lambda L}{n\varepsilon_0}$ (ε_0 = permittivity of free space), then the value of n is :   **[JEE Adv 2015, P-1]**

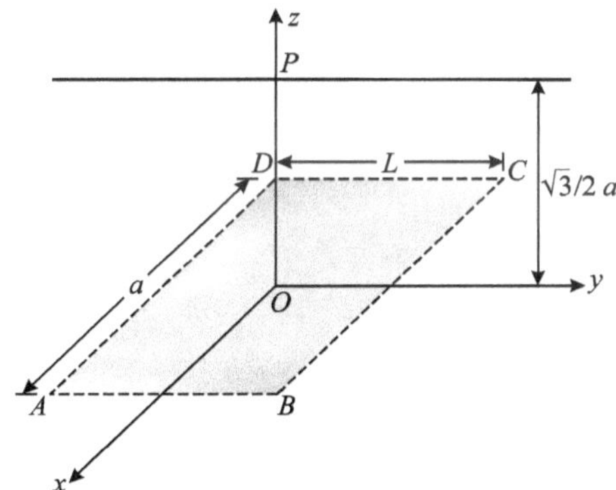

53. A particle, of mass 10^{-3} kg and charge 1.0 C, is initially at rest. At time $t = 0$, the particle comes under the influence of an electric field $\vec{E}(t) = E_0 \sin \omega t\, \hat{i}$ where $E_0 = 1.0$ N C^{-1} and $\omega = 10^3$ rad s^{-1}. Consider the effect of only the electrical force on the particle. Then the maximum speed, in ms^{-1}, attained by the particle at subsequent times is _______ .

[JEE Adv 2018, P-2]

54. One end of a spring of negligible unstretched length and spring constant k is fixed at the origin $(0,0)$. A point particle of mass m carrying a positive charge q is attached at its other end. The entire system is kept on a smooth horizontal surface.

When a point dipole $\vec{p}$ pointing towards the charge q is fixed at the origin, the spring gets stretched to a length l and attains a new equilibrium position (see figure below). If the point mass is now displaced slightly by $\Delta l \ll l$ from its equilibrium position and released, it is found to oscillate at frequency $\dfrac{1}{\delta}\sqrt{\dfrac{k}{m}}$. The value of δ is _______ .   **[JEE Adv 2020, P-1]**

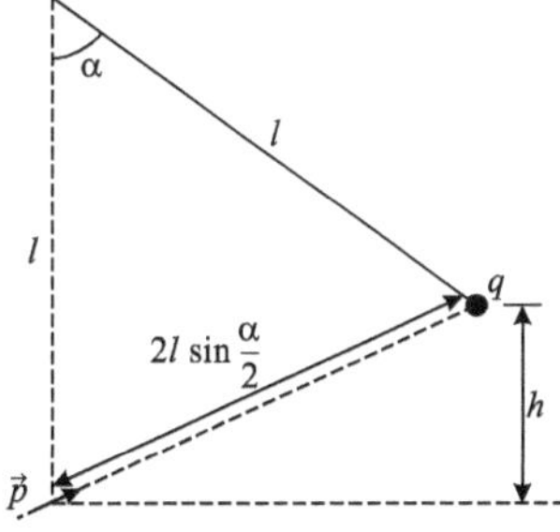

55. A circular disc of radius R carries surface charge density $\sigma(r) = \sigma_0\left(1 - \dfrac{r}{R}\right)$, where σ_0 is a constant and r is the distance from the centre of the disc. Electric flux through a large spherical surface that encloses the charged disc completely is ϕ_0. Electric flux through another spherical surface of radius $\dfrac{R}{4}$ and concentric with the disc is ϕ. Then the ratio $\dfrac{\phi_0}{\phi}$ is _______ .

[JEE Adv 2020, P-1]

56. A point charge q of mass m is suspended vertically by a string of length. A point dipole of dipole moment $\vec{p}$ is now brought towards q from infinity so that the charge moves away. The final equilibrium position of the system including the direction of the dipole, the angles and distances is shown in the figure below. If the work done in bringing the dipole to this position is $N \times (mgh)$, where g is the acceleration due to gravity, then the value of N is _______ . (Note that for three coplanar forces keeping a point mass in equilibrium, $\dfrac{F}{\sin\theta}$ is the same for all forces, where F is any one of the forces and θ is the angle between the other two forces).   **[JEE Adv 2020, P-2]**

57. Two large circular discs separated by a distance of 0.01 m are connected to a battery via a switch as shown in the figure. Charged oil drops of density 900 kg m^{-3} are released through a tiny hole at the center of the top disc. Once some oil drops achieve terminal velocity, the switch is closed to apply a voltage of 200 V across the discs. As a result, an oil drop of radius 8×10^{-7} m stops moving vertically and floats between the discs. The number of electrons present in this oil drop is ______. (neglect the buoyancy force, take acceleration due to gravity $=10$ ms^{-2} and charge on an electron $(e) = 1.6 \times 10^{-19}$ C)

[JEE Adv 2020, P-2]

58. A charge q is surrounded by a closed surface consisting of an inverted cone of height h and base radius R, and a hemisphere of radius R as shown in the figure. The electric flux through the conical surface is $\dfrac{nq}{6 \in_0}$ (in SI units). The value of n is ______.

[JEE Adv 2022, P-2]

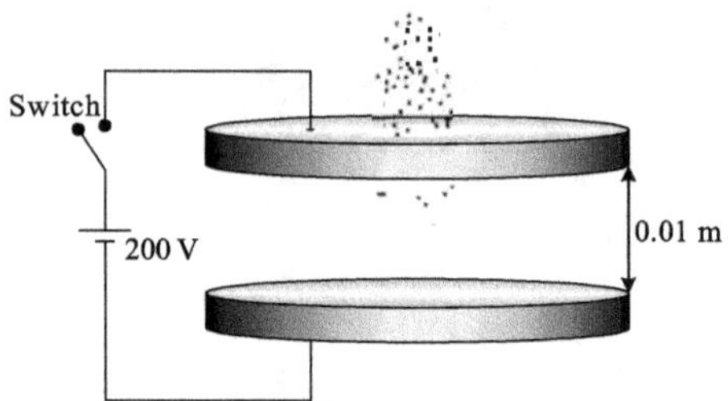

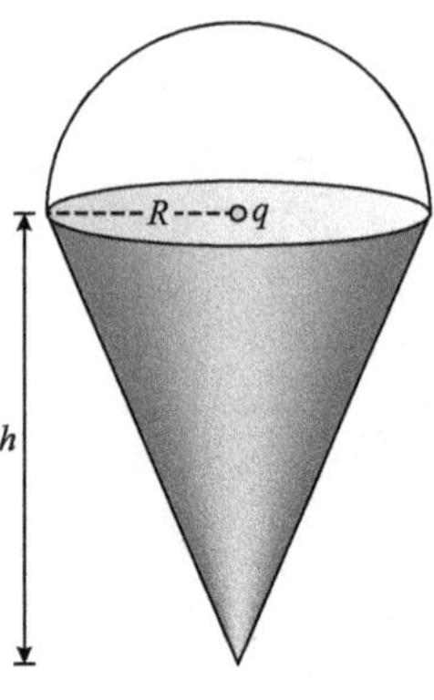

$*$ $*$ $*$ $*$ $*$

13 CAPACITANCE

MCQ with Single Option Correct

1. A circuit is connected as shown in the figure with the switch S open. When the switch is closed, the total amount of charge that flows from Y to X is : **[JEE Adv 2007, P-1]**

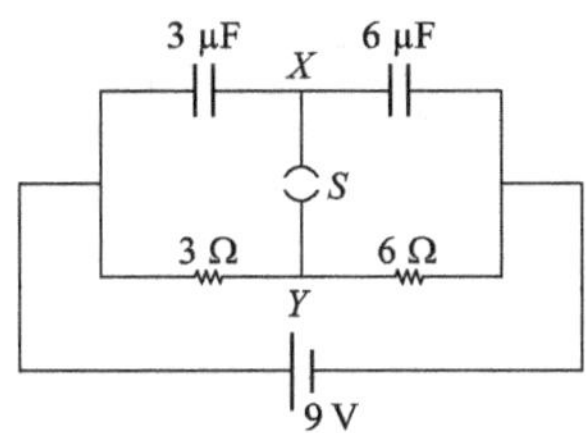

(A) 0
(B) 54 μC
(C) 27 μC
(D) 81 μC

2. A parallel plate capacitor C with plates of unit area and separation d is filled with a liquid of dielectric constant $K = 2$. The level of liquid is $d/3$ initially. Suppose the liquid level decreases at a constant speed V, the time constant as a function of time t is : **[JEE Adv 2008, P-2]**

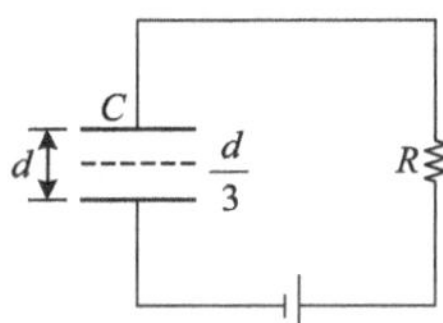

(A) $\dfrac{6\varepsilon_0 R}{5d + 3Vt}$

(B) $\dfrac{(15d + 9Vt)\varepsilon_0 R}{2d^2 - 3dVt - 9V^2t^2}$

(C) $\dfrac{6\varepsilon_0 R}{5d - 3Vt}$

(D) $\dfrac{(15d - 9Vt)\varepsilon_0 R}{2d^2 + 3dVt - 9V^2t^2}$

3. A 2 μF capacitor is charged as shown in figure. The percentage of its stored energy dissipated after the switch S is turned to position 2 is : **[JEE Adv 2011, P-1]**

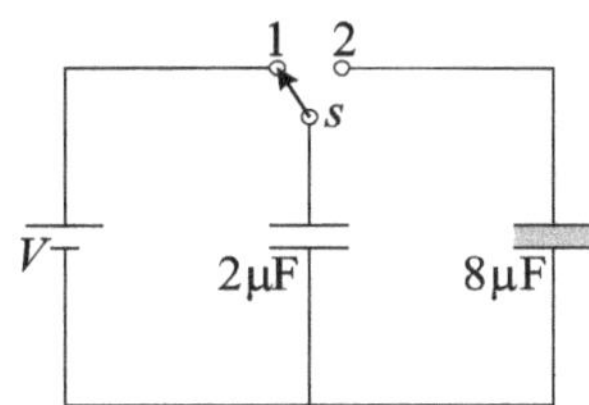

(A) 0 %
(B) 20 %
(C) 75 %
(D) 80%

4. In the given circuit, a charge of +80 μC is given to the upper plate of the 4 μF capacitor. Then in the steady state, the charge on the upper plate of the 3 μF capacitor is : **[JEE Adv 2012, P-2]**

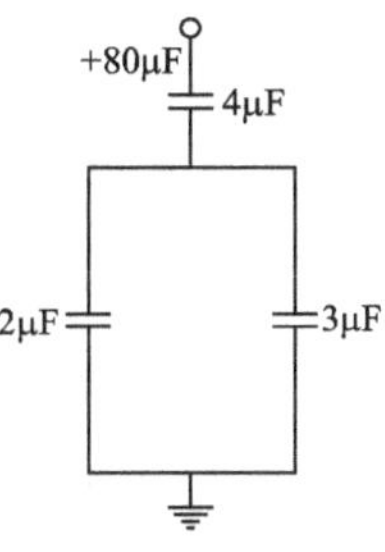

(A) $+32\ \mu C$
(B) $+40\ \mu C$
(C) $+48\ \mu C$
(D) $+80\ \mu C$

5. A medium having dielectric constant $K > 1$ fills the space between the plates of a parallel plate capacitor. The plates have large area, and the distance between them is d. The capacitor is connected to a battery of voltage V, as shown in Figure-(a).

Now, both the plates are moved by a distance of $\dfrac{d}{2}$ from their original positions, as shown in Figure-(b) :

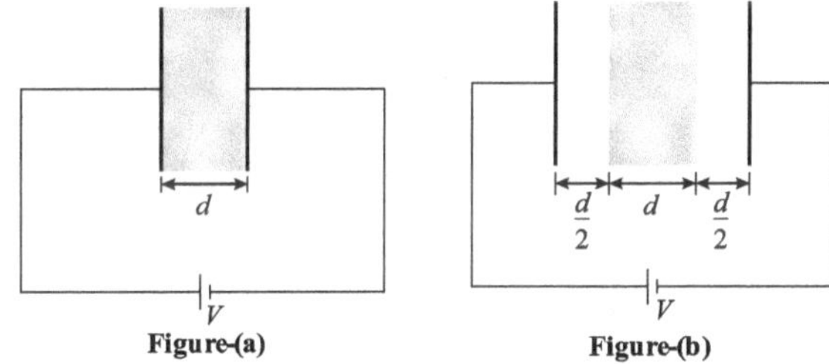

Figure-(a)   Figure-(b)

In the process of going from the configuration depicted in Figure-(a) to that in Figure-(b), which of the following statement(s) is(are) correct ? **[JEE Adv 2022, P-1]**

(A) The electric field inside the dielectric material is reduced by a factor of $2K$

(B) The capacitance is decreased by a factor of $\dfrac{1}{K+1}$

(C) The voltage between the capacitor plates is increased by a factor of $(K+1)$

(D) The work done in the process **DOES NOT** depend on the presence of the dielectric material

6. A container has a base of 50 cm × 5 cm and height 50 cm, as shown in the figure. It has two parallel electrically conducting walls each of area 50 cm × 50 cm. The remaining walls of the container are thin and non-conducting. The container is being filled with a liquid of dielectric constant 3 at a uniform rate of

$250 \text{ cm}^3 \text{ s}^{-1}$. What is the value of the capacitance of the container after 10 seconds?

[Given: Permittivity of free space $\in_0 = 9 \times 10^{-12} \text{ C}^2 \text{ N}^{-1} \text{ m}^{-2}$, the effects of the non-conducting walls on the capacitance are negligible]

[JEE Adv 2023, P-1]

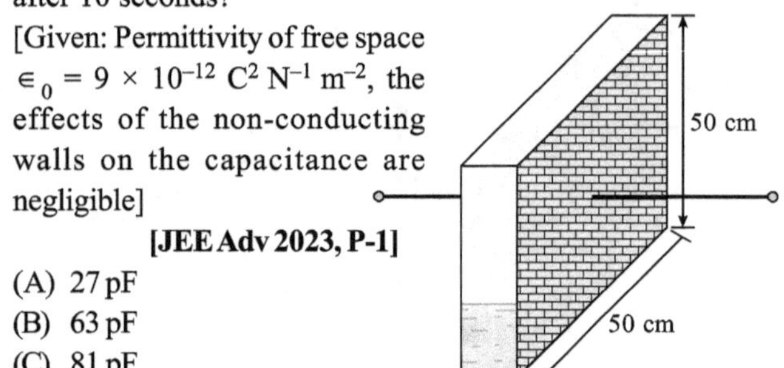

(A) 27 pF

(B) 63 pF

(C) 81 pF

(D) 135 pF

MCQ with One or More than One Options Correct

7. In the circuit shown in the figure, there are two parallel plate capacitors each of capacitance C. The switch S_1 is pressed first to fully charge the capacitor C_1 and then released. The switch S_2 is then pressed to charge the capacitor C_2. After some time, S_2 is released and then S_3 is pressed. After some time : **[JEE Adv 2013, P-1]**

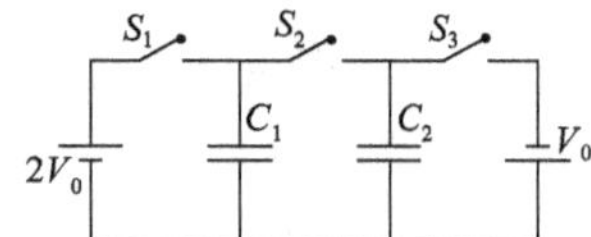

(A) The charge on the upper plate of C_1 is $2CV_0$

(B) The charge on the upper plate of C_1 is CV_0

(C) The charge on the upper plate of C_2 is 0

(D) The charge on the upper plate of C_2 is $- CV_0$

8. A parallel plate capacitor has a dielectric slab of dielectric constant K between its plates that covers 1/3 of the area of its plates, as shown in the figure. The total capacitance of the capacitor is C while that of the portion with dielectric in between is C_1. When the capacitor is charged, the plate area covered by the dielectric gets charge Q_1 and the rest of the area gets charge Q_2. The electric field in the dielectric is E_1 and that in the other portion is E_2. Choose the correct option/options, ignoring edge effect : **[JEE Adv 2014, P-1]**

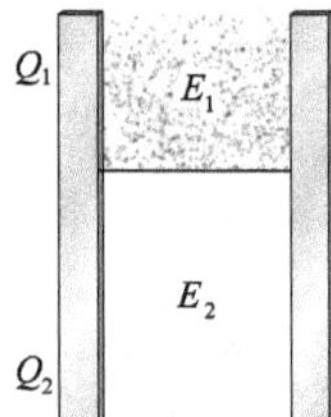

(A) $\dfrac{E_1}{E_2} = 1$

(B) $\dfrac{E_1}{E_2} = \dfrac{1}{K}$

(C) $\dfrac{Q_1}{Q_2} = \dfrac{3}{K}$

(D) $\dfrac{C}{C_1} = \dfrac{2+K}{K}$

9. A parallel plate capacitor having plates of area S and plate separation d, has capacitance C_1 in air. When two dielectrics of different relative permittivities ($\varepsilon_1 = 2$ and $\varepsilon_2 = 4$) are introduced between the two plates as shown in the figure, the capacitance becomes C_2. The ratio $\dfrac{C_2}{C_1}$ is : **[JEE Adv 2015, P-2]**

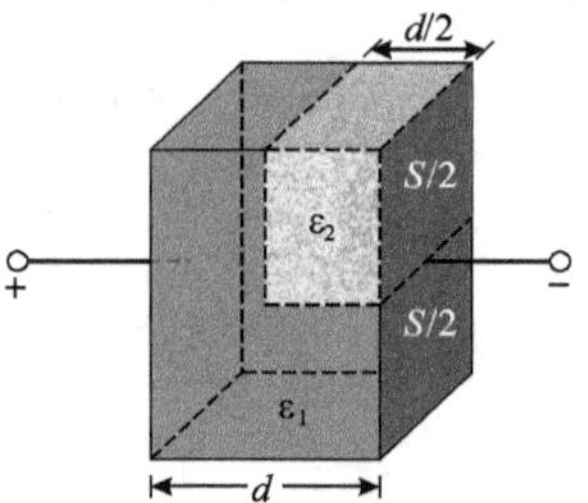

(A) 6/5

(B) 5/3

(C) 7/5

(D) 7/3

10. In the circuit shown, initially there is no charge on capacitors and keys S_1 and S_2 are open. The values of the capacitors are $C_1 = 10 \ \mu F$, $C_2 = 30 \ \mu F$ and $C_3 = C_4 = 80 \ \mu F$: **[JEE Adv 2019, P-1]**

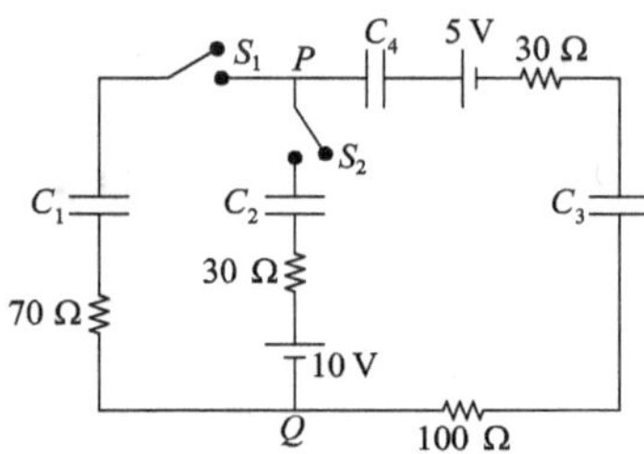

Which of the statement(s) is/are correct ?

(A) The keys S_1 is kept closed for long time such that capacitors are fully charged. Now key S_2 is closed, at this time, the instantaneous current across 30 Ω resistor (between points P and Q) will be 0.2 A (round off to 1st decimal place).

(B) If key S_1 is kept closed for long time such that capacitors are fully charged, the voltage difference between points P and Q will be 10 V.

(C) At time $t = 0$, the key S_1 is closed, the instantaneous current in the closed circuit will be 25 mA.

(D) If key S_1 is kept closed for long time such that capacitors are fully charged, the voltage across the capacitors C_1 will be 4 V.

Comprehension based MCQ

Paragraph-1 (Q. No. Sol. 11-12)

In the circuit shown below, the switch S is connected to position P for a long time so that the charge on the capacitor becomes $q_1 \ \mu C$. Then S is switched to position Q. After a long time, the charge on the capacitor is $q_2 \ \mu C$. **[JEE Adv 2021, P-1]**

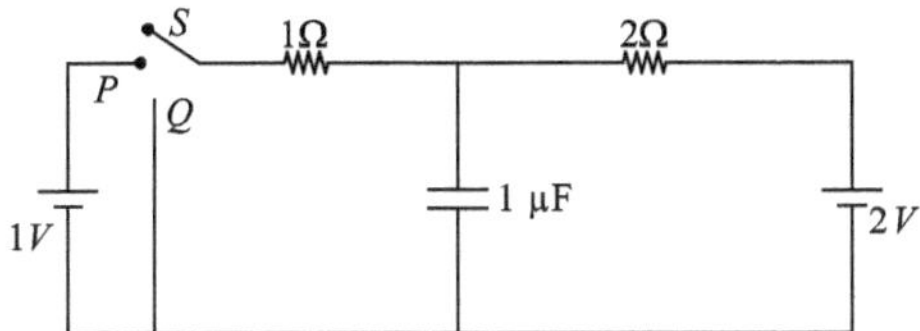

11. The magnitude of q_1 is _________ .

12. The magnitude of q_2 is _________ .

Integer Answer based Questions

13. At time $t = 0$, a battery of 10 V is connected across points A and B is the given circuit. If the capacitors have no charge initially, at what time (in seconds) does the voltage across them become 4 V ?   [Take : $\ln 5 = 1.6, \ln 3 = 1.1$]

[JEE Adv 2010, P-2]

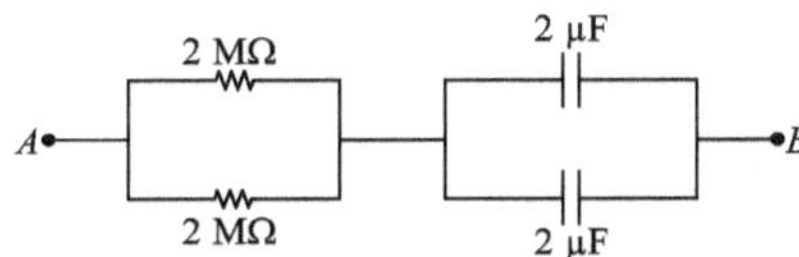

14. Three identical capacitors C_1, C_2 and C_3 have a capacitance of 1.0 μF each and they are uncharged initially. They are connected in a circuit as shown in the figure and C_1 is then filled completely with a dielectric material of relative permittivity $\in_r$. The cell electromotive force (emf) $V_0 = 8$V. First the switch S_1 is closed while the switch S_2 is kept open. When the capacitor C_3 is fully charged, S_1 is opened and S_2 is closed simultaneously. When all the capacitors reach equilibrium, the charge on C_3 is found to be 5 μC. The value of $\in_r$.   **[JEE Adv 2018, P-1]**

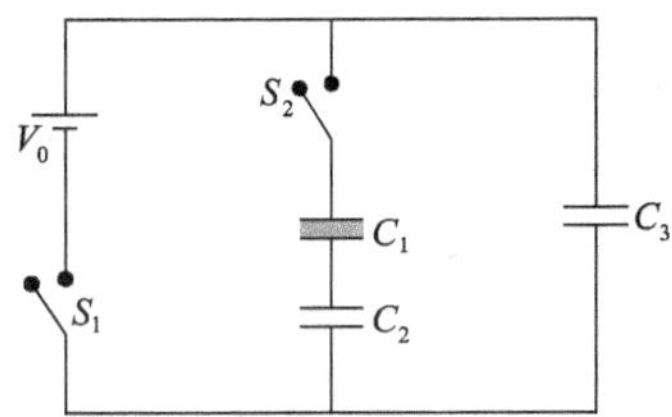

15. A parallel plate capacitor of capacitance C has spacing d between two plates having area A. The region between the plates is filled with N dielectric layers, parallel to its plates, each with thickness $\delta = \dfrac{d}{N}$. The dielectric constant of the mth layer is $K_m = K\left(1 + \dfrac{m}{N}\right)$. For a very large N ($> 10^3$), the capacitance C is $\alpha\left(\dfrac{K \in_0 A}{d \ln 2}\right)$. The value of α will be _______ :

[$\in_0$ is the permittivity of free space]   **[JEE Adv 2019, P-1]**

16. Two capacitors with capacitance values $C_1 = 2000 \pm 10$ pF and $C_2 = 3000 \pm 15$ pF are connected in series. The voltage applied across this combination is $V = 5.00 \pm 0.02$ V. The percentage error in the calculation of the energy stored in this combination of capacitors is _______ .   **[JEE Adv 2020, P-2]**

17. In the following circuit $C_1 = 12$ μF, $C_2 = C_3 = 4$ μF and $C_4 = C_5 = 2$ μF. The charge stored in C_3 is _______ μC.

[JEE Adv 2022, P-1]

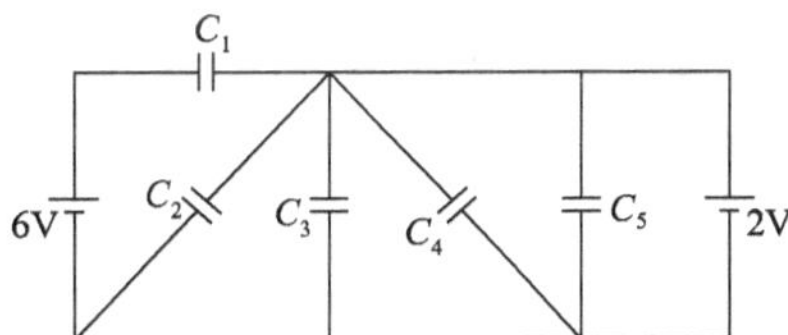

* * * * *

14 CURRENT ELECTRICITY

MCQ with Single Option Correct

[JEE Adv 2010, P-1]

1. A resistance of 2 Ω is connected across one gap of a meter-bridge (the length of the wire is 100 cm) and an unknown resistance, greater than 2 Ω, is connected across the other gap. When these resistances are interchanged, the balance point shifts by 20 cm. Neglecting any corrections, the unknown resistance is : **[JEE Adv 2007, P-1]**

(A) 3 Ω (B) 4 Ω
(C) 5 Ω (D) 6 Ω

2. Figure shows three resistor configurations R_1, R_2 and R_3 connected to 3V battery. If the power dissipated by the configuration R_1, R_2 and R_3 is P_1, P_2 and P_3, respectively, then : **[JEE Adv 2008, P-1]**

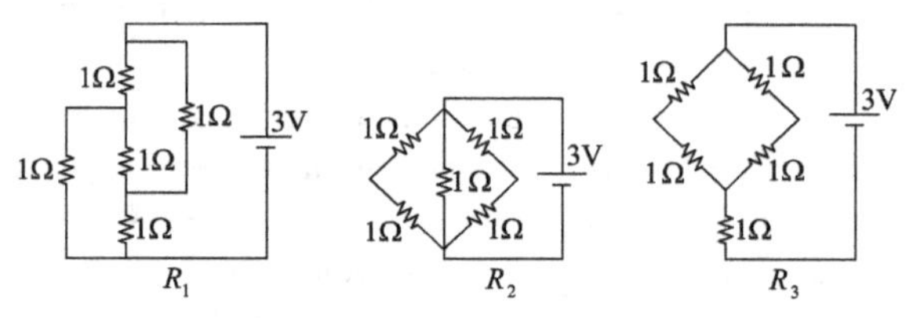

(A) $P_1 > P_2 > P_3$ (B) $P_1 > P_3 > P_2$
(C) $P_2 > P_1 > P_3$ (D) $P_3 > P_2 > P_1$

3. Consider a thin square sheet of side L and thickness t, made of a material of resistivity ρ. The resistance between two opposite faces, shown by the shaded areas in the figure is : **[JEE Adv 2010, P-1]**

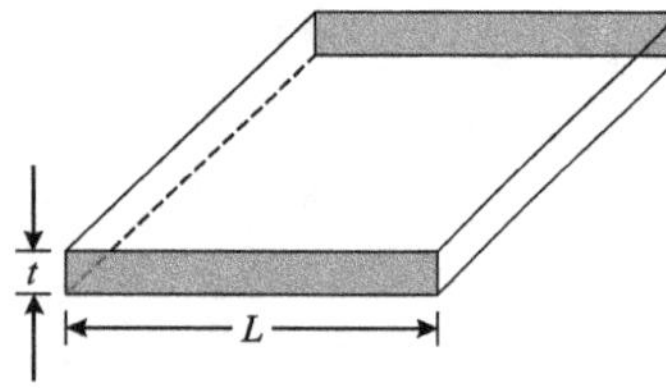

(A) Directly proportional to L
(B) Directly proportional to t
(C) Independent of L
(D) Independent of t

4. Incandescent bulbs are designed by keeping in mind that the resistance of their filament increases with the increase in temperature. If at room temperature, 100 W, 60 W and 40 W bulbs have filament resistances R_{100}, R_{60} and R_{40}, respectively, the relation by between these resistance is :

(A) $\dfrac{1}{R_{100}} = \dfrac{1}{R_{40}} + \dfrac{1}{R_{60}}$ (B) $R_{100} = R_{40} + R_{60}$

(C) $R_{100} > R_{60} > R_{40}$ (D) $\dfrac{1}{R_{100}} > \dfrac{1}{R_{60}} > \dfrac{1}{R_{40}}$

5. To verify Ohm's law, a student is provided with a test resistor R_T, a high resistance R_1, a small resistance R_2, two identical galvanometers G_1 and G_2, and a variable voltage source V. The correct circuit to carry out the experiment is : **[JEE Adv 2010, P-1]**

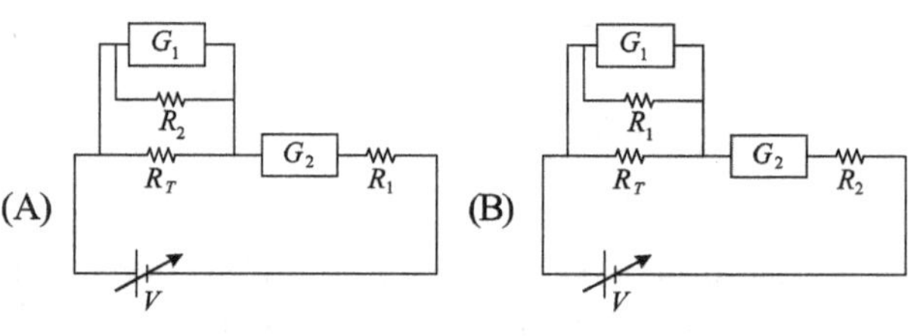

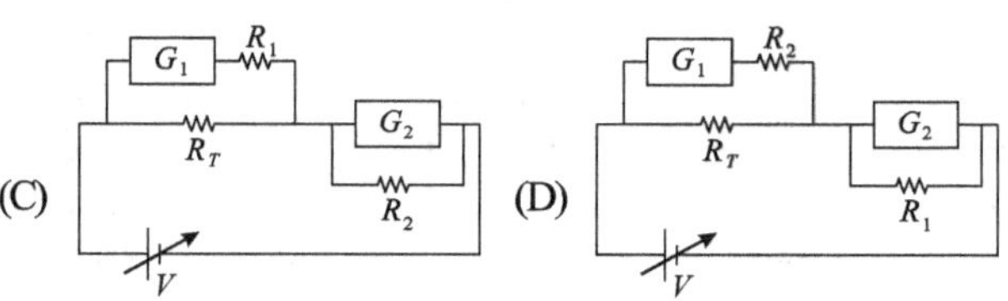

6. A meter bridge is set-up as shown, to determine an unknown resistance X using a standard 10 Ω resistor. The galvanometer shows null point when tapping-key is at 52 cm mark. The end-corrections are 1 cm and 2 cm respectively for the ends A and B. The determined value of X is : **[JEE Adv 2011, P-1]**

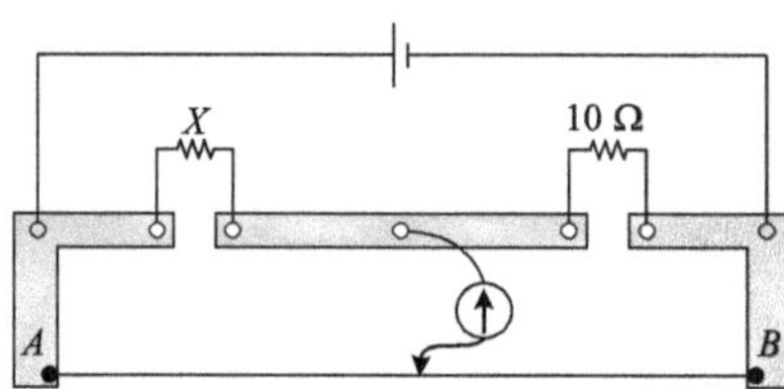

(A) 10.2 Ω (B) 10.6 Ω
(C) 10.8 Ω (D) 11.1 Ω

7. Which of the field patterns given below is valid for electric field as well as for magnetic field : **[JEE Adv 2011, P-2]**

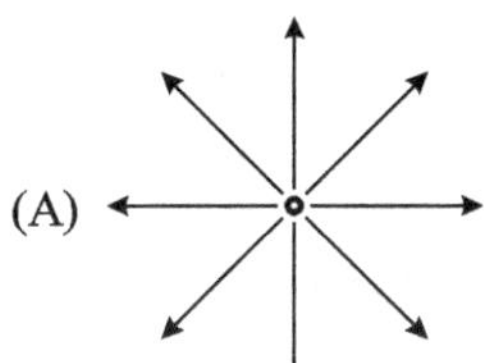
(A)

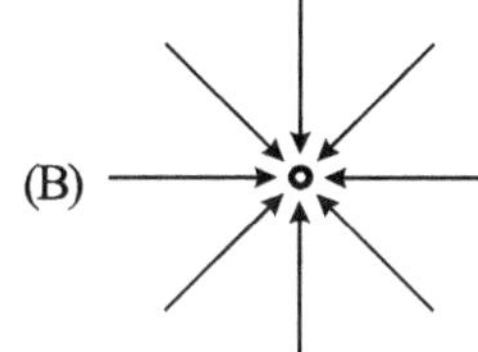
(B)

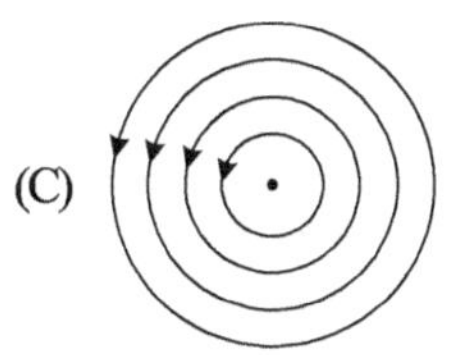
(C)

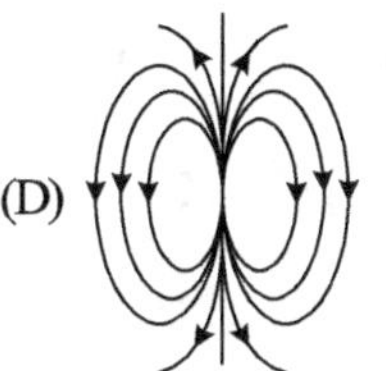
(D)

8. During an experiment with a metre bridge, the galvanometer shows a null point when the jockey is pressed at 40.0 cm using a standard resistance of 90 Ω, as shown in the figure. The least count of the scale used in the meter bridge is 1 mm. The unknown resistance is : **[JEE Adv 2014, P-2]**

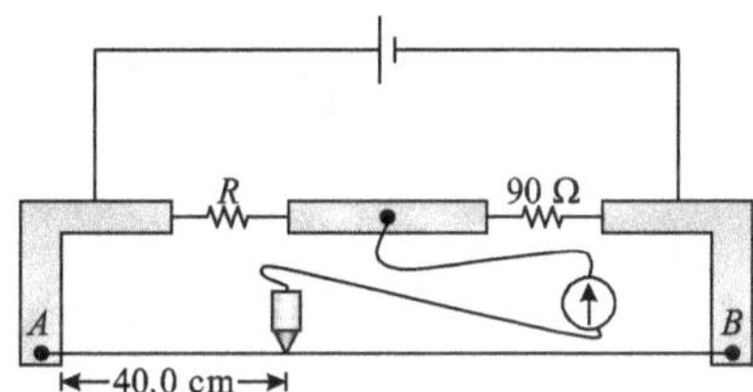

(A) $60 \pm 0.15\,\Omega$ (B) $135 \pm 0.56\,\Omega$
(C) $60 \pm 0.25\,\Omega$ (D) $135 \pm 0.23\,\Omega$

9. An infinite line charge of uniform electric charge density λ lies along the axis of an electrically conducting infinite cylindrical shell of radius R. At time $t = 0$, the space inside the cylinder is filled with a material of permittivity ε and electrical conductivity σ. The electrical conduction in the material follows Ohm's law. Which one of the following graphs best describes the subsequent variation of the magnitude of current density $j(t)$ at any point in the material ? **[JEE Adv 2016, P-1]**

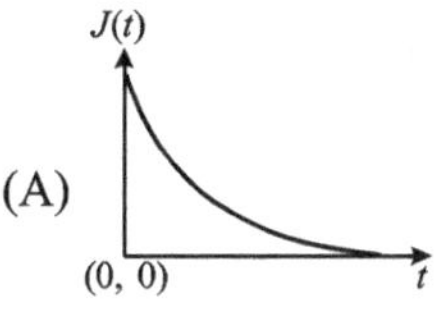
(A)

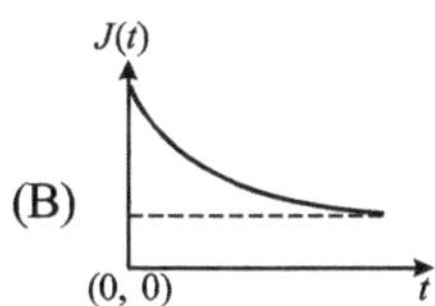
(B)

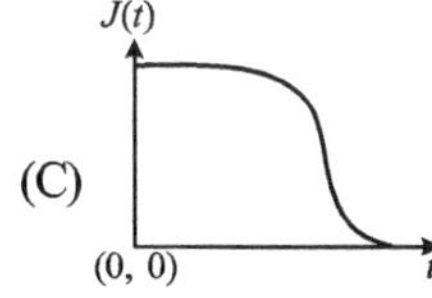
(C)

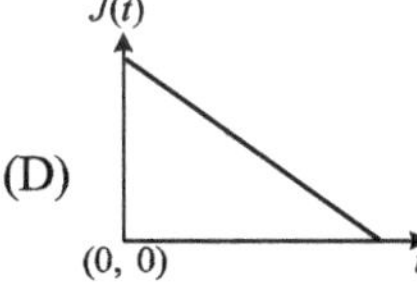
(D)

MCQ with One or More than One Options Correct

10. For the circuit shown in the figure : **[JEE Adv 2009, P-1]**

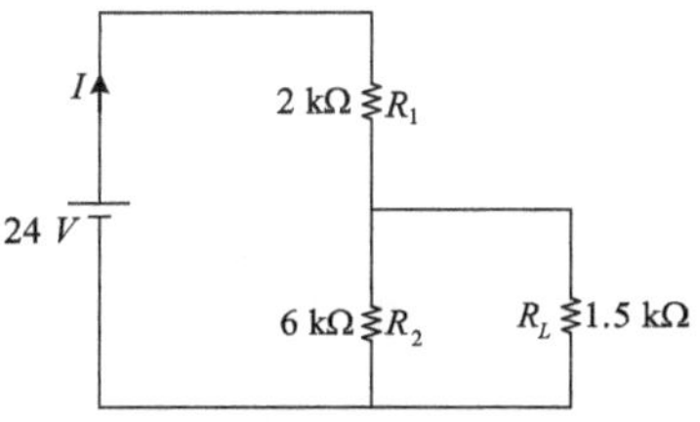

(A) The current I through the battery is 7.5 mA
(B) The potential difference across R_L is 18 V
(C) Ratio of powers dissipated in R_1 and R_2 is 3
(D) If R_1 and R_2 are interchanged, magnitude of the power dissipated in R_L will decrease by a factor of 9

11. For the resistance network shown in the figure, choose the correct option : **[JEE Adv 2012, P-1]**

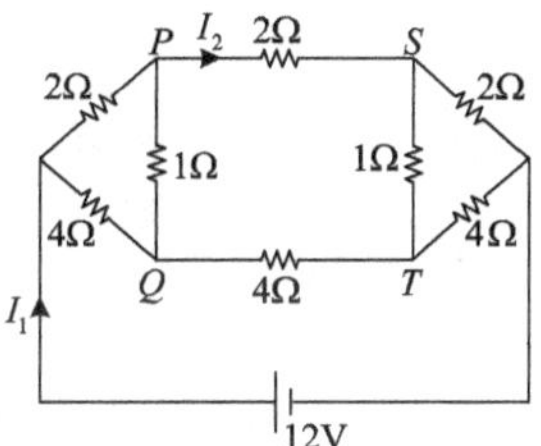

(A) The current through PQ is zero
(B) $I_1 = 3$ A
(C) The potential at S is less than that at Q
(D) $I_2 = 2$ A

12. Heater of an electric kettle is made of a wire of length L and diameter d. It takes 4 minutes to raise the temperature of 0.5 kg water by 40 K. This heater is replaced by a new heater having two wires of the same material, each of length L and diameter $2d$. The way these wires are connected is given in the options. How much time in minutes will it take to raise the temperature of the same amount of water by 40 K : **[JEE Adv 2014, P-1]**

(A) 4 if wires are in parallel   (B) 2 if wires are in series
(C) 1 if wires are in series   (D) 0.5 if wires are in parallel

13. Two ideal batteries of emf V_1 and V_2 and three resistance R_1, R_2 and R_3 are connected as shown in the figure. The current in resistance R_2 would be zero if : **[JEE Adv 2014, P-1]**

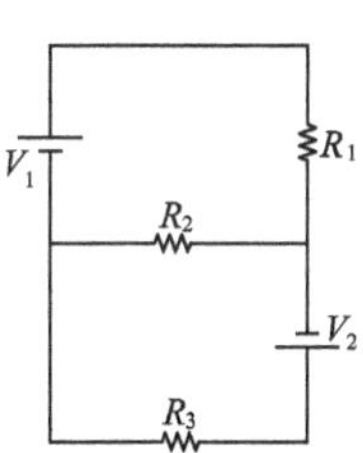

(A) $V_1 = V_2$ and $R_1 = R_2 = R_3$
(B) $V_1 = V_2$ and $R_1 = 2R_2 = R_3$
(C) $V_1 = 2V_2$ and $2R_1 = 2R_2 = R_3$
(D) $2V_1 = V_2$ and $2R_1 = R_2 = R_3$

14. In an aluminum (Al) bar of square cross section, a square hole is drilled and is filled with iron (Fe) as shown in the figure. The electrical resistivities of Al and Fe are 2.7×10^{-8} Ωm and 1.0×10^{-7} Ωm, respectively. The electrical resistance between the two faces P and Q of the composite bar is :

[JEE Adv 2015, P-1]

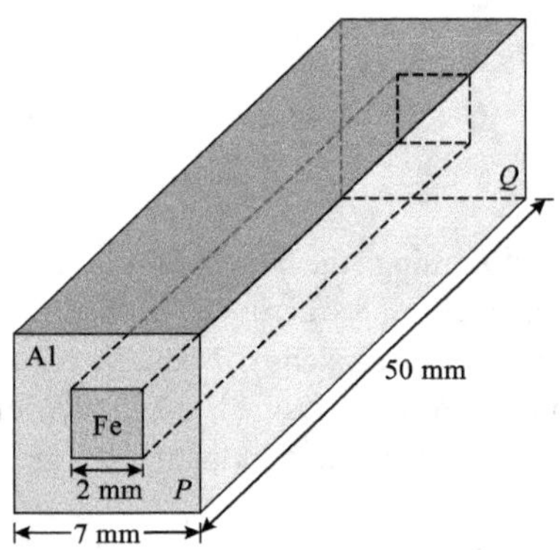

(A) $\dfrac{2475}{64} \, \mu\Omega$

(B) $\dfrac{1875}{64} \, \mu\Omega$

(C) $\dfrac{1875}{49} \, \mu\Omega$

(D) $\dfrac{2475}{132} \, \mu\Omega$

15. An incandescent bulb has a thin filament of tungsten that is heated to high temperature by passing an electric current. The hot filament emits black-body radiation. The filament is observed to break up at random locations after a sufficiently long time of operation due to non-uniform evaporation of tungsten from the filament. If the bulb is powered at constant voltage, which of the following statement(s) is (are) true?

[JEE Adv 2016, P-1]

(A) The temperature distribution over the filament is uniform

(B) The resistance over small sections of the filament decreases with time

(C) The filament emits more light at higher band of frequencies before it breaks up

(D) The filament consumes less electrical power towards the end of the life of the bulb

16. Consider two identical galvanometers and two identical resistors with resistance R. If the internal resistance of the galvanometers $R_C < R/2$, which of the following statement(s) about any one of the galvanometers in(are) true?

[JEE Adv 2016, P-2]

(A) The maximum voltage range is obtained when all the components are connected in series

(B) The maximum voltage range is obtained when the two resistors and one galvanometer are connected in series, and the second galvanometer is connected in parallel to the first galvanometer

(C) The maximum current range is obtained when all the components are connected in parallel

(D) The maximum current range is obtained when the two galvanometers are connected in series and the combination is connected in parallel with both the resistors

17. In the circuit shown below, the key is pressed at time $t = 0$. Which of the following statement(s) is(are) true ?

[JEE Adv 2016, P-2]

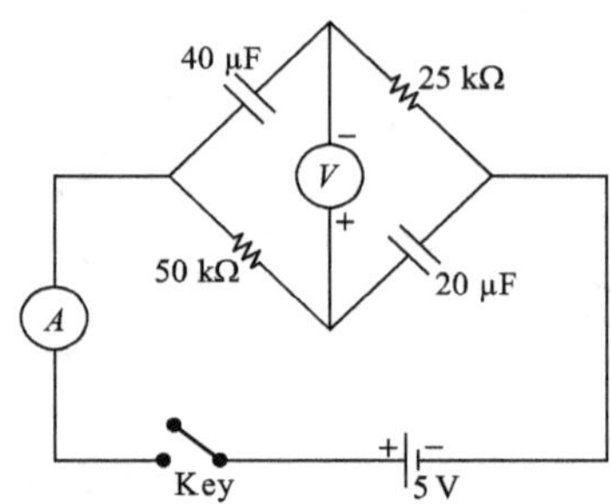

(A) The voltmeter displays –5 V as soon as the key is pressed, and displays +5 V after a long time

(B) The voltmeter will display 0 V at time $t = \ln 2$ seconds

(C) The current in the ammeter becomes $1/e$ of the initial value after 1 second

(D) The current in the ammeter becomes zero after a long time

18. Two identical moving coil galvanometer have 10 Ω resistance and full scale deflection at 2 μA current. One of them is converted into a voltmeter of 100 mV full scale reading and the other into an Ammeter of 1 μA full scale current using appropriate resistors. These are then used to measure the voltage and current in the Ohm's law experiment with $R = 1000\,\Omega$ resistor by using an ideal cell. Which of the following statement(s) is/are correct : **[JEE Adv 2019, P-1]**

(A) The measured value of R will be $978\,\Omega < R < 982\,\Omega$.

(B) The resistance of the Voltmeter will be 100 kΩ.

(C) The resistance of the Ammeter will be 0.02 Ω. (round off to 2nd decimal place)

(D) If the ideal cell is replaced by a cell having internal resistance of 5 Ω then the measured value of R will be more than 1000 Ω.

19. The figure shows a circuit having eight resistances of 1 Ω each, labelled R_1 to R_8, and two ideal batteries with voltages $\varepsilon_1 = 12$ V and $\varepsilon_2 = 6$ V.

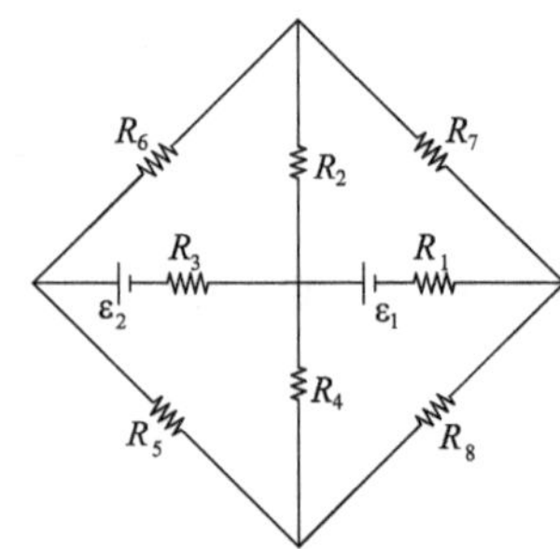

Which of the following statement(s) is(are) correct ?

[JEE Adv 2022, P-1]

(A) The magnitude of current flowing through R_1 is 7.2 A

(B) The magnitude of current flowing through R_2 is 1.2 A

(C) The magnitude of current flowing through R_3 is 4.8 A

(D) The magnitude of current flowing through R_5 is 2.4 A

20. In Circuit-1 and Circuit-2 shown in the figures, $R_1 = 1\Omega$, $R_2 = 2\Omega$, and $R_3 = 3\Omega$. P_1 and P_2 are the power dissipations in Circuit-1 and Circuit-2 when the switches S_1 and S_2 are in open conditions, respectively. Q_1 and Q_2 are the power dissipations in Circuit-1 and Circuit-2 when the switches S_1 and S_2 are in closed conditions, respectively.

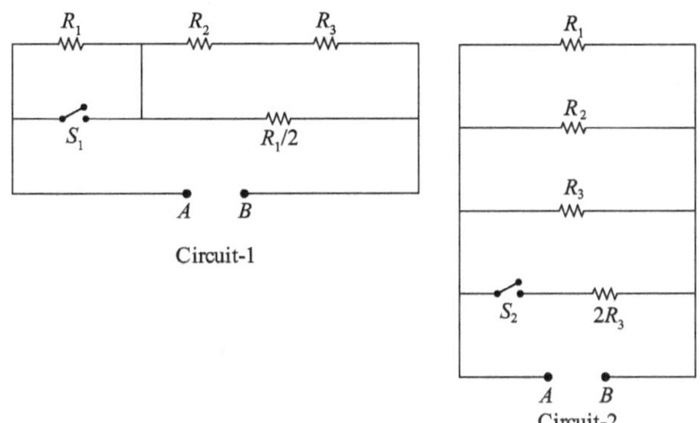

Circuit-1

Circuit-2

Which of the following statement(s) is (are) correct?

[JEE Adv 2022, P-2]

(A) When a voltage source of $6V$ is connected across A and B in both circuits, $P_1 < P_2$

(B) When a constant current source of 2 Amp is connected across A and B in both circuits, $P_1 > P_2$

(C) When a voltage source of $6V$ is connected across A and B is Circuit-1, $Q_1 > P_1$

(D) When a constant current source of 2 Amp is connected across A and B in both circuits, $Q_2 < Q_1$

21. In a circuit shown in the figure, the capacitor C is initially uncharged and the key K is open. In this condition, a current of 1 A flows through the 1 Ω resistor. The key is closed at time $t = t_0$. Which of the following statement(s) is(are) correct? [Given : $e^{-1} = 0.36$]

[JEE Adv 2023, P-1]

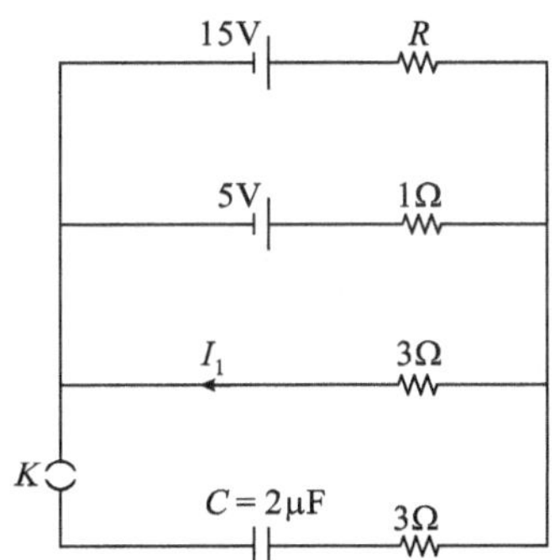

(A) The value of the resistance R is 3 Ω

(B) For $t < t_0$, the value of current I_1 is 2 A

(C) At $t = t_0 + 7.2$ μs, the current in the capacitor is 0.6 A

(D) For $t \to \infty$, the charge on the capacitor is 12 μC

Assertion Reason based on MCQ

22. STATEMENT-1 **[JEE Adv 2008, P-1]**

In a Meter Bridge experiment, null point for an unknown resistance is measured. Now, the unknown resistance is put inside an enclosure maintained at a higher temperature. The null point can be obtained at the same point as before by decreasing the value of the standard resistance.

because

STATEMENT-2

Resistance of a metal increases with increase in temperature :

(A) Statement-1 is True, Statement-2 is True; Statement-2 is a correct explanation for Statement-1

(B) Statement-1 is True, Statement-2 is True, Statement-2 is **NOT** a correct explanation for Statement-2

(C) Statement-1 is True, Statement-2 is False

(D) Statement-1 is False, Statement-2 is True

Matrix Match MCQ

23. Column-I gives some devices and **Column-II** gives some process on which the functioning of these devices depend. Match the devices in **Column-I** with the processes in **Column-II** and indicate your answer by darkening appropriate bubbles in the 4×4 matrix given in the ORS : **[JEE Adv 2007, P-2]**

Column-I	Column-II
(A) Bimetallic strip	(P) Radiation from a hot body
(B) Steam engine	(Q) Energy conversion
(C) In candescent lamp	(R) Melting
(D) Electric fuse	(S) Thermal expansion of solids

Comprehension based MCQ

Paragraph-1 (Q. No. 24-25)

A thermal power plant produces electric power of 600 kW at 4000 V, which is to be transported to a place 20 km away from the power plant for consumer's usage. It can be transported either directly with a cable of large current carrying capacity or by using a combination of step-up and step-down transformers at the two ends. The drawback of the direct transmission is the large energy dissipation. In this method using transformers, the dissipation is much smaller. In this method, a step-up transformer is used at the plant side so that the current is reduced to smaller value. At the consumer's end, a step-down transformer is used to supply power to the consumers at the specified lower voltage. It is reasonable to assume that the power cable is purely resistive and the transformers are ideal with a power factor unity. All the currents and voltages mentioned are rms values.   **[JEE Adv 2013, P-2]**

24. If the direct transmission method with a cable of resistance 0.4 Ωkm^{-1} is used, the power dissipation (in%) during transmission is :

(A) 20   (B) 30

(C) 40   (D) 50

25. In the method using the transformers, assume that the ratio of the number of turns in the primary to that in the secondary in the step-up transformer is 1 : 10. If the power to the consumers has to be supplied at 200 V, the ratio of the number of turns in the primary to that in the secondary in the step-down transformer is :

(A) 200 : 1   (B) 150 : 1

(C) 100 : 1   (D) 50 : 1

Paragraph-2 (Q. No. 26-27)

Consider an evacuated cylindrical chamber of height h having rigid conducting plates at the ends and an insulating curved surface as shown in the figure. A number of spherical balls made of a light weight and soft material and coated with a conducting material are placed on the bottom plate. The balls have a radius $r \ll h$. Now a high voltage source (HV) is connected across the conducting plates such that the bottom plate is at $+V_0$ and the top plate at $-V_0$. Due to their conducting surface, the balls will get charged, will become equipotential with the plate and are repelled by it. The balls will eventually collide with the top plate, where the coefficient of restitution can be taken to be zero due to the soft nature of the material of the balls. The electric field in the chamber can be considered to be that of a parallel plate capacitor. Assume that there are no collisions between the balls and the interaction between them is negligible. (Ignore gravity) **[JEE Adv 2016, P-2]**

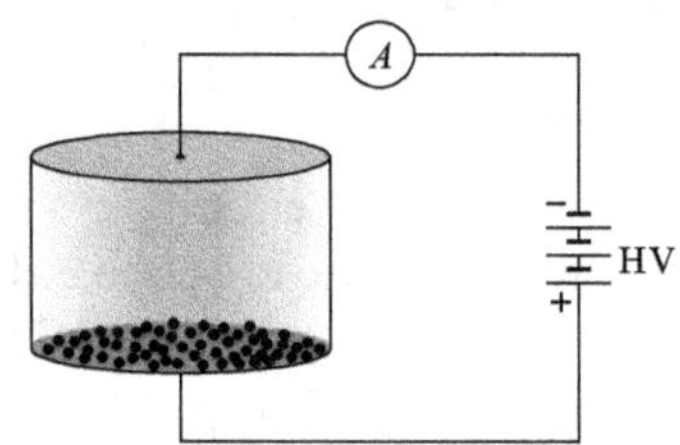

26. Which one of the following statements is correct ?

(A) The balls will bounce back to the bottom plate carrying the opposite charge they went up with

(B) The balls will execute simple harmonic motion between the two plates

(C) The balls will bounce back to the bottom plate carrying the same charge they went up with

(D) The balls will stick to the top plate and remain there

27. The average current in the steady state registered by the ammeter in the circuit will be :

(A) Proportional to $V_0^{1/2}$

(B) Proportional to V_0^2

(C) Proportional to the potential V_0

(D) Zero

Integer Answer based Questions

28. When two identical batteries of internal resistance 1 Ω each are connected in series across a resistor R, the rate of heat produced in R is J_1. When the same batteries are connected in parallel across R, the rate is J_2. If $J_1 = 2.25 J_2$ then the value of R in Q is ?   **[JEE Adv 2010, P-1]**

29. Two batteries of different emfs and different internal resistances are connected as shown. The voltage across AB in volts is ?   **[JEE Adv 2011, P-2]**

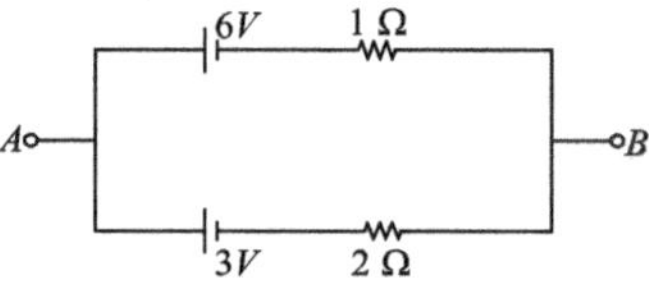

30. A galvanometer gives full scale deflection with 0.006 A current. By connecting it to a 4990 Ω resistance, it can be converted into a voltmeter of range 0 – 30 V. If connected to a $\dfrac{2n}{249}\Omega$ resistance, it becomes an ammeter of range 0 – 1.5 A. The value of n is ?   **[JEE Adv 2014, P-1]**

31. In the following circuit, the current through the resistor $R = 2\Omega$ is I Amperes. The value of I is :   **[JEE Adv 2015, P-2]**

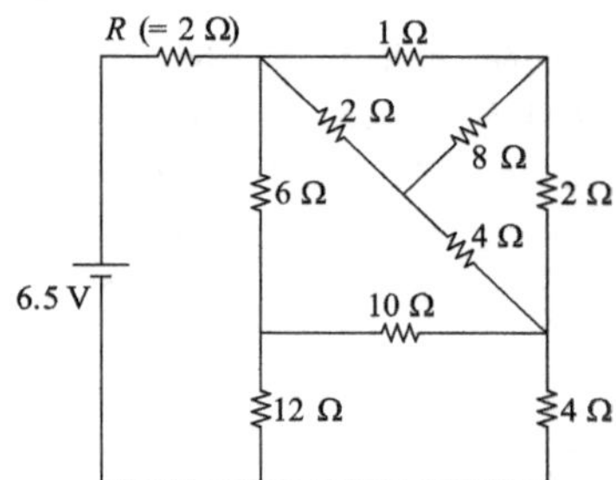

32. A moving coil galvanometer has 50 turns and each turn has an area 2×10^{-4} m^2. The magnetic field produced by the magnet inside the galvanometer is 0.02 T. The torsional constant of the suspension wire is 10^{-4} N m rad^{-1}. When a current flows through the galvanometer, a full scale deflection occurs if the coil rotates by 0.2 rad. The resistance of the coil of the galvanometer is 50 Ω. This galvanometer is to be converted into an ammeter capable of measuring current in the range $0 - 1.0$ A. For this purpose, a shunt resistance is to be added in parallel to the galvanometer. The value of this shunt resistance, in ohms, is ______.   **[JEE Adv 2018, P-2]**

33. In the balanced condition, the values of the resistances of the four arms of a Wheatstone bridge are shown in the figure below. The resistance R_3 has temperature coefficient $0.0004°C^{-1}$. If the temperature of R_3 is increased by $100°C$, the voltage developed between S and T will be ______ volt.

[JEE Adv 2020, P-2]

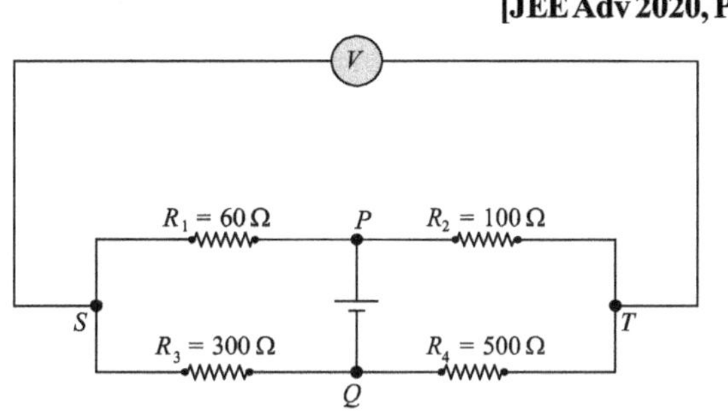

34. In order to measure the internal resistance r_1 of a cell of emf E, a meter bridge of wire resistance $R_0 = 50\ \Omega$, a resistance $R_0/2$, another cell of emf $E/2$ (internal resistance r) and a galvanometer G are used in a circuit, as shown in the figure. If the null point is

found at $l = 72$ cm, then the value of $r_1 =$ ______ Ω.

[JEE Adv 2021, P-2]

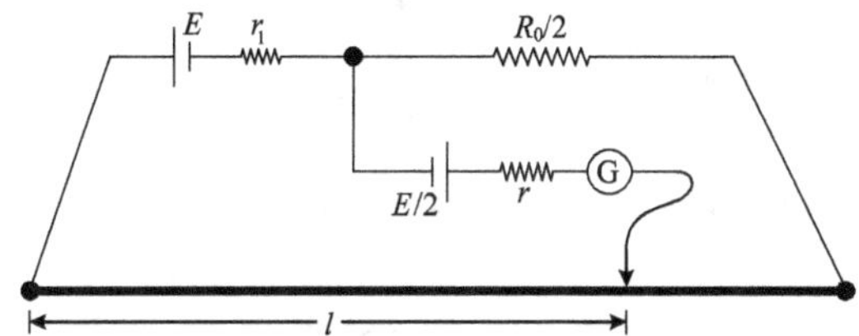

35. Two resistances $R_1 = X\ \Omega$ and $R_2 = 1\ \Omega$ are connected to a wire AB of uniform resistivity, as shown in the figure. The radius of the wire varies linearly along its axis from 0.2 mm at A to 1 mm at B. A galvanometer (G) connected to the center of the wire, 50 cm from each end along its axis, shows zero deflection when A and B are connected to a battery. The value of X is ______.

[JEE Adv 2022, P-2]

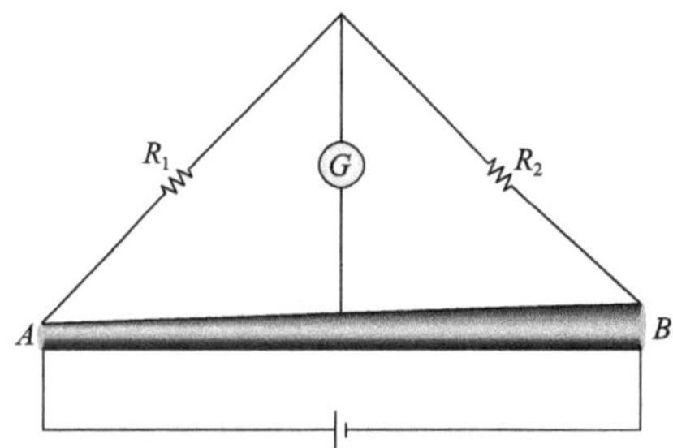

*   *   *   *   *

MCQ with Single Option Correct

1. A magnetic field $\vec{B} = B_0\hat{j}$ exists in the region $a < x < 2a$ and $\vec{B} = -B_0\hat{j}$, in the region $2a < x < 3a$, where B_0 is a positive constant. A positive point charge moving with a velocity $\vec{v} = v_0\hat{i}$, where v_0 is a positive constant, enters the magnetic field at $x = a$. The trajectory of the charge in this region can be like :

[JEE Adv 2007, P-2]

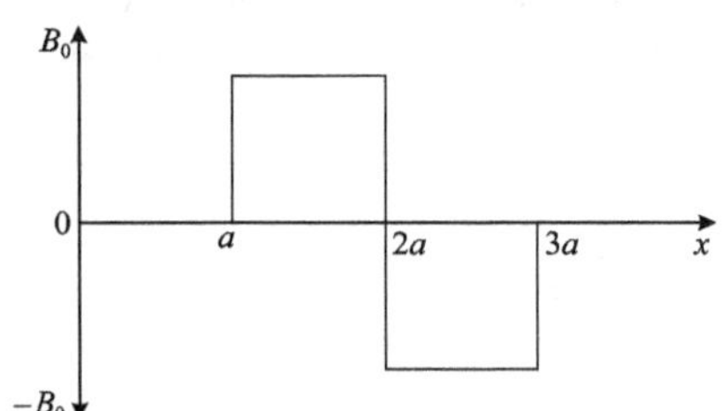

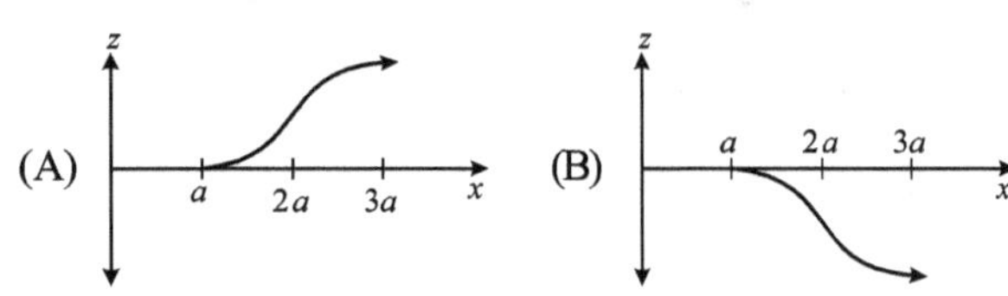

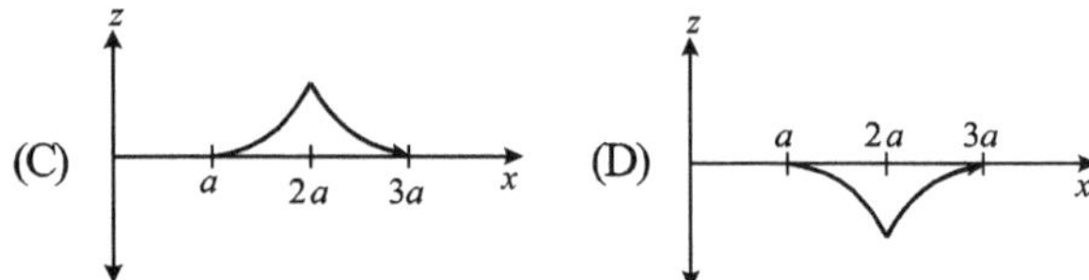

2. The figure shows certain wire segments joined together to from a coplanar loop. The loop is placed in a perpendicular magnetic field in the direction going into the plane of the figure. The magnitude of the field increases with time I_1 and I_2 are the currents in the segments ab and cd. Then, :

[JEE Adv 2009, P-1]

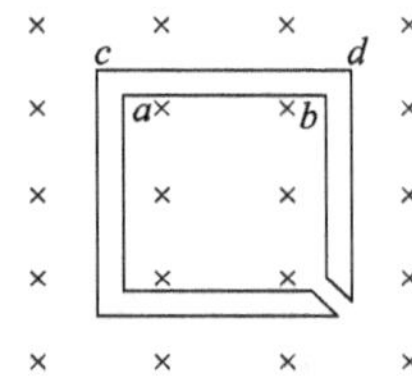

(A) $I_1 > I_2$
(B) $I_1 < I_2$
(C) I_1 is in the direction ba and I_2 is in the direction cd
(D) I_1 is in the direction ab and I_2 is in the direction dc

3. A thin flexible wire of length L is connected to two adjacent fixed points and carries a current I in the clockwise direction, as shown in the figure. When the system is put in a uniform magnetic field of strength B going into the plane of the paper, the wire takes the shape of a circle. The tension in the wire is :

[JEE Adv 2010, P-1]

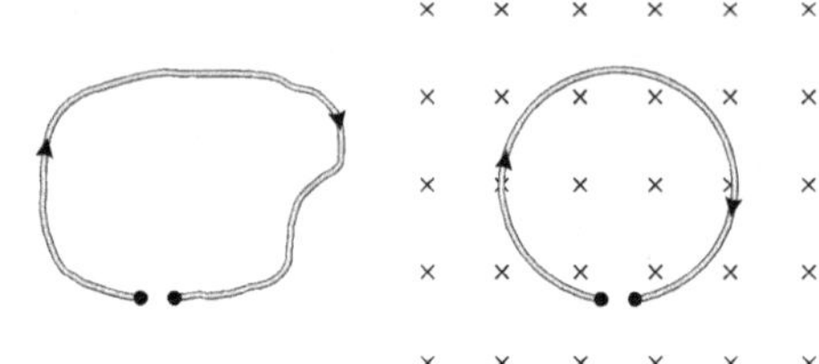

(A) IBL

(B) $\dfrac{IBL}{\pi}$

(C) $\dfrac{IBL}{2\pi}$

(D) $\dfrac{IBL}{4\pi}$

4. A long insulated copper wire is closely wound as a spiral of N turns. The spiral has inner radius a and outer radius b. The spiral lies in the X-Y plane and a steady current I flow through the wire. The Z-component of the magnetic field at the center of the spiral is :

[JEE Adv 2011, P-2]

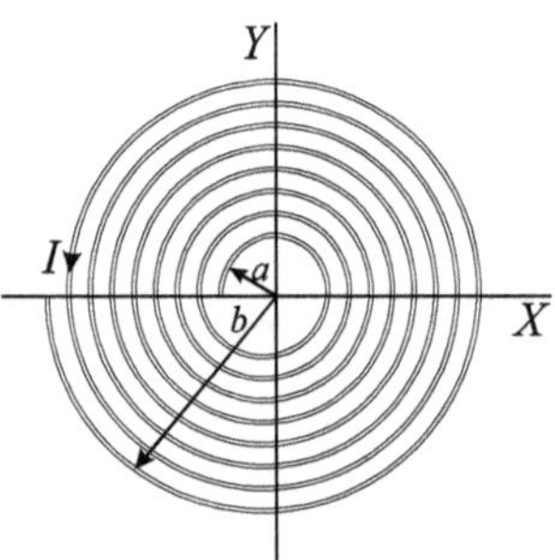

(A) $\dfrac{\mu_0 NI}{2(b-a)}\ln\left(\dfrac{b}{a}\right)$

(B) $\dfrac{\mu_0 NI}{2(b-a)}\ln\left(\dfrac{b+a}{b-a}\right)$

(C) $\dfrac{\mu_0 NI}{2b}\ln\left(\dfrac{b}{a}\right)$

(D) $\dfrac{\mu_0 NI}{2b}\ln\left(\dfrac{b+a}{b-a}\right)$

5. An infinitely long hollow conducting cylinder with inner radius $R/2$ and outer radius R carries a uniform current density along its length. The magnitude of the magnetic field, $|\vec{B}|$ as a function of the radial distance r from the axis is best represented by : **[JEE Adv 2012, P-2]**

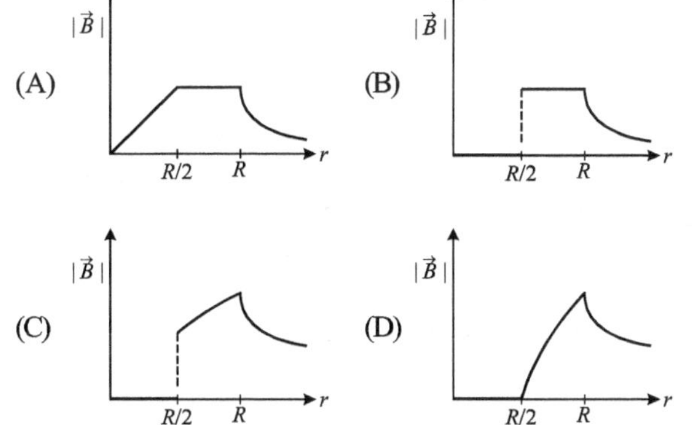

(A)

(B)

(C)

(D)

6. A loop carrying current I lies in the x-y plane as shown in the figure. The unit vector $\hat{k}$ is coming out of the plane of the paper. The magnetic moment of the current loop is :

[JEE Adv 2012, P-2]

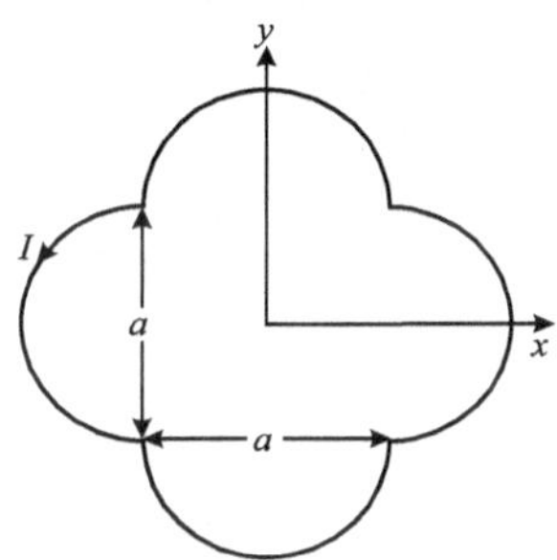

(A) $a^2 I\,\hat{k}$

(B) $\left(\dfrac{\pi}{2}+1\right)a^2 I\hat{k}$

(C) $-\left(\dfrac{\pi}{2}+1\right)a^2 I\hat{k}$

(D) $(2\pi+1)\,a^2 I\,\hat{k}$

7. A symmetric star shaped conducting wire loop is carrying a steady state current I as shown in the figure. The distance between the diametrically opposite vertices of the star is $4a$. The magnitude of the magnetic field at the center of the loop is:

[JEE Adv 2017, P-2]

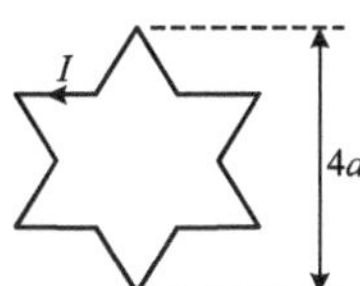

(A) $\dfrac{\mu_0 I}{4\pi a}3[\sqrt{3}-1]$

(B) $\dfrac{\mu_0 I}{4\pi a}6[\sqrt{3}-1]$

(C) $\dfrac{\mu_0 I}{4\pi a}6[\sqrt{3}+1]$

(D) $\dfrac{\mu_0 I}{4\pi a}3[2-\sqrt{3}]$

8. A circular coil of radius R and N turns has negligible resistance. As shown in the schematic figure, its two ends are connected to two wires and it is hanging by those wires with its plane being vertical. The wires are connected to a capacitor with charge Q through a switch. The coil is in a horizontal uniform magnetic field B_0 parallel to the plane of the coil. When the switch is closed, the capacitor gets discharged through the coil in a very short time. By the time the capacitor is discharged fully, magnitude of the angular momentum gained by the coil will be (assume that the discharge time is so short that the coil has hardly rotated during this time)

[JEE Adv 2020, P-1]

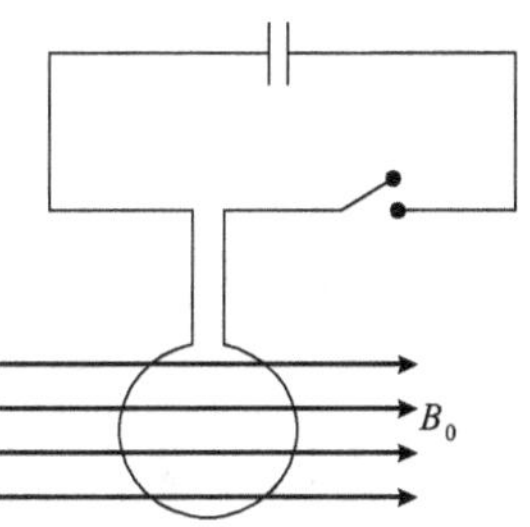

(A) $\dfrac{\pi}{2}\,NQB_0 R^2$

(B) $\pi NQB_0 R^2$

(C) $2\pi NQB_0 R^2$

(D) $4\pi NQB_0 R^2$

9. Which one of the following options represents the magnetic field $\vec{B}$ at O due to the current flowing in the given wire segments lying on the xy plane ? **[JEE Adv 2022, P-2]**

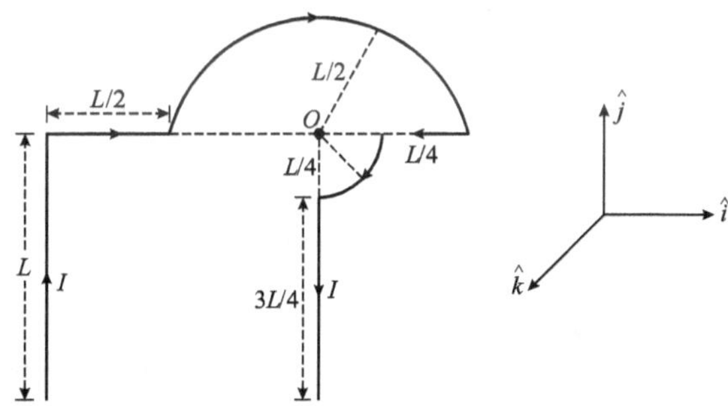

(A) $\vec{B} = \dfrac{-\mu_0 I}{L}\left(\dfrac{3}{2}+\dfrac{1}{4\sqrt{2}\pi}\right)\hat{k}$

(B) $\vec{B} = \dfrac{-\mu_0 I}{L}\left(\dfrac{3}{2}+\dfrac{1}{2\sqrt{2}\pi}\right)\hat{k}$

(C) $\vec{B} = \dfrac{-\mu_0 I}{L}\left(1+\dfrac{1}{4\sqrt{2}\pi}\right)\hat{k}$

(D) $\vec{B} = \dfrac{-\mu_0 I}{L}\left(1+\dfrac{1}{4\pi}\right)\hat{k}$

MCQ with One or More than One Options Correct

10. A particle of mass m and charge q, moving with velocity V enters Region II normal to the boundary as shown in the figure. Region II has a uniform magnetic field B perpendicular to the plane of the paper. The length of the Region II is l. Choose the correct choice(s) : **[JEE Adv 2008, P-1]**

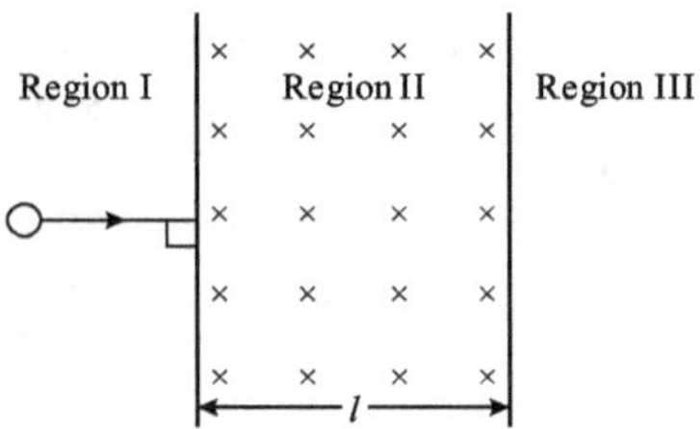

(A) The particle enters Region III only if its velocity $V > \dfrac{qlB}{m}$

(B) The particle enters Region III only if its velocity $V > \dfrac{qlB}{m}$

(C) Path length of the particle in Region II is maximum when velocity $V = \dfrac{qlB}{m}$

(D) Time spent in Region II is same for any velocity V as long as the particle returns to Region I

11. A electron and a proton are moving on straight parallel paths with same velocity. They enter a semi-infinite region of uniform magnetic field perpendicular to the velocity. Which of the following statements is/are true : **[JEE Adv 2011, P-1]**
(A) They will never come out of the magnetic field region
(B) They will come out travelling along parallel paths
(C) They will come out at the same time
(D) They will come out at different times

12. Consider the motion of a positive point charge in a region where there are simultaneous uniform electric and magnetic fields $\vec{E} = E_0 \hat{j}$ and $\vec{B} = B_0 \hat{j}$. At time $t = 0$, this charge has velocity $\vec{v}$ in the x-y plane, making an angle θ with the x-axis. Which of the following option is (are) correct for time $t > 0$:
[JEE Adv 2012, P-1]
(A) If $\theta = 0°$, the charge moves in a circular path in the x-z plane
(B) If $\theta = 0°$, the charge undergoes helical motion with constant pitch along the y-axis
(C) If $\theta = 10°$, the charge undergoes helical motion with its pitch increasing with time, along the y-axis
(D) If $\theta = 90°$, the charge undergoes linear but accelerated motion along the y-axis

13. A particle of mass M and positive charge Q, moving with a constant velocity $\vec{u}_1 = 4\,\hat{i}$ ms^{-1}, enters a region of uniform static magnetic field normal to the x-y plane. The region of the magnetic field extends from $x = 0$ to $x = L$ for all values of y. After passing through this region, the particle emerges on the other side after 10 milliseconds with a velocity $\vec{u}_2 = 2\,(\sqrt{3}\hat{i} + \hat{j})$ ms^{-1}. The correct statement (s) is (are) :

[JEE Adv 2013, P-1]

(A) The direction of the magnetic field is $-z$ direction
(B) The direction of the magnetic field is $+z$ direction

(C) The magnitude of the magnetic field $\dfrac{50\pi M}{3Q}$ units

(D) The magnitude of the magnetic field is $\dfrac{100\pi M}{3Q}$ units

14. A steady current I flows along an infinitely long hollow cylindrical conductor of radius R. This cylinder is placed coaxially inside an infinite solenoid of radius $2R$. The solenoid has n turns per unit length and carries a steady current I. Consider a point P at a distance r from the common axis. The correct statement(s) is (are) : **[JEE Adv 2013, P-2]**
(A) In the region $0 < r < R$, the magnetic field is non-zero.
(B) In the region $R < r < 2R$, the magnetic field is along the common axis.
(C) In the region $R < r < 2R$, the magnetic field is tangential to the circle of radius r, centered on the axis.
(D) In the region $r > 2R$, the magnetic field is non-zero.

15. A conductor (shown in the figure) carrying constant current I is kept in the x-y plane in a uniform magnetic field $\vec{B}$. If F is the magnitude of the total magnetic force acting on the conductor, then the correct statement(s) is(are) : **[JEE Adv 2015, P-1]**

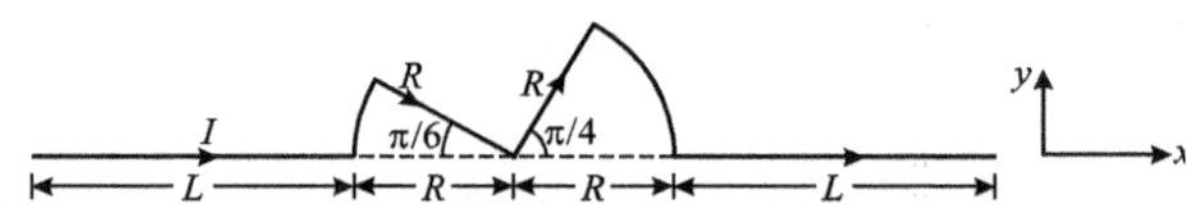

(A) If $\vec{B}$ is along $\hat{z}$, $F \propto (L + R)$

(B) If $\vec{B}$ is along $\hat{x}$, $F = 0$

(C) If $\vec{B}$ is along $\hat{y}$, $F \propto (L + R)$

(D) If $\vec{B}$ is along $\hat{z}$, $F = 0$

16. A uniform magnetic field B exists in the region between $x = 0$ to $x = \dfrac{3R}{2}$ (region 2 in the figure) pointing normally into the plane of the paper. A particle with charge $+Q$ and momentum p directed along x-axis enters region 2 from region 1 at point P_1 $(y = -R)$. Which of the following option(s) is/are correct :

[JEE Adv 2017, P-2]

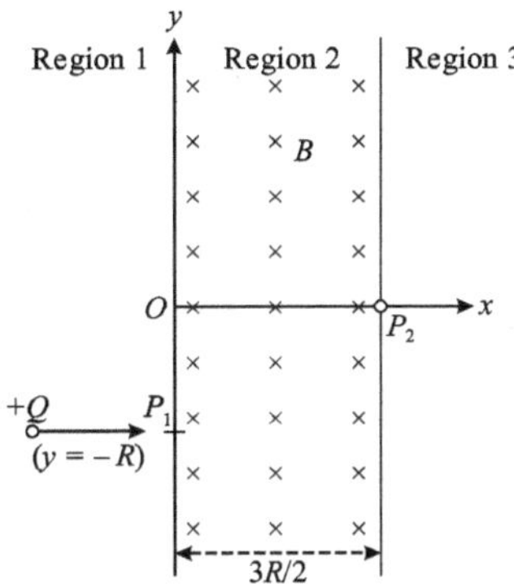

(A) For $B = \dfrac{8}{13}\dfrac{p}{QR}$, the particle will enter region 3 through the point P_2 on x-axis

(B) For $B > \dfrac{2}{3}\dfrac{p}{QR}$, the particle will re-enter region 1

(C) For a fixed B, particles of same charge Q and same velocity v, the distance between the point P_1 and the point of re-entry into region 1 is inversely proportional to the mass of the particle

(D) When the particle re-enters region 1 through the longest possible path in region 2, the magnitude of the change in its linear momentum between point P_1 and the farthest point from y-axis is $p / \sqrt{2}$.

17. Two infinitely long straight wires lie in the xy-plane along the lines $x = \pm R$. The wire located at $x = +R$ carries a constant current I_1 and the wire located at $x = -R$ carries a constant current I_2. A circular loop of radius R is suspended with its centre at $(0, 0, \sqrt{3}R)$ and in a plane parallel to the xy-plane. This loop carries a constant current I in the clockwise direction as seen from above the loop. The current in the wire is taken to be positive if it is in the $+\hat{j}$ direction. Which of the following statements regarding the magnetic field $\vec{B}$ is (are) true ?

[JEE Adv 2018, P-1]

(A) If $I_1 = I_2$, then $\vec{B}$ cannot be equal to zero at the origin $(0, 0, 0)$

(B) If $I_1 > 0$ and $I_2 < 0$, then $\vec{B}$ can be equal to zero at the origin $(0, 0, 0)$

(C) If $I_1 < 0$ and $I_2 > 0$, then $\vec{B}$ can be equal to zero at the origin $(0, 0, 0)$

(D) If $I_1 = I_2$, then the z-component of the magnetic field at the centre of the loop is $\left(-\dfrac{\mu_0 I}{2R} \right)$

18. A conducting wire of parabolic shape, initially $y = x^2$, is moving with velocity $\vec{V} = V_0 \hat{i}$ in a non-uniform magnetic field $\vec{B} = B_0 \left(1 + \left(\dfrac{y}{L} \right)^{\beta} \right) \hat{k}$, as shown in figure. If V_0, B_0, L and β are positive constants and $\Delta\phi$ is the potential difference developed between the ends of the wire, then the correct statement(s) is/are :

[JEE Adv 2019, P-1]

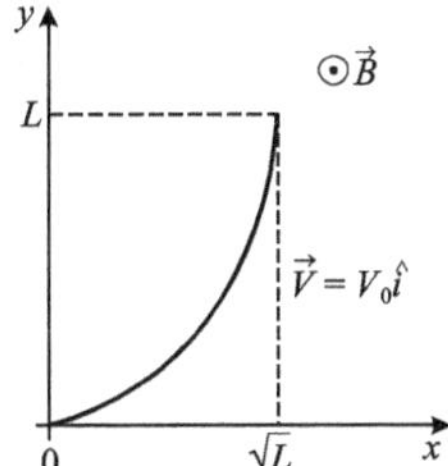

(A) $|\Delta\phi|$ remains the same if the parabolic wire is replaced by a straight wire, $y = x$ initially, of length $\sqrt{2}L$

(B) $|\Delta\phi|$ is proportional to the length of the wire projected on the y-axis.

(C) $|\Delta\phi| = \dfrac{1}{2} B_0 V_0 L$ For $\beta = 0$

(D) $|\Delta\phi| = \dfrac{4}{3} B_0 V_0 L$ For $\beta = 2$

19. A long straight wire carries a current, $I = 2$ ampere. A semi-circular conducting rod is placed beside it on two conducting parallel rails of negligible resistance. Both the rails are parallel to the wire. The wire, the rod and the rails lie in the same horizontal plane, as shown in the figure. Two ends of the semi-circular rod are at distances 1 cm and 4 cm from the wire. At time $t = 0$, the rod starts moving on the rails with a speed $v = 3.0$ m/s (see the figure).

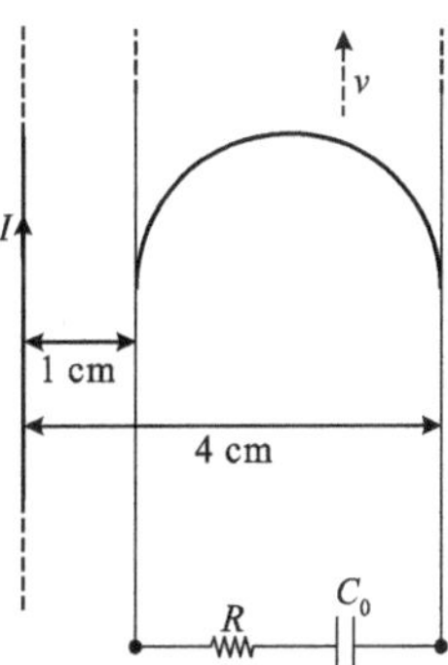

A resistor $R = 1.4\ \Omega$ and a capacitor $C_0 = 5.0\ \mu F$ are connected in series between the rails. At time $t = 0$, C_0 is uncharged. Which of the following statement(s) is(are) correct? [$\mu_0 = 4\pi \times 10^{-7}$ SI units. Take $\ln 2 = 0.7$]   **[JEE Adv 2021, P-1]**

(A) Maximum current through R is 1.2×10^{-6} ampere

(B) Maximum current through R is 3.8×10^{-6} ampere

(C) Maximum charge on capacitor C_0 is 8.4×10^{-12} coulomb

(D) Maximum charge on capacitor C_0 is 2.4×10^{-12} coulomb

20. Two concentric circular loops, one of radius R and the other of radius $2R$, lie in the xy-plane with the origin as their common center, as shown in the figure. The smaller loop carries current I_1 in the anti-clockwise direction and the larger loop carries current I_2 in the clockwise direction, with $I_2 > 2I_1$. $\vec{B}(x,y)$ denotes the magnetic field at a point (x, y) in the xy-plane. Which of the following statement(s) is(are) correct?

[JEE Adv 2021, P-2]

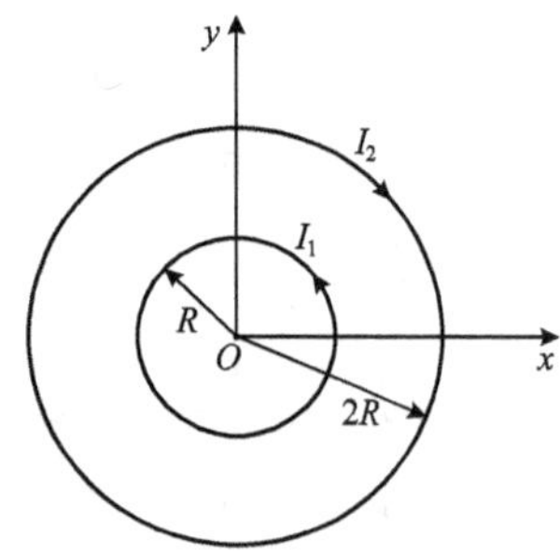

(A) $\vec{B}(x, y)$ is perpendicular to the xy-plane at any point in the plane

(B) $|\vec{B}(x,y)|$ depends on x and y only through the radial distance $r = \sqrt{x^2 + y^2}$

(C) $|\vec{B}(x,y)|$ is non-zero at all points for $r < R$

(D) $\vec{B}(x, y)$ points normally outward from the xy-plane for all the points between the two loops

Assertion Reason based on MCQ

21. STATEMENT-1   **[JEE Adv 2008, P-2]**
The sensitivity of a moving coil galvanometer is increased by placing a suitable magnetic material as core inside the coil.

because

STATEMENT-2
Soft iron has a high magnetic permeability and cannot be easily magnetized or demagnetized :
(A) Statement-1 is True, Statement-2 is True; Statement-2 is a correct explanation for Statement-1
(B) Statement-1 is True, Statement-2 is True; Statement-2 is NOT a correct explanation for Statement-1
(C) Statement-1 is True, Statement-2 is False
(D) Statement-1 is False, Statement-2 is True

Matrix Match MCQ

22. Two wires each carrying a steady current I are shown in four configurations in **Column-I**. Some of the resulting effects are described in **Column-II**. Match the statements in **Column-I** with the statements in **Column-II** and indicate your answer by darkening appropriate bubbles in the 4×4 matrix given in the ORS :   **[JEE Adv 2007, P-2]**

Column-I

(A) Point P is situated midway between the wires.

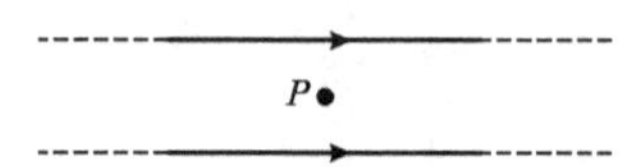

(B) Point P is situated at the mid-point of the line joining the centers of the circular wires, which have same radii.

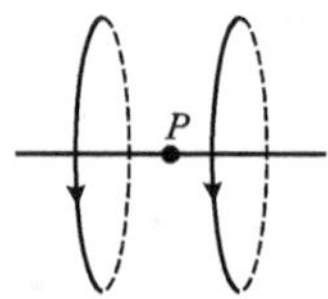

(C) Point P is situated at the mid-point of the line joining the centers of the circular wires, which have same radii.

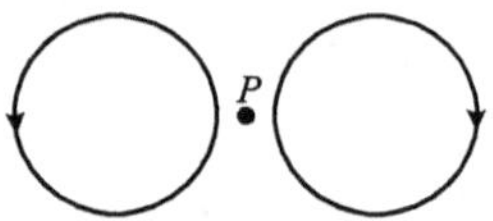

(D) Point P is situated at the common center of the wires.

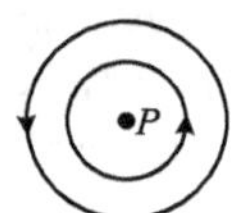

Column-II

(p) The magnetic fields (B) at P due to the currents in the wires are in the same direction.
(q) The magnetic fields (B) at P due to the currents in the wires are in opposite directions.
(r) There is no magnetic field at P.
(s) The wire repel each other.

Answer Q.23, Q.24 and Q.25 by appropriately matching the information given in the three columns of the following table.

A charged particle (electron or proton) is introduced at the origin $(x = 0, y = 0, z = 0)$ with a given initial velocity $\vec{v}$. A uniform electric field $\vec{E}$ and a uniform magnetic field $\vec{B}$ exist everywhere. The velocity $\vec{v}$, electric field $\vec{E}$ and magnetic field $\vec{B}$ are given in column 1, 2 and 3, respectively. The quantities E_0, B_0 are positive in magnitude.   **[JEE Adv 2017, P-1]**

Column I	Column 2	Column 3
(I) Electron with $\vec{v} = 2\dfrac{E_0}{B_0}\hat{x}$	(i) $\vec{E} = E_0\hat{z}$	(P) $\vec{B} = -B_0\hat{x}$
(II) Electron with $\vec{v} = \dfrac{E_0}{B_0}\hat{y}$	(ii) $\vec{E} = -E_0\hat{y}$	(Q) $\vec{B} = B_0\hat{x}$
(III) Proton with $\vec{v} = 0$	(iii) $\vec{E} = -E_0\hat{x}$	(R) $\vec{B} = B_0\hat{y}$
(IV) Proton with $\vec{v} = 2\dfrac{E_0}{B_0}\hat{x}$	(iv) $\vec{E} = E_0\hat{x}$	(S) $\vec{B} = B_0\hat{z}$

23. In which case will the particle move in a straight line with constant velocity :

(A) (II)(iii)(S)   (B) (IV)(i)(S)
(C) (III)(ii)(R)   (D) (III)(iii)(P)

24. In which case will the particle describe a helical path with axis along the positive z-direction ?

(A) (II)(ii)(R)   (B) (IV)(ii)(R)
(C) (IV)(i)(S)   (D) (III)(iii)(P)

25. In which case would the particle move in a straight line along the negative direction of y-axis (i.e., move along $-\hat{y}$) :

(A) (IV)(ii)(S)   (B) (III)(ii)(P)
(C) (II)(iii)(Q)   (D) (III)(ii)(R)

Comprehension based MCQ

Paragraph-1 (Q. No. 26-27)

Electrical resistance of certain materials, known as superconductors, changes abruptly from a nonzero value to zero as their temperature is lowered below a critical temperature $T_C(0)$. An interesting property of superconductors is that their critical temperature becomes smaller than $T_C(0)$ if they are placed in a magnetic field, i.e., the critical temperature $T_C(B)$ is a function of the magnetic field strength B. The dependence of $T_C(B)$ on B is shown in the figure.   **[JEE Adv 2010, P-1]**

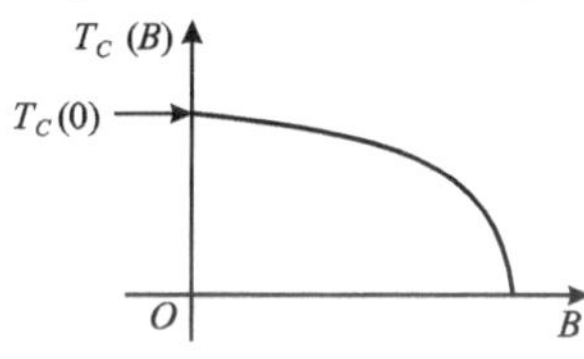

26. In the graphs below, the resistance R of a superconductor is shown as a function of its temperature T for two different magnetic fields B_1 (solid line) and B_2 (dashed line). If B_2 is larger than B_1, which of the following graphs shows the correct variation of R with T in these fields ?

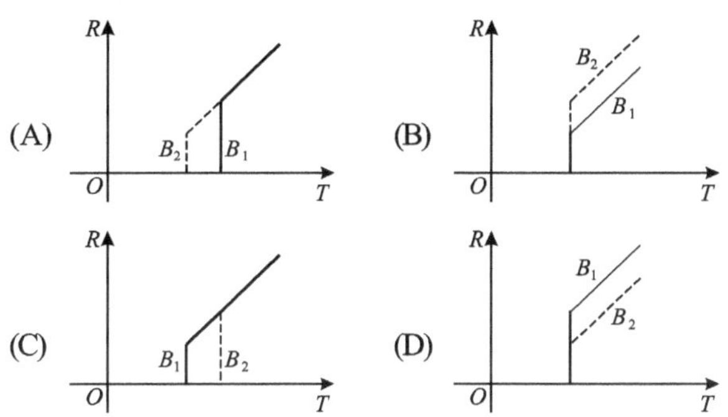

27. A superconductor has $T_C(0) = 100$ K. When a magnetic field of 7.5 Tesla is applied, its T_C decreases to 75 K. For this material one can definitely say that when :

(A) $B = 5$ Tesla, $T_C(B) = 80$ K
(B) $B = 5$ Tesla, 75 K $< T_C(B) < 100$ K
(C) $B = 10$ Tesla, 75 K $< T_C(B) < 100$ K
(D) $B = 10$ Tesla, $T_C(B) = 70$ K

Paragraph-2 (Q. No. 28-29)

A point charge Q is moving in a circular orbit of radius R in the x-y plane with an angular velocity ω. This can be considered as equivalent to a loop carrying a steady current $\dfrac{Q\omega}{2\pi}$. A uniform magnetic field along the positive z-axis is now switched on, which increases at a constant rate B. The application of the magnetic field induces an emf in the orbit. The induced emf is defined as the work done by an induced electric field in moving a unit positive charge around a closed loop. It is known that, for an orbiting charge, the magnetic dipole moment is proportional to the angular momentum with a proportionality constant γ.   **[JEE Adv 2013, P-2]**

28. The magnitude of the induced electric field in the orbit at any instant of time during the time interval of the magnetic field change is :

(A) $\dfrac{BR}{4}$ (B) $\dfrac{BR}{2}$

(C) BR (D) $2BR$

29. The change in the magnetic dipole moment associated with the orbit, at the end of the time interval to the magnetic field change, is :

(A) $-\gamma BQR^2$ (B) $-\gamma\dfrac{BQR^2}{2}$

(C) $\gamma\dfrac{BQR^2}{2}$ (D) γBQR^2

Paragraph-3 (Q. No. 30-31)

The figure shows a circular loop of radius a with two long parallel wires (numbered 1 and 2) all in the plane of the paper. The distance of each wire from the centre of the loop is d. The loop and the wires are carrying the same current I. The current in the loop is in the counterclockwise direction if seen from above.   **[JEE Adv 2014, P-2]**

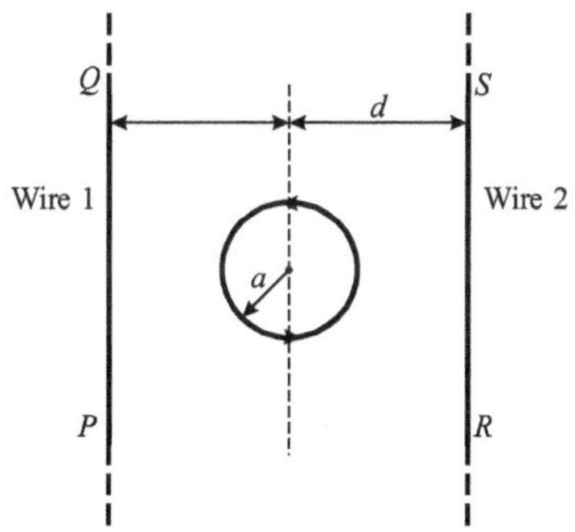

30. When $d \approx a$ but wires are not touching the loop, it is found that the net magnetic field on the axis of the loop is zero at a height h above the loop. In that case

(A) Current in wire 1 and wire 2 is the direction PQ and RS, respectively and $h \approx a$

(B) Current in wire 1 and wire 2 is the direction PQ and SR, respectively and $h \approx a$

(C) Current in wire 1 and wire 2 is the direction PQ and SR, respectively and $h \approx 1.2a$

(D) Current in wire 1 and wire 2 is the direction PQ and RS, respectively and $h \approx 1.2a$

31. Consider $d >> a$, and the loop is rotated about its diameter parallel to the wires by $30°$ from the position shown in the figure. If the currents in the wires are in the opposite directions, the torque on the loop at its new position will be (assume that the net field due to the wires is constant over the loop) :

(A) $\dfrac{\mu_0 I^2 a^2}{d}$

(B) $\dfrac{\mu_0 I^2 a^2}{2d}$

(C) $\dfrac{\sqrt{3}\mu_0 I^2 a^2}{d}$

(D) $\dfrac{\sqrt{3}\mu_0 I^2 a^2}{2d}$

Paragraph-4 (Q. No. 32-33)

In a thin rectangular metallic strip a constant current I flows along the positive x-direction, as shown in the figure. The length, width and thickness of the strip are l, w and d respectively.

A uniform magnetic field $\vec{B}$ is applied on the strip along the positive y-direction. Due to this, the charge carriers experience a net deflection along the z-direction. This results in accumulation of charge carriers on the surface $PQRS$ and appearance of equal and opposite charges on the face opposite to $PQRS$. A potential difference along the z-direction is thus developed. Charge accumulation continues until the magnetic force is balanced by the electric force. The current is assumed to be uniformly distributed on the cross section of the strip and carried by electrons. **[JEE Adv 2015, P-2]**

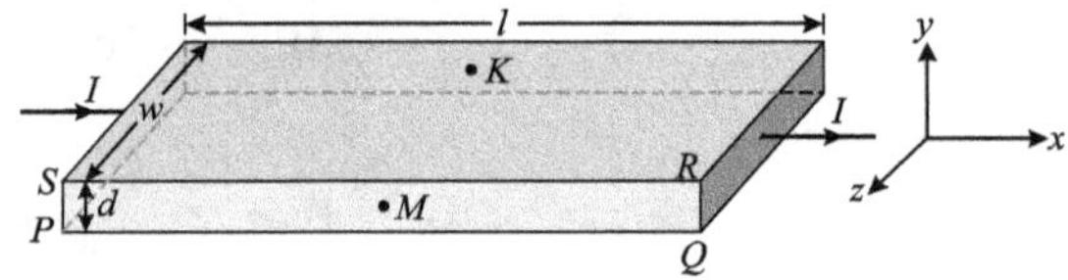

32. Consider two different metallic strips (1 and 2) of the same material. Their lengths are the same, widths are w_1 and w_2 and thicknesses are d_1 and d_2, respectively. Two points K and M are symmetrically located on the opposite faces parallel to the x-y plane (see figure). V_1 and V_2 are the potential differences between K and M in strips 1 and 2, respectively. Then, for a given current I flowing through them in a given magnetic field strength B, the correct statement(s) is(are) :

(A) If $w_1 = w_2$ and $d_1 = 2d_2$, then $V_2 = 2V_1$

(B) If $w_1 = w_2$ and $d_1 = 2d_2$, then $V_2 = V_1$

(C) If $w_1 = 2w_2$ and $d_1 = d_2$, then $V_2 = 2V_1$

(D) If $w_1 = 2w_2$ and $d_1 = d_2$, then $V_2 = V_1$

33. Consider two different metallic strips (1 and 2) of same dimensions (length l, width w and thickness d) with carrier densities n_1 and n_2, respectively. Strip 1 is placed in magnetic field B_1 and strip 2 is placed in magnetic field B_2, both along positive y-directions. Then V_1 and V_2 are the potential differences developed between K and M in strips 1 and 2, respectively. Assuming that the current I is the same for both the strips, the correct option(s) is(are) :

(A) If $B_1 = B_2$ and $n_1 = 2n_2$, then $V_2 = 2V_1$

(B) If $B_1 = B_2$ and $n_1 = 2n_2$, then $V_2 = V_1$

(C) If $B_1 = 2B_2$ and $n_1 = n_2$, then $V_2 = 0.5V_1$

(D) If $B_1 = 2B_2$ and $n_1 = n_2$, then $V_2 = V_1$

Integer Answer based Questions

34. A steady current I goes through a wire loop PQR having shape of a right angle triangle with $PQ = 3x$, $PR = 4x$ and $QR = 5x$. If the magnitude of the magnetic field at P due to this loop is

$k\left(\dfrac{\mu_0 I}{48\pi x}\right)$, find the value of k.   **[JEE Adv 2009, P-2]**

35. A long circular tube of length 10 m and radius 0.3 m carries a current I along its curved surface as shown. A wire-loop of resistance 0.005 Ω and of radius 0.1 m is placed inside the tube with its axis coinciding with axis of the tube. The current varies as $I = I_0 \cos (300t)$ where I_0 is constant. If the magnetic moment of the loop is $N\mu_0 I_0 \sin (300t)$, then N is ? **[JEE Adv 2011, P-1]**

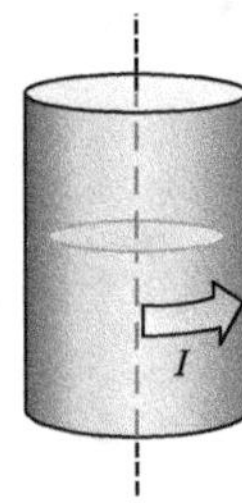

36. A cylindrical cavity of diameter a exists inside a cylinder of diameter $2a$ as shown in the figure. Both the cylinder and the cavity are infinitely long. A uniform current density J flows along the length. If the magnitude of the magnetic field at the

point P is given by $\dfrac{N}{12}\mu_0 aJ$, then the value of N is :

[JEE Adv 2012, P-1]

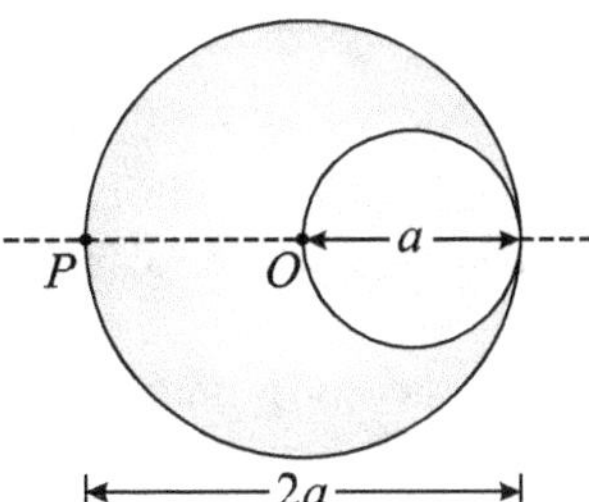

37. A circular wire loop of radius R is placed in the x-y plane centered at the origin O. A square loop of side a ($a << R$) having two turns is placed with its center at $z = \sqrt{3}R$ along the axis of the circular wire loop, as shown in figure. The plane of the square loop makes an angle of 45° with respect to the z-axis. If the mutual inductance between the loops is given by

$\dfrac{\mu_0 a^2}{2^{p/2} R}$, then the value of p is :   [JEE Adv 2012, P-1]

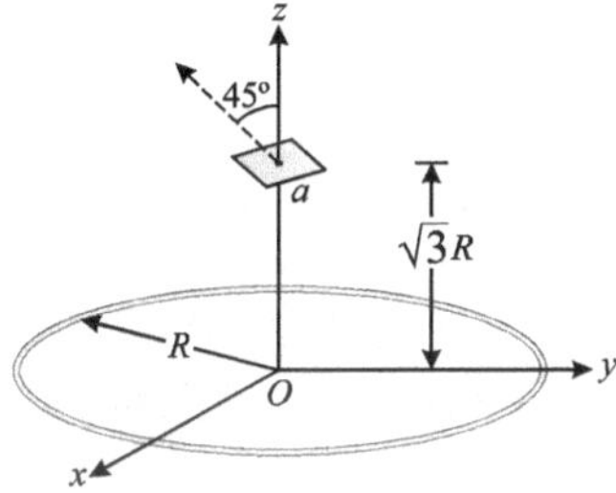

38. Two parallel wires in the plane of the paper are distance x_0 apart. A point charge is moving with speed u between the wires in the same plane at a distance x_1 from one of the wires. When the wires carry current of magnitude I in the same direction, the radius of curvature of the path of the point charge is R_1. In contrast, if the currents I in the two wires have directions opposite to each other, the radius of curvature of

the path is R_2. If $\dfrac{x_0}{x_1} = 3$, the value of $\dfrac{R_1}{R_2}$ is :

[JEE Adv 2014, P-1]

39. In the xy-plane, the region $y > 0$ has a uniform magnetic field $B_1\hat{k}$ and the region $y < 0$ has a another uniform magnetic field $B_2\hat{k}$. A positively charged particle is projected from the origin along the positive y-axis with speed $v_0 = \pi$ ms^{-1} at $t = 0$, as shown in the figure. Neglect gravity in this problem. Let $t = T$ be the time when the particle crosses the x-axis from below for the first time. If $B_2 = 4B_1$, the average speed of the particle, in ms^{-1}, along the x-axis in the time interval T is ______.

[JEE Adv 2018, P-1]

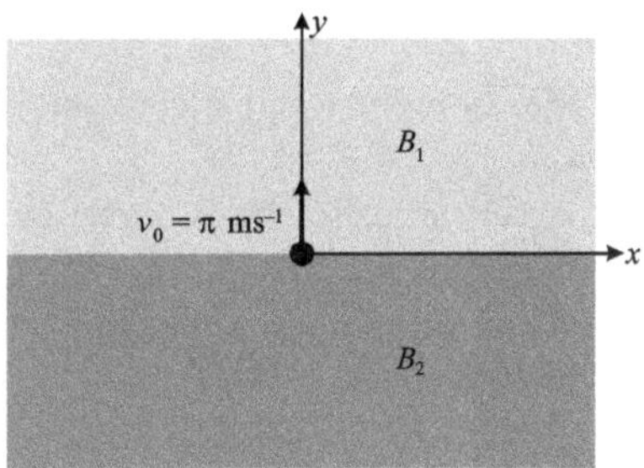

40. An α-particle (mass 4 amu) and a singly charged sulfur ion (mass 32 amu) are initially at rest. They are accelerated through a potential V and then allowed to pass into a region of uniform magnetic field which is normal to the velocities of the particles. Within this region, the α-particle and the sulfur ion move in circular orbits of radii r_α and r_s, respectively. The ratio (r_s/r_α) is ______.   [JEE Adv 2021, P-1]

* * * * *

16 ELECTROMAGNETIC INDUCTION

MCQ with Single Option Correct

1. A light disc made of aluminum (a nonmagnetic material) is kept horizontally and is free to rotate about its axis as shown in the figure. A strong magnet is held vertically at a point above the disc away from its axis. On revolving the magnet about the axis of the disc, the disc will (figure is schematic and not drawn to scale) **[JEE Adv 2020, P-1]**

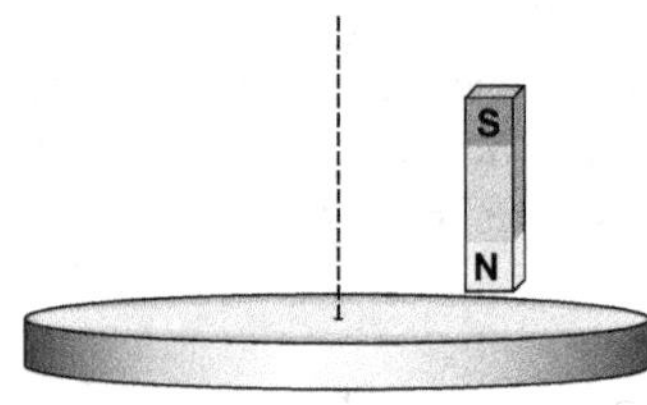

(A) Rotate in the direction opposite to the direction of magnet's motion
(B) Rotate in the same direction as the direction of magnet's motion
(C) Not rotate and its temperature will remain unchanged
(D) Not rotate but its temperature will slowly rise

MCQ with One or More than One Options Correct

2. Two metallic rings A and B, identical in shape and size but having different resistivities ρ_A and ρ_B, are kept on top of two identical solenoids as shown in the figure. When current I is switched on in both the solenoids in identical manner, the rings A and B jump to heights h_A and h_B, respectively, with $h_A > h_B$. The possible relations(s) between their resistivities and their masses m_A and m_B is (are) : **[JEE Adv 2009, P-2]**

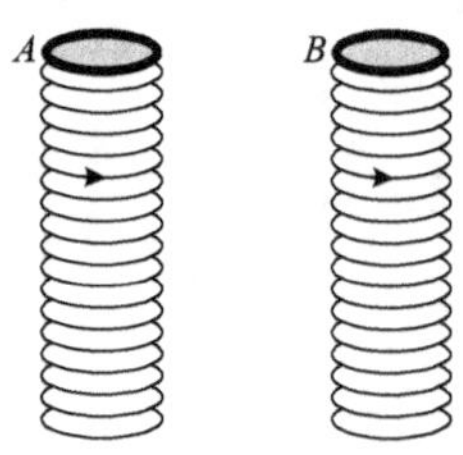

(A) $\rho_A > \rho_B$ and $m_A = m_B$ (B) $\rho_A < \rho_B$ and $m_A = m_B$
(C) $\rho_A > \rho_B$ and $m_A > m_B$ (D) $\rho_A < \rho_B$ and $m_A < m_B$

3. A Current carrying infinitely long wire is kept along the diameter of a circular wire loop, without touching it. The correct statement (s) is (are) : **[JEE Adv 2012, P-2]**

(A) The emf induced in the loop is zero if the current is constant
(B) The emf induced in the loop is finite if the current is constant
(C) The emf induced in the loop is zero if the current decreases at a steady rate
(D) The emf induced in the loop is finite if the current decreases at a steady rate

4. A conducting loop in the shape of a right angled isosceles triangle of height 10 cm is kept such that the 90° vertex is very close to an infinitely long conducting wire (see the figure). The wire is electrically insulated from the loop. The hypotenuse of the triangle is parallel to the wire. The current in the triangular loop is in counterclockwise direction and increased at a constant rate of 10 As^{-1}. Which of the following statement(s) is(are) true? **[JEE Adv 2016, P-1]**

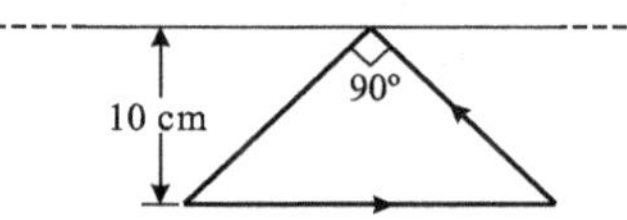

(A) The induced current in the wire is in opposite direction to the current along the hypotenuse
(B) There is a repulsive force between the wire and the loop
(C) If the loop is rotated at a constant angular speed about the wire, an additional emf of $\left(\dfrac{\mu_0}{\pi}\right)$ volt is induced in the wire
(D) The magnitude of induced emf in the wire is $\left(\dfrac{\mu_0}{\pi}\right)$ volt

5. A rigid wire loop of square shape having side of length L and resistance R is moving along the x-axis with a constant velocity v_0 in the plane of the paper. At $t = 0$, the right edge of the loop enters a region of length $3L$ where there is a uniform magnetic field B_0 into the plane of the paper, as shown in the figure. For sufficiently large v_0, the loop eventually crosses the region. Let x be the location of the right edge of the loop Let $v(x)$, $I(x)$ and $F(x)$ represent the velocity of the loop, current in the loop, and force on the loop, respectively, as a function of x. Counter-clockwise current is taken as positive.

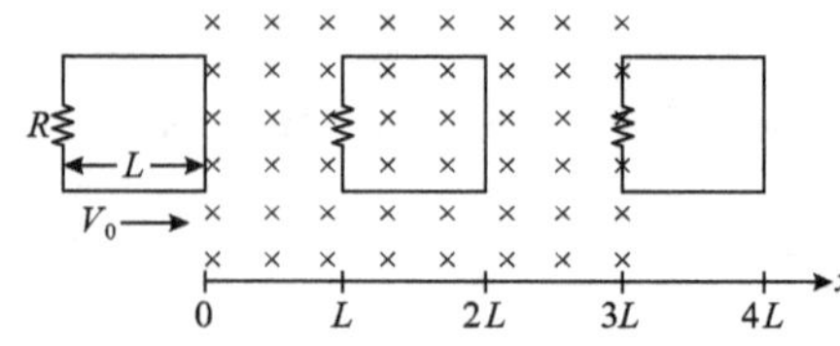

Which of the following schematic plot(s) is(are) correct ? (Ignore gravity) **[JEE Adv 2016, P-2]**

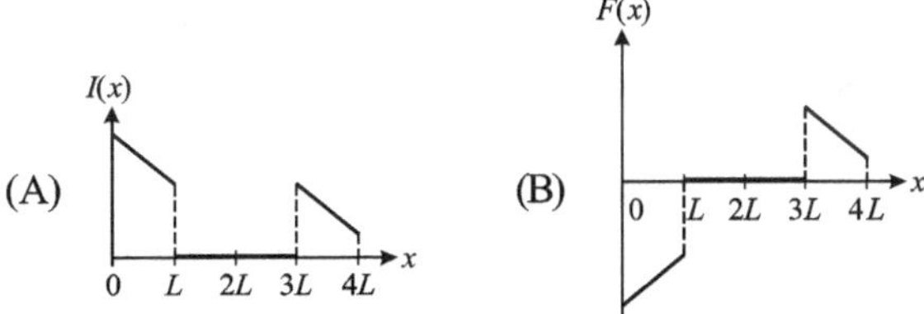

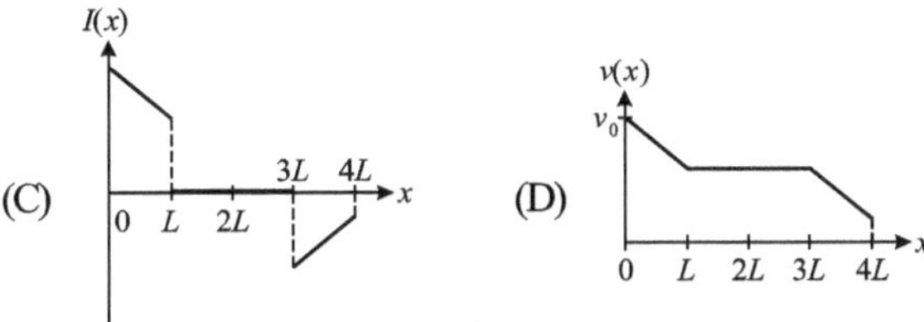

6. A circular insulated copper wire loop is twisted to form two loops of area A and $2A$ as shown in the figure. At the point of crossing the wires remain electrically insulated from each other. The entire loop lies in the plane (of the paper). A uniform magnetic field $\vec{B}$ points into the plane of the paper. At $t = 0$, the loop starts rotating about the common diameter as axis with a constant angular velocity ω in the magnetic field. Which of the following options is/are correct : **[JEE Adv 2017, P-1]**

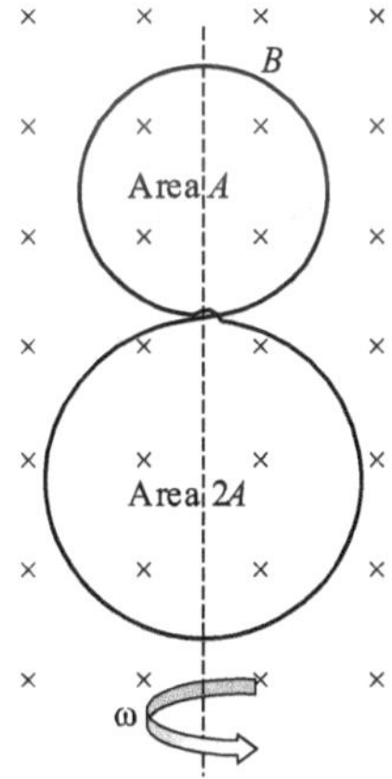

(A) The rate of change of the flux is maximum when the plane of the loops is perpendicular to plane of the paper.
(B) The net emf induced due to both the loops is proportional to $\cos\omega t$.
(C) The emf induced in the loop is proportional to the sum of the areas of the two loops.
(D) The amplitude of the maximum net emf induced due to both the loops is equal to the amplitude of maximum emf induced in the smaller loop alone.

Assertion Reason based on MCQ

7.   STATEMENT-1   **[JEE Adv 2007, P-2]**
A vertical iron rod has a coil of wire wound over it at the bottom end. An alternating current flows in the coil. The rod goes through a conducting ring as shown in the figure. The ring can float at a certain height above the coil.

because

STATEMENT-2
In the above situation, a current is induced in the right which interacts with the horizontal component of the magnetic field to produce an average force in the upward direction :

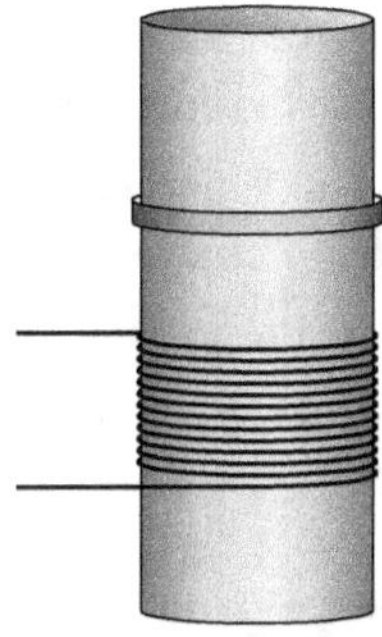

(A) Statement-1 is True, Statement-2 is True; Statement-2 is a correct explanation for Statement-1
(B) Statement-1 is True, Statement-2 is True; Statement-2 is **NOT** a correct explanation for Statement-1
(C) Statement-1 is True, Statement-2 is False
(D) Statement-1 is False, Statement-2 is True

Matrix Match MCQ

8.   Column-II gives certain systems undergoing a process. **Column-I** suggests changes in some of the parameters related to the system. Match the statements in **Column-I** to the appropriate process(es) from **Column-II** : **[JEE Adv 2009, P-2]**

Column-I	**Column-II**
(A) The energy of the system is increased	(p) **System:** A capacitor, initially uncharged. Process: It is connected to a battery.
(B) Mechanical energy is provided to the system, which converted into energy of random motion of its parts.	(q) **System:** A gas in an adiabatic container fitted with an adiabatic piston. **Process:** The gas is compressed by pushing the piston.
(C) Internal energy of the system is converted into its mechanical energy.	(r) **System:** A gas in a rigid container. **Process:** A gas is gets cooled due to colder atmosphere surrounding it.

(D) Mass of the system is decreased

(s) **System:** A heavy nucleus, initially at rest.
Process: The nucleus fissions into two fragments of nearly equal masses and some neutrons are emitted.

(t) **System:** A resistive wire loop.
Process: The loop is placed in a time varying magnetic field perpendicular to its plane.

9. A small circular loop of area A and resistance R is fixed on a horizontal xy-plane with the center of the loop always on the axis $\hat{n}$ of a long solenoid. The solenoid has m turns per unit length and carries current I counterclockwise as shown in the figure. The magnetic field due to the solenoid is in $\hat{n}$ direction. List-I gives time dependences of $\hat{n}$ in terms of a constant angular frequency ω. List-II gives the torques experienced by the circular loop at time $t = \dfrac{\pi}{6\omega}$. Let $\alpha = \dfrac{A^2 \mu_0^2 m^2 I^2 \omega}{2R}$

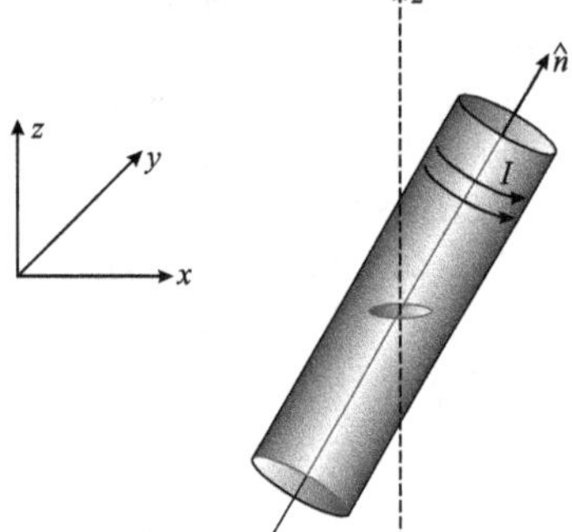

List-I		List-II
(I) $\dfrac{1}{\sqrt{2}} (\sin \omega t\, \hat{j} + \cos \omega t\, \hat{k})$		(P) 0
(II) $\dfrac{1}{\sqrt{2}} (\sin \omega t\, \hat{i} + \cos \omega t\, \hat{j})$		(Q) $-\dfrac{\alpha}{4}\hat{i}$
(III) $\dfrac{1}{\sqrt{2}} (\sin \omega t\, \hat{i} + \cos \omega t\, \hat{k})$		(R) $\dfrac{3\alpha}{4}\hat{i}$
(IV) $\dfrac{1}{\sqrt{2}} (\cos \omega t\, \hat{j} + \sin \omega t\, \hat{k})$		(S) $\dfrac{\alpha}{4}\hat{j}$
		(T) $-\dfrac{3\alpha}{4}\hat{i}$

Which one of following options is correct ?

[JEE Adv 2022, P-1]

(A) I → Q, II → P, III → S, IV → T
(B) I → S, II → T, III → Q, IV → P
(C) I → Q, II → P, III → S, IV → R
(D) I → T, II → Q, III → P, IV → R

10. A thin conducting rod MN of mass 20 gm, length 25 cm and resistance 10 Ω is held on frictionless, long, perfectly conducting vertical rails as shown in the figure. There is a uniform magnetic field $B_0 = 4\, T$ directed perpendicular to the plane of the rod-rail arrangement. The rod is released from rest at time $t = 0$ and it moves down along the rails. Assume air drag is negligible. Match each quantity in List-I with an appropriate value from List-II, and choose the correct option. **[JEE Adv 2023, P-1]**
[Given: The acceleration due to gravity $g = 10\ \text{m s}^{-2}$ and $e^{-1} = 0.4$]

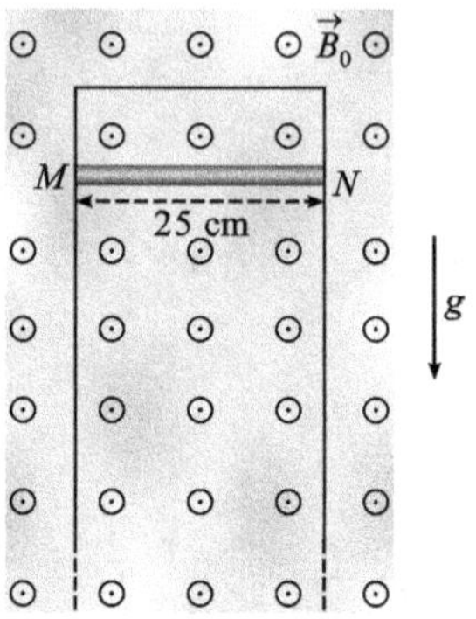

List-I		List-II
(P) At $t = 0.2$ s, the magnitude of the induced emf in Volt		(1) 0.07
(Q) At $t = 0.2$ s, the magnitude of the magnetic force in Newton		(2) 0.14
(R) At $t = 0.2$ s, the power dissipated as heat in Watt		(3) 1.20
(S) The magnitude of terminal velocity of the rod in m s^{-1}		(4) 0.12
		(5) 2.00

(A) (P) → (5), (Q) → (2), (R) → (3), (S) → (1)
(B) (P) → (3), (Q) → (1), (R) → (4), (S) → (5)
(C) (P) → (4), (Q) → (3), (R) → (1), (S) → (2)
(D) (P) → (3), (Q) → (4), (R) → (2), (S) → (5)

Comprehension based MCQ

Paragraph-1 (Q. No. 11-12)

A special metal S conducts electricity without any resistance. A closed wire loop, made of S, does not allow any change in flux through itself by inducing a suitable current to generate a compensating flux. The induced current in the loop cannot decay due to its zero resistance. This current gives rise to a magnetic moment which in turn repels the source of magnetic field or flux. Consider such a loop, of radius a, with its center at the origin. A magnetic dipole of moment m is brought along the axis of this loop from infinity to a point at distance $r\ (>> a)$ from the center of the loop with its north pole always facing the loop, as shown in the figure below.

The magnitude of magnetic field of a dipole m, at a point on its axis at distance r, is $\dfrac{\mu_0}{2\pi}\dfrac{m}{r^3}$, where μ_0 is the permeability of free space. The magnitude of the force between two magnetic dipoles with moments, m_1 and m_2, separated by a distance r on the common axis, with their north poles facing each other, is $\dfrac{k\,m_1 m_2}{r^4}$, where k is a constant of appropriate dimensions. The direction of this force is along the line joining the two dipoles.

[JEE Adv 2021, P-2]

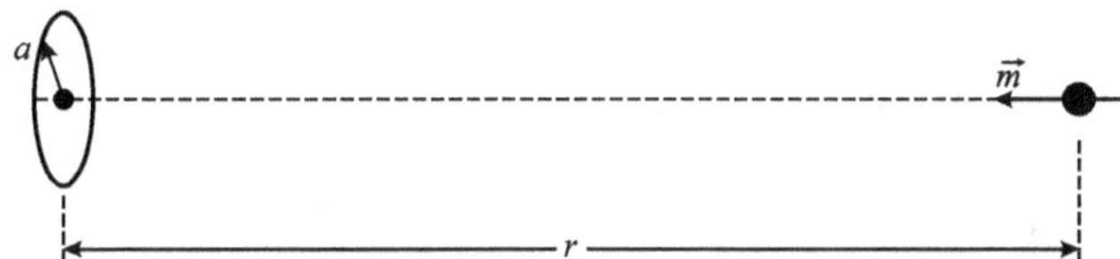

11. When the dipole m is placed at a distance r from the center of the loop (as shown in the figure), the current induced in the loop will be proportional to :

(A) $\dfrac{m}{r^3}$ (B) $\dfrac{m^2}{r^2}$

(C) $\dfrac{m}{r^2}$ (D) $\dfrac{m^2}{r}$

12. The work done in bringing the dipole from infinity to a distance r from the center of the loop by the given process is proportional to :

(A) $\dfrac{m}{r^5}$ (B) $\dfrac{m^2}{r^5}$

(C) $\dfrac{m^2}{r^6}$ (D) $\dfrac{m^2}{r^7}$

Integer Answer based Questions

13. A 10 cm long perfectly conducting wire PQ is moving, with a velocity 1 cm/s on a pair of horizontal rails of zero resistance. One side of the rails is connected to an inductor $L = 1$ mH and a resistance $R = 1\ \Omega$ as shown in figure. The horizontal rails, L and R lie in the same plane with a uniform magnetic field $B = 1$ T perpendicular to the plane. If the key S is closed at certain instant, the current in the circuit after 1 millisecond is $x \times 10^{-3}$ A, where the value of x is________.
[Assume the velocity of wire PQ remains constant (1 cm/s) after key S is closed. Given : $e^{-1} = 0.37$, where e is base of the natural logarithm] **[JEE Adv 2019, P-2]**

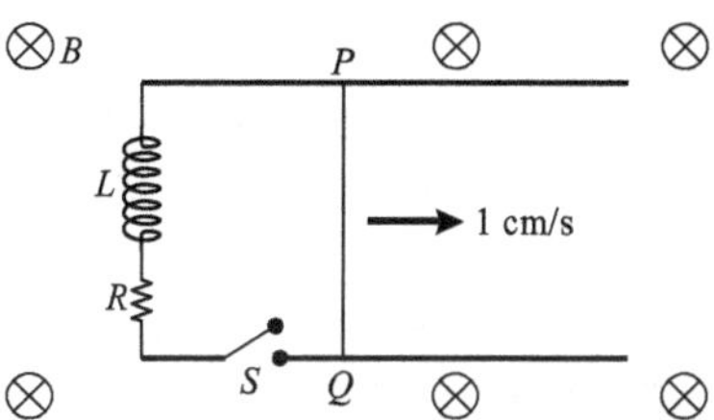

14. The inductors of two LR circuits are placed next to each other, as shown in the figure. The values of the self-inductance of the inductors, resistances, mutual-inductance and applied voltages are specified in the given circuit. After both the switches are closed simultaneously, the total work done by the batteries against the induced EMF in the inductors by the time the currents reach their steady state values is________ mJ.

[JEE Adv 2020, P-2]

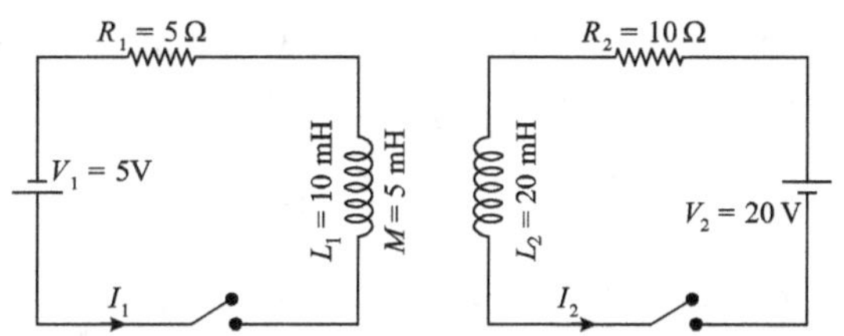

15. Consider an LC circuit, with inductance $L = 0.1$ H and capacitance $C = 10^{-3}\,F$, kept on a plane. The area of the circuit is 1 m². It is placed in a constant magnetic field of strength B_0 which is perpendicular to the plane of the circuit. At time $t = 0$, the magnetic field strength starts increasing linearly as $B = B_0 + \beta t$ with $\beta = 0.04$ T s⁻¹. The maximum magnitude of the current in the circuit is________ mA. **[JEE Adv 2022, P-1]**

16. A rectangular conducting loop of length 4 cm and width 2 cm is in the xy-plane, as shown in the figure. It is being moved away from a thin and long conducting wire along the direction $\dfrac{\sqrt{3}}{3}\hat{x}+\dfrac{1}{2}\hat{y}$ with a constant speed v. The wire is carrying a steady current $I = 10$ A in the positive x-direction. A current of 10 μA flows through the loop when it is at a distance $d = 4$ cm from the wire. If the resistance of the loop is 0.1 Ω, then the value of v is________ ms⁻¹. **[JEE Adv 2023, P-2]**
[Given: The permeability of free space $\mu_0 = 4\pi \times 10^{-7}\,\mathrm{N\,A^{-2}}$]

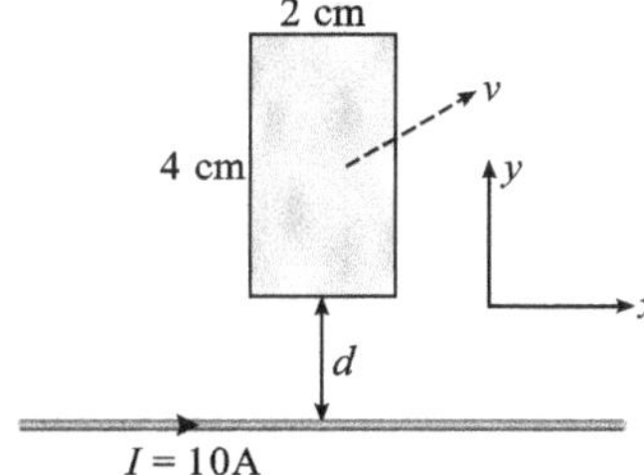

* * * * *

MCQ with Single Option Correct

1. An AC voltage source of variable angular frequency ω and fixed amplitude V_0 is connected in series with a capacitance C and an electric bulb of resistance R (inductance zero). When ω is increased : **[JEE Adv 2010, P-1]**
(A) The bulb glows dimmer
(B) The bulb glows brighter
(C) Total impedance of the circuit is unchanged
(D) Total impedance of the circuit increases

2. A point mass is subjected to two simultaneous sinusoidal displacement in x-direction $x_1(t) = A \sin\omega t$ and $x_2(t) = A \sin\left(\omega t + \dfrac{2\pi}{3}\right)$. Adding a third sinusoidal displacement $x_3(t) = B \sin(\omega t + \phi)$ brings the mass to a complete rest. The values of B and ϕ are : **[JEE Adv 2011, P-2]**

(A) $\sqrt{2}A, \dfrac{3\pi}{4}$

(B) $A, \dfrac{4\pi}{3}$

(C) $\sqrt{3}A, \dfrac{5\pi}{6}$

(D) $A, \dfrac{\pi}{3}$

MCQ with One or More than One Options Correct

3. A series R-C circuit is connected to AC voltage source. Consider two cases; (A) when C is without a dielectric medium and (B) when C is filled with dielectric of constant 4. The current I_R through the resistor and voltage V_C across the capacitor are compared in the two cases. Which of the following is/are true : **[JEE Adv 2011, P-2]**

(A) $I_R^A > I_R^B$

(B) $I_R^A < I_R^B$

(C) $V_C^A > V_C^B$

(D) $V_C^A < V_C^B$

4. In the given circuit, the AC source has $\omega = 100$ rad/s. Considering the inductor and capacitor to be ideal, the correct choice(s) is (are) : **[JEE Adv 2012, P-2]**

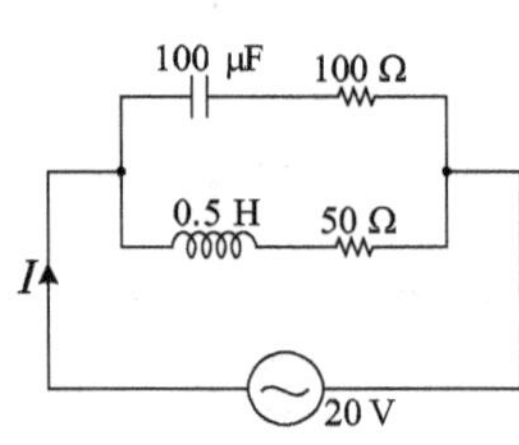

(A) The current through the circuit, I is 0.3 A
(B) The current through the circuit, I is $0.3\sqrt{2}$ A.
(C) The voltage across $100\,\Omega$ resistor $= 10\sqrt{2}$ V
(D) The voltage across $50\,\Omega$ resistor $= 10$ V

5. At time $t = 0$, terminal A in the circuit shown in the figure is connected to B by a key and an alternating current $I(t) = I_0 \cos(\omega t)$, with $I_0 = 1$A and $\omega = 500$ rad s^{-1} starts flowing in it with the initial direction shown in the figure. At $t = \dfrac{7\pi}{6\omega}$, the key is switched from B to D. Now onwards only A and D are connected. A total charge Q flows from the battery to charge the capacitor fully. If $C = 20$ μF, $R = 10$ Ω and the battery is ideal with emf of 50 V, identify the correct statement(s) : **[JEE Adv 2014, P-1]**

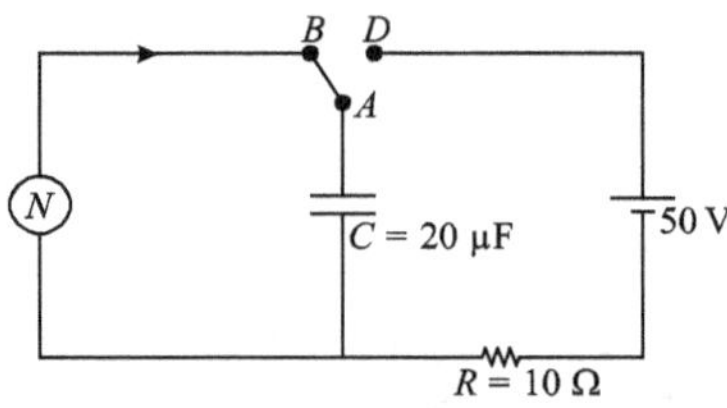

(A) Magnitude of the maximum charge on the capacitor before $t = \dfrac{7\pi}{6\omega}$ is 1×10^{-3} C

(B) The current in the left part of the circuit just before $t = \dfrac{7\pi}{6\omega}$ is clockwise

(C) Immediately after A is connected to D, the current in R is 10 A
(D) $Q = 2 \times 10^{-3}$ C

6. In the circuit shown, $L = 1$ μH, $C = 1$ μF and $R = 1$ kΩ. They are connected in series with an a.c. source $V = V_0 \sin\omega t$ as shown. Which of the following options is/are correct : **[JEE Adv 2017, P-1]**

(A) The frequency at which the current will be in phase with the voltage is independent of R

(B) At $\omega \sim 0$ the current flowing through the circuit becomes nearly zero

(C) At $\omega \gg 10^6$ rad s^{-1}, the circuit behaves like a capacitor

(D) The current will be in phase with the voltage if $\omega = 10^4$ rad s^{-1}

7. A source of constant voltage V is connected to a resistance R and two ideal inductors L_1 and L_2 through a switch S as shown. There is no mutual inductance between the two inductors. The switch S is initially open. At $t = 0$, the switch is closed and current begins to flow. Which of the following options is/are correct : **[JEE Adv 2017, P-2]**

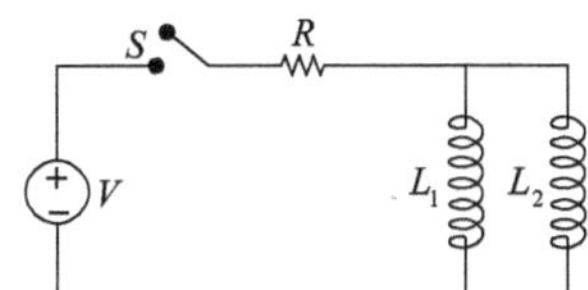

(A) The ratio of the currents through L_1 and L_2 is fixed at all times $(t > 0)$

(B) After a long time, the current through L_1 will be $\dfrac{V}{R}\dfrac{L_2}{L_1+L_2}$

(C) After a long time, the current through L_2 will be $\dfrac{V}{R}\dfrac{L_2}{L_1+L_2}$

(D) At $t = 0$, the current through the resistance R is $\dfrac{V}{R}$

8. The instantaneous voltages at three terminals marked X, Y and Z are given by

$$V_X = V_0 \sin\omega t, \quad V_Y = V_0 \sin\left(\omega t + \frac{2\pi}{3}\right) \text{ and } V_Z = V_0 \sin\left(\omega t + \frac{4\pi}{3}\right)$$

An ideal voltmeter is configured to read rms value of the potential difference between its terminals. It is connected between points X and Y and then between Y and Z. The reading(s) of the voltmeter will be : **[JEE Adv 2017, P-2]**

(A) $V_{XY}^{\text{rms}} = V_0$

(B) $V_{YZ}^{\text{rms}} = V_0\sqrt{\dfrac{1}{2}}$

(C) Independent of the choice of the two terminals

(D) $V_{XY}^{\text{rms}} = V_0\sqrt{\dfrac{3}{2}}$

9. In the figure below, the switches S_1 and S_2 are closed simultaneously at $t = 0$ and a current starts to flow in the circuit. Both the batteries have the same magnitude of the electromotive force (emf) and the polarities are as indicated in the figure.

Ignore mutual inductance between the inductors. The current I in the middle wire reaches its maximum magnitude $I_{\max}$ at time $t = \tau$. Which of the following statement(s) is (are) true? **[JEE Adv 2018, P-1]**

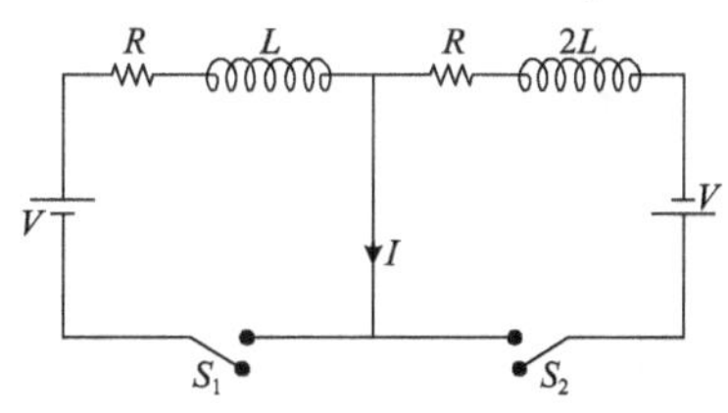

(A) $I_{\max} = \dfrac{V}{2R}$

(B) $I_{\max} = \dfrac{V}{4R}$

(C) $\tau = \dfrac{L}{R}\ln 2$

(D) $\tau = \dfrac{2L}{R}\ln 2$

Matrix Match MCQ

10. You are given many resistance, capacitors and inductors. These are connected to variable DC voltage source (The first two circuits) or an AC voltage source of 50 Hz frequency (the next three circuits) in different ways as shown in **Column-II**. When a current (steady state for DC or rms for AC) flows through the circuit, the corresponding voltage V_1 and V_2. (indicated in circuits) are related as shown in **Column-I**. Match the two. **[JEE Adv 2010, P-2]**

    Column-I   **Column-II**

(A) $I \neq 0$, V_1 is proportional to I (p) 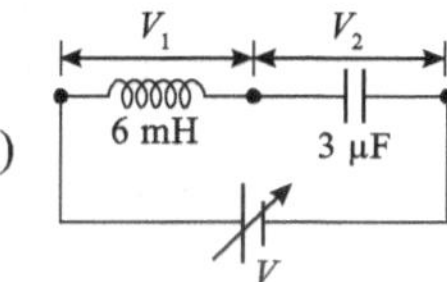

(B) $I \neq 0$, $V_2 > V_1$ (q) 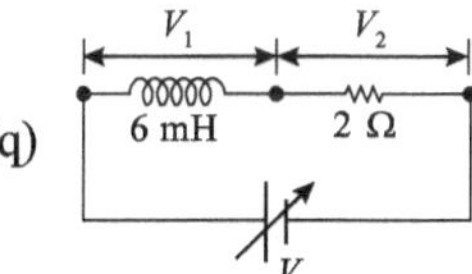

(C) $V_1 = 0$, $V_2 = V$ (r) 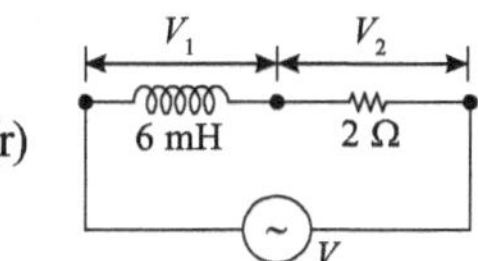

(D) $I \neq 0$, V_2 is proportional to I (s) 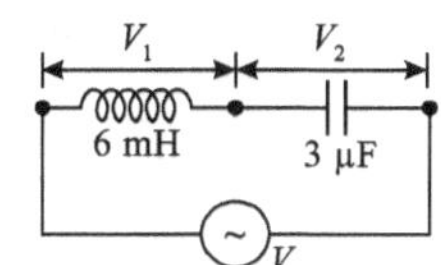

                         (t) 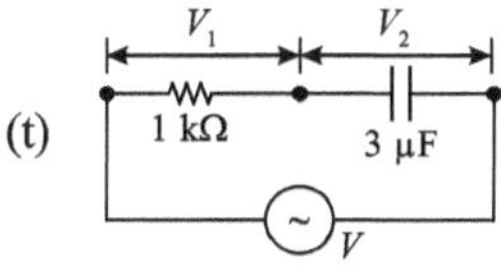

11. A series *LCR* circuit is connected to a 45 sin(ωt) Volt source. The resonant angular frequency of the circuit is 10^5 rad s^{-1} and current amplitude at resonance is I_0. When the angular frequency of the source is $\omega = 8 \times 10^4$ rad s^{-1}, the current amplitude in the circuit is 0.05 I_0. If $L = 50$ mH, match each entry in List-I with an appropriate value from List-II and choose the correct option.

[JEE Adv 2023, P-1]

List-I		List-II
(P) I_0 in mA	(1)	44.4
(Q) The quality factor of the circuit	(2)	18
(R) The bandwidth of the circuit in rad s^{-1}	(3)	400
(S) The peak power dissipated at	(4)	2250
resonance in Watt	(5)	500

(A) (P) → (2), (Q) → (3), (R) → (5), (S) → (1)
(B) (P) → (3), (Q) → (1), (R) → (4), (S) → (2)
(C) (P) → (4), (Q) → (5), (R) → (3), (S) → (1)
(D) (P) → (4), (Q) → (2), (R) → (1), (S) → (5)

Comprehension based MCQ

Paragraph-1 (Q. No. 12-13)

Consider a simple *RC* circuit as shown in figure 1.

Process 1: In the circuit the switch *S* is closed at $t = 0$ and the capacitor is fully charged to voltage V_0 (i.e., charging continues for time $T >> RC$). In the process some dissipation (E_D) occurs across the resistance *R*. The amount of energy finally stored in the fully charged capacitor is E_C.

Process 2: In a different process the voltage is first set to $\dfrac{V_0}{3}$ and maintained for a charging time $T >> RC$. Then the voltage is raised to $\dfrac{2V_0}{3}$ without discharging the capacitor and again maintained for a time $T >> RC$. The process is repeated one more time by raising the voltage to V_0 and the capacitor is charged to the same final voltage V_0 as in Process 1.

These two processes are depicted in Figure 2.

[JEE Adv 2017, P-2]

12. In Process 1, the energy stored in the capacitor E_C and heat dissipated across resistance E_D are related by :
(A) $E_C = E_D$ (B) $E_C = 2E_D$
(C) $E_C = \dfrac{1}{2}E_D$ (D) $E_C = E_D \ln 2$

13. In Process 2, total energy dissipated across the resistance E_D is :

(A) $E_D = \dfrac{1}{3}\left(\dfrac{1}{2}CV_0^2\right)$ (B) $E_D = 3\left(\dfrac{1}{2}CV_0^2\right)$

(C) $E_D = \left(\dfrac{1}{2}CV_0^2\right)$ (D) $E_D = 3CV_0^3$

Paragraph-2 (Q. No. 14-15)

In a circuit, a metal filament lamp is connected in series with a capacitor of capacitance $C\ \mu F$ across a 200 V, 50 Hz supply. The power consumed by the lamp is 500 W while the voltage drop across it is 100 V. Assume that there is no inductive load in the circuit. Take *rms* values of the voltages. The magnitude of the phase-angle (in degrees) between the current and the supply voltage is φ. Assume, $P\sqrt{3} \approx 5$. **[JEE Adv 2021, P-2]**

14. The value of *C* is __________.

15. The value of φ is __________.

Integer Answer based Questions

16. A series *R-C* combination is connected to an AC voltage of angular frequency $\omega = 500$ radian/s. If the impedance of the *R-C* circuit is $R\sqrt{1.25}$, the time constant (in milli second) of the circuit is ? **[JEE Adv 2011, P-2]**

17. Two inductors L_1 (inductance 1 mH, internal resistance 3 Ω) and L_2 (inductance 2 mH, internal resistance 4 Ω), and a resistor *R* (resistance 12 Ω) are all connected in parallel across a 5V battery. The circuit is switched on at time $t = 0$. The ratio of the maximum to the minimum current (I_{max}/I_{min}) drawn from the battery is ? **[JEE Adv 2016, P-1]**

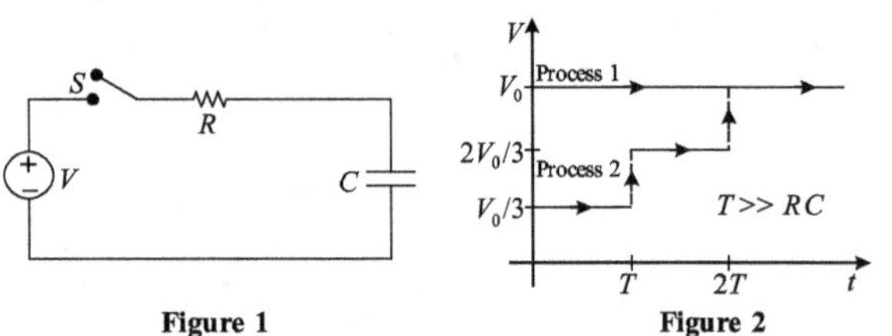

Figure 1   **Figure 2**

*   *   *   *   *

MCQ with Single Option Correct

1. In an experiment to determine the focal length (f) of a concave mirror by the u-v method, a student places the object pin A on the principal axis at a distance x from the pole P. The student looks at the pin and its inverted image from a distance keeping his/her eye in line with PA. When the student shifts his/her eye towards left, the image appears to the right of the object pin. Then, : **[JEE Adv 2007, P-1]**
(A) $x < f$
(B) $f < x < 2f$
(C) $x = 2f$
(D) $x > 2f$

2. A ray of light traveling in water is incident on its surface open to air. The angle of incidence is θ, which is less than the critical angle. Then there will be : **[JEE Adv 2007, P-1]**
(A) Only a reflected ray and no refracted ray
(B) Only a refracted ray and no reflected ray
(C) A reflected ray and a refracted ray and the angle between them would be less than $180° - 2\theta$
(D) A reflected ray and a refracted ray and the angle between them would be greater than $180° - 2\theta$

3. Two beams of red and violet colours are made to pass separately through a prism (angle of the prism is $60°$). In the position of minimum deviation, the angle of refraction will be : **[JEE Adv 2008, P-1]**
(A) $30°$ for both the colours
(B) Greater for the violet colour
(C) Greater for the red colour
(D) Equal but not $30°$ for both the colours

4. A light beam is traveling from Region I to Region IV (Refer Figure). The refractive index in Regions I, II, III and IV are n_0, $\dfrac{n_0}{2}$, $\dfrac{n_0}{6}$ and $\dfrac{n_0}{8}$, respectively. The angle of incidence θ for which the beam just misses entering Region IV is : **[JEE Adv 2008, P-2]**

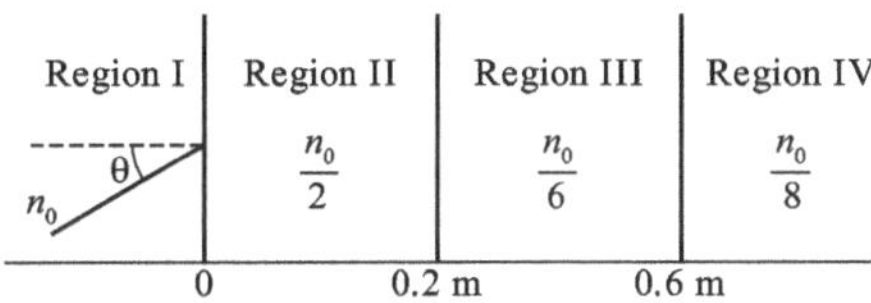

(A) $\sin^{-1}\left(\dfrac{3}{4}\right)$
(B) $\sin^{-1}\left(\dfrac{1}{8}\right)$
(C) $\sin^{-1}\left(\dfrac{1}{4}\right)$
(D) $\sin^{-1}\left(\dfrac{1}{3}\right)$

5. A ball is dropped from a height of 20 m above the surface of water in a lake. The refractive index of water is $4/3$. A fish inside the lake, in the line of fall of the ball, is looking at the ball. At an instant, when the ball is 12.8 m above the water surface, the fish sees the speed of ball as : [Take $g = 10$ m/s^2]
[JEE Adv 2009, P-1]
(A) 9 m/s
(B) 12 m/s
(C) 16 m/s
(D) 21.33 m/s

6. A biconvex lens of focal length 15 cm is in front of a plane mirror. The distance between the lens and the mirror is 10 cm. A small object is kept at a distance of 30 cm from the lens. The final image is : **[JEE Adv 2010, P-2]**
(A) virtual and at a distance of 16 cm from the mirror
(B) real and at a distance of 16 cm from the mirror
(C) virtual and at a distance of 20 cm from the mirror
(D) real and at a distance of 20 cm from the mirror

7. A light ray traveling in glass medium is incident on glass-air interface at an angle of incidence θ. The reflected (R) and transmitted (T) intensities, both as function of θ, are plotted. The correct sketch is : **[JEE Adv 2011, P-2]**

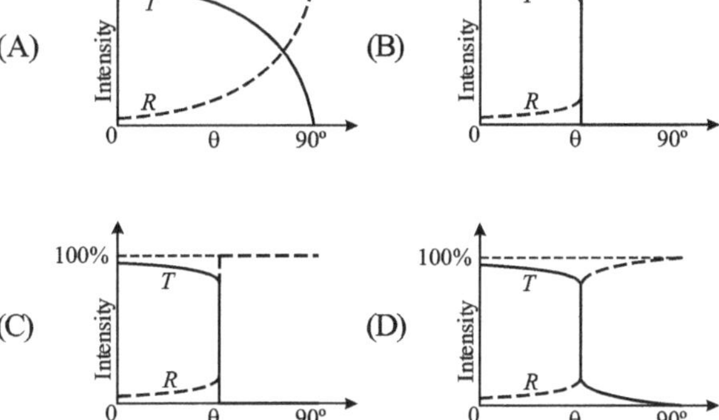

8. A bi-convex lens is formed with two thin plano-convex lenses as shown in the figure. Refractive index n of the first lens is 1.5 and that of the second lens is 1.2. Both the curved surfaces are of the same radius of curvature $R = 14$ cm. For this bi-convex lens, for an object distance of 40 cm, the image distance will be : **[JEE Adv 2012, P-1]**

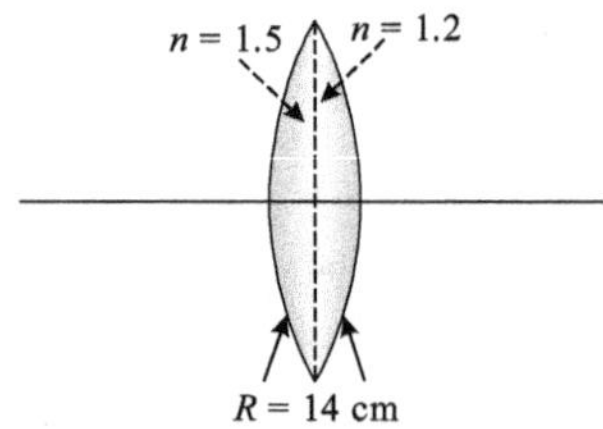

(A) −280.0 cm (B) 40.0 cm
(C) 21.5 cm (D) 13.3 cm

9. A ray of light travelling in the direction $\frac{1}{2}(\hat{i} + \sqrt{3}\hat{j})$ is incident on a plane mirror. After reflection, it travels along the direction $\frac{1}{2}(\hat{i} - \sqrt{3}\hat{j})$. The angle of incidence is :

[JEE Adv 2013, P-1]

(A) 30° (B) 45°
(C) 60° (D) 75°

10. The image of an object, formed by a plano-convex lens at a distance of 8 m behind the lens, is real and is one-third the size of the object. The wavelength of light inside the lens is 2/3 times the wavelength in free space. The radius of the curved surface of the lens is : **[JEE Adv 2013, P-1]**

(A) 1 m (B) 2 m
(C) 3 m (D) 6 m

11. A point source S is placed at the bottom of a transparent block of height 10 mm and refractive index 2.72. It is immersed in a lower refractive index liquid as shown in the figure. It is found that the light emerging from the block to the liquid forms a circular bright spot of diameter 11.54 mm on the top of the block. The refractive index of the liquid is :

[JEE Adv 2014, P-2]

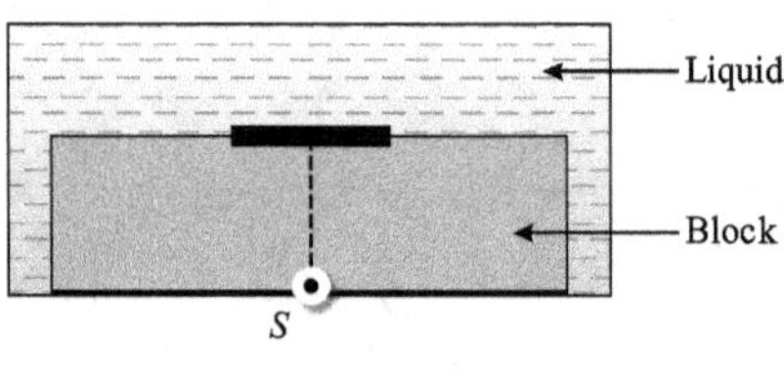

(A) 1.21 (B) 1.30
(C) 1.36 (D) 1.42

12. A parallel beam of light is incident from air at an angle α on the side PQ of a right angled triangular prism of refractive index $n = \sqrt{2}$. Light undergoes total internal reflection in the prism at the face PR when α has a minimum value of 45°. The angle θ of the prism is : **[JEE Adv 2016, P-1]**

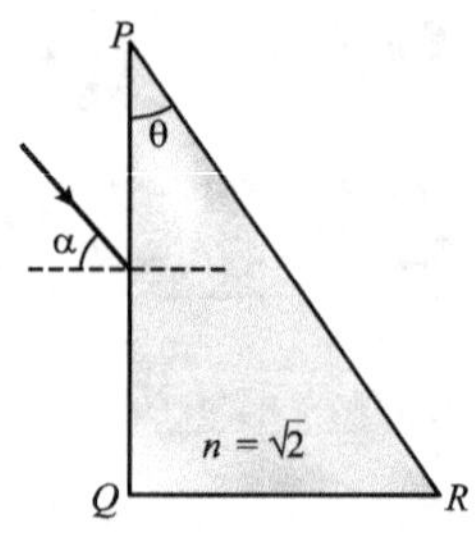

(A) 15° (B) 22.5°
(C) 30° (D) 45°

13. A small object is placed 50 cm to the left of a thin convex lens of focal length 30 cm. A convex spherical mirror of radius of curvature 100 cm is placed to the right of the lens at a distance of 50 cm. The mirror is tilted such that the axis of the mirror is at an angle $\theta = 30°$ to the axis of the lens, as shown in the figure. If the origin of the coordinate system is taken to be at the centre of the lens, the coordinates (in cm) of the point (x, y) at which the image is formed are : **[JEE Adv 2016, P-2]**

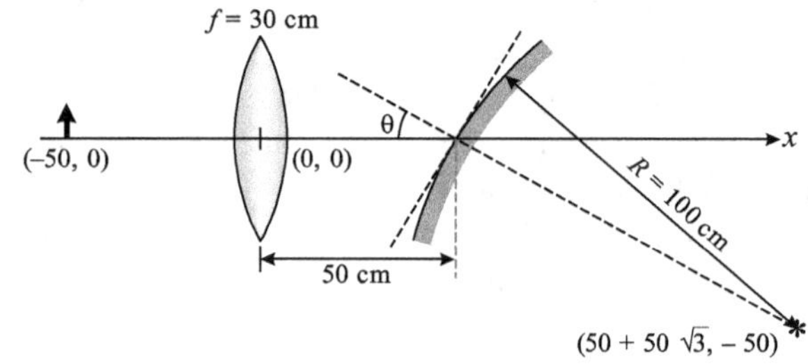

(A) $(25, 25\sqrt{3})$ (B) $(125/3, 25/\sqrt{3})$
(C) $(50 - 25\sqrt{3}, 25)$ (D) $(0, 0)$

14. An extended object is placed at point O, 10 cm in front of a convex lens L_1 and a concave lens L_2 is placed 10 cm behind it, as shown in the figure. The radii of curvature of all the curved surfaces in both the lenses are 20 cm. The refractive index of both the lenses is 1.5. The total magnification of this lens system is : **[JEE Adv 2021, P-1]**

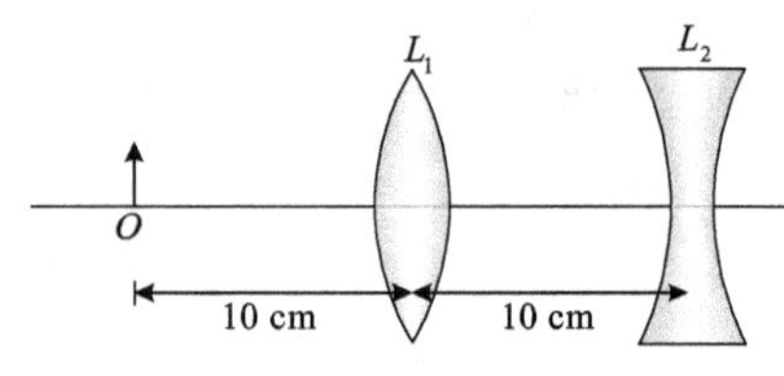

(A) 0.4 (B) 0.8
(C) 1.3 (D) 1.6

MCQ with One or More than One Options Correct

15. A student performed the experiment of determination of focal length of a concave mirror by u-v method using an optical bench of length 1.5 meter. The focal length of the mirror used is 24 cm. The maximum error in the location of the image can be 0.2 cm. The 5 sets of (u, v) values recorded by the student (in cm) are: (42, 56), (48, 48), (60, 40), (66, 33), (78, 39). The date set(s) that cannot come from experiment and is (are) incorrectly recorded, is (are) :   **[JEE Adv 2009, P-1]**

(A) (42, 56)   (B) (48, 48)

(C) (66, 33)   (D) (78, 39)

16. A ray OP of monochromatic light is incident on the face AB of prism $ABCD$ near vertex B at an incident angle of 60° (see figure). If the refractive index of the material of the prism is $\sqrt{3}$, which of the following is (are) correct ?   **[JEE Adv 2010, P-1]**

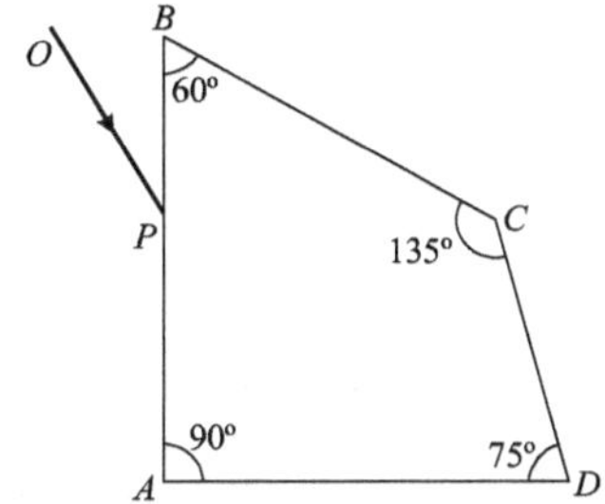

(A) The ray gets totally internally reflected at face CD

(B) The ray comes out through face AD

(C) The angle between the incident ray and the emergent ray is 90°

(D) The angle between the incident ray and the emergent ray is 120°

17. A transparent thin film of uniform thickness and refractive index $n_1 = 1.4$ is coated on the convex spherical surface of radius R at one end of a long solid glass cylinder of refractive index $n_2 = 1.5$, as shown in the figure. Rays of light parallel to the axis of the cylinder traversing through the film from air to glass get focused at distance f_1 from the film, while rays of light traversing from glass to air get focused at distance f_2 from the film. Then :   **[JEE Adv 2014, P-1]**

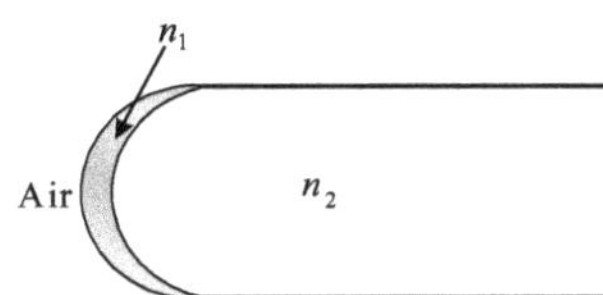

(A) $|f_1| = 3R$ (B) $|f_1| = 2.8R$

(C) $|f_2| = 2R$ (D) $|f_2| = 1.4R$

18. Two identical glass rods S_1 and S_2 (refractive index = 1.5) have one convex end of radius of curvature 10 cm. They are placed with the curved surfaces at a distance d as shown in the figure, with their axes (shown by the dished line) aligned. When a point source of light P is placed inside rod S_1 on its axis at a

distance of 50 cm from the curved face, the light rays emanating from it are found to be parallel to the axis inside S_2. The distance d is :   **[JEE Adv 2015, P-1]**

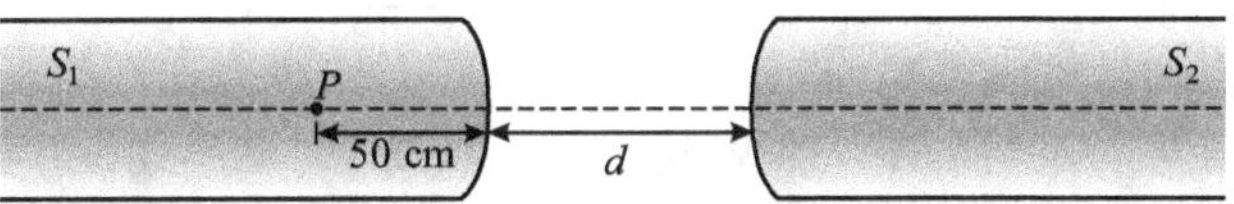

(A) 60 cm   (B) 70 cm

(C) 80 cm   (D) 90 cm

19. A transparent slab of thickness d has refractive index $n(z)$ that increases with z. Here z is the vertical distance inside the slab, measured from the top. The slab is placed between two media with uniform refractive indices n_1 and n_2 ($> n_1$), as shown in the figure. A ray of light is incident with angle θ_i from medium 1 and emerges in medium 2 with refraction angle θ_f with a lateral displacement l.   **[JEE Adv 2016, P-1]**

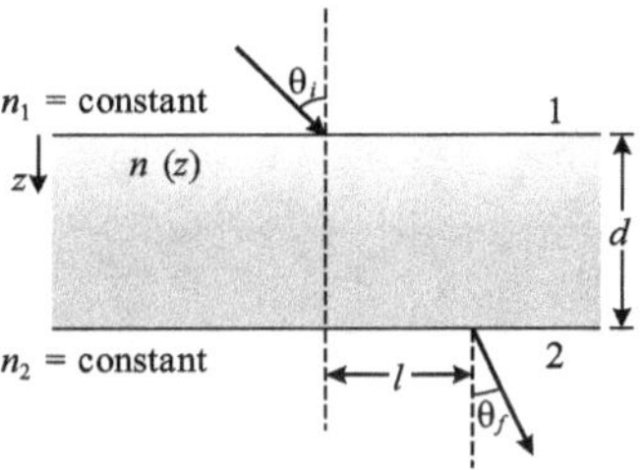

Which of the following statement(s) is(are) true ?

(A) l is independent of n_2 (B) l is dependent on $n(z)$

(C) $n_1 \sin\theta_i = (n_2 - n_1)\sin\theta_f$ (D) $n_1 \sin\theta_i = n_2 \sin\theta_f$

20. A plano-convex lens is made of a material of refractive index n. When a small object is placed 30 cm away in front of the curved surface of the lens, an image of double the size of the object is produced. Due to reflection from the convex surface of the lens, another faint image is observed at a distance of 10 cm away from the lens. Which of the following statement(s) is (are) true ?   **[JEE Adv 2016, P-1]**

(A) The refractive index of the lens is 2.5

(B) The radius of curvature of the convex surface is 45 cm

(C) The faint image is erect and real

(D) The focal length of the lens is 20 cm

21. For an isosceles prism of angle A and refractive index μ, it is found that the angle of minimum deviation $\delta_m = A$. Which of the following options is/are correct :   **[JEE Adv 2017, P-1]**

(A) At minimum deviation, the incident angle i_1 and the refracting angle r_1 at the first refracting surface are related by $r_1 = (i_1/2)$.

(B) For this prism, the refractive index μ and the angle of prism A are related as $A = \dfrac{1}{2}\cos^{-1}\left(\dfrac{\mu}{2}\right)$

(C) For this prism, the emergent ray at the second surface will be tangential to the surface when the angle of incidence at the first surface is $i_1 = \sin^{-1}\left[\sin A\sqrt{4\cos^2\dfrac{A}{2}-1}-\cos A\right]$

(D) For the angle of incidence $i_1 = A$, the ray inside the prism is parallel to the base of the prism

22. A wire is bent in the shape of a right angled triangle and is placed in front of a concave mirror of focal length f, as shown in the figure. Which of the figures shown in the four options qualitatively represent(s) the shape of the image of the bent wire ? (These figures are not to scale.)   **[JEE Adv 2018, P-2]**

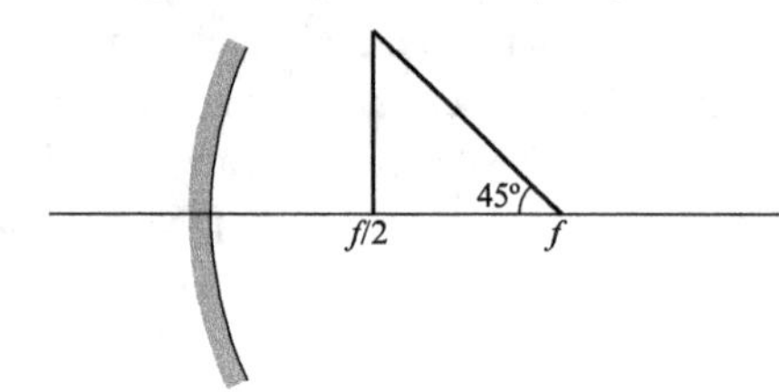

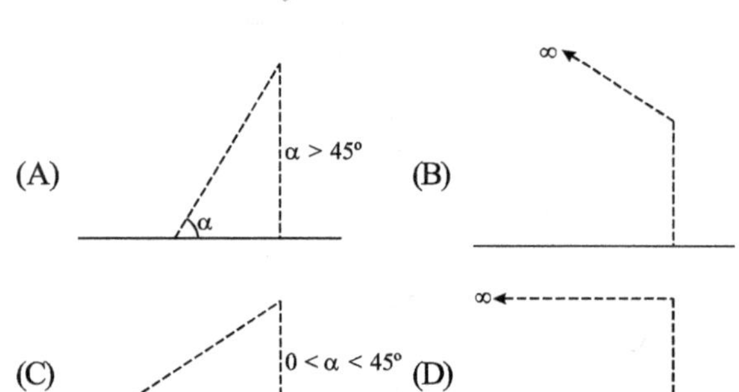

23. A thin convex lens is made of two materials with refractive indices n_1 and n_2, as shown in figure. The radius of curvature of the left and right spherical surfaces are equal. f is the focal length of the lens when $n_1 = n_2 = n$. The focal length is $f + \Delta f$ when $n_1 = n$ and $n_2 = n + \Delta n$. Assuming $\Delta n << (n-1)$ and $1 < n < 2$, the correct statement(s) is/are : **[JEE Adv 2019, P-1]**

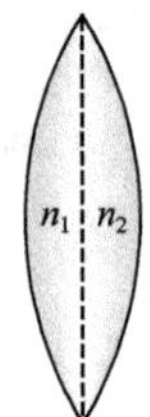

(A) The relation between $\dfrac{\Delta f}{f}$ and $\dfrac{\Delta n}{n}$ remains unchanged if both the convex surfaces are replaced by concave surfaces of the same radius of curvature.

(B) $\left|\dfrac{\Delta f}{f}\right| < \left|\dfrac{\Delta n}{n}\right|$

(C) For $n = 1.5$, $\Delta n = 10^{-3}$ and $f = 20$ cm, the value of $|\Delta f|$ will be 0.02 cm (round off to 2nd decimal place)

(D) If $\dfrac{\Delta n}{n} < 0$ then $\dfrac{\Delta f}{f} > 0$

24. Three glass cylinders of equal height $H = 30$ cm and same refractive index $n = 1.5$ are placed on a horizontal surfaces shown in figure. Cylinder I has a flat top, cylinder II has a convex top and cylinder III has a concave top. The radii of curvature of the two curved tops are same ($R = 3$m). If H_1, H_2 and H_3 are the apparent depths of a point X on the bottom of the three cylinders, respectively, the correct statement(s) is/are : **[JEE Adv 2019, P-2]**

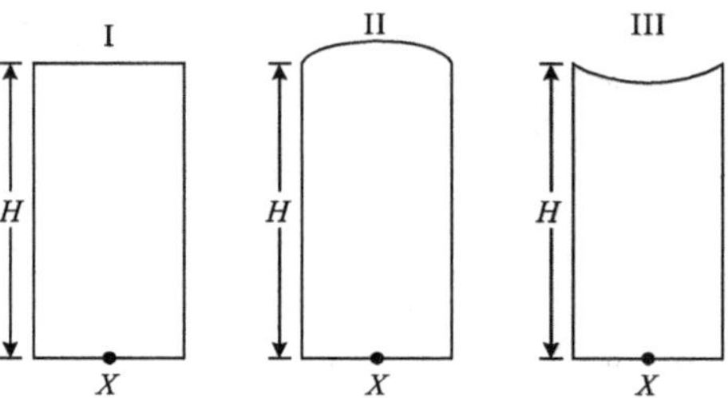

(A) $H_3 > H_1$

(B) $0.8\,\text{cm} < (H_2 - H_1) < 0.9\,\text{cm}$

(C) $H_2 > H_3$

(D) $H_2 > H_1$

25. A beaker of radius r is filled with water (refractive index 4/3) up to a height H as shown in the figure on the left. The beaker is kept on a horizontal table rotating with angular speed ω. This makes the water surface curved so that the difference in the height of water level at the center and at the circumference of the beaker is h ($h << H$, $h << r$), as shown in the figure on the right. Take this surface to be approximately spherical with a radius of curvature R. Which of the following is/are correct? (g is the acceleration due to gravity)   **[JEE Adv 2020, P-2]**

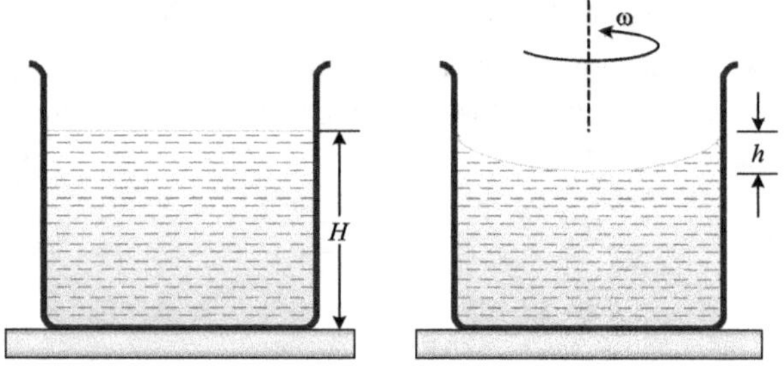

(A) $R = \dfrac{h^2 + r^2}{2h}$

(B) $R = \dfrac{3r^2}{2h}$

(C) Apparent depth of the bottom of the beaker is close to $\dfrac{3H}{2}\left(1 + \dfrac{\omega^2 H}{2g}\right)^{-1}$

(D) Apparent depth of the bottom of the beaker is close

$$\text{to } \frac{3H}{4}\left(1+\frac{\omega^2 H}{4g}\right)^{-1}$$

26. A wide slab consisting of two media of refractive indices n_1 and n_2 is placed in air as shown in the figure. A ray of light is incident from medium n_1 to n_2 at an angle θ, where $\sin\theta$ is slightly larger than $1/n_1$. Take refractive index of air as 1. Which of the following statement(s) is (are) correct?

[JEE Adv 2021, P-1]

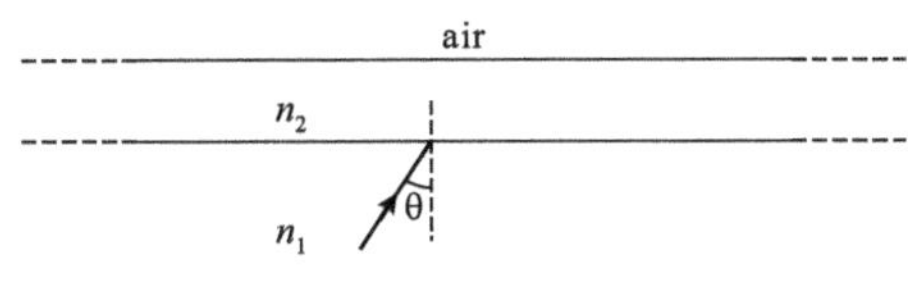

(A) The light ray enters air if $n_2 = n_1$
(B) The light ray is finally reflected back into the medium of refractive index n_1 if $n_2 < n_1$
(C) The light ray is finally reflected back into the medium of refractive index n_1 if $n_2 > n_1$
(D) The light ray is reflected back into the medium of refractive index n_1 if $n_2 = 1$

27. For a prism of prism angle $\theta = 60°$, the refractive indices of the left half and the right half are, respectively, n_1 and n_2 ($n_2 = n_1$) as shown in the figure. The angle of incidence i is chosen such that the incident light rays will have minimum deviation if $n_1 = n_2 = n = 1.5$. For the case of unequal refractive indices, $n_1 = n$ and $n_2 = n + \Delta n$ (where $\Delta n << n$), the angle of emergence $e = i + \Delta e$. Which of the following statement(s) is(are) correct?

[JEE Adv 2021, P-2]

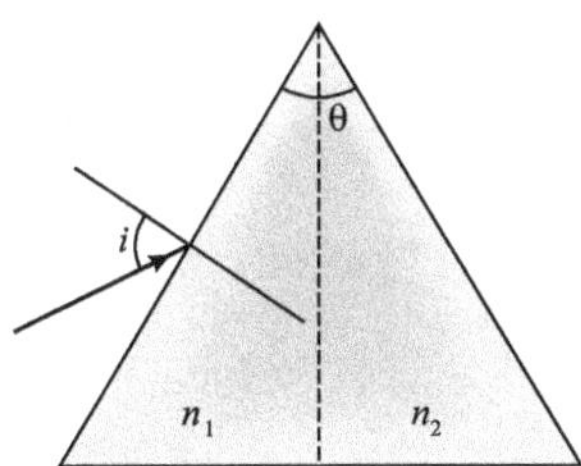

(A) The value of Δe (in radians) is greater than that of Δn
(B) Δe is proportional to Δn
(C) Δe lies between 2.0 and 3.0 milliradians, if $\Delta n = 2.8 \times 10^{-3}$
(D) Δe lies between 1.0 and 1.6 milliradians, if $\Delta n = 2.8 \times 10^{-3}$

28. Three plane mirrors form an equilateral triangle with each side of length L. There is a small hole at a distance $l > 0$ from one of the corners as shown in the figure. A ray of light is passed through the hole at an angle θ and can only come out through the same hole. The cross section of the mirror configuration and the ray of light lie on the same plane.

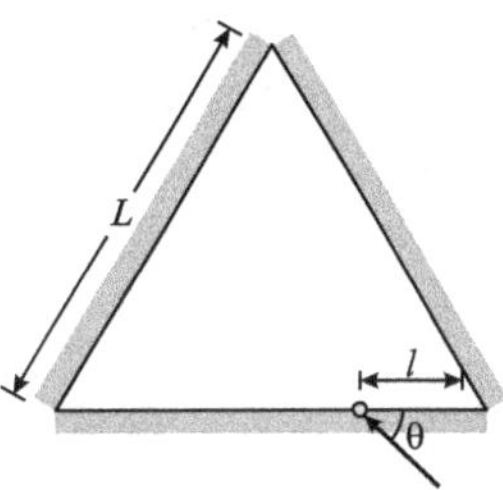

Which of the following statement(s) is(are) correct ?

[JEE Adv 2022, P-1]

(A) The ray of light will come out for $\theta = 30°$, for $0 < l < L$

(B) There is an angle for $l = \dfrac{L}{2}$ at which the ray of light will come out after two reflections

(C) The ray of light will NEVER come out for $\theta = 60°$, and $l = \dfrac{L}{3}$

(D) The ray of light will come out for $\theta = 60°$, and $0 < l < \dfrac{L}{2}$ after six reflections

29. A plane polarized blue light ray is incident on a prism such that there is no reflection from the surface of the prism. The angle of deviation of the emergent ray is $\delta = 60°$ (see figure-1). The angle of minimum deviation for red light from the same prism is $\delta_{min} = 30°$ (see figure-2). The refractive index of the prism material for blue light is $\sqrt{3}$. Which of the following statement(s) is(are) correct?

[JEE Adv 2023, P-1]

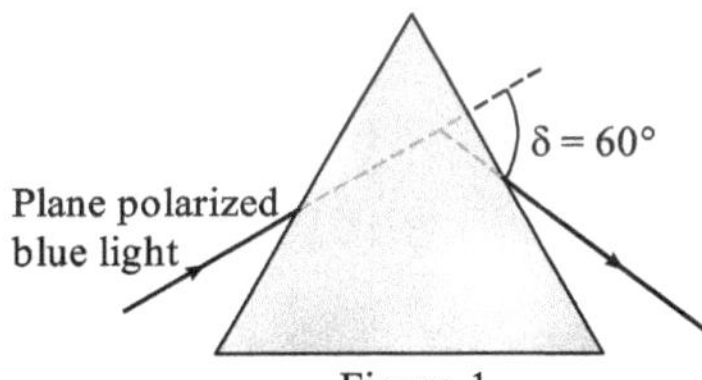

(A) The blue light is polarized in the plane of incidence.
(B) The angle of the prism is $45°$.
(C) The refractive index of the material of the prism for red light is $\sqrt{2}$.
(D) The angle of refraction for blue light in air at the exit plane of the prism is $60°$.

30. A monochromatic light wave is incident normally on a glass slab of thickness d, as shown in the figure. The refractive index of the slab increases linearly from n_1 to n_2 over the height h. Which of the following statement(s) is(are) true about the light wave emerging out of the slab?　　　**[JEE Adv 2023, P-2]**

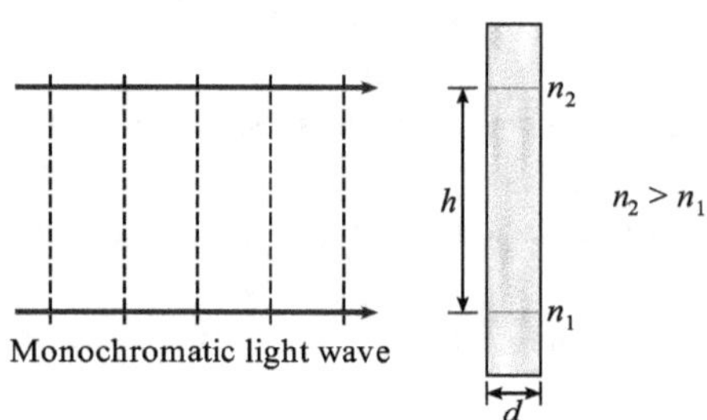

(A) It will deflect up by an angle $\tan^{-1}\left[\dfrac{(n_2^2 - n_1^2)d}{2h}\right]$

(B) It will deflect up by an angle $\tan^{-1}\left[\dfrac{(n_2 - n_1)d}{h}\right]$

(C) It will not deflect

(D) The deflection angle depends only on $(n_2 - n_1)$ and not on the individual values of n_1 and n_2

Assertion Reason based on MCQ

31. STATEMENT-1　　　　　　　　**[JEE Adv 2007, P-1]**
The formula connecting u, v and f for a spherical mirror is valid only for mirrors whose sizes are very small compared to their radii of curvature.

because

STATEMENT-2
Laws of reflection are strictly valid for plane surface, but not for large spherical surfaces :
(A) Statement-1 is True, Statement-2 is True; Statement-2 is a correct explanation for Statement-1
(B) Statement-1 is True, Statement-2 is True; Statement-2 is **NOT** a correct explanation for Statement-2
(C) Statement-1 is True, Statement-2 is False
(D) Statement-1 is False, Statement-2 is True

Matrix Match MCQ

32. An optical component and an object S placed along its optic axis are given in **Column-I.** The distance between the object and the component can be varied. The properties of images are given in **Column-II.** Match all the properties of images from **Column-II** with the appropriate components given in **Column-I.** Indicate your answer by darkening the appropriate bubbles of the 4×4 matrix given in the ORS :

[JEE Adv 2008, P-2]

Column-I　　　　　　　　　**Column-II**

(A) 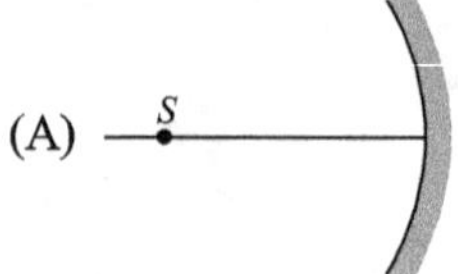　　(p) Real image

(B) 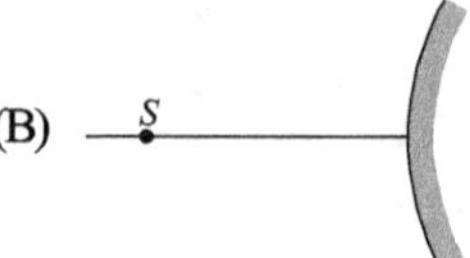　　(q) Virtual image

(C) 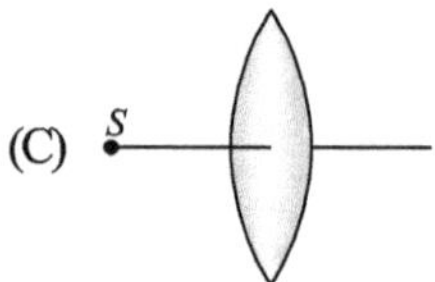　　(r) Magnified image

(D) 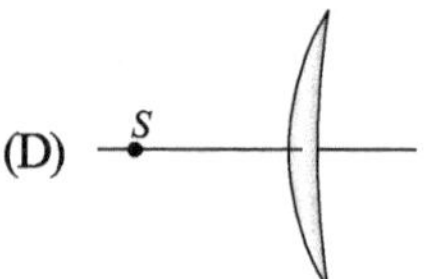　　(s) Image at infinity

33. Two transparent media of refractive indices μ_1 and μ_3 have a solid lens shaped transparent material of refractive index μ_2 between them as shown in figures in **Column-II**. A traversing these media is also shown in the figure. In **Column-I** different relationship between μ_1, μ_2 and μ_3 are given. Match them to the ray diagrams shown in Column :　　**[JEE Adv 2010, P-2]**

Column-I　　　　　　　　　**Column-II**

(A) $\mu_1 < \mu_2$　　(p) 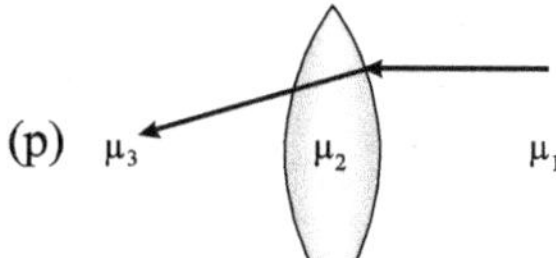

(B) $\mu_1 > \mu_2$　　(q) 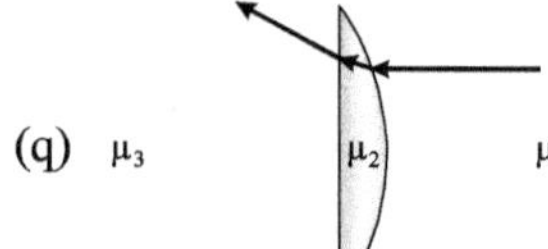

(C) $\mu_2 = \mu_3$　　(r) 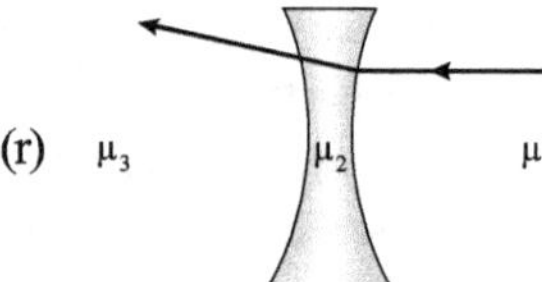

(D) $\mu_2 > \mu_3$　　(s) 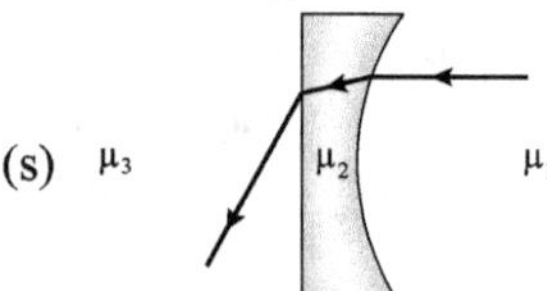

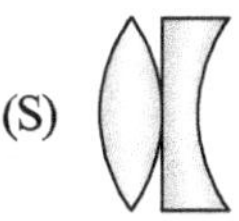

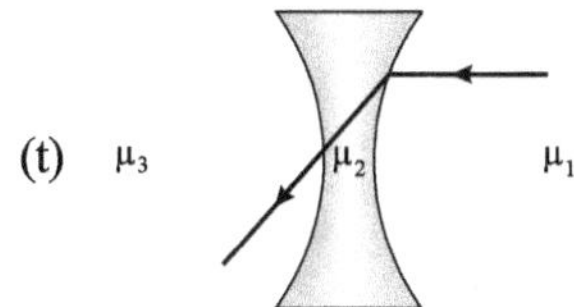

34. A right angled prism of refractive index μ_1 is placed in a rectangular block of refractive index μ_2, which is surrounded by a medium of refractive index μ_3, as shown in the figure. A ray of light 'e' enters the rectangular block at normal incidence. Depending upon the relationships between μ_1, μ_2 and μ_3, it takes one of the four possible paths 'ef', 'eg', 'eh' or 'ei' :

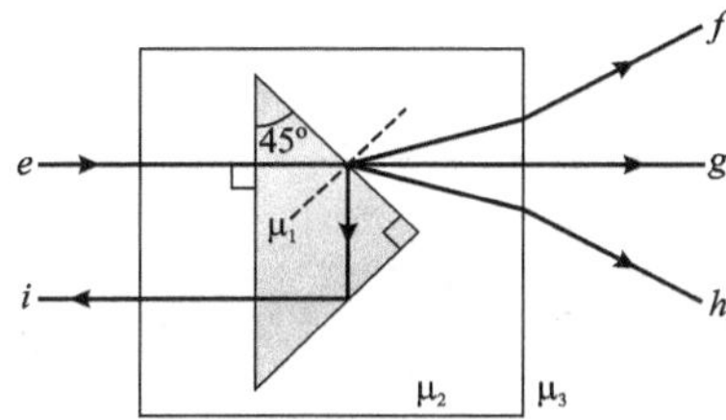

Match the paths in **Coloum-I** with conditions of refractive indices in **Coloum-II** and select the correct answer using the codes given below the lists :   [**JEE Adv 2013, P-2**]

Coloum-I	**Coloum-II**
(P) $e \to f$	(1) $\mu_1 > \sqrt{2}\mu_2$
(Q) $e \to g$	(2) $\mu_2 > \mu_1$ and $\mu_2 > \mu_3$
(R) $e \to h$	(3) $\mu_1 = \mu_2$
(S) $e \to i$	(4) $\mu_2 < \mu_1 < \sqrt{2}\mu_2$ and $\mu_2 > \mu_3$

Codes :

	P	Q	R	S
(A)	2	3	1	4
(B)	1	2	4	3
(C)	4	1	2	3
(D)	2	3	4	1

35. Four combinations of two thin lenses are given in **Column-I**. The radius of curvature of all curved surfaces is r and the refractive index of all the lenses is 1.5. Match lens combinations in **Column-I** with their focal length in **Column-II** and select the correct answer using the code given below the lists.   [**JEE Adv 2014, P-2**]

Column-I	**Column-II**
(P) 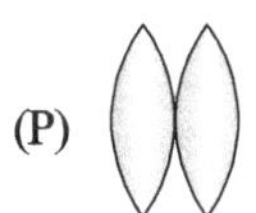	(1) $2r$
(Q) 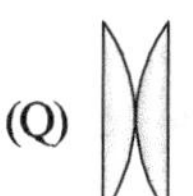	(2) $r/2$

(R) 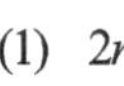

(R)   (3) $-r$

(S)   (4) 4

Code :
(A) P → 1, Q → 2, R → 3, S → 4
(B) P → 2, Q → 4, R → 3, S → 1
(C) P → 4, Q → 1, R → 2, S → 3
(D) P → 2, Q → 1, R → 3, S → 4

36. List-I contains four combinations of two lenses (1 and 2) whose focal lengths (in cm) are indicated in the figures. In all cases, the object is placed 20 cm from the first lens on the left, and the distance between the two lenses is 5 cm. List-II contains the positions of the final images.   [**JEE Adv 2022, P-1**]

List-I	**List-II**
(I) 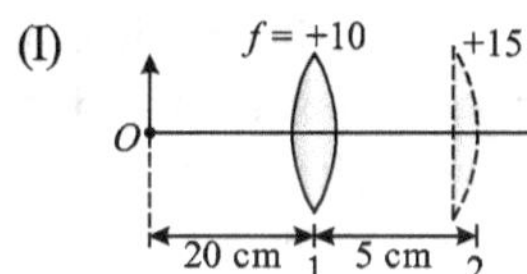	(P) Final image is formed at 7.5 cm on the right side of lens 2
(II) 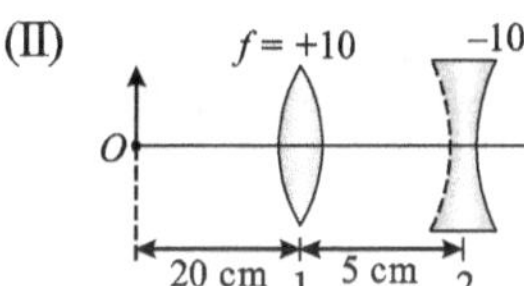	(Q) Final image is formed at 60.0 cm on the right side of lens 2
(III) 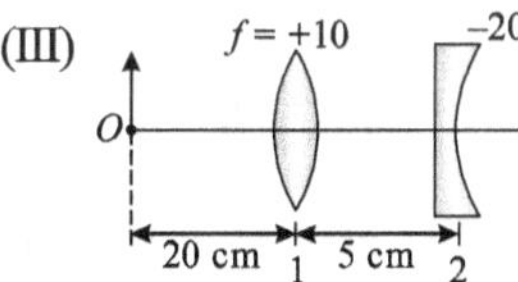	(R) Final image is formed at 30.0 cm on the left side of lens 2
(IV) 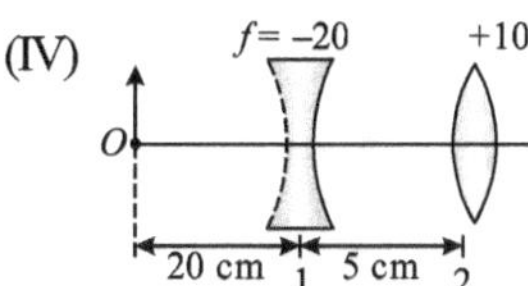	(S) Final image is formed at 6.0 cm on the right side of lens 2
	(T) Final image is formed at 30.0 cm on the right side of lens 2

Which one of the following options is correct?

(A) I → P, II → R, III → Q, IV → T
(B) I → Q, II → P, III → T, IV → S
(C) I → P, II → T, III → R, IV → Q
(D) I → T, II → S, III → Q, IV → R

Comprehension based MCQ

Paragraph-1 (Q. No. 37-38)

Most materials have the refractive index, $n > 1$. So, when a light ray from air enters a naturally occurring material, then by Snell's law, $\dfrac{\sin\theta_1}{\sin\theta_2} = \dfrac{n_2}{n_1}$, it is understood that the refracted ray bends towards the normal. But it never emerges on the same side of the normal as the incident ray. According to electromagnetism, the refractive index of the medium is given by the relation, $n = \left(\dfrac{c}{v}\right) = \pm\sqrt{\varepsilon_r\mu_r}$, where c is the speed of electromagnetic waves in vacuum, v its speed in the medium, ε_r and μ_r are the relative permittivity and permeability of the medium respectively.

In normal materials, both ε_r and μ_r are positive, implying positive n for the medium. When both ε_r and μ_r are negative, one must choose the negative root of n. Such negative refractive index materials can now be artificially prepared and are called meta-materials. They exhibit significantly different optical behavior, without violating any physical laws. Since n is negative, it results in a change in the direction of propagation of the refracted light. However, similar to normal materials, the frequency of light remains unchanged upon refraction even in meta-materials. **[JEE Adv 2012, P-2]**

37. For light incident from air on a meta-material, the appropriate ray diagram is :

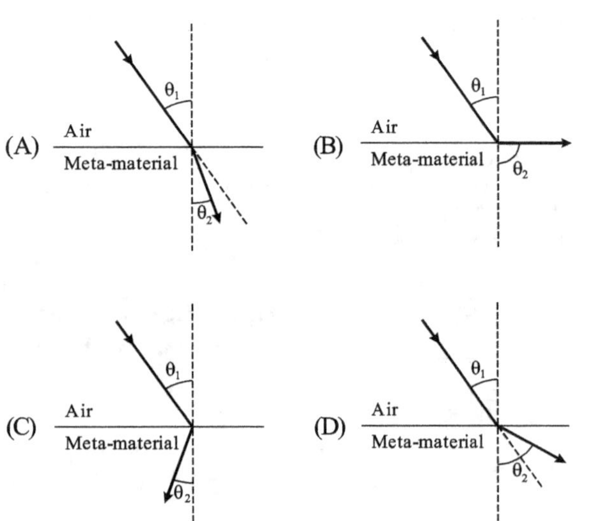

38. Choose the correct statement :
(A) The speed of light in the meta-material is $v = c|n|$
(B) The speed of light in the meta-material is $v = \dfrac{c}{|n|}$
(C) The speed of light in the meta-material is $v = c$

(D) The wavelength of the light in the meta-material (λ_m) is given by $\lambda_m = \lambda_{air}|n|$, where λ_{air} is the wavelength of the light in air.

Paragraph-2 (Q. No. 39-40)

Light guidance in an optical fiber can be understood by considering a structure comprising of thin solid glass cylinder of refractive index n_1 surrounded by a medium of lower refractive index n_2. The light guidance in the structure takes place due to successive total internal reflections at the interface of the media n_1 and n_2 as shown in the figure. All rays with the angle of incidence i less than a particular value i_m are confined in the medium of refractive index n_1. The numerical aperture (NA) of the structure is defined as $\sin i_m$. **[JEE Adv 2015, P-2]**

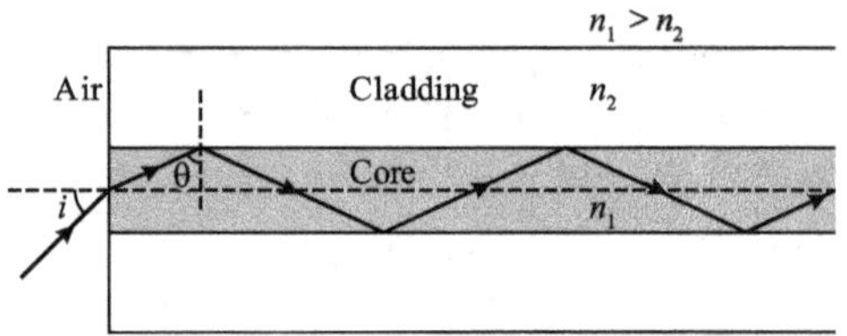

39. For two structures namely S_1 with $n_1 = \sqrt{45}/4$ and $n_2 = 3/2$, and S_2 with $n_1 = 8/5$ and $n_2 = 7/5$ and taking the refractive index of water to be $4/3$ and that of air to be 1, the correct option(s) is(are)
(A) NA of S_1 immersed in water is the same as that of S_2 immersed in a liquid of refractive index $\dfrac{16}{3\sqrt{15}}$

(B) NA of S_1 immersed in liquid of refractive index $\dfrac{6}{\sqrt{15}}$ is the same as that of S_2 immersed in water
(C) NA of S_1 placed in air is the same as that of S_2 immersed in liquid of refractive index $\dfrac{4}{\sqrt{15}}$
(D) NA of S_1 placed in air is the same as that of S_2 placed in water

40. If two structures of same cross-sectional area, but different numerical apertures NA_1 and NA_2 ($NA_2 < NA_1$) are joined longitudinally, the numerical aperture of the combined structure is :
(A) $\dfrac{NA_1 NA_2}{NA_1 + NA_2}$
(B) $NA_1 + NA_2$
(C) NA_1
(D) NA_2

Integer Answer based Questions

41. The focal length of a thin biconvex lens is 20 cm. When an object is moved from a distance of 25 cm in front of it to 50 cm, the magnification of its image changes from m_{25} to m_{50}. The ratio $\dfrac{m_{25}}{m_{50}}$ is ?   **[JEE Adv 2010, P-1]**

42. A large glass slab ($\mu = 5/3$) of thickness 8 cm is placed over a point source of light on a plane surface. It is seen that light emerges out of the top surface of the slab from a circular area of radius R cm. What is the value of R?   **[JEE Adv 2010, P-2]**

43. Image of an object approaching a convex mirror of radius of curvature 20 m along its optical axis is observed to move from $\dfrac{25}{3}$ m to $\dfrac{50}{7}$ m in 30 seconds. What is the speed of the object in km per hour ?   **[JEE Adv 2010, P-2]**

44. Water (with refractive index = 4/3) in a tank is 18 cm deep. Oil of refractive index 7/4 lies on water making a convex surface of radius of curvature $R = 6$ cm as shown. Consider oil to act as a thin lens. An object S is placed 24 cm above water surface. The location of its image is at x cm above the bottom of the tank. Then x is ?   **[JEE Adv 2011, P-2]**

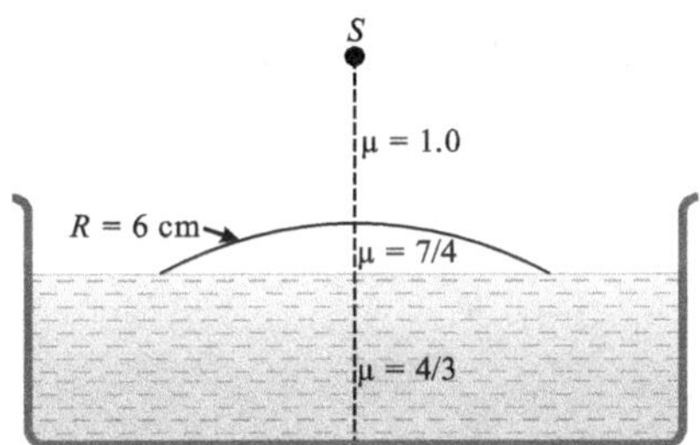

45. Consider a concave mirror and a convex lens (refractive index = 1.5) of focal length 10 cm each, separated by a distance of 50 cm in air (refractive index = 1) as shown in the figure. An object is placed at a distance of 15 cm from the mirror. Its erect image formed by this combination has magnification M_1. When the set-up is kept in a medium of refractive index 7/6 the magnification becomes M_2. The magnitude $\left|\dfrac{M_2}{M_1}\right|$ is :

[JEE Adv 2015, P-1]

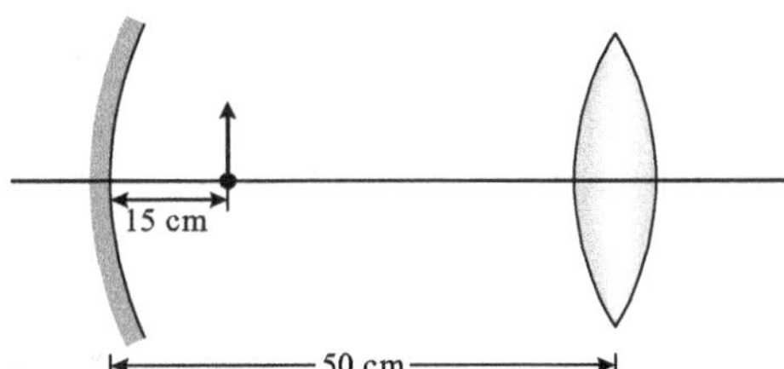

46. A monochromatic beam of light is incident at 60° on one face of an equilateral prism of refractive index n and emerges from the opposite face making an angle $\theta(n)$ with the normal (see the figure). For $n = \sqrt{3}$ the value of θ is 60° and $\dfrac{d\theta}{dn} = m$. The value of m is :   **[JEE Adv 2015, P-2]**

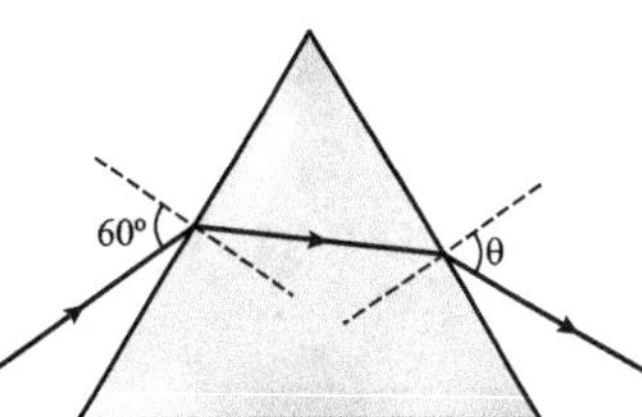

47. A monochromatic light is travelling in a medium of refractive index $n = 1.6$. It enters a stack of glass layers from the bottom side at an angle $\theta = 30°$. The interfaces of the glass layers are parallel to each other. The refractive indices of different glass layers are monotonically decreasing as $n_m = n - m\Delta n$, where n_m is the refractive index of the mth slab and $\Delta n = 0.1$ (see the figure). The ray is refracted out parallel to the interface between the $(m-1)^{\text{th}}$ and m^{th} slabs from the right side of the stack. What is the value of m?   **[JEE Adv 2017, P-1]**

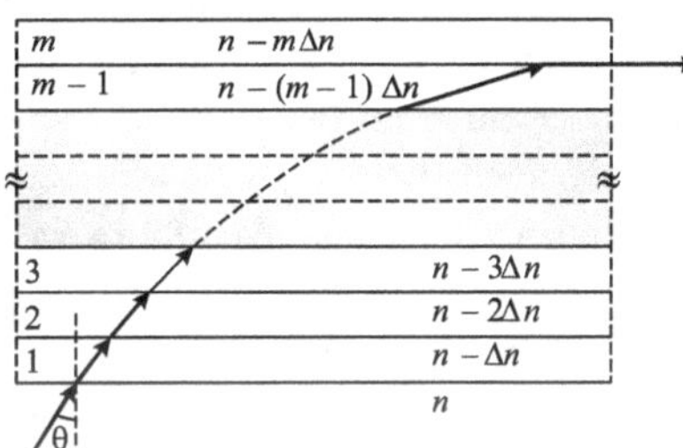

48. A planar structure of length L and width W is made of two different optical media of refractive indices $n_1 = 1.5$ and $n_2 = 1.44$ as shown in figure. If $L >> W$, a ray entering from end AB will emerge from end CD only if the total internal reflection condition is met inside the structure. For $L = 9.6$ m, if the incident angle θ is varied, the maximum time taken by a ray to exit the plane CD is $t \times 10^{-9}$ s, where t is ________.   **[JEE Adv 2019, P-1]**
[Speed of light $c = 3 \times 10^8$ m/s]

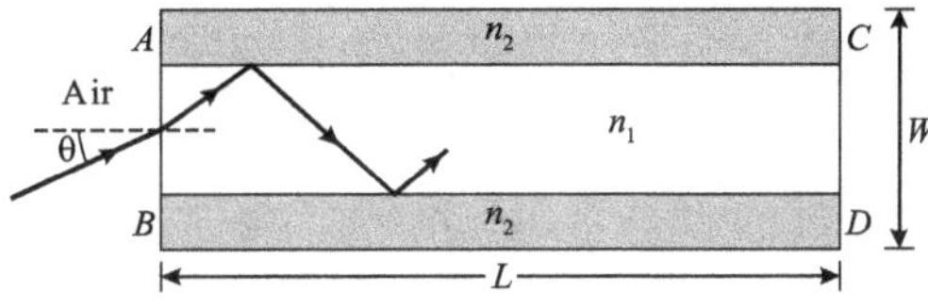

49. A monochromatic light is incident from air on a refracting surface of a prism of angle 75° and refractive index $n_0 = \sqrt{3}$. The other refracting surface of a prism is coated by a thin film of material of refractive index n as shown in figure. The light suffers total internal reflection at the coated prism surface for an incidence angle of $\theta \le 60°$. The value of n^2 is _______.

[JEE Adv 2019, P-2]

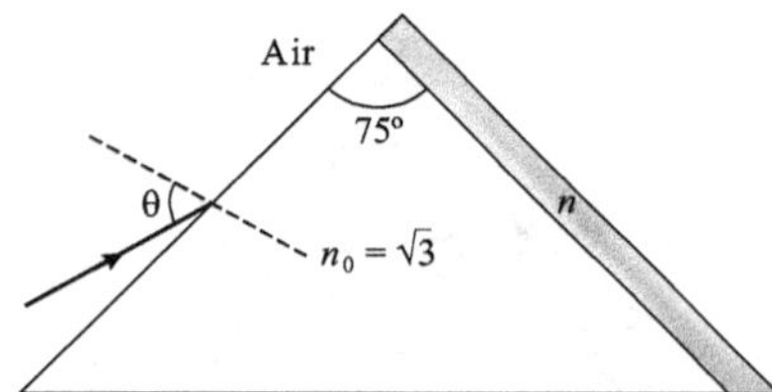

50. An optical bench has 1.5 m long scale having four equal divisions in each cm. While measuring the focal length of a convex lens, the lens is kept at 75 cm mark of the scale and the object pin is kept at 45 cm mark. The image of the object pin on the other side of the lens overlaps with image pin that is kept at 135 cm mark. In this experiment, the percentage error in the measurement of the focal length of the lens is _______.

[JEE Adv 2019, P-2]

51. A large square container with thin transparent vertical walls and filled with water (refractive index 4/3) is kept on a horizontal table. A student holds a thin straight wire vertically inside the water 12 cm from one of its corners, as shown schematically in the figure. Looking at the wire from this corner, another student sees two images of the wire, located symmetrically on each side of the line of sight as shown. The separation (in cm) between these images is _______.

[JEE Adv 2020, P-2]

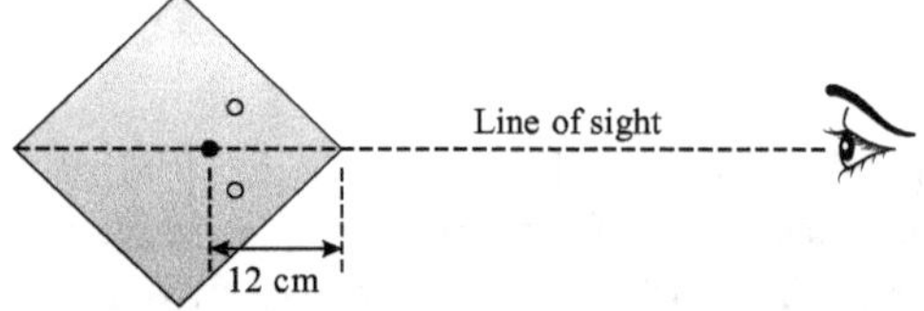

52. A rod of length 2 cm makes an angle $\dfrac{2\pi}{3}$ rad with the principal axis of a thin convex lens. The lens has a focal length of 10 cm and is placed at a distance of $\dfrac{40}{3}$ cm from the object as shown in the figure. The height of the image is $\dfrac{30\sqrt{3}}{13}$ cm and the angle made by it with respect to the principal axis is α rad. The value of α is $\dfrac{\pi}{n}$ rad, where n is _______.

[JEE Adv 2022, P-1]

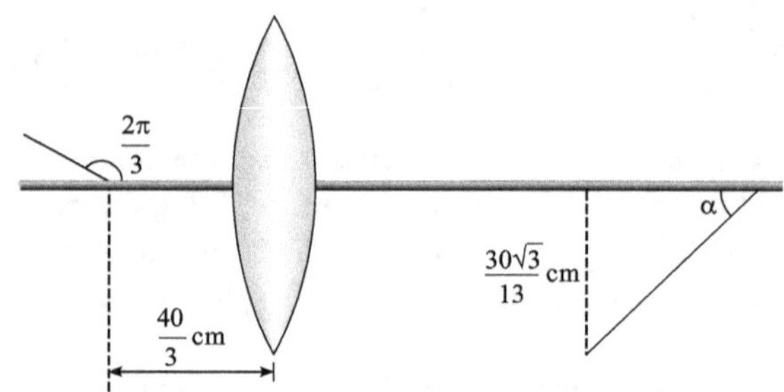

53. Consider a configuration of n identical units, each consisting of three layers. The first layer is a column of air of height $h = \dfrac{1}{3}$ cm, and the second and third layers are of equal thickness $d = \dfrac{\sqrt{3}-1}{2}$ cm, and refractive indices $\mu_1 = \sqrt{\dfrac{3}{2}}$ and $\mu_2 = \sqrt{3}$, respectively. A light source O is placed on the top of the first unit, as shown in the figure. A ray of light from O is incident on the second layer of the first unit at an angle of $\theta = 60°$ to the normal. For a specific value of n, the ray of light emerges from the bottom of the configuration at a distance $l = \dfrac{8}{\sqrt{3}}$ cm, as shown in the figure. The value of n is _______.

[JEE Adv 2022, P-2]

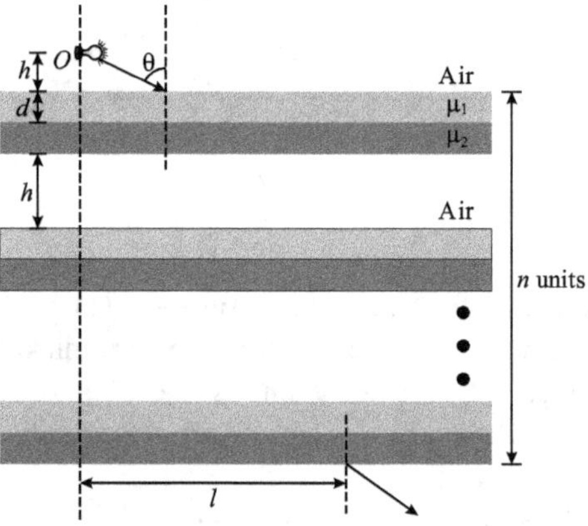

54. An object and a concave mirror of focal length $f = 10$ cm both move along the principal axis of the mirror with constant speeds. The object moves with speed $V_0 = 15$ cm s^{-1} towards the mirror with respect to a laboratory frame. The distance between the object and the mirror at a given moment is denoted by u. When $u = 30$ cm, the speed of the mirror V_m is such that the image is instantaneously at rest with respect to the laboratory frame, and the object forms a real image. The magnitude of V_m is _______ cm s^{-1}.　　**[JEE Adv 2022, P-2]**

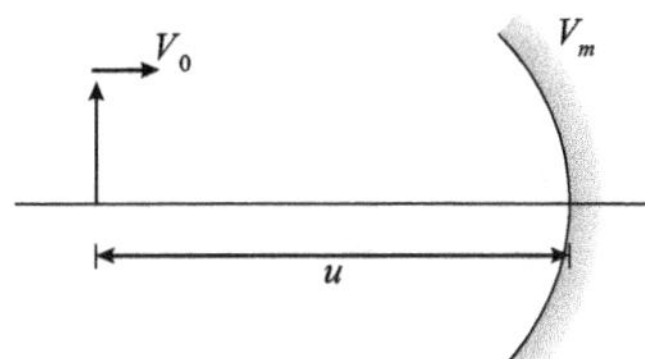

55. An optical arrangement consists of two concave mirrors M_1 and M_2, and a convex lens L with a common principal axis, as shown in the figure. The focal length of L is 10 cm. The radii of curvature of M_1 and M_2 are 20 cm and 24 cm, respectively. The distance between L and M_2 is 20 cm. A point object S is placed at the mid-point between L and M_2 on the axis. When the distance between L and M_1 is $n/7$ cm, one of the images coincides with S. The value of n is _______.

[JEE Adv 2023, P-1]

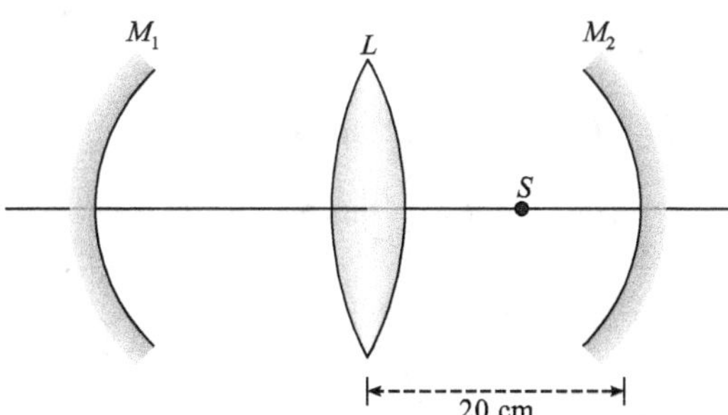

* * * * *

WAVE OPTICS & ELECTROMAGNETIC WAVE

MCQ with Single Option Correct

1. Young's double slit experiment is carried out by using green, red and blue light, one color at a time. The fringe widths recorded are β_G, β_R and β_B, respectively. Then :

[JEE Adv 2012, P-1]

(A) $\beta_G > \beta_B > \beta_R$ (B) $\beta_B > \beta_G > \beta_R$
(C) $\beta_R > \beta_B > \beta_G$ (D) $\beta_R > \beta_G > \beta_B$

2. In the Young's double slit experiment using a monochromatic light of wavelength λ, the path difference (in terms of an integer n) corresponding to any point having half the peak intensity is : **[JEE Adv 2013, P-1]**

(A) $(2n+1)\dfrac{\lambda}{2}$ (B) $(2n+1)\dfrac{\lambda}{4}$

(C) $(2n+1)\dfrac{\lambda}{8}$ (D) $(2n+1)\dfrac{\lambda}{16}$

3. While conducting the Young's double slit experiment, a student replaced the two slits with a large opaque plate in the x-y plane containing two small holes that act as two coherent point sources (S_1, S_2) emitting light of wavelength 600 nm. The student mistakenly placed the screen parallel to the x-z plane (for $z > 0$) at a distance $D = 3$ from the mid-point of $S_1 S_2$, as shown schematically in the figure. The distance between the sources $d = 0.6003$ mm. The origin O is at the intersection of the screen and the line joining $S_1 S_2$. Which of the following is (are) true of the intensity pattern on the screen ?

[JEE Adv 2016, P-2]

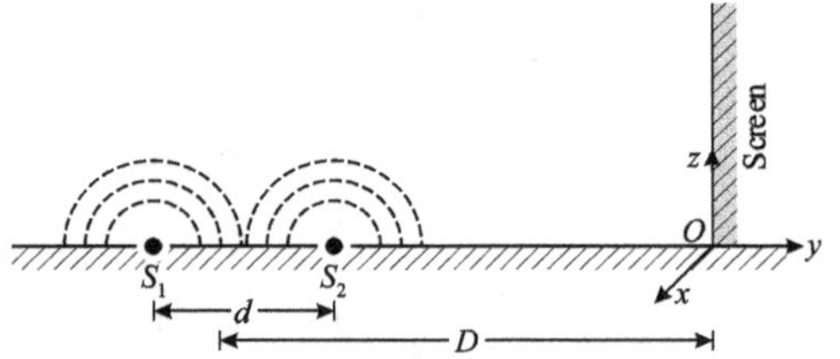

(A) Hyperbolic bright and dark bands with foci symmetrically placed about O in the x-direction
(B) Semi circular bright and dark bands centered at point O
(C) The region very close to the point O will be dark
(D) Straight bright and dark bands parallel to the x-axis

4. A parallel beam of light strikes a piece of transparent glass having cross section as shown in the figure below. Correct shape of the emergent wavefront will be (figures are schematic and not drawn to scale) : **[JEE Adv 2020, P-1]**

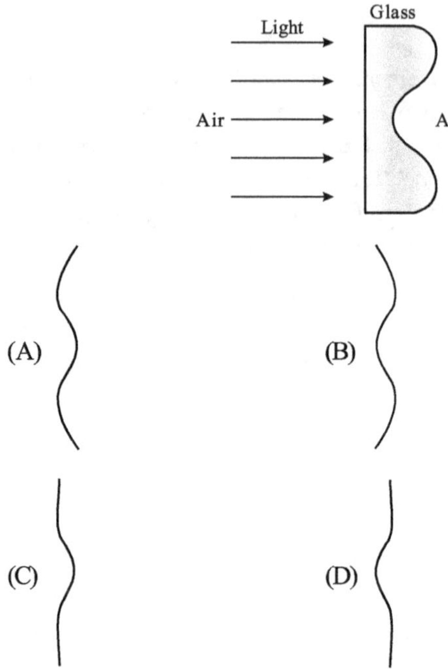

MCQ with One or More than One Options Correct

5. In a Young's double slit experiment, the separation between the two slits is d and the wavelength of the light is λ. The intensity of light on slit 1 is four times the intensity of light falling on slit 2. Choose the correct choice (s) :

[JEE Adv 2008, P-1]

(A) If $d = \lambda$, the screen will contain only one maximum
(B) If $\lambda < d < 2\lambda$, at least one more maximum (besides the central maximum) will be observed on the screen
(C) In the intensity of light falling on slit 1 is reduced so that it becomes equal to that of slit 2, the intensities of the observed dark and bright fringes will increase
(D) If the intensity of light falling on slit 2 is increased so that it becomes equal to that of slit 1, the intensities of the observed dark and bright fringes will increase

6. A light source, which emits two wavelengths $\lambda_1 = 400$ nm and $\lambda_2 = 600$ nm, is used in a Young's double slit experiment. If recorded fringe widths for λ_1 and λ_2 are β_1 and β_2 and the number of fringes for them within a distance y on one side of the central maximum are m_1 and m_2, respectively, then : **[JEE Adv 2014, P-1]**

(A) $\beta_2 > \beta_1$
(B) $m_1 > m_2$

(C) From the central maximum, 3rd maximum of λ_2 overlaps with 5th minimum of λ_1

(D) The angular separation of fringes for λ_1 is greater than λ_2

7. Two coherent monochromatic point sources S_1 and S_2 of wavelength $l = 600$ nm are placed symmetrically on either side of the center of the circle as shown. The sources are separated by a distance $d = 1.8$ mm. This arrangement produces interference fringes visible as alternate bright and dark spots on the circumference of the circle. The angular separation between two consecutive bright spots is $\Delta\theta$. Which of the following options is/are correct ? **[JEE Adv 2017, P-2]**

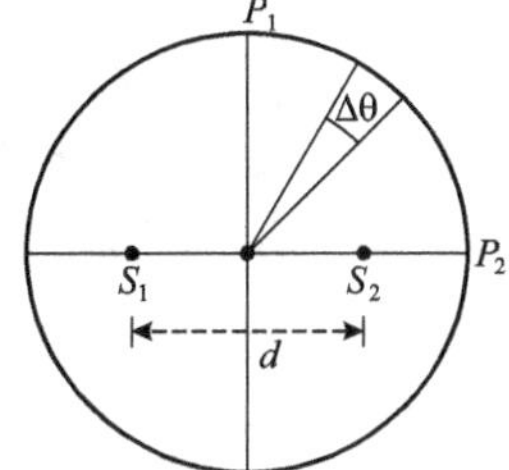

(A) A dark spot will be formed at the point P_2

(B) The angular separation between two consecutive bright spots decreases as we move from P_1 to P_2 along the first quadrant

(C) At P_2 the order of the fringe will be maximum

(D) The total number of fringes produced between P_1 and P_2 in the first quadrant is close to 3000

8. In a Young's double slit experiment, the slit separation d is 0.3 mm and the screen distance D is 1 m. A parallel beam of light of wavelength 600 nm is incident on the slits at angle α as shown in figure. On the screen, the point O is equidistant from the slits and distance PO is 11.0 mm. Which of the following statement(s) is/are correct : **[JEE Adv 2019, P-2]**

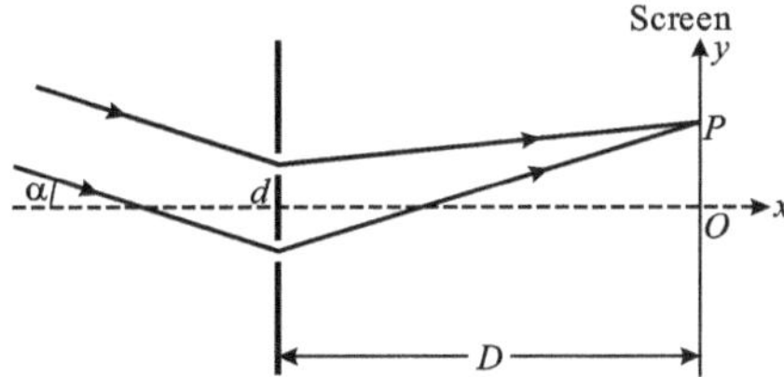

(A) For $\alpha = \dfrac{0.36}{\pi}$ degree, there will be destructive interference at point O.

(B) Fringe spacing depends on α

(C) For $\alpha = \dfrac{0.36}{\pi}$ degree, there will be destructive interference at point P

(D) For $\alpha = 0$, there will be constructive interference at point P.

9. A double slit setup is shown in the figure. One of the slits is in medium 2 of refractive index n_2. The other slit is at the interface of this medium with another medium 1 of refractive index n_1 ($\neq n_2$). The line joining the slits is perpendicular to the interface and the distance between the slits is d. The slit widths are much smaller than d. A monochromatic parallel beam of light is incident on the slits from medium 1. A detector is placed in medium 2 at a large distance from the slits, and at an angle θ from the line joining them, so that θ equals the angle of refraction of the beam. Consider two approximately parallel rays from the slits received by the detector.

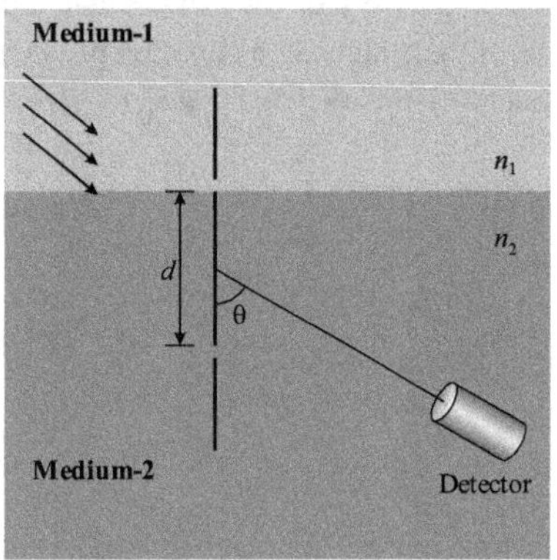

Which of the following statement(s) is(are) correct?

[JEE Adv 2022, P-2]

(A) The phase difference between the two rays is independent of d

(B) The two rays interfere constructively at the detector

(C) The phase difference between the two rays depends on n_1 but is independent of n_2

(D) The phase difference between the two rays vanishes only for certain values of d and the angle of incidence of the beam, with θ being the corresponding angle of refraction

10. The electric field associated with an electromagnetic wave propagating in a dielectric medium is given by

$$\vec{E} = 30(2\hat{x} + \hat{y})\sin\left[2\pi\left(5\times10^{14}t - \frac{10^7}{3}z\right)\right]\text{Vm}^{-1}$$

Which of the following option(s) is(are) correct ?

[Given: The speed of light in vacuum, $c = 3 \times 10^8$ m s^{-1}]

[JEE Adv 2023, P-2]

(A) $B_x = -2 \times 10^{-7}\sin\left[2\pi\left(5\times10^{14}t - \frac{10^7}{3}z\right)\right]$ Wb m^{-2}

(B) $B_y = 2 \times 10^{-7}\sin\left[2\pi\left(5\times10^{14}t - \frac{10^7}{3}z\right)\right]$ Wb m^{-2}

(C) The wave is polarized in the xy-plane with polarization angle 30° with respect to the x-axis

(D) The refractive index of the medium is 2

Matrix Match MCQ

11. **Column-I** shows four situations of standard Young's double slit arrangement with the screen placed far away from the slits S_1 and S_2. In each of these cases $S_1P_0 = S_2P_0$, $S_1P_1 - S_2P_1 = \lambda/4$ and $S_1P_2 - S_2P_2 = \lambda/3$, where λ is the wavelength of the light used. In the cases B, C and D, a transparent sheet of refractive index μ and thickness t is pasted on slit S_2. The thicknesses of the sheets are different in different cases. The phase difference between the light waves reaching a point P on the screen from the two slits is denoted by $\delta(P)$ and the intensity by $I(P)$. Match each situation given in **Column-I** with the statement(s) in **Column-II** valid for the situation :

[JEE Adv 2009, P-2]

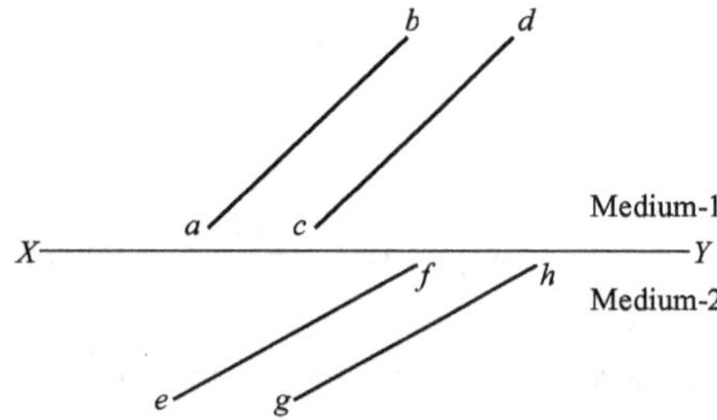

Column-I

(A)

(B) $(\mu - 1)t = \lambda/4$

(C) $(\mu - 1)t = \lambda/2$

(D) $(\mu - 1)t = 3\lambda/4$

Column-II

(p) $\delta(P_0) = 0$

(q) $\delta(P_1) = 0$

(r) $I(P_1) = 0$

(s) $I(P_0) > I(P_1)$

(t) $I(P_2) > I(P_1)$

Comprehension based MCQ

Paragraph-1 (Q. No. 12-14)

The figure shows a surface XY separating two transparent media, medium-1 and medium-2. The lines ab and cd represent wavefronts of a light wave travelling in medium-1 and incident on XY. The lines of end gh represent wavefronts of the light wave in medium-2 after refraction. **[JEE Adv 2007, P-2]**

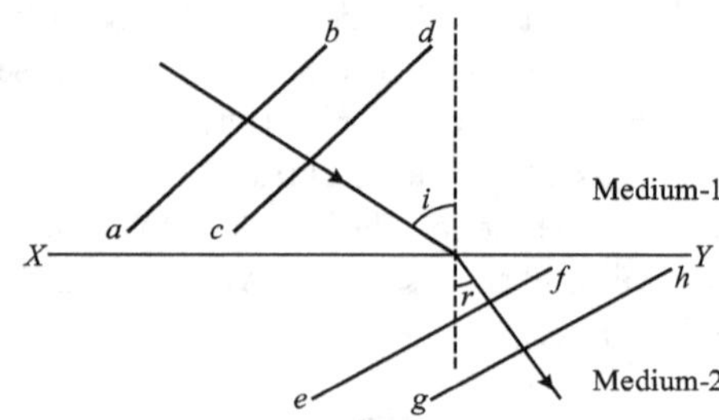

12. Light travels as a :

(A) Parallel beam in each medium

(B) Convergent beam in each medium

(C) Divergent beam in each medium

(D) Divergent beam in one medium and convergent beam in the other medium

13. The phases of the light wave at c, d, e and f are ϕ_c, ϕ_d, ϕ_e and ϕ_f respectively. If is given that $\phi_c \neq \phi_f$:

(A) ϕ_c cannot be equal to ϕ_d

(B) ϕ_d can be equal to ϕ_e

(C) $(\phi_d - \phi_f)$ is equal to $(\phi_c - \phi_e)$

(D) $(\phi_d - \phi_c)$ is not equal to $(\phi_f - \phi_e)$

14. Speed of light is :

(A) Same in medium-1 and medium-2

(B) Larger in medium-1 than in medium-2

(C) Larger in medium-2 than in medium-1

(D) Different at b and d

Integer Answer based Questions

15. A Young's double slit interference arrangement with slits S_1 and S_2 is immersed in water (refractive index $= 4/3$) as shown in the figure. The positions of maxima on the surface of water are given by $x^2 = p^2 m^2 \lambda^2 - d^2$, where λ is the wavelength of light in air (refractive index = 1), $2d$ is the separation between the slits and m is an integer. The value of p is : **[JEE Adv 2015, P-1]**

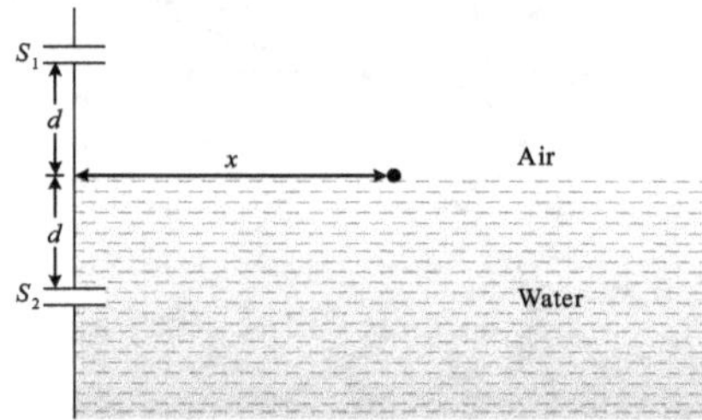

16. Sunlight of intensity 1.3 kW m^{-2} is incident normally on a thin convex lens of focal length 20 cm. Ignore the energy loss of light due to the lens and assume that the lens aperture size is much smaller than its focal length. The average intensity of light, in kW m^{-2}, at a distance 22 cm from the lens on the other side is _______. **[JEE Adv 2018, P-1]**

* * * * *

DUAL NATURE OF RADIATION, MATTER AND X-RAYS

MCQ with Single Option Correct

1. Electrons with de-Broglie wavelength λ fall on the target in an X-ray tube. The cut-off wavelength of the emitted X-rays is :

[JEE Adv 2007, P-2]

(A) $\lambda_0 = \dfrac{2mc\lambda^2}{h}$

(B) $\lambda_0 = \dfrac{2h}{mc}$

(C) $\lambda_0 = \dfrac{2m^2c^2\lambda^3}{h^2}$

(D) $\lambda_0 = \lambda$

2. Which one of the following statements is **WRONG** in the context of X-rays generated from X-ray tube ?

[JEE Adv 2008, P-1]

(A) Wavelength of characteristic X-rays decreases when the atomic number of the target increases

(B) Cut-off wavelength of the continuous X-rays depends on the atomic number of the target

(C) Intensity of the characteristic X-ray depends on the electrical power given to the X-ray tube

(D) Cut-off wavelength of the continuous X-rays depends on the energy of the electrons in the X-ray tube

3. Photoelectric effect experiments are performed using three different metal plates p, q and r having work functions $\phi_p = 2.0$ eV, $\phi_q = 2.5$ eV and $\phi_r = 3.0$ eV, respectively. A light beam containing wavelengths of 550 nm, 450 nm and 350 nm with equal intensities illuminates each of the plates. The correct $I\text{-}V$ graph for the experiment is : [Take $hc = 1240$ eV nm]

[JEE Adv 2009, P-2]

(A) 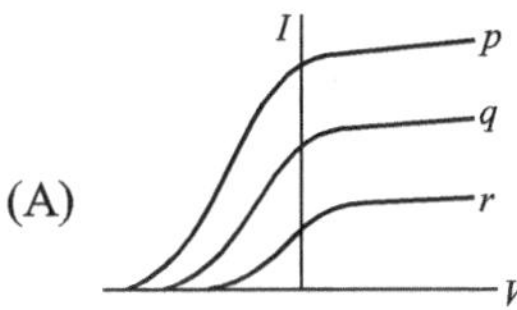

(B) 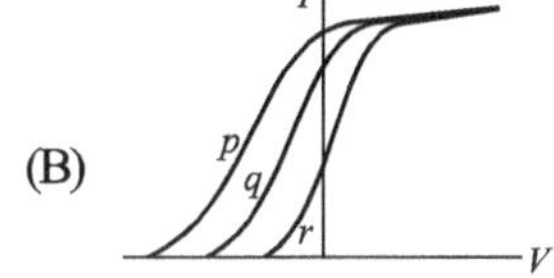

(C) 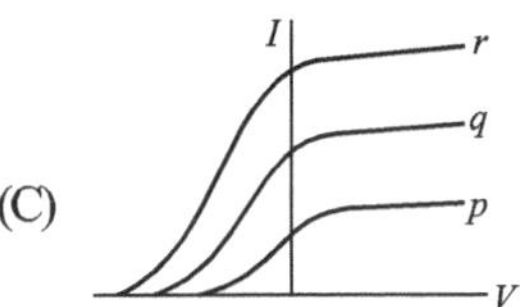

(D) 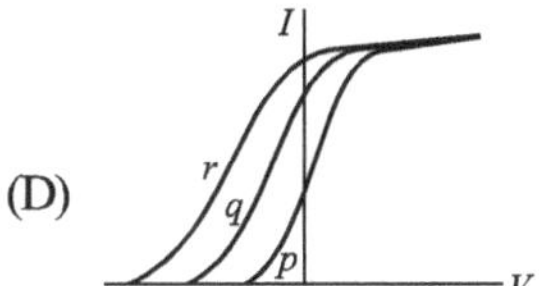

4. A pulse of light of duration 100 ns is absorbed completely by a small object initially at rest. Power of the pulse is 30 mW and the speed of light is 3×10^8 ms^{-1}. The final momentum of the object is :

[JEE Adv 2013, P-1]

(A) 0.3×10^{-17} kg ms^{-1}

(B) 1.0×10^{-17} kg ms^{-1}

(C) 3.0×10^{-17} kg ms^{-1}

(D) 9.0×10^{-17} kg ms^{-1}

5. If λ_{Cu} is the wavelength of K_α X-ray line of copper (atomic number 29) and λ_{Mo} is the wavelength of the K_α X-ray line of molybdenum (atomic number 42), then the ratio $\lambda_{Cu} / \lambda_{Mo}$ is close to :

[JEE Adv 2014, P-2]

(A) 1.99

(B) 2.14

(C) 0.50

(D) 0.48

6. A metal surface is illuminated by light of two different wavelengths 248 nm and 310 nm. The maximum speeds of the photoelectrons corresponding to these wavelengths are u_1 and u_2, respectively. If the ratio $u_1 : u_2 = 2 : 1$ and $hc = 1240$ eV nm, the work function of the metal is nearly : **[JEE Adv 2014, P-2]**

(A) 3.7 eV

(B) 3.2 eV

(C) 2.8 eV

(D) 2.5 eV

7. In a historical experiment to determine Planck's constant, a metal surface was irradiated with light of different wavelengths. The emitted photoelectron energies were measured by applying a stopping potential. The relevant data for the wavelength (λ) of incident light and the corresponding stopping potential (V_0) are given below : **[JEE Adv 2016, P-1]**

$\lambda(\mu m)$	$V_0(\text{Volt})$
0.3	2.0
0.4	1.0
0.5	0.4

Given that $c = 3 \times 10^8$ ms^{-1} and $e = 1.6 \times 10^{-19}$ C, Planck's constant (in units of Js) found from such an experiment is :

(A) 6.0×10^{-34}

(B) 6.4×10^{-34}

(C) 6.6×10^{-34}

(D) 6.8×10^{-34}

8. A photoelectric material having work-function ϕ_0 is illuminated with light of wavelength $\lambda \left(\lambda < \dfrac{hc}{\phi_0} \right)$. The fastest photoelectron has a de Broglie wavelength λ_d. A change in wavelength of the incident light by $\Delta\lambda$ results in a change $\Delta\lambda_d$

in λ_d. Then the ratio $\dfrac{\Delta\lambda_a}{\Delta\lambda}$ is proportional to :

[JEE Adv 2017, P-2]

(A) $\dfrac{\lambda_d^3}{\lambda^2}$

(B) $\dfrac{\lambda_d^3}{\lambda}$

(C) $\dfrac{\lambda_d^2}{\lambda^2}$

(D) $\dfrac{\lambda_d}{\lambda}$

9. When light of a given wavelength is incident on a metallic surface, the minimum potential needed to stop the emitted photoelectrons is 6.0 V. This potential drops to 0.6 V if another source with wavelength four times that of the first one and intensity half of the first one is used. What are the wavelength of the first source and the work function of the metal, respectively?

[Take $\dfrac{hc}{e} = 1.24 \times 10^{-6}\,\mathrm{Jm\,C^{-1}}$]   **[JEE Adv 2022, P-2]**

(A) $1.72 \times 10^{-7}\,\mathrm{m}, 1.20\,\mathrm{eV}$ (B) $1.72 \times 10^{-7}\,\mathrm{m}, 5.60\,\mathrm{eV}$

(C) $3.78 \times 10^{-7}\,\mathrm{m}, 5.60\,\mathrm{eV}$ (D) $3.78 \times 10^{-7}\,\mathrm{m}, 1.20\,\mathrm{eV}$

MCQ with One or More than One Options Correct

10. The radius of the orbit of an electron in a Hydrogen-like atom is $4.5a_0$, where a_0 is the Bohr radius. Its orbital angular momentum is $3h/2\pi$. It is given that h is Planck's constant and R is Rydberg constant. The possible wavelength(s), when the atom de-excites, is (are) :   **[JEE Adv 2013, P-2]**

(A) $\dfrac{9}{32R}$

(B) $\dfrac{9}{16R}$

(C) $\dfrac{9}{5R}$

(D) $\dfrac{4}{3R}$

11. For photo-electric effect with incident photon wavelength λ the stopping potential is V_0. Identify the correct variation(s) of V_0 with λ and $1/\lambda$:   **[JEE Adv 2015, P-1]**

(A) 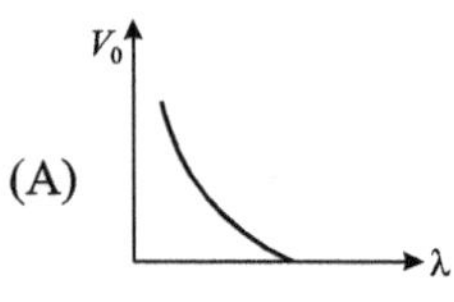

(B) 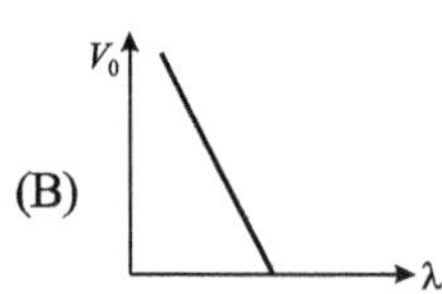

(C) 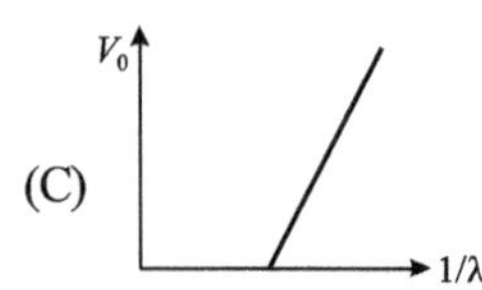

(D) 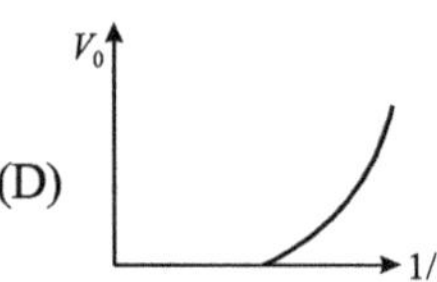

12. Light of wavelength λ_{ph} falls on a cathode plate inside a vacuum tube as shown in the figure. The work function of the cathode surface is ϕ and the anode is a wire mesh of conducting material kept at a distance d from the cathode. A potential

difference V is maintained between the electrodes. If the minimum de-Broglie wavelength of the electrons passing through the anode is λ_e, which of the following statement(s) is(are) true?   **[JEE Adv 2016, P-2]**

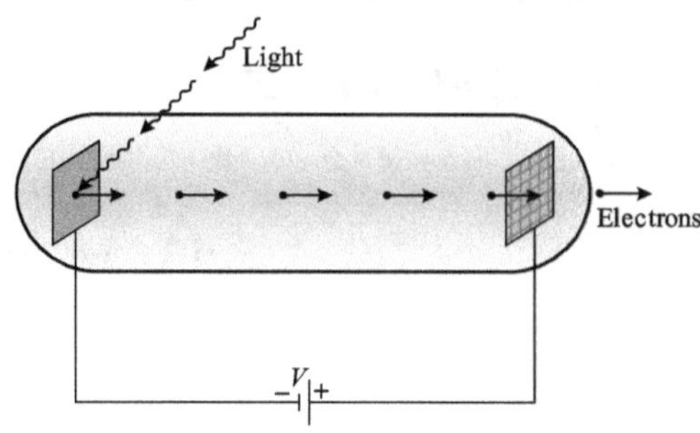

(A) For large potential difference $(V \gg \phi/e)$, λ_e is approximately halved if V is made four times

(B) λ_e increases at the same rate as λ_{ph} for $\lambda_{ph} < hc/\phi$

(C) λ_e is approximately halved, if d is doubled

(D) λ_e decreases with increase in ϕ and λ_{ph}

13. In an X-ray tube, electrons emitted from a filament (cathode) carrying current I hit a target (anode) at a distance d from the cathode. The target is kept at a potential V higher than the cathode resulting in emission of continuous and characteristic X-rays. If the filament current I is decreased to $I/2$, the potential difference V is increased to $2V$, and the separation distance d is reduced to $d/2$, then :   **[JEE Adv 2020, P-2]**

(A) The cut-off wavelength will reduce to half, and the wavelengths of the characteristic X-rays will remain the same

(B) The cut off wavelength as well as the wavelengths of the characteristic X-rays will remain the same

(C) The cut-off wavelength will reduce to half, and the intensities of all the X-rays will decrease

(D) The cut-off wavelength will become two times larger, and the intensity of all the X-rays will decrease

Assertion Reason based on MCQ

14. STATEMENT-1   **[JEE Adv 2007, P-1]**

If the accelerating potential in ax X-ray tube is increased, the wavelength of the characteristic X-ray do not change.

because

STATEMENT-2

When an electron beam strikes the target in an X-ray tube, part of the kinetic energy is converted into X-ray energy :

(A) Statement-1 is True, Statement-2 is True; Statement-2 is a correct explanation for Statement-1

(B) Statement-1 is True, Statement-2 is True; Statement-2 is **NOT** a correct explanation for Statement-1

(C) Statement-1 is True, Statement-2 is False

(D) Statement-1 is False, Statement-2 is True

Integer Answer based Questions

15. An α-particle and a proton are accelerated from rest by a potential difference of 100 V. After this, their de-Broglie wavelengths are λ_α and λ_p respectively. The ratio $\dfrac{\lambda_p}{\lambda_\alpha}$, to the nearest integer, is ?   **[JEE Adv 2010, P-1]**

16. A silver sphere of radius 1 cm and work function 4.7 eV is suspended from an insulating thread in free-space. It is under continues illumination of 200 nm wavelength of light. As photoelectrons are emitted, the sphere gets charged and acquires a potential. The maximum number of photoelectrons emitted from the sphere is $A \times 10^Z$ (where $1 < A < 10$). The value of Z is ?   **[JEE Adv 2011, P-2]**

17. A proton is fired from very far away towards a nucleus with charge $Q = 120\,e$, where e is the electronic charge. It makes a closest approach of 10 fm to the nucleus. The de-Broglie wavelength (in units of fm) of the proton at its starts is : (take the proton mass, $m_p = (5/3) \times 10^{-27}$ kg; $h/e = 4.2 \times 10^{-15}$ J.s/C;

$\dfrac{1}{4\pi\varepsilon_0} = 9 \times 10^9$ m/F; 1 fm $= 10^{-15}$ m).   **[JEE Adv 2012, P-1]**

18. The work functions of Silver and Sodium are 4.6 and 2.3 eV, respectively. The ratio of the slope of the stopping potential versus frequency plot for Silver to that of Sodium is ?   **[JEE Adv 2013, P-1]**

19. Consider a hydrogen atom with its electron in the nth orbital. An electromagnetic radiation of wavelength 90 nm is used to ionize the atom. If the kinetic energy of the ejected electron is 10.4 eV, then the value of n is ($hc = 1242$ eV nm)   **[JEE Adv 2015, P-1]**

20. An electron in an excited state of Li^{2+} ion has angular momentum $3h/2\pi$. The de Broglie wavelength of the electron in this state is $p\pi a_0$ (where a_0 is the Bohr radius). The value of p is :   **[JEE Adv 2015, P-2]**

21. In a photoelectric experiment a parallel beam of monochromatic light with power of 200 W is incident on a perfectly absorbing cathode of work function 6.25 eV. The frequency of light is just above the threshold frequency so that the photoelectrons are emitted with negligible kinetic energy. Assume that the photoelectron emission efficiency is 100% A potential difference of 500 V is applied between the cathode and the anode. All the emitted electrons are incident normally on the anode and are absorbed. The anode experiences a force $F = n \times 10^{-4}$ N due to the impact of the electrons. The value of n is______ Mass of the electron $m_e = 9 \times 10^{-31}$ kg and 1.0 eV $= 1.6 \times 10^{-19}$ J ?   **[JEE Adv 2018, P-2]**

22. A perfectly reflecting mirror of mass M mounted on a spring constitutes a spring-mass system of angular frequency Ω such that $\dfrac{4\pi M\Omega}{h} = 10^{24}\,\text{m}^{-2}$ with h as Planck's constant. N photons of wavelength $\lambda = 8\pi \times 10^{-6}$ m strike the mirror simultaneously at normal incidence such that the mirror gets displaced by 1 μm. If the value of N is $x \times 10^{12}$, then the value of x is______. [Consider the spring as massless]   **[JEE Adv 2019, P-2]**

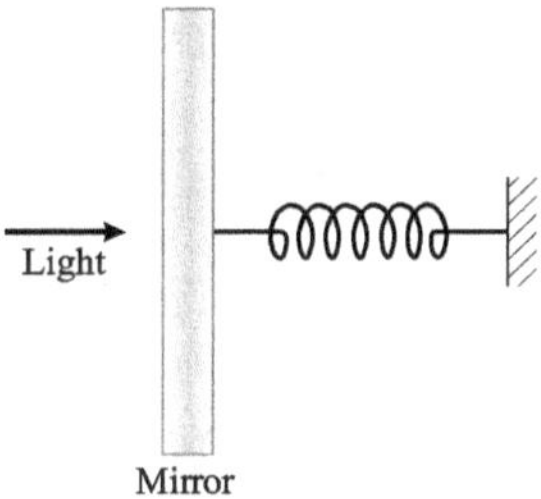

23. A small object is placed at the center of a large evacuated hollow spherical container. Assume that the container is maintained at 0 K. At time $t = 0$, the temperature of the object is 200 K. The temperature of the object becomes 100 K at $t = t_1$ and 50 K at $t = t_2$. Assume the object and the container to be ideal black bodies. The heat capacity of the object does not depend on temperature. The ratio (t_2/t_1) is______.   **[JEE Adv 2021, P-1]**

24. In a photoemission experiment, the maximum kinetic energies of photoelectrons from metals P, Q and R are E_P, E_Q and E_R, respectively, and they are related by $E_P = 2E_Q = 2E_R$. In this experiment, the same source of monochromatic light is used for metals P and Q while a different source of monochromatic light is used for the metal R. The work functions for metals P, Q and R are 4.0 eV, 4.5 eV and 5.5 eV, respectively. The energy of the incident photon used for metal R, in eV, is :   **[JEE Adv 2021, P-2]**

* * * * *

MCQ with Single Option Correct

1. The largest wavelength in the ultraviolet region of the hydrogen spectrum is 122 nm. The smallest wavelength in the infrared region of the hydrogen spectrum (to the nearest integer) is : **[JEE Adv 2007, P-1]**
(A) 802 nm
(B) 823 nm
(C) 1882 nm
(D) 1648 nm

2. The wavelength of the first spectral line in the Balmer series of hydrogen atom is 6561 Å. The wavelength of the second spectral line in the Balmer series of singly-ionized helium atom is : **[JEE Adv 2011, P-1]**
(A) 1215 Å
(B) 1640 Å
(C) 2430 Å
(D) 4687 Å

MCQ with One or More than One Options Correct

3. Highly excited states for hydrogen like atoms (also called Rydberg states) with nuclear charge Ze are defined by their principal quantum number n, where $n \gg 1$. Which of the following statement(s) is (are) true ? **[JEE Adv 2016, P-1]**
(A) Relative change in the radii of two consecutive orbitals does not depend on Z
(B) Relative change in the radii of two consecutive orbitals varies as $1/n$
(C) Relative change in the energy of two consecutive orbitals varies as $1/n^3$
(D) Relative change in the angular momenta of two consecutive orbitals varies as $1/n$

4. A free hydrogen atom after absorbing a photon of wavelength λ_a gets excited from the state $n = 1$ to the state $n = 4$. Immediately after that the electron jumps to $n = m$ state by emitting a photon of wavelength λ_e. Let the change in momentum of atom due to the absorption and the emission are Δp_a and Δp_e, respectively. If $\lambda_a/\lambda_e = 1/5$. Which of the option(s) is/are correct ? [Use $hc = 1242$ eV nm; 1 nm = 10^{-9} m, h and c are Planck's constant and speed of light, respectively]
[JEE Adv 2019, P-2]
(A) $\lambda_e = 418$ nm
(B) The ratio of kinetic energy of the electron in the state $n = m$ to the state $n = 1$ is 1/4
(C) $m = 2$
(D) $\Delta p_a/\Delta p_e = 1/2$

5. A particle of mass m moves in circular orbits with potential energy $V(r) = Fr$, where F is a positive constant and r is its distance from the origin. Its energies are calculated using the Bohr model. If the radius of the particle's orbit is denoted by R and its speed and energy are denoted by v and E, respectively, then for the nth orbit (here h is the Planck's constant) :
[JEE Adv 2020, P-1]
(A) $R \propto n^{1/3}$ and $v \propto n^{2/3}$
(B) $R \propto n^{2/3}$ and $v \propto n^{1/3}$
(C) $E = \dfrac{3}{2}\left(\dfrac{n^2 h^2 F^2}{4\pi^2 m}\right)^{1/3}$
(D) $E = 2\left(\dfrac{n^2 h^2 F^2}{4\pi^2 m}\right)^{1/3}$

6. Which of the following statement(s) is (are) correct about the spectrum of hydrogen atom? **[JEE Adv 2021, P-1]**
(A) The ratio of the longest wavelength to the shortest wavelength in Balmer series is 9/5
(B) There is an overlap between the wavelength ranges of Balmer and Paschen series
(C) The wavelengths of Lyman series are given by $\left(1 + \dfrac{1}{m^2}\right)\lambda_0$, where λ_0 is the shortest wavelength of Lyman series and m is an integer
(D) The wavelength ranges of Lyman and Balmer series do not overlap

Matrix Match MCQ

7. Some laws/processes are given is **Column-I**. Match these with the physical phenomena given in **Column-II** and indicate your answer by darkening appropriate bubbles in the 4×4 matrix given in the ORS : **[JEE Adv 2007, P-1]**

Column-I	Column-II
(A) Transition between two atomic energy levels	(p) Characteristic X-rays
(B) Electron emission from a material	(q) Photoelectric effect
(C) Moseley's lay	(r) Hydrogen spectrum
(D) Change of photon energy into kinetic energy of electrons	(s) β-decay

Comprehension based MCQ

Paragraph-1 (Q. No. 8-10)

In a mixture H – He$^+$ gas (He$^+$ is singly ionized He atom), H atoms and He$^+$ ions are excited to their respective first excited states. Subsequently, H atoms transfer their total excitation energy to He$^+$ ions (by collisions). Assume that the Bohr model of atom is exactly valid.   **[JEE Adv 2008, P-1]**

8. The quantum number n of the state finally populated in He$^+$ ions is :

(A) 2   (B) 3

(C) 4   (D) 5

9. The wavelength of light emitted in the visible region by He$^+$ ions after collisions with H-atoms is :

(A) 6.5×10^{-7} m   (B) 5.6×10^{-7} m

(C) 4.8×10^{-7} m   (D) 4.0×10^{-7} m

10. The ratio of the kinetic energy of the $n = 2$ electron for the H atom to that of He$^+$ ion is :

(A) $\dfrac{1}{4}$ (B) $\dfrac{1}{2}$

(C) 1   (D) 2

Paragraph-2 (Q. No. 11-13)

When a particle is restricted to move along x-axis between $x = 0$ and $x = a$, where a is of nanometer dimension, its energy can take only certain specific values. The allowed energies of the particle moving in such a restricted region, correspond to the formation of standing waves with nodes at such a restricted region, correspond to the formation of standing waves with nodes at its ends $x = 0$ and $x = a$. The wavelength of this standing wave is related to the linear momentum p of the particle according to the de-Broglie relation. The energy of the particle of mass m is related to its linear momentum as $E = \dfrac{p^2}{2m}$. Thus, the energy of the particle can be denoted by a quantum number 'n' taking value 1, 2, 3,... ($n = 1$, called the ground state) corresponding to the number of loops in the standing wave. Use the model described above to answer the following three questions for a particle moving in the line $x = 0$ to $x = a$. Take $h = 6.6 \times 10^{-34}$ J s and $e = 1.6 \times 10^{-19}$ C.   **[JEE Adv 2009, P-1]**

11. The allowed energy for the particle for a particular value of n is proportional to :

(A) a^{-2} (B) $a^{-3/2}$

(C) a^{-1} (D) a^2

12. If the mass of the particle is $m = 1.0 \times 10^{-30}$ kg and $a = 6.6$ nm, the energy of the particle in its ground state is closest to :

(A) 0.8 meV   (B) 8 meV

(C) 80 meV   (D) 800 meV

13. The speed of the particle, that can take discrete values, is proportional to :

(A) $n^{-3/2}$ (B) n^{-1}

(C) $n^{1/2}$ (D) n

Paragraph-3 (Q. No. 14-16)

The key feature of Bohr's theory of spectrum of hydrogen atom is the quantization of angular momentum when an electron is revolving around a proton. We will extend this to a general rotational motion to find quantized rotational energy of a diatomic molecule assuming it to be rigid. The rule to be applied is Bohr's quantization condition.   **[JEE Adv 2010, P-2]**

14. A diatomic molecule has moment of inertia I. By Bohr's quantization condition its rotational energy in the nth level ($n = 0$ is not allowed) is :

(A) $\dfrac{1}{n^2}\left(\dfrac{h^2}{8\pi^2 I}\right)$ (B) $\dfrac{1}{n}\left(\dfrac{h^2}{8\pi^2 I}\right)$

(C) $n\left(\dfrac{h^2}{8\pi^2 I}\right)$ (D) $n^2\left(\dfrac{h^2}{8\pi^2 I}\right)$

15. It is found that the excitation frequency from ground to the first excited state of rotation for the CO molecule is close to $\dfrac{4}{\pi} \times 10^{11}$ Hz. Then the moment of inertia of CO molecule about its center of mass is close to (Take $h = 2\pi \times 10^{-34}$ J s) :

(A) 2.76×10^{-46} kg m^2 (B) 1.87×10^{-46} kg m^2

(C) 4.67×10^{-47} kg m^2 (D) 1.17×10^{-47} kg m^2

16. In a CO molecule, the distance between C (mass = 12 a.m.u.) and O (mass = 16 a.m.u.), where 1 a.m.u. = $\dfrac{5}{3} \times 10^{-27}$ kg, is close to :

(A) 2.4×10^{-10} m   (B) 1.9×10^{-10} m

(C) 1.3×10^{-10} m   (D) 4.4×10^{-11} m

Integer Answer based Questions

17. A hydrogen atom in its ground state is irradiated by light of wavelength 970 Å. Taking $hc/e = 1.237 \times 10^{-6}$ eV m and the ground state energy of hydrogen atom as -13.6 eV, the number of lines present in the emission spectrum is ?

[JEE Adv 2016, P-1]

18. An electron in a hydrogen atom undergoes a transition from an orbit with quantum number n_i to another with quantum number n_f. V_i and V_f are respectively the initial and final potential energies of the electron. If $\dfrac{V_i}{V_f} = 6.25$, then the smallest possible n_f is ?

[JEE Adv 2017, P-1]

19. Consider a hydrogen-like ionized atom with atomic number Z with a single electron. In the emission spectrum of this atom, the photon emitted in the $n = 2$ to $n = 1$ transition has energy 74.8 eV higher than the photon emitted in the $n = 3$ to $n = 2$ transition. The ionization energy of the hydrogen atom is 13.6 eV. The value of Z is _______. **[JEE Adv 2018, P-2]**

20. A Hydrogen-like atom has atomic number Z. Photons emitted in the electronic transitions from level $n = 4$ to level $n = 3$ in these atoms are used to perform photoelectric effect experiment on a target metal. The maximum kinetic energy of the photoelectrons generated is 1.95 eV. If the photoelectric threshold wavelength for the target metal is 310 nm, the value of Z is _______. **[JEE Adv 2023, P-1]**
[Given: $hc = 1240$ eV-nm and $Rhc = 13.6$ eV, where R is the Rydberg constant, h is the Planck's constant and c is the speed of light in vacuum]

* * * * *

CHAPTER 22 — NUCLEI

MCQ with Single Option Correct

1. In the options given below, let E denote the rest mass energy of a nucleus and n a neutron. The correct option is :

[JEE Adv 2007, P-1]

(A) $E\left(^{236}_{92}U\right) > E\left(^{137}_{53}I\right) + E\left(^{97}_{99}Y\right) + 2E(n)$

(B) $E\left(^{236}_{92}U\right) < E\left(^{137}_{53}I\right) + E\left(^{97}_{99}Y\right) + 2E(n)$

(C) $E\left(^{236}_{92}U\right) < E\left(^{140}_{56}Ba\right) + E\left(^{94}_{36}Kr\right) + 2E(n)$

(D) $E\left(^{236}_{92}U\right) = E\left(^{140}_{56}Ba\right) + E\left(^{94}_{36}Kr\right) + 2E(n)$

2. A radioactive sample S_1 having an activity of 5 µCi has twice the number of nuclei as another sample S_2 which has an activity of 10 µCi. The half lives of S_1 and S_2 can be :

[JEE Adv 2008, P-2]

(A) 20 years and 5 years, respectively
(B) 20 years and 10 years, respectively
(C) 10 years each
(D) 5 years each

3. An accident in a nuclear laboratory resulted in deposition of a certain amount of radioactive material of half-life 18 days inside the laboratory. Tests revealed that the radiation was 64 times more than the permissible level required for safe operation of the laboratory. What is the minimum number of days after which the laboratory can be considered safe for use ?

[JEE Adv 2016, P-2]

(A) 64
(B) 90
(C) 108
(D) 120

4. The electrostatic energy of Z protons uniformly distributed throughout a spherical nucleus or radius R is given by

$$E = \frac{3}{5}\frac{Z(Z-1)e^2}{4\pi\varepsilon_0 R}$$

The measured masses of the neutron, ^1_1H, $^{15}_7N$ and $^{15}_8O$ are 1.008665 u, 1.007825 u, 15.000109 u and 15.003065 u, respectively. Given that the radii of both the $^{15}_7N$ and $^{15}_8O$ nuclei are same, 1u = 931.5 MeV/c^2 (c is the speed of light) and $e^2/(4\pi\varepsilon_0)$ = 1.44 MeV fm. Assuming that the difference between the binding energies of $^{15}_7N$ and $^{15}_8O$ is purely due to the electrostatic energy, the radius of either of the nuclei is :
(1 fm = 10^{-15} m)

[JEE Adv 2016, P-2]

(A) 2.85 fm
(B) 3.03 fm
(C) 3.42 fm
(D) 3.80 fm

5. In a radioactive sample, $^{40}_{19}K$ nuclei either decay into stable $^{40}_{20}Ca$ nuclei with decay constant 4.5×10^{-10} per year or into stable $^{40}_{18}Ar$ nuclei with decay constant 0.5×10^{-10} per year. Given that in this sample all the stable $^{40}_{20}Ca$ and $^{40}_{18}Ar$ nuclei are produced by the $^{40}_{19}K$ nuclei only. In time $t \times 10^9$ years, if the ratio of the sum of stable $^{40}_{20}Ca$ and $^{40}_{18}Ar$ nuclei to the radioactive $^{40}_{19}K$ nuclei is 99, the value of t will be :

[Given ln 10 = 2.3]   **[JEE Adv 2019, P-1]**

(A) 9.2
(B) 1.15
(C) 4.6
(D) 2.3

6. A heavy nucleus Q of half-life 20 minutes undergoes alpha-decay with probability of 60% and beta-decay with probability of 40%. Initially, the number of Q nuclei is 1000. The number of alpha-decays of Q in the first one hour is : **[JEE Adv 2021, P-1]**

(A) 50
(B) 75
(C) 350
(D) 525

MCQ with One or More than One Options Correct

7. Assume that the nuclear binding energy per nucleon (B/A) versus mass number (A) is as shown in the figure. Use this plot to choose the correct choice (s) given below :

[JEE Adv 2008, P-1]

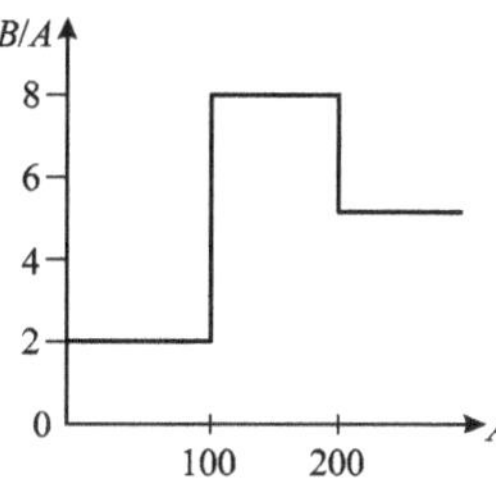

(A) Fusion of two nuclei with mass numbers lying in the range of $1 < A < 50$ will release energy

(B) Fusion of two nuclei with mass numbers lying in the range of $51 < A < 100$ will release energy

(C) Fission of a nucleus lying in the mass range of $100 < A < 200$ will release energy when broken into equal fragments

(D) Fission of a nucleus lying in the mass range of $200 < A < 260$ will release energy when broken into two equal fragments

8. A fission reaction is given by $^{236}_{92}U \rightarrow {}^{140}_{54}Xe + {}^{94}_{38}Sr + x + y$, where x and y are two particles. Considering $^{236}_{92}U$ to be at rest, the kinetic energies of the products are denoted by K_{Xe}, K_{Sr}, K_x (2 MeV) and K_y (2 MeV), respectively. Let the binding energies per nucleon of $^{236}_{92}U$, $^{140}_{54}Xe$ and $^{94}_{38}Sr$ be 7.5 MeV, 8.5 MeV and 8.5 MeV, respectively. Considering different conservation laws, the correct option(s) is (are) : **[JEE Adv 2015, P-2]**
(A) $x = n, y = n, K_{Sr} = 129$ MeV, $K_{Xe} = 86$ MeV
(B) $x = p, y = e^-, K_{Sr} = 129$ MeV, $K_{Xe} = 86$ MeV
(C) $x = p, y = n, K_{Sr} = 129$ MeV, $K_{Xe} = 86$ MeV
(D) $x = n, y = n, K_{Sr} = 86$ MeV, $K_{Xe} = 129$ MeV

9. In a radioactive decay chain, $^{232}_{90}Th$ nucleus decays to $^{212}_{82}Pb$ nucleus. Let N_α and N_β be the number of α and β^- particles, respectively, emitted in this decay process. Which of the following statements is (are) true ? **[JEE Adv 2018, P-2]**
(A) $N_\alpha = 5$ (B) $N_\alpha = 6$
(C) $N_\beta = 2$ (D) $N_\beta = 4$

10. A heavy nucleus N, at rest, undergoes fission $N \rightarrow P + Q$, where P and Q are two lighter nuclei. Let $\delta = M_N - M_P - M_Q$, where M_P, M_Q and M_N are the masses of P, Q and N, respectively. E_P and E_Q are the kinetic energies of P and Q, respectively. The speeds of P and Q are v_P and v_Q, respectively. If c is the speed of light, which of the following statement(s) is(are) correct ?
[JEE Adv 2021, P-2]

(A) $E_P + E_Q = c^2 \delta$ (B) $E_P = \left(\dfrac{M_P}{M_P + M_Q} \right) c^2 \delta$

(C) $\dfrac{v_P}{v_Q} = \dfrac{M_Q}{M_P}$

(D) The magnitude of momentum for P as well as Q is $c\sqrt{2\mu\delta}$, where $\mu = \dfrac{M_P M_Q}{(M_P + M_Q)}$

11. The binding energy of nucleons in a nucleus can be affected by the pairwise Coulomb repulsion. Assume that all nucleons are uniformly distributed inside the nucleus. Let the binding energy of a proton be E_b^p and the binding energy of a neutron be E_b^n in the nucleus. Which of the following statement(s) is(are) correct ?
[JEE Adv 2022, P-1]
(A) $E_b^p - E_b^n$ is proportional to $Z(Z-1)$ where Z is the atomic number of the nucleus
(B) $E_b^p - E_b^n$ is proportional to $A^{-1/3}$ where A is the mass number of the nucleus
(C) $E_b^p - E_b^n$ is positive
(D) E_b^p increases if the nucleus undergoes a beta decay emitting a positron

Matrix Match MCQ

12. Match **Coloum-I** of the nuclear processes with **Coloum-II** containing parent nucleus and one of the end products of each process and then select the correct answer using the codes given below the lists : **[JEE Adv 2013, P-2]**

Coloum-I	**Coloum-II**
(P) Alpha decay	(1) $^{15}_{8}O \rightarrow {}^{15}_{7}N + ...$
(Q) β^+ decay	(2) $^{238}_{92}U \rightarrow {}^{234}_{90}Th + ...$
(R) Fission	(3) $^{185}_{83}Bi \rightarrow {}^{184}_{82}Pb + ...$
(S) Proton emission	(4) $^{239}_{94}Pu \rightarrow {}^{140}_{57}La + ...$

Codes :

	P	Q	R	S
(A)	4	2	1	3
(B)	1	3	2	4
(C)	2	1	4	3
(D)	4	3	2	1

13. Match the nuclear processes given in **Column-I** with the appropriate option(s) in **Column-II**. **[JEE Adv 2015, P-1]**

Column-I	**Column-II**
(A) Nuclear fusion	(p) Absorption of thermal neutrons by $^{235}_{92}U$
(B) Fission in a nuclear reactor	(q) $^{60}_{27}Co$ nucleus
(C) β-decay	(r) Energy production in stars via hydrogen conversion to helium
(D) γ-ray emission	(s) Heavy water
	(t) Neutrino emission

14. List-I shows different radioactive decay processes and List-II provides possible emitted particles. Match each entry in List-I with an appropriate entry from List-II, and choose the correct option. **[JEE Adv 2023, P-1]**

List-I	**List-II**
(P) $^{238}_{92}U \rightarrow {}^{234}_{91}Pa$	(1) one α particle and one β^+ particle
(Q) $^{214}_{82}Pb \rightarrow {}^{210}_{82}Pb$	(2) three β^- particle and one α particle
(R) $^{210}_{81}Tl \rightarrow {}^{206}_{82}Pb$	(3) two β^- particles and one α particle
(S) $^{228}_{91}Pa \rightarrow {}^{224}_{88}Ra$	(4) one α particle and two β^- particle
	(5) one α particle and two β^+ particle

(A) $(P) \rightarrow (4), (Q) \rightarrow (3), (R) \rightarrow (2), (S) \rightarrow (1)$
(B) $(P) \rightarrow (4), (Q) \rightarrow (1), (R) \rightarrow (2), (S) \rightarrow (5)$
(C) $(P) \rightarrow (5), (Q) \rightarrow (3), (R) \rightarrow (1), (S) \rightarrow (4)$
(D) $(P) \rightarrow (5), (Q) \rightarrow (1), (R) \rightarrow (3), (S) \rightarrow (2)$

Comprehension based MCQ

Paragraph-1 (Q. No. 15-17)

Scientists are working hard to develop nuclear fusion reactor. Nuclei of heavy hydrogen, $^{2}_{1}\text{H}$, known as deuteron and denoted by D, can be thought of as a candidate for fusion reactor. The D-D reaction is $^{2}_{1}\text{H} + ^{2}_{1}\text{H} \rightarrow ^{3}_{2}\text{He} + n +$ energy. In the core of fusion reactor, a gas of heavy hydrogen is fully ionized into deuteron nuclei and electrons. This collection of $^{2}_{1}\text{H}$ nuclei and electrons is known as plasma. The nuclei move randomly in the reactor core and occasionally come close enough for nuclear fusion to take place. Usually, the temperatures in the reactor core are too high and no material wall can be used to confine the plasma. Special techniques are used which confine the plasma for a time t_0 before the particles fly away from the core. If n is the density (number/volume) of deuterons, the product nt_0 is called Lawson number. In one of the criteria, a reactor is termed successful if Lawson number is greater than 5×10^{14} s/cm^2.

In may be helpful to use the following : Boltzmann constant $k = 8.6 \times 10^{-5}$ eV/k; $\dfrac{e^2}{4\pi\varepsilon_0} = 1.44 \times 10^{-9}$ eVm :

[JEE Adv 2009, P-1]

15. In the core of nuclear fusion reactor, the gas becomes plasma because of :
(A) Strong nuclear force acting between the deuterons
(B) Coulomb force acting between the deuterons
(C) Coulomb force acting between deuteron-electron pairs
(D) The high temperature maintained inside the reactor core

16. Assume that two deuteron nuclei in the core of fusion reactor at temperature T are moving towards each other, each with kinetic energy 1.5 kT, when the separation between them is large enough to neglect Coulomb potential energy. Also neglect any interaction from other particles in the core. The minimum temperature T required for them to reach a separation of 4×10^{-15} m is in the range :
(A) 1.0×10^9 K $< T < 2.0 \times 10^9$ K
(B) 2.0×10^9 K $< T < 3.0 \times 10^9$ K
(C) 3.0×10^9 K $< T < 4.0 \times 10^9$ K
(D) 4.0×10^9 K $< T < 5.0 \times 10^9$ K

17. Results of calculations for four different designs of a fusion reactor using D-D reaction are given below. Which of these is most promising based on Lawson criterion ?
(A) Deuteron density = 2.0×10^{12} cm^{-3}, confinement time = 5.0×10^{-3} s
(B) Deuteron density = 8.0×10^{14} cm^{-3}, confinement time = 9.0×10^{-1} s
(C) Deuteron density = 4.0×10^{23} cm^{-3}, confinement time = 1.0×10^{-11} s
(D) Deuteron density = 1.0×10^{24} cm^{-3}, confinement time = 4.0×10^{-12} s

Paragraph-2 (Q. No. 18-19)

The β-decay process, discovered around 1900, is basically the decay of a neutron (n). In the laboratory, a proton (p) and an electron (e^-) are observed as the decay products of the neutron. Therefore, considering the decay of a neutron as a two-body decay process, it was predicted theoretically that the kinetic energy of the electron should be a constant. But experimentally, it was observed that the electron kinetic energy has a continuous spectrum. Considering a three-body decay process, i.e. $n \rightarrow p + e^- + \overline{v}_e$, around 1930, Pauli explained the observed electron energy spectrum. Assuming the anti-neutrino ($\overline{v}_e$) to be massless and possessing negligible energy, and the neutron to be at rest, momentum and energy conservation principles are applied. From this calculation, the maximum kinetic energy of the electron is 0.8×10^6 eV. The kinetic energy carried by the proton is only the recoil energy. **[JEE Adv 2012, P-2]**

18. What is the maximum energy of the anti-neutrino :
(A) Zero
(B) Much less than 0.8×10^6 eV
(C) Nearly 0.8×10^6 eV
(D) Much larger than 0.8×10^6 eV

19. If the anti-neutrino had a mass of 3 eV/c^2 (where c is the speed of light) instead of zero mass, what should be the range of the kinetic energy, K, of the electron :
(A) $0 \leq K \leq 0.8 \times 10^6$ eV
(B) $3.0 \, \text{eV} \leq K \leq 0.8 \times 10^6$ eV
(C) $3.0 \, \text{eV} \leq K < 0.8 \times 10^6$ eV
(D) $0 \leq K < 0.8 \times 10^6$ eV

Paragraph-3 (Q. No. 20-21)

The mass of a nucleus $^{A}_{Z}\text{X}$ is less than the sum of the masses of $(A$-$Z)$ number of neutrons and Z number of protons in the nucleus. The energy equivalent to the corresponding mass difference is known as the binding energy of the nucleus. A heavy nucleus of mass M can break into two light nuclei of masses m_1 and m_2 only if $(m_1 + m_2) < M$. Also two light nuclei of masses m_3 and m_4 can undergo complete fusion and form a heavy nucleus of mass M' only if $(m_3 + m_4) > M'$. The masses of some neutral atom are given in the table below.

[JEE Adv 2013, P-2]

$^{1}_{1}\text{H}$	$^{6}_{3}\text{Li}$	$^{152}_{64}\text{Gd}$
1.007825u	6.015123u	151.919803u
$^{2}_{1}\text{H}$	$^{7}_{3}\text{Li}$	$^{206}_{82}\text{Pb}$
2.014102u	7.016004u	205.974455u
$^{3}_{1}\text{H}$	$^{70}_{30}\text{Zn}$	$^{209}_{83}\text{Bi}$
3.016050u	69.925325u	208.980388u
$^{4}_{2}\text{He}$	$^{82}_{34}\text{Se}$	$^{210}_{84}\text{Po}$
4.002603u	81.916709u	209.982876u

$$(1u = 932 \text{ MeV/c}^2)$$

20. The correct statement is :

(A) The nucleus $_{3}^{6}\text{Li}$ can emit an alpha particle

(B) The nucleus $_{84}^{210}\text{Po}$ can emit a proton

(C) Deuteron and alpha particle can undergo complete fusion

(D) The nuclei $_{30}^{70}\text{Zn}$ and $_{34}^{82}\text{Se}$ can undergo complete fusion

21. The kinetic energy (in keV) of the alpha particle, when the nucleus $_{84}^{210}\text{Po}$ at rest undergoes alpha decay, is :

(A) 5319   (B) 5422
(C) 5707   (D) 5818

Integer Answer based Questions

22. To determine the half life of a radioactive element, a student plots a graph of $\ln\left|\dfrac{dN(t)}{dt}\right|$ versus t. Here $\dfrac{dN(t)}{dt}$ is the rate of radioactive decay at time t. If the number of radioactive nuclei of this element decreases by a factor of p after 4.16 years, the value of p is ?   **[JEE Adv 2010, P-2]**

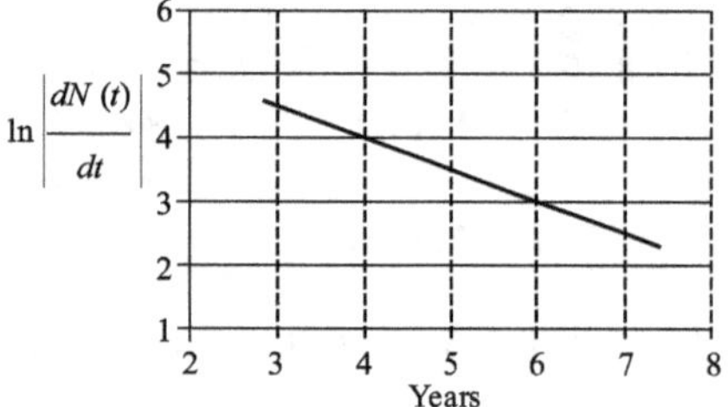

23. The activity of a freshly prepared radioactive sample is 10^{10} disintegrations per second, whose mean life is 10^{9} s. The mass of an atom of this radioisotope is 10^{-25} kg. The mass (in mg) of the radioactive sample is ?   **[JEE Adv 2011, P-1]**

24. A freshly prepared sample of a radioisotope of half-life 1386 s has activity 10^{3} disintegrations per second. Given that $\ln 2 = 0.693$, the fraction of the initial number of nuclei (expressed in nearest integer percentage) that will decay in the first 80 s after preparation of the sample is ?

25. A nuclear power plant supplying electrical power to a village uses a radioactive material of half life T years as the fuel. The amount of fuel at the beginning is such that the total power requirement of the village is 12.5% of the electrical power available from the plant at that time. If the plant is able to meet the total power needs of the village for a maximum period of nT years, then the value of n is ?   **[JEE Adv 2015, P-1]**

26. For a radioactive material, its activity A and rate of change of its activity R are defined as $A = -\dfrac{dN}{dt}$ and $R = -\dfrac{dA}{dt}$, where $N(t)$ is the number of nuclei at time t. Two radioactive sources P (mean life τ) and Q (mean life 2τ) have the same activity at $t = 0$. Their rates of change of activities at $t = 2\tau$ are R_P and R_Q, respectively. If $\dfrac{R_P}{R_Q} = \dfrac{n}{e}$, then the value of n is :

[JEE Adv 2015, P-2]

27. The isotope $_{6}^{12}\text{B}$ having a mass 12.014 u undergoes β-decay to $_{6}^{12}\text{C}$. $_{6}^{12}\text{C}$ has an excited state of the nucleus ($_{6}^{12}\text{C*}$) at 4.041 MeV above its ground state. If $_{6}^{12}\text{B}$ decays to $_{6}^{12}\text{C*}$, the maximum kinetic energy of the β-particle in units of MeV is ? ($1u = 931.5$ MeV/c², where c is the speed of light in vacuum)

[JEE Adv 2016, P-1]

28. ^{131}I is an isotope of Iodine that β decays to an isotope of Xenon with a half-life of 8 days. A small amount of a serum labelled with ^{131}I is injected into the blood of a person. The activity of the amount of ^{131}I injected was 2.4×10^{5} Becquerel (Bq). It is known that the injected serum will get distributed uniformly in the blood stream in less than half an hour. After 11.5 hours, 2.5 ml of blood is drawn from the person's body, and gives an activity of 115 Bq. The total volume of blood in the person's body, in liters is approximately (you may use $e^x \approx 1+x$ for $|x| \ll 1$ and $\ln 2 \approx 0.7$) ?   **[JEE Adv 2017, P-1]**

29. Suppose a $_{88}^{226}\text{Ra}$ nucleus at rest and in ground state undergoes a-decay to a $_{86}^{222}\text{Rn}$ nucleus in its excited state. The kinetic energy of the emitted a particle is found to be 4.44 MeV. $_{86}^{222}\text{Rn}$ nucleus then goes to its ground state by γ-decay. The energy of the emitted γ-photon is _______ keV.

[Given : Atomic mass of $_{86}^{222}\text{Rn}$ = 226.005 u, atomic mass of $_{86}^{222}\text{Rn}$ = 222.000 u, atomic mass of α particle = 4.000 u, $1u = 931$ MeV/c², c is speed of the light]   **[JEE Adv 2019, P-2]**

30. The minimum kinetic energy needed by an alpha particle to cause the nuclear reaction $_{7}^{16}\text{N} + _{2}^{4}\text{He} \rightarrow _{1}^{1}\text{H} + _{8}^{19}\text{O}$ in a laboratory frame is n (in MeV). Assume that $_{7}^{16}\text{N}$ is at rest in the laboratory frame. The masses of $_{7}^{16}\text{N}$, $_{2}^{4}\text{H}$ and $_{8}^{19}\text{O}$ can be taken to be $16.006u$, $4.003u$, $1.008u$ and $19.003u$, respectively, where $1u = 930$ MeV c⁻². The value of n is _______.   **[JEE Adv 2022, P-1]**

31. In a radioactive decay chain reaction, $^{230}_{30}$Th nucleus decays into $^{214}_{84}$Po nucleus. The ratio of the number of α to number of β^- particles emitted in this process is ________.

[JEE Adv 2022, P-2]

32. In a radioactive decay process, the activity is defined as $A = -\dfrac{dN}{dt}$, where $N(t)$ is the number of radioactive nuclei at time t. Two radioactive sources, S_1 and S_2 have same activity at time $t = 0$. At a later time, the activities of S_1 and S_2 are A_1 and A_2, respectively. When S_1 and S_2 have just completed their 3rd and 7th half-lives, respectively, the ratio A_1/A_2 is ________.

[JEE Adv 2023, P-2]

* * * * *

CHAPTER 23 ERRORS AND EXPERIMENTS

1. A student performs an experiment to determine the Young's modulus of a wire, exactly 2 m long, by Searle's method. In a particular reading, the student measures the extension in the length of the wire to be 0.8 mm with an uncertainty of $\pm\, 0.05$ mm at a load of exactly 1.0 kg. The student also measures the diameter of the wire to be 0.4 mm with an uncertainty of $\pm\, 0.01$ mm. Take $g = 9.8$ m/s^2 (exact). The Young's modulus obtained from the reading is : **[JEE Adv 2007, P-2]**
(A) $(2.0 \pm 0.3) \times 10^{11}\,$N/m^2
(B) $(2.0 \pm 0.2) \times 10^{11}\,$N/m^2
(C) $(2.0 \pm 0.1) \times 10^{11}\,$N/m^2
(D) $(2.0 \pm 0.05) \times 10^{11}\,$N/m^2

2. Students I, II and III perform an experiment for measuring the acceleration due to gravity (g) using a simple pendulum. They use different lengths of the pendulum and/or record time for different number of oscillations. The observations are shown in the table :

Least count for length = 0.1 cm
Least count for time = 0.1 s

Student	Length of the pendulum (cm)	Number of oscillations (n)	Total time for (n) oscillations(s)	Time period (s)
I	64.0	8	128.0	16.0
II	64.0	4	64.0	16.0
III	20.0	4	36.0	9.0

If E_I, E_{II} and E_{III} are the percentage errors in g i.e., $\left(\dfrac{\Delta g}{g} \times 100 \right)$ for students I, II and III, respectively : **[JEE Adv 2008, P-1]**
(A) $E_I = 0$
(B) E_I is minimum
(C) $E_I = E_{II}$
(D) E_{II} is maximum

3. A Vernier calipers has 1 mm marks on the main scale. It has 20 equal divisions on the Vernier scale which match with 16 main scale divisions. For this Vernier calipers, the least count is : **[JEE Adv 2010, P-2]**
(A) 0.02 mm
(B) 0.05 mm
(C) 0.1 mm
(D) 0.2 mm

4. The density of a solid ball is to be determined in an experiment. The diameter of the ball is measured with a screw gauge, whose pitch is 0.5 mm and there are 50 divisions on the circular scale. The reading on the main scale is 2.5 mm and that on the circular scale is 20 divisions. If the measured mass of the ball has a relative error of 2%, the relative percentage error in the density is : **[JEE Adv 2011, P-2]**
(A) 0.9 %
(B) 2.4 %
(C) 3.1 %
(D) 4.2 %

5. In the determination of Young's modulus $\left(Y = \dfrac{4MLg}{\pi l d^2} \right)$ by using Searle's method, a wire of length $L = 2$ m and diameter $d = 0.5$ mm is used. For a load $M = 2.5$ kg, an extension $l = 0.25$ mm in the length of wire is observed. Quantities d and l are measured using a screw gauge and a micrometer, respectively. They have the same pitch of 0.5 mm. The number of divisions on their circular scale is 100. The contributions to the maximum probable error of the Y measurement : **[JEE Adv 2012, P-1]**
(A) Due to the errors in the measurements of d and l are the same.
(B) Due to the error in the measurement of d is twice that due to the error in the measurements of l.
(C) Due to the error in the measurement of l is twice that due to the error in the measurements of d.
(D) Due to the error in the measurements of d is four times that due to the error in the measurement of l.

6. The diameter of a cylinder is measured using a Vernier callipers with no zero error. It is found that the zero of the Vernier scale lies between 5.10 cm and 5.15 cm of the main scale. The Vernier scale has 50 division equivalent to 2.45 cm. The 24th division of the vernier scale exactly coincides with one of the main scale divisions. The diameter of the cylinder is : **[JEE Adv 2013, P-1]**
(A) 5.112 cm
(B) 5.124 cm
(C) 5.136 cm
(D) 5.148 cm

7. Using the expression $2d \sin \theta = \lambda$, one calculates the values of d by measuring the corresponding angles θ in the range 0 to 90°. The wavelength λ is exactly known and the error in θ is constant for all values of θ. As θ increases from 0° : **[JEE Adv 2013, P-2]**
(A) The absolute error in d remains constant
(B) The absolute error in d increases
(C) The fractional error in d remains constant
(D) The fractional error in d decreases

8. There are two Vernier calipers both of which have 1 cm divided into 10 equal divisions on the main scale. The Vernier scale of one of the calipers (C_1) has 10 equal divisions that correspond to 9 main scale divisions. The Vernier scale of the other caliper (C_2) has 10 equal divisions that correspond to 11 main scale divisions. The readings of the two calipers are shown in the figure. The measured values (in cm) by calipers C_1 and C_2, respectively, are : **[JEE Adv 2016, P-2]**

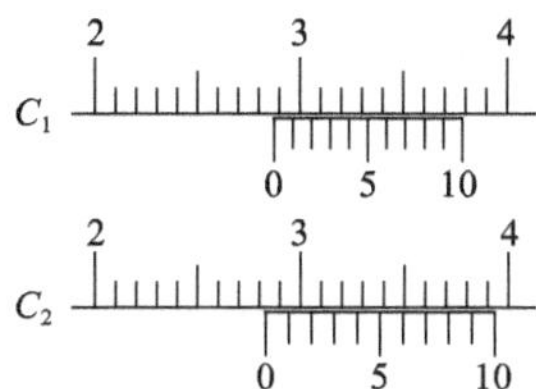

(A) 2.87 and 2.86   (B) 2.87 and 2.87
(C) 2.87 and 2.83   (D) 2.85 and 2.82

9. A person measures the depth of a well by measuring the time interval between dropping a stone and receiving the sound of impact with the bottom of the well. The error in his measurement of time is $\delta T = 0.01$ seconds and he measures the depth of the well to be $L = 20$ meters. Take the acceleration due to gravity $g = 10$ ms^{-2} and the velocity of sound is 300 ms^{-1}. Then the fractional error in the measurement, $\dfrac{\delta L}{L}$, is closest to :

[JEE Adv 2017, P-2]

(A) 0.2%   (B) 5%
(C) 3%   (D) 1%

10. The smallest division on the main scale of a Vernier calipers is 0.1 cm. Ten divisions of the Vernier scale correspond to nine divisions of the main scale. The figure below on the left shows the reading of this calipers with no gap between its two jaws. The figure on the right shows the reading with a solid sphere held between the jaws. The correct diameter of the sphere is :

[JEE Adv 2021, P-1]

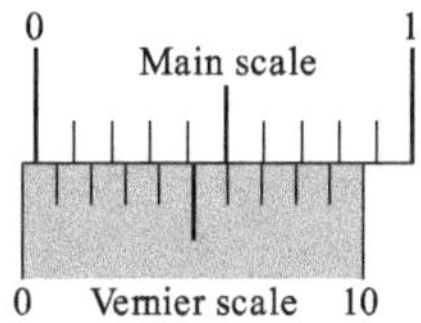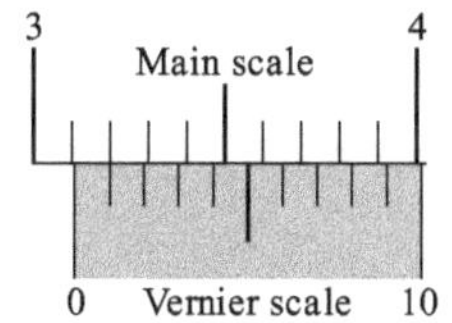

(A) 3.07 cm   (B) 3.11 cm
(C) 3.15 cm   (D) 3.17 cm

11. Area of the cross-section of a wire is measured using a screw gauge. The pitch of the main scale is 0.5 mm. The circular scale has 100 divisions and for one full rotation of the circular scale, the main scale shifts by two divisions. The measured readings are listed below.

Measurement Condition	Main scale reading	Circular scale reading
Two arms of gauge touching each other without wire	0 division	4 divisions
Attempt-1: With wire	4 divisions	20 divisions
Attempt-2: With wire	4 divisions	16 divisions

What are the diameter and cross-sectional area of the wire measured using the screw gauge? **[JEE Adv 2022, P-2]**
(A) 2.22 ± 0.02 mm, $\pi(1.23 \pm 0.02)$ mm^2
(B) 2.22 ± 0.01 mm, $\pi(1.23 \pm 0.01)$ mm^2
(C) 2.14 ± 0.02 mm, $\pi(1.14 \pm 0.02)$ mm^2
(D) 2.14 ± 0.01 mm, $\pi(1.14 \pm 0.01)$ mm^2

MCQ with One or More than One Options Correct

12. A student uses a simple pendulum of exactly 1 m length to determine g, the acceleration due to gravity. He uses a stop watch with the least count of 1 s for this and records 40 seconds for 20 oscillations. For this observation, which of the following statement(s) is (are) true ? **[JEE Adv 2010, P-1]**
(A) Error ΔT in measuring T, the time period, is 0.05 seconds
(B) Error ΔT in measuring T, the time period, is 1 second
(C) Percentage error in the determination of g is 5%
(D) Percentage error in the determination of g is 2.5%

13. Consider a Vernier callipers in which each 1 cm on the main scale is divided into 8 equal divisions and a screw gauge with 100 divisions on its circular scale with one division of length 0.5 mm. In the Vernier callipers, 5 divisions of the Vernier scale coincide with 4 divisions on the main scale and in the screw gauge, one complete rotation of the circular scale moves it by 100 divisions on the linear scale. Then : **[JEE Adv 2015, P-1]**
(A) It the pitch of the screw gauge is twice the least count of the Vernier callipers, the least count of the screw gauge is 0.01 mm.
(B) If the pitch of the screw gauge is twice the least count of the Vernier callipers, the least count of the screw gauge is 0.005 mm.
(C) If the least count of the linear scale of the screw gauge is twice the least count of the Vernier callipers, the least count of the screw gauge is 0.01 mm.
(D) If the least count of the linear scale of the screw gauge is twice the least count of the Vernier callipers, the least count of the screw gauge is 0.005 mm.

14. In an experiment to determine the acceleration due to gravity g, the formula used for the time period of a periodic motion is $T = 2\pi\sqrt{\dfrac{7(R-r)}{5g}}$. The values of R and r are measured to be (60 ± 1) mm and (10 ± 1) mm, respectively. In five successive measurements, the time period is found to be 0.52 s, 0.56 s, 0.57 s, 0.54 s and 0.59 s. The least count of the watch used for the measurement of time period is 0.01 s. Which of the following statement(s) is(are) true ?   **[JEE Adv 2016, P-2]**

(A) The error in the measurement of r is 10%

(B) The error in the measurement of T is 3.57%

(C) The error in the measurement of T is 2%

(D) The error in the determined value of g is 11%

Comprehension based MCQ

Paragraph-1 (Q. No. 15-16)

If the measurement errors in all the independent quantities are known, then it is possible to determine the error in any dependent quantity. This is done by the use of series expansion and truncating the expansion at the first power of the error. For example, consider the relation $z = x/y$. If the errors in x, y and z are Δx, Δy and Δz, respectively, then

$$z \pm \Delta z = \frac{x \pm \Delta x}{y \pm \Delta y} = \frac{x}{y}\left(1 \pm \frac{\Delta x}{x}\right)\left(1 \pm \frac{\Delta y}{y}\right)^{-1}$$

The series expansion for $\left(1 \pm \dfrac{\Delta y}{y}\right)^{-1}$, to first power in $\Delta y/y$, is $1 \mp (\Delta y/y)$. The relative errors in independent variables are always added. So the error in z will be

$$\Delta z = z\left(\frac{\Delta x}{x} + \frac{\Delta y}{y}\right)$$

The above derivation makes the assumption that $\dfrac{\Delta x}{x} \ll 1$, $\dfrac{\Delta y}{y} \ll 1$. Therefore, the higher powers of these quantities are neglected.   **[JEE Adv 2018, P-1]**

15. Consider the ratio $r = \dfrac{(1-a)}{(1+a)}$ to be determined by measuring a dimensionless quantity a. If the error in the measurement of a is $\Delta a(\Delta a/a \ll 1)$, then what is the error Δr in determining r ?

(A) $\dfrac{\Delta a}{(1+a)^2}$ (B) $\dfrac{2\Delta a}{(1+a)^2}$

(C) $\dfrac{2\Delta a}{(1-a^2)}$ (D) $\dfrac{2a\Delta a}{(1-a^2)}$

16. In an experiment the initial number of radioactive nuclei is 3000. It is found that 1000 ± 40 nuclei decayed in the first 1.0 s. For $|x| \ll 1$, $ln(1+x) = x$ up to first power in x. The error $\Delta\lambda$, in the determination of the decay constant λ, in s^{-1}, is :

(A) 0.04   (B) 0.03

(C) 0.02   (D) 0.01

Integer Answer based Questions

17. During Searle's experiment, zero of the Vernier scale lies between 3.20×10^{-2} m and 3.25×10^{-2} m of the main scale. The 20th division of the Vernier scale exactly coincides with one of the main scale divisions. When an additional load of 2 Kg is applied to the wire, the zero of the Vernier scale still lies between 3.20×10^{-2} m and 3.25×10^{-2} m of the main scale but now the 45th division of Vernier scale coincides with one of the main scale divisions. The length of the thin metallic wire is 2 m and its cross-sectional area is 8×10^{-7} m^2. the least count of the Vernier scale is 1.0×10^{-5} m. The maximum percentage error in the Young's modulus of the wire is :   **[JEE Adv 2014, P-1]**

18. The energy of a system as a function of time t is given as $E(t) = A^2 \exp(-\alpha t)$, where $\alpha = 0.2$ s^{-1}. The measurement of A has an error of 1.25%. If the error in the measurement of time is 1.50%, the percentage error in the value of $E(t)$ at $t = 5$ s is :   **[JEE Adv 2015, P-2]**

19. In an experiment for determination of the focal length of a thin convex lens, the distance of the object from the lens is 10 ± 0.1 cm and the distance of its real image from the lens is 20 ± 0.2 cm. The error in the determination of focal length of the lens is n %. The value of n is ______.   **[JEE Adv 2023, P-1]**

* * * * *

Ch-1 Units & Dimensions

1. **(A)** 2. (A, C, D) 3. (A, C) 4. (B, D)
5. (A, B, C) 6. (A, B) 7. (B, D)
8. [A (p, q); B (r, s); C (r, s); D (r, s)] 9. (C)
10. (D) 11. (3) 12. (3) 13. (4)

Ch-2 Kinematics & Laws of Motion

1. (B) 2. (D) 3. (B) 4. (B) 5. (A)
6. (A) 7. (D) 8. (D) 9. (C) 10. (A)
11. (A) 12. (A, C) 13. (C, D) 14. (A, B, C, D)
15. (A, C, D) 16. (C) 17. (B) 18. (B)
19. (B) 20. [A (p, t); B (q, s, t); C (p, r, t); D (q)]
21. (D) 22. (0.5) 23. (7.5) 24. (5) 25. (5)
26. (2) 27. (5) 28. (30) 29. (4) 30. (0.95)
31. (40)

Ch-3 Work Energy Power & Circular Motion

1. (D) 2. (C) 3. (C) 4. (D) 5. (A)
6. (D) 7. (B) 8. (B, C) 9. (A, B, D)
10. (A, D) 11. [A (p, s); B (q, r, s); C (s); D (q)]
12. [A (p, q, r, t); (B) (q, s); (C) (p, q, r, s); (D) (p, r, t)]
13. (A) 14. (B) 15. (A) 16. (0.18) 17. (0.16)
18. (8) 19. (4) 20. (5) 21. (5) 22. (2)
23. (0.75) 24. (3)

Ch-4 System of Particles and Rotational Motion

1. (D) 2. (A) 3. (C) 4. (C) 5. (D)
6. (B) 7. (C) 8. (C, D) 9. (A) 10. (C)
11. (A) 12. (B) 13. **(B)** 14. (A) 15. (A, D)
16. (B, C) 17. (A, C) 18. (A, C) 19. (D) 20. (A, B)
21. (D) 22. (A, B, D) 23. (A, D) 24. (A, C)
25. (A, B, D) 26. (A, B, C) 27. (C)
28. (A, C) 29. (A, C, D)
30. (A, C, D) 31. (B, D) 32. (A, B, C)
33. (A, B, D) 34. (A, B, C, D) 35. (B)
36. (D) 37. (D) 38. (C) 39. (A) 40. (B)
41. (B) 42. (B) 43. (C) 44. (D) 45. (D)
46. (C) 47. (A) 48. (D) 49. (D) 50. (C)
51. (A) 52. (B) 53. (4) 54. (4) 55. (9)
56. (3) 57. (5) 58. (8) 59. (4) 60. (2)
61. (7) 62. (6) 63. (0.75) 64. (2.09) 65. (25.60)
66. (49) 67. (0.52) 68. (2.86) 69. (30)

Ch-5 Gravitation

1. (C) 2. (A) 3. (B) 4. (B) 5. (C)
6. (C) 7. (D) 8. (A) 9. (B, D) 10. (B)
11. (A) 12. (B) 13. (6) 14. (3) 15. (2)
16. (7) 17. (9) 18. (2.30)

Ch-6 Mechanical Properties of Solids

1. (C) 2. (A, B) 3. (4) 4. (3) 5. (2)
6. (0.23 to 0.24)

Ch-7 Mechanical Properties of Fluids

1. (B) 2. (B) 3. (A) 4. (D) 5. (B)
6. (A, B, D) 7. (A, D) 8. (B, C) 9. (A, D)
10. (A, C) 11. (A, C, D) 12. (A, C, D)
13. (A, C) 14. (C, D) 15. (A) 16. (C) 17. (A)
18. (D) 19. (C) 20. (C) 21. (A) 22. (B)
23. (C) 24. (A) 25. (0.3) 26. (10) 27. (6)
28. (6) 29. (3) 30. (6) 31. (6.30) 32. (3.74)
33. (9) 34. (4) 35. (2.05) 36. (25)

Ch-8 Thermal Properties of Matter

1. (C) 2. (A) 3. (A) 4. (B) 5. (A)
6. (A) 7. (A, C, D) 8. (A, B, C, D)
9. (A, B, C) 10. (B, C, D) 11. (C)
12. (C) 13. (9) 14. (9) 15. (8) 16. (2)
17. (9) 18. (4) 19. (270) 20. (8.33)

Ch-9 Thermodynamics & Kinetic Theory of Gases

1. (C) 2. (D) 3. (A) 4. (D) 5. (D)
6. (D) 7. (D) 8. (C) 9. (C)
10. (A) 11. (C) 12. (B, D) 13. (B, D) 14. (A, B)
15. (A, B, D) 16. (B) 17. (B, C, D)
18. (A, B) 19. (A, C, D) 20. (B, C)
21. (A, B, C) 22. (B) 23. (B, C, D)
24. (B) 25. [A (q); B (p, r); C (p, s); D (q, s)]
26. [A (p, r, t); B (p, r); C (q, s); D (r, t)] 27. (A)
28. (B) 29. (A) 30. (D) 31. (C) 32. (C)
33. (C) 34. (D) 35. (B) 36. (B) 37. (D)
38. (D) 39. (A) 40. (B) 41. (47.1 or 60.8)
42. (18 or 30) 43. (4) 44. (2) 45. (900)
46. (1.77 to 1.78) 47. (6) 18. (121) 49. (2)

Ch-10 Oscillations

1. (D) 2. (D) 3. (A) 4. (A, D) 5. (A, D)
6. (B, D) 7. (A, B, D) 8. (C)
9. [A (q); B (q, r); C (p); D (r, q)] 10. (C) 11. (B, C)
12. (B) 13. (D) 14. (D) 15. (C) 16. (B)
17. (6) 18. (10)

Ch-11 Waves

1. (A)	**2.** (A)	**3.** (A)	**4.** (B)	**5.** (A)
6. (B)	**7.** (A, D)	**8.** (B, D)	**9.** (B, C)	**10.** (A, B)
11. (A, C, D)		**12.** (A, C, D)		
13. (A, B, D)		**14.** (A, B, C)		**15.** (A, D)

16. [**A** (p, t); **B** (p, s); **C** (p, s); **D** (q, r)]   **17.** (A)

18. (B)	**19.** (A)	**20.** (A)	**21.** (648)	**22.** (8.2)
23. (5)	**24.** (7)	**25.** (5)	**26.** (3)	**27.** (6)
28. (5)	**29.** (8.12 to 8.13)		**30.** (0.62 to 0.63)	
31. (5)				

Ch-12 Electric Charges, Field & Potential

1. (D)	**2.** (A)	**3.** (B)	**4.** (C)	**5.** (C)
6. (B)	**7.** (A)	**8.** (D)	**9.** (A)	**10.** (C)
11. (C)	**12.** (D)	**13.** (C)	**14.** (C)	**15.** (A)
16. (B)	**17.** (A)	**18.** (A, D)	**19.** (A, B, C, D)	
20. (C, D)	**21.** (A, C, D)		**22.** (A, B, C)	
23. (B, D)	**24.** (C, D)	**25.** (C)	**26.** (D)	**27.** (A, B)
28. (A, B)	**29.** (A, B, D)		**30.** (A, D)	**31.** (B, C)
32. (A, C, D)		**33.** (A, C)	**34.** (A, B, C)	
35. (B)	**36.** (A, C, D)		**37.** (B)	

38. [**A** (q); **B** (r, s); **C** (r, s); **D** (p, q, r)]

39. [**A** (p, r, s); **B** (r, s); **C** (p, q, t); **D** (r, s)]   **40.** (A)

41. (B)	**42.** (A)	**43.** (B)	**44.** (C)	**45.** (C)
46. (B)	**47.** (1.73)	**48.** (3)	**49.** (2)	**50.** (3)
51. (6)	**52.** (6)	**53.** (2)	**54.** (3.14)	**55.** (6.40)
56. (2)	**57.** (6)	**58.** (3)		

Ch-13 Capacitance

1. (C)	**2.** (A)	**3.** (D)	**4.** (C)	**5.** (B)
6. (B)	**7.** (B, D)	**8.** (A, D)	**9.** (D)	**10.** (C, D)
11. (1.33)	**12.** (0.67)	**13.** (2)	**14.** (1.50)	**15.** (1)
16. (1.30)	**17.** (8)			

Ch-14 Current Electricity

1. (A)	**2.** (C)	**3.** (C)	**4.** (D)	**5.** (C)
6. (B)	**7.** (C)	**8.** (C)	**9.** (A)	**10.** (A, D)
11. (A, B, C, D)		**12.** (B, D)	**13.** (A, B, D)	
14. (B)	**15.** (C, D)	**16.** (A, C)	**17.** (A, B, C, D)	
18. (A, C)	**19.** (A, B, C, D)		**20.** (A, B, C)	
21. (A, B, C, D)		**22.** (D)		

23. [**A** (S); **B** (Q); **C** (P); **D** (R)]   **24.** (B)   **25.** (A)

26. (A)	**27.** (B)	**28.** (4)	**29.** (5)	**30.** (5)
31. (1)	**32.** (5.55)	**33.** (0.26 to 0.27)		**34.** (3)
35. (5)				

Ch-15 Moving Charges and Magnetism

1. (A)	**2.** (D)	**3.** (C)	**4.** (A)	**5.** (D)
6. (B)	**7.** (B)	**8.** (B)	**9.** (C)	
10. (A, C, D)		**11.** (B, D)	**12.** (C, D)	**13.** (A, C)
14. (A, D)	**15.** (A, B, C)		**16.** (A, B)	
17. (A, B, D)		**18.** (A, B, D)		**19.** (A, C)
20. (A, B)	**21.** (C)	**22.** [**A** (q, r); **B** (p); **C** (q, r); **D** (q)]		
23. (A)	**24.** (C)	**25.** (D)	**26.** (A)	**27.** (B)
28. (B)	**29.** (B)	**30.** (C)	**31.** (B)	**32.** (A, D)
33. (A, C)	**34.** (7)	**35.** (6)	**36.** (5)	**37.** (7)
38. (3)	**39.** (2.00)	**40.** (4)		

Ch-16 Electromagnetic Induction

1. (B)	**2.** (B, D)	**3.** (A, C)	**4.** (B, D)
5. (B, C, D)		**6.** (A, D)	**7.** (A)

8. [**A** (p, q, t); **B** (q); **C** (s); **D** (s)]   **9.** (C)   **10.** (D)

11. (A)	**12.** (C)	**13.** (0.63)	**14.** (55)	**15.** (4)
16. (4)			

Ch-17 Alternating Current

1. (B)	**2.** (B)	**3.** (B, C)	**4.** (A, C)	**5.** (C, D)
6. (A, B)	**7.** (A, B, C)		**8.** (C, D)	**9.** (B, D)

10. [**A** (r, s, t,); **B** (q, r, s, t); **C** (p, q); **D** (q, r, s, t)]   **11.** (B)

12. (A)	**13.** (A)	**14.** (100)	**15.** (60)	**16.** (4)
17. (8)				

Ch-18 Ray Optics and Optical Instruments

1. (B)	**2.** (C)	**3.** (A)	**4.** (B)	**5.** (C)
6. (B)	**7.** (C)	**8.** (B)	**9.** (A)	**10.** (C)
11. (C)	**12.** (A)	**13.** (A)	**14.** (B)	**15.** (C, D)
16. (A, B, C)		**17.** (A, C)	**18.** (B)	
19. (A, B, D)		**20.** (A, D)	**21.** (A, C, D)	
22. (D)	**23.** (A, C, D)		**24.** (C, D)	**25.** (A, D)
26. (B, C, D)		**27.** (B, C)	**28.** (A, B)	
29. (A, C, D)		**30.** (B, D)	**31.** (C)	

32. [**A** (p, q, r, s); **B** (q); **C** (p, q, r, s); **D** (p, q, r, s)]

33. [**A** (p, r); **B** (q, s, t); **C** (p, r, t); **D** (q, s)]   **34.** (D)

35. (B)	**36.** (A)	**37.** (C)	**38.** (B)	**39.** (A, C)
40. (D)	**41.** (6)	**42.** (6)	**43.** (3)	**44.** (2)
45. (7)	**46.** (2)	**47.** (8)	**48.** (50.00)	**49.** (1.50)
50. (0.69)	**51.** (2)	**52.** (6)	**53.** (4)	**54.** (3)
55. (80 or 150 or 220)				

Ch-19 Wave Optics & Electromagnetic Wave

1. (D)	**2.** (B)	**3.** (B, C)	**4.** (A)	**5.** (A, B)
6. (A, B, C)		**7.** (C, D)	**8.** (C)	**9.** (A, B)
10. (A, D)		**11.** [**A** (p, s); **B** (q); **C** (t); **D** (r, s, t)]		
12. (A)	**13.** (C)	**14.** (B)	**15.** (3)	**16.** (130)

Ch-20 Dual Nature of Radiation, Matter & X-Rays

1. (A)	2. (B)	3. (A)	4. (B)	5. (B)
6. (A)	7. (B)	8. (A)	9. (A)	10. (A, C)
11. (A, C)	12. (A)	13. (A, C)	14. (B)	15. (3)
16. (7)	17. (7)	18. (1)	19. (2)	20. (2)
21. (24)	22. (1.00)	23. (9)	24. (6)	

Ch-21 Atoms

1. (B)	2. (A)	3. (A, B, D)		4. (B, C)
5. (B, C)	6. (A, D)	7. [A (q, r); B (q, s); C (p); D (q)]		
8. (C)	9. (C)	10. (A)	11. (A)	12. (B)
13. (D)	14. (D)	15. (B)	16. (C)	17. (6)
18. (5)	19. (3)	20. (3)		

Ch-22 Nuclei

1. (A)	2. (A)	3. (C)	4. (C)	5. (A)
6. (D)	7. (A, D)	8. (A)	9. (A, C)	
10. (A, C, D)		11. (A, B, D)		12. (C)
13. [(A) r, t; (B) p, q, s, t; (C) q, r, t; (D) p, q, r]				14. (A)
15. (D)	16. (A)	17. (B)	18. (C)	19. (D)
20. (C)	21. (A)	22. (8)	23. (1)	24. (4)
25. (3)	26. (2)	27. (9)	28. (5)	29. (135)
30. (2.32 to 2.33)		31. (2)	32. (16)	

Ch-23 Errors and Experiments

1. (B)	2. (B)	3. (D)	4. (C)	5. (A)
6. (B)	7. (D)	8. (C)	9. (D)	10. (C)
11 (C)	12. (A, C)	13. (B, C)	14. (A, C)	15. (B)
16. (C)	17. (4)	18. (4)	19. (1)	

* * * * *

Ch-1 Units & Dimensions

Sol. 1 Modulus of elasticity Y is expressed as
$$Y = c^\alpha h^\beta G^\gamma$$
In terms of dimensions of MLT, LHS & RHS of above expression is written as
$$[ML^{-1}T^{-2}] = [LT^{-1}]^\alpha [ML^2T^{-1}]^\beta [M^{-1}L^3T^{-2}]^\gamma$$
Comparing dimensions of M, L and T on both side gives

$$1 = \beta - \gamma \qquad \ldots(1)$$
$$-1 = \alpha + 2\beta + 3\gamma \qquad \ldots(2)$$
$$-2 = -\alpha - \beta - 2\gamma \qquad \ldots(3)$$
$$\Rightarrow \quad -3 = \beta + \gamma$$
$$\Rightarrow \quad 1 = \beta - \gamma$$
$$\Rightarrow \quad -2 = 2\beta$$
$$\Rightarrow \quad \beta = -1$$
$$\text{and} \quad \gamma = -2$$
$$\Rightarrow \quad -1 = \alpha - 2 - 6$$
$$\Rightarrow \quad \alpha = 7 \qquad \qquad \textbf{Ans. (A)}$$

Sol. 2 Energy of a photon of frequency v is given as
$$E = hv$$
$$\Rightarrow \quad [h] = [E][T]$$
$$[h] = ML^2\,T^2\,T$$
$$[h] = ML^2T^{-1}$$

Dimensions of speed of light is given as
$$[c] = LT^{-1}$$
Dimensions of universal gravitational constant is given as
$$[G] = [\frac{FR^2}{M^2}] = MLT^{-2}L^2M^{-2}$$
$$[G] = M^{-1}L^3T^{-2}$$
If dimensions of G, h and c are considered for defining unit of length, we have
$$[L] = [G]^\alpha [h]^\beta [c]^\gamma$$
$$\Rightarrow \quad [L] = [M^{-1}L^3T^{-2}]^\alpha [ML^2T^{-1}]^\beta [LT^{-1}]^\gamma$$
Comparing LHS and RHS, we get
$$\Rightarrow \quad 3\alpha + 2\beta + \gamma = 1$$
$$\Rightarrow \quad -\alpha + \beta = 0$$
$$\Rightarrow \quad -2\alpha - \beta - \gamma = 0$$
$$\Rightarrow \quad \gamma = -3\alpha$$
$$\Rightarrow \quad \beta = \frac{1}{2}, \alpha = \beta = \frac{1}{2}$$
$$\Rightarrow \quad L \propto \sqrt{G}$$
$$\text{and} \quad L \propto \sqrt{h}$$
Hence option (C) and (D) are correct.
If dimensions of G, h and c are considered for defining unit of mass, we have

$$[M] = [G]^\alpha [h]^\beta [c]^\gamma$$
$$\Rightarrow \quad [M] = [M^{-1}L^3T^{-2}]^\alpha [ML^2T^{-1}]^\beta [LT^{-1}]^\gamma$$
Comparing LHS and RHS, we get
$$\Rightarrow \quad -\alpha + \beta = 1$$
$$\Rightarrow \quad 3\alpha + 2\beta + \gamma = 0$$
$$\Rightarrow \quad -2\alpha - \beta - \gamma = 0$$
$$\Rightarrow \quad \gamma = -2\alpha - \beta$$
$$\Rightarrow \quad -\alpha + \beta = 1$$
$$\Rightarrow \quad \alpha + \beta = 0$$
$$\Rightarrow \quad 2\beta = 1$$
$$\Rightarrow \quad \beta = \frac{1}{2}, \alpha = -\frac{1}{2}, \gamma = \frac{1}{2}$$
$$\Rightarrow \quad M \propto \sqrt{c} \quad \text{and} \quad M \propto \frac{1}{\sqrt{G}}$$
Hence option (A) is correct and (B) is NOT correct.
$$\textbf{Ans. (A, C, D)}$$

Sol. 3 The dimensions of the given parameters in question are listed below

$$\mu_0 = MLT^{-2}A^{-2}$$
$$V = ML^2T^{-3}A^{-1}$$
$$\varepsilon_0 = M^{-1}L^{-3}T^4A^2$$
$$c = LT^{-1}$$
$$I = A$$
Substituting these values in each equation given in the options of question, we can see that options (A) and (C) are correct.
$$\textbf{Ans. (A, C)}$$

Sol. 4 **(B):** $\quad \epsilon = \dfrac{q^2}{Fm^2} \, ; \quad T = \theta$

$$n = \frac{1}{m^3} \, ; \quad k_B = \frac{Fm}{\theta}$$

Hence $\quad \epsilon k_B T = \dfrac{q^2}{m}$

$$\Rightarrow \quad \sqrt{\frac{\epsilon k_B T}{nq^2}} = \sqrt{\frac{q^2}{m \times \dfrac{1}{m^3} \times q^2}} = m = l$$

(D): $\quad \sqrt{\dfrac{q^2}{\epsilon k_B T n^{1/3}}} = \sqrt{\dfrac{m \times q^2}{q^2 \times \dfrac{1}{m}}} = \sqrt{m^2} = m = l$

(A): $\quad \sqrt{\dfrac{nq^2}{\epsilon_0 \, k_B T}} = \sqrt{L^{-3}L} = L^{-1}$

(C): $\sqrt{\dfrac{q^2}{\epsilon_0\, k_B T n^{2/3}}} = \sqrt{\dfrac{L}{L^{-2}}} = L^{3/2}$ **Ans (B, D)**

Sol. 5 As per situation given in the question we will consider mass and angular momentum dimensionless in new system so we use

$$\text{Mass} = M^0 L^0 T^0$$
$$mvr = M^0 L^0 T^0$$

substituting the dimensions of m, v and r in above relation, we have

$$M^0 \frac{L^1}{T^1} \cdot L^1 = M^0 L^0 T^0$$
$$\Rightarrow \qquad L^2 = T^1 \qquad\qquad \dots(1)$$

In SI units dimensions of force is given as
$$[F] = M^1 L^1 T^{-2}$$
In new system we use
$$[F] = M^0 L^1 L^{-4}$$
$$\Rightarrow \qquad [F] = L^{-3}$$
In SI units dimensions of energy is given as
$$[E] = M^1 L^2 T^{-2}$$
In new system we use
$$[E] = M^0 L^2 L^{-4}$$
$$\Rightarrow \qquad [E] = L^{-2}$$
As $\qquad \text{Power} = \dfrac{\text{Energy}}{\text{Time}}$

In SI units dimensions of power is given as
$$[P] = M^1 L^2 T^{-3} \qquad\qquad \text{(in SI)}$$
In new system we use
$$[P] = M^0 L^2 L^{-6}$$
$$\Rightarrow \qquad [P] = L^{-4}$$
In SI units dimensions of linear momentum is given as
$$[p] = M^1 L^1 T^{-1}$$
In new system we use
$$[p] = M^0 L^1 L^{-2}$$
$$\Rightarrow \qquad [p] = L^{-1} \qquad\qquad \textbf{Ans. (A, B, C)}$$

Sol. 6 As per information given in the question for dimensions of below given physical quantities, we use

Length $\qquad L = X^\alpha \qquad\qquad \dots(1)$

Speed $\qquad LT^{-1} = X^\beta \qquad\qquad \dots(2)$

Acceleration
$$LT^{-2} = X^p \qquad\qquad \dots(3)$$

Linear momentum
$$MLT^{-1} = X^q \qquad\qquad \dots(4)$$

Force
$$MLT^{-2} = X^r \qquad\qquad \dots(5)$$

Dividing equation-(1) by (2) gives
$$T = X^{\alpha - \beta}$$

From equation-(3), we have
$$\frac{x^\alpha}{x^{2(\alpha-\beta)}} = x^p$$
$$\Rightarrow \qquad \alpha + p = 2\beta$$
Thus option-(A) is correct.
From equation-(4), we have
$$M = x^{q-\beta}$$
From equation-(5), we have
$$x^q = x^r\, x^{\alpha-\beta}$$
$$\Rightarrow \qquad \alpha + r - q = \beta \qquad\qquad \dots(6)$$
Replacing value 'α' in equation-(6) from option (A), we get
$$2\beta - p + r - q = \beta$$
$$\Rightarrow \qquad p + q - r = \beta$$
Thus option-(B) is correct.
Replacing value 'β' in equation-(6) from option (A), we get
$$2\alpha + 2r - 2q = \alpha + p$$
$$\alpha = p + 2q - 2r$$
Thus option-(C) is not correct. $\qquad$ **Ans. (A, B)**

Sol. 7 Given physical quantity is called Poynting vector which is defined as the power of an electromagnetic wave per unit cross sectional area. This can be analysed by using dimensions of electric field, magnetic field and μ_0 also.

$$[S] = \frac{\text{Power}}{\text{Area}} = \frac{\text{Force}}{\text{Length} \times \text{Time}} \qquad \textbf{Ans. (B, D)}$$

Sol. 8 (A): By Newton's law of gravitation, we have
$$F = \frac{GM_e M_s}{R^2} \quad\Rightarrow\quad GM_e M_s = FR^2$$
SI unit of F is kg, SI unit of R^2 is m^2. So we use
$$GM_e M_s = Nm^2$$
Using dimensions on LHS & RHS, we have
$$[GM_e M_s] = [\text{work} \times \text{length}]$$
$$\Rightarrow \qquad [GM_e M_s] = [\text{coulomb} \times \text{volt} \times \text{metre}]$$
So option (p) and (q) correct match.

(B): RMS speed of gas molecules is given as
$$v_{\text{rms}} = \sqrt{\frac{3RT}{m}}$$
$$\Rightarrow \qquad \frac{3RT}{m} = v^2_{\text{rms}}$$
$$\Rightarrow \qquad \left[\frac{3RT}{m}\right] = m^2\, s^{-2}$$
To compare with other units we use energy of capacitor as
$$U = \frac{1}{2} CV^2 \ \text{kg m}^2\, \text{s}^{-2}$$
$$\Rightarrow \qquad \frac{\text{Farad(volt)}^2}{\text{kg}} = \left(\frac{m}{s}\right)^2 = \left[\frac{3RT}{m}\right]$$
$$\Rightarrow \qquad \left[\frac{3RT}{m}\right] = m^2\, s^{-2}$$
Correct option is (r) and (s)

(C) : Force on a charge in magnetic field is given as
$$F = qvB$$

$$\Rightarrow \qquad \frac{F^2}{q^2 B^2} = v^2$$

Dimensions of LHS and RHS can be written as

$$\left[\frac{F^2}{q^2 B^2}\right] = [\text{m}^2\,\text{s}^{-2}]$$

From option (B) $\text{m}^2\,\text{s}^{-2} = \text{farad } v^2\,\text{kg}^{-1}$

Here dimensions of $\left[\dfrac{F^2}{q^2 B^2}\right] = [\text{farad } v^2\,\text{kg}^{-1}]$

Correct option is (r) and (s)

(D) : Gravitational force on

$$F = \frac{G M_e M}{R_e^{\,2}}$$

$$\Rightarrow \qquad \frac{G M_e}{R_e} = \frac{F R_e}{M}$$

$$U = F.R = \text{Energy} = \text{kg m}^2\,\text{s}^{-2}$$

$$\Rightarrow \qquad \frac{F R_e}{m} = \frac{W}{M} = \text{m}^2\,\text{second}^{-2}$$

$$\left[\frac{G M_e}{R_e}\right] = \text{farad (volt)}^2\,(\text{kg})^{-1}$$

So correct match is (r) and (s).

$$\textbf{Ans. } [\mathbf{A}\,(p, q);\ \mathbf{B}\,(r, s);\ \mathbf{C}\,(r, s);\ \mathbf{D}\,(r, s)]$$

Sol. 9 The expression of velocity of wave is given as

$$c = \frac{E}{B}$$

Where c is the speed of light. Now using dimensions of physical quantities in above expression, we have

$$[E] = [c][B] = [LT^{-1}][B] \qquad\qquad \textbf{Ans. (C)}$$

Sol. 10 We have the speed of light in terms of permittivity and permeability, given as

$$c = \frac{1}{\sqrt{\mu_0\,\epsilon_0}}$$

$$\Rightarrow \qquad c^2 = \frac{1}{\mu_0\,\epsilon_0}$$

$$\Rightarrow \qquad [\mu_0] = [\epsilon_0^{-1}]\,[L^{-2}\,T^2] \qquad\qquad \textbf{Ans. (D)}$$

Sol. 11 The distance d can be considered to depend on ρ, S and f with dimensions a, b and c. So we have

$$d \ \alpha\ \rho^a S^b f^c$$

Substituting the dimensional relations of all physical quantities in above expression, we have

$$\Rightarrow \qquad [L] = [MT^{-3}]^a \left[\frac{M}{T^3}\right]^b \left[\frac{1}{T}\right]^c$$

$$\Rightarrow \qquad [LT^{-1}] = M^{a+b}\,L^{-3a}T^{\,-3b-c}$$

Comparing dimensions of LHS and RHS, we get

$$a + b = 0, \quad \Rightarrow b = -a$$

$$-3a = 1 \quad \Rightarrow a = -1/3$$

$$\Rightarrow \qquad b = 1/3$$

$$\Rightarrow \qquad n = 3 \qquad\qquad \textbf{Ans. (3)}$$

Sol. 12 Extension in steel wire is given as

$$\Delta l = \frac{Fl}{AY}$$

$$\Rightarrow \qquad \Delta l = \frac{1.2 \times 10 \times 1}{\pi \left(\dfrac{5 \times 10^{-4}}{2}\right)^2 \times 2 \times 10^{11}} = 0.3\,\text{mm}$$

So here the third marking of vernier scale will coincide with the main scale because least count of vernier scale is 0.1 mm.

$$\textbf{Ans. (3)}$$

Sol. 13 Substituting dimensions in given dimensional expression of magnetic field, we have

$$[B] = [e]^\alpha\,[m_e]^\beta\,[h]^\gamma\,[k]^\delta$$

$$\Rightarrow \quad [M^1 T^{-2} A^{-1}] = [AT]^\alpha\,[m]^\beta\,[ML^2 T^{-1}]^\gamma\,[ML^3 A^{-2} T^{-4}]^\delta$$

$$\Rightarrow \quad M^1 T^{-2} A^{-1} = m^{\beta+\gamma+\delta}\,L^{2r+3\delta}\,T^{\alpha-\gamma-4\delta}\,A^{\alpha-25}$$

Comparing dimensions in LHS and RHS gives

$$\beta + \gamma + \delta = 1$$

$$2\gamma + 3\delta = 0$$

$$\alpha - \gamma - 4\delta = -2$$

$$\alpha - 2\delta = -1$$

Solving above equations, we get

$$\alpha = 3,\ \beta = 2,\ \gamma = -3,\ \delta = 2$$

$$\Rightarrow \qquad \alpha + \beta + \gamma + \delta = 4 \qquad\qquad \textbf{Ans. (4)}$$

Ch-2 Kinematics & Laws of Motion

Sol. 1 As shown in diagram when particles are at a separation x from the centre line of force, resolving the forces along the line of force and perpendicular to it, let acceleration is 'a' when separation is $2x$, we get

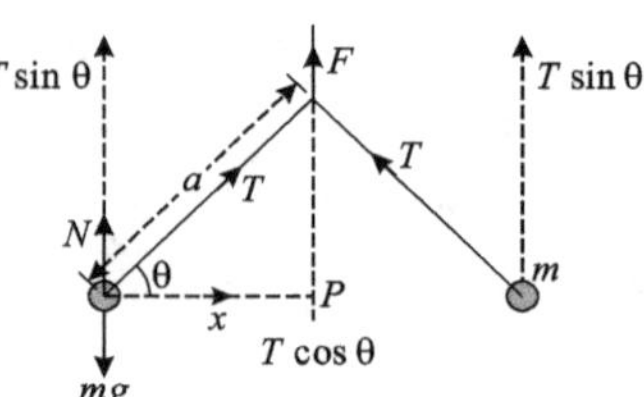

$$2T \sin\theta = F$$

and $\qquad T \cos\theta = ma$

$$\Rightarrow \qquad 2 \tan \theta = \frac{F}{mA}$$

$$\Rightarrow \qquad a = \frac{F}{2m}\left(\frac{x}{\sqrt{a^2 - x^2}}\right) \qquad \textbf{Ans. (B)}$$

Sol. 2 Momentum of particle is given as

$$\vec{P}(k) = A\,(\hat{i}\cos kt - \hat{j}\sin kt)$$

Thus force on particle is given as

$$F = \frac{dP(t)}{dt}$$

$$\Rightarrow \qquad F = \frac{d}{dt}A(-\hat{i}\cos kt - \hat{j}\sin kt)$$

$$\Rightarrow \qquad F = A\,(-\hat{i}\,k\sin kt - \hat{j}k\cos kt)$$

$$\Rightarrow \qquad F = Ak\,(-\hat{i}\,k\sin kt - \hat{j}\cos kt)$$

Let angle between two vector is θ, we use

$$\cos\theta = \frac{\vec{F}\cdot\vec{P}}{|F||P|}$$

As here for the force and momentum

$$\vec{F}\cdot\vec{P} = 0$$

$$\Rightarrow \qquad \cos\theta = 0$$

$$\Rightarrow \qquad \theta = 90° \qquad \textbf{Ans. (D)}$$

Sol. 3 Figure below shows the block placed on inclined plane with the weight acting on it.

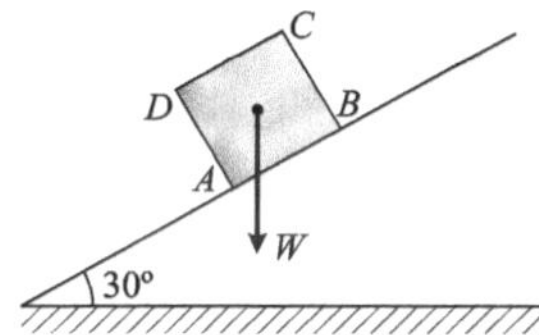

At $\theta = 30°$, being less than $45°$, the weight W of the block passes through the base AB, and hence the block will not topple.

For sliding the angle of repose for the friction coefficient given in question is $\phi = \tan^{-1}(\sqrt{3}) = 60°$. At $\theta = 30°$, being less than $60°$, it will not slide.

As θ is increased the block will topple when θ exceeds $45°$ when line of action of weight cross over left edge of the block so due to its anticlockwise torque it will topple. Thus option (B) is the only correct option. **Ans. (B)**

Sol. 4 Figure below shows the free body diagram of the bead sliding on the parabolic shaped wire. For motion of bead its equations can be written as

$$N\sin\theta = ma$$

$$N\cos\theta = mg$$

$$\Rightarrow \qquad \tan\theta = \frac{a}{g}$$

Slope of tangent in the figure can be calculated as

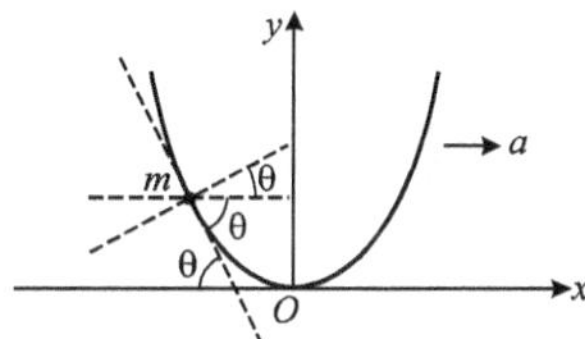

$$\text{Slope} = \tan(\pi - \theta) = -\tan\theta = \frac{dy}{dx} = 2kx$$

$$\Rightarrow \qquad x = -\frac{a}{2kg}$$

Hence option (B) is correct. **Ans. (B)**

Sol. 5 As in the given range of applied force block is in equilibrium so we use

$$P - mg\sin\theta + f = 0$$

$$\Rightarrow \qquad f = mg\sin\theta - P$$

Variation with P, it is an equation of straight line with negative slope hence option (A) is correct. **Ans. (A)**

Sol. 6 Time of flight for projectile is calculated as

$$\Rightarrow \qquad T = \frac{2u\sin\theta}{g} = 1\text{ s}$$

$$\Rightarrow \qquad T = \frac{2u\sin 45}{g} = 1\text{ s}$$

$$\Rightarrow \qquad u = \frac{g}{\sqrt{2}} = \sqrt{50}\text{ m/s} \qquad \textbf{Ans. (A)}$$

Sol. 7 Initially speed of bead is low so to balance inward radial component of gravity, normal force on bead will act in outward direction thus force by bead on wire is radially inward. After covering some angle speed of bead increases and after a point the contact force between wire and bead becomes zero and after this point force on bead is in radially inward direction so force by bead on wire acts radially outward. Thus option (D) is correct. **Ans. (D)**

Sol. 8 Figure below shows the forces acting on the stick. As the stick is at rest, net force along X & Y direction acting on stick is zero so we use along Y direction

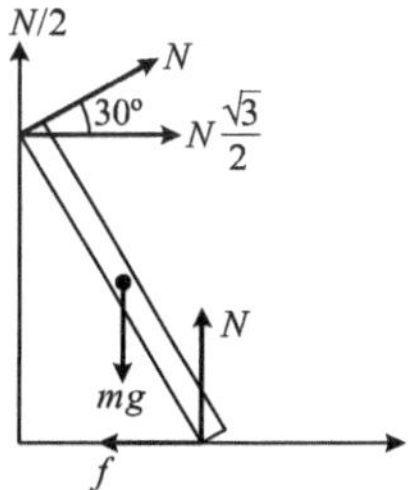

$$mg - N - \frac{N}{2} = 0$$

$$\Rightarrow \quad N = \frac{2}{3}mg = \frac{2}{3} \times 1.6 \times 10 = \frac{32}{3}\,\text{N}$$

Along X-direction, we use

$$f = \frac{N\sqrt{3}}{2} = \frac{16\sqrt{3}}{3}$$

Balancing torque about the bottom point of stick for its static equilibrium, we have

$$mg \times \left(\frac{l}{2}\sin 30°\right) = N \times \frac{h}{\cos 30°}$$

$$\Rightarrow \quad 4l = \left(\frac{32}{3}\right) \times \left(\frac{2h}{\sqrt{3}}\right)$$

$$\Rightarrow \quad \frac{h}{l} = \frac{3\sqrt{3}}{16} \qquad\qquad \textbf{Ans. (D)}$$

Sol. 9 Here we use

$$\vec{P} + b\,\vec{R} = \vec{S}$$

$$\Rightarrow \quad \vec{R} = \frac{\vec{S} - \vec{P}}{b}$$

Also w have

$$\vec{R} = \vec{Q} - \vec{P}$$

$$\Rightarrow \quad \frac{\vec{S} - \vec{P}}{b} = \vec{Q} - \vec{P}$$

$$\Rightarrow \quad \vec{S} - \vec{P} = b\,\vec{Q} - b\,\vec{P}$$

$$\Rightarrow \quad \vec{S} = b\,\vec{Q} + (1-b)\,\vec{P}$$

By use of section formula, directly we can also write as

$$\vec{S} = (1-b)\,\vec{P} + b\,(\vec{Q}) \qquad\qquad \textbf{Ans. (C)}$$

Sol. 10 Velocity components along x and y directions are given as

$$v_x = \alpha y$$
$$v_y = 2\alpha x$$

Acceleration of particle along x and y direction are given as

$$\frac{dv_x}{dt} = \alpha\frac{dy}{dt} = 2\alpha^2 x$$

and

$$\frac{dv_y}{dt} = 2\alpha v_x = 2\alpha^2 y$$

Force acting on the particle is calculated as

$$\vec{F} = m\vec{a} = 2m\alpha^2(x\hat{x} + y\hat{y}) \qquad \textbf{Ans. (A)}$$

Sol. 11 For inertial frame of reference by Newton's law we have

$$F = \frac{dp}{dt}$$

So for $\sum \vec{F}_{ext} = \vec{0}$ linear momentum will not change in time hence option (A) is correct. Due to internal forces kinetic energy of system can alter along with potential energy so that total energy will remain constant so options (B) and (D) are NOT be correct. External forces are zero but their couple can be non zero hence angular momentum must not remain constant in such cases. Thus option (C) is NOT be correct. **Ans. (A)**

Sol. 12 Figure below shows the free body diagram of the block

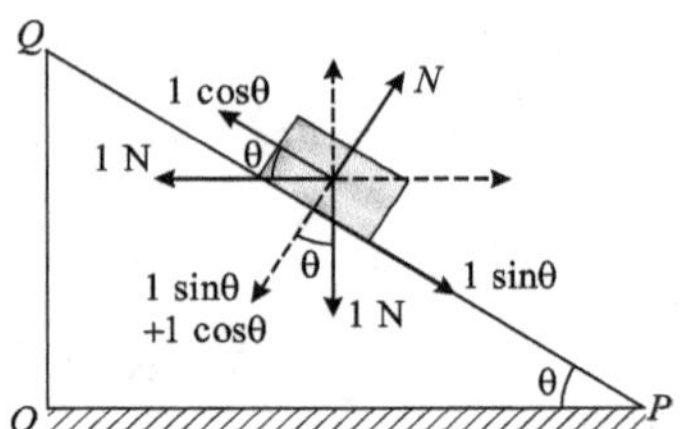

In above figure, if friction is zero and

$$\sin\theta = \cos\theta$$

$$\Rightarrow \quad \theta = 45°$$

Hence option (A) is correct. If friction on block acts toward P that it indicates $\sin\theta < \cos\theta$ thus $\theta < 45°$. Similarly if friction acts toward Q then it indicates $\sin\theta > \cos\theta$ thus $\theta > 45°$. Hence option (C) is also correct. **Ans. (A, C)**

Sol. 13 As ladder is in static equilibrium, μ_2 cannot be zero as if $\mu_2 = 0$, reaction on wall N_1 cannot be balanced and rod can not stay in equilibrium. Hence option (B) is NOT correct. We use balancing of forces acting on it in both X and Y direction. Forces in Y-direction are given as

$$\mu_1 N_1 + N_2 = mg$$

Forces in X-direction are given as

$$N_1 = \mu_2 N_2$$

$$\Rightarrow \quad N_2 = \frac{mg}{1 + \mu_1\mu_2}$$

For the case when $\mu_1 = 0$, the forces are shown in figure below. Balancing torques about point A for static equilibrium of rod, we have

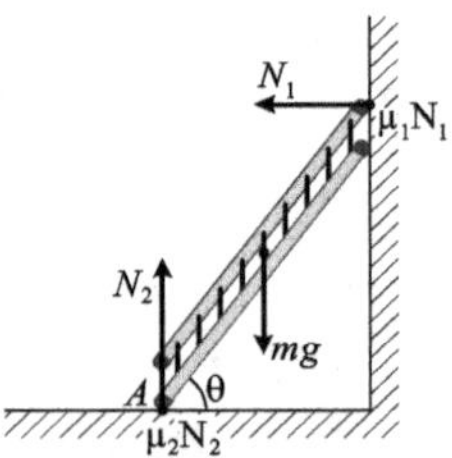

$$mg\left(\frac{L}{2}\cos\theta\right) = N_1\,(L\sin\theta)$$

$$\Rightarrow \quad \frac{mg}{2} = N_1\tan\theta \qquad\qquad \textbf{Ans. (C, D)}$$

Sol. 14 Path of particle follows

$$y = \frac{x^2}{2} \qquad \qquad \ldots(1)$$

At $t = 0$, given that at origin speed is 1 m/s. Differentiating equation-(1), with respect to time, we get

$$\frac{dy}{dt} = \frac{1}{2} \cdot 2x \, \frac{dx}{dt}$$

$$\Rightarrow \qquad v_y = x v_x$$

Further differentiating with respect to time, we get

$$a_y = \frac{dx}{dt} \cdot v_x + x a_x = v_x^2 + x a_x$$

$$a_y = v_x^2 + x a_x$$

We can check all given options now with above equations

Option-(A) : If $a_x = 1$ m/s^2 and particle is at origin ($x = 0$, $y = 0$), so we have

$$a_y = v_x^2$$

$$a_y = 1^2 = 1 \text{ m/s}^2$$

Hence option (A) is correct.

Option-(B) : If $a_x = 0$, we use

$$a_y = v_x^2 + x a_x$$

$$\Rightarrow \qquad a_y = v_x^2 = 1 \text{ m/s}^2$$

Hence option (B) is correct.

Option-(C) : At $t = 0$, $x = 0$, speed = 1 m/s

$$v_y = x v_x$$

$$v_y = 0$$

So at $t = 0$ particle has velocity only in x-direction hence option (C) is correct.

Option-(D) : At $t = 1$ s

$$a_y = v_x^2 + x a_x$$

$$\Rightarrow \qquad a_y = v_x^2$$

If $a_x = 0 \Rightarrow v_x = $ constant = 1 m/s

$$\Rightarrow \qquad a_y = 1^2 = 1 \text{ m/s}^2$$

At $t = 1$ s

$$v_y = 0 + a_y t = 1 \text{ m/s}$$

If θ is the angle made by velocity vector with x axis, we use

$$\Rightarrow \qquad \tan \theta = \frac{v_y}{v_x} = 1$$

$$\Rightarrow \qquad \theta = 45°$$

Hence option (D) is correct. **Ans. (A, B, C, D)**

Sol. 15 Situation of question is shown in figure below. When ball leaves the slide its horizontal speed is gained due to work done by gravity for a height h of slide so this speed is given as $\sqrt{2gh}$ hence option (A) is correct.

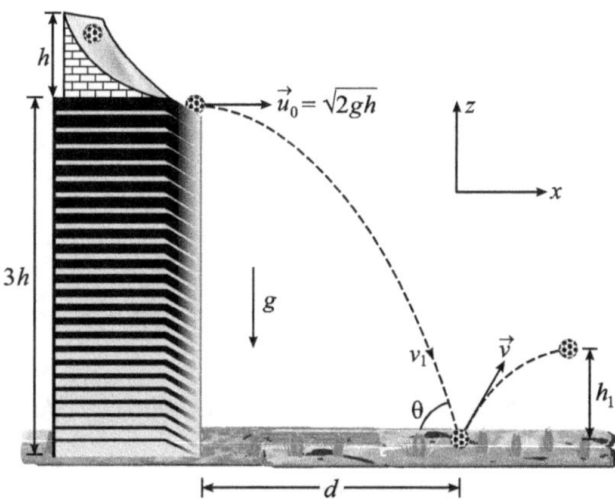

When ball strikes the ground, it attains a vertically downward velocity $\sqrt{6gh}$ so the velocity of ball when it strikes the ground is given as

$$\vec{v}_1 = \sqrt{2gh}\,\hat{i} - \sqrt{6gh}\,\hat{k}$$

Angle at which ball strikes the ground is given as

$$\tan \theta = \frac{\sqrt{6gh}}{\sqrt{2gh}} = \sqrt{3}$$

$$\Rightarrow \qquad \theta = 60°$$

Hence option (C) is correct.

When ball rebounds, its vertical component gets changed due to coefficient of restitution, given as

$$\vec{v} = \sqrt{2gh}\,\hat{i} + \sqrt{6gh} \times \frac{1}{\sqrt{3}}\,\hat{k}$$

$$\Rightarrow \qquad \vec{v} = \sqrt{2gh}\,\hat{i} + \sqrt{2gh}\,\hat{k} \qquad \ldots(1)$$

Hence option (B) is NOT correct.

After rebound ball's vertical velocity component is given by equation-(1) so vertical height attained by ball after collision is given as

$$h_1 = \frac{v_y^2}{2g} = \frac{2gh}{2g} = h$$

Horizontal range of ball d is calculated as

$$d = u_0 t = \sqrt{2gh} \times \sqrt{\frac{2 \times (3h)}{g}}$$

$$\Rightarrow \qquad d = \sqrt{2gh}\,\sqrt{\frac{6h}{g}} = 2\sqrt{3}\,h$$

$$\Rightarrow \qquad d = \frac{d}{h_1} = 2\sqrt{3}$$

Hence option (D) is correct. **Ans. (A, C, D)**

Sol. 16 Below figure shows the two cases as described in statement-I.

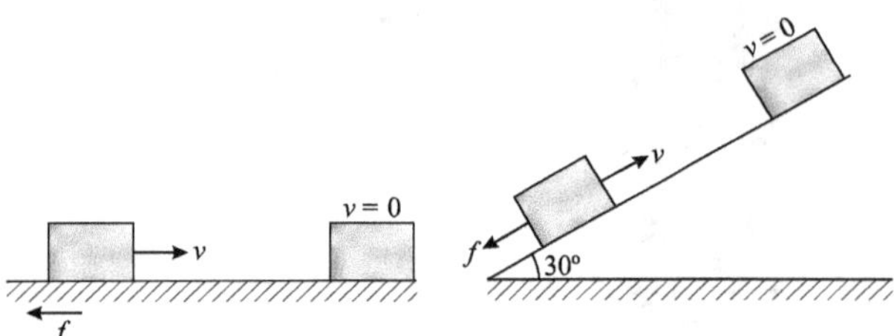

Decrease in mechanical energy in first case can be calculated as

$$E_i - E_f = \frac{1}{2}mv^2 - 0 = \frac{1}{2}mv^2$$

Decrease in mechanical energy in second case can be calculated as

$$E_i - E_f = \frac{1}{2}mv^2 - mgh$$

So statement-1 is correct.

In statement-2 μ does not depend on angle of inclination, it only depend on nature of surface so statement-2 is false.

Ans. (C)

Sol. 17 When the cloth is pulled with a high jerk then it can come out and all the dishes will remain at rest on table due to their inertia and cloth can be pulled out safely hence statement-1 is correct. Statement-2 is stating Newton's third law hence this is also correct but not related to statement-1 in any way.

Ans. (B)

Sol. 18 In pulling case when force is applied at some angle to horizontal on a body then its vertical upward component reduces the normal reaction so limiting friction will be less in the case compared to the case of pushing because in case of pushing the vertical component of force increases the normal reaction on body and the limiting friction increases.

So if is easier to pull a heavy object than to push so, statement-1 is right and of friction force also depends on the nature of surface. Therefore statement-1 & statement-2 both are right & statement-2 is not the correct explanation of statement-1

Ans. (B)

Sol. 19 Figure below shows the motion of an observer located at a distance y and it covered a distance d on ground so relative to object observer moves ahead a distance d. In this case the relative angular displacement of object with respect to observer is given as

$$\tan \theta = \left[\frac{d}{y}\right]$$

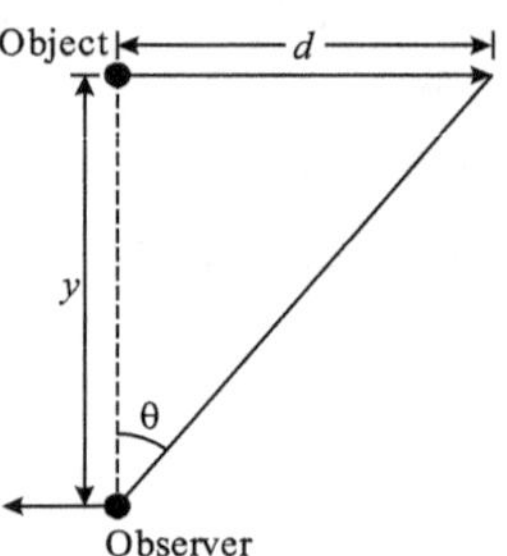

If y is very large, then angle subtended by displacement d in a given time is very small as compare to nearer object so distant object appear to be almost at rest to moving observer. Hence statement-1 is correct. By definition of relative velocity, statement-2 is also correct but there is no direct relation between these two statements.

Ans. (B)

Sol. 20 (p) As body is moving at uniform speed, its acceleration is zero hence force applied on it by X is equal to Mg. Gravitational potential energy of X is constant here as it is fixed. Due to some friction or opposing force speed of Y is kept constant hence total mechanical energy of system $(X + Y)$ must be decreasing. As line of weight of Y is not passing through P, its torque about P is non-zero. Hence option (A) and (C) are correctly related here.

(q) Force on Y by $Z = Mg$ downward and weight of Y is also Mg acting downward on X. As system is going up, gravitational potential energy of X continuously increases and mechanical energy of system is continuously increasing. Torque of weight of Y about point P in this case will be zero. Hence option (B) and (D) are correctly related here.

(r) Resultant of tension $\sqrt{2}\,T$ is acting on pulley Y and same is the force which is exerted by X on Y and tension is equal to Mg. System is going down so gravitational potential energy decreases and hence total mechanical energy also decreases. Line of action of weight does not pass through P hence torque is non zero. Hence option (C) is correctly related here.

(s) As sphere starts moving down means force on Y by X is less than Mg. Due to displacement of Y downward X is going up hence gravitational potential energy of X continuously increases and total mechanical energy of system remain constant as system is isolated. Line of action of weight of Y is not passing through P hence torque is non zero.

(t) As Y is falling down, due to the same reason as explained in previous part gravitational potential energy of X continuously increases. As Y is moving at terminal velocity, net force on it is zero hence force exerted by X on Y is equal to Mg. Due to viscous forces continuously total mechanical energy of system decreases. Line of action of weight of Y is not passing through P hence torque is non zero.

Ans. [A (p, t); B (q, s, t); C (p, r, t); D (q)]

Sol. 21 Blocks will move when

$$\mu m_2\, g\cos\theta = (m_1 + m_2)\, g\sin\theta$$

$$\frac{\mu m_2}{m_1 + m_2} = \tan\theta = 0.2$$

$$\Rightarrow \qquad \theta = 11.5°$$

P : $\theta = 5°$

Friction will be static and balancing the downward force so

$$f = (m_1 + m_2)g\sin\theta$$

Q : $\theta = 10°$

Friction will be static and balancing the downward force so

$$f = (m_1 + m_2)g\sin\theta$$

R : $\theta = 15°$

Blocks will move so friction will be kinetic friction

$$f = \mu(m_2 g\cos\theta)$$

S : $\theta = 20°$

Blocks will move so friction will be kinetic friction

$$f = \mu(m_2 g\cos\theta) \qquad\qquad\textbf{Ans. (D)}$$

Sol. 22-23 For the given projectile the time of flight is given as

$$t = \frac{2\times 5}{10} = 1\text{ s}$$

Range of projectile is given as

$$R = 5\sqrt{2}\cos 45° \times 1 = 5\text{ m}$$

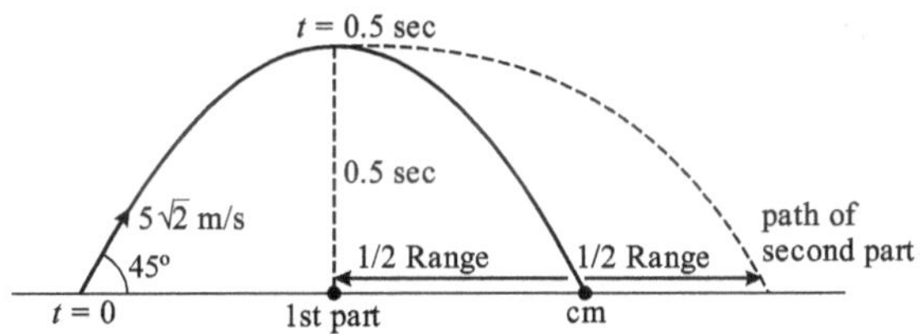

In this case center of mass follows the same projectile path and reach at ground 0.5 s after the splitting. If first part reaches ground at this instant, second also hit the ground at the same time instant so distance of second part from O is given from above figure as

$$x = \frac{3}{2}\times\text{Range}$$

$$\Rightarrow \qquad x = \frac{3}{2}\times 5\times 1 = \frac{15}{2} = 7.5\text{ m}$$

Sol. 24 The normal reaction acting on the block on inclined plane is given as

$$R = mg\cos\theta$$

Force required to slide the block up the plane is given as

$$F_{up} = mg\sin\theta + \mu mg\cos\theta$$

Force required to slide the block down the plane is given as

$$F_{down} = mg\sin\theta - \mu mg\cos\theta$$

It is given that

$$F_{up} = F_{down}$$

$$\Rightarrow \quad mg\sin\theta + \mu mg\cos\theta = 3\,(mg\sin\theta - \mu mg\cos\theta)$$

$$\Rightarrow \quad \frac{1}{\sqrt{2}} + \frac{\mu}{\sqrt{2}} = \frac{3}{\sqrt{2}} - \frac{3\mu}{\sqrt{2}}$$

$$\Rightarrow \quad \frac{4\mu}{\sqrt{2}} = \frac{2}{\sqrt{2}}$$

$$\Rightarrow \quad \mu = \frac{1}{2}$$

$$\Rightarrow \quad N = 10\mu = 10\left(\frac{1}{2}\right) = 5\text{ N} \qquad\textbf{Ans. (5)}$$

Sol. 25 Time taken by projectile is given as

$$T = \frac{2u\sin\theta}{g}$$

$$\Rightarrow \qquad T = \frac{2\times 10\times\sqrt{3}}{2\times 10} = \sqrt{3}\text{ s}$$

Range of projectile in inertial frame is given as

$$x = 10\cos 60°\,(T) = 5\sqrt{3}\text{ m}$$

In frame of train, we use

$$5\sqrt{3}\text{ m} = \frac{1}{2}a\,(\sqrt{3}\,)^2 + 1.15$$

$$a = 5\text{ m/s}^2 \qquad\textbf{Ans. (5)}$$

Sol. 26 As both balls are moving relative to rocket in it, relative speed of approach of the two balls is given as

$$0.2 + 0.3 = 0.5\text{ m/s}$$

Time after which the two balls will hit is given as

$$t = \frac{4}{0.5} = 2\text{ s} \qquad\textbf{Ans. (2)}$$

Sol. 27 Figure below shows the situation which observer in A sees the plane B and using this we analyse the relative motion of B with respect to A.

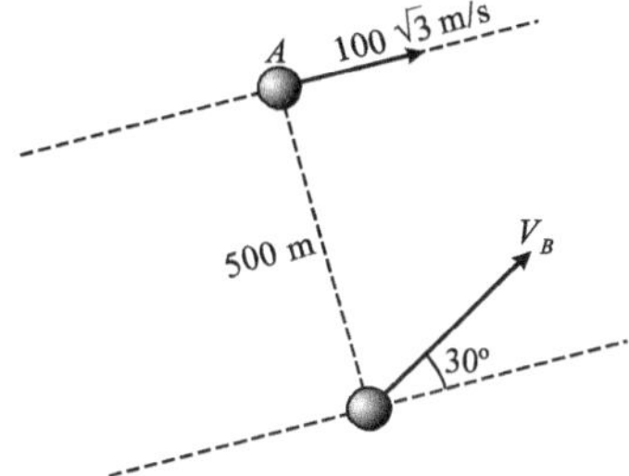

As V_{BA} is perpendicular to the line of motion of A so we use

$$V_B\cos 30° = 100\sqrt{3}$$

$$\Rightarrow \qquad V_B = \frac{100\sqrt{3} \times 2}{\sqrt{3}}$$

$$\Rightarrow \qquad V_B = 200 \text{ m/s}$$

Time after which collision may occur is given as

$$t_0 = \frac{500}{V_B \sin 30°}$$

$$\Rightarrow \qquad t_0 = \frac{500}{100} = 5 \text{ s} \qquad \textbf{Ans. (5)}$$

Sol. 28 Maximum height of projectile is given as

$$H = \frac{u^2 \sin^2 \theta}{2g} \quad \Rightarrow \quad 120 = \frac{u^2\left(\frac{1}{2}\right)}{2g}$$

$$\Rightarrow \qquad u^2 = 480\, g$$

$$\Rightarrow \qquad \text{KE}_{\text{initial}} = \frac{1}{2} m u^2 = 240\, mg$$

$$\Rightarrow \qquad \text{KE}_{\text{final}} = \frac{1}{2}(240\, mg) = 120\, mg$$

$$\Rightarrow \qquad \frac{1}{2} m v^2 = 120\, mg$$

$$\Rightarrow \qquad v^2 = 240\, g$$

After bounce, maximum height attained by the projectile is given as

$$H' = \frac{v^2 \sin^2 \theta}{2g} = \frac{240g \times \left(\frac{1}{4}\right)}{2g} = 30 \text{ m} \qquad \textbf{Ans. (30)}$$

Sol. 29 Average velocity of entire motion for long time as specified in the question is given as

$$\text{Average Velocity} = \frac{\text{Total displacement}}{\text{Total time}}$$

$$\text{Total time} = t_1 + t_2 + t_3 + \ldots = t_1 + \frac{t_1}{\alpha} + \frac{t_1}{\alpha^2} + \ldots$$

$$\Rightarrow \qquad \text{Total time} = \frac{t_1}{1 - \dfrac{1}{\alpha}}$$

If average velocity for the first projectile is v_1 then it is equal to $u\cos\theta$, thus for the second projectile it will be v_1/α, for the third projectile it will be v_1/α^2 and so on. Thus total displacement is given as

$$\text{Total displacement} = v_1 t_1 + \frac{v_1}{\alpha} \cdot \frac{t_1}{\alpha} + \ldots = \frac{v_1 t_1}{1 - \dfrac{1}{\alpha^2}}$$

Solving for average velocity, it gives

$$<v> = \frac{v_1 \alpha}{\alpha + 1} = 0.8\, v_1$$

$$\Rightarrow \qquad \alpha = 4 \qquad \textbf{Ans. (4)}$$

Sol. 30 Figure below shows the situation described in the question. After covering half the range $d/2$ particle reaches the maximum height h and now onward it will experience change in gravity from g to $g/0.81$ due to which its time of fall will decrease and it is given as

$$t_{\text{fall}} = \sqrt{\frac{2h}{g/0.81}} = 0.9\sqrt{\frac{2h}{g}}$$

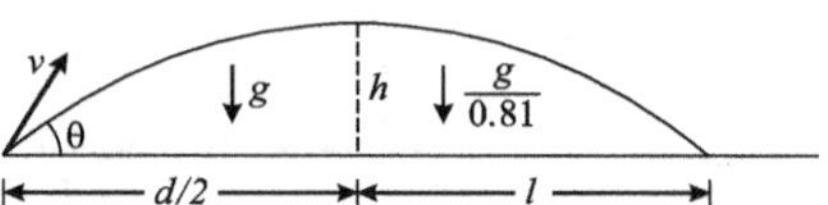

Original range of projectile was

$$d = u\left(2\sqrt{\frac{2h}{g}}\right)$$

Now new range of projectile will become

$$d' = \frac{d}{2} + u \times 0.9\sqrt{\frac{2h}{g}} = \frac{d}{2} + 0.9\frac{d}{2} = 0.95d$$

$$\Rightarrow \qquad n = 0.95 \qquad \textbf{Ans. (0.95)}$$

Sol. 31 Figure below shows the situation described in the question.

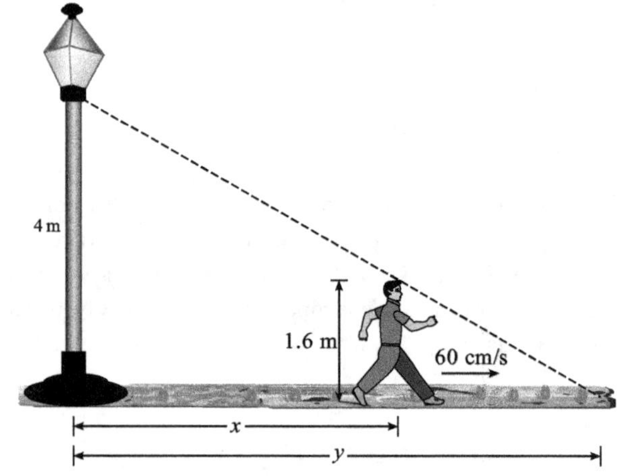

From the figure, using similar triangles we have

$$\frac{4}{y} = \frac{1.6}{y - x}$$

$$\Rightarrow \qquad 4y - 4x = 1.6y$$

$$\Rightarrow \qquad 2.4y = 4x$$

$$\Rightarrow \qquad x = 0.6y$$

Differentiating with respect to time gives

$$\frac{dx}{dt} = 0.6 \times \frac{dy}{dt}$$

$$\Rightarrow \qquad 60 = 0.6 \times \frac{dy}{dt}$$

$$\Rightarrow \qquad \frac{dy}{dt} = 100 \,\text{cm/s}$$

Speed of tip of person's shadow with respect to the person is given as

$$v_{sp} = 100 - 60 = 40 \,\text{cm/s} \qquad \textbf{Ans. (40)}$$

Ch-3 Work Energy Power & Circular Motion

Sol. 1 Minimum velocity required at A to reach point B is given as

$$V = \sqrt{5gL}$$

As total energy is conserved, we use

$$\frac{1}{2} m (5gL) = \frac{1}{2} m \left(\frac{5gL}{4}\right) + mgh$$

$$\Rightarrow \qquad h = \frac{15L}{8} = L + \frac{7L}{8}$$

$$\Rightarrow \quad L(1 - \cos\theta) = L\left(1 + \frac{7}{8}\right)$$

$$\Rightarrow \qquad \cos\theta = -\frac{7}{8} = -0.875$$

Here we can state that $\cos\theta$ is less than -0.707 (which is $-\frac{1}{\sqrt{2}}$).

This value is chosen to match with the most appropriate answer out of given options. So we use

$$-1 < \cos\theta < -\frac{1}{\sqrt{2}}$$

$$\Rightarrow \qquad \frac{3\pi}{4} < \theta < \pi \qquad \textbf{Ans. (D)}$$

Sol. 2 In the given situation when block B is displaced, supports will get displaced by the same distance as these do not have any mass so have no inertia and will move along with the spring and springs will not be elongated in any case. Here in the two directions total system energy will remain conserved when block B is at rest in either direction so we use

$$\Rightarrow \qquad \frac{1}{2} Kx^2 = \frac{1}{2}(4K)y^2$$

$$\Rightarrow \qquad x = 2y$$

$$\Rightarrow \qquad \frac{y}{x} = \frac{1}{2} \qquad \textbf{Ans. (C)}$$

Sol. 3 In the given situation the area under force time graph

gives the total impulse or the change in momentum of body which is calculated as

$$\text{Total Impulse } J = \left[\frac{1}{2} \times 3 \times 4\right] - \left[\frac{1}{2} \times 2 \times 1.5\right]$$

$$= 6 - 1.5 = 4.5 \,\text{N-s}$$

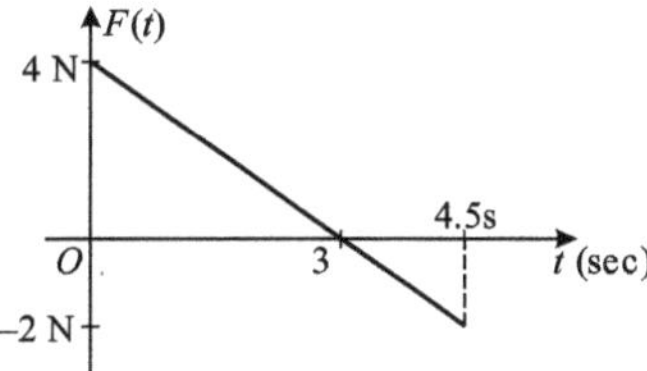

If velocity gained is v, we use

$$\Rightarrow \qquad 4.5 = 2\,[v - 0]$$

$$\Rightarrow \qquad v = \frac{4.5}{2} = 2.25 \,\text{m/s}$$

Thus gain in kinetic energy is given as

$$K = \frac{1}{2} \times 2\,(2.25)^2 = 5.06 \,\text{J} \qquad \textbf{Ans. (C)}$$

Sol. 4 According to free body diagram shown in figure below

$$T\cos\theta = mg$$

and $\quad T\sin\theta = m\omega^2 L \sin\theta$

$$\Rightarrow \qquad T = m\omega^2 L$$

$$\Rightarrow \qquad \omega_{max}^2 = \frac{T_{max}}{mL}$$

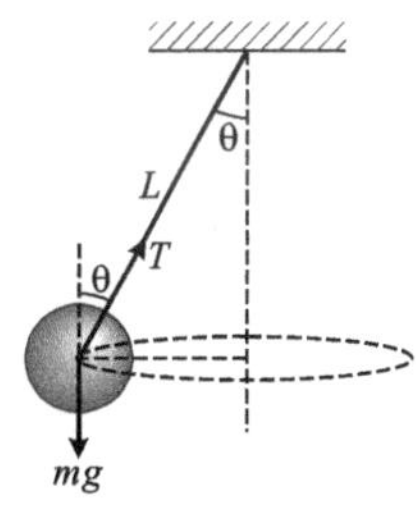

$$\Rightarrow \qquad \omega_{max} = \sqrt{\frac{T_{max}}{mL}} = \sqrt{\frac{324}{0.5 \times 0.5}} = \sqrt{324 \times 4}$$

$$\omega_{max} = 36 \,\text{rad/s} \qquad \textbf{Ans. (D)}$$

Sol. 5 Figure below shows the velocities of the two particles after time t.

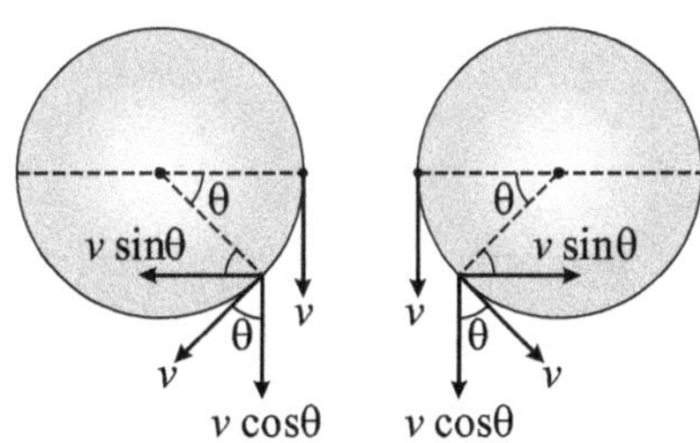

Relative velocity of one with respect to another is given as

$$v_r = |\,2\,v\sin\theta\,| = |\,2\,v\sin\omega t\,|$$

Corresponding graph is drawn as shown in below figure

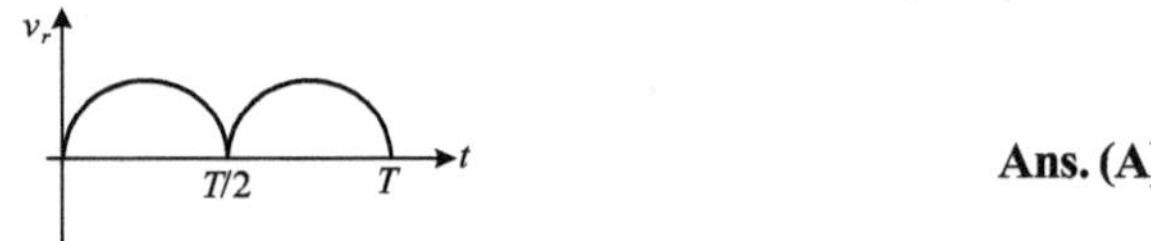

Ans. (A)

Sol. 6 For the small displacement $dr = dx\,\hat{i} + dy\,\hat{j}$ work done is given as

$$dW = \vec{F}\cdot\vec{dr} = \vec{F}\cdot(dx\,\hat{i} + dy\,\hat{j})$$

$$\Rightarrow \qquad W = K\int \frac{x\,dx}{(x^2+y^2)^{3/2}} + \frac{y\,dy}{(x^2+y^2)^{3/2}}$$

Using $x^2 + y^2 = a^2$, total workdone can be calculated as

$$W = \frac{K}{a^3}\int_a^0 x\,dx + \int_a^0 y\,dy = \frac{K}{a^3}\left(\frac{-a^2}{2} + \frac{a^2}{2}\right) = 0$$

Alternatively it can be directly stated that the force is a central force so it is acting in direction normal to velocity of particle so work done by this force is zero. **Ans. (D)**

Sol. 7 Kinetic energy in downward motion will increase as

$$K = \frac{1}{2}mv^2 = \frac{1}{2}mg^2t^2$$

$$\Rightarrow \qquad K\,\alpha\,t^2$$

During collision kinetic energy will convert into deformation energy for a short time during contact and regained as kinetic energy then ball bounces back and kinetic energy decreases so graph (B) is the most appropriate option here. **Ans. (B)**

Sol. 8 Potential energy of the particle is given as

$$V = \frac{kr^2}{2}$$

Force on particle is given as

$$F = -\frac{dV}{dr}$$

$$\Rightarrow \qquad F = -kr \text{ (towards centre)}$$

At $r = R$, the centripetal force for circular motion is provided by this force, so we use

$$kR = \frac{mv^2}{R}$$

Where v is speed of particle, given as

$$v = \sqrt{\frac{kR^2}{m}} = \sqrt{\frac{k}{m}}\,R$$

Angular momentum of the particle is given as

$$L = mvR = m\sqrt{\frac{k}{m}}\cdot R^2 = \sqrt{mK}\,R$$

So option (B) and (C) correct. **Ans. (B, C)**

Sol. 9 From the given expression of rate of change of kinetic energy which is given proportional to time, this indicates that kinetic energy will be proportional to square of time. Hence speed of particle is proportional to time which indicates constant acceleration so force will also be a constant. Thus options (A) and (B) are correct. As speed is directly proportional to time, distance will be dependent on square of time hence option (C) is wrong. As force is constant in magnitude and direction, it is a conservative force so option (D) is also correct.

Ans. (A, B, D)

Sol. 10 By applying conservation of energy at bottom point and point y, we have

$$\frac{1}{2}mv_0^2 = mgh + \frac{1}{2}mv_1^2$$

$$\Rightarrow \qquad v_1^2 = v_0^2 - 2gh \qquad\qquad \ldots(1)$$

Now at point y the centripetal force is provided by the components of mg, so we have

$$\Rightarrow \qquad mg\sin 30^\circ = \frac{mv_1^2}{R}$$

$$\Rightarrow \qquad v_1^2 = \frac{gR}{2}$$

$\Rightarrow$ From equation-(1), we get

$$\frac{gR}{2} = v_0^2 - 2gh$$

At point x and z of circular path, the points are at same height but less then h. So the velocity at these points will be more than that compared to point y.

So required centripetal force $\dfrac{mv^2}{r}$ at points x and z will be more. **Ans. (A, D)**

Sol. 11 (A) : Potential energy of the pendulum bob at a displacement x from mean position is given as

$$U = U_0 + \frac{1}{2}kx^2$$

Here U_0 is potential energy taken at mean position which can be considred any constant or zero.

Hence option (p) and (s) are correctly related.

(B) : In one dimensional motion when acceleration of particle is zero and body is moving with uniform velocity then its displacement is given as

$$x = x_0 + vt$$

Which is corresponding to options (q) and (r) and when body is having acceleration then displacement will vary as

$$y = x_0 + v_0 t + \frac{1}{2} a t^2$$

(C) : Range of projectile is given as $R \propto u^2$ hence option (s) is correctly related.

(D) : Square of time period of simple pendulum can be expressed as $T^2 \propto L$ hence option (q) is correctly related.

Ans. [A (p, s); B (q, r, s); C (s); D (q)]

Sol. 12 (A) : $U_i(x) = \dfrac{U_0}{2}\left[1 - \left(\dfrac{x}{a}\right)^2\right]^2$

Force acting on the particle is given as

$$F = -\frac{dU}{ax} = -\left[\frac{U_0}{2} \times 2\left(1 - \frac{x^2}{a^2}\right)\cdot\left(0 - \frac{2x}{a^2}\right)\right]$$

$$\Rightarrow \qquad F = -U_0\left(1 - \frac{x^2}{a^2}\right)\left(-\frac{2x}{a^2}\right)$$

$$\Rightarrow \qquad F(x = a) = 0$$

$$\Rightarrow \qquad F(x = 0) = 0$$

$$\Rightarrow \qquad F(x = -a) = 0$$

$$\Rightarrow \qquad F(x < a) = +ve$$

Hence option (p), (q), (r) and (t) are correctly related.

(B) : $\qquad U_2(x) = \dfrac{U_0}{2}\left(\dfrac{x}{a}\right)^2$

Force acting on the particle is given as

$$F = -\frac{dU_2}{dx} = -\frac{U_0}{2} 2\left(\frac{x}{a}\right) = -\frac{U_0 x}{a}$$

Hence option (q) and (s) are correctly related.

(C) : $\qquad U_3(x) = \dfrac{U_0}{2}\left(\dfrac{x^2}{a^2}\right)e^{-\frac{x^2}{a^2}}$

Force acting on the particle is given as

$$F = -\frac{dU_3}{dx} = -\left[\frac{U_0}{2} \times \frac{x^2}{a^2} e^{-\frac{x^2}{a^2}} \times \frac{-2x}{a^2} + \frac{U_0}{2} e^{-\frac{x^2}{a}} \times \frac{2x}{a^2}\right]$$

$$\Rightarrow F = -e^{-\frac{x^2}{x^2}} \frac{U_0}{2} \times \frac{2x}{a^2}\left[-\frac{x^2}{a} + 1\right]$$

$$\Rightarrow F = -\frac{U_0 x}{a^2} e^{-\frac{x^2}{a^2}}\left[1 - \frac{x^2}{a^2}\right]$$

$$\Rightarrow \quad F \text{ at } (x = a) = 0$$

$$\Rightarrow \quad F \text{ at } (x = 0) = 0$$

$$\Rightarrow \quad F \text{ at } (x = -a) = 0$$

F at $|x| < a$ will be negative.

Hence option (p), (q), (r) and (s) are correctly related.

(D) : $\qquad U_4(x) = \dfrac{U_0}{2}\left[\dfrac{x}{a} - \dfrac{1}{3}\left(\dfrac{x}{a}\right)^3\right]$

Force acting on the particle is given as

$$F_4 = -\frac{U_0}{2}\left[\frac{1}{a} - \frac{3}{3} \times \frac{x^2}{a^3}\right] = -\frac{U_0}{2a}\left[1 - \frac{x^2}{a^2}\right]$$

$$\Rightarrow \quad F \text{ at } (x = a) = 0$$

$$\Rightarrow \quad F \text{ at } (x = -a) = 0$$

Hence option (p), (r) and (t) are correctly related.

Ans. [A (p, q, r, t); (B) (q, s); (C) (p, q, r, s); (D) (p, r, t)]

Sol. 13 (P) : Velocity of particle is given as

$$\vec{v} = \frac{d\vec{r}}{dt} = \alpha\,\hat{i} + \beta\,\hat{j} = \text{Constant}$$

$$\Rightarrow \qquad \vec{a} = 0$$

Further $\vec{P} = m\vec{v}$ is constant and kinetic energy $K = \dfrac{1}{2}mv^2$ is also constant. As acceleration is zero. So force on particle will also be zero.

As $\qquad \vec{F} = -\left(\dfrac{\partial U}{\partial x}\hat{i} + \dfrac{\partial U}{\partial y}\hat{j}\right) = 0$

$$\Rightarrow \qquad U = \text{constant}$$

Also $E = K + U$ will also remain constant. As force is zero, net torque will also be zero hence we use

$$\frac{d\vec{L}}{dt} = \vec{\tau} = 0$$

Thus angular momentum will also remain conserved so for option (P) all 1, 2, 3, 4 and 5 are correctly related.

(Q) : Velocity of particle is given as

$$\vec{v} = \frac{d\vec{r}}{dt} = -\alpha\omega(\sin\omega t)\,\hat{i} + \beta\omega(\cos\omega t)\,\hat{j}$$

$$\Rightarrow \quad \vec{a} = \frac{d\vec{v}}{dt} = -\omega^2[\alpha\cos\omega t\,\hat{i} + \beta\sin\omega t\,\hat{j}] = -\omega^2\vec{r}$$

As acceleration vector is parallel to position vector of particle so force is also parallel to position vector hence, we use

$$\vec{\tau} = \vec{r} \times \vec{F} = 0$$

Hence angular momentum of the particle will remain conserved. Potential energy of particle is calculated as

$$\Delta U = \int \vec{F} \cdot d\vec{r} = \int_0^r m\omega^2 r\,dr = \frac{m\omega^2 r^2}{2}$$

$$\Rightarrow \qquad U \propto r^2$$

Magnitude of r is given as

$$r = \sqrt{\alpha^2 \cos^2\omega t + \beta^2 \sin^2\omega t}$$

Magnitude of v is given as

$$v = \omega\sqrt{\alpha^2 \sin^2 \omega t + \beta^2 \cos^2 \omega t}$$

Thus potential energy is given as

$$U = \frac{1}{2}m\omega^2 (\alpha^2 \cos^2 \omega t + \beta^2 \sin^2 \omega t)$$

Kinetic energy of particle is given as

$$K = \frac{1}{2}mv^2 = \frac{1}{2}m\omega^2 (\alpha^2 \sin^2 \omega t + \beta^2 \cos^2 \omega t)$$

From above expressions of potential and kinetic energy, we have expression of total energy given as

$$E = U + K = \text{constant}$$

Thus for option (Q), only 2 and 5 will remain conserved. Here only in answer option (A) it is given so no need to check other options in column-I. If students wish then continue to check and verify in the same manner we did here for (P) and (Q).

Ans. (A)

Sol. 14 By work energy theorem, we use

$$mg\,R \sin 30^\circ + W_f = \frac{1}{2}mv^2$$

$$\Rightarrow \qquad 200 - 150 = \frac{v^2}{2}$$

$$\Rightarrow \qquad\qquad v = 10\text{ m/s} \qquad\qquad \textbf{Ans. (B)}$$

Sol. 15 Net force on block at point Q can be calculated from the figure given below as

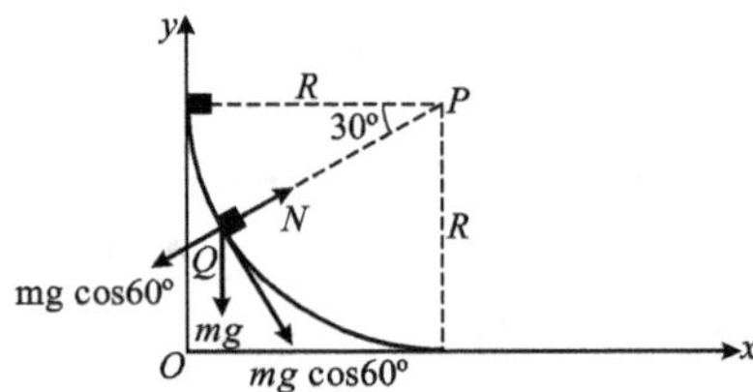

$$N - mg \cos 60^\circ = \frac{mv^2}{R}$$

$$\Rightarrow \qquad N = 5 + \frac{5}{2} = 7.5\text{ N} \qquad\qquad \textbf{Ans. (A)}$$

Sol. 16 Figure below shows the situation described in the question.

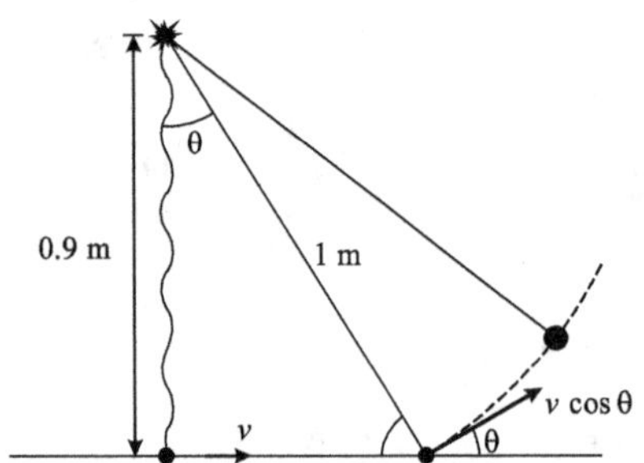

When the bob breaks off the ground, angle θ is given as

$$\cos \theta = \frac{0.9}{1} = \frac{9}{10}$$

Initial speed of bob v is given as

$$P = mv$$

$$\Rightarrow \qquad 0.2 = 0.1\,v$$

$$\Rightarrow \qquad v = 2\text{ m/s}$$

Velocity just after string become taut will be $v \cos \theta$ thus angular momentum of the bob just before it lifts off from the ground is given as

$$J = m(v\cos\theta)r = (0.1)(2)(0.9)(1) = 0.18 \qquad \textbf{Ans. (0.18)}$$

Sol. 17 The kinetic energy just after the bob lifts off the ground is given as

$$K = \frac{1}{2}m(v \cos \theta)^2$$

$$\Rightarrow \qquad K = \frac{1}{2}(0.1)\left(2 \times \frac{9}{10}\right)^2$$

$$\Rightarrow \qquad K = \frac{1}{20}\frac{(18)^2}{100} = 0.16 \qquad \textbf{Ans. (0.16)}$$

Sol. 18 Acceleration of blocks is given as

$$a = \frac{(m_2 - m_1)g}{m_1 + m_2} = \frac{0.36 \times 10}{1.08} = \frac{10}{3}\text{ m/s}^2$$

Displacement of blocks during f.0irst second is given as

$$s = \frac{1}{2}gt^2 = \frac{1}{2} \times \frac{10}{3} \times (1)^2 = \frac{5}{3}\text{ m}$$

Tension in string of given Atwood's machine is given as

$$T = \frac{2m_1 m_2 g}{m_1 + m_2} = \frac{2 \times 0.36 \times 0.72 \times 10}{3 \times 0.36}\text{ N}$$

$$\Rightarrow \qquad T = 2 \times 2.4\text{ N} = 4.8\text{ N}$$

Work done by string on block of mass 0.36 kg is given as

$$\Rightarrow \qquad W = T.S = 1.6 \times \frac{5}{3} = 4.8 \times \frac{5}{3} = 8\text{ J} \qquad \textbf{Ans. (8)}$$

Sol. 19 Block comes to rest after losing its kinetic energy in work done against friction and a part of it goes into the potential energy of spring.

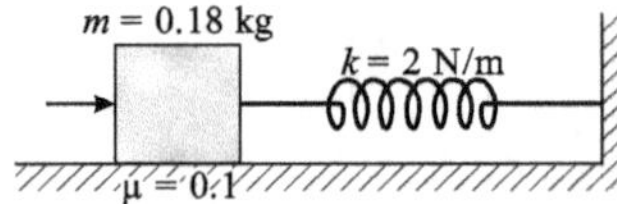

Using work energy theorem, from the instant of impulse to the time it comes to rest, we use

$$\frac{1}{2}mu^2 = \frac{1}{2}Kx^2 + \mu mg\,(x)$$

$$\Rightarrow \quad \frac{1}{2}(0.18)u^2 = \frac{1}{2} \times 2 \times 36 \times 10^{-4} + 0.1 \times 0.18 \times 10 \times 0.06$$

$$\Rightarrow \quad u = 0.4 \text{ m/s}$$

$$\Rightarrow \quad u = \frac{4}{10} \text{ m/s} \qquad \qquad \textbf{Ans. (4)}$$

Sol. 20 For a constant power force, the energy imparted by the force in 5 s is given as

$$E = 0.5 \times 5 = 2.5 = K_f - K_i$$

$$\Rightarrow \quad 2.5 = \frac{M}{2}(v_f^2 - v_i^2)$$

$$\Rightarrow \quad v_f = 5 \text{ m/s} \qquad \qquad \textbf{Ans. (5)}$$

Sol. 21 By work energy theorem in motion of block from P to Q, we have

$$\Rightarrow \quad W = -mgh + Fx$$

$$\Rightarrow \quad W = -10 \times 4 + 18 \times 5$$

$$\Rightarrow \quad W = 50 \text{ J}$$

$$\Rightarrow \quad n = 5 \qquad \qquad \textbf{Ans. (5)}$$

Sol. 22 Substituting the resultant magnitude in the given relation

$$|\vec{A} + \vec{B}| = \sqrt{3}|\vec{A} - \vec{B}|$$

$$\Rightarrow \quad |a\hat{i} + a\cos\omega t\,\hat{i} + a\sin\omega t\,\hat{j}| = \sqrt{3}|a\hat{i} - a\cos\omega t\,\hat{i} - a\sin\omega t\,\hat{j}|$$

$$\Rightarrow \quad |(1 + \cos\omega t)\hat{i} + \sin\omega t\,\hat{j}| = \sqrt{3}|(1 - \cos\omega t)\hat{i} - \sin\omega t\,\hat{j}|$$

$$\Rightarrow \quad \sqrt{2 + 2\cos\omega t} = \sqrt{3}\sqrt{2 - 2\cos\omega t}$$

$$\Rightarrow \quad 1 + \cos\omega t = 3(1 - \cos\omega t)$$

$$\Rightarrow \quad 4\cos\omega t = 2$$

$$\Rightarrow \quad \cos\omega t = \frac{1}{2}$$

$$\Rightarrow \quad \omega t = \frac{\pi}{3}$$

$$\Rightarrow \quad \frac{\pi}{6} \times \tau = \frac{\pi}{3}$$

$$\Rightarrow \quad \tau = 2 \text{ s} \qquad \qquad \textbf{Ans. (2)}$$

Sol. 23 Force on the particle is given as

$$F = (\alpha y\,\hat{i} + 2\alpha x\,\hat{j})$$

Here work done along AB is given as

$$W_{AB} = (-1\hat{i}) \cdot (1\hat{i}) = -1 \text{ J}$$

Work done along BC is given as

$$W_{BC} = 1 \text{ J}$$

Work done along CD is given as

$$W_{CD} = 0.25 \text{ J}$$

Work done along DE is given as

$$W_{DE} = 0.5 \text{ J}$$

Work done along EF and FA is given as

$$W_{EF} = W_{FA} = 0 \text{ J}$$

$$\Rightarrow \quad \text{Net work done in cycle} = 0.75 \text{ J} \qquad \textbf{Ans. (0.75)}$$

Sol. 24 As the given force is central force and its line of action is passing through origin so torque about origin is zero so angular momentum about origin remains conserved. At $t = 0$ position vector of particle and velocity are given as

$$\vec{r} = \left(\frac{1}{2}\hat{i} + \sqrt{2}\hat{j}\right)\text{m}$$

and

$$\vec{v} = \left(-\sqrt{2}\hat{i} + \sqrt{2}\hat{j} + \frac{2}{\pi}\hat{k}\right)\text{m/s}$$

If at any instant position and velocity coordinates are (x, y, z) and (v_x, v_y, v_z) then angular momentum of particle is given as

$$\overrightarrow{L_0} = m(\vec{r} \times \vec{v})$$

$$\Rightarrow \quad \overrightarrow{L_0} = (yv_z - zv_y)\hat{i} + (zv_x - xv_z)\hat{j} + (xv_y - yv_x)\hat{k} \,...(1)$$

From the given values of $\vec{r}$ and $\vec{v}$ and taking $m = 1$ kg, we have

$$\overrightarrow{L_0} = \hat{i}\left[\sqrt{2} \times \frac{2}{\pi}\right] - \hat{j}\left[\frac{\sqrt{2}}{\pi}\right] + \hat{k}\,[1 + 2] \qquad ...(2)$$

Comparing equations (1) and (2), we have

$$xv_y - yv_x = 3 \qquad \qquad \textbf{Ans. (3)}$$

Ch-4 System of Particles and Rotational Motion

Sol. 1 Using conservation of energy for object rolling in upward direction, all the kinetic energy transforms to potential energy at maximum height so, we use

$$KE_i = PE_F$$

$$\Rightarrow \quad KE_{\text{translational}} + KE_{\text{rotational}} = PE\,(Mgh_{\text{Max}})$$

$$\Rightarrow \quad \frac{1}{2}mv^2 + \frac{1}{2}I_{\text{cm}}\left(\frac{v}{R}\right)^2 = mg\left(\frac{3v^2}{4g}\right)$$

$$\Rightarrow \quad \frac{1}{2}I_{\text{cm}}\left(\frac{v}{R}\right)^2 = \frac{3}{4}mv^2 - \frac{1}{2}mv^2$$

$$\Rightarrow \quad \frac{1}{2}I_{\text{cm}}\left(\frac{v}{R}\right)^2 = \frac{1}{4}mv^2$$

$$\Rightarrow \quad I_{\text{cm}} = \frac{mR^2}{2}$$

From the given option it is the moment of inertia for a disc so option (D) is correct. $\qquad \textbf{Ans. (D)}$

Sol. 2 Figure below shows the locations of centre of mass of all the ink pieces as described in the question.

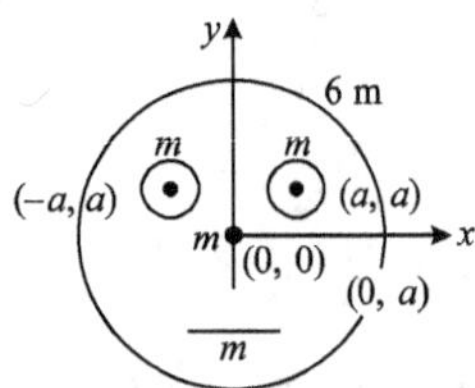

By symmetry we can see that x-coordinate of centre of mass of this system will be located at $x = 0$ and y-coordinate of centre of mass is calculated as

$$y_{cm} = \frac{7m \times 0 + 2m \times a + m(-a)}{10m} = \frac{ma}{10m} = \frac{a}{10}$$

Thus option (A) is correct. **Ans. (A)**

Sol. 3 Figure below shows the situation described in question after particle starts moving and colliding sequentially.

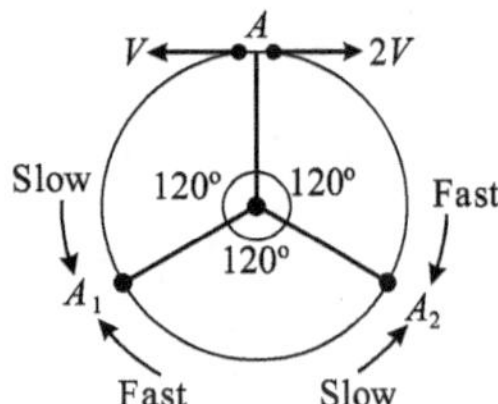

The first collision takes place at A_1 as the particle moving in anticlockwise sense covers half the distance covered by the other one. As collision is elastic, they exchange velocities and the second collision takes place at A_2. In the same manner we can define that the third collision takes place at A again. Thus option (C) is correct. **Ans. (C)**

Sol. 4 When the rod is rotated by a slight angle θ, the restoring torque on the rod due to spring forces is given as

$$\text{Restoring torque } \tau_r = 2 \times F_{spring} \times \frac{L}{2}$$

Where spring force is given as

$$F_{spring} = K\delta x$$

For small angular displacement θ, δx is given as

$$\delta x = \frac{L}{2}\theta$$

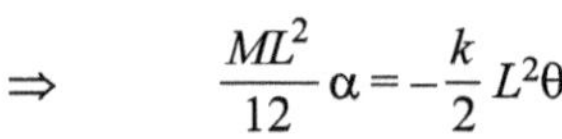

$$\Rightarrow \quad \tau_r = 2 \times k \frac{L}{2}\theta \times \frac{L}{2}$$

As $\tau_r = I\alpha$, we us

$$\Rightarrow \quad \frac{ML^2}{12}\alpha = -\frac{k}{2}L^2\theta$$

Here $-$ve sign is considered for opposite direction of torque and angular displacement. Further we have

$$\alpha = -\frac{6k}{M}\theta$$

Thus frequency of oscillations is given as

$$f = \frac{1}{2\pi}\sqrt{\frac{6k}{M}}$$

Thus option (C) is correct. **Ans. (C)**

Sol. 5 In the situation described in question, the time taken to reach the ground for both bullet and ball is given as

$$T = \sqrt{\frac{2H}{g}} = 1 \text{ s}$$

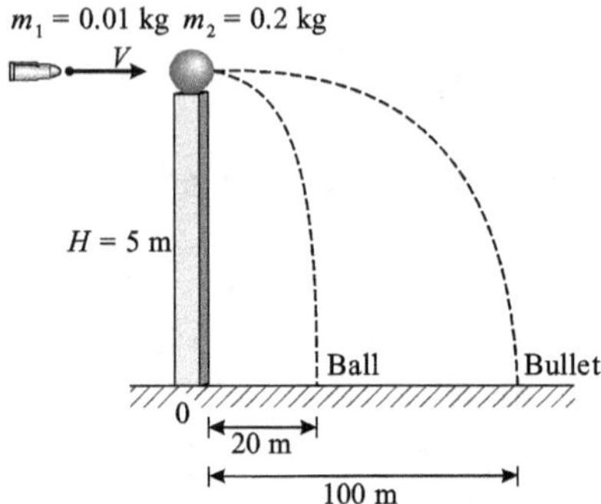

If v_1 and v_2 are the velocities of the bullet and ball respectively just after collision, we use

$$v_2 \times 1 = 20$$
$$\text{and} \quad v_1 \times 1 = 100$$
$$\Rightarrow \quad v_2 = 20 \text{ m/s}$$
$$\text{and} \quad v_1 = 100 \text{ m/s}$$

If initial velocity of the bullet is v, by conservation of momentum when bullet hits the ball, we have

$$0.01 \times V = (0.01 \times 100) + (0.2 \times 20)$$
$$\Rightarrow \quad 0.01 V = 1 + 4 = 5$$
$$\Rightarrow \quad V = \frac{5}{10^{-2}} = 500 \text{ m/s} \qquad \textbf{Ans. (D)}$$

Sol. 6 As rod is thin, we can neglect the mass of rod in this case. Thus angular momentum of the rod with insect is given as

$$L = I\omega$$

Here $I = mr^2$ and $r = vt$, we use

$$L = [m(vt)^2]\omega$$
$$\Rightarrow \quad L = mv^2\omega t^2$$

The magnitude of torque on this system is given as

$$\tau = \frac{dL}{dt} = 2mv^2\omega t$$
$$\Rightarrow \quad \tau \propto t$$

Thus the graph of torque as a function of time is best represented by a straight line passing through $(0, 0)$. **Ans. (B)**

Sol. 7 Angular momentum of particle about point P is given as

$$\vec{L} = (\vec{r} \times \vec{p})$$

$$\overrightarrow{L_P} = m(\overrightarrow{PA} \times \vec{v})$$

This vector is in the direction perpendicular to the plane containing the length of string and velocity vector of the mass which rotates as the mass revolves in the circle hence $\overrightarrow{L_P}$ changes with time in direction but remain constant in magnitude. The angular momentum of the mass about point O is given as

$$\overrightarrow{L_0} = m(\overrightarrow{OA} \times \vec{v})$$

This vector is always in direction normal to the plane of circle in which mass is revolving so it remains constant in magnitude as well as in direction. Hence option (C) is correct.   **Ans. (C)**

Sol. 8 During flight the rightward velocity component of particle P is always more than the rightward velocity components of the points on disc below point P hence with respect to disc particles on initial position of line PR, particle P will be moving toward right hence it will land on unshaded region.

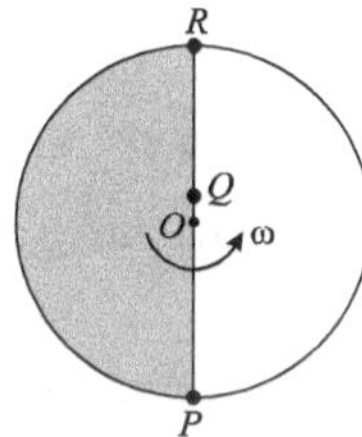

During flight the leftward velocity component of particle Q is less compared to all particles on the disc below particle Q along line PR thus with respect to line PR on disc, particle Q would be moving toward right hence it will also land on the unshaded region of the disc. Hence option (C) is correct.

Ans. (C, D)

Sol. 9 Velocity of particle performing projectile motion at highest point is given as

$$v_1 = u_0 \cos\alpha$$

Velocity of particle thrown vertically upwards at the point of collision is given as

$$v_2^2 = u_0^2 - 2g\left(\frac{u_0^2 \sin^2\alpha}{2g}\right) = u_0 \cos\alpha$$

After collision final momentum of the combined particle after inelastic collision in horizontal and vertical direction will remain same as before collision. If the combined particle is moving at an angle θ with the horizontal then we have

$$\tan\theta = \frac{v_y}{v_x} = \frac{u_0 \cos\alpha}{u_0 \cos\alpha} = 1$$

$$\Rightarrow \qquad \theta = \frac{\pi}{4} \qquad\qquad \textbf{Ans. (A)}$$

Sol. 10 For triangular polygon $(n = 3)$

$$h = \left(\frac{a}{2\sqrt{3}}\right)$$

$$\Delta h = \left[\frac{a}{\sqrt{3}} - \frac{a}{2\sqrt{3}}\right] = \left(\frac{a}{2\sqrt{3}}\right) = h$$

For cube $(n = 4)$

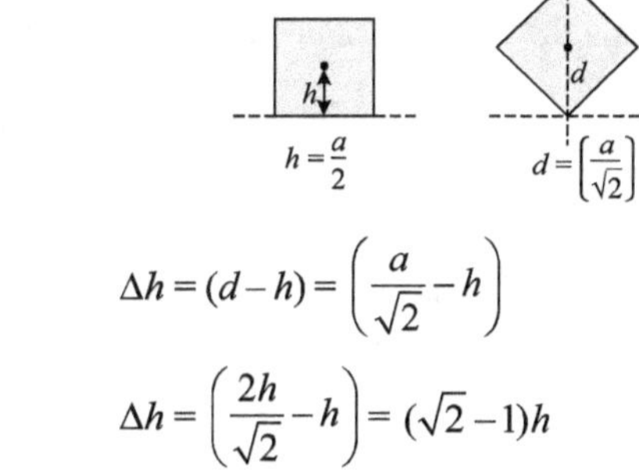

$$\Delta h = (d - h) = \left(\frac{a}{\sqrt{2}} - h\right)$$

$$\Rightarrow \qquad \Delta h = \left(\frac{2h}{\sqrt{2}} - h\right) = (\sqrt{2} - 1)h$$

$$\Rightarrow \qquad \Delta h = h\left[\frac{1}{\cos\left(\frac{\pi}{4}\right)} - 1\right] = h(\sqrt{2} - 1)$$

This result for all polygons can be expressed by the option (C) hence this is correct.   **Ans. (C)**

Sol. 11 Figure below shows the forces acting on the football and for football to roll down the plank its line of action of weight must cross the bottom edge of hole toward right so that it will fall due to the torque of its weight.

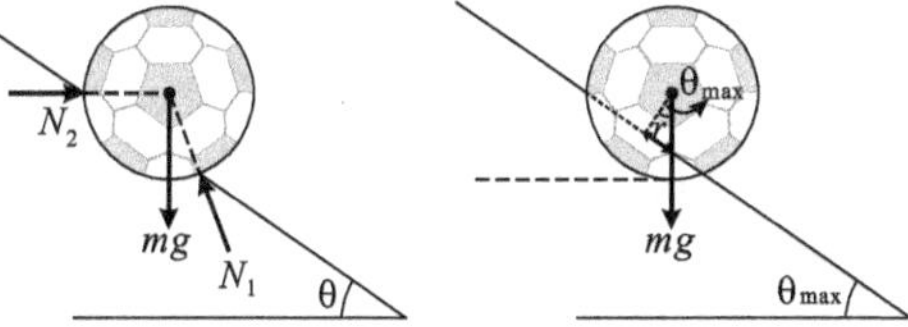

For θ_{max}, the football is about to roll, then $N_2 = 0$ and all the forces (Mg and N_1) must pass through bottom contact point as explained, so we use

$$\cos(90° - \theta_{max}) = \frac{r}{R}$$

$$\Rightarrow \qquad \sin\theta_{max} = \frac{r}{R} \qquad\qquad \textbf{Ans. (A)}$$

Sol. 12 For no slipping at the ground, if R is the roller radius, we use

$$V_{centre} = \omega R$$

If r is the radius of axle then the velocity of scale can be given as

$$v = (V_{center} + \omega r)$$

As the centre of the roller has moved by 50 cm, we use

$$V_{center} \times t = 50 \, cm$$

In this time the distance moved by scale is given as

$$s = (V_{center} + \omega r)t$$

$$\Rightarrow \quad s = \left(V_{center} + \frac{V_{center}r}{R} \right) t = \frac{3V_{center}}{2} \times t = 75 \, cm$$

Thus relative displacement of scale with respect to centre of roller is $(75 - 50)$ cm $= 25$ cm. Hence option (B) is correct.

Ans. (B)

Sol. 13 Figure below shows the angular speed of the disk B.

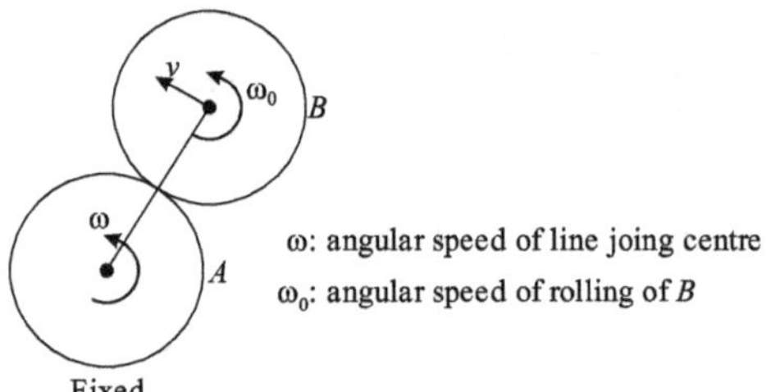

The linear speed of its centre of mass is given as

$$v = \omega(2R)$$

If disk B is rotating at angular speed ω_0, for its pure rolling, the speed of its centre of mass is given as

$$v = \omega_0 R$$

$$\Rightarrow \quad \omega_0 = 2\omega$$

The angular momentum of the disk B about center of A is given as

$$\vec{L} = m(\vec{r} \times \vec{v}_c) + I_c \vec{\omega}_0$$

$$\Rightarrow \quad L = M(2R)v + \frac{1}{2}MR^2\omega_0$$

$$\Rightarrow \quad L = 4MR^2\omega + \frac{1}{2}MR^2(2\omega) = 5MR^2\omega$$

$$\Rightarrow \quad n = 5$$

Ans. (B)

Sol. 14 Figure below shows the situation described in the question.

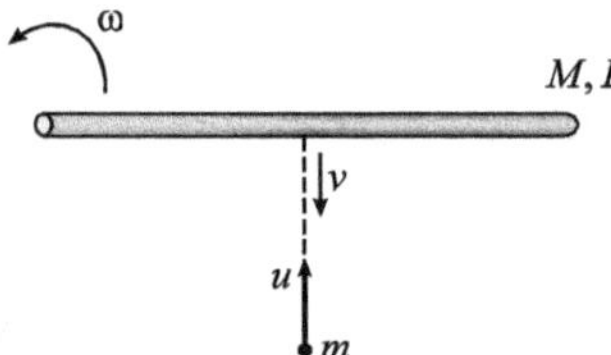

Applying angular momentum conservation about hinge, we use

$$mu\frac{L}{2} = -mv\frac{L}{2} + \frac{ML^2}{3}\omega \qquad \ldots(1)$$

Also using coefficient of restitution, we have

$$e = 1 = \frac{\omega\left(\dfrac{L}{2}\right) + v}{u}$$

$$\Rightarrow \quad u = \omega\left(\frac{L}{2}\right) + v \qquad \ldots(2)$$

Solving equations-(1) & (2), we have

$$\omega \approx 6.98 \, rad/s$$

& $$v = 4.30 \, m/s$$

Hence option (A) is correct.

Ans. (A)

Sol. 15 For the given conditions, initial momentum of the balls

$$\vec{p}_1 = p\,\hat{i}$$

$$\vec{p}_2 = -p\,\hat{i}$$

Net linear momentum just before collision is given as

$$\vec{p}_i = \vec{p}_1 + \vec{p}_2 = p\,\hat{i} - p\,\hat{i} = 0$$

As there is no external force acting on the balls, hence net linear momentum will remain conserved and will be equal to zero, hence

$$p'_f = \vec{p}'_1 + \vec{p}'_2 = 0$$

In option (A), we have

$$\vec{p}'_1 + \vec{p}'_2 = (a_1 + a_2)\,\hat{i} + (b_1 + b_2)\,\hat{j} + c_1\,\hat{k} \neq 0$$

As c_1 is non zero, it can't be zero. Similarly in option (D) also we have

$$\vec{p}'_1 + \vec{p}'_2 = (a_1 + a_2)\,\hat{i} + 2b_1\,\hat{j} \neq 0$$

Here b_1 is non zero so this cannot be zero. In options (B) and (C) values of constants can be adjusted for final momentum to be zero hence these are possible cases. **Ans. (A, D)**

Sol. 16 Figure below shows the velocities of points A, B and C in the sphere rolling with slipping as described in question.

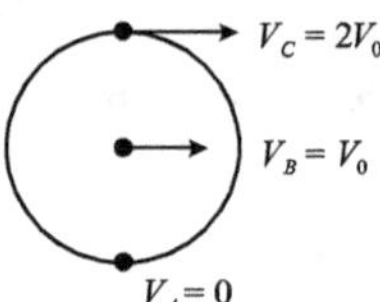

From above figure, we have

$$\vec{V}_B - \vec{V}_A = \vec{V}_0$$

$$\vec{V}_C - \vec{V}_B = \vec{V}_0$$

$$|\vec{V}_C - \vec{V}_A| = 2V_0$$

$$|\vec{V}_C - \vec{V}_B| = V_0$$

Thus options (B) and (C) are correct. **Ans. (B, C)**

Sol. 17 Figure below shows the situation described in the question.

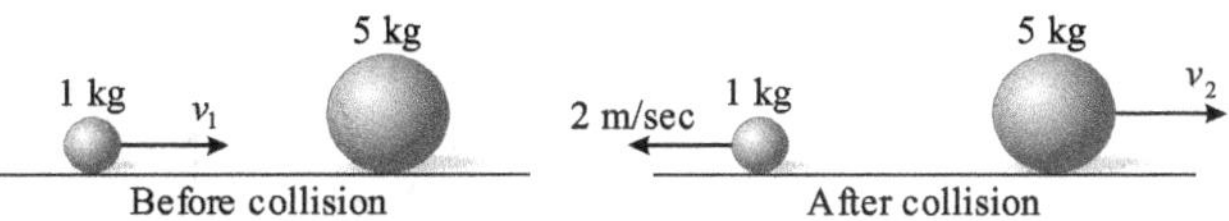

As collision is elastic, we use restitution equal to unity so we have

$$v_2 + 2 = v_1 \qquad \ldots(1)$$

Using conservation of momentum, we have

$$1 \times v_1 + 0 = -2 \times 1 + 5 \times v_2 \qquad \ldots(2)$$

Solving equations (1) and (2), we get

$$v_1 = 3 \text{ m/s}$$

$$v_2 = 1 \text{ m/s}$$

Total momentum of system is given as

$$\vec{P}_{\text{system}} = 1 \times v_1 = 3 \text{ kg-m/s}$$

Momentum of 5 kg mass is given as

$$p = 5 \times v_2 = 5 \text{ kg-m/s}$$

Velocity of centre of mass of system is calculated as

$$v_{\text{CM}} = \frac{1 \times 3 \times 5 \times 0}{6} = 0.5 \text{ m/s}$$

Kinetic energy of centre of mass is given as

$$K_{\text{cm}} = \frac{1}{2} \times (M_1 + M_2)\, v_{\text{CM}}^2 = 0.75 \text{ J}$$

Total kinetic energy of system is given as

$$K_{\text{system}} = \frac{1}{2} \times 1 \times 9 = 4.5 \text{ J} \qquad \textbf{Ans. (A, C)}$$

Sol. 18 By linear momentum conservation in horizontal direction, after collision the right will come to instantaneous rest so its final velocity will be zero. Thus its centre of mass becomes stationary after collision. Hence option (A) is correct. During impact linear impulses acting on ring due to ball are calculated as

(1) In horizontal direction

$$J_1 = \Delta p = 0.1 \times 20 = 2 \text{ N-s}$$

(2) In vertical direction

$$J_2 = \Delta p = 0.1 \times 10 = 1 \text{ N-s}$$

Writing equation about centre of mass, we have

Angular impulse = Change in angular momentum

$$1 \times \left(\frac{\sqrt{3}}{2} \times \frac{1}{2} \right) - 2 \times 0.5 \times \frac{1}{2} = 2 \times (0.5)^2 \left(\omega - \frac{1}{0.5} \right)$$

Solving above equation gives positive value of ω so just after collision ball would be rotating in the anticlockwise direction as before. Thus friction acts leftwards. So option (C) is also correct. **Ans. (A, C)**

Sol. 19 As most of mass of P is concentrated near its surface, its moment of inertia will be higher than that of Q, so we have

$$I_P > I_Q$$

Acceleration of bodies rolling down the inclined plane in case of pure rolling is given as

$$a = \frac{g \sin\theta}{I_P + mR^2}$$

$$\Rightarrow \qquad a_P = \frac{g \sin\theta}{I_P + mR^2} \; ; a_P = \frac{g \sin\theta}{I_Q + mR^2}$$

$$\Rightarrow \qquad a_P < a_Q$$

$$\Rightarrow \qquad t_P > t_Q$$

$$\text{As} \qquad v^2 = u^2 + 2as$$

$$\Rightarrow \qquad v_P < v_Q$$

$$\Rightarrow \qquad K_P < K_Q$$

$$\text{As} \qquad v = \omega R$$

$$\Rightarrow \qquad \omega \propto v$$

$$\Rightarrow \qquad \omega_P < \omega_Q$$

Thus cylinder Q reaches ground first and has larger angular speed. **Ans. (D)**

Sol. 20 Figure below shows the velocity vectors in the particle P on the inner disc.

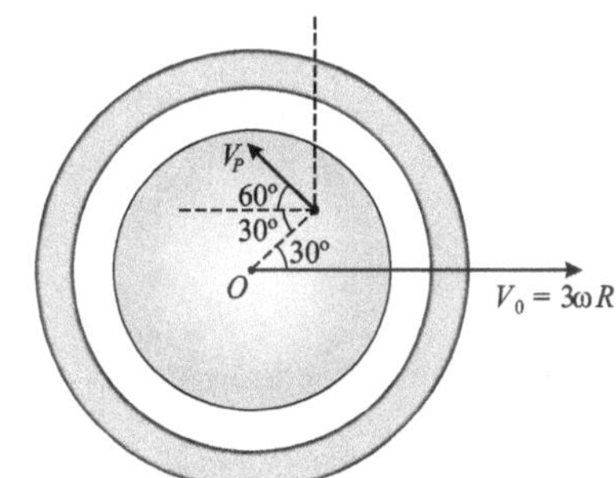

As outer ring is in pure rolling, velocity of centre is given as

$$\vec{V_O} = 3\,\omega R\,\hat{i}$$

Velocity of point P can be given as

$$\vec{V_P} = \left(3\,\omega R - \frac{\omega R}{2} \cos 60^\circ\right) \hat{i} + \frac{\omega R}{2} \sin 60\, \hat{k}$$

$$\Rightarrow \qquad \vec{V_P} = \frac{11\omega R}{4}\hat{i} + \frac{\sqrt{3}\omega R}{4}\hat{k} \qquad \textbf{Ans. (A, B)}$$

Sol. 21 Initial moment of inertia of the system is given as

$$I_1 = MR^2 \text{ (for Ring)}$$

Final moment of inertia of the system is given as

$$I_2 = MR^2 + \frac{M}{8} \left(\frac{3}{5} R \right)^2 + \frac{M}{8} x^2$$

Using conservation of angular momentum about the given axis, we have

$$I_1\omega_1 = I_2\omega_2$$

$$\Rightarrow \quad MR^2\omega_0 = \left[MR^2 + \frac{M}{8}\cdot\left(\frac{3}{5}R\right)^2 + \frac{M}{8}x^2\right]\left[\frac{8}{9}\omega\right]$$

$$\Rightarrow \quad x = \frac{4}{5}R \qquad\qquad\qquad \textbf{Ans. (D)}$$

Sol. 22 Position vector $\vec{r}$ of particle of mass m is given by

$$\vec{r} = \alpha t^3\,\hat{i} + \beta t^2\,\hat{j}$$

(A) The velocity vector of the particle is given as

$$\vec{v} = \frac{d\vec{r}}{dt} = 3at^2\,\hat{i} + 2\beta t\,\hat{j}$$

$$\Rightarrow \quad \vec{v} = 3\times\frac{10}{3}t^2\hat{i} + 2\times 5t\,\hat{j}$$

$$\Rightarrow \quad \vec{v} = 10\times 1^2\hat{i} + 10\,\hat{j} = (10\,\hat{i} + 10\,\hat{j})\,\text{ms}^{-1}$$

(B) Angular momentum of particle is given as

$$\vec{L} = \vec{r}\times m\vec{v}$$

Here $\vec{r} = \dfrac{10}{3}\hat{i} + 5\hat{j}$ so angular momentum is calculated as

$$\Rightarrow \quad \vec{L} = 0.1\begin{vmatrix} \hat{i} & \hat{j} & \hat{k} \\ \dfrac{10}{3} & 5 & 0 \\ 10 & 10 & 0 \end{vmatrix}$$

$$\Rightarrow \quad \vec{L} = 0.1\left[\hat{k}\left[\frac{100}{3} - 50\right]\right]$$

$$\Rightarrow \quad \vec{L} = -\frac{50\times 0.1}{3}\hat{k} = -\frac{5}{3}\hat{k}\;\text{Nm/s}$$

(D) The acceleration of particle is given as

$$\vec{a} = 6\alpha t\,\hat{i} + 2\beta\,\hat{j}$$

The acceleration at $t = 1$ s is calculated as

$$\Rightarrow \quad \vec{a} = 6\times\frac{10}{3}\hat{i} + 2\times 5\,\hat{j}$$

$$\Rightarrow \quad \vec{a} = 20\,\hat{i} + 10\,\hat{j}$$

The force acting on the particle is given as

$$\vec{F} = 2\,\hat{i} + \hat{j}$$

Torque is calculated as

$$\vec{\tau}_0 = \vec{r}\times\vec{F} = \begin{vmatrix} \hat{i} & \hat{j} & \hat{k} \\ \dfrac{10}{3} & 5 & 0 \\ 2 & 1 & 0 \end{vmatrix}$$

$$\Rightarrow \quad = \hat{k}\left(\frac{10}{3} - 10\right) = -\frac{20}{3}\hat{k}\,\text{Nmv} \quad \textbf{Ans. (A, B, D)}$$

Sol. 23 Figure below shows the direction of all velocities in objects given in the question.

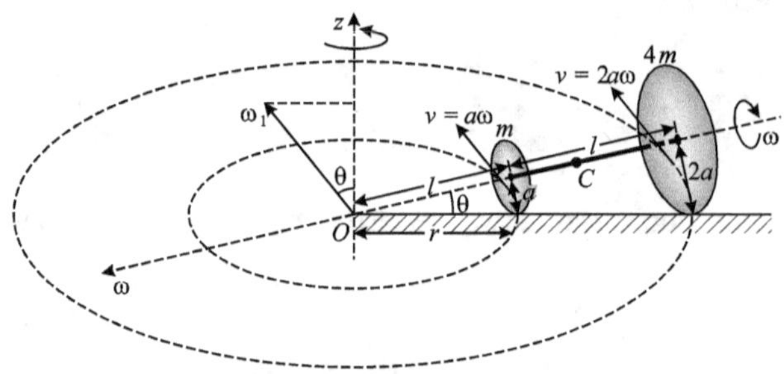

If the whole system is rotating about the given central axis, the angular speed of rotation of the axle is calculated as

$$r = \sqrt{l^2 + a^2} = \sqrt{24a^2 + a^2} = 5a$$

Time taken to complete one revolution is given as

$$t = \frac{2\pi r}{a\omega} = \frac{2\pi(5a)}{a\omega}$$

Thus angular speed of system assembly about point O and z-axis is given as

$$\omega_1 = \frac{2\pi}{t} = \frac{\omega}{5}$$

Position of centre of mass from point O is given as

$$l_C = \frac{ml + (4m\times 2l)}{m+4m} = \frac{9l}{5}$$

Velocity of center of mass is given as

$$v_C = \frac{m(a\omega) + 4m(2a\omega)}{m+4m} = \frac{9}{5}a\omega$$

Angular velocity of centre of mass w.r.t. z-axis is same as calculated above

$$\omega'_z = \frac{\omega}{5}$$

Hence option (D) is correct.

Angular momentum of system w.r.t. centre of mass is given as

$$L_{\text{system}} = I_{\text{CM}}\omega$$

$$\Rightarrow \quad L_{\text{system}} = \frac{ma^2}{2}\omega + \frac{(4m)(2a)^2}{2}\omega$$

$$\Rightarrow \quad L_{\text{system}} = \frac{17}{2}ma^2\omega$$

Hence option (A) is correct.

Angular momentum of centre of mass about O is given as

$$L_{co} = 5mv_C l_C$$

$$\Rightarrow \quad L_{co} = 5m\left(\frac{9}{5}a\omega\right)\left(\frac{9}{5}l\right) = \frac{81}{5}ma\omega l$$

$$\Rightarrow \quad L_{co} = \frac{81}{5}\sqrt{24}\,ma^2\omega$$

Hence option (C) is NOT correct.

Total angular momentum of the assembly about z-axis can be calculated by taking components of the two angular momentum vectors of system as calculated above of which directions are shown in figure below.

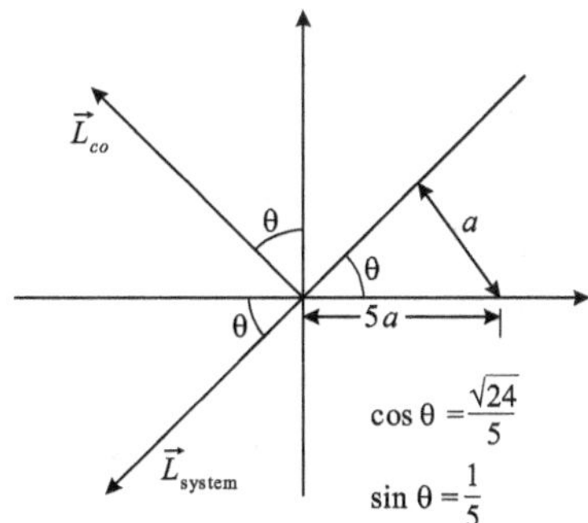

Total angular momentum of the assembly is given by sum of these two angular momenta, calculated as

$$\vec{L} = \vec{L}_{system} + \vec{L}_{co}$$

z-component of the angular momentum can be calculated from the above figure as

$$L_z = L_{co} \cos \theta - L_{system} \sin \theta$$

$$\Rightarrow \qquad L_z = \frac{81}{5}\left(\frac{24}{5}\right) ma^2\omega - \frac{17}{2} ma^2\omega \times \frac{1}{5}$$

$$\Rightarrow \qquad L_z = \frac{81}{25} \times 24\, ma^2\omega - \frac{17}{10} ma^2\omega$$

$$\Rightarrow \qquad L_z = \frac{(81 \times 24 \times 2 - 17 \times 5)}{50} ma^2\omega$$

$$\Rightarrow \qquad L_z \cong 76\, ma^2\omega$$

Hence option (B) is NOT correct. **Ans. (A, D)**

Sol. 24 Let the block be displaced by x. If initially the centre of mass of the system is at origin then displacement of centre of mass will be zero so we have

$$0 = \frac{M \times x + m(x + R)}{M + m}$$

$$0 = Mx + mx + mR$$

$$\Rightarrow \qquad x = \frac{-mR}{m + M}$$

Hence option (A) is correct.

If v is the velocity of mass m as it leaves the block and V is the velocity of block at that instant then by linear momentum conservation, we have

$$mv = MV$$

By energy conservation, we have

$$mgR = \frac{1}{2}mv^2 + \frac{1}{2}mv'^2$$

$$\Rightarrow \qquad 2gR = v^2\left[\frac{M + m}{M}\right]$$

$$\Rightarrow \qquad v = \sqrt{\frac{2gR}{1 + \dfrac{m}{M}}}$$

Hence option (C) is correct. **Ans. (A, C)**

Sol. 25 Figure below shows the molecules of the gas striking the plate from the two sides. A and B are two molecules considered on the left and right side of plate colliding with average speed u normally to the plate. We've considered their final speed after collisions as shown in below figure as v_1 and v_2.

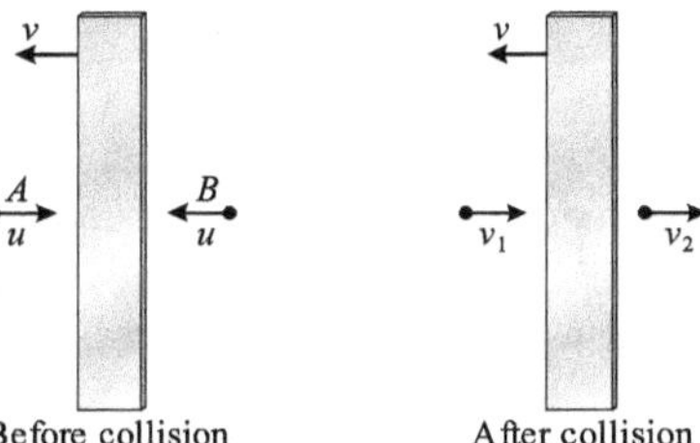

As collision is elastic, we use restitution equal to unity so for the two molecules considered, we use

For A $\qquad 1 = \dfrac{v_1 - v}{v + u}$

For B $\qquad 1 = \dfrac{v + v_2}{u - v}$

$$\Rightarrow \qquad v_1 = u + 2v$$

and $\qquad v_2 = u - 2v$

$$\Rightarrow \qquad \Delta v_1 = 2u + 2v$$

and $\qquad \Delta v_2 = 2u - 2v$

Force on the two sides due to collision can be given by rate of change of linear momentum in molecules due to collisions so for area of plate A, we have

$$F_1 = \rho A(u + v)(2u + 2v)$$

$$\Rightarrow \qquad F_1 = 2\rho A (u + v)^2$$

and $\qquad F_2 = \rho A(u - v)(2u - 2v)$

$$\Rightarrow \qquad F_2 = 2\rho A (u - v)^2$$

Resistive force on plate due to collisions can be calculated as

$$\Delta F = F_1 - F_2 = 8\rho Auv$$

$$\Rightarrow \qquad P = \frac{\Delta F}{A} = 8\rho uv$$

As resistive force is increasing with speed of plate v so after sometime it will balance the external force and then onward plate will move with terminal speed. Hence options (A), (B) and (D) are correct. **Ans. (A, B, D)**

Sol. 26 As no external horizontal force is acting on the rod, the center of mass of rod will fall vertically down. Thus the displacement of its centre of mass at the given instant in question is calculated as

$$\Delta y_{CM} = \frac{l}{2} - \frac{l}{2}\cos\theta$$

$$\Rightarrow \quad \Delta y_{CM} = \frac{l}{2}(1 - \cos\theta)$$

The line of action of weight is acting along the initial line of rod thus horizontal distance of point of contact of rod from the point O is given as

$$r = l\sin\theta$$

Thus torque about this point due to weight is proportional to $\sin\theta$. **Ans. (A, B, C)**

Sol. 27 Torque due to applied force at X decreases as wheel climbs up as the separation between the line of force and point Q decreases. Thus option (A) is NOT correct.

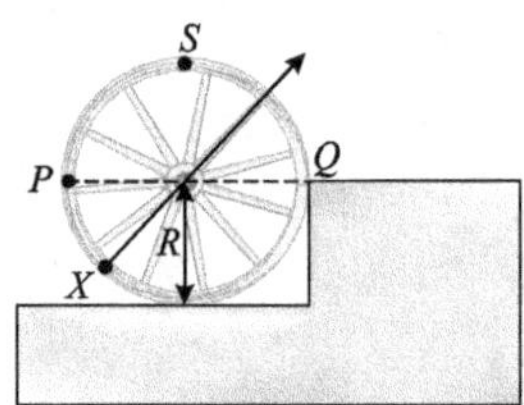

When force is applied tangentially at point S then due to the torque of this force wheel can climb up and as it climbs, torque increases as the distance between line of force and point Q increases. Thus option (B) is NOT correct.

When applied forces passes through point P and acts normal to circumference then line of force passes through point Q so torque is zero. Thus option (C) is correct.

When force is applied tangentially at P then torque about Q will remain constant as wheel climbs up because the distance between line of force and point Q remain same and equal to diameter of the wheel. Thus option (D) is NOT correct. **Ans. (C)**

Sol. 28 Given force is given as

$$\vec{F} = t\hat{i} + \hat{j}$$

$$\Rightarrow \quad \frac{m d\vec{v}}{dt} = t\hat{i} + \hat{j}$$

$$\Rightarrow \quad d\vec{v} = t\,dt\,\hat{i} + dt\,\hat{j}$$

$$\Rightarrow \quad \int_0^v d\vec{v} = \int_0^t t\,dt\hat{i} + \int_0^t dt\hat{j}$$

$$\Rightarrow \quad \vec{v} = \frac{t^2}{2}\hat{i} + t\hat{j}$$

Hence option (C) is correct.

At $t = 1$s, velocity is given as

$$\vec{v} = \frac{1}{2}\hat{i} + \hat{j} = \frac{1}{2}(\hat{i} + 2\hat{j})\,\text{ms}^{-1}$$

$$\Rightarrow \quad \frac{d\vec{r}}{dt} = \frac{t^2}{2}\hat{i} + t\hat{j}$$

$$\Rightarrow \quad d\vec{r} = \frac{t^2}{2}dt\hat{i} + t\,dt\,\hat{j}$$

$$\Rightarrow \quad \int_0^r d\vec{r} = \int_0^t \frac{t^2}{2}dt\hat{i} + \int_0^t t\,dt\,\hat{j}$$

$$\Rightarrow \quad \vec{r} = \frac{t^3}{6}\hat{i} + \frac{t^2}{2}\hat{j}$$

At $t = 1$ s, position vector of body is given as

$$\vec{r} = \frac{1}{6}\hat{i} + \frac{1}{2}\hat{j}$$

$$\Rightarrow \quad |\vec{r}| = \sqrt{\frac{1}{36} + \frac{1}{4}} = \sqrt{\frac{10}{36}}\,\text{m}$$

Hence option (D) is NOT correct.

At $t = 1$ s torque acting is calculated as

$$\vec{\tau} = \vec{r} \times \vec{F} = \left(\frac{1}{6}\hat{i} + \frac{1}{2}\hat{j}\right) \times (\hat{i} + \hat{j})$$

$$\vec{\tau} = \begin{vmatrix} \hat{i} & \hat{j} & \hat{k} \\ \frac{1}{6} & \frac{1}{2} & 0 \\ 1 & 1 & 0 \end{vmatrix} = \hat{i}(0-0) - \hat{j}(0-0) + \hat{k}\left(\frac{1}{6} - \frac{1}{2}\right) = -\frac{1}{3}\hat{k}$$

$$\Rightarrow \quad |\vec{\tau}| = \frac{1}{3}\,\text{Nm}$$

Hence option (A) is correct and (B) is NOT correct. **Ans. (A, C)**

Sol. 29 The axis of rotation of rod is considered at the bottom contact point in this case. Using work energy theorem, we have from the initial state of rod to the state when it makes an angle 60° with the vertical, it gives

$$mg\frac{l}{4} = \frac{1}{2}\left(\frac{ml^2}{3}\right)\omega^2$$

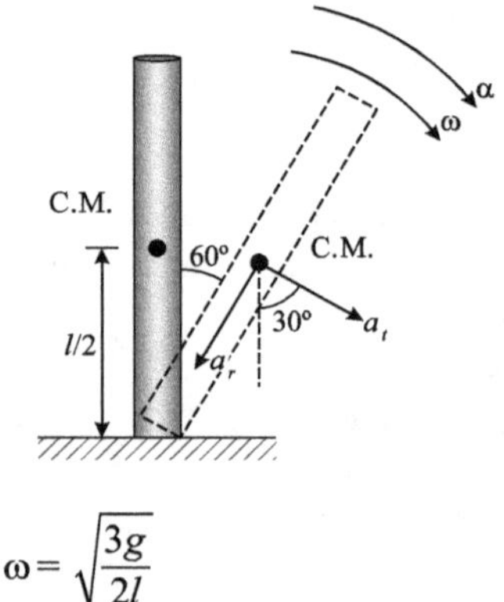

$$\Rightarrow \quad \omega = \sqrt{\frac{3g}{2l}}$$

Hence option (C) is correct.

Radial acceleration of centre of mass of rod is given as

$$a_r = \left(\frac{l}{2}\right)\omega^2 = \frac{3g}{4}$$

Hence option (A) is correct.

Using $\tau = I\alpha$ about bottom contact point gives

$$\frac{Mgl}{2}\sin 60° = \frac{Ml^2}{3}\alpha$$

$$\Rightarrow \qquad \alpha = \frac{3\sqrt{3}}{4l}g$$

Hence option (B) is NOT correct.

Thus tangential acceleration of centre of mass of rod is given as

$$a_t = \alpha \times \frac{l}{2}$$

Total acceleration of centre of mass of rod in vertical direction is given as

$$a_v = a_r \cos 60° + a_t \cos 30°$$

$$\Rightarrow \qquad a_v = \left(\frac{3g}{4}\right)\left(\frac{1}{2}\right) + \left(\alpha\frac{l}{2}\right)\cos 30°$$

$$\Rightarrow \qquad a_v = \frac{3g}{8} + \frac{3\sqrt{3}g}{4l}\left(\frac{l}{2}\right)\left(\frac{\sqrt{3}}{2}\right)$$

$$\Rightarrow \qquad a_v = \frac{3g}{8} + \frac{9g}{16} = \frac{15}{16}g$$

In vertical direction on rod, we use

$$Mg - N = Ma_v = M\left(\frac{15}{16}g\right)$$

$$\Rightarrow \qquad N = \frac{Mg}{16}$$

Hence option (D) is correct. $\qquad$ **Ans. (A, C, D)**

Sol. 30 By the angular momentum conservation about the suspension point, we have

$$mvx = \left(\frac{mL^2}{3} + mx^2\right)\omega$$

$$\Rightarrow \qquad \omega = \frac{mvx}{\dfrac{mL^2}{3} + mx^2} = \frac{3vx}{L^2 + 3x^2}$$

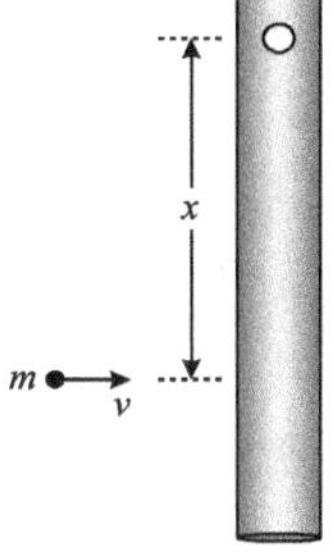

Hence option (A) is correct.

For maximum value of ω, we use

$$\frac{d\omega}{dx} = 0$$

$$\Rightarrow \qquad \frac{d}{dx}\left(\frac{3vx}{L^2 + 3x^2}\right) = 0$$

$$\Rightarrow \qquad 3v\frac{d}{dx}\left(\frac{x}{L^2 + 3x^2}\right) = 0$$

$$\Rightarrow \qquad \frac{d}{dx}\left(\frac{1}{\dfrac{L^2}{x} + 3x}\right) = 0$$

$$\Rightarrow \qquad \frac{d}{dx}\left(\frac{L^2}{x} + 3x\right)^{-2}\left(-\frac{L^2}{x^2} + 3\right) = 0$$

$$\Rightarrow \qquad \frac{L^2}{x^2} = 3$$

$$\Rightarrow \qquad x = \frac{L}{\sqrt{3}}$$

Hence option (C) is correct.

$$\Rightarrow \qquad \omega_{max} = \frac{3v\left(\dfrac{L}{\sqrt{3}}\right)}{L^2 + 3\left(\dfrac{L^2}{3}\right)} = \frac{\sqrt{3}v}{2L}$$

Hence option (D) is correct.. $\qquad$ **Ans. (A, C, D)**

Sol. 31 Considering friction acting at the bottom contact in leftward direction as shown in figure below, writing equation of motion for the body, we have

$$F - f_S = ma$$

$$f_S R = I\alpha$$

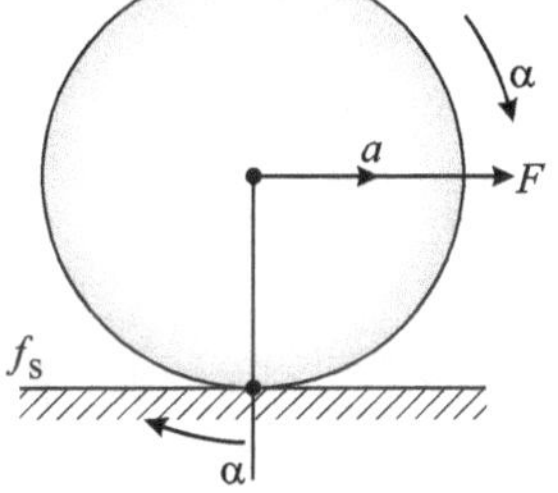

Using $a = R\alpha$, we have

$$f_S = \frac{I\alpha}{R} = \left(\frac{I}{R^2}\right)a \qquad \qquad \ldots(1)$$

and $\qquad F = \left(m + \frac{I}{R^2}\right)a \qquad \qquad \ldots(2)$

Here value of acceleration depends upon moment of inertia of body so option (A) is not correct.

For a solid cylinder, we use $I = \frac{1}{2}mR^2$ so from equations (1) and (2), we have

$$a = \frac{2F}{3m} = \frac{2f_S}{m}$$

Maximum value of friction is its limiting value equal to μmg thus maximum possible acceleration is given by equation (1) as

$$a_{max} = 2\mu g$$

Hence option (B) is correct.

For pure rolling the friction on ground is between 0 to limiting value so option (C) is not correct.

For a thin walled hollow cylinder, we use $I = mR^2$, so from equation (2), we have

$$a = \frac{F}{2m}$$

Hence option (D) is correct.   **Ans. (B, D)**

Sol. 32 (A) Displacement of particle is given as

$$s = \frac{1}{2}at^2 = \frac{1}{2}(10)t^2$$

$$\Rightarrow \qquad\qquad t = 2 \text{ s}$$

(B) Torque with respect to origin for the given location of particle is calculated as

$$\vec{\tau} = \vec{r} \times \vec{F} = (10\hat{i} - \hat{j}) \times (0.2 \times 10\hat{i}) = 2\,\hat{k}$$

(C) Angular momentum of particle with respect to origin is calculated as

$$\vec{L} = \vec{r} \times \vec{p} = (10\hat{i} - \hat{j}) \times (0.2 \times 20\hat{i}) = 4\,\hat{k}$$

(D) Torque with respect to origin for the given location of particle is calculated as

$$\vec{\tau} = \vec{r} \times \vec{F} = (-\hat{j}) \times (0.2 \times 10\hat{i}) = 2\,\hat{k} \qquad \textbf{Ans. (A, B, C)}$$

Sol. 33 Figure below shows the forces acting on the beam. For equilibrium of system in horizontal direction, we have

$$R_1 = T\cos 45°$$

$$\Rightarrow \qquad\qquad R_1 = \frac{T}{\sqrt{2}} \qquad\qquad \dots(1)$$

For equilibrium in vertical direction, we use

$$R_2 + T\sin 45° = W + \alpha W$$

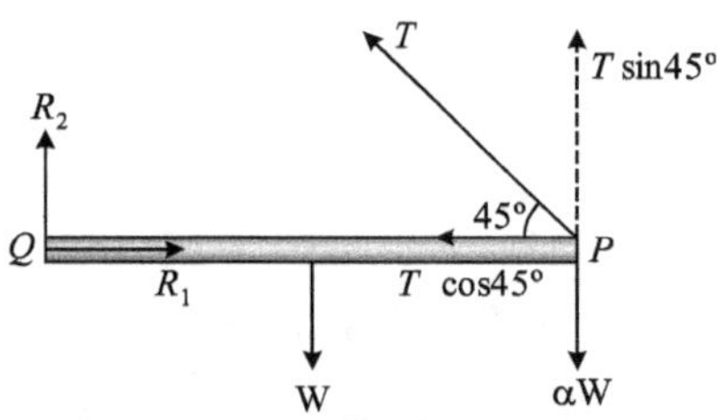

$$\Rightarrow \qquad\qquad R_2 + \frac{T}{\sqrt{2}} = W(1 + \alpha) \qquad\qquad \dots(2)$$

As beam is in static equilibrium, net torque on it about point Q is equal to zero, so we use

$$W \times \frac{L}{2} + \alpha W L = \frac{T}{\sqrt{2}} \times L$$

$$\Rightarrow \qquad\qquad T = \sqrt{2}\,W\left(\alpha + \frac{1}{2}\right) \qquad\qquad \dots(3)$$

From equations (2) and (3), we have

$$R_2 + W\left(\alpha + \frac{1}{2}\right) = W(1 + \alpha)$$

$$\Rightarrow \qquad\qquad R_2 = \frac{W}{2}$$

Thus option (A) is correct.
From equations (1) and (3), we have

$$R_1 = W\left(\alpha + \frac{1}{2}\right)$$

For $\alpha = 0.5$

$$\Rightarrow \qquad\qquad R_1 = W$$

Thus option (B) is correct.
From equation-(3) if $\alpha = 0.5$, we have

$$T = \sqrt{2}\,W$$

Thus option (C) is not correct.

As $T_{\max} = 2\sqrt{2}\,W$ so for rope to break, we need

$$T > 2\sqrt{2}\,W$$

$$\Rightarrow \qquad \sqrt{2}\,W\left(\alpha + \frac{1}{2}\right) > 2\sqrt{2}\,W$$

$$\Rightarrow \qquad\qquad \alpha > \frac{3}{2}$$

Thus option (D) correct.   **Ans. (A, B, D)**

Sol. 34 Due to impulse if disk attains an initial linear speed v and angular speed ω, we use

$$J_0 = mv \qquad\qquad \dots(1)$$

$$J_0 h = I_c \omega \qquad\qquad \dots(2)$$

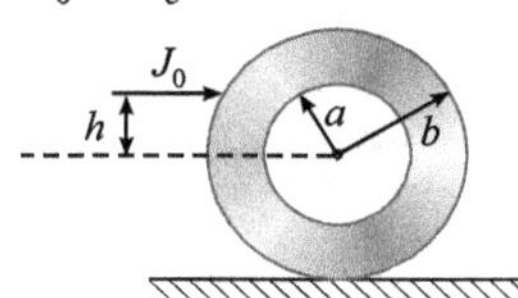

At $h = h_m$ disk rolls without slipping so we use

$$v = \omega b \qquad\qquad \dots(3)$$

$$\Rightarrow \qquad\qquad h_m = \frac{I_c}{mb} \qquad\qquad \dots(4)$$

(A) If $a = 0$ we have $I_c = \frac{1}{2}mb^2$ so from equation-(4), it gives

$$h_m = \frac{b}{2}$$

(B) If $a = b$ we have $I_c = mb^2$ so from equation-(4), it gives

$$h_m = b$$

(C) At $h = h_m$ the initial angular velocity is given as

$$\omega = \frac{v}{b} = \frac{J_0}{mb}$$

(D) In absence of friction if the impulse is acting at centre of mass, it will not impart any angular speed so body will be in pure translational motion, no rotation.   **Ans. (A, B, C, D)**

Sol. 35 In collision, momentum remain conserved both in elastic and inelastic collisions. For elastic collision as restitution is unity relative speed before and after collision remain same hence both statements are true but second statement is not explaining statement-1 **Ans. (B)**

Sol. 36 Statement-1 is false because velocity of centre of mass of a body remain constant if there is no external force acting on the body and it is not directly related to external torque whereas statement-2 is true because for an isolated system as no external force is acting on system, linear momentum will remain conserved. **Ans. (D)**

Sol. 37 By conservation of energy, we have

$$\frac{1}{2}mv_c^2 + \frac{1}{2}I_c\omega^2 = mgh$$

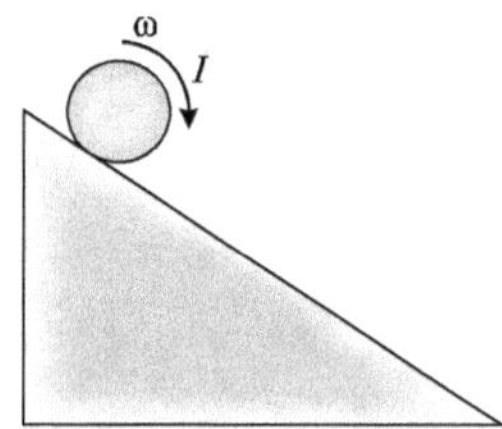

Moment of inertia of solid and hollow cylinders are given as

$$I_{\text{solid}} = \frac{MR^2}{2}$$

$$I_{\text{hollow}} = MR^2$$

For pure rolling, we have

$$\omega = v_c/R$$

As

$$I_{\text{solid}} < I_{\text{hollow}}$$

$$\Rightarrow \quad v_{\text{solid}} > v_{\text{hollow}}$$

Hence solid cylinder will reach the bottom first. **Ans. (D)**

Sol. 38 Entire potential energy of spring is transformed to rotational kinetic energy of disc-1, so we use

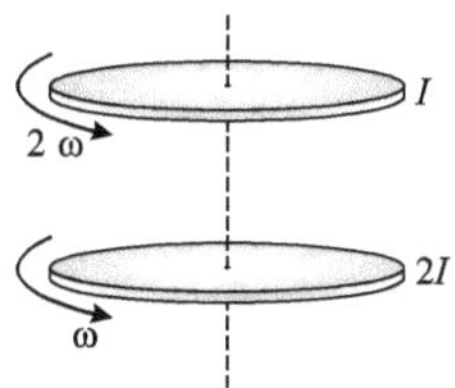

$$\frac{1}{2}kx_1^2 = \frac{1}{2}I(2\omega)^2 \qquad \ldots(1)$$

When compressed by x_2, potential energy is transferred to rotational kinetic energy of disc-2, so we use

$$\frac{1}{2}kx_2^2 = \frac{1}{2}(2I)(\omega)^2 \qquad \ldots(2)$$

By solving equation (1) and (2), we get

$$\frac{x_1}{x_2} = \sqrt{2} \qquad\qquad \textbf{Ans. (C)}$$

Sol. 39 Applying conservation of angular momentum, we have

$$I_1(2\omega) + I_2(\omega) = I'\omega'$$

$$\Rightarrow \quad I(2\omega) + 2I(\omega) = 3I\omega'$$

$$\Rightarrow \quad \omega' = \frac{I(2\omega) + 2I(\omega)}{3I} = \frac{4\omega}{3} \qquad \ldots(1)$$

$$\Rightarrow \quad \omega' = \omega + \frac{\tau}{2I}t \qquad \ldots(2)$$

From equation-(1) and (2), $\tau = \dfrac{2I\omega}{3t}$ **Ans. (A)**

Sol. 40 Loss of kinetic energy

$$\Delta E = K_f - K_i$$

$$\Rightarrow \quad \Delta E = \frac{1}{2}I\left(2\omega - \frac{4\omega}{3}\right)^2 + \frac{1}{2}(2I)\left(\omega - \frac{4\omega}{3}\right)^2$$

$$\Rightarrow \quad \Delta E = \frac{1}{2}I\left(\frac{2\omega}{3}\right)^2 + \frac{1}{2}(2I)\left(-\frac{\omega}{3}\right)^2$$

$$\Rightarrow \quad \Delta E = \frac{2}{9}I\omega^2 + \frac{1}{9}I\omega^2 = \frac{1}{3}I\omega^2 \qquad \textbf{Ans. (B)}$$

Sol. 41 In the figure shown below, from $\triangle ABD$, we have

$$\tan 60^\circ = \frac{AD}{BD}$$

$$\Rightarrow \quad AD = BD\tan 60^\circ = \sqrt{3} \times \sqrt{3}\ \text{m} = 3\ \text{m}$$

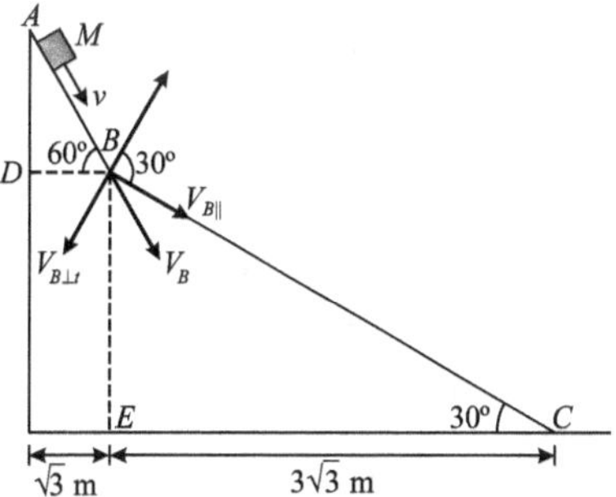

Speed of block at B just before collision with inline BC is V_B

$$\frac{1}{2}MV_B^2 = Mg(AD)$$

$$\Rightarrow \quad V_B = \sqrt{60}\,\text{m/s}$$

Collision between block and inline is perfectly inelastic. Just after collision with incline BC component of velocity of block perpendicular to incline BC becomes zero and component of velocity of block parallel to incline BC is

$$V'_B = V_B\cos 30^\circ = \sqrt{45}\ \text{m/s}$$

Speed of block just after collision with incline BC is $\sqrt{45}$ m/s

Ans. (B)

Sol. 42 The height BD is given as

$$BD = 3\sqrt{3}\tan 30^\circ = 3 \text{ m}$$

By energy conservation, we have

$$\frac{1}{2}M(\sqrt{45})^2 + Mg(3) = \frac{1}{2}MV_C^2$$

$$\Rightarrow \qquad V_C = \sqrt{105} \text{ m/s} \qquad\qquad \textbf{Ans. (B)}$$

Sol. 43 If collision at B is elastic then situation is shown in figure below as block B will bounce off the plane such that its velocity component along the incline remain same and normal to incline get reversed.

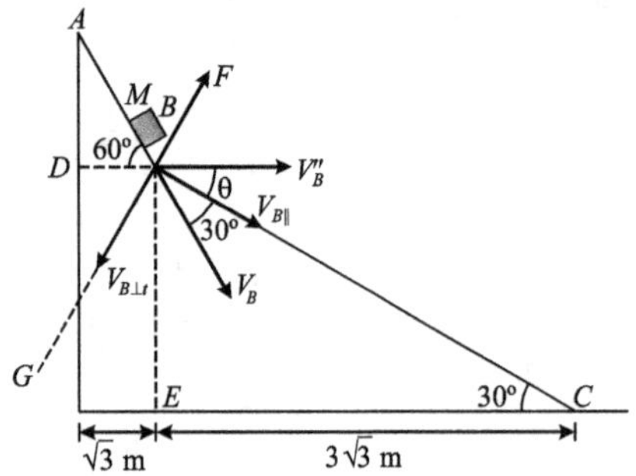

So just after collision with incline BC, component of velocity of block along BC is

$$V''_{B\|} = V_B\cos 30^\circ = \sqrt{45} \text{ m/s}$$

Component of velocity perpendicular to BC is

$$V''_{B\perp} = V_B\sin 30^\circ = \sqrt{15} \text{ m/s}$$

The angle made by the velocity of ball V''_B after collision with the plane is θ then we have

$$\tan\theta = \frac{V''_{B\perp r}}{V''_{B\|}} = \frac{\sqrt{15}}{\sqrt{15}} = \frac{1}{\sqrt{3}}$$

$$\Rightarrow \qquad \theta = 30^\circ$$

Thus $\overrightarrow{V''_B}$ is in horizontal direction and hence vertical component

of $\overrightarrow{V''_B}$ is zero. **Ans. (C)**

Sol. 44 For translational motion, we use

$$2kx - F = Ma \qquad\qquad\qquad \ldots(1)$$

For rotational motion, we use

$$FR = I\alpha = \frac{MR^2}{2}\left(\frac{a}{R}\right) \qquad\qquad \ldots(2)$$

From equations (1) and (2), we have

$$F = \frac{Ma}{2}$$

$$\Rightarrow \qquad a = -\frac{4kx}{3M}$$

External force on disk (which is friction in this case) is given as

$$F_{\text{ext}} = Ma = -\frac{4kx}{3} \qquad\qquad \textbf{Ans. (D)}$$

Sol. 45 From the above question, the restoring force is given as

$$F = -\frac{4kx}{3M} = -\omega^2 x$$

$$\Rightarrow \qquad \omega = \sqrt{\frac{4k}{3M}} \qquad\qquad \textbf{Ans. (D)}$$

Sol. 46 For motion of disk, we have friction acting on disk is given as

$$F = \frac{Ma}{2}$$

For slipping so start F should have its maximum value i.e. limiting friction, so we use

$$F = \frac{Ma}{2} = \mu Mg$$

$$\Rightarrow \qquad a = 2\mu g$$

As already calculated, we have

$$a = \frac{4kx}{3m}$$

$$\Rightarrow \qquad \frac{4kx}{3m} = 2\mu g$$

$$\Rightarrow \qquad x = \frac{6\mu Mg}{4k}$$

Thus at this value of x slipping will start. The velocity required to attain this displacement is given by energy conservation, used as

$$2 \times \frac{1}{2}kx^2 = \frac{1}{2}mv^2 + \frac{1}{2}I\omega^2$$

$$\Rightarrow \qquad k\left(\frac{6\mu Mg}{4k}\right)^2 = mv^2 + \frac{MR^2}{2}\frac{v^2}{R^2}$$

$$\Rightarrow \qquad v = \mu g\sqrt{\frac{3M}{k}} \qquad\qquad \textbf{Ans. (C)}$$

Sol. 47 Since z-coordinate of any particle is not changing with time so axis will be parallel to z-axis. **Ans. (A)**

Sol. 48 Angular velocity of rigid body about any axes which are parallel to each other is same. So angular velocity is ω.

Ans. (D)

Sol. 49 In rotating frame, force on block is given as

$$F = m\omega^2 r$$

$$\Rightarrow \quad mv\frac{dv}{dr} = m\omega^2 r$$

$$\Rightarrow \quad \int_0^v v\,dv = \int_{R/2}^r \omega^2 r\,dr$$

$$\Rightarrow \quad v = \omega\sqrt{r^2 - \frac{R^2}{4}}$$

$$\Rightarrow \quad \int_{R/2}^r \frac{dr}{\sqrt{r^2 - \frac{R^2}{4}}} = \omega\int_0^t dt$$

$$\Rightarrow \quad \log e\left(\frac{2r}{R} + \sqrt{\left(\frac{2r}{R}\right)^2 - 1}\right) = \omega t$$

$$\Rightarrow \quad \omega t = \ln\left(\frac{2r}{R} + \frac{\sqrt{4r^2 - R^2}}{R}\right)$$

$$\Rightarrow \quad r = \frac{R}{4}(e^{\omega t} + e^{-\omega t}) \qquad \textbf{Ans. (D)}$$

Sol. 50 One reaction on block is acting at base in upward direction along $\hat{k}$ which balances the weight of block so it will be equal to the weight. Another reaction will act on the block due to one side wall due to rotational motion of disc which will act along $\hat{j}$ as Coriolis force given as

$$\vec{F}_{cor} = 2mv\omega\,\hat{j} = 2m\omega^2 r\,\hat{j}$$

$$\Rightarrow \quad \vec{F}_{cor} = m\frac{\omega^2 R}{2}(e^{\omega t} - e^{-\omega t})\,\hat{j}$$

Net reaction force exerted by disc on the block is

$$\vec{F} = \frac{m\omega^2 R}{2}(e^{\omega t} - e^{-\omega t})\,\hat{j} + mg\,\hat{k} \qquad \textbf{Ans. (C)}$$

Sol. 51 Figure below shows the top view of rotating ring and here point of contact A is instantaneous axis of rotation of ring and angular speed of ring ω_0 so its kinetic energy is given as

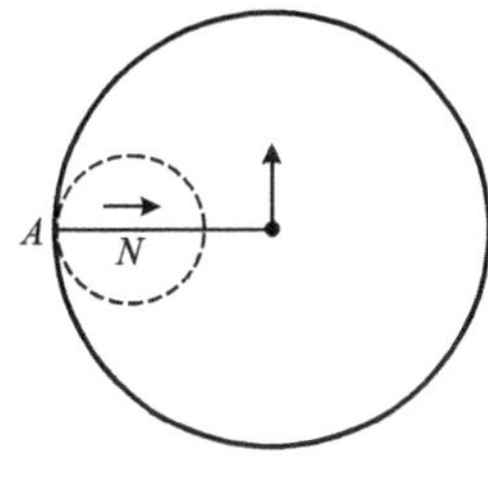

$$K = \frac{1}{2}I_A\omega_0^2$$

$$\Rightarrow \quad K = \frac{1}{2}2MR^2\omega_0^2$$

$$\Rightarrow \quad K = MR^2\omega_0^2 \qquad \textbf{Ans. (A)}$$

Sol. 52 During rotation of ring, its centre of mass revolves in a circle of radius $(R - r)$, the normal force by finger on ring due to its angular velocity ω_0 is given as

$$N = M\omega_0^2(R - r)$$

To hold the ring in vertical equilibrium, the limiting friction on ring at point of contact with finger should balance the weight of ring, so we use

$$\mu M\omega_0^2(R - r) = Mg$$

$$\Rightarrow \quad \omega_0 = \sqrt{\frac{g}{\mu(R - r)}}$$

If angular speed goes down below this value then friction will not be able to hold the ring and it will fall. **Ans. (B)**

Sol. 53 For collision between A and B, by conservation of momentum, we have

$$m \times 9 + 2\,m \times 0 = mv_1 + 2\,mv_2$$

$$\Rightarrow \quad 9 = v_1 + 2\,v_2 \qquad \ldots(1)$$

$$e = 1$$

So $$9 = v_2 - v_1 \qquad \ldots(2)$$

From equations (1) and (2), we get

$$v_2 = 6 \text{ m/s}$$

For collision between B and D, we have

$$2\,m \times 6 = (2\,m + m)v$$

$$\Rightarrow \quad v = \frac{2 \times 6}{3} = 4 \text{ m/s} \qquad \textbf{Ans. (4)}$$

Sol. 54 Figure below shows the forces acting on the situation described in the question on the ring

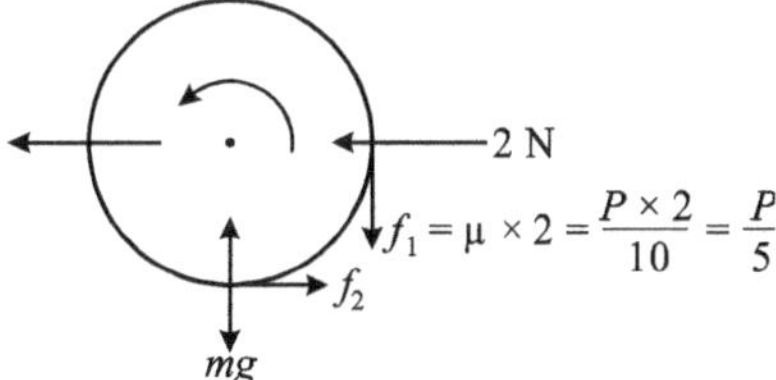

Net force in x-direction is given as

$$2 - f_2 = Ma_{cm} \qquad \ldots(1)$$

$$f_2 = 2 - 2 \times 0.3 = 1.4 \text{ N}$$

For rotational motion of ring, we use

$$(f_2 - f_1)R = I_{cm}\alpha$$

As the ring is in pure rolling, we use

$$(f_2 - f_1)R = MR^2 \times \frac{a_{cm}}{R}$$

$$\Rightarrow \quad f_2 - f_1 = Ma_{cm}$$

$$\Rightarrow \quad f_1 = f_2 - Ma_{cm} = 1.4 - 2 \times 0.3 = 0.8 \text{ N}$$

$$\Rightarrow \qquad 0.8 = \frac{P}{5}$$

$$\Rightarrow \qquad P = 4 \qquad \text{Ans. (4)}$$

Sol. 55 For the given situation shown in figure, we have

$$r = \frac{\sqrt{5}}{2}\,\text{cm} = \frac{\sqrt{5}}{2} \times 10^{-2}\,\text{m}$$

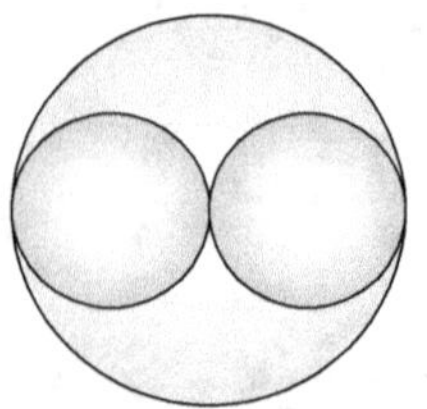

and $\qquad m = \frac{1}{2}\,\text{kg}$

and $\qquad l = 4 \times 10^{-2}\,\text{m}$

Using parallel axes theorem, we have

$$I_{\text{total}} = \left[4 \times \frac{2}{5} \times \frac{1}{2} \times \frac{5}{4} \times 10^{-4} \right] + \left[2 \times \frac{1}{2} \times 8 \times 10^{-4} \right]$$

$$\Rightarrow \qquad I_{\text{total}} = 10^{-4} + 8 \times 10^{-4} = 9 \times 10^{-4}\,\text{kg m}^2 \qquad \text{Ans. (9)}$$

Sol. 56 If whole disc without hole is considered to be of mass $4m$, the mass of removed part will be m. The moment of inertia about axis passing through O is given as

$$I_0 = \frac{(4m)(2R)^2}{2} - \frac{3}{2}\,mR^2$$

$$\Rightarrow \qquad I_0 = mR^2 \left[8 - \frac{3}{2} \right]$$

$$\Rightarrow \qquad I_0 = \frac{13}{2}\,mR^2$$

Moment of inertia about axis passing through P

$$I_P = \frac{3}{2}(4m)(2R)^2 - \left[\frac{mR^2}{2} + m[(2R)^2 + R^2] \right]$$

$$\Rightarrow \qquad I_P = 24\,mR^2 - \frac{11}{2}\,mR^2$$

$$\Rightarrow \qquad I_P = \frac{37}{2}\,mR^2$$

$$\Rightarrow \qquad \frac{I_P}{I_O} = \frac{\frac{37}{2}}{\frac{13}{2}} = \frac{37}{13} \approx 3 \qquad \text{Ans. (3)}$$

Sol. 57 The initial speed of first bob suspended by a string of length l_1 is $\sqrt{5gl_1}$. The speed of this bob its highest point will be $\sqrt{gl_1}$. When this bob collides elastically with the other bob there speeds will be interchanged so for second bob to complete its vertical circle, we use

$$\sqrt{gl_1} = \sqrt{5gl_2}$$

$$\Rightarrow \qquad \frac{l_1}{l_2} = 5 \qquad \text{Ans. (5)}$$

Sol. 58 By conservation of angular momentum about vertical axis of disc, we have

$$I_i\,\omega_i = I_f\,\omega_f$$

Figure below shows the initial and final system after adding two rings

Initial moment of inertia of system is given as

$$I_i = \frac{1}{2}\,MR^2$$

Final moment of inertia of system is given as

$$I_f = \frac{1}{2}\,MR^2 + 2 \times (I_{\text{cm}} + mr^2)$$

$$\Rightarrow \qquad I_f = \frac{1}{2}\,MR^2 + 2 \times (mr^2 + mr^2)$$

$$\Rightarrow \qquad I_f = \frac{1}{2}\,MR^2 + 4mr^2$$

By conservation of angular momentum, we have

$$\frac{50(0.4)^2}{2} \times 10 = \left[\frac{50(0.4)^2}{2} + 4(6.25)(0.2)^2 \right] \omega$$

$$\Rightarrow \qquad \omega = 8\,\text{rad/s} \qquad \text{Ans. (8)}$$

Sol. 59 Moment of inertia of the platform is

$$I = \frac{mR^2}{2}$$

Final angular momentum of the balls after firing is given as

$$L_f = 2mvr$$

By conservation of angular momentum about axis of rotation, we have

$$\frac{(0.45)(0.5)^2}{2}\,\omega = 2[0.05 \times 9 \times 0.25]$$

$$\Rightarrow \qquad \frac{45 \times 0.25}{2}\,\omega = 2[45 \times 0.25]$$

$$\Rightarrow \qquad \omega = 4\,\text{rad/s} \qquad \text{Ans. (4)}$$

Sol. 60 Torque on disc due to applied forces is given as

$$\tau = r \times f$$

$$\Rightarrow \qquad \tau = 3 \cdot F(0.25)$$

$$\Rightarrow \qquad \tau = 3 \times 0.5 \times 0.25 = \frac{3}{8}\,\text{N-m}$$

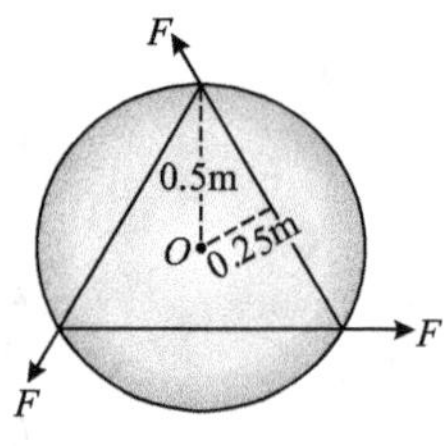

Angular acceleration of the disc is given as

$$\alpha = \frac{3/8}{\dfrac{1.5\times(0.5)^2}{2}} = \frac{3/8}{1.5\times1/8} = 2 \text{ rad/s}^2$$

Angular speed after 1 s is given as
$$\omega = \alpha t = 2 \text{ rad/s} \qquad\qquad \textbf{Ans. (2)}$$

Sol. 61 Using energy conservation in both situation as described in question, we get

$$\frac{1}{2}mv_1^2 + \frac{1}{2}\left(\frac{1}{2}mR^2\right)\frac{v_1^2}{R^2} + mg\,(30)$$

$$= \frac{1}{2}mv^2 + \frac{1}{2}\left(\frac{1}{2}mR^2\right)\frac{v^2}{R^2}$$

$$\Rightarrow \quad \frac{1}{2}\times\frac{3}{2}mv_1^2 + mg\times 30 = \frac{1}{2}\times\frac{3}{2}mv^2 \qquad\ldots(1)$$

Similarly for second case, we have

$$\frac{1}{2}\times\frac{3}{2}mv_2^2 + mg\times 27 = \frac{1}{2}\times\frac{3}{2}mv^2 \qquad\ldots(2)$$

From equation-(1) & (2), we have

$$\frac{1}{2}\times\frac{3}{2}mv_1^2 + mg\times 30 = \frac{1}{2}\times\frac{3}{2}mv_2^2 + mg\times 27$$

$$\Rightarrow \quad \frac{3\times9}{4} + 300 = \frac{3}{4}v_2^2 + 270$$

$$\Rightarrow \quad \frac{27}{4} + 30 = \frac{3}{4}v_2^2$$

$$\Rightarrow \quad 3\left[\frac{9}{4}+10\right] = \frac{3}{4}v_2^2 \Rightarrow 3\times\frac{49}{4} = \frac{3}{4}v_2^2$$

$$\Rightarrow \quad v_2 = 7 \text{ m/s} \qquad\qquad \textbf{Ans. (7)}$$

Sol. 62 As we know that moment of inertia of hollow sphere is $\frac{2}{3}mr^2$ so considering a thin shell of width dr at radius r from centre of sphere. The mass of thin shell considered inside the sphere A is $\rho_A(r).4\pi r^2 dr$. The moment of inertia of this elemental shell is given as

$$dI = \frac{2}{3}dm\,r^2$$

Moment of inertia of sphere A is calculated as

$$I_A = \int \frac{2}{3}dm\,r^2$$

$$\Rightarrow \quad I_A = \frac{2}{3}\left[\int_0^R \frac{kr}{R}\times(4\pi r^2 dr)\times r^2\right]$$

$$\Rightarrow \quad I_A = \frac{2}{3}\times\frac{k(4\pi)}{R}\left[\frac{r^6}{6}\right]_0^R = \frac{8\pi kR^5}{18}$$

Similarly moment of inertia of sphere B is given as

$$I_B = \frac{2}{3}\int_0^R k\left(\frac{r}{R}\right)^5 (4\pi r^2 dr)\times r^2$$

$$\Rightarrow \quad I_B = \frac{2}{3}\frac{k}{R^5}(4\pi)\left[\frac{r^{10}}{10}\right]_0^R = \frac{4\pi kR^5}{15}$$

The ratio of moment of inertias of A and B is given as

$$\frac{I_B}{I_A} = \frac{4/15}{8/18} = \frac{6}{10}$$

$$\Rightarrow \quad n = 6 \qquad\qquad \textbf{Ans. (6)}$$

Sol. 63 The time taken to reach the ground is given by

$$t = \frac{1}{\sin\theta}\sqrt{\frac{2h}{g}\left(1+\frac{I_C}{MR^2}\right)}$$

For ring $\quad t_1 = \frac{1}{\sin 60°}\sqrt{\frac{2h}{g}\left(1+\frac{MR^2}{MR^2}\right)} = \frac{4}{\sqrt3}\sqrt{\frac{h}{g}}$

For disc $\quad t_2 = \frac{1}{\sin 60°}\sqrt{\frac{2h}{g}\left(1+\frac{\frac{1}{2}MR^2}{MR^2}\right)} = \frac{2}{\sqrt3}\sqrt{\frac{3h}{g}}$

Given $\quad t_1 - t_2 = \dfrac{2-\sqrt3}{\sqrt{10}}$

$$\Rightarrow \quad \frac{4}{\sqrt3}\sqrt{\frac{h}{g}} - \frac{2}{\sqrt3}\sqrt{\frac{3h}{g}} = \frac{2-\sqrt3}{\sqrt{10}}$$

$$\Rightarrow \quad 2\sqrt{\frac{h}{10}} - \sqrt{\frac{3h}{10}} = \frac{(2-\sqrt3)}{\sqrt{10}}\left(\frac{\sqrt3}{2}\right)$$

$$\Rightarrow \quad 2\sqrt h - \sqrt{3h} = \sqrt3 - \frac{3}{2}$$

$$\Rightarrow \quad \sqrt h\,(2-1.732) = 1.732 - 1.5 \Rightarrow \sqrt h = \frac{0.232}{0.268}$$

$$\Rightarrow \quad h \approx 0.75 \text{ m} \qquad\qquad \textbf{Ans. (0.75)}$$

Sol. 64 As the collision is head on and elastic, final speeds of the bodies are given as

$$v_1 = \frac{(m_1-m_2)u_1}{m_1+m_2} + \frac{2m_2u_2}{m_1+m_2} = \frac{(1-2)2}{1+2} = \frac{-2}{3}\text{ ms}^{-1}$$

and $\quad v_2 = \dfrac{(m_2-m_1)u_2}{m_1+m_2} + \dfrac{2m_1u_1}{m_1+m_2} = \dfrac{2\times1\times2}{1+2} = \dfrac{4}{3}\text{ ms}^{-1}$

The time period of oscillations of mass 2 kg after collision is given as

$$T = 2\pi\sqrt{\frac{m}{k}} = 2\pi\sqrt{\frac{2}{2}} = 2\pi$$

Thus the time taken for spring to return to the original unstretched position is half of time period, equal to π s. Thus distance between the two blocks is equal to the distance travelled by the 1 kg mass in this period, given as

$$s = \frac{2}{3} \times \pi = \frac{2}{3} \times \frac{22}{7} = 2.09 \text{ m} \qquad \textbf{Ans. (2.09)}$$

Sol. 65 Below figure shows the forces acting on the fingers. Initially after some displacement, we consider that left finger stops at a distance x_L as shown in figure then right finger starts moving. Initially the normal reactions are at the fingers are such that

$$N_1 + N_2 = Mg \qquad \qquad \dots(1)$$

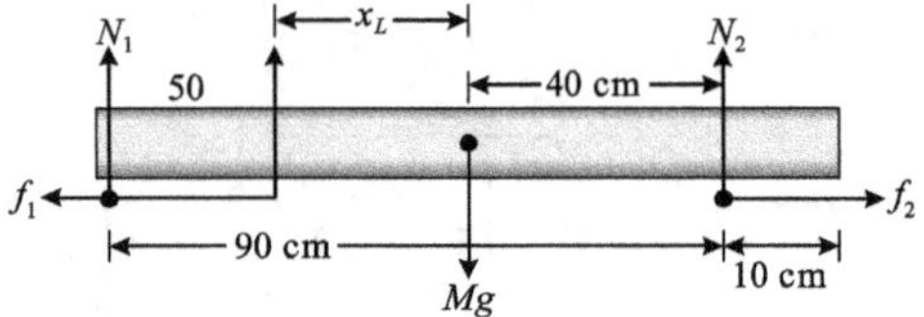

For static equilibrium of scale we consider net torque about centre is zero so we have

$$N_1(50) = N_2(40) \qquad \qquad \dots(2)$$

From equations (1) and (2), we have

$$N_1 = \frac{4Mg}{9} \text{ and } N_2 = \frac{5Mg}{9}$$

$$\Rightarrow \qquad 5N_1 = 4N_2$$

Kinetic and static frictions at the two fingers are taken as

$$f_{1_K} = \mu_k N_1 \qquad \qquad f_{1_L} = \mu_s N_1$$
$$f_{1_K} = 0.32\,N_1 \qquad \qquad f_{1_L} = 0.4\,N_1$$
$$f_{2_K} = 0.32\,N_2 \qquad \qquad f_{2_L} = 0.4\,N_2$$

At a distance x_L of left finger from centre when right finger starts moving, we use kinetic friction on left finger is balanced by limiting friction of right finger, so we have

$$f_{K_1} = f_L$$

$$\Rightarrow \qquad 0.32\,N_1 = 0.40\,N_2$$

$$\Rightarrow \qquad 4N_1 = 5N_2 \qquad \qquad \dots(3)$$

At this position again balancing torque about centre, we get

$$N_1 x_L = N_2(40) \qquad \qquad \dots(4)$$

From equation (3) and (4), we have

$$N_1 x_L = \frac{4N_1}{5}(40)$$

$$\Rightarrow \qquad x_L = 32 \text{ cm}$$

Now if x_R is the distance when right finger stops and left finger starts moving so similar to above case we use net torque at

this point on scale is zero so we have

$$N_1 x_L = N_2(x_R)$$

and $\qquad f_{L_1} = f_{K_2}$

$$\Rightarrow \qquad 0.4\,N_1 = 0.32\,N_2$$

$$\Rightarrow \qquad 5N_1 = 4N_2$$

$$\Rightarrow \qquad \frac{4N_2}{5}(32) = N_2 x_R$$

$$\Rightarrow \qquad x_R = \frac{128}{5} = 25.6 \text{ cm} \qquad \textbf{Ans. (25.60)}$$

Sol. 66 Angular momentum of system about the given axis is calculated as

$$L = \frac{Ma^2}{3}\,\Omega + \frac{M(a/4)^2}{2}\,4\Omega + \frac{M(3a/4)^2}{4}\,\Omega$$

$$\Rightarrow \qquad L = Ma^2\Omega\left(\frac{1}{3} + \frac{1}{8} + \frac{9}{16}\right) = Ma^2\Omega\left[\frac{16+6+27}{48}\right]$$

$$\Rightarrow \qquad L = \frac{49}{48}Ma^2\Omega \qquad \textbf{Ans. (49)}$$

Sol. 67 Figure below shows the motion of particle relative to rolling disk. Actually this will be moving in right ward direction due to the net velocity of stone with respect to ground but analysing the case relative to disk makes it very easy to understand and solve.

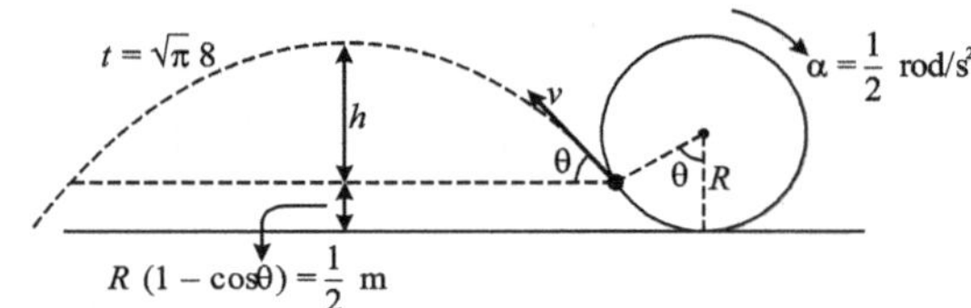

At time $t = \sqrt{\pi}$ the angle rotated by disk is calculated as

$$\theta = \frac{1}{2}\alpha t^2 = \frac{1}{2}\left(\frac{2}{3}\right)(\sqrt{\pi})^2 = \frac{\pi}{3} = 60^\circ$$

At $t = \sqrt{\pi}$ angular speed is given as

$$\omega = \alpha t = \frac{2}{3}\sqrt{\pi} \text{ rad/s}$$

At this instant tangential speed of stone relative to disk is given as

$$u = \omega r = \frac{2}{3}\sqrt{\pi} \text{ m/s}$$

Height of stone above ground when it gets detached from the disk is given as

$$h = R(1 - \cos\theta) = 1 - \cos 60^\circ = \frac{1}{2} \text{ m}$$

As shown in figure above the maximum height attained by the stone above ground can be given as

$$h = \frac{1}{2} + \frac{u^2 \sin^2 \theta}{2g}$$

$$\Rightarrow \qquad h = \frac{1}{2} + \frac{(4\pi/9)^2 \sin^2(\pi/3)}{20}$$

$$\Rightarrow \qquad h = \frac{1}{2} + \frac{\pi}{60} = \frac{1}{2} + \frac{x}{10}$$

$$\Rightarrow \qquad x = \frac{\pi}{6} = 0.52 \qquad \textbf{Ans. (0.52)}$$

Sol. 68 Figure below shows all forces acting on the sphere while it is rolling down the inclined plane.

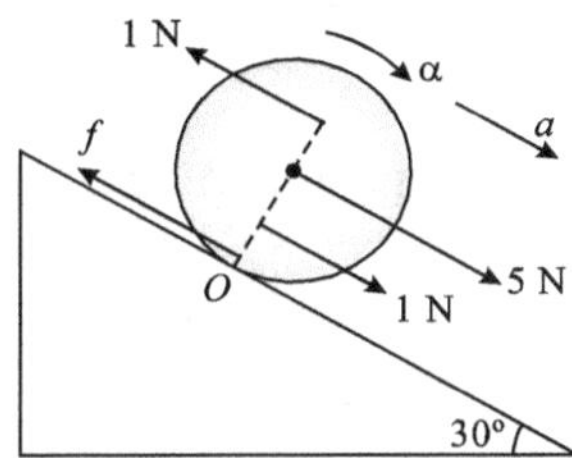

To find its acceleration, we write its torque equation about the bottom contact point as

$$\tau_0 = 5 \times 1 + 1 \times 0.5 - 1 \times 1.5 = \left(\frac{7}{5}MR^2\right)\alpha = \frac{7}{5}\alpha$$

$$\Rightarrow \quad \alpha = \frac{20}{7} = 2.857 \approx 2.86 \text{ rad/s}^2$$

Thus acceleration of sphere rolling down is given as

$$a = R\alpha = 2.86 \text{ m/s}^2 \qquad \textbf{Ans. (2.86)}$$

Sol. 69 Due to impulse imparted if the coin attains a linear speed v and angular speed about its diameter at ω as shown in figure below then these are calculated by impulse momentum equations.

$$J = mv$$

$$\Rightarrow \qquad v = \frac{J}{m} = \frac{\sqrt{\dfrac{\pi}{2}} \times 10^{-2}}{5 \times 10^{-3}} = \sqrt{2\pi} \text{ m/s}$$

And by angular impulse, we have

$$Jr = I_c \omega$$

$$\Rightarrow \qquad Jr = \frac{1}{4}mR^2 \omega$$

$$\Rightarrow \qquad \omega = \frac{4Jr}{mR^2} = \frac{4 \times \sqrt{\dfrac{\pi}{2}} \times 10^{-2} \times 0.66 \times 10^{-2}}{5 \times 10^{-3} \times \left(1.33 \times 10^{-2}\right)^2}$$

$$\Rightarrow \qquad \omega = 150\sqrt{2\pi} \text{ rad/s}$$

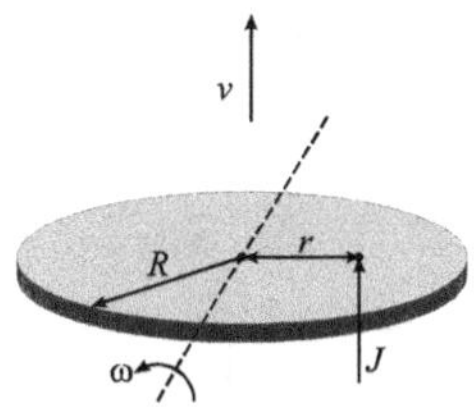

Time taken by coin to come back to initial position is given as

$$t = \frac{2v}{g} = \frac{2\sqrt{2\pi}}{10} = \frac{\sqrt{2\pi}}{5} \text{ s}$$

In this time number of rotations by coin are calculated as

$$N = \frac{\omega t}{2\pi} = \frac{150\sqrt{2\pi} \times \sqrt{2\pi}}{2\pi \times 5} = 30 \ \textbf{Ans. (30)}$$

Ch-5 Gravitation

Sol. 1 As gravitational force depends on density for the point inside the spherical body, we use

For $\qquad r < R$

$$\frac{mv^2}{r} = \frac{GMm}{r^2} \qquad \qquad \text{...(1)}$$

Mass of system is taken as

$$M = \left(\rho_0 \times \frac{4}{3}\pi r^3\right)$$

Thus by equation-(1), we have

$$v^2 \propto r^2 \text{ or } v \propto r$$

For $r < R$, we have

$$\frac{mv^2}{r} = \frac{GMm}{r^2}$$

$$\Rightarrow \qquad v^2 \propto \frac{1}{r}$$

$$\Rightarrow \qquad v \propto \frac{1}{\sqrt{r}} \qquad \textbf{Ans. (C)}$$

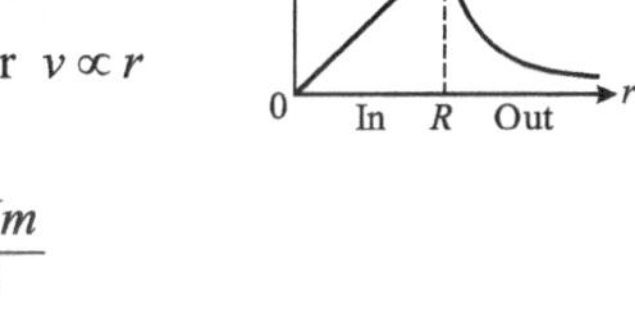

Sol. 2 Work required to take a unit mass from P to infinity is given as

$$\Delta W_{\text{ext}} = -V_P,$$

Here V_P is the gravitational potential at P due to the annular disc. To find V_P we take a small element of thickness dr at distance r from centre of disc. The mass of this elemental ring is given as

$$dm = \frac{M(2\pi r dr)}{\pi(4R)^2 - \pi(3R)^2} = \frac{2Mr dr}{7R^2}$$

Gravitational potential at point P is given by integration of potential at P due to this elemental ring, calculated as

$$V_P = \int dV = \int -\frac{Gdm}{(r^2 + 16R^2)^{1/2}}$$

$$\Rightarrow \qquad V_P = \int -\frac{GM\,2\pi r\,dr}{7\pi R^2\,(r^2+16R^2)^{1/2}}$$

Substituting
$$r^2 + 16R^2 = t^2$$

$$V_P = -\frac{2GM}{7R^2}\int_{5R}^{4\sqrt{2}R} dt = -\frac{2GM}{7R}(4\sqrt{2}-5)$$

Work done from P to infinity is given as

$$\Rightarrow \qquad \Delta W_{\text{ext}} = -V_P = \frac{2GM}{7R}(4\sqrt{2}-5) \qquad \textbf{Ans. (A)}$$

Sol. 3 Here centripetal force on satellite is provided by gravitational force

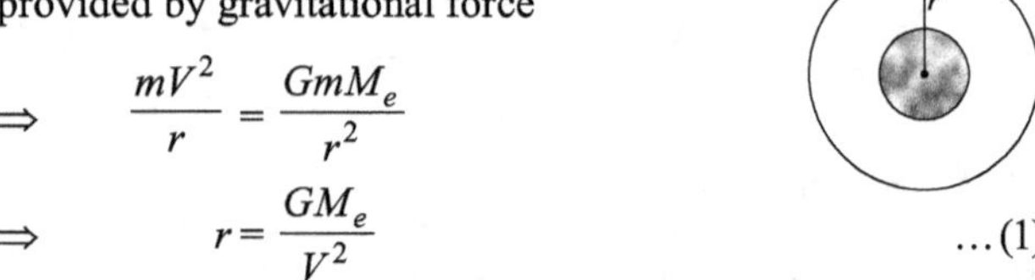

$$\Rightarrow \qquad \frac{mV^2}{r} = \frac{GmM_e}{r^2}$$

$$\Rightarrow \qquad r = \frac{GM_e}{V^2} \qquad\qquad \dots(1)$$

If kinetic energy of mass m is K then for escaping from gravitational pull, total energy of object should be equal to zero, thus we have

$$E = K - \frac{GmM_e}{r} = 0$$

$$\Rightarrow \qquad K = m\left(\frac{GM_e}{r}\right) = mV^2 \qquad \textbf{Ans. (B)}$$

Sol. 4 Each point of wire experiences different g given as

$$g_y = \frac{MGy}{R^3}$$

Force acting on an element of width dy of the wire due to gravitational pull is given as

$$dF = (\lambda dy)\frac{MGy}{R^3}$$

Total gravitational pull on wire is given as

$$F = \int dF = \frac{\lambda MG}{R^3}\int_{\frac{4R}{5}}^{R} y\,dy$$

$$\Rightarrow \qquad F = \frac{\lambda MG}{R^3}\left[\frac{R^2 - \dfrac{16R^2}{25}}{2}\right]$$

$$\Rightarrow \qquad F = \frac{\lambda MG}{R}\left[\frac{9}{50}\right] = \frac{9\lambda MG}{50R}$$

$$\Rightarrow \qquad F = \frac{9\lambda G}{50}\frac{M_e}{\dfrac{R_e}{10}\,1000}$$

$$\Rightarrow \qquad F = \frac{9\lambda GM_e}{5000\,R_e}$$

$$\Rightarrow \qquad F = \frac{9\lambda g R_e}{5000}$$

$$\Rightarrow \qquad F = \frac{9\times10^{-3}\times10\times6\times10^6}{5000} = \frac{54\times10^4}{5\times10^3} = 108\,\text{N}$$

Ans. (B)

Sol. 5 By energy conservation, we have

$$\left[\frac{-GM_e}{R_e} - \frac{GM_{\text{Sun}}}{d}\right]m + \frac{1}{2}mv_e^2 = 0$$

$$\Rightarrow \qquad \sqrt{2\left(\frac{GM_e}{R_e} + \frac{GM_{\text{Sun}}}{d}\right)} = v_s$$

$$\Rightarrow \qquad \sqrt{2\frac{GM_e}{R_e}\left(1 + \frac{M_{\text{Sun}}}{M_e}\frac{R_e}{d}\right)} = v_s$$

$$\Rightarrow \qquad v_s = 11.2\sqrt{1 + \frac{3\times10^5}{2.5\times10^4}}$$

$$\Rightarrow \qquad v_s = 11.2\,(1+12)^{1/2}$$

$$\Rightarrow \qquad v_s = 40.38\,\text{km/s}$$

Closes match is 42 km/s in the options given. **Ans. (C)**

Sol. 6 Mass in terms of density is given as

$$m = \rho\left(\frac{4}{3}\pi r^3\right)$$

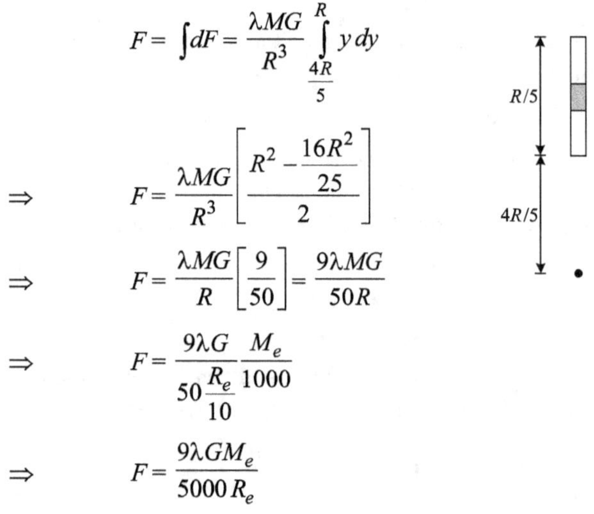

$$\Rightarrow \qquad \frac{3m}{4\pi} = \rho r^3$$

By differentiating this expression with respect to time, we get

$$\Rightarrow \qquad \rho 3r^2\frac{dr}{dt} + r^3\frac{d\rho}{dt} = 0$$

$$\Rightarrow \qquad \frac{dr}{dt} = -\frac{r^3\dfrac{d\rho}{dt}}{3\rho r^2}$$

$$\Rightarrow \qquad \frac{dr}{dt} = -\frac{r}{3\rho}\frac{d\rho}{dt}$$

$$\Rightarrow \qquad v = -\frac{r}{3}k \qquad\qquad \textbf{Ans. (C)}$$

Sol. 7 If mass of cloud in a sphere of radius r is M, then for a particle of mass m on the surface of this sphere, we have

$$\frac{GMm}{r^2} = \frac{mv^2}{r}$$

$$\Rightarrow \qquad \frac{GMm}{r} = 2K$$

$$\Rightarrow \qquad M = \frac{2Kr}{Gm}$$

For an elemental shell of radius r, thickness dr and mass dM, we use

$$dM = \frac{2K\,dr}{Gm}$$

If density of cloud is $\rho(r)$, we have

$$(4\pi r^2 dr)\,\rho(r) = \frac{2K\,dr}{Gm}$$

$$\Rightarrow \qquad \rho(r) = \frac{K}{2\pi r^2 Gm}$$

$$\Rightarrow \qquad n(r) = \frac{\rho(r)}{m} = \frac{K}{2\pi r^2 m^2 G} \qquad \textbf{Ans. (D)}$$

Sol. 8 Figure below shows the situation described in the question.

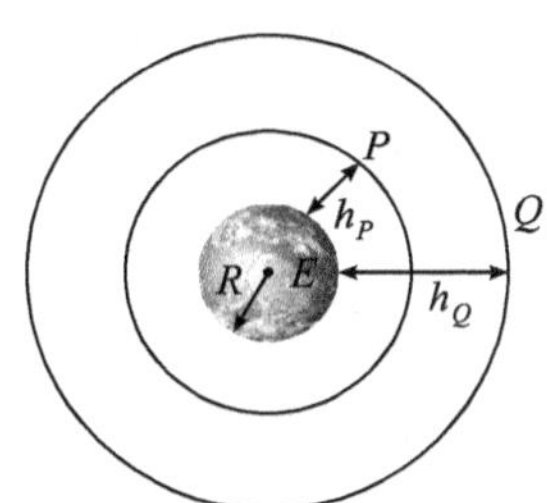

Ratio of earth's gravity at location of satellites P and Q are given as

$$\frac{g_P}{g_Q} = \frac{\dfrac{GM}{r_P^2}}{\dfrac{GM}{r_Q^2}} = \left(\frac{r_Q}{r_P}\right)^2$$

$$\Rightarrow \qquad \frac{36}{25} = \left(\frac{r_Q}{r_P}\right)^2$$

$$\Rightarrow \qquad \frac{r_Q}{r_P} = \frac{6}{5}$$

$$\Rightarrow \qquad r_Q = \frac{6}{5}r_P$$

$$\Rightarrow \qquad R + h_Q = \frac{6}{5}\left(R + \frac{R}{3}\right)$$

$$\Rightarrow \qquad h_Q = \frac{24}{15}R - R = \frac{9}{15}R = \frac{3}{5}R \qquad \textbf{Ans. (A)}$$

Sol. 9 Escape velocity from the surface of a planet is given as

$$V_e = \sqrt{\frac{2GM}{R}} = \sqrt{\frac{2 \cdot G\rho \cdot \frac{4}{3}\pi R^3}{R}} = \sqrt{\frac{4G\rho}{3}}\,R$$

$$\Rightarrow \qquad V_e \propto R$$

Surface area of planet P is

$$A_P = 4\pi R_P^2$$

Surface area of planet Q is

$$A_Q = 4A = 4\pi R_Q^2$$

$$\Rightarrow \qquad R_Q = 2R_P$$

Mass of planet R is

$$M_R = M_P + M_Q$$

$$\rho\,\frac{4}{3}\pi R_R^3 = \rho\,\frac{4}{3}\pi R_P^3 + \rho\,\frac{4}{3}\pi R_Q^3$$

$$\Rightarrow \qquad R_R^3 = R_P^3 + R_Q^3 = 9R_P^3$$

$$R_R = 9^{1/3}\,R_P$$

$$\Rightarrow \qquad R_R > R_Q > R_P$$

Thus we have

$$V_R > V_Q > V_P$$

$$\Rightarrow \qquad \frac{V_R}{V_P} = 9^{1/3} \ \text{ and } \ \frac{V_P}{V_Q} = \frac{1}{2} \qquad \textbf{Ans. (B, D)}$$

Sol. 10 To escape the particle from gravitational pull, we use

$$KE + PE = 0$$

$$\Rightarrow \qquad \frac{-2GMm}{L} + \frac{1}{2}mv^2 = 0$$

$$\Rightarrow \qquad v = 2\sqrt{\frac{GM}{L}} \qquad \textbf{Ans. (B)}$$

Sol. 11 Normal force created by astronaut an orbiting space station is zero so apparent weight of astronaut in orbiting space station is zero. Hence statement-1 is true. Because astronaut and spaceship both are in free fall motion so both statements are correct and reason is correct explanation for assertion.

$$\textbf{Ans. (A)}$$

Sol. 12 Orbital velocity around the planet is given as

$$V_0 = \sqrt{\frac{GM}{R}},$$

$$\Rightarrow \qquad \frac{V_1}{V_2}\sqrt{\frac{R_2}{R_1}} = \frac{2}{1}$$

Ratio of angular momenta of satellite is given as

$$\frac{L_1}{L_2} = \frac{m_1 v_1 R_1}{m_1 v_2 R_2} = \frac{2 \times 2 \times 1}{1 \times 1 \times 4} = \frac{1}{1}$$

Kinetic energy of satellite is given as

$$K = \frac{GMm}{2R}$$

Therefore $\dfrac{k_1}{k_2} = \dfrac{m_1}{m_2} \times \dfrac{R_1}{R_2} = \dfrac{2 \times 4}{1 \times 1} = \dfrac{8}{1}$

By Kepler's law, we have

$$T^2 \propto R^3$$

$$\Rightarrow \qquad \frac{T_1}{T_2} = \left(\frac{R_1}{R_2}\right)^{3/2} = \frac{1}{8} \qquad\qquad \textbf{Ans. (B)}$$

Sol. 13 Figure below shows the situation described in the question for the binary star comprising two stars A and B.

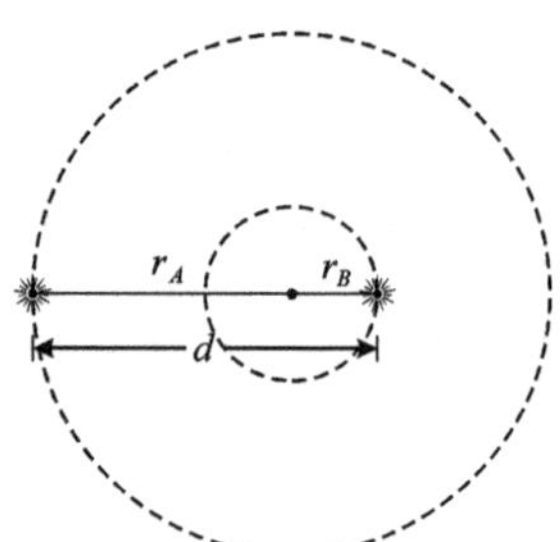

Angular momentum of A is given as

$$L_A = m_A \omega r_A^2$$

Angular momentum of B is given as

$$L_B = m_B \omega r_B^2$$

Ratio of total angular momentum to that of star B is given as

$$K = \frac{L_A + L_B}{L_B} = \frac{L_A}{L_B} + 1 = \frac{m_A r_A^2}{m_B r_B^2} + 1$$

The radii of their orbit around centre of mass is inversely proportional to their masses, which are given as

$$\frac{r_A}{r_B} = \frac{m_B}{m_A} = \frac{11}{2.2} = 5$$

$$\Rightarrow \qquad K = \frac{1}{5} \times 5^2 + 1 = 6 \qquad\qquad \textbf{Ans. (6)}$$

Sol. 14 Ratio of escape velocities at planet and earth is given as

$$\frac{v_p}{v_e} = \sqrt{\frac{2g_p R_p}{2g_e R_e}} = \sqrt{\frac{g_p}{g_e} \times \frac{R_p}{R_e}} \qquad \ldots(1)$$

Given that mass density of planet is (2/3) times that of the mass density of earth so we use

$$\frac{M_p}{\frac{4}{3}\pi R_p^3} = \frac{2}{3} \frac{M_e}{\frac{4}{3}\pi R_e^3}$$

$$\Rightarrow \qquad \frac{M_p}{M_e} = \frac{2}{3} \frac{R_p^3}{R_e^3} \qquad\qquad \ldots(2)$$

Gravitational acceleration on planet $\dfrac{\sqrt{6}}{11}$ acceleration due to gravity, so we use

$$\frac{GM_p}{R_p^2} = \frac{\sqrt{6}}{11} \frac{GM_e}{R_e^2}$$

$$\Rightarrow \qquad \frac{M_p}{M_e} = \frac{\sqrt{6}}{11} \frac{R_p^2}{R_e^2} \qquad\qquad \ldots(3)$$

From equations (2) and (3), we have

$$\frac{2}{3}\frac{R_p^3}{R_e^3} = \frac{\sqrt{6}}{11}\frac{R_p^2}{R_e^2}$$

$$\Rightarrow \qquad \frac{R_p}{R_e} = \frac{3\sqrt{6}}{22} \qquad\qquad \ldots(4)$$

From equations (1) and (4), we have

$$\frac{v_p}{v_e} = \sqrt{\frac{\sqrt{6}}{11} \times \frac{3\sqrt{6}}{22}} = \sqrt{\frac{18}{242}} = \frac{3}{11}$$

$$\Rightarrow \qquad v_p = 3 \text{ km/s} \qquad\qquad \textbf{Ans. (3)}$$

Sol. 15 Gravity at the surface of earth is given as

$$g_{\text{surface}} = \frac{GM}{R^2}$$

Gravity at a height h above the surface of earth is given as

$$g' = \frac{GM}{(R+h)^2}$$

Given that $\dfrac{GM}{(R+h)^2} = \dfrac{GM}{4R^2}$

$$\Rightarrow \qquad \left(\frac{R+h}{R}\right)^2 = 4$$

$$\Rightarrow \qquad \frac{R+h}{R} = 2$$

$$\Rightarrow \qquad R + h = 2R$$

$$\Rightarrow \qquad h = R$$

By conservation of energy, we use

$$-\frac{GMm}{R} + \frac{1}{2}mv^2 = -\frac{GMm}{2R}$$

$$\Rightarrow \qquad \frac{1}{2}mv^2 = \frac{GMm}{2R}$$

If v_e is the escape velocity, we use

$$-\frac{GMm}{R} + \frac{1}{2}mv_e^2 = 0$$

$$\Rightarrow \qquad \frac{1}{2}mv_e^2 = \frac{GMm}{R} = mv^2$$

$$\Rightarrow \qquad v_e = v\sqrt{2}$$

$$\Rightarrow \qquad N = 2 \qquad\qquad \textbf{Ans. (2)}$$

Sol. 16 Figure below shows the forces acting on the masses

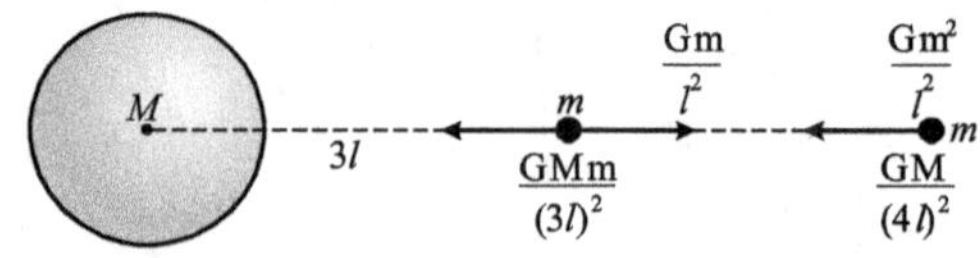

Net force acting on the masses will be zero at the given separation, so we use

$$\frac{GMm}{(3l)^2} - \frac{Gm^2}{l^2} = \frac{GMm}{(4l)^2} + \frac{Gm^2}{l^2}$$

$$\Rightarrow \quad M\left[\frac{1}{9} - \frac{1}{16}\right] = 2m$$

$$\Rightarrow \quad M\frac{7}{288} = m$$

$$\Rightarrow \quad k = 7 \qquad\qquad \textbf{Ans. (7)}$$

Sol. 17 Let both the stars rotate about their common COM with angular velocity ω then for star A

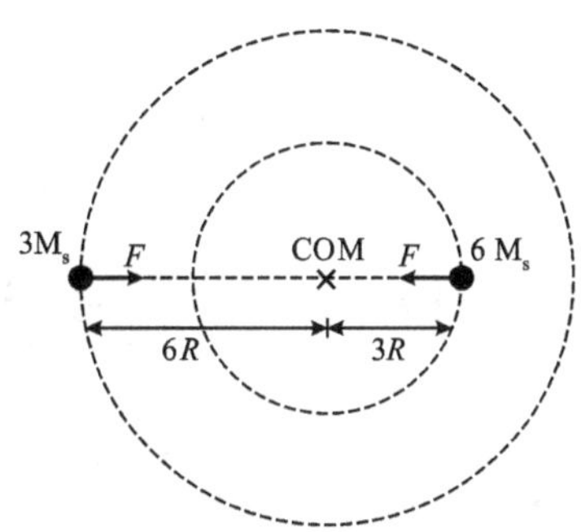

Gravitational force between two masses provides them the necessary centripetal force for revolution, so we use

$$F_G = 3M_S\,\omega^2\,(6R)$$

$$\Rightarrow \quad \frac{G(3M_S)(6M_S)}{(9R)^2} = 3M_S\omega^2(6R)$$

$$\Rightarrow \quad \omega = \sqrt{\frac{GM_S}{81R^3}}$$

$$\Rightarrow \quad T' = 2\pi\sqrt{\frac{81R^3}{GM_S}} = 9T \qquad \textbf{Ans. (9)}$$

Sol. 18 Given that radius of both planets are equal

$$R_A = R_B = R$$

and $$M_B = 2M_A$$

When mass is shifted from A to B, final radius of star A will become $\dfrac{R_A}{2}$ and mass of remaining star A will become

$$m_A = \rho_A \times \frac{4}{3}\pi\left(\frac{R_A}{2}\right)^3 = \frac{M_A}{8}$$

Thus escape velocity for A is given as

$$v_A = \sqrt{\frac{2G(M_A/8)}{R_A/2}} = \sqrt{\frac{GM_A}{2R}} \qquad \ldots(1)$$

Mass after shifting over B, new mass of B will become

$$m_B = 2M_A + \frac{7}{8}M_A = \frac{23}{8}M_A$$

If the radius of B now becomes r, then additional volume added over it can be written as

$$\frac{4}{3}\pi(r^3 - R_B^3)\rho_A = \frac{7}{8}\rho_A \times \frac{4}{3}\pi R_A^3$$

$$\Rightarrow \quad r^3 = \frac{7}{8}R_A^3 + R_B^3 = \frac{(15)^{1/3}R}{2}$$

Escape velocity for planet B is given as

$$V_B = \sqrt{\frac{2(23GM_A/8)}{(15^{1/3}R/2)}}$$

$$\Rightarrow \quad \frac{V_B}{V_A} = \sqrt{\frac{23}{15^{1/3}}} = \sqrt{\frac{10 \times 2.30}{15^{1/3}}}$$

$$\Rightarrow \quad n = 2.30 \qquad\qquad \textbf{Ans. (2.30)}$$

Ch-6 Mechanical Properties of Solids

Sol. 1 Figure below shows the situation described in question.

F ←————[2L, 2R | L, R]————→ F

Both wires of copper so the equivalent force constants of the two wires is given as

$$k_1 = \frac{\pi 4R^2}{2L}, \quad k_2 = \frac{\pi R^2}{L}$$

Here x and y are elongation in two wires

$$\Rightarrow \quad F = k_1 x = k_2 y$$

$$\Rightarrow \quad \frac{y}{x} = \frac{k_1}{k_2} = 2 \qquad\qquad \textbf{Ans. (C)}$$

Sol. 2 P can have more stress then Q before falling after proportional limit so P is more ductile than Q. Hence (B) is correct. For same stress S strain in P is higher than Q. From figure, we can see that P breaks later compared to Q hence option (A) is also correct.

As $Y = \dfrac{\text{Stress}}{\text{Strain}}$ will be lower for P so option (D) incorrect.

Ans. (A, B)

Sol. 3 For the suspended mass, we have

$$\text{strain} = \frac{x}{l}$$

$$\frac{\text{stress}}{\text{strain}} = Y \text{ (Young's modulus)}$$

$$\Rightarrow \quad \text{stress} = Yx \qquad\qquad (l = 1\text{ m})$$

$$\Rightarrow \quad \frac{F}{A} = Yx$$

$$\Rightarrow \quad F = Ayx$$

$$Ayx = ma$$

$$a = \frac{AYx}{m}; \quad \omega = \sqrt{\frac{AY}{m}}$$

$$\Rightarrow \quad 140 = \sqrt{\dfrac{4.9 \times 10^{-7} \times n \times 10^9}{0.1}}$$

$$\Rightarrow \quad 140 = 70\sqrt{n}$$

$$\Rightarrow \quad n = 4 \qquad \text{Ans. (4)}$$

Sol. 4 Change in length by Young's modulus

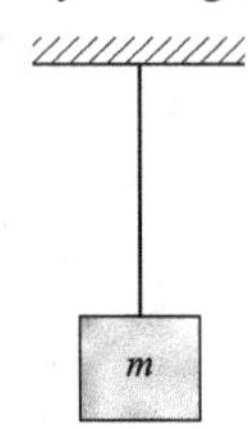

$$\Delta L = \dfrac{mgL}{AY} = L\alpha\,(\Delta\theta)$$

$$\Rightarrow \quad m = \dfrac{AY\alpha(\Delta\theta)}{g} = \dfrac{\pi \times 10^{-6} \times 10^{11} \times 10^{-5} \times 10}{10}$$

$$\Rightarrow \quad m = 3.14\,\text{kg} \cong 3\,\text{kg} \qquad \text{Ans. (3)}$$

Sol. 5 The tensions in the two wires are taken as

$$T_S = \text{tension in steel wire}$$
$$T_C = \text{Tension in copper wire}$$

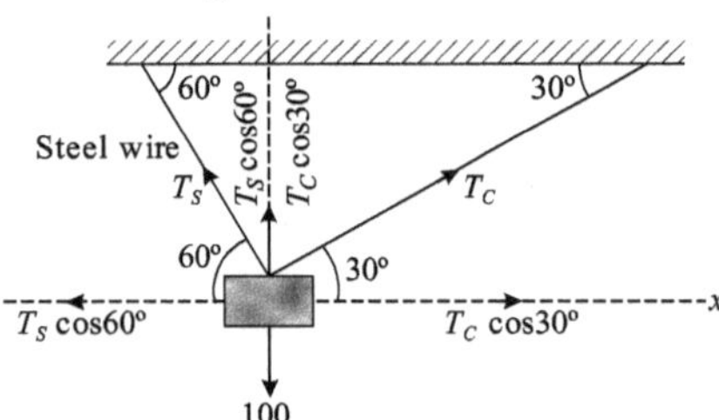

For equilibrium of block In x-direction, we have

$$T_C\cos30° = T_S\cos60°$$

$$T_C \times \dfrac{\sqrt{3}}{2} = T_S \times \dfrac{1}{2}$$

$$\Rightarrow \quad \sqrt{3}\,T_C = T_S \qquad \ldots(1)$$

For equilibrium in y-direction, we have

$$T_C\sin30° + T_S\sin60° = 100$$

$$\Rightarrow \quad \dfrac{T_C}{2} + \dfrac{T_S\sqrt{3}}{2} = 100 \qquad \ldots(2)$$

Solving equation-(1) & (2), gives

$$T_C = 50\,\text{N}$$

$$T_S = 50\sqrt{3}\,\text{N}$$

We know by definition of Young's modulus

$$\Delta l = \dfrac{Fl}{AY}$$

$$\Rightarrow \quad \Delta l = \dfrac{\Delta l_C}{\Delta l_S} = \dfrac{T_C l_C}{A_C Y_C} \times \dfrac{A_S Y_S}{T_S l_S}$$

Solving above equation

$$\Rightarrow \quad \dfrac{\Delta l_C}{\Delta l_S} = 2 \qquad \text{Ans. (2)}$$

Sol. 6 If a is the edge length of the cubical solid, change in its volume is given as

$$\dfrac{dV}{V} = \dfrac{3\Delta a}{a}$$

Bulk modulus of the wire is given as

$$B = -V\dfrac{dP}{dV} = \dfrac{-V(\rho gh)}{dV} = \dfrac{-\rho gh}{3\Delta a}\,a$$

$$\Rightarrow \quad 70 \times 10^9 = \dfrac{1 \times 5000 \times 10^3 \times 10 \times 1}{3 \times \Delta a}$$

$$\Rightarrow \quad \Delta a = \dfrac{5}{21} \times 10^{-2}\,\text{m} = 2.38\,\text{mm}$$

$$\text{Ans. (0.23 to 0.24)}$$

Ch-7 Mechanical Properties of Fluids

Sol. 1 Pressure at a depth x, from the surface of water due to weight of liquid is given as ρgx. Thus net force on each surface of $ABCD$ is calculated by considering an element as shown in figure below, given as

$$\int_0^h (P_0 + \rho gx)2R\,dx - 2RT = F$$

$$\Rightarrow \quad 2P_0 Rh + R\rho gh^2 - 2RT = F$$

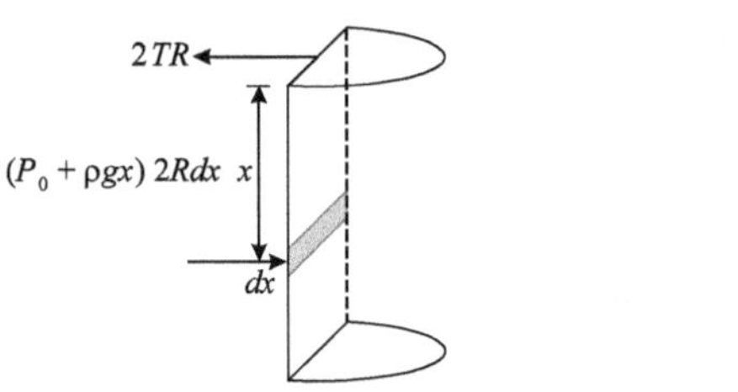

$$\text{Ans. (B)}$$

Sol. 2 Let the radius of the bubble at end 2 be R. Then $R > r$ as the shape is sub-hemispherical means it is less than hemisphere so radius of curvature will be more. Now, excess pressures inside this is given as

$$P_2 - P_0 = \dfrac{4T}{R}$$

$$\Rightarrow \quad P_2 = P_0 + \dfrac{4T}{R}$$

and pressure inside first one is given as

$$P_1 = P_0 + \dfrac{4T}{r}$$

$$\Rightarrow \quad P_1 > P_2$$

Thus air will flow from end 1 to 2, and as a result volume at end 1 decreases. **Ans. (B)**

Sol. 3 Let outer volume of shell is V_0 and inner volume of shell is V_i and volume of water inside the shall is V, so we have

$$\Rightarrow \quad V(1)g + \rho_c(V_0 - V_i)g = (1)\frac{V_0}{2}g$$

$$\Rightarrow \quad V + \rho_c(V_0 - V_i) = \frac{V_0}{2}$$

$$\Rightarrow \quad \rho_c(V_0 - V_i) = \frac{V_0}{2} - V$$

$$\Rightarrow \quad \rho_c = \frac{\dfrac{V_0}{2} - V}{V_0 - V_i}$$

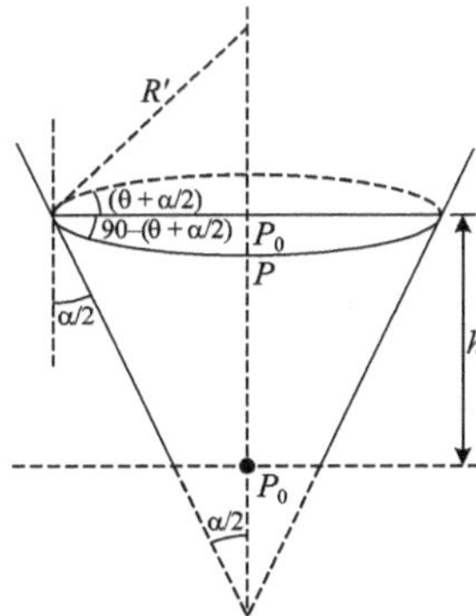

If $\rho_c < \dfrac{1}{2}$ then we use

$$\Rightarrow \quad \frac{\dfrac{V_0}{2} - V}{V_0 - V_i} < \frac{1}{2}$$

$$\Rightarrow \quad \frac{V_0}{2} - V < \frac{V_0}{2} - \frac{V_i}{2}$$

$$\Rightarrow \quad -V < -\frac{V_i}{2}$$

$$\Rightarrow \quad V > \frac{V_i}{2} \qquad \textbf{Ans. (A)}$$

Sol. 4 As R' is the radius of curvature of meniscus formed as shown in figure below, we use

$$\cos\left(\theta + \frac{\alpha}{2}\right) = \frac{b}{R'}$$

$$\Rightarrow \quad R' = \frac{b}{\cos\left(\theta + \dfrac{\alpha}{2}\right)}$$

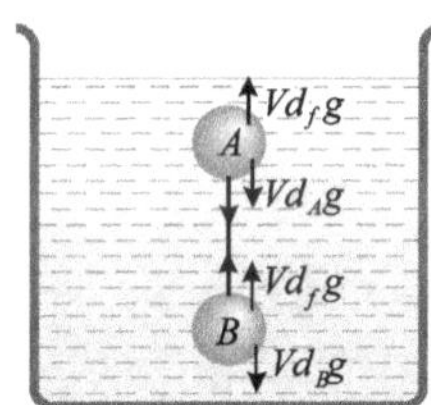

Excess pressure on concave side of meniscus is taken as

$$P_0 - P = \frac{2S}{R'}$$

$$\Rightarrow \quad P_0 - P = \frac{2S}{b}\cos\left(\theta + \frac{\alpha}{2}\right)$$

$$\Rightarrow \quad P = P_0 - \frac{2S}{b}\cos\left(\theta + \frac{\alpha}{2}\right)$$

$$P + \rho gh = P_0$$

$$\Rightarrow \quad P_0 - \frac{2S}{b}\cos\left(\theta + \frac{\alpha}{2}\right) + \rho gh = P_0$$

$$\Rightarrow \quad h = \frac{2S}{b\rho g}\cos\left(\theta + \frac{\alpha}{2}\right) \qquad \textbf{Ans. (D)}$$

Sol. 5 Final sum of heights in the two arms of tube is given as

$$h_1 + h_2 = 0.29 \times 2 + 0.1$$

$$h_1 + h_2 = 0.68 \qquad \qquad \ldots(1)$$

If ρ_k is the density of kerosene & ρ_w is the density of water then we use Pascal's equation as

$$P_0 + \rho_k g(0.1) + \rho_w g(h_1 - 0.1) - \rho_w gh_2 = P_0$$

$$\Rightarrow \quad \rho_k g(0.1) + \rho_w gh_1 - \rho_k g \times (0.1) = \rho_w gh_2$$

$$\Rightarrow \quad 800 \times 10 \times 0.1 + 1000 \times 10 \times h_1 - 1000 \times 10 \times 0.1$$
$$= 1000 \times 10 \times h_2$$

$$\Rightarrow \quad 10000(h_1 - h_2) = 200$$

$$\Rightarrow \quad h_1 - h_2 = 0.02 \qquad \qquad \ldots(2)$$

$$\Rightarrow \quad h_1 = 0.35$$

$$\Rightarrow \quad h_2 = 0.33$$

$$\Rightarrow \quad \frac{h_1}{h_2} = \frac{35}{33} \qquad \textbf{Ans. (B)}$$

Sol. 6 Figure below shows the forces acting on the spheres

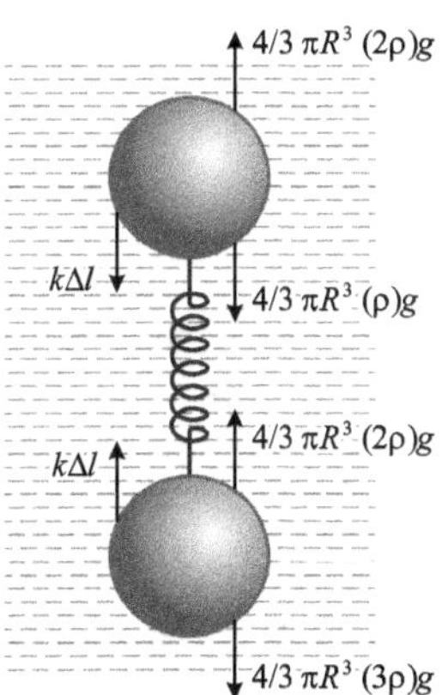

System will be in equilibrium with tension in string only if $d_f > d_A$ and $d_B > d_f$. If both A and B are considered as a system then we use

$$2Vd_f g = V(d_A + d_B)g$$

$$\Rightarrow \quad d_A + d_B = 2d_f \qquad \textbf{Ans. (A, B, D)}$$

Sol. 7 At equilibrium, we have

$$\frac{4}{3}\pi R^3 2\rho g = \frac{4}{3}\pi R^3 \rho g + k\Delta l$$

$$\Rightarrow \quad k\Delta l = \frac{4}{3}\pi R^3 \rho g$$

$$\Rightarrow \quad k\Delta l = \frac{4}{3k}\pi R^3 \rho g$$

For equilibrium of the complete system, net force of buoyancy must be equal to the total weight of the sphere which holds true in the given problem. So both the spheres are completely submerged.

Ans. (A, D)

Sol. 8 Force acting on an element shell of width dr at a radius r is given as

$$dF = \frac{GM}{R^3} r \, (\rho dS \, dr)$$

Pressure on this elemental shell is

$$dp = \frac{dF}{dS} = \frac{GM\rho}{R^3} r \, dr$$

Net pressure is given as

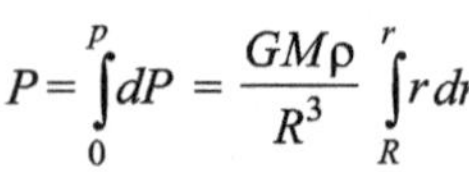

$$P = \int_0^p dP = \frac{GM\rho}{R^3} \int_R^r r \, dr$$

$$\Rightarrow \qquad P = -\frac{GM\rho}{R^3} \left[\frac{r^2}{2}\right]_R^r$$

Here $P(r)$ is pressure at $r < R$

$$\Rightarrow \qquad P = +\frac{GM\rho}{2R^3} [R^2 - r^2]$$

$$\Rightarrow \quad \frac{P\left(\dfrac{3R}{4}\right)}{P(2R/3)} = \frac{\dfrac{GM\rho}{2R^3}\left[R^2 - \dfrac{9R^2}{16}\right]}{\left[R^2 - \dfrac{4R^2}{9}\right]} = \frac{\dfrac{7R^2}{16}}{\dfrac{5R^2}{9}} = \frac{63}{80}$$

$$\Rightarrow \quad \frac{P(3R/5)}{P(2R/5)} = \frac{\dfrac{GM\rho}{2R^3}\left[R^2 - \dfrac{9R^2}{25}\right]}{\dfrac{GM\rho}{2R^3}\left[R^2 - \dfrac{4R^2}{25}\right]} = \frac{16}{25} \times \frac{25}{21} = \frac{16}{21}$$

$$\Rightarrow \quad \frac{P(R/2)}{P(R/3)} = \frac{\dfrac{GM\rho}{2R^3}\left[R^2 - \dfrac{R^2}{4}\right]}{\dfrac{GM\rho}{2R^3}\left[R^2 - \dfrac{R^2}{9}\right]} = \frac{\dfrac{3R^2}{4}}{\dfrac{8R^2}{9}} = \frac{27}{32}$$ **Ans. (B, C)**

Sol. 9 For equilibrium of spheres, we use below free body diagrams of the spheres

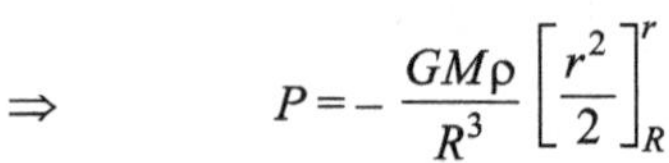

For P $\qquad\qquad T = B_1 - M_1 g,$

For Q $\qquad\qquad T = M_2 g - B_2$

From above equations, we have

$$B_1 - M_1 g = M_2 g - B_2$$

As both spheres are completely submerged, we use

$$\sigma_1 - \rho_1 = \rho_2 - \sigma_2$$

Terminal velocity for a ball of density ρ in a liquid of density σ is given as

$$V_T = \frac{\dfrac{4}{3}\pi r^3 g(\rho - \sigma)}{6\pi \eta r}$$

$$\Rightarrow \qquad V_T = \frac{2}{9} \frac{(\rho - \sigma)r^2 g}{\eta}$$

$$\Rightarrow \qquad V_P = \frac{2}{9} \frac{(\rho_1 - \sigma_1)r^2 g}{\eta_1}$$

and $\qquad\qquad V_Q = \dfrac{2}{9} \dfrac{(\rho_2 - \sigma_2)r^2 g}{\eta_2}$

As we have $\sigma_1 - \rho_1 = \rho_2 - \sigma_2$ we have from above terminal speeds

$$\Rightarrow \qquad \left|\frac{V_P}{V_Q}\right| = \frac{\eta_2}{\eta_1}$$

Thus option (A) is correct. From the equilibrium state of the two spheres where string is taut, it means if string is cut, the two balls will be moving in opposite directions hence the terminal speeds of the two spheres are in opposite directions hence option (D) is also correct. **Ans. (A, D)**

Sol. 10 Capillary height is given as

$$h = \frac{2\sigma \cos\theta}{r\rho g_{eff}}$$

As r increases, h decreases and $h \propto \sigma$. Further if lift is going up with an acceleration a then $g_{eff} = g + a$. As g_{eff} increases, h decreases. Also h is not proportional to θ but $h \propto \cos\theta$.

Ans. (A, C)

Sol. 11 Viscous force between layers of a flowing liquid is given as

$$|F| = \eta A \frac{u_0}{h}$$

Where $\dfrac{u_0}{h}$ is the velocity gradient. The shear stress on the given plate can be calculated as

$$\frac{|F|}{A} = \eta \frac{u_0}{h} \qquad\qquad \textbf{Ans. (A, C, D)}$$

Sol. 12 Height raised in the capillary tube is given as

$$h = \frac{2T \cos\theta}{\rho g R}$$

If only tube T1 is inserted then capillary height is calculated as

$$h_1 = \frac{2 \times 0.075 \times \cos 0°}{1000 \times 10 \times 0.2 \times 10^{-3}} = 75 \text{ mm}$$

If only tube T2 is inserted then capillary height is calculated as

$$h_2 = \frac{2 \times 0.075 \times \cos 60°}{1000 \times 10 \times 0.2 \times 10^{-3}} = 37.5 \text{ mm}$$

Now we can check the given option.

(A) : Since contact angles are different so correction in the height of water column raised in the tube will be different in both the cases, hence option (A) is correct.

(B) : If joint is 5 cm is above water surface, then water crosses the joint by height h in T2 so we use

$$P_0 - \frac{2T}{r} + \rho gh + \rho g \times 5 \times 10^{-2} = P_0$$

For the given capillary tube, at meniscus we use

$$r = \frac{R}{\cos\theta}$$

$$\Rightarrow \quad \rho g\,(h + 5 \times 10^{-2}) = \frac{2T\cos\theta}{R}$$

$$\Rightarrow \quad h = \frac{2 \times 0.075 \times \cos 60}{0.2 \times 10^{-3} \times 1000 \times 10} - 5 \times 10^{-2}$$

Above value of h is negative which is not possible, so liquid will not cross the interface but to balance the pressure, at interface radius of curvature of liquid changes. Hence option (B) is NOT correct.

(C) : If interface is 8 cm above water then water will not even reach the interface, and water will rise till 7.5 cm only in T1, hence option (C) is correct.

(D) : If interface is 5 cm above the water in vessel, then water in capillary will not even reach the interface. Water will reach only till 3.75 cm, hence option (D) is correct.   **Ans. (A, C, D)**

Sol. 13 For acceleration a the pressure difference between points 2 and 1 can be calculated as

$$P_2 + \rho d\left(g - \frac{a}{\sqrt{2}}\right) - \rho\frac{a}{\sqrt{2}}\,d = P_1$$

$$\Rightarrow \quad P_1 - P_2 = \rho d\,(g - \sqrt{2}\,a)$$

$$\Rightarrow \quad \frac{P_1 - P_2}{\rho gd} = \left(1 - \frac{\sqrt{2}\,a}{g}\right)$$ **Ans. (A, C)**

Sol. 14 For a bubble, gas pressure inside is given by atmospheric pressure plus the excess pressure due to surface tension, given as

$$P_{gas} = P_a + \frac{4S}{r}$$

For adiabatic process, we use

$$PV^\gamma = \text{Constant}$$

$$\Rightarrow \quad \left(P_{a1} + \frac{4S}{r_1}\right)\left(\frac{4}{3}\pi r_1^3\right)^{5/3} = \left(P_{a2} + \frac{4S}{r_2}\right)\left(\frac{4}{3}\pi r_2^3\right)^{5/3}$$

$$\Rightarrow \quad \frac{r_1^3}{r_2^3} = \left(\frac{P_{a2} + \dfrac{4S}{r_2}}{P_{a1} + \dfrac{4S}{r_1}}\right)$$

Hence option (A) is NOT correct and option (C) is correct. As atmospheric pressure is involved in work option (B) is NOT correct.

For adiabatic process, we also have

$$P^{1-\gamma}\,T^\gamma = \text{Constant}$$

$$\Rightarrow \quad \left(P_{a2} + \frac{4S}{r_2}\right)^{1-5/3} T_2^{5/3} = \left(P_{a1} + \frac{4S}{r_1}\right)^{1-5/3} T_1^{5/3}$$

$$\Rightarrow \quad \left(\frac{T_2}{T_1}\right)^{5/3} = \left(\frac{P_{a1} + \dfrac{4S}{r_1}}{P_{a2} + \dfrac{4S}{r_2}}\right)^{-2/3}$$

$$\Rightarrow \quad \left(\frac{T_2}{T_1}\right)^{5/3} = \left(\frac{P_{a2} + \dfrac{4S}{r_2}}{P_{a1} + \dfrac{4S}{r_1}}\right)$$

Hence option (D) is correct.   **Ans. (C, D)**

Sol. 15 According to equation of continuity, volume flow rate of liquid 'Av' remain constant. When hose pipe is held vertically up, its velocity decreases hence cross sectional area increases and when held vertically down, its velocity increases and hence cross-sectional area decreases. Thus both statement-1 and 2 are correct and statement-2 is the correct explanation. **Ans. (A)**

Sol. 16 When Lift at rest efflux velocity of water from hole is given as

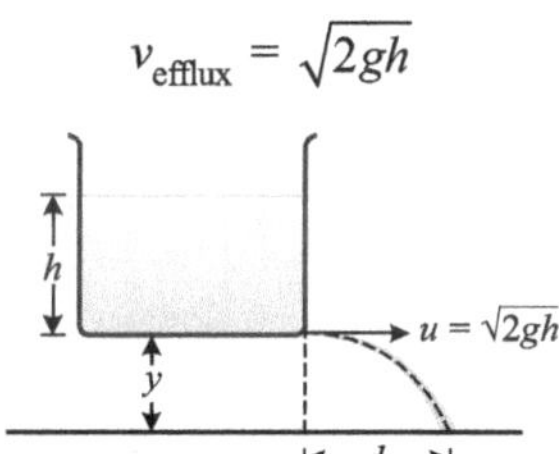

Distance on floor where water jet hits is calculated as

$$d = v_{efflux} \times t$$

$$\Rightarrow \quad d = \sqrt{2gh}\,\sqrt{\frac{2y}{g}}$$

$$\Rightarrow \quad d = \sqrt{2gy} = 1.2\,\text{m}$$

Now we can check all the cases mentioned in **Column-I.**

(P) : As Lift is accelerating upwards with respect to lift, effective gravity is taken as

$$g_{eff} = g + a$$

Thus the distance on floor where water jet hits is now calculated as

$$d' = \sqrt{2(g+a)h}\,\sqrt{\frac{2y}{g+a}}$$

$$\Rightarrow \quad d' = 1.2\,\text{m}$$

(Q) : As Lift is accelerates downward with respect to lift, effective gravity is taken as

$$g_{\text{eff}} = g - a$$

Thus the distance on floor where water jet hits is now calculated as

$$d' = \sqrt{2(g-a)h}\,\sqrt{\frac{2y}{g-a}}$$

$$\Rightarrow \qquad d' = 1.2\,\text{m}$$

(R) : When lift moves at constant speed then we use $a = 0$, hence $d = 1.2$ m

(S) : When lift is falling freely then $a = g$ and in this case fluid will not come out of jar so no efflux

Hence option (C) is correct. **Ans. (C)**

Sol. 17 As cylinder has a hole at its top, it is open to atmosphere. So pressure in the cylinder between its top and the piston will be equal to atmospheric pressure P_0. Thus option (A) is correct.

Ans. (A)

Sol. 18 Pressure inside piston when the piston is sealed at a distance of $2L$ is P_0.

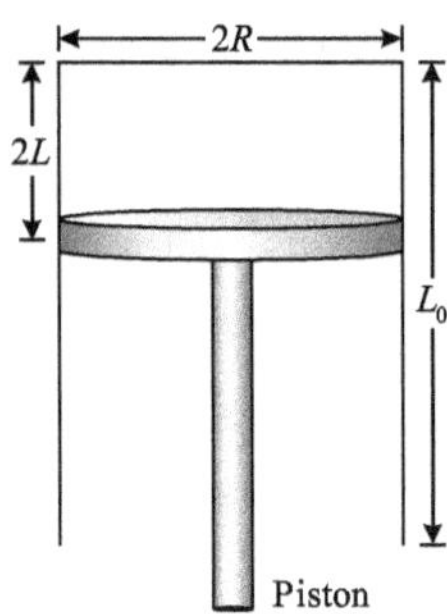

If P_f is the pressure at equilibrium so we use

$$P_f \cdot (Ax) = P_0\,(2AL)$$

$$\Rightarrow \qquad P_f(x\pi R^2) = P_0\,(2L\pi R^2)$$

$$\Rightarrow \qquad P_f = \frac{2P_0 L}{x}$$

At equilibrium of piston, we use

piston weight + down ward force due to air pressure = upward force due to atmospheric pressure

$$\Rightarrow \qquad Mg + P_f(\pi R^2) = P_0 \pi R^2$$

$$\Rightarrow \qquad x = \left(\frac{P_0 \pi R^2}{\pi R^2 P_0 - Mg}\right)(2L) \qquad \textbf{Ans. (D)}$$

Sol. 19 Pressure inside piston must be equal to the pressure at the bottom of the piston exerted by water to stay in equilibrium

$$P = P_0 + \rho g\,(L_0 - H)$$

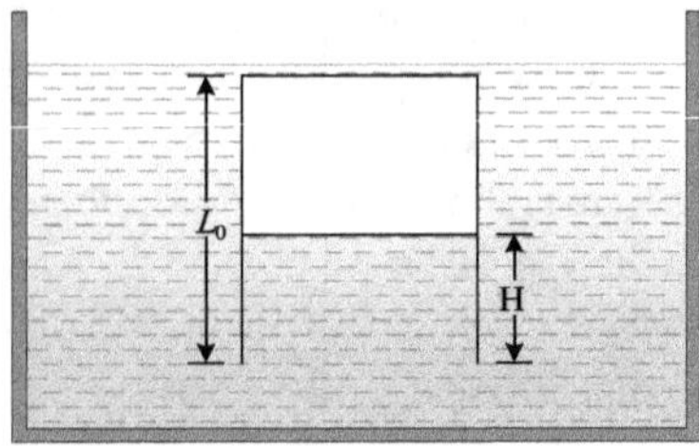

Applying Boyle's law $P_1 V_1 = P_2 V_2$, we have

$$P_0\,(AL_0) = [P_0 + (L_0 - H)\,\rho g]\,[A\,(L_0 - H)]$$

$$\Rightarrow \quad \rho g\,(L_0 - H)^2 + P_0\,(L_0 - H) - L_0 P_0 = 0$$

Thus option (C) is correct. **Ans. (C)**

Sol. 20 Figure below shows the drop formed below the opening of dropper. The force exerted by surface tension on the drop is

$$F_T = 2\pi r T$$

Net vertically upward force on drop

$$F_V = F_T \sin\theta$$

For small angle as $r \ll R$, we can use

$$F = F_T \tan\theta$$

$$\Rightarrow \qquad F = 2\pi r T\left(\frac{r}{R}\right) = \frac{2\pi r^2 T}{R} \quad \textbf{Ans. (C)}$$

Sol. 21 Drop will detach from dropper when

$$mg = \rho v g$$

$$\Rightarrow \qquad \frac{2\pi r^2 T}{R} = \frac{4}{3}\pi R^3 \times \rho \times g$$

$$\Rightarrow \qquad \frac{2 \times 25 \times 10^{-8} \times 0.11}{R} = \frac{4}{3} \times R^3 \times 10^3 \times 10$$

$$\Rightarrow \qquad R^4 = \frac{50 \times 3 \times 0.11 \times 10^{-8}}{4 \times 10^4}$$

$$\Rightarrow \qquad R^4 = 4.125 \times 10^{-12}$$

$$\Rightarrow \qquad R = 1.4 \times 10^{-3}\,\text{m} \qquad \textbf{Ans. (A)}$$

Sol. 22 Surface energy of a liquid drop is given as

$$E_S = T \times 4\pi R^2$$

$$\Rightarrow \qquad E_S = 0.11 \times 4 \times 3.14 \times 1.96 \times 10^{-6}$$

$$\Rightarrow \qquad E_S = 2.7 \times 10^{-6}\,\text{J} \qquad \textbf{Ans. (B)}$$

Sol. 23 By continuity equation in this case, we have

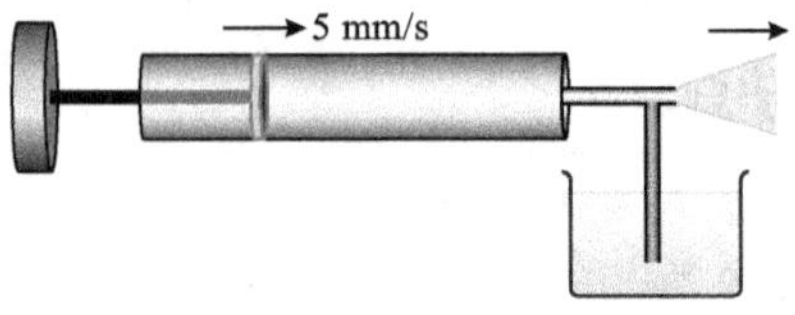

$$A_1 v_1 = A_2 v_2$$

$$\Rightarrow \qquad v_2 = \frac{A_1}{A_2} \cdot v_1$$

$$\Rightarrow \qquad v_2 = 400 \times 5 \times 10^{-3} = 2 \text{ m/s} \qquad \textbf{Ans. (C)}$$

Sol. 24 If P_1 is the pressure inside the gun, P_2 at the inside of nozzle and P_0 is the atmospheric pressure, when air comes out of nozzle with water after travelling some distance it expands in atmosphere and its speed reduces to zero. By Bernoulli's theorem for air we use

$$P_2 + \frac{1}{2}\rho_a v_2^2 = P_0 \qquad \ldots (1)$$

Liquid rises in the thin tube due to pressure difference $P_0 - P_2$ and if liquid rises at a speed v_l by Bernoulli's theorem for liquid from container to nozzle, we have

$$P_2 + \frac{1}{2}\rho_l v_l^2 = P_0 \qquad \ldots (2)$$

From equations-(1) and (2), we have

$$\rho_a v_2^2 = \rho_l v_l^2$$

By continuity equation, we use $v_2 = \left(\dfrac{A_1}{A_2}\right) v_1$

$$\Rightarrow \qquad \rho_a \left(\frac{A_1}{A_2}\right)^2 v_1^2 = \rho_l v_l^2$$

$$\Rightarrow \qquad v_l = \sqrt{\frac{\rho_a}{\rho_\ell}} \left(\frac{A_1}{A_2}\right) v_1$$

Volume flow rate of liquid is proportional to v_l hence option (A) is correct. **Ans. (A)**

Sol. 25 Test tube will start to sink when total buoyance on it is equal to its weight. Volume of test tube glass is

$$V_g = \frac{5}{2.5} = 2 \text{ cc}$$

Initially total volume of water displaced by test tube is

$$V = 2 + 3.3 = 5.3 \text{ cc}$$

Thus buoyancy force on test tube initially is given as 5.3 gm force which is more than its weight so test tube is supported by bottle cap at the top. When volume of inside trapped air in test tube decreases to 3 cc then buoyancy will exactly balances its weight and further it will start to sink hence the volume of trapped air inside becomes

$$v_0 - \Delta v = 3$$

$$\Rightarrow \qquad 3.3 - \Delta v = 3$$

$$\Rightarrow \qquad \Delta v = 0.3 \text{ cc} \qquad \textbf{Ans. (0.3)}$$

Sol. 26 For isothermal process, we use

$$P_0 V_0 = PV$$

$$10^5 \times 3.3 = P(3)$$

$$\Rightarrow \qquad P = 1.1 \times 10^5$$

$$\Delta P = 0.1 \times 10^5 = 10 \times 10^3 \text{ Pa}$$

$$\Rightarrow \qquad Y = 10 \qquad \textbf{Ans. (10)}$$

Sol. 27 Pressure due to falling water level at 200 mm is given as

$$P_2 + \rho gh = P_0$$

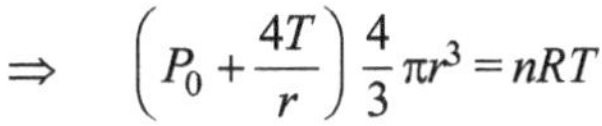

At constant temperature, we use

$$P_1 V_1 = P_2 V_2$$

$$P_0 \times A (0.5 - H) = (P_0 - \rho g \times 0.2) A \times 0.3$$

$$\Rightarrow \quad 10^5 (0.5 - H) = (10^5 - 2 \times 10^3) \times 0.3$$

$$\Rightarrow \quad 100 (0.5 - H) = (100 - 2) \times 0.3$$

$$\Rightarrow \qquad 0.5 - H = \frac{29.4}{100}$$

$$\Rightarrow \qquad H = 0.5 - .294$$

$$\Rightarrow \qquad H = 0.206$$

$$\Rightarrow \qquad H = 206 \text{ mm}$$

So fall in height is 6 mm **Ans. (6)**

Sol. 28 Excess pressure inside soap bubble is given as

$$\Delta P = \frac{4T}{r}$$

Here T is the surface tension of liquid

Thus net pressure inside the bubble is given as

$$P = P_0 + \frac{4T}{r}$$

From gas law, we use

$$P \times \frac{4}{3}\pi r^3 = nRT$$

$$\Rightarrow \quad \left(P_0 + \frac{4T}{r}\right) \frac{4}{3}\pi r^3 = nRT$$

For the two bubbles A and B, we use

$$\frac{\left(P_0 + \dfrac{4S}{r}\right) r_A^3}{\left(P_0 + \dfrac{4S}{r_B}\right) r_B^3} = \frac{n_A}{n_B}$$

$$\Rightarrow \quad \frac{\left(8 + \dfrac{4 \times 0.04}{2 \times 10^{-2}}\right)(2 \times 10^{-2})^3}{\left(8 + \dfrac{4 \times 0.04}{4 \times 10^{-2}}\right)(4 \times 10^{-2})^3} = \frac{n_A}{n_B}$$

$$\Rightarrow \qquad \frac{n_B}{n_A}=6 \qquad \textbf{Ans. (6)}$$

Sol. 29 By Stokes law, terminal velocity is given as

$$v=\frac{\frac{4}{3}r^2 g(\rho_0-\rho_L)}{6\eta}$$

$$\Rightarrow \qquad \frac{v_P}{v_Q}=\left(\frac{r_P}{r_Q}\right)^2\times\frac{\eta_Q}{\eta_P}\times\frac{(\rho_P-\rho_{L_1})}{(\rho_Q-\rho_{L_2})}$$

$$\Rightarrow \qquad \frac{v_P}{v_Q}=4\times\frac{2}{3}\times\frac{(8-0.8)}{(8-1.6)}=\frac{8}{3}\times\frac{7.2}{6.4}=3 \qquad \textbf{Ans. (3)}$$

Sol. 30 Volume of K smaller drop = volume of bigger drop

$$K\left(\frac{4}{3}\pi r^3\right)=\frac{4}{3}\pi R^3$$

$$\Rightarrow \qquad r=\left[\frac{R}{(K)^{1/3}}\right]$$

$$\Rightarrow \qquad A=4\pi r^2 K-4\pi R^2$$

Change in surface energy is given as

$$E=10^{-3}=A\times\left(\frac{0.1}{4\pi}\right)$$

$$\Rightarrow \qquad 10^{-3}=(4\pi r^2 K-4\pi R^2)\left[\frac{0.1}{4\pi}\right]$$

$$\Rightarrow \qquad 10^{-3}=(r^2 K-R^2)(0.1)$$

$$\Rightarrow \qquad 10^{-2}=R^2\left(\frac{K}{K^{2/3}}-1\right)$$

$$\Rightarrow \qquad 10^{-2}=10^{-4}(K^{1/3}-1)$$

$$\Rightarrow \qquad K=10^6$$

$$\Rightarrow \qquad \alpha=6 \qquad \textbf{Ans. (6)}$$

Sol. 31 Impulse causes an initial speed v_0 so we use

$$J=mv_0$$

$$\Rightarrow \qquad v_0=\frac{J}{m}=\frac{1}{0.4}=2.5 \text{ m/s}$$

As block moves at speed $v=v_0 e^{-t/\tau}$ we use

$$\frac{ds}{dt}=v_0 e^{-t/\tau}$$

$$\Rightarrow \qquad ds=v_0 e^{-t/\tau}\,dt$$

$$\Rightarrow \qquad s=v_0\int_0^\tau e^{-t/\tau}\,dt$$

$$\Rightarrow \qquad s=v_0\tau(1-e^{-1})=2.5\times4\times0.63=6.30\text{ m} \qquad \textbf{Ans. (6.30)}$$

Sol. 32 Pressure at the bottom of disc is due to the surface tension which can be given as

$$\rho gh=\frac{T}{R}$$

Here R is the radius of the sides of the disc which can be considered as $h/2$

$$\Rightarrow \qquad \rho gh=\frac{T}{h/2}$$

$$\Rightarrow \qquad h^2=\frac{2T}{\rho g}$$

$$\Rightarrow \qquad h=\sqrt{\frac{2T}{\rho g}}=\sqrt{\frac{2\times0.07}{10^3\times10}}=\sqrt{\frac{14\times100}{10^4\times100}}$$

$$\Rightarrow \qquad h=\sqrt{14}\text{ mm}=3.741 \qquad \textbf{Ans. (3.74)}$$

Sol. 33 Using Bernoulli's equation for moving train, we have

$$P_0+\frac{1}{2}\rho v_t^2=P+\frac{1}{2}\rho v^2$$

$$\Rightarrow \qquad P_0-P=\frac{1}{2}\rho(v^2-v_t^2) \qquad \ldots(1)$$

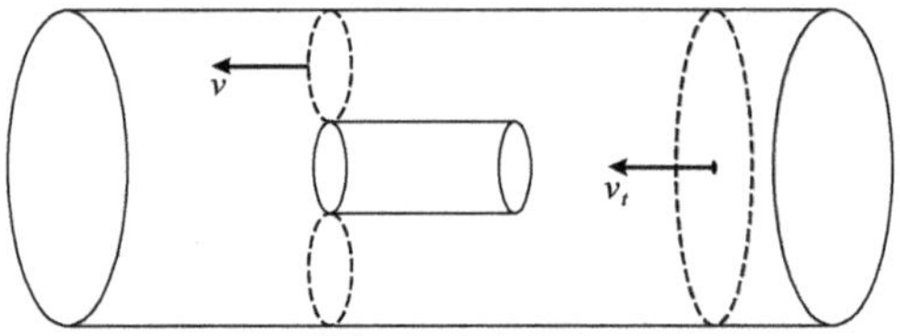

From equation of continuity, we have

$$4S_t v_t=v(3S_t)$$

$$\Rightarrow \qquad v=\frac{4}{3}v_t \qquad \ldots(2)$$

From equation-(1) and (2), we have

$$P_0-P=\frac{1}{2}\rho\left(\frac{16}{9}v_t^2-v_t^2\right)=\frac{1}{2}\rho\frac{7v_t^2}{9}$$

$$\Rightarrow \qquad N=9 \qquad \textbf{Ans. (9)}$$

Sol. 34 For the floating balloon is in equilibrium its weight is balanced by buoyant force acting force on it

$$480\times g=v\rho_1 g$$

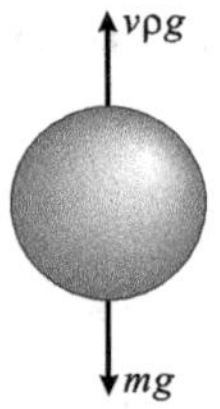

When N sand bags thrown out

$$\Rightarrow \qquad (480-N)g=v\rho_2 g$$

$$\Rightarrow \qquad \frac{480-N}{480}=\frac{\rho_2}{\rho_1}$$

$$\Rightarrow \qquad \left(1-\frac{N}{480}\right)=\frac{e^{-h_2/h_0}}{e^{-h_1/h_0}}=e^{\frac{h_1-h_2}{h_0}}=e^{-\frac{50}{6000}}$$

$$\Rightarrow \quad 1-\frac{N}{480}=1-\frac{50}{6000} \quad \Rightarrow N=\frac{50\times480}{6000}=4 \quad \textbf{Ans. (4)}$$

Sol. 35 Work done in the given process is calculated as

$$W=(\Delta P)_{\text{avg}}\times4\pi R^2a$$

For small change $(\Delta P)_{\text{avg}}$ can be taken as mean pressure, so we use

$$\Rightarrow \quad W=\left|\frac{dP}{2}\cdot4\pi R^2a\right|$$

For adiabatic process we use $PV^{\gamma}=c$

$$\Rightarrow \quad dP=-\gamma\frac{P}{V}dV=-\frac{\gamma P_0}{V}4\pi R^2a$$

$$\Rightarrow \quad W=\frac{\gamma P_0}{2V}\times4\pi R^2a\times4\pi R^2a$$

$$\Rightarrow \quad W=\frac{\gamma P_0}{2\times4\pi R^3}4\pi R^2a\times4\pi R^2a$$

$$\Rightarrow \quad W=(4\pi RP_0a^2)\frac{3\gamma}{2}$$

$$\Rightarrow \quad X=2.05 \quad\quad \textbf{Ans. (2.05)}$$

Sol. 36 Initial capillary height of liquid in capillary is calculated as

$$h_0=\frac{2T\cos\theta}{\rho gr}=\frac{2\times0.075\times1}{10^3\times10\times10^{-4}}=15\text{ cm}$$

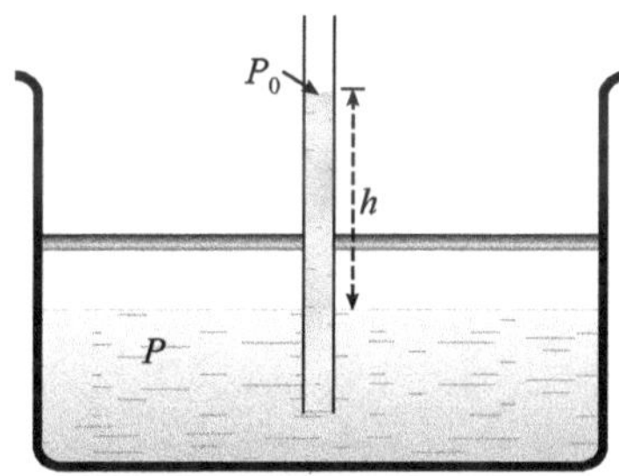

After piston compresses the air to the volume $\frac{100}{101}V_0$, the pressure above the liquid surface P is calculated as

$$P_0V_0=P\left(\frac{100}{101}\right)V_0$$

$$\Rightarrow \quad P=\frac{101}{100}P_0$$

Using Pascal's equation from the bottom point of meniscus of liquid in capillary to the liquid surface, we have

$$P_0-\frac{2T\cos\theta}{r}+\rho gh=\frac{101}{100}P_0$$

$$\Rightarrow \quad -\rho gh_0+\rho gh=\frac{P_0}{100}$$

$$\Rightarrow \quad h=h_0+\frac{P_0}{100\rho g}$$

$$\Rightarrow \quad h=15\text{ cm}+\frac{10^5}{100\times10^3\times10}$$

$$\Rightarrow \quad h=25\text{ cm} \quad\quad \textbf{Ans. (25)}$$

Ch-8 Thermal Properties of Matter

Sol. 1 In steady state energy absorbed by middle plate is equal to energy released by middle plate, so we use

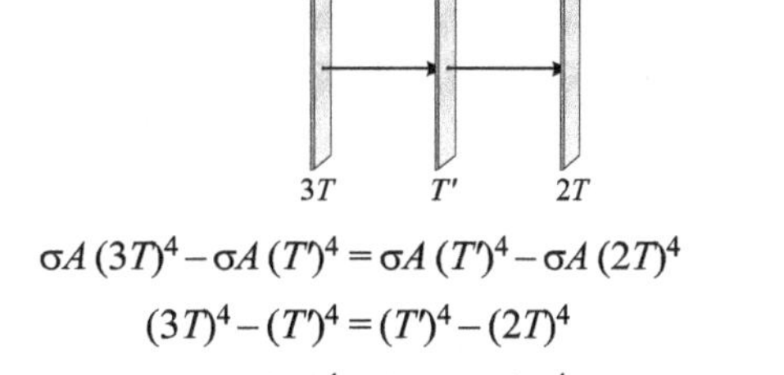

$$\sigma A(3T)^4-\sigma A(T')^4=\sigma A(T')^4-\sigma A(2T)^4$$

$$\Rightarrow \quad (3T)^4-(T')^4=(T')^4-(2T)^4$$

$$\Rightarrow \quad (2T')^4=(16+81)T^4$$

$$\Rightarrow \quad T'=\left(\frac{97}{2}\right)^{1/4}T \quad\quad \textbf{Ans. (C)}$$

Sol. 2 Thermal resistance in the configuration-I given in question is calculated as

$$R_1=\frac{L}{\kappa A}+\frac{L}{2\kappa A}=\frac{3L}{2\kappa A} \quad\quad \ldots(1)$$

Thermal resistance in configuration-II is calculated as

$$\frac{1}{R_2}=\frac{1}{\left(\frac{L}{\kappa A}\right)}+\frac{1}{\left(\frac{L}{2\kappa A}\right)}=\frac{3\kappa A}{L} \quad\quad \ldots(2)$$

$$\Rightarrow \quad R_2=\frac{L}{3\kappa A}$$

Temperature difference between the ends is same in both cases, so for same amount of heat transfer through the two cases, we have

$$\Delta Q_1=\Delta Q_2$$

$$\Rightarrow \quad \frac{\Delta T}{R_1}t_1=\frac{\Delta T}{R_2}t_2$$

$$\Rightarrow \quad t_2=\frac{R_2}{R_1}t_1=2\text{ s} \quad\quad \textbf{Ans. (A)}$$

Sol. 3 In steady state the amount of heat absorbed by the body is equal to the amount of heat radiated, so we use

$$IA=\sigma[T^4-T_0^4]A$$

$$\Rightarrow \quad I\cdot\pi r^2=\sigma[T^4-T_0^4]4\pi r^2$$

$$\Rightarrow \quad T^4-T_0^4=\frac{I}{\sigma\cdot4}$$

$$\Rightarrow \quad T^4-(300)^4=\frac{912}{4\times5.67\times10^{-8}}$$

$$\Rightarrow \quad T^4 - (300)^4 = \frac{912 \times 10^8}{22 \cdot 68}$$

$$\Rightarrow \quad T^4 - 81 \times 10^8 = 40 \times 10^8$$

$$\Rightarrow \quad T^4 = (40 + 81) \times 10^8$$

$$\Rightarrow \quad T^4 = [121 \times 10^8]$$

$$\Rightarrow \quad T = [121 \times 10^8]^{1/4}$$

$$\Rightarrow \quad T = 330 \, \text{K} \qquad \textbf{Ans. (A)}$$

Sol. 4 Heat generated in 3 hrs is given as

$$Q_1 = 3 \times (60 \times 60) \times 3 \times 10^3$$

Heat absorbed by water cooler is given as

$$Q_2 = ms\Delta T = 120 \times 4.2 \times 10^3 \times 20$$

Heat absorbed by coolant is given as

$$= P \times t = P \times 3 \times 60 \times 60$$

$$\Rightarrow \quad P \times 3 \times 60 \times 60 + 120 \times 4.2 \times 10^3 \times 20$$

$$= 3 \times 10^3 \times 3 \times 60 \times 60$$

$$\Rightarrow \quad P = 2066.67 = 2067 \, \text{W} \qquad \textbf{Ans. (B)}$$

Sol. 5 Let temperature of junction is T then rate of heat transfer

$$\frac{dQ}{dT} = \frac{2KA(10-T)}{1} = \frac{KA(T-400)}{1}$$

$$\Rightarrow \quad 20 - 2T = T - 400$$

$$\Rightarrow \quad T = \frac{420}{3} = 140$$

$$10°C \quad 2K \quad QR \quad K \quad 400°C$$

Now for wire PQ, let us imagine a small length Δx at a distance x from the junction

$$\Rightarrow \quad \frac{dT}{dx} = \frac{140 - 10}{1} = 130$$

Thus temperature at distance x, is given as

$$T = 10 + 130x$$

$$T - 10 = 130x$$

Increase in length of the small element Δx is expressed as

$$\frac{dy}{dx} = \alpha \, \Delta T = \alpha \, (T - 10)$$

$$\Rightarrow \quad \frac{dy}{dx} = \alpha(130)x$$

Integrating both side

$$\int_0^{\Delta L} dy = 130\alpha \int_0^L x\,dx$$

$$\Rightarrow \quad \Delta L = 130 \, \alpha \left[\frac{x^2}{2} \right]_0^L$$

$$\Rightarrow \quad \Delta L = \frac{130 \times 1.2 \times 10^{-5} \times 1}{2} = 0.78 \, \text{mm} \quad \textbf{Ans. (A)}$$

Sol. 6 Power is rate of flow of heat

$$P = \frac{dQ}{dt}$$

$$\Rightarrow \quad \frac{dQ}{dt} = ms\frac{dT}{dt}$$

The heat capacity of metal rod is given as

$$C = \frac{P}{\left(\dfrac{dT}{dt}\right)}$$

$$\Rightarrow \quad \frac{dT}{dt} = T_0\left[0 + \beta\frac{1}{4} \cdot t^{-3/4} \right] = \frac{\beta T_0}{4} \cdot t^{-3/4}$$

$$\Rightarrow \quad C = \frac{P}{(dT/dt)} = \frac{4P}{\beta T_0} \cdot t^{3/4}$$

$$\Rightarrow \quad C = \frac{4P}{\beta}\left[\frac{t^{3/4}}{T_0} \right]$$

$$\Rightarrow \quad \frac{T(t)}{T_0} = (1 + \beta t^{1/4})$$

$$\Rightarrow \quad \beta t^{1/4} = \frac{T(t)}{T_0} - 1 = \frac{T(t) - T_0}{T_0}$$

$$\Rightarrow \quad t^{3/4} = \left(\frac{T(t) - T_0}{\beta \cdot T_0} \right)^3$$

$$\Rightarrow \quad C = \frac{4P}{T_0\beta}\left[\frac{T(t) - T_0}{\beta \cdot T_0} \right]^3 = \frac{4P}{\beta^4 T_0^4}[T(t) - T_0]^3 \quad \textbf{Ans. (A)}$$

Sol. 7 Figure below shows the conduction of heat through the given slabs

All the three system shown are in series hence rate of heat flow will be same through both A and E. Hence option (A) is correct. Thermal resistances of the rods are calculated as

$$R_A = \frac{L}{8(KA)} \; ; R_B = \frac{4L}{3KA} \; ; R_C = \frac{4L}{8KA} \; ; R_D = \frac{4L}{5KA} \; ; R_E = \frac{L}{24KA}$$

If H is the heat flow rate through this entire system then same heat flow rate will be there through the slab A and E and through parallel combination of B, C and D. Through the parallel combination heat will flow rate for individual slabs will be inversely proportional to their thermal resistances so, the heat flow rate can be given as

$$H_B = \frac{3H}{16}\,;\, H_C = \frac{H}{2} \text{ and } H_D = \frac{5H}{16}$$

From above values of heat flow rate, we can analyse that Rate of heat flow across C = Rate of heat flow through B
+ Rate of heat flow through D.

Hence option (D) is correct. The temperature differences across different slabs can be calculated as

$$\Delta\theta_A = HR_A = \frac{HL}{8KA}$$

$$\Delta\theta_B = \frac{3H}{16}R_B = \frac{3H}{16}\left(\frac{4L}{3KA}\right) = \frac{HL}{4KA}$$

$$\Delta\theta_C = \frac{H}{2}(R_C) = \frac{H}{2}\left(\frac{4L}{8KA}\right) = \frac{HL}{4KA}$$

$$\Delta\theta_D = \frac{5H}{16}\left(\frac{4L}{5KA}\right) = \frac{HL}{4KA}$$

$$\Delta\theta_E = H\left(\frac{L}{24KA}\right) = \frac{HL}{24KA}$$

Here least temperature difference is across slab E hence option (C) is correct. **Ans. (A, C, D)**

Sol. 8 Option (A) is correct because the graph between $(0 - 100 \text{ K})$ appears to be a straight line upto a reasonable approximation. Option (B) is correct because area under the curve in the temperature range $(0 - 100 \text{ K})$ is less than in range $(400 - 500 \text{ K})$. Option (C) is correct because the graph of C versus T is constant in the temperature range $(400 - 500 \text{ K})$. Option (D) is correct because in the temperature range $(200 - 300 \text{ K})$ specific heat capacity increases with temperature. **Ans. (A, B, C, D)**

Sol. 9 Assuming black body, the rate of heat transfer from the body can be given as

$$\frac{d\dot{Q}}{dt} = 4\sigma T_0^3(T - T_0)$$

$$\Rightarrow \qquad \frac{d\dot{Q}}{dt} = 4\frac{460}{300}(1)(10) = 60 \text{ W}$$

Hence option (A) is correct. If surrounding temperature decreases by ΔT_0 the total heat radiated by body will be

$$\left(\frac{dQ}{dt}\right)_{new} = 4\sigma T_0^3(T - (T_0 - \Delta T_0))$$

$$\Rightarrow \left(\frac{dQ}{dt}\right)_{new} = 4\sigma T_0^3(T - T_0) + 4\sigma T_0^3 \Delta T_0$$

Thus to maintain same body temperature at T, extra heat needed to be radiated is same as given in answer option (B) hence this is correct. When human body is curled up, body surface area is reduced hence for same body temperature total heat flow rate reduces, hence option (C) is correct. **Ans. (A, B, C)**

Sol. 10 (A) : Power radiated by the filament is calculated by Stefan's law as

$$P = \sigma A e T^4$$

$$\Rightarrow \qquad P = 5.67 \times 10^{-8} \times 64 \times 10^{-6} \times 1 \times (2500)^4$$

$$\Rightarrow \qquad P = 141.75 \text{ W}$$

Thus option (A) is NOT correct.

(B) : Power entering into the eye of observer is given as

$$P_e = \frac{P}{4\pi d^2} \times (\pi R_e^2)$$

$$\Rightarrow \qquad P_e = \frac{141.75}{4\pi \times (100)^2} \times \pi \times (3 \times 10^{-3})^2$$

$$\Rightarrow \qquad P_e = 3.189375 \times 10^{-8} \text{ W}$$

Thus option (B) is correct

(C) : By Wein's displacement law, we have

$$\lambda_m T = b$$

$$\Rightarrow \qquad \lambda_m \times 2500 = 2.9 \times 10^{-3}$$

$$\Rightarrow \qquad \lambda_m = 1.16 \times 10^{-6}$$

$$\Rightarrow \qquad \lambda_m = 1160 \text{ nm}$$

Thus option (C) is correct

(D) : If N are the number of photons entering into eye per second then power received by one eye of observer can be written as

$$P = \left(\frac{hc}{\lambda}\right) \times N$$

$$\Rightarrow 3.189375 \times 10^{-8} = \frac{6.63 \times 10^{-34} \times 3 \times 10^8}{1740 \times 10^{-9}} \times N$$

$$\Rightarrow \qquad N = 2.79 \times 10^{11}$$

Thus option (D) is correct. **Ans. (B, C, D)**

Sol. 11 P $\rightarrow$ (4); Q $\rightarrow$ (2); R $\rightarrow$ (1); S $\rightarrow$ (3)

(P) : Using molecular kinetic energy relation, we have

$$E = \frac{3}{2}kT$$

Writing dimensions on the two sides, we have

$$[ML^2T^{-2}] = [k]\,[K]$$

$$\Rightarrow \qquad [k] = [ML^2T^{-2}K^{-1}]$$

(Q) : Using Stokes rule, we have

$$F = 6\pi\eta rv$$

Writing dimensions on the two sides, we have

$$[MLT^{-2}] = [\eta]\,[L]\,[LT^{-1}]$$

$$\Rightarrow \qquad [\eta] = [ML^{-1}T^{-1}]$$

(R) : Using relation of energy of a photon, we have

$$E = h\nu$$

Writing dimensions on the two sides, we have

$$[ML^2T^{-2}] = \frac{[h]}{[T]}$$

$$\Rightarrow \qquad [h] = [ML^2T^{-1}]$$

(S) : Using relation of steady state of heat conduction, we have

$$\frac{dQ}{dt} = \frac{kA(\Delta T)}{\Delta x}$$

$$\frac{[ML^2T^{-2}]}{[T]} = \frac{[k][L^2][K]}{[L]}$$

$$[k] = [MLT^{-3}K^{-1}] \qquad\qquad \textbf{Ans. (C)}$$

Sol. 12 (P) temperature is minimum hence wavelength at peak intensity λ_m will be maximum compared to all other temperatures in other options. Central maxima of single slit diffraction has a width proportional to the wavelength of light so in this option, it is widest. Hence correct option is (C).

(Q) At temperature $T = 3000$ K the power emitted per unit area by a blackbody is given as

$$P_{3000} = \sigma A\,(3000)^4$$

At 6000 K temperature, it is given as

$$P_{6000} = \sigma A\,(6000)^4$$

$$\Rightarrow \qquad \frac{P_{3000}}{P_{6000}} = \left(\frac{1}{2}\right)^4 = \frac{1}{16}$$

$$P_{3000} = \frac{1}{16} P_{6000}$$

Hence option (D) is correct.

(R) At temperature $T = 5000$ K, radiation at peak wavelength is calculated as

$$\lambda_m = \frac{2.9 \times 10^{-3}}{5000} = 0.58 \times 10^{-6} = 580\,\text{nm}$$

This is range of visible radiation hence option (B) is correct.

(S) At temperature $T = 10000$ K emitted wavelength at peak intensity will be minimum compared to all other given options so for single slit diffraction central maxima will be narrowest. Thus option (C) cannot be correct. So the other option (A) would be correct answer which can also be verified by calculating the wavelength at peak intensity as

$$\lambda_m = \frac{2.9 \times 10^{-3}}{10000} = 0.29 \times 10^{-6} = 290\,\text{nm}$$

Photon energy for this wavelength is given as

$$E = \frac{hc}{\lambda_m e} = \frac{1.24 \times 10^{-6}}{0.29 \times 10^{-6}} = 4.27\,\text{eV}$$

Hence option (A) is correct.   **Ans. (C)**

Sol. 13 It is given that equal amount of water is evaporated as

that of ice melts so we use

$$m \times 80 = \left(\frac{\Delta Q}{\Delta t}\right)_{\text{ice}}$$

$$m \times 540 = \left(\frac{\Delta Q}{\Delta t}\right)_{\text{water}}$$

In steady state of heat conduction through the rod, we use

$$\frac{\Delta Q}{\Delta t} = \frac{KA\Delta T}{x}$$

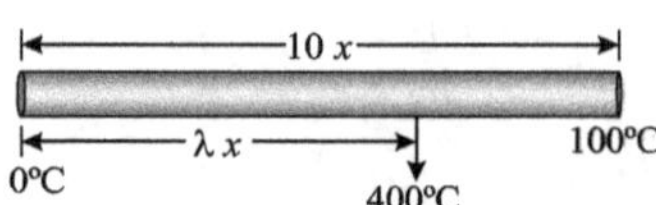

For water being evaporated, we use

$$\left(\frac{\Delta Q}{\Delta t}\right)_{\text{water}} = \frac{300}{\dfrac{10x - \lambda x}{KA}} = mL_v \qquad\qquad \ldots(1)$$

For ice being melted, we use

$$\left(\frac{\Delta Q}{\Delta t}\right)_{\text{ice}} = \frac{400}{\dfrac{\lambda x}{KA}} = mL_f \qquad\qquad \ldots(2)$$

Dividing equation (1) and (2), we have

$$\frac{300}{10x - \lambda x} \times \frac{\lambda x}{400} = \frac{L_v}{L_f}$$

$$\Rightarrow \qquad \frac{3}{4}\frac{\lambda}{(10 - \lambda)} = \frac{540}{80}$$

$$\Rightarrow \qquad \lambda = 9\,(10 - \lambda)$$

$$\Rightarrow \qquad 10\lambda = 90$$

$$\Rightarrow \qquad \lambda = 9\,m \qquad\qquad \textbf{Ans. (9)}$$

Sol. 14 Maximum intensities occur at wavelengths

$$\lambda_A = 500\,\text{nm}$$

$$\lambda_B = 1500\,\text{nm}$$

By Wein's law we use

$$\lambda T = \text{constant}$$

$$\Rightarrow \qquad \lambda_A T_A = \lambda_B T_B$$

$$\Rightarrow \qquad \frac{T_A}{T_B} = 3 \qquad\qquad \ldots(1)$$

From Stefan's law the ratio of rate of total energy radiated by A to that of B is given as

$$\Rightarrow \quad \frac{E_A}{E_B} = \frac{\sigma(4\pi r_{A^2})(T_A^4)}{\sigma(4 g r_{B^2})(T_B^4)} = \left(\frac{1}{3}\right)^2 \times (3)^4 = 9 \qquad \textbf{Ans. (9)}$$

Sol. 15 The amount of heat required to raise the temperature of ice from $-5°C$ to $0°C$.

$$Q_1 = m \times 2100 \times 10^{-3} \times 5 = 10.5\,m\,\text{Joule}$$

The amount of heat required to melt 1 gm of ice is given as

$$Q_2 = 10^{-3} \times 3.36 \times 10^5 = 336 \, J$$

As total 420 J of heat is provided, we have

$$420 = 336 + 10.5 \, m$$

$$\Rightarrow \quad 10.5 \, m = 84$$

$$\Rightarrow \quad m = 8 \, gm \qquad \textbf{Ans. (8)}$$

Sol. 16 For the two stars it is given that

$$R_A = 400 \, R_B$$

$$P_A = 10^4 \, P_B$$

By Stefan's law, we have

$$\left(\frac{\Delta\theta}{\Delta t}\right)_A = \left(\frac{\Delta\theta}{\Delta t}\right)_B$$

$$\sigma A_A T_A^4 = 10^4 \cdot \sigma A_B T_B^4$$

$$\Rightarrow \quad R_A^2 \, T_A^4 = 10^4 \, R_B^2 \, T_B^4$$

$$\Rightarrow \quad 16 T_A^4 = T_B^4$$

$$\Rightarrow \quad T_B = 2 \, TA$$

By Wein's displacement law, we have

$$\lambda_A T_A = \lambda_B T_B$$

$$\Rightarrow \quad \frac{\lambda_A}{\lambda_B} = \frac{T_B}{T_A} = 2 \qquad \textbf{Ans. (2)}$$

Sol. 17 Using Stefan's law, the power radiated by metal is given as

$$P = \sigma A e t^4$$

$$\Rightarrow \quad P \propto T^4$$

The two temperature in the situations described in question are given as

$$T_1 = 487^\circ C = 487 + 273 = 760 \, K,$$

$$T_2 = 2767^\circ C = 2767 + 273 = 3040 \, K$$

If sensor scale reads R_1 and R_2 in the two cases, we use the sensor display given as

$$R = \log_2\left(\frac{P}{P_0}\right)$$

$$\Rightarrow \quad R_2 - R_1 = \log_2\left(\frac{P_2}{P_1}\right) = \log_2\left(\frac{T_2}{T_1}\right)^4$$

$$\Rightarrow \quad R_2 - R_1 = \log_2\left(\frac{3040}{760}\right)^4$$

$$\Rightarrow \quad R_2 - R_1 = 4\log_2 4 = 8$$

$$\Rightarrow \quad R_2 = 8 + 1 = 9 \qquad \textbf{Ans. (9)}$$

Sol. 18 The intermediate temperature of slabs is given by the formula

$$T = \frac{\dfrac{k_1 A_1 T_1}{l_1} + \dfrac{k_2 A_2 T_2}{l_2}}{\dfrac{k_1 A_1}{l_1} + \dfrac{k_2 A_2}{l_2}}$$

$$\Rightarrow \quad 200 = \frac{k_1 \pi r^2 \times 300 + k_2 \pi (4r^2) 100}{k_1 \pi r^2 + k_2 \pi (4r^2)}$$

$$\Rightarrow \quad 200 = \frac{300 k_1 + 400 k_2}{k_1 + 4 k_2}$$

$$\Rightarrow \quad 200 k_1 + 800 k_2 = 300 k_1 + 400 k_2$$

$$\Rightarrow \quad 400 k_2 = 100 k_1$$

$$\Rightarrow \quad \frac{k_1}{k_2} = 4 \qquad \textbf{Ans. (4)}$$

Sol. 19 First 5 g of liquid at 30° is poured to calorimeter at 110°C so we use

$$m \times x \times (110 - 80) = 5 \times s \times (80 \times 30) + 5L$$

$$\Rightarrow \quad mx \times 30 = 250 \, s + 5L \qquad \ldots(1)$$

Now, 80 g of liquid at 30° is poured into calorimeter at 80°C, the equilibrium temperature reaches to 50°C.

$$m \times x \times (80 - 30) = 80 \times s \times (50 - 30)$$

$$\Rightarrow \quad mx \times 30 = 1600 \, s \qquad \ldots(2)$$

From equations (1) & (2), we use

$$250 \, s + 5L = 1600 \, s$$

$$\Rightarrow \quad 5L = 1350 \, s$$

$$\Rightarrow \quad \frac{L}{s} = 270 \qquad \textbf{Ans. (270)}$$

Sol. 20 The amount of heat absorbed by the water can be calculated as

$$Q_1 = 700 \times 0.05 = 35 \, J/s$$

Amount of heat radiated by water can be calculated by Newton's law of cooling, given as

$$Q_2 = msK\Delta T$$

After a long time when water is at equilibrium temperature, we use

$$Q_1 = Q_2$$

$$35 = 1 \times 4200 \times 10^{-3} \times \Delta T$$

$$\Rightarrow \quad \Delta T = \frac{50}{6} = \frac{25}{3} = 8.33 \, K \qquad \textbf{Ans. (8.33)}$$

Ch-9 Thermodynamics & Kinetic Theory of Gases

Sol. 1 For the process PT^2 = constant, using gas law we can write

$$\Rightarrow \qquad \frac{nRT^3}{V} = C$$

$$\Rightarrow \qquad V = \frac{nRT^3}{C}$$

Differentiating above equation we get

$$\frac{dV}{dT} = \frac{3nRT^2}{C} = \frac{3V}{T}$$

Coefficient of volume expansion of gas can be written as

$$\frac{\left(\dfrac{dV}{dT}\right)}{V} = \frac{3}{T} \qquad\qquad\qquad \textbf{Ans. (C)}$$

Sol. 2 A real gas behaves like an ideal one at very low pressure and very high temperature. **Ans. (D)**

Sol. 3 For adiabatic process, we use

$$T_1 V_1^{\gamma-1} = T_2 V_2^{\gamma-1}$$

$$\Rightarrow \qquad T_2 = T_1 \left(\frac{V_1}{V_2}\right)^{\gamma-1}$$

$$\Rightarrow \qquad T_2 = T_1 \left(\frac{5.7}{0.7}\right)^{\frac{5}{3}-1} = T_1 (8)^{2/3} = 4T_1$$

5.6 litre of helium gas at STP will have 0.25 mole of gas so work done by gas is given as

$$W = \frac{nR(T_1 - T_2)}{\gamma - 1} = \frac{0.25 \times R(4T_1 - T_1)}{2/3} = \frac{9}{8}RT_1$$

$$\textbf{Ans. (A)}$$

Sol. 4 Ratio of rms speeds of the gases is given as

$$\frac{v_{\text{rms}_{\text{He}}}}{v_{\text{rms}_{\text{Ar}}}} = \frac{\sqrt{\dfrac{3RT}{m_{\text{He}}}}}{\sqrt{\dfrac{3RT}{m_{\text{Ar}}}}} = \sqrt{\frac{m_{\text{Ar}}}{m_{\text{He}}}} = \sqrt{\frac{40}{4}} = \sqrt{10} \approx 3.16$$

$$\textbf{Ans. (D)}$$

Sol. 5 For isobaric process, heat supplied to gas is given as

$$\Delta Q = nC_P \Delta T$$

$$\Rightarrow \qquad \Delta Q = 2\left(\frac{f}{2}R + R\right)\Delta T$$

$$\Rightarrow \qquad \Delta Q = 2\left[\frac{3}{2}R + R\right] \times 5$$

$$\Rightarrow \qquad \Delta Q = 2 \times \frac{5}{2} \times 8.31 \times 5 = 208 \text{ J} \qquad \textbf{Ans. (D)}$$

Sol. 6 By ideal gas equation, we have

$$PV = nRT = \frac{m}{M}RT$$

$$\Rightarrow \qquad PM = \rho RT$$

$$\Rightarrow \qquad \frac{\rho_1}{\rho_2} = \frac{P_1 M_1}{P_2 M_2} = \left(\frac{P_1}{P_2}\right) \times \left(\frac{M_1}{M_2}\right) = \frac{4}{3} \times \frac{2}{3} = \frac{8}{9}$$

Here ρ_1 and ρ_2 are the densities of gases in the vessel containing the mixture. **Ans. (D)**

Sol. 7 For the resonance tube if L is the first resonance length, the speed of sound is given as

$$\sqrt{\frac{\gamma RT}{M}} = f(4L)$$

If gas is monoatomic, we use $\gamma = 1.67$ and molar mass if taken in grams, so we have

$$v = \sqrt{\frac{167RT \times 10}{M}} = 244 \times 4 \times 0.350 = 341.6 \text{ m/s}$$

$$\Rightarrow \qquad v = 640\sqrt{\frac{10}{M}} = 341.6 \text{ m/s}$$

If gas is diatomic, we use $\gamma = 1.4$ and molar mass if taken in grams, so we have

$$v = \sqrt{\frac{140RT \times 10}{M}} = 244 \times 4 \times 0.350 = 341.6 \text{ m/s}$$

$$\Rightarrow \qquad v = 590\sqrt{\frac{10}{M}} = 341.6 \text{ m/s}$$

Error in calculation of sound speed can be given as

$$\Delta\left(\sqrt{\frac{\gamma RT}{M}}\right) = 4f\Delta L = 4.88 \text{ m/s}$$

Hence the speed of sound should be in range from 336.72 to 346.48 m/s. Now we can check for the given options in the questions for this

For Neon gas $\quad v = 640 \times \dfrac{7}{10} = 448$ m/s

For Argon gas $\quad v = 640 \times \dfrac{17}{32} = 340$ m/s

For Oxygen gas $v = 590 \times \dfrac{9}{16} = 331.8$ m/s

For Nitrogen gas $v = 590 \times \dfrac{3}{5} = 354$ m/s

Thus answer is option (D) only. **Ans. (D)**

Sol. 8 For first process, the ratio of specific heats of gases is given as

$$\gamma = \frac{5}{3}$$

$$\Rightarrow \qquad C_P = \frac{5}{2}R \ \text{ and } C_v = \frac{3}{2}R$$

Amount of heat supplies to system in second process is given as

$$Q = nC_p(\Delta T) + nC_v(\Delta T')$$

$$\Rightarrow \qquad Q = n\frac{5}{2}R\Delta T + n\frac{3}{2}R\Delta T'$$

$$\Rightarrow \qquad Q = \frac{5}{2}[10^5 \times 8 \times 10^{-3} - 10^5 \times 10^{-3}]$$

$$+ \frac{3}{2}[\frac{1}{32} \times 10^5 \times 8 \times 10^{-3} - 10^5 \times 8 \times 10^{-3}]$$

$$\Rightarrow \qquad Q = \frac{5}{2}[800 - 100] + \frac{3}{2}[25 - 800]$$

$$\Rightarrow \qquad Q = \frac{5}{2} \times 700 + \frac{3}{2} \times -775 = 587.5\,\text{J} = 588\,\text{J} \qquad \textbf{Ans. (C)}$$

Sol. 9 Here process 1 is the isobaric expansion in which heat will be supplied and similarly in process 4 which is isochoric heating of gas in which also heat will be supplied to gas. In process 2 and 3 heat will be released hence option (C) is correct.

Ans. (C)

Sol. 10 The processes given in question are shown in indicator diagram as shown below

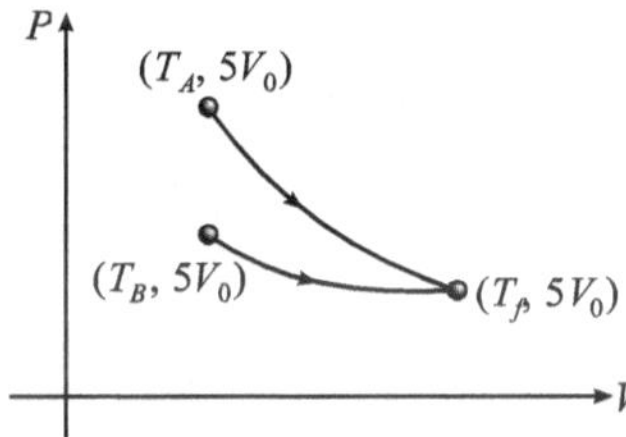

For the adiabatic process, we use

$$T_A V_0^{\gamma-1} = T_f (5V_0)^{\gamma-1}$$

For isothermal process, we have $T_B = T_f$ so we have

$$\frac{T_A}{T_f} = 5^{\gamma-1} = \frac{T_A}{T_B} \qquad\qquad \textbf{Ans. (A)}$$

Sol. 11 Internal energy of one mole of a gas with f degrees of freedom is calculated as

$$U = \frac{f}{2}RT$$

Thus internal energy is more if degrees of freedom are more hence options (A) and (B) are NOT correct.
Speed of sound in the gas is calculated as

$$v_{\text{sound}} = \sqrt{\frac{\gamma RT}{M}} = \sqrt{\left(\frac{2}{f}+1\right)\frac{RT}{M}}$$

Thus higher the degrees of freedom, lesser will be the speed of

sound hence option (C) is correct. Ans. (C)

Sol. 12 C_p and C_V for diatomic is greater than monoatomic. So, $C_p + C_V$ and $C_p C_V$ is greater for diatomic ideal gas.

Ans. (B, D)

Sol. 13 As given cycle is clockwise, net work is done by the gas hence option (D) is correct. In process $B \to C \to D$ gas is being compressed and heat is rejected by the gas hence option (B) is correct. Ans. (B, D)

Sol. 14 From the given figure process AB is isothermal so at points A and B internal energies are same hence option (A) is correct.

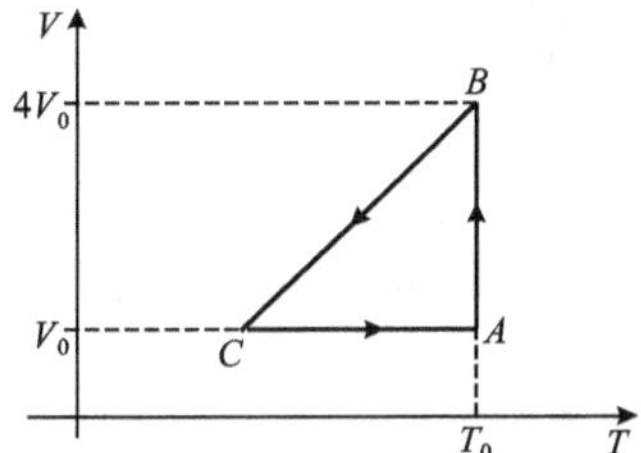

Work done in the process AB is calculated as

$$W_{AB} = nRT_0 \ln\left(\frac{V_2}{V_1}\right) = P_0 V_0 \ln 4$$

Hence option (B) is correct. About line BC it is not specified that it passes through origin so we cannot calculate the pressure or temperature at point C. Ans. (A, B)

Sol. 15 Total internal energy of gaseous mixture is given as

$$E = \frac{5}{2}RT + \frac{3}{2}RT = 4RT$$

Average energy/mole can be given as $2RT$.

For the mixture effective value of γ_{mix} is given as

$$\frac{n_1 + n_2}{\gamma_{\text{mix}} - 1} = \frac{n_1}{\gamma_1 - 1} + \frac{n_2}{\gamma_2 - 1}$$

$$\Rightarrow \qquad \gamma_{\text{mix}} = \frac{3}{2}$$

Equivalent molar mass for mixture of gases is given as

$$M_{\text{mix}} = \frac{2+4}{2} = 3$$

$$\Rightarrow \qquad \frac{v_{\text{mix}}}{v_{\text{He}}} = \sqrt{\frac{\gamma_{\text{mix}}}{M_{\text{mix}}} \cdot \frac{M_{\text{He}}}{\gamma_{\text{He}}}}$$

$$\Rightarrow \qquad \frac{v_{\text{mix}}}{v_{\text{He}}} = \sqrt{\frac{3/2}{3} \cdot \frac{4}{5/3}} = \sqrt{\frac{6}{5}}$$

Root mean square speed of helium molecules is given as

$$v_{\text{rmsHe}} = \sqrt{\frac{3RT}{M}}$$

$$\Rightarrow \quad \frac{v_{\text{rmsHe}}}{v_{\text{rm H}_2}} = \sqrt{\frac{M_{H_2}}{M_{He}}} = \sqrt{\frac{1}{2}} \qquad \textbf{Ans. (A, B, D)}$$

Sol. 16 Change in internal energy of gas can be given as

$$\Delta U = nC_v \Delta T$$

$$\Rightarrow \quad \Delta U = \frac{3}{2} nR\Delta T$$

$$\Rightarrow \quad \Delta U = \frac{3}{2} nR(2T_1) = 3nRT_1 = 3P_1 V_1$$

Hence option (B) is correct. When spring is compressed by x, considering vacuum on the spring side of piston, we use for equilibrium of piston

$$P_2 A = Kx$$

Energy stored in spring in this state is given as

$$\Delta W = \frac{1}{2} Kx^2$$

By mole conservation of gas in initial and final state, we use

$$\frac{P_1 V_1}{T_1} = \frac{P_2 V_2}{T_2} \qquad \qquad \dots (1)$$

Using $V_2 = 2V_1$ and $T_2 = 3T_1$ we have

$$\frac{P_1 V_1}{T_1} = \frac{P_2 2V_1}{3T_1}$$

$$\Rightarrow \quad P_2 = \frac{3}{2} P_1$$

$$\Rightarrow \quad \Delta W = \frac{1}{2}(Kx)\frac{\Delta V}{A}$$

$$\Rightarrow \quad \Delta W = \frac{1}{2}(P_2 A) \times \frac{V_1}{A} = \frac{1}{2} \times \frac{3}{2} P_1 V_1 = \frac{3}{4} P_1 V_1$$

Hence option (A) is NOT correct.

In equation-(1) using $V_2 = 3V_1$ and $T_2 = 4T_1$ we have

$$\frac{P_1 V_1}{T_1} = \frac{P_2 V_2}{T_2}$$

$$\frac{P_1 V_1}{T_1} = \frac{P_2 3V_1}{4T_1}$$

$$\Rightarrow \quad P_2 = \frac{4}{3} P_1$$

$$\Rightarrow \quad \Delta W = \frac{1}{2} \times \frac{4}{3} P_1 \times 2V_1 = \frac{4}{3} P_1 V_1$$

Hence option (C) is NOT correct. In this case change in internal energy can be calculated as

$$\Delta U = \frac{3}{2} nR\Delta T$$

$$\Rightarrow \quad \Delta U = \frac{3}{2} nR(3T_1) = \frac{9}{2} nRT_1 = \frac{9}{2} P_1 V_1$$

In this case total heat supplied to gas is calculated as

$$\Delta Q = \frac{9}{2} P_1 V_1 + \frac{4}{3} P_1 V_1 = \frac{35}{6} P_1 V_1$$

Hence option (D) is NOT correct.   **Ans. (B)**

Sol. 17 In process I, volume is changing. Therefore it is not isochoric. Hence option (A) is NOT correct. In process II, $q = \Delta U + W$ and $\Delta U = 0$ as temperature is constant so $\Delta Q = W$. Here gas is expanding so work done is positive thus ΔQ is positive i.e. heat is absorbed by the gas. Hence option (B) is correct.

For process IV, $\Delta Q = W$ as $\Delta U = 0$ and W is negative as gas is being compressed so ΔQ is negative i.e., gas is rejecting or releasing heat. Hence option (C) is correct. For an isobaric process, $V \propto T$ i.e. graph should be a straight inclined line in T–V graph so graphs I and II are NOT isobaric. Hence option (D) is correct.   **Ans. (B, C, D)**

Sol. 18 From graph we can directly state that

Process $1 \rightarrow 2$ is isobaric with $P = \dfrac{RT_0}{V_0}$

Process $2 \rightarrow 3$ is isochoric with $V = 2V_0$

Process $3 \rightarrow 4$ is isobaric with $P = \dfrac{RT_0}{2V_0}$

Process $4 \rightarrow 1$ is isochoric with $V = V_0$

Work in cycle is calculated as

$$W = \frac{RT_0}{V_0} \cdot V_0 - \frac{RT_0}{2V_0} \cdot V_0 = \frac{RT_0}{2}$$

Hence option (A) is correct.

Heat supplied in processes $1 \rightarrow 2$ and $2 \rightarrow 3$ are calculated as

$$Q_{1-2} = nC_P \Delta T = n\left(\frac{5R}{2}\right)T_0$$

$$Q_{2-3} = nC_V \Delta T = n\left(\frac{3R}{2}\right)T_0$$

$$\Rightarrow \quad \left|\frac{Q_{1-2}}{Q_{2-3}}\right| = \frac{5}{3}$$

Hence option (B) is correct.

Heat supplied in process $3 \rightarrow 4$ is calculated as

$$Q_{3-4} = nC_P \Delta T = n\left(\frac{5R}{2}\right)\left(\frac{T_0}{2}\right)$$

$$\Rightarrow \quad \left|\frac{Q_{1-2}}{Q_{3-4}}\right| = 2$$

Hence option (D) is NOT correct.

The cycle shown does not have any adiabatic process.

Hence option (C) is NOT correct.   **Ans. (A, B)**

Sol. 19 Equivalent C_V for gaseous mixture is given as

$$(C_V)_{mix} = \frac{n_1 C_{V_1} + n_2 C_{V_2}}{n_1 + n_2}$$

$$\Rightarrow \quad (C_V)_{mix} = \frac{n_1 C_{V_1} + n_2 C_{V_2}}{n_1 + n_2} = \frac{5R}{3}$$

$$\Rightarrow \quad (C_P)_{mix} = \frac{5R}{3} + R = \frac{8R}{3}$$

$$\Rightarrow \quad \gamma_m = \frac{(C_P)_{mix}}{(C_V)_{mix}} = \frac{8}{5} = 1.6$$

Thus option (D) is correct.

For adiabatic process, we use

$$P_0 V_0^{\gamma} = P \left(\frac{V_0}{4} \right)^{\gamma}$$

$$\Rightarrow \quad P = P_0 (4)^{8/5} = 9.2\, P_0$$

This is between $9P_0$ and $10P_0$. Hence option (A) is correct. Average kinetic energy of gaseous mixture is given as

$$K = 5 \times \frac{3}{2} RT + 1 \times \frac{5}{2} RT = 10RT$$

By using gas law from initial to final state of gas, we have

$$\frac{P_0 V_0}{T_0} = 9.2\, P_0 \times \frac{V_0}{4 \times T}$$

$$\Rightarrow \quad T = \frac{9.2}{4} T_0$$

After compression, average kinetic energy of the gas is given as

$$K = 10R \times 9.2 \frac{T_0}{4} = 23 RT_0$$

Thus option (B) is NOT correct.

Work done during the process is given as

$$W = \frac{P_1 V_1 - P_2 V_2}{\gamma - 1}$$

$$\Rightarrow \quad W = \frac{P_0 V_0 - 9.2\, P_0 \times \dfrac{V_0}{4}}{3/5} = -13 RT_0$$

Hence option (C) is correct.   **Ans. (A, C, D)**

Sol. 20 The rate at which particle collides the piston is given as

$$\text{Average rate of collision} = \frac{2L}{v}$$

Hence option (A) is NOT correct.

Speed of particle after collision is given as

$$v = 2V + v_0$$

Thus change in speed at each collision is $2V$. Hence option (B) is correct.

Number of collision per unit time of particle with piston are $\dfrac{v}{2L}$.

Thus we can calculate the change in speed of particle in time dt is given as $2V \times$ number of collision in dt time, expressed as

$$dv = 2V \left(\frac{v}{2L} \right) \cdot \left(-\frac{dL}{V} \right)$$

In above expression, we used $dt = \left(-\dfrac{dL}{V} \right)$ as L is decreasing

$$\Rightarrow \quad dv = -\frac{v\, dL}{L}$$

Hence option (D) is NOT correct. Now integrating above expression, we have

$$\int_{v_0}^{v} \frac{dv}{v} = -\int_{L_0}^{L_0/2} \frac{dL}{L}$$

$$\Rightarrow \quad [\ln v]_{v_0}^{v} = -[\ln L]_{L}^{L_0/2}$$

$$\Rightarrow \quad v = 2v_0$$

$$\Rightarrow \quad \frac{KE_{L_0/2}}{KE_0} = 4$$

Hence option (C) is correct.   **Ans. (B, C)**

Sol. 21 As the solutions are considered as ideal gases, pressure in the two vessels is given as

$$P_1 = \frac{n_1 RT}{N_A} \text{ and } p_2 = \frac{n_2 RT}{N_A}$$

Force due to pressure difference across the tube is given as

$$F = (n_1 - n_2)\, k_B TS = \Delta n k_B TS$$

Hence option (A) is correct. If the diffusion velocity of molecules is v, by given viscous force, it is calculated as

$$v = \frac{\Delta n k_B TS}{\beta}$$

$$\Rightarrow \quad \Delta n k_B TS = \ln_1 S \beta v$$

$$\Rightarrow \quad n_1 \beta v l = \Delta n k_B T$$

Hence option (B) is correct.

Total number of molecules flowing per second is given as

$$N = \frac{(n_1 v\, dt) S}{dt}$$

$$\Rightarrow \quad N = n_1 v S = \frac{\Delta n k_B T v S}{\beta v l}$$

$$\Rightarrow \quad N = \left(\frac{\Delta n}{l} \right) \left(\frac{k_B T}{\beta} \right) S$$

Hence option (C) is correct.

As Δn will decrease with time therefore rate of molecules getting transfer decreases with time hence option (D) is NOT correct.

Ans. (A, B, C)

Sol. 22 Figure below shows the situation described in question. In this case as density of flowing gas is varying at the two ends of chimney, we cannot directly use continuity equation rather we use constant mass flow rate of gas at the two ends for steady flow.

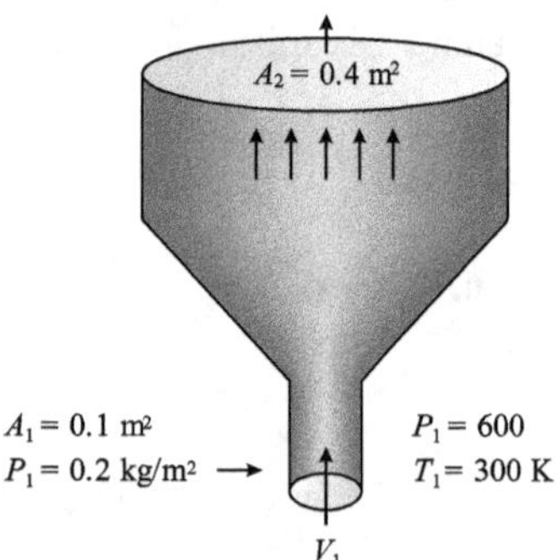

For steady mass flow rate of gas we use

$$\frac{dm}{dt} = \rho_1 A_1 v_1 = 0.8 \text{ kg/s}$$

$$\Rightarrow \qquad v_1 = \frac{0.8}{0.2 \times 0.1} = 40 \text{ m/s}$$

Also we can use

$$\rho_2 A_2 v_2 = 0.8$$

$$\Rightarrow \qquad v_2 = \frac{0.8}{0.1 \times 0.4} = 20 \text{ m/s}$$

Hence option (B) is correct.

Gas undergoes adiabatic expansion with $\gamma = 2$, we use

$$p^{1-\gamma} T^\gamma = \text{Constant}$$

$$\Rightarrow \qquad \frac{P_2}{P_1} = \left(\frac{T_1}{T_2}\right)^{\frac{r}{1-\gamma}}$$

$$\Rightarrow \qquad P_2 = \left(\frac{300}{150}\right)^{\frac{2}{-1}} \times 600$$

$$\Rightarrow \qquad P_2 = \frac{600}{4} = 150 \text{ Pa}$$

Hence option (A) is NOT correct.

By gas law density of gas is given as

$$\rho = \frac{PM}{RT}$$

$$\Rightarrow \qquad \rho \propto \frac{P}{T}$$

$$\Rightarrow \qquad \frac{\rho_1}{\rho_2} = \left(\frac{P_1}{P_2}\right)\left(\frac{T_1}{T_2}\right) = \left(\frac{150}{600}\right)\left(\frac{300}{150}\right) = \frac{1}{2}$$

$$\Rightarrow \qquad \rho_2 = \frac{\rho_1}{2} = 0.1 \text{ kg/m}^3$$

Hence option (D) is NOT correct.

In this case we cannot use Bernoulli's equation as gas is expanding during flow so we use compressible flow equation for the flowing gas under adiabatic expansion which is given as

$$\frac{v^2}{2} + gh + \left(\frac{\gamma}{\gamma-1}\right)\frac{P}{\rho} = \text{Constant} \qquad \dots(1)$$

IMPORTANT : Above equation-(1) is derived by Ashish Sir in speed solutions of JEE Advanced 2022. To watch this derivation search in youtube for "*JEE Advanced 2022 Paper 1 Physics Speed Solutions*".

For bottom and top of chimney, we use

$$\frac{(40)^2}{2} + 10 \times 0 + \left(\frac{2}{2-1}\right)\frac{600}{0.2} = \frac{(20)^2}{2} + 10h + \left(\frac{2}{2-1}\right)\frac{150}{0.1}$$

$$\Rightarrow \qquad 800 + 6000 = 200 + 10h + 3000$$

$$\Rightarrow \qquad h = 360 \text{ m} \qquad\qquad \textbf{Ans. (B)}$$

Sol. 23 For adiabatic process $A \to B$, we use

$$P_A V_A^\gamma = P_B V_B^\gamma$$

$$\Rightarrow \qquad 10^5 \times (0.8)^{5/3} = 3 \times 10^5 (V_B)^{5/3}$$

$$\Rightarrow \qquad V_B = 0.8 \times \left(\frac{1}{3}\right)^{0.6} = 0.4 \text{ m}^3$$

Work done in process $A \to B$ is given as

$$W_{AB} = \frac{P_A V_A - P_B V_B}{\gamma - 1}$$

$$\Rightarrow \qquad W_{AB} = \frac{10^5 \times 0.8 - 3 \times 10^5 \times 0.4}{\frac{5}{3} - 1}$$

$$\Rightarrow \qquad W_{AB} = -60 \text{ kJ}$$

$$\Rightarrow \qquad |W_{AB}| = 60 \text{ kJ}$$

Hence option (C) is correct.

For isothermal process $B \to C$, final pressure can be taken as 150 kPa and Work done in process $B \to C$ is given as

$$W_{BC} = nRT \ln \frac{V_C}{V_B} = P_B V_B \ln \frac{V_C}{V_B}$$

$$\Rightarrow \qquad W_{BC} = 3 \times 10^5 \times 0.4 \ln \frac{0.8}{0.4}$$

$$\Rightarrow \qquad W_{BC} = 84 \text{ kJ}$$

Hence option (B) is correct.

As process $C \to A$ is isochoric work done is zero in this.

Hence option (D) is correct.

Total work done in the process $A \to B \to C$ is calculated as

$$W_{ABC} = W_{AB} + W_{BC} + W_{CA} = -60 + 84 + 0$$

$$\Rightarrow \qquad W_{ABC} = 24 \text{ kJ}$$

Hence option (A) is NOT correct.   **Ans. (B, C, D)**

Although the figure given in question is not proper but with the given data question can be solved. However in exam bonus marks were awarded to all for this question.

Sol. 24 Total translational kinetic energy of all the molecules of a gas is given as

$$E = \frac{3}{2}nRT = \frac{3}{2}PV$$

Thus statement-1 is correct. In a gas, molecule are in Brownian motion and travel randomly in all directions and at every collision direction of motion changes so velocity changes. Thus statement-1 and 2 are true but statement-2 is not explanation for statement-1. **Ans. (B)**

Sol. 25 (A) : Free expansion under adiabatic conditions

$$\Delta Q = 0 \ \& \ W = 0$$

$$\Rightarrow \qquad \Delta U = 0$$

$$\Rightarrow \ \text{Temperature remains constant}$$

(B) : For $P \propto \dfrac{1}{V^2}$ or $P = \dfrac{k}{V^2}$ we use

$$PV = nRT$$

$$\Rightarrow \qquad \frac{K}{V} = nRT$$

If gas expands from volume $V \to 2V$ then from above relations

temperature of gas changes from $T \to \dfrac{T}{2}$

$$\Rightarrow \qquad \Delta U = \frac{3}{2}nR\Delta T = \frac{3K}{4V}$$

$$\Rightarrow \qquad \Delta W = \int\limits_{V}^{2V} PdV = R\int\limits_{V}^{2V}\frac{dV}{V^2} = \frac{K}{2V}$$

$$\Rightarrow \qquad \Delta Q = \Delta U + \Delta W < 0$$

(C) : For $P \propto \dfrac{1}{V^{4/3}}$ or $P = \dfrac{K}{V^{4/3}}$ from gas law, we have

$$\frac{K}{V^{1/3}} = nRT$$

If gas expands from volume $V \to 2V$ then from above relation

gas temperature changes from $T \to \dfrac{T}{2^{1/3}}$

$$\Rightarrow \qquad \Delta U = \frac{3}{2}nR\Delta T = \frac{3K}{2V^{1/3}}\left[\frac{1}{2^{1/3}} - 1\right]$$

$$\Rightarrow \qquad \Delta W = \int\limits_{V}^{2V}\frac{KdV}{V^{4/3}} = \frac{3K}{V^{1/3}}\left[1 - \frac{1}{2^{1/3}}\right]$$

$$\Rightarrow \qquad \Delta Q = \Delta U + \Delta W > 0$$

(D) : For the gas process shown by the diagram given below, we can use

$$PV = nRT$$

$$\text{and} \qquad 2P'V = nRT'$$

$$\Rightarrow \qquad \frac{T'}{T}\left(\frac{2P'}{P}\right) > 1$$

$$\Rightarrow \qquad \Delta W > 0$$

$$\Rightarrow \qquad \Delta U = \frac{3}{2}nR\Delta T = \frac{3}{2}V[2P' - P] > 0$$

$$\Rightarrow \qquad \Delta Q = \Delta U + \Delta W > 0$$

Ans. [A (q); B (p, r); C (p, s); D (q, s)]

Sol. 26 In process $A \to B$ we have

If $T_A = T$ then $T_B = \dfrac{T}{3}$ and in the process by first law of thermodynamics, we have

$$\Delta U = nC_V\Delta T \to \text{Negative}$$

$$\Delta W = nR\Delta T = \text{Negative}$$

$$\Delta Q = \Delta U + \Delta W = \text{Negative}$$

In process $B \to C$ as volume is constant, we have

If $T_B = \dfrac{T}{3}$ then $T_C = \dfrac{T}{9}$ and by first law of thermodynamics, we have

$$\Delta U = nC_V\Delta T \to \text{Negative}$$

$$\Delta W = \text{Zero}$$

$$\Delta Q = \text{Negative}$$

In process $C \to D$ as pressure is constant, we have

If $T_C = \dfrac{T}{9}$ then $T_D = T$ and by first law of thermodynamics, we have

$$\Delta U = nC_V\Delta T \to \text{positive}$$

$$\Delta W = \text{positive}$$

$$\Delta Q = \text{positive}$$

In process $D \to A$ if $T_D = T$ and $T_A = T$ and by first law of thermodynamics, we have

$$\Delta U = 0$$

$$\Delta W = \text{negative}$$

$$\Delta Q = \text{negative}$$

Ans. [A (p, r, t); B (p, r); C (q, s); D (r, t)]

Sol. 27 From the given curve here process FH is an adiabatic process and FG is an isothermal process.

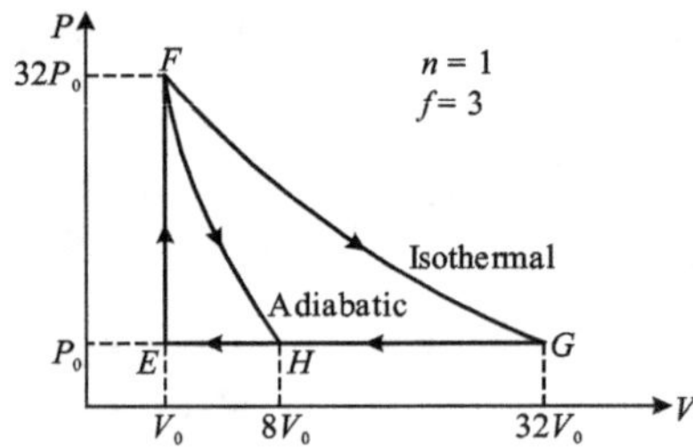

For the process FH, we can use

$$PV^{5/3} = \text{constant}$$

$$\Rightarrow \quad (32P_0)\,V_0^{5/3} = P_0 V_H^{5/3}$$

$$\Rightarrow \quad V_H = 8V_0$$

For process FG, we can use

$$PV = \text{constant}$$

$$\Rightarrow \quad (32P_0)\,V_0 = P_0 V_G$$

$$\Rightarrow \quad V_G = 32V_0$$

Work done in process GE is calculated as

$$W_{GE} = 31\,P_0 V_0$$

Work done in process GH is calculated as

$$W_{GH} = 24\,P_0 V_0$$

Work done in process FH is calculated as

$$W_{FH} = \frac{P_H V_H - P_F V_F}{(-2/f)} = 36\,P_0 V_0$$

Work done in process FG is calculated as

$$W_{FG} = RT \ln\left(\frac{V_G}{V_F}\right) = 160\,P_0 V_0 \ln 2 \qquad \textbf{Ans. (A)}$$

Sol. 28 In the given expression work done is $P\Delta V$ which is valid in case of isobaric process hence correct in the three columns is $II \to iii \to P$ **Ans. (B)**

Sol. 29 Out of given options in question correct combination for $W_{1\to 2} = 0$ is that process is isochoric and it is represented by S $III \to ii \to S$ **Ans. (A)**

Sol. 30 In correction of speed of sound process used is adiabatic hence correct option is $I \to iv \to Q$ **Ans. (D)**

Sol. 31 **Process-I** is an adiabatic so we use $\Delta Q = 0$

Process-II is isobaric so work done is calculated as

$$W = P(V_2 - V_1) = 3P\,(3V_0 - V_0) = 6\,P_0 V_0$$

Process-III is isochoric so work done is 0

Process-IV is isothermal so temperature is constant and hence internal energy change is zero. $\Delta U = 0$ **Ans. (C)**

Sol. 32 (I) : Work done in any process = Area under P–V graph

$$W = P_0 V_0$$

$$\Rightarrow \qquad W = \frac{RT_0}{3}$$

Hence option (Q) is correct.

(II) : Change in internal energy $1 \to 2 \to 3$

$$\Delta U = nC_v \Delta T$$

$$\Rightarrow \qquad \Delta U = \frac{f}{2} nR\Delta T$$

$$\Rightarrow \qquad \Delta U = \frac{f}{2}(P_f V_f - P_i V_i)$$

$$\Rightarrow \qquad \Delta U = \frac{3}{2}\left(\frac{3P_0}{2} 2V_0 - P_0 V_0\right)$$

$$\Rightarrow \qquad \Delta U = 3P_0 V_0$$

$$\Rightarrow \qquad \Delta U = RT_0$$

Hence option (R) is correct.

(III) : Heat absorbed in $1 \to 2 \to 3$

for any process, I^{st} law of thermodynamics is stated as

$$\Delta Q = \Delta W + W$$

$$\Rightarrow \qquad \Delta Q = RT_0 + \frac{RT_0}{3}$$

$$\Rightarrow \qquad \Delta Q = \frac{4RT_0}{3}$$

Hence option (S) is correct.

(IV) : Heat absorbed in process $1 \to 2$ is given as

$$\Delta Q = \Delta U + W$$

$$\Delta Q = \frac{f}{2}(P_f V_f - P_i V_i) + W$$

$$\Rightarrow \qquad \Delta Q = \frac{3}{2}(P_0 2V_0 - P_0 V_0) + P_0 V_0$$

$$\Rightarrow \qquad \Delta Q = \frac{5}{2} P_0 V_0$$

$$\Rightarrow \qquad \Delta Q = \frac{5}{2}\left(\frac{RT_0}{3}\right)$$

$$\Rightarrow \qquad \Delta Q = \frac{5RT_0}{6}$$

Hence option (U) is correct.   **Ans. (C)**

Sol. 33 (I) : By first law of thermodynamics, we have

$$\Delta U = \Delta Q - \Delta W$$

$$\Rightarrow \qquad \Delta U = \left\{(10^{-3} \times 2250) - \frac{10^5(10^{-3} - 10^{-6})}{10^3}\right\} \text{kJ}$$

$\Rightarrow \qquad \Delta U = (2.25 - 0.0999)\,\text{kJ}$

$\Rightarrow \qquad \Delta U = 2.1501\,\text{kJ}$

Hence closest option (P) is correctly related here.

(II) : As volume becomes $3V$ so temperature will also become three times hence final temperature will be 1500K. So change in internal energy is given as

$$\Delta U = nC_V\Delta T$$

$\Rightarrow \qquad \Delta U = \dfrac{5}{2}nR\Delta T$

$\Rightarrow \qquad \Delta U = \dfrac{5}{2}\cdot(0.2)(8)(1500-500)\,\text{J}$

$\Rightarrow \qquad \Delta U = 4\,\text{kJ}$

Hence option (R) is correctly related here.

(III) : For adiabatic process, we can use

$$P_1 V_2^\gamma = P_2 V_2^\gamma$$

$\Rightarrow \qquad 2\left(\dfrac{1}{2}\right)^{5/3} = P_2\left(\dfrac{1}{24}\right)^{5/3}$

$\Rightarrow \qquad P_2 = 64\,\text{kPa}$

Change in internal energy is calculated as

$$\Delta U = nC_V\Delta T = \dfrac{3}{2}(P_2 V_2 - P_1 V_1)$$

$\Rightarrow \qquad \Delta U = \dfrac{3}{2}\left(64\times\dfrac{1}{24}-2\times\dfrac{1}{3}\right)\,\text{kJ}$

$\Rightarrow \qquad \Delta U = 3\,\text{kJ}$

Hence option (T) is correctly related here.

(IV) : $\qquad \Delta U = nC_V\Delta T$

$\Rightarrow \qquad \Delta U = \dfrac{7}{2}nR\Delta T$

$\Rightarrow \qquad \Delta U = \dfrac{7}{9}\Delta Q = 7\,\text{kJ}$

Hence option (Q) is correctly related here. **Ans. (C)**

Sol. 34 Free body diagram of gas bubble is shown below

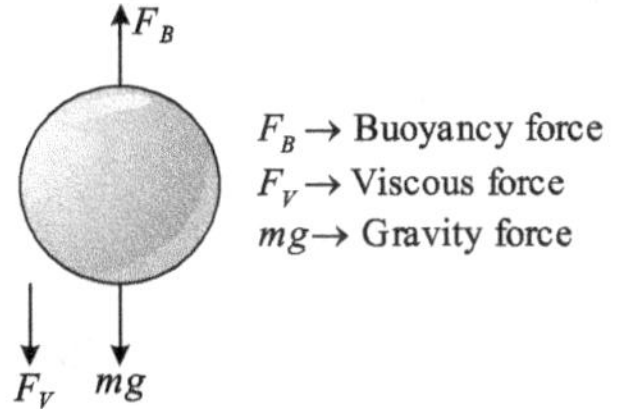

Buoyancy force is due to pressure difference and as it moves up, it experiences the viscous force as well. **Ans. (D)**

Sol. 35 Using mole conservation for gas inside bubble, we have

$$n_i = n_f$$

$\Rightarrow \qquad \dfrac{P_i V_i}{T_i} = \dfrac{P_f V_f}{T_f}$

$\Rightarrow \qquad T_f\,\dfrac{P_f V_f}{T_f}\cdot T_i \qquad\qquad \ldots(1)$

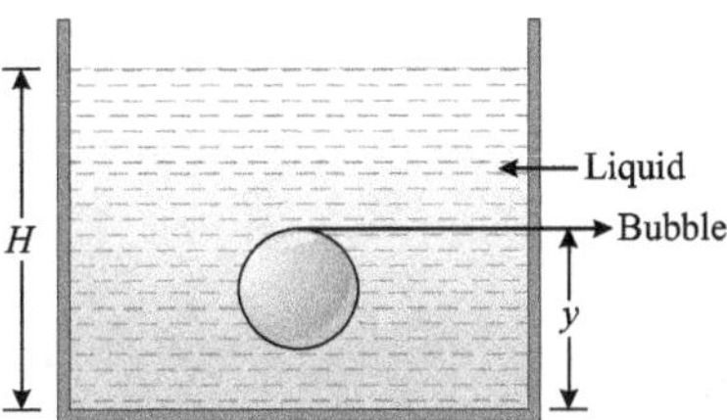

As bubble does not exchange heat hence process is adiabatic in nature, so we use

$$P_i V_i^\gamma = P_i V_f^\gamma$$

$$V_f/V_i = (P_i/P_f)^{1/\gamma} \qquad\qquad \ldots(2)$$

From equations (1) and (2), we have

$$T_f = \left(\dfrac{P_f}{P_i}\right)\left(\dfrac{P_i}{P_f}\right)^{1/\gamma}\cdot T_i$$

$\Rightarrow \qquad T_f = \left(\dfrac{P_f}{P_i}\right)^{1-1/\gamma}\cdot T_i$

$\Rightarrow \qquad P_i = P_0 + \rho_L gH$

$\Rightarrow \qquad P_f = P_0 + \rho_L g(H-y)$

$\Rightarrow \qquad T_f = \left[\dfrac{P_0+\rho_L g(H-y)}{P_0\rho_L gH}\right]^{2/5} T_0 \qquad$ **Ans. (B)**

Sol. 36 The buoyant force on bubble is given as

$$F_B = \rho_L V_f g$$

$\Rightarrow \qquad F_B = \rho_L\left(\dfrac{nRT_f}{P_f}\right)g$

$\Rightarrow \qquad F_B = \dfrac{\rho_L nR}{P_f}\left(\dfrac{P_f}{P_i}\right)\left(\dfrac{P_i}{P_f}\right)^{1/\gamma}T_i$

$\Rightarrow \qquad F_B = \dfrac{\rho_L nR}{P_i^{1-1/\gamma}}\cdot\dfrac{1}{P_f^{1/\gamma}}\cdot T_i$

$\Rightarrow \qquad F_B = \dfrac{\rho_L nR}{P_i^{2/5}P_f^{3/5}}\cdot T_i$

$\Rightarrow \qquad F_B = \dfrac{\rho_L nR}{(P_0+\rho_L gH)^{2/5}}\dfrac{T_0}{[P_0+\rho_L g(H-y)]^{3/5}}$

Ans. (B)

Sol. 37 Upper portion of gas follow isobaric process and lower follow isochoric process and as piston is thermally conducting, we use

$$\Delta Q_{\text{isobaric}} = \Delta Q_{\text{isochoric}}$$

$$2 \times \frac{7}{2} R(T - 400) = 2 \times \frac{3}{2} R(700 - T)$$

$$\Rightarrow \quad 7T - 2800 = 2100 - 3T$$

$$\Rightarrow \quad 10T = 4900$$

$$\Rightarrow \quad T = 490\,\text{K} \qquad \textbf{Ans. (D)}$$

Sol. 38 Partition is free to move without friction so that pressure of gases in both compartments is same so both gases follow isobaric process

$$2 \times \frac{7}{2} R(T - 400) = 2 \times \frac{5}{2} R(700 - T)$$

$$\Rightarrow \quad 7T - 2800 = 3500 - 5T$$

$$\Rightarrow \quad 12T = 6300$$

$$\Rightarrow \quad T = \frac{6300}{12} = \frac{2100}{4} = 525\,\text{K}$$

Total work done by gas is calculated as

$$W = nR\Delta T_1 + nR\Delta T_2$$

$$\Rightarrow \quad W = 2R[125 - 175] = -100\,R \qquad \textbf{Ans. (D)}$$

Sol. 39 After displacement of piston, for gas in right side using adiabatic process, we have

$$TV^{\gamma-1} = \text{constant}$$

$$\Rightarrow \quad T_1 V_1^{\gamma-1} = T_2 V_2^{\gamma-1}$$

$$\Rightarrow \quad T_0 V_0^{1/2} = T_R (V_0/2)^{1/2}$$

$$\Rightarrow \quad T_R = T_0 \sqrt{2}$$

$$\Rightarrow \quad \frac{T_R}{T_0} = \sqrt{2} \qquad \textbf{Ans. (A)}$$

Sol. 40 For gas in right side, we can use

$$PV^{\gamma} = \text{constant}$$

$$\Rightarrow \quad P_0 V_0^{3/2} = P\left(\frac{V_0}{2}\right)^{3/2}$$

$$\Rightarrow \quad P = P_0 (2)^{3/2} \qquad \dots(1)$$

Using mole conservation for left side gas, we have

$$n = \frac{P_0 V_0}{RT_0} = \frac{P_0 (2)^{3/2}\left(\dfrac{3V_0}{2}\right)}{RT_R}$$

$$\Rightarrow \quad T_R = 3\sqrt{2}\, T_0 \qquad \dots(2)$$

For the system of two gases total work done is zero so by first law of thermodynamics, we have

$$\Delta Q = \Delta U = C_V \Delta T$$

$$\Rightarrow \quad \Delta Q = \Delta U = 2R\Delta T_L + 2R\Delta T_R$$

$$\Rightarrow \quad \Delta Q = 2R\,[(3\sqrt{2}\, T_0 - T_0) + (\sqrt{2}\, T_0 - T_0)]$$

$$\Rightarrow \quad \frac{\Delta Q}{RT_0} = 4(2\sqrt{2} - 1) \qquad \textbf{Ans. (B)}$$

Sol. 41 Given that inside the furnace pressure is same at atmospheric pressure so for the atmospheric air entering the furnace, using ideal gas law we can use

$$P = \frac{\rho RT}{M}$$

As pressure remain constant we use

$$\rho T = \text{constant}$$

$$\Rightarrow \quad \rho_0 T_0 = \rho T$$

$$\Rightarrow \quad 1.2 \times 300 = \rho(360)$$

$$\Rightarrow \quad \rho = 1\,\text{kg/m}^3$$

As inside the furnace pressure is constant so within the height H ideal gas(air) is considered to be in brownian motion so within the furnace Bernoulli's equation cannot be applied. Here we apply Bernoulli's equation at a point A in furnace (having diameter D) just below the mouth of chimney and at the topmost point B of chimney in atmosphere as shown in figure below.

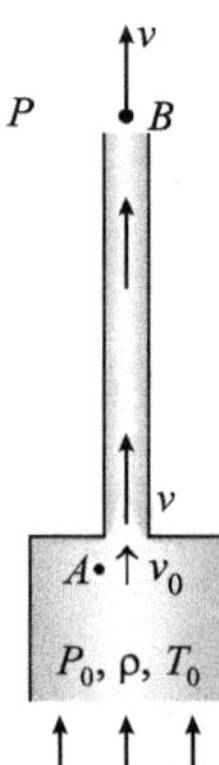

Between points A & B by Bernoulli's theorem, we use

$$P_0 + \frac{1}{2}\rho v_0^2 = P + \frac{1}{2}\rho v^2 + \rho g h \qquad \dots(1)$$

By continuity equation between same points, we have

$$\left(\frac{\pi D^2}{4}\right) v_0 = \left(\frac{\pi d^2}{4}\right) v \qquad \dots(2)$$

The air speed changes when it enters the chimney at A to v and the air flow speed v remain constant throughout chimney height as flow is considered streamline

$$P + \frac{1}{2}\rho V^2 = P_0 - \rho_0 g(H + h) + \frac{1}{2}\rho V^2 \qquad \dots(3)$$

From equations-(1) & (2) we have

$$\Rightarrow \quad P_0 + \frac{1}{2}\rho\left(v\frac{d^2}{D^2}\right)^2 = P + \frac{1}{2}\rho v^2 + \rho gh$$

$$\Rightarrow \quad P_0 - P = \frac{1}{2}\rho v^2\left[1 - \frac{d^4}{D^4}\right] + \rho gh \qquad \ldots(4)$$

Here the calculation of pressure difference $P_0 - P$ is tricky due to the conditions given in the question. There are two possible cases to solve this case from this point.

Case I: We cannot apply Bernoulli's theorem for the height of furnace H. It can also not be applied outside the chimney in atmosphere which may be due to the turbulent flow with brownian motion due to air flow from outside of chimney to inside of furnace. In such a case we consider atmospheric pressure same upto mouth of chimney outside of furnace in atmosphere. In this case we use

$$P_0 - P = h\rho_0 g$$

Thus from equation (4) we have

$$h\rho_0 g = \frac{1}{2}\rho v^2\left[1 - \frac{d^4}{D^4}\right] + \rho gh$$

As $d \ll D$ we use

$$v^2 = 2gh(\rho_0 - \rho)$$

$$\Rightarrow \quad v^2 = 2 \times 10 \times 9\,(1.2 - 1) = 36$$

$$\Rightarrow \quad v = 6\,\text{m/s}$$

Volume flow rate of air from chimney can be calculated as

$$Q = Av$$

$$Q = \rho\left(\frac{\pi d^2}{4}\right)v = 1 \times \frac{\pi}{4} \times 10^{-2} \times 6$$

$$Q = 47.1\,\text{gm/s}$$

Case II: If the question is only solved theoretically (which cannot be analysed under practical conditions) then we consider pressure outside the atmosphere is constant from the base of furnace to the top of chimney. This is similar to application of Bernoulli's theorem from base of furnace to the top of chimney but in this case pressure inside furnace cannot be considered constant. In this case, we use

$$P_0 - P = (h + H)\rho_0 g$$

Thus from equation (4) we have

$$(H+h)\rho_0 g = \frac{1}{2}\rho v^2\left[1 - \frac{d^4}{D^4}\right] + \rho gh$$

As $d \ll D$ we use

$$\Rightarrow \quad v^2 = \frac{2\rho_0}{\rho}g(H+h) - 2gh$$

$$\Rightarrow \quad v^2 = 2 \times 1.2 \times 10 \times 10 - 2 \times 10 \times 9$$

$$\Rightarrow \quad v^2 = 240 - 180 = 60$$

$$\Rightarrow \quad v = \sqrt{60}\,\text{m/s}$$

Volume flow rate of air from chimney can be calculated as

$$Q = \rho\left(\frac{\pi d^2}{4}\right)v = 1 \times \frac{\pi}{4} \times 10^{-2} \times \sqrt{60}$$

$$\Rightarrow \quad Q = 60.80\,\text{gm/s}$$

IIT Guwahati conducted this exam in 2023 and first they've given answer to this question 47.1 gm/s which is practically feasible and explainable but later due to many students who only study and apply the theoretical laws of physics and solved as analysed in case II above. The question was dropped by IIT and bonus marks were awarded to all because case II is not a correct solution. Its only a theoretical solution under assumptions given in question. **Ans. (47.1 or 60.8)**

Sol. 42 Similar to previous question here also two cases can be considered for solving this question. When the top is closed by a cap as shown in figure below, air flow stops and inside chimney air column will be considered as a static fluid only. If pressure at the top of chimney inside the cap is considered as P_i this pressure can be calculated as

$$P_i = P_0 - \rho gh$$

If outside pressure of atmosphere is considered as P then it is calculated under two cases as explained in previous question.

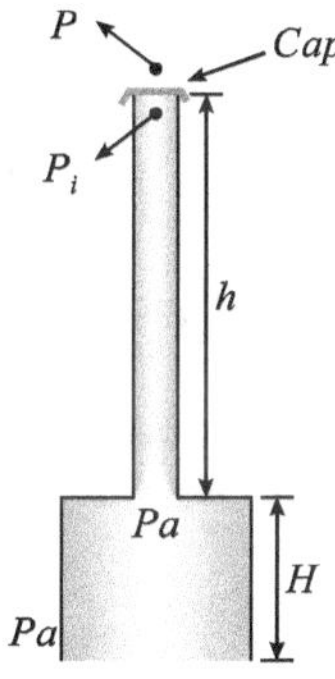

Case I: Pressure outside the cap in atmosphere is calculated as

$$P = P_0 - \rho_0 gh$$

In this case the pressure difference is calculated as

$$\Delta P = gh(\rho_0 - \rho)$$

$$\Rightarrow \quad \Delta P = 10 \times 9 \times (1.2 - 1) = 18\,\text{N/m}^2$$

Case II: Pressure outside the cap in atmosphere is calculated as

$$P = P_0 - \rho_0 g(h + H)$$

In this case the pressure difference is calculated as

$$\Delta P = \rho_0 g(h + H) - \rho gh$$

$$\Rightarrow \quad \Delta P = 1.2 \times 10 \times 10 - 1 \times 10 \times 9$$

$$\Rightarrow \quad \Delta P = 120 - 90 = 30\,\text{N/m}^2 \quad \textbf{Ans. (18 or 30)}$$

Sol. 43 For adiabatic process, we use

$$TV^{\gamma-1} = \text{constant}$$

$$\Rightarrow \quad T_i V^{\frac{7}{5}-1} = aT_i\left(\frac{V}{32}\right)^{\frac{7}{5}-1}$$

$$\Rightarrow \quad a = 4 \qquad \textbf{Ans. (4)}$$

Sol. 44 Change in internal energy of system is given as

$$U_f - U_i = 500 - 200 = 300\,\text{J}$$

$$\Rightarrow \quad U_f = 400\,\text{J}$$

For the process *ib*, we use

$$U_b - 100 = Q_{ib} - W_{ib}$$

$$\Rightarrow \quad 100 + 50 = Q_{ib}$$

$$\Rightarrow \quad Q_{ib} = 150\,\text{J}$$

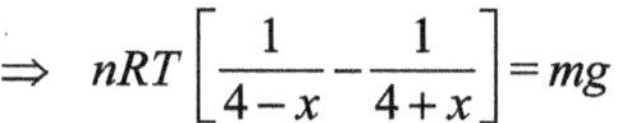

for the process *bf*, we use

$$Q_{bf} = (U_f - U_b) + W_{bf}$$

$$\Rightarrow \quad Q_{bf} = (200) + 100 = 300\,\text{J}$$

$$\Rightarrow \quad \frac{Q_{bf}}{Q_{ib}} = 2 \qquad \textbf{Ans. (2)}$$

Sol. 45 As the given process is adiabatic process and for monoatomic ideal gas we use $\gamma = 5/3$, which gives

$$TV^{\gamma-1} = T_2(8V)^{\gamma-1}$$

$$\Rightarrow \quad T_2 = \frac{T}{4}$$

Change in internal energy of gas is given as

$$\Delta U = nC_V\Delta T = n\left(\frac{f}{2}R\right)\Delta T = \frac{nfR}{2}\left(\frac{-3T}{4}\right)$$

$$\Rightarrow \quad \Delta U = -\frac{1\times 3\times 8}{2} \times \frac{3}{4} \times 100 = -900\,\text{J} \qquad \textbf{Ans. (900)}$$

Sol. 46 For adiabatic process, we use

$$\frac{P_1}{4}(4V_1)^{5/3} = P_2(32V_1)^{5/3}$$

$$\Rightarrow \quad P_2 = \frac{P_1}{4}\left(\frac{1}{8}\right)^{5/3} = \frac{P_1}{128}$$

Figure below shows the indicator diagram for the processes described in the question

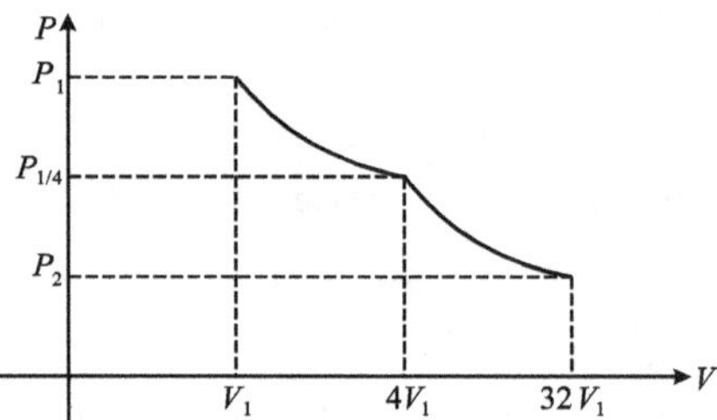

Work done in adiabatic process is calculated as

$$W = \frac{P_1V_1 - P_2V_2}{\gamma - 1} = \frac{P_1V_1 - \dfrac{P_1}{128}(32V_1)}{\dfrac{5}{3} - 1}$$

$$\Rightarrow \quad W = \frac{P_1V_1(3/4)}{2/3} = \frac{9}{8}P_1V_1$$

Work done in isothermal process is calculated as

$$W_{\text{iso}} = P_1V_1\ln\left(\frac{4V_1}{V_1}\right) = 2P_1V_1\ln 2$$

$$\Rightarrow \quad \frac{W_{\text{iso}}}{W_{\text{adio}}} = \frac{2P_1V_1\ln 2}{\dfrac{9}{8}P_1V_1} = \frac{16}{9}\ln 2 = f\ln 2$$

$$\Rightarrow \quad f = \frac{16}{9} = 1.7778 \approx 1.78 \qquad \textbf{Ans. (1.77 to 1.78)}$$

Sol. 47 As the piston is diathermic, we can consider that temperature remains constant at 300 K so we use

$$P_1V_1 = P_2V_2$$

If piston displaces by a distance x, we use

$$\frac{P_1\left(\dfrac{V_0}{2}\right)}{T} = \frac{P_1'\left(\dfrac{V_0}{2} - Ax\right)}{T}$$

For equilibrium of piston, we have

$$(P_1' - P_2')A = mg$$

$$\Rightarrow \quad \left[\frac{P_1\left(\dfrac{V_0}{2}\right)}{\dfrac{V_0}{2} - Ax} - \frac{P_2\left(\dfrac{V_0}{2}\right)}{\dfrac{V_0}{2} + Ax}\right]A = mg$$

$$\Rightarrow \quad nRT\left[\frac{1}{4-x} - \frac{1}{4+x}\right] = mg$$

$$\Rightarrow \quad (0.1)(8.3)\left[\frac{4+x-4+x}{16-x^2}\right] = mg$$

$$\Rightarrow \quad 3\left(\frac{2x}{16-x^2}\right) = 1$$

$$\Rightarrow \quad 6x = 16 - x^2$$

$$\Rightarrow \quad x^2 + 6x - 16 = 0$$

$$x = 2\,\text{m}$$

Final distance of piston from top is given as

$$l = 4 + 2 = 6\,\text{m} \qquad \textbf{Ans. (6)}$$

Sol. 48 At constant pressure work done by gas is given as

$$W = nR\Delta T = 66\,\text{J}$$

Change in internal energy of gas is calculated as

$$\Delta U = n(C_V)_{\text{mix}}\Delta T \qquad \ldots(1)$$

Here molar specific heat of mixture at constant volume is given as

$$(C_V)_{\text{mix}} = \frac{n_1 C_{V_1} + n_2 C_{V_2}}{n_1 + n_2}$$

$$\Rightarrow \qquad (C_V)_{\text{mix}} = \frac{2 \times \frac{3}{2} R + 1 \times \frac{5}{2} R}{3}$$

$$\Rightarrow \qquad (C_V)_{\text{mix}} = \frac{11}{6} R$$

Thus from equation-(1), we have

$$\Delta U = \frac{11}{6} nR\Delta T$$

$$\Rightarrow \qquad \Delta U = \frac{11}{6} \times 66 = 121 \text{ J} \qquad \textbf{Ans. (121)}$$

Sol. 49 Total work done in first cycle is calculated as

$$W_1 = W_a + W_b + W_c + W_d$$

$$\Rightarrow \qquad W_1 = 4P_0V_0 + 8P_0V_0 \ln 2 - 6P_0V_0 - 0$$

Total work done in second cycle is calculated as

$$W_2 = W_{a'} + W_{b'} + W_{c'} + W_{d'}$$

$$\Rightarrow \qquad W_2 = 4P_0V_0 \ln 2 - 0 - P_0V_0 + 0$$

$$\Rightarrow \qquad \frac{W_{\text{I}}}{W_{\text{II}}} = \frac{4P_0V_0 + 8P_0V_0 \ln 2 - 6P_0V_0 - 0}{4P_0V_0 \ln 2 - 0 - P_0V_0 + 0}$$

$$\Rightarrow \qquad \frac{W_{\text{I}}}{W_{\text{II}}} = \frac{8\ln 2 - 2}{4\ln 2 - 1} = 2 \qquad \textbf{Ans. (2)}$$

Ch-10 Oscillations

Sol. 1 Position of particle in simple harmonic motion is given as

$$x = 1 \sin\left(\frac{2\pi}{8} t\right) \text{ cm}$$

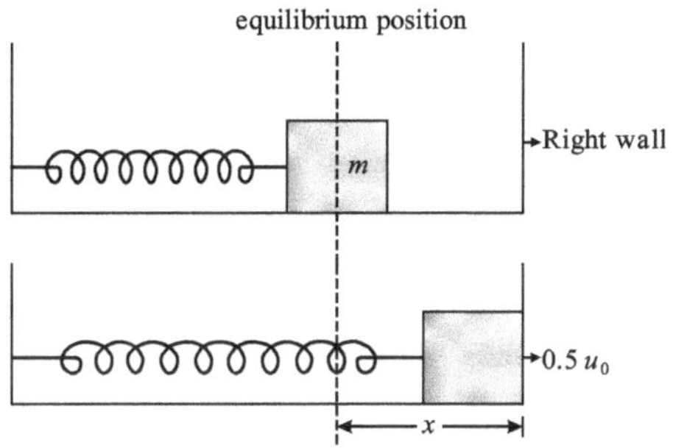

Its acceleration is given as

$$a = \left| \frac{d^2 x}{dt^2} \right|_{t=4/3} = -\left(\frac{\pi}{4}\right)^2 \sin\left(\frac{\pi t}{4}\right)\Big|_{t=4/3}$$

$$\Rightarrow \qquad a = -\frac{\pi^2}{16} \times \frac{\sqrt{3}}{2} = -\frac{\sqrt{3}\pi^2}{32} \text{ cm/s}^2 \qquad \textbf{Ans. (D)}$$

Sol. 2 Net extension in spring is equal to the amplitude A. If x_1 and x_2 are the extensions in first and second part of springs then we use

$$x_1 + x_2 = A$$

Throughout spring tension remain same so we use

$$k_1\, x_1 = k_2\, x_2$$

$$\Rightarrow \qquad A = F\left(\frac{1}{k_1} + \frac{1}{k_2}\right)$$

$$\Rightarrow \qquad F = A\left(\frac{k_1 k_2}{k_1 + k_2}\right)$$

Thus amplitude at P is given as

$$x_1 = \frac{F}{k_1} = \frac{k_2 A}{k_1 + k_2} \qquad \textbf{Ans. (D)}$$

Sol. 3 In order to have net force zero at mean position, the mean position will be shifted towards right. As electric force is constant so it will not affect the frequency of oscillations thus the time period will remain unaffected. **Ans. (A)**

Sol. 4 Restoring torque is same is both cases because weight of disk and rod acts at their centres which are at same location in both the cases. After release the angular acceleration of the system is given as

$$\alpha = \frac{\tau}{I} = -\omega^2\theta$$

In case (A) moment of inertia of system is more as compared to case (B) because in second case disc will act like a point mass because it is in translation motion so we use

$$\omega_B > \omega_A$$

Thus options (A) and (D) are correct. **Ans. (A, D)**

Sol. 5 By energy conservation, we have

$$\frac{1}{2} mu_0^2 = \frac{1}{2} kx^2 + \frac{1}{2} m\,(0.25\, u_0^2) \qquad \ldots (1)$$

After elastic collision speed of block is $0.5\, u_0$. So when it comes back to equilibrium position its speed will be u_0, thus option (A) is correct.

For leftward half oscillations, Amplitude of oscillation can be given as

$$\frac{1}{2}mu_0^2 = \frac{1}{2}kx^2$$

$$\Rightarrow \qquad x = u_0\sqrt{\frac{m}{k}} = A$$

Value of (x) from (i)

$$\frac{3}{4} \times \frac{1}{2}mu_0^2 = \frac{1}{2}kx^2$$

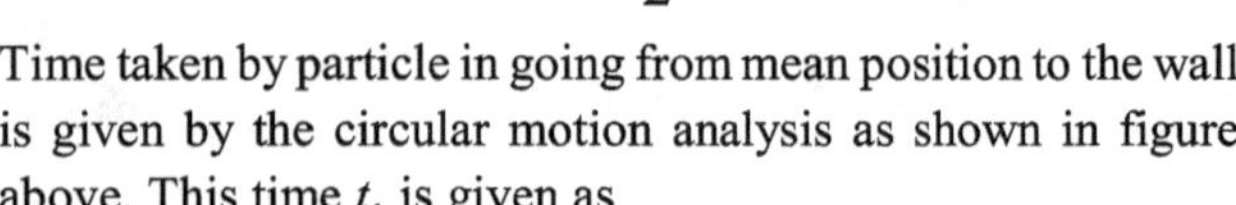

$$\Rightarrow \qquad x = \frac{\sqrt{3}u_0}{2}\sqrt{\frac{m_2}{k}} = \frac{\sqrt{3}}{2}A$$

Time taken by particle in going from mean position to the wall is given by the circular motion analysis as shown in figure above. This time t_1 is given as

$$t_1 = \frac{\pi}{3\omega} = \frac{\pi}{3}\sqrt{\frac{m}{k}}$$

Time to reach equilibrium position first time will be double of this, given as

$$2t_1 = \frac{2\pi}{3}\sqrt{\frac{m}{k}}$$

Second time it will reach mean position after completing half oscillation toward left at time

$$t = \frac{2\pi}{3}\sqrt{\frac{m}{k}} + \frac{T}{2} = \frac{2\pi}{3}\sqrt{\frac{m}{k}} + \frac{2\pi}{2}\sqrt{\frac{m}{k}} = \frac{5\pi}{3}\sqrt{\frac{m}{k}}$$

Hence option (D) is correct. **Ans. (A, D)**

Sol. 6 Total energy of oscillation 1 is given as

$$\frac{1}{2}m\omega_1^2 a^2 = E_1 \qquad \ldots(1)$$

Total energy of oscillation 2 is given as

$$\frac{1}{2}m\omega_2^2 R^2 = E_2 \qquad \ldots(2)$$

From equations (1) and (2), we have

$$\frac{\omega_1}{\omega_2}\frac{a}{R} = \sqrt{\frac{E_1}{E_2}}$$

$$\Rightarrow \qquad \frac{\omega_1}{\omega_2}n = \sqrt{\frac{E_1}{E_2}} \qquad \ldots(3)$$

By energy momentum relation, we have at $x = 0$ for oscillator 1

$$\frac{b^2}{2m} = E_1$$

Similarly for oscillator 2, we use

$$\frac{R^2}{2m} = E_2$$

$$\Rightarrow \qquad \frac{b^2}{R^2} = \frac{E_1}{E_2} \qquad \ldots(4)$$

From equations (3) and (4), we have

$$\frac{\omega_1}{\omega_2}n = \frac{b}{R} = \frac{1}{n}$$

$$\Rightarrow \qquad \frac{\omega_1}{\omega_2} = \frac{1}{n^2}$$

$$\Rightarrow \qquad \frac{\omega_2}{\omega_1} = n^2$$

$$\Rightarrow \qquad \frac{E_1}{E_2} = \frac{1}{n^2}$$

$$\Rightarrow \qquad E_1\omega_2 = E_2\omega_1 \qquad \textbf{Ans. (B, D)}$$

Sol. 7 For case-I, by momentum and energy conservation when mass m is added, we use

$$Mv_0 = (m + M)v$$

At extreme end kinetic energy is converted into potential energy, so we have

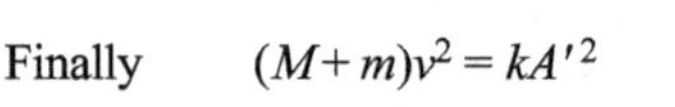

Initially $\qquad Mv_0^2 = kA^2$

Finally $\qquad (M+m)v^2 = kA'^2$

$$\Rightarrow \quad \frac{A'}{A} = \sqrt{\left(\frac{M+m}{M}\right)} \times \frac{v}{v_0} = \sqrt{\left(\frac{M}{M+m}\right)}$$

For case-II, energy remain unchanged because mass is added when the block was at rest at extreme position.

Hence option (A) is correct and option (C) is NOT correct.

In both cases after addition of mass time period will be given as

$$T' = 2\pi\sqrt{\left(\frac{M+m}{k}\right)}$$

Hence option (D) is correct.

At mean position as angular frequency of oscillations is decreased, speed will be less in both cases, hence option (D) is also correct. **Ans. (A, B, D)**

Sol. 8 For mass $2m$, we have

$$kx \leftarrow \boxed{2m} \rightarrow 2T$$

$$2T - kx = 2ma_1 \qquad \ldots(1)$$

Tension in the string is given as

$$T = \frac{2(2m)(m)}{3m}(g - a_1) = \frac{4m}{3}(g - a_1)$$

From equation (1), we have

$$\frac{8m}{3}(g - a_1) - kx = 2ma_1$$

$$\Rightarrow \quad \frac{8Mg}{3} - \frac{8ma_1}{3} - kx = 2ma_1$$

$$\Rightarrow \quad \frac{8Mg}{3} - kx = \frac{14ma_1}{3}$$

$$\Rightarrow \quad a_1 = \frac{8Mg - 3kx}{14m}$$

$$\Rightarrow \quad \frac{vdv}{dx} = \left(\frac{8Mg}{14m} - \frac{3kx}{14m}\right)$$

$$\Rightarrow \quad \int vdv = \frac{1}{14m}\int(8Mg - 3kx)dx$$

For maximum elongation in spring, we use final velocity of block to be zero, so we use

$$0 = \frac{1}{14m}\int_0^{x_0}(8Mg - 3kx)dx$$

$$\Rightarrow \quad 0 = \frac{1}{14m}\left(8Mgx_0 - \frac{3kx_0^2}{2}\right)$$

$$\Rightarrow \quad 8Mgx_0 = \frac{3kx_0^2}{2}$$

$$\Rightarrow \quad x_0 = \frac{16Mg}{3k}$$

Hence option (A) is NOT correct. At $x = \dfrac{x_0}{2}$, we have

$$\int_0^v vdv = \frac{1}{14m}\int_0^{x_0/2}(8Mg - 3kx)dx$$

$$\Rightarrow \quad \frac{v^2}{2} = \frac{1}{14m}\left(\frac{8Mgx_0}{2} - \frac{3kx_0^2}{2\times4}\right)$$

$$\Rightarrow \quad v^2 = \frac{1}{7m}\left(\frac{8Mg}{2}\times\frac{16Mg}{3x} - \frac{3x}{8}\times\frac{16M^2g^2}{3x\times3x}\right)$$

$$\Rightarrow \quad v^2 = \frac{1}{7m}\left(\frac{64M^2g^2}{3x} - \frac{2M^2g^2}{3x}\right)$$

$$\Rightarrow \quad v^2 = \frac{62Mg^2}{21k}$$

Hence option (B) is NOT correct. For inextensible string, we can use $a_2 - a_1 = a_1 - a_3$ hence option (C) is correct.

$$a_1 = \frac{8Mg - 3k\,x_0/4}{14m}$$

$$\Rightarrow \quad a_1 = \frac{8g}{14} - \frac{3kx_0}{14m\times4}$$

$$\Rightarrow \quad a_1 = \frac{8g}{14} - \frac{3x}{14m\times4}\times\frac{16Mg}{3x}$$

$$\Rightarrow \quad a_1 = \frac{8g}{14} - \frac{4g}{14} = \frac{4g}{14} = \frac{2g}{7}$$

Hence option (D) is NOT correct.   **Ans. (C)**

Sol. 9 (A): Given that

$$v = c_1\sqrt{c^2 - x^2}$$

This expression matches with velocity of particle in SHM given as

$$v = \omega\sqrt{A^2 - x^2}$$

Thus option (P) is correctly related.

(B): From the given equation $v = -kx$. Here if at $v = 0, x = 0$ so object comes to rest at $x = 0$. Object is starting from negative x-values comes to rest at $x = 0$ so its velocity decreases with time and so kinetic energy decreases. So option (Q) and (R) are correctly related.

(C): When elevator is considered frame of reference, pseudo force acts so motion of object will remain SHM so option (P) is correctly related.

(D): Velocity of object is given as

$$v = 2\sqrt{\frac{aM_e}{R}}$$

$$\Rightarrow \quad v = \sqrt{2}\sqrt{\frac{2aM_e}{R}} = \sqrt{2}\,v_e$$

where v_e is escape velocity. As other forces are neglected, the direction of motion of an object does not change and speed increases so option (Q) and (R) are correctly related.

Ans. [A (q); B (q, r); C (p); D (r, q)]

Sol. 10 (I): Relative velocity of A with respect to B is given as

$$\vec{v}_{BA} = \vec{v}_B - \vec{v}_A = \sqrt{2}\text{ m/s}$$

Hence option (S) is correctly related.

(II): As $0.1 < \dfrac{\pi}{3}$ so we consider velocities of the particles at $t = 0.1$ s only as this time onward relative velocity will not change. At $t = 0.1$ s velocities of A and B are given as

$$\vec{v}_A = \frac{5\pi}{2}\hat{i} + \left(\frac{5\pi}{2} - 1\right)\hat{j}$$

$$\vec{v}_B = -\frac{5\pi}{2}\hat{i} + \frac{5\pi}{2}\hat{j}$$

$$\Rightarrow \quad \vec{v}_{BA} = -5\pi\hat{i} - \hat{j}$$

$$\Rightarrow \quad |\vec{v}_{BA}| = -\sqrt{25\pi^2 + 1}$$

Hence option (T) is correctly related here.

(III) : Position coordinates of A and B as a function of time are given as

$$x_A = \sin t$$

and
$$x_B = \cos t$$

Velocities of the two particles at time $t = \dfrac{\pi}{3}$ s are given as

$$v_A = \cos t = \frac{1}{2}\ \text{m/s}$$

and
$$v_B = -\sin t = -\frac{\sqrt{3}}{2}\ \text{m/s}$$

$$\Rightarrow \qquad v_{BA} = -\frac{\sqrt{3}}{2} - \frac{1}{2}$$

$$\Rightarrow \qquad |v_{BA}| = \frac{\sqrt{3}}{2} + \frac{1}{2}$$

Hence option (P) is correctly related here.

(IV) : In this case $\vec{v}_A$ & $\vec{v}_B$ are always perpendicular so relative velocity magnitude at any time instant is given as

$$|\vec{v}_{BA}| = \sqrt{v_A^2 + v_B^2} = \sqrt{10}\ \text{m/s}$$

Hence option (R) is correctly related here. **Ans. (C)**

Sol. 11 Total energy should be less than maximum potential energy, so we have $E < V_0$ and $E > 0$. If $E > V_0$ particle will escape. **Ans. (B, C)**

Sol. 12 Potential energy of particle is given as
$$V(x) = \alpha x^4$$

$$\Rightarrow \qquad [\alpha] = \frac{[V(x)]}{[x]^4} = \frac{[ML^2T^{-2}]}{[L^4]} = [ML^{-2}T^{-2}]$$

Time period α (Amplitude)^x $(\alpha)^y$ (Mass)^z

$$\Rightarrow \qquad [T] = [L]^x\,[ML^{-2}T^{-2}]^y\,[M]^2$$

Solving for dimensions in LHS & RHS, we get

$$x = -1,\ y = -\frac{1}{2},\ z = \frac{1}{2}$$

$$\Rightarrow \qquad T = A^{-1}\,\alpha^{-1/2}\,M^{1/2} = \frac{1}{A}\sqrt{\frac{M}{\alpha}} \qquad \textbf{Ans. (B)}$$

Sol. 13 For $|x| > X_0$
$$U = \text{constant}$$

$$\Rightarrow \qquad F = -\frac{dU}{dx} = 0$$

Hence acceleration will also be zero. **Ans. (D)**

Sol. 14 From conservation of energy, we have

$$\frac{1}{2}mv^2 + mgx = \frac{1}{2}\,mu^2$$

$$\Rightarrow \qquad m^2v^2 - m^2u^2 = 2m^2\,gx$$

$$\Rightarrow \qquad p^2 - p_0^2 = 2m^2\,gx$$

$$\Rightarrow \qquad p^2 = p_0^2 + 2m^2\,gx \qquad \textbf{Ans. (D)}$$

Sol. 15

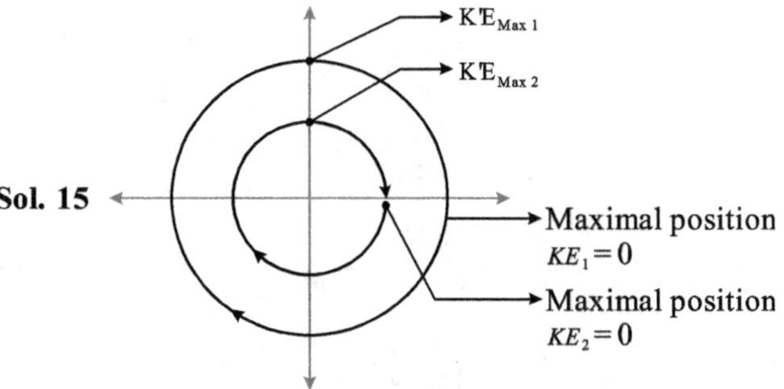

Energy in oscillator is potential energy so we have

$$E = \frac{1}{2}kx^2$$

$$\Rightarrow \qquad \frac{E_1}{E_2} = \frac{\dfrac{1}{2}k(2a)^2}{\dfrac{1}{2}k(a)^2} = 4$$

$$\Rightarrow \qquad E_1 = 4E_2 \qquad \textbf{Ans. (C)}$$

Sol. 16 Block starts from above mean position so initial position is positive. As it move downward momentum first increases then decreases in negative direction. **Ans. (B)**

Sol. 17 For the given situation described in question the force constant of spring is different in case of compression or elongation state given as

$$l > l_0 \to k = k_1$$
$$l < l_0 \to k = k_2$$

So for the two half of oscillations on the two sides of mean position, total time period of oscillation is given as

$$T = \pi\sqrt{\frac{m}{k_1}} + \pi\sqrt{\frac{m}{k_2}}$$

$$\Rightarrow \qquad T = \pi\sqrt{\frac{0.1}{0.009}} + \pi\sqrt{\frac{0.1}{0.016}}$$

$$\Rightarrow \qquad T = \frac{\pi}{0.3} + \frac{\pi}{0.4}$$

$$\Rightarrow \qquad T = \frac{0.7}{0.12}\,\pi \Rightarrow T = 5.83\,\pi$$

$$\Rightarrow \qquad T \approx 6\pi$$

$$\Rightarrow \qquad n = 6 \qquad \textbf{Ans. (6)}$$

Sol. 18 Centre of mass of the rod is located at a distance of 4 cm and 6 cm from the two masses as shown in figure below.

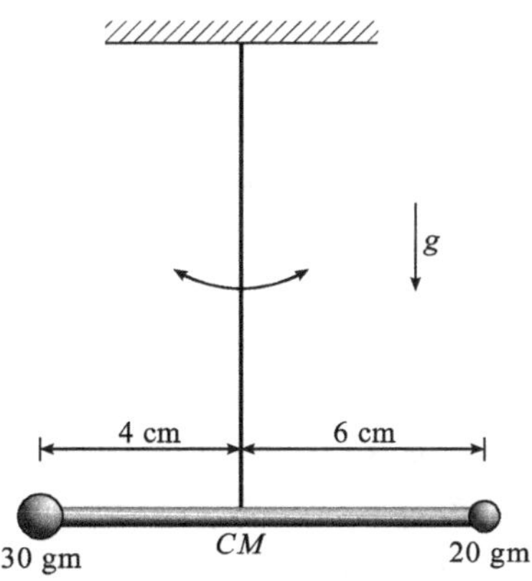

Time period of torsional pendulum *is given as*

$$T = 2\pi\sqrt{\frac{I}{C}}$$

$$\Rightarrow \qquad \omega = \sqrt{\frac{C}{I}}$$

Moment of inertia of the rod is calculated as

$$I = (30)(4)^2 + (20)(6)^2$$

$$\Rightarrow \qquad I = 1200 \text{ gm-cm}^2 = 1.2 \times 10^{-4} \text{ kg-m}^2$$

$$\Rightarrow \qquad \omega = \sqrt{\frac{1.2 \times 10^{-8}}{1.2 \times 10^{-4}}}$$

$$\Rightarrow \qquad \omega = \sqrt{10^{-4}} = 10^{-2} \text{ rad/s}$$

$$\Rightarrow \qquad n \times 10^{-3} = 10^{-2}$$

$$\Rightarrow \qquad n = 10 \qquad\qquad \textbf{Ans. (10)}$$

Ch-11 Waves

Sol. 1 To determine the speed of sound using resonance column, prongs are kept in a vertical plane so that both prongs can send sound wave inside tube. In one resonance, length of resonating air column is

$$l_1 = \frac{\lambda}{4}$$

In another resonance, length of resonating air column is

$$l_2 = \frac{3\lambda}{4}$$

Thus option (A) is correct. **Ans. (A)**

Sol. 2 Third harmonic in closed pipe is given as

$$f = \frac{3v}{4L} = \frac{3 \times 340}{4 \times 0.75} = 340 \text{ Hz}$$

The string has the same frequency of increasing T, f increases

and the number of beats with n decreases so it is given as

$$n - 340 = 4$$

$$\Rightarrow \qquad n = 344 \text{ Hz} \qquad\qquad \textbf{Ans. (A)}$$

Sol. 3 For a travelling wave at any point, we use

Particle velocity $v_p = -$ (slope of y-x graph)

Here velocity is positive as wave is travelling in positive x direction and at point P slope is negative. Here velocity of particle P is in positive y-direction, given as

$$v_P = \omega\sqrt{A^2 - y^2}$$

$$\Rightarrow \qquad v_P = 2\pi f\sqrt{A^2 - y^2}$$

$$\Rightarrow \qquad v_P = 2\pi \frac{C}{\lambda}\sqrt{A^2 - y^2}$$

$$\Rightarrow \qquad v_P = \frac{2\pi \times 0.1}{0.5}\sqrt{(0.1)^2 - (0.05)^2}$$

$$\Rightarrow \qquad v_P = \frac{\sqrt{3}\pi}{50} \text{ m/s} \qquad\qquad \textbf{Ans. (A)}$$

Sol. 4 Fundamental frequency of closed pipe is given as

$$n_0 = \frac{v}{4l}$$

$$\Rightarrow \qquad n_0 = \frac{320}{4 \times 0.8} = \frac{320}{3.2} = 100 \text{ Hz}$$

Frequency of 2nd Harmonic of string

$$n_2 = \frac{v}{l} = \frac{1}{l}\sqrt{\frac{T}{\mu}}$$

$$100 = \frac{1}{l}\sqrt{\frac{50}{m/l}}$$

$$\Rightarrow \qquad 100 = \sqrt{\frac{50}{m \times 0.5}} = \sqrt{\frac{100}{m}}$$

$$\Rightarrow \qquad 10000 = \frac{100}{m} \Rightarrow m = 10^{-2} \text{ kg} = 10 \text{ gm} \qquad \textbf{Ans. (B)}$$

Sol. 5 Velocity of source is given as

$$v_s = \frac{36 \times 10^3}{3600} \text{ m/s} = 10 \text{ m/s}$$

For motion of car toward wall car itself will act as an observer for the reflected sound so observer velocity for reflected sound is given as

$$v_0 = 10 \text{ m/s}$$

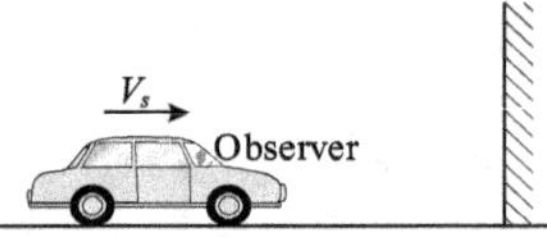

Frequency of siren heard by car driver in reflected sound is given as

$$v' = \left(\frac{V+V_0}{V-V_s'}\right)v$$

$$\Rightarrow \qquad v' = \left(\frac{320+10}{320-10}\right)8\,\text{KHz}$$

$$\Rightarrow \qquad v' = \frac{330}{310}\times 8 = 8.51\,\text{KHz} \qquad\qquad \textbf{Ans. (A)}$$

Sol. 6 With end correction, frequency of air column is given as

$$\frac{V}{4(l+e)} = f$$

$$\Rightarrow \qquad l+e = \frac{V}{4f}$$

$$\Rightarrow \qquad l = \frac{V}{4f} - e$$

$$\Rightarrow \qquad l = \frac{336\times 10^2}{4\times 512} - 1.2 = 15.2\,\text{cm} \qquad \textbf{Ans. (B)}$$

Sol. 7 As length of air-column increases, intensity decreases Hence option (A) is correct. Including end correction the length of air column at first resonance l is related to wavelength is given as

$$l+e = \frac{\lambda}{4}$$

$$\Rightarrow \qquad l < \frac{\lambda}{4}$$

Hence option (D) is correct. $\qquad\qquad$ **Ans. (A, D)**

Sol. 8 At open end phase of pressure wave changes by π so compression returns as refraction. While at closed end phase of pressure wave does not change so compression return as compression. Hence options (B) and (D) are correct.

$$\textbf{Ans. (B, D)}$$

Sol. 9 Equation of wave is given as

$$y = 0.01\,\text{m} \sin(20\,\pi x)\cos 200\pi t$$

As string is vibrating in firth harmonic, total number of nodes will be 6, hence option (A) is NOT correct. From the wave equation, we have

$$20\,\pi = \frac{2\pi}{\lambda}$$

$$\Rightarrow \qquad \lambda = \frac{1}{10}\,\text{m} = 0.1$$

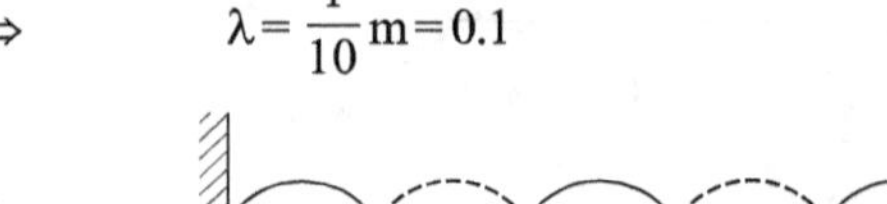

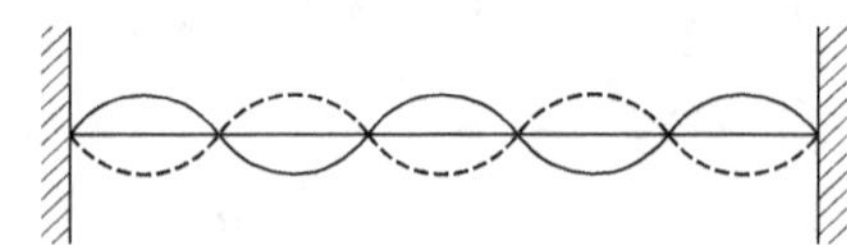

Length of the string is given as

$$l = 0.5\times \frac{1}{2} = 0.25\,\text{m}$$

Hence option (B) is correct.

Mid point of the string is the antinode in the given oscillation. Hence option (C) is correct.

Frequency of string at this note is given as

$$f = \frac{200\pi}{2\pi} = 100\,\text{Hz}$$

Thus fundamental frequency is given as

$$f_0 = \frac{100}{5} = 20\,\text{Hz}$$

Hence option (D) is NOT correct. $\qquad$ **Ans. (B, C)**

Sol. 10 If wind blows from source to observer, the apparent frequency is given as

$$f_2 = f_1\left(\frac{V+w+u}{V-w-u}\right)$$

When wind blows from observer towards source, the apparent frequency is given as

$$f_2 = f_1\left(\frac{V-w+u}{V-w-u}\right)$$

In both cases, $\;f_2 > f_1$ $\qquad\qquad$ **Ans. (A, B)**

Sol. 11 As at one end string is fixed where node is formed and at other end where it is vibrating antinode is formed so length of string is written as

$$\frac{n\lambda}{2} + \frac{\lambda}{4} = L$$

$$\Rightarrow \qquad \lambda\left(\frac{2n+1}{4}\right) = L$$

$$\Rightarrow \qquad \frac{2\pi}{k}\left(\frac{2n+1}{4}\right) = 3$$

$$\Rightarrow \qquad k = \frac{2\pi(2n+1)}{12}, n = 0,1,2\ldots$$

$$\Rightarrow \qquad k = \frac{\pi}{6},\frac{3\pi}{6},\frac{5\pi}{6},\frac{7\pi}{6},\frac{9\pi}{6}\ldots$$

For above values of k, equations in options (A), (C) and (D), it matches with

$$k = \frac{\pi}{6},\frac{5\pi}{6},\frac{5\pi}{2}$$

Oscillation frequency of string is given as

$$\Rightarrow \qquad f = \frac{v}{\lambda} = \frac{v}{\dfrac{4L}{2n+1}} = \frac{v(2n+1)}{4L}$$

$$\Rightarrow \qquad \omega = 2\pi f = \frac{2\pi v(2n+1)}{24} = \frac{\pi(100)}{2\times 3}(2n+1)$$

$$\Rightarrow \qquad \omega = \frac{100\pi(2n+1)}{6}$$

$$\omega = \frac{50\pi}{3}, 50\pi, \frac{250\pi}{3} \ ......$$

For $n = 0, 2$ and 7 it matches with options (A), (C) and (D). Thus all these three options can be the correct equations under different resonating conditions of the string. **Ans. (A, C, D)**

Sol. 12 By doppler's effect beat frequency is given as

$$\Delta f = f_N\left(\frac{v+v_1\cos\theta}{v}\right) - f_M\left(\frac{v+v_1\cos\theta}{v}\right)$$

$$\Rightarrow \qquad \Delta f = (f_N - f_M)\left(\frac{v+v_1\cos\theta}{v}\right)$$

$$\Rightarrow \qquad \Delta v_P = (f_N - f_M)\left(\frac{330 + \dfrac{50}{3}\times\cos\theta}{330}\right)$$

$$\Rightarrow \qquad \Delta v_R = (f_N - f_M)\left(\frac{330 - \dfrac{50}{3}\times\cos\theta}{330}\right)$$

$$\Rightarrow \qquad \Delta v_Q = (f_N - f_M)\left(\frac{330 - 0}{330}\right) \qquad \textbf{Ans. (A, C, D)}$$

Sol. 13 Wave Speed in string at a distance x below the top end is given as

$$v = \sqrt{\frac{T}{\mu}} = \sqrt{\frac{\left[M + \left(\dfrac{m}{l}\right)(l-x)\right]g}{\mu}}$$

At any point on rope the velocity is only a function of x hence time taken to travel along the rope in either side will be same hence option (A), (B) and (D) are correct. At point A tension is less hence velocity is less hence for a given frequency of pulse wavelength at A will be less. Hence option (C) is NOT correct.

Ans. (A, B, D)

Sol. 14 For the two successive resonance lengths obtained in experiment, we use

$$(2n+1)\frac{\lambda}{4} = 50.7 + e$$

and $\qquad (2n+3)\dfrac{\lambda}{4} = 83.9 + e$

For $n = 1$, we use

$$\frac{3\lambda/4}{5\lambda/4} = \frac{50.7+e}{83.9+e}$$

$$\Rightarrow \qquad 3\times 83.9 \times 3e = 5\times 50.7 + 5e$$

$$\Rightarrow \qquad 2e = 1.8$$

$$\Rightarrow \qquad e = 0.9\,\text{cm}$$

$$\Rightarrow \qquad \frac{3\lambda}{4} = 50.7 + 0.9 = 51.6$$

$$\Rightarrow \qquad \lambda = 66.4\,\text{cm}$$

Sound velocity measured in the experiment is given as

$$v = v\lambda = 500 \times 0.664\,\text{ms}^{-1}$$

$$\Rightarrow \qquad v = 332.0\,\text{ms}^{-1}$$

Here we solved above case for $n = 1$ which is an assumption but answers are matching with the given options for this.

Ans. (A, B, C)

Sol. 15 In closed pipe resonance happen when apparent frequency matches with the resonating frequency of the pipe. Figure below shows the situation described in question.

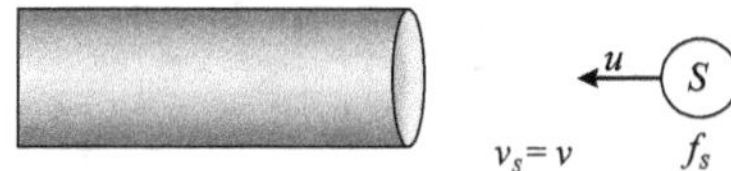

Apparent frequency received by pipe is given as

$$f' = f_s\left(\frac{v}{v-u}\right)$$

$$\Rightarrow \qquad f' = (2n+1)f_0$$

$$\Rightarrow \qquad f_s\left(\frac{v}{v-u}\right) = (2n+1)f_0$$

For $u = 0.8\,v$ and $f_s = f_0$ we have

$$f_0 \times \frac{(v)}{0.2v} = (2n+1)f_0$$

$$\Rightarrow \qquad f_0(5) = (2n+1)f_0$$

Hence option (A) is correct

For $u = 0.8\,v$ and $f_s = 2f_0$ we have

$$2f_0 \times \frac{(v)}{0.2v} = (2n+1)f_0$$

$$\Rightarrow \qquad f_0(10) = (2n+1)f_0$$

Hence option (B) is NOT correct. Similarly we can check that option (C) is NOT correct

For $u = 0.5v$ and $f_s = 1.5f_0$ we have

$$f_s\left(\frac{v}{v-0.5v}\right) = (2n+1)f_0$$

$$\Rightarrow \qquad 1.5f_0 \times 2 = (2n+1)f_0$$

$$\Rightarrow \qquad f_0(3) = (2n+1)f_0$$

Hence option (D) is correct. **Ans. (A, D)**

Sol. 16 (A) For the organ pipe waves are longitudinal and fundamental mode of oscillation for displacement is shown in figure below.

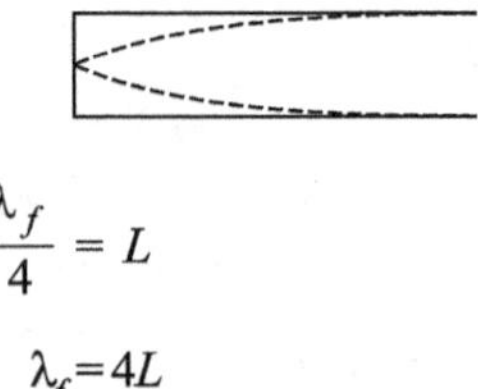

$$\frac{\lambda_f}{4} = L$$

$$\Rightarrow \qquad \lambda_f = 4L$$

(B) For the organ pipe waves are longitudinal and fundamental mode of oscillation for displacement is shown in figure below.

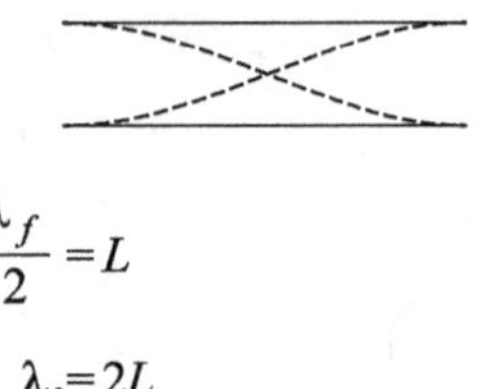

$$\frac{\lambda_f}{2} = L$$

$$\Rightarrow \qquad \lambda_f = 2L$$

(C) In the stretched wire clamped at both ends, transverse standing waves are formed as shown in figure below.

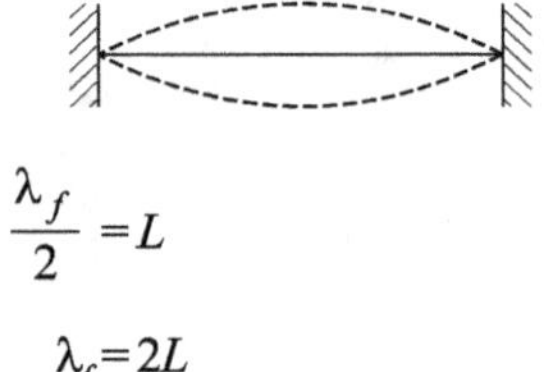

$$\frac{\lambda_f}{2} = L$$

$$\Rightarrow \qquad \lambda_f = 2L$$

(D) In the stretched wire clamped at both ends and mid point the transverse standing wave formed as shown in figure below.

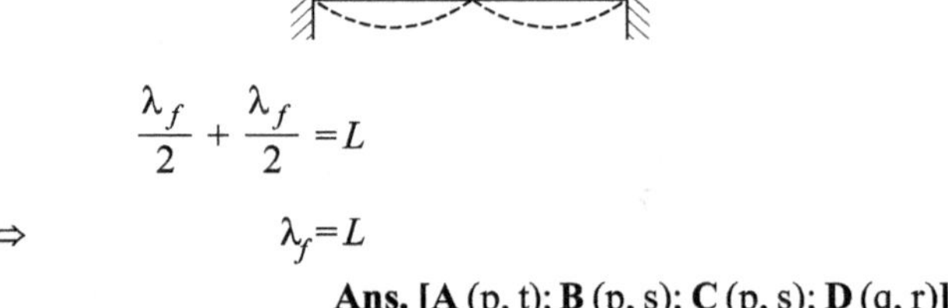

$$\frac{\lambda_f}{2} + \frac{\lambda_f}{2} = L$$

$$\Rightarrow \qquad \lambda_f = L$$

Ans. [A (p, t); B (p, s); C (p, s); D (q, r)]

Sol. 17 For string (A) as length of string is L_0 and it is vibrating in Ist harmonic or fundamental mode so its frequency is given as

$$f_0 = \frac{1}{2L_0}\sqrt{\frac{T_0}{\mu}}$$

Thus tension in this string is T_0

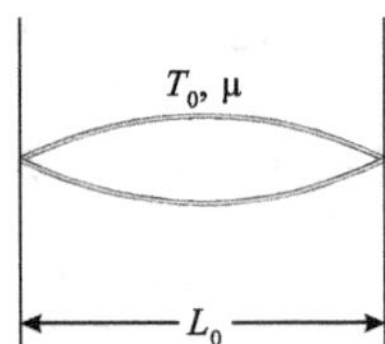

For string (2) as it is oscillating in 3rd harmonic as shown in figure below. The length of string is $\frac{3L_0}{2}$ so its oscillation frequency is given as

$$f_0 = \frac{3v}{2L}$$

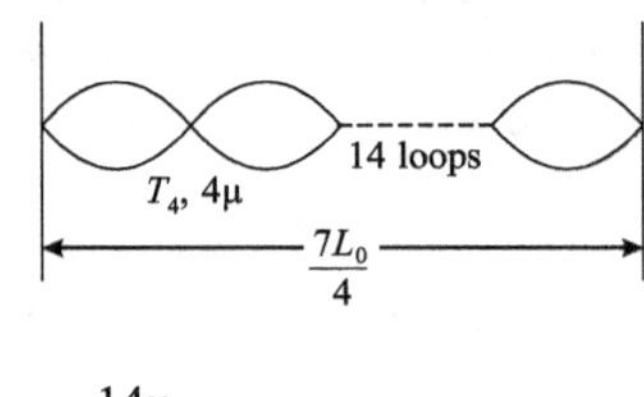

$$\Rightarrow \qquad f_0 = \frac{3}{2\left(\frac{3L_0}{2}\right)}\sqrt{\frac{T_2}{2\mu}}$$

$$\Rightarrow \qquad f_0 = \frac{1}{L_0}\sqrt{\frac{T_2}{2\mu}} = \frac{1}{2L_0}\sqrt{\frac{T_0}{\mu}}$$

$$\Rightarrow \qquad T_2 = \frac{T_0}{2}$$

For string (3) length of string is $\frac{5L_0}{4}$ and it is vibrating in 5th harmonic and frequency is still f_0 so we use

$$f_0 = \frac{5V}{2L}$$

$$\Rightarrow \qquad f_0 = \frac{5}{2\left(\frac{5L_0}{4}\right)}\sqrt{\frac{T_3}{3\mu}} = \frac{1}{2L_0}\sqrt{\frac{T_0}{\mu}}$$

$$\Rightarrow \qquad \frac{2}{L_0}\sqrt{\frac{T_3}{3\mu}} = \frac{1}{2L_0}\sqrt{\frac{T_0}{\mu}}$$

$$T_3 = \frac{3T_0}{16} \quad \Rightarrow \quad (T)$$

For string (4) length of string is $\frac{7L_0}{4}$ and it is vibrating in 14th harmonic and frequency is still f_0 so we use

$$f_0 = \frac{14v}{2L}$$

$$\Rightarrow \qquad f_0 = \frac{14}{2\left(\frac{7L_0}{4}\right)}\sqrt{\frac{T_4}{4\mu}} = \frac{1}{2L_0}\sqrt{\frac{T_0}{\mu}}$$

$$\Rightarrow \quad \frac{4}{L_0}\sqrt{\frac{T_4}{4\mu}} = \frac{1}{2L_0}\sqrt{\frac{T_0}{\mu}}$$

$$\Rightarrow \quad T_4 = \frac{T_0}{16} \qquad \textbf{Ans. (A)}$$

Sol. 18 Relative velocity of B wrt A is given as

$$v_{BA} = 30 - 20 = 10 \text{ m/s}$$

Speed of sound for passenger in A is given as

$$v_0 = 340 + 20 = 360 \text{ m/s}$$

Speed of sound for passenger in B is given as

$$v_0 = 340 - 30 = 310 \text{ m/s}$$

So option (B) is correct. **Ans. (B)**

Sol. 19 For passenger in train A there is no relative motion between source and observer as both are moving with 20 m/s so there is no change in observed frequencies and no change in their intensities. **Ans. (A)**

Sol. 20 For passenger in trains B, observer is receding with $V = 30$ m/s and source is approaching with velocity 20 m/s hence the frequencies observed are given as

$$f_1' = 800\left(\frac{340-30}{340-20}\right) = 775$$

$$f_2' = 1120\left(\frac{340-30}{340-20}\right) = 1085$$

Spread of frequency range $= 1085 - 775 = 310 \text{ Hz}$ **Ans. (A)**

Sol. 21 Figure below shows the situation described in question.

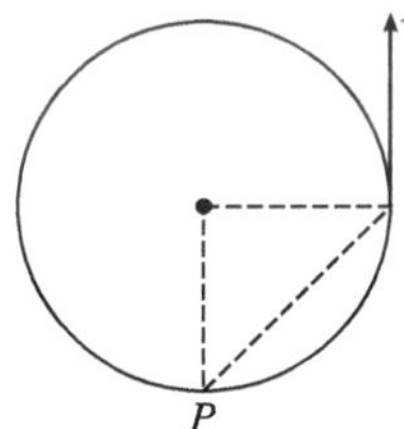

At this position of source S_2, the apparent frequency received by the detector is given as

$$f_{ap} = \frac{c}{c + v\cos 45°}f$$

$$\Rightarrow \quad f_{ap} = \frac{324}{324 + 4\sqrt{2}\times\dfrac{1}{\sqrt{2}}}\times 656$$

$$\Rightarrow \quad f_{ap} = 648 \text{ Hz} \qquad \textbf{Ans. (648)}$$

Sol. 22 When S_2 is at R, as it is moving perpendicular to line joining with the detector, detector will receive its actual frequency given as

$$f_{S_2} = 656 \text{ Hz}$$

As source S_1 is moving toward detector, the apparent frequency

received by detector from S_1 is given as

$$f_{S_1} = \left(\frac{c}{c-v}\right)f$$

$$\Rightarrow \quad f_{S_1} = \left(\frac{324}{324-4}\right)\times 656 = 664.2 \text{ Hz}$$

Beat frequency received by the detector is given as

$$\Delta f = 664.2 - 656 = 8.2 \text{ Hz} \qquad \textbf{Ans. (8.2)}$$

Sol. 23 Mass per unit length of the string is given as

$$\mu = \frac{1\times 10^{-3}}{20\times 10^{-2}} = \frac{1}{2}\times 10^{-2}\text{ kg/m}$$

Wave velocity in string is given as

$$V = \sqrt{\frac{T}{\mu}} = \sqrt{\frac{0.5}{0.5\times 10^{-2}}} = 10 \text{ m/s}$$

Wavelength of wave is calculated as

$$\lambda = \frac{V}{f} = \frac{10}{100} = 0.1 \text{ m} = 10 \text{ cm}$$

Separation between successive nodes $= \dfrac{\lambda}{2} = \dfrac{10}{2} = 5 \text{ cm}$

Ans. (5)

Sol. 24 Car which is approaching source will be treated as observer, then it will be treated as source which is moving in direction of sound hence the two reflected frequencies are given as

$$f_1 = f_0\left(\frac{v+v_1}{v-v_1}\right)$$

and

$$f_2 = f_0\left(\frac{v+v_2}{v-v_2}\right)$$

$$\Rightarrow \quad f_1 - f_2 = \left(\frac{1.2}{100}\right)f_0 = f_0\left(\frac{v+v_1}{v-v_1} - \frac{v+v_2}{v-v_2}\right)$$

$$\Rightarrow \quad \left(\frac{1.2}{100}\right)f_0 = \frac{2v(v_1-v_2)}{(v-v_1)(v-v_2)}f_0$$

As v_1 and v_2 are very less than v, we can use

$$(v-v_1)(v-v_2) = v^2$$

$$\Rightarrow \quad v_1 - v_2 = \frac{v\times 1.2}{200} = \frac{330\times 1.2}{200} = 1.98 \text{ m/s} = 7.12 \text{ km/hr}$$

Ans. (7)

Sol. 25 Equations of two progressive waves

$$y_1 = 4\sin(2x - 6t)$$

$$y_2 = 3\sin(2x - 6t - \pi/2)$$

Phase difference between the two waves is

$$\phi = \frac{\pi}{2}$$

Thus resulting amplitude is given as

$$A_{res} = \sqrt{A_1^2 + A_2^2 + 2A_1 A_2 \cos\phi}$$

$$A_{res} = \sqrt{3^2 + 4^2 + 0} = 5 \qquad \textbf{Ans. (5)}$$

Sol. 26 If the amplitude of each wave is A figure below shows the phasor diagram for superposition of these waves. The one having phases of 0 or π will cancel each other and resultant of other two is having angle $\dfrac{\pi}{3}$ between them is given as

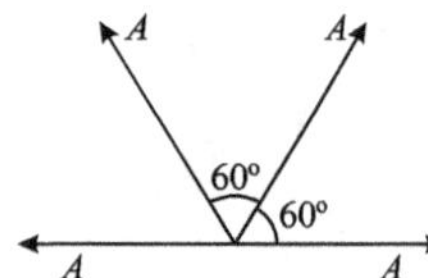

$$2A \cos\frac{\pi}{6} = \sqrt{3}\,A$$

Resulting intensity is given as

$$I \propto A^2$$

$$I = 3kA^2 = 3I_0$$

$$\Rightarrow \qquad n = 3 \qquad \textbf{Ans. (3)}$$

Sol. 27 Figure below shows the situation described in the question.

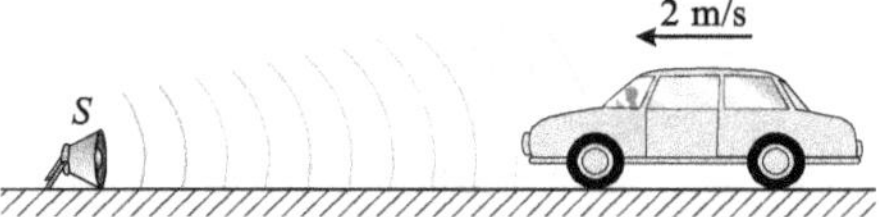

If f_1 is the frequency reflected by the car then by doppler's effects it is given as

$$f_i = \left(\frac{v + v_0}{v - v_s}\right) f_0 = \frac{330 + 2}{330 - 2} \times f_0$$

$$\Rightarrow \qquad f_1 = \frac{332}{328} f_0$$

Beat frequency after superposition with original sound is given as

$$f_B = \left(\frac{332}{328} - 1\right) f_0$$

$$\Rightarrow \qquad f_B = \frac{4}{328} \times 492 = 6\,\text{Hz} \qquad \textbf{Ans. (6)}$$

Sol. 28 Figure below shows the situation described in the question.

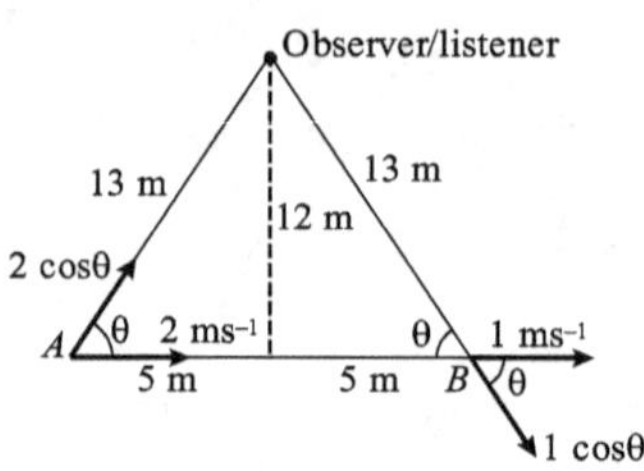

The frequency received by observer from the two sources are given as

$$v_A = v\left[\frac{v}{v - 2\cos\theta}\right]$$

and

$$v_B = v\left[\frac{v}{v + 1\cos\theta}\right]$$

Beat frequency is calculated as

$$f_B = v\left[\frac{v}{v - 2\cos\theta}\right] - v\left[\frac{v}{v + \cos\theta}\right]$$

$$\Rightarrow \qquad f_B = v\,v\left[\frac{1}{v - 2\cos\theta} - \frac{1}{v + \cos\theta}\right]$$

$$\Rightarrow \qquad f_B = 1430 \times 330\left[\frac{1}{330 - 2\times\dfrac{5}{13}} - \frac{1}{330 + \dfrac{5}{13}}\right]$$

$$\Rightarrow \qquad f_B = 1430 \times 330 \times 13\left[\frac{1}{330\times13 - 10} - \frac{1}{330\times13 + 5}\right]$$

$$\Rightarrow \qquad f_B = 1430 \times 330 \times 13\left[\frac{1}{4280} - \frac{1}{4295}\right] \approx 5\,\text{Hz}$$

$$\textbf{Ans. (5.00 Hz)}$$

Sol. 29 Figure below shows the situation described in question with velocity components of observer and train S1.

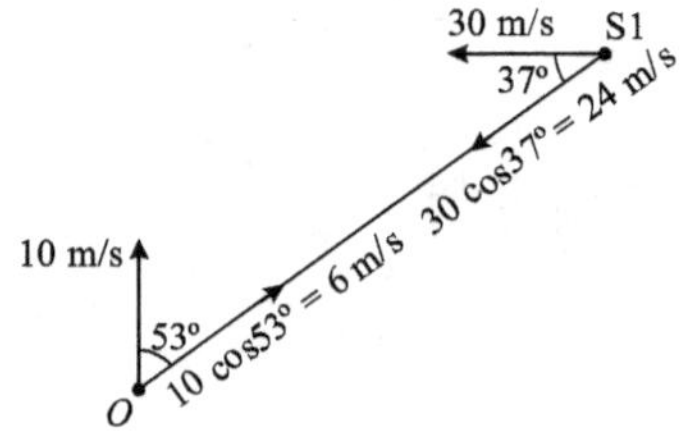

Frequency observed by O from S2 is given as

$$f_2 = \frac{330 + 10}{330} \times 120 = \frac{340}{330} \times 120 = 123.63\,\text{Hz}$$

Frequency observed by O from S1 is given as

$$f_1 = \frac{330 + 6}{330 - 24} \times 120 = \frac{336}{306} \times 120 \approx 131.76\,\text{Hz}$$

Beat frequency is calculated as

$$f_B = 131.76 - 123.63 = 8.128\,\text{Hz} \quad \textbf{Ans. (8.12 to 8.13)}$$

Sol. 30 When fork is stationary, for resonance its frequency will be matching with that of the pipe. If the length of pipe is l_1, its frequency will be inversely proportional to the length, so we use

$$f = \frac{k}{l_1} \qquad \ldots(1)$$

When fork is moving, its frequency which resonate with the pipe is given by Doppler's effect. If the new length of pipe is l_2, we use

$$\left(\frac{v}{v - v_T}\right) f = \frac{k}{l_2} \qquad \ldots(2)$$

Equation-(1) divided by equation-(2) gives

$$\Rightarrow \qquad \frac{v - v_T}{v} = \frac{l_2}{l_1}$$

$$\Rightarrow \qquad \frac{l_2}{l_1} - 1 = \frac{v - v_T}{v} - 1$$

$$\Rightarrow \qquad \frac{l_2 - l_1}{l_1} = -\frac{v_T}{v}$$

$$\Rightarrow \qquad \frac{l_2 - l_1}{l_1} \times 100 = \frac{-2}{320} \times 100 = -0.625$$

There smallest value of percentage change required in the length of pipe is 0.625. **Ans. (0.62 to 0.63)**

Sol. 31 If the string oscillates in p loops, the oscillation frequency is given as

$$f = \frac{p}{2l}\sqrt{\frac{T}{\mu}}$$

$$\Rightarrow \qquad 750 = \frac{P}{2}\sqrt{\frac{T}{\mu}} \qquad \ldots(1)$$

And for next harmonic, we use

$$1000 = \frac{p+1}{2}\sqrt{\frac{T}{\mu}} \qquad \ldots(2)$$

From equations-(1) and (2), we use

$$\frac{4}{3} = \frac{p+1}{p}$$

$$\Rightarrow \qquad p = 3$$

$$\Rightarrow \qquad 1000 = \frac{4}{2}\sqrt{\frac{T}{2 \times 10^{-5}}}$$

$$\Rightarrow \qquad T = 5\,\text{N} \qquad \qquad \textbf{Ans. (5)}$$

Ch-12 Electric Charges, Field & Potential

Sol. 1 Sphere is neutral and conducting as positive point charge placed near it equal charge separation takes place so net charge will be zero.

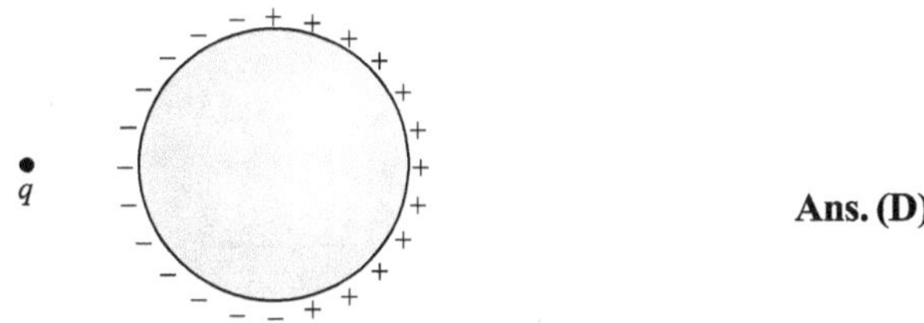

Ans. (D)

Sol. 2 Figure below shows the situation described in the question.

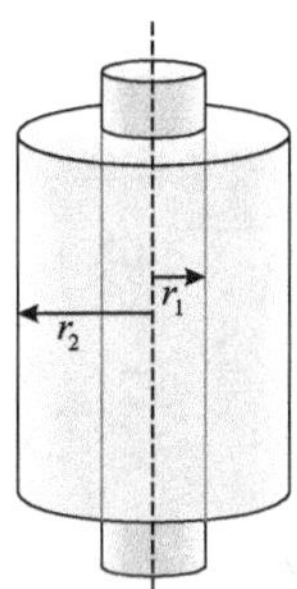

A potential difference appears between the two cylinders only when there exist some electric field between the two cylinders. In case of situations given in options (A), (C) and (D) it happens thus only option (A) is correct. **Ans. (A)**

Sol. 3 If a gaussian surface is constructed within the cavity then by Gauss law, we have

$$\oint \vec{E} \cdot \vec{ds} = 0$$

If P is a point inside cavity and ρ is the charge density then net electric field at point P is given as

$$\vec{E} = \frac{\rho}{3\varepsilon_0}\vec{b} - \frac{\rho}{3\varepsilon_0}\vec{a}$$

$$\Rightarrow \qquad \vec{E} = \frac{\rho}{3\varepsilon_0}(\vec{b} - \vec{a}) = \frac{\rho}{3\varepsilon_0}\vec{r}$$

Thus electric field is non zero and uniform within cavity.
Ans. (B)

Sol. 4 Electric potential at point $(-a, 0, a)$ is given as

$$V_1 = \frac{kq_1}{r_1} + \frac{kq_2}{r_2}$$

$$\Rightarrow \quad V_1 = \frac{kq}{\sqrt{a^2 + \left(\frac{a}{2}\right)^2}} + \frac{(-kq)}{\sqrt{a^2 + \left(\frac{a}{2}\right)^2}} = 0$$

Electric potential at $(0, a, 0)$ is given as

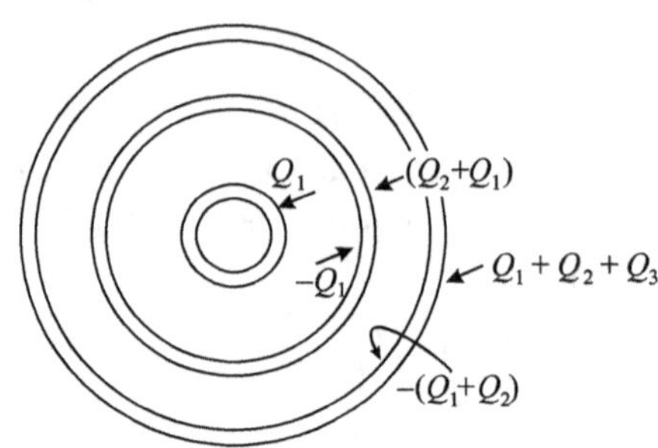

$$V_2 = \frac{kq_1}{r_1} + \frac{kq_2}{r_2}$$

$$\Rightarrow \quad V_2 = \frac{kq}{\sqrt{a^2 + \left(\frac{a}{2}\right)^2}} + \frac{(-kq)}{\sqrt{a^2 + \left(\frac{a}{2}\right)^2}} = 0$$

As Potential difference $\Delta V = V_1 - V_2 = 0$ so work done $q\Delta V = 0$ hence option (C) is correct.   **Ans. (C)**

Sol. 5 Electric field at O is given as

$$E = \frac{2q/3}{4\pi\varepsilon_0 R^2} = \frac{q}{6\pi\varepsilon_0 R^2}$$

Hence option (A) is NOT correct.

Potential energy of system of charges is calculated as

$$U = K\left[\frac{q^2/9}{AB} + \frac{(-2q^2/9)}{BC} + \frac{(-2q^2/9)}{AC}\right]$$

$$\Rightarrow \quad U = K\left[\frac{q^2/9}{2R} + \frac{(-2q^2/9)}{2R(\sqrt{3}/2)} + \frac{(-2q^2/9)}{2R\left(\frac{1}{2}\right)}\right]$$

$$\Rightarrow \quad U \neq 0$$

Hence option (B) is NOT correct.

Force between charges at B and C is given as

$$F_{C-B} = \frac{(2q/3)(q/3)}{4\pi\varepsilon_0(3R^2)} = \frac{q^2}{54\pi\varepsilon_0 R^2}$$

Hence option (C) is correct.

Electric potential at O is given as

$$\Rightarrow \quad V = K\left[\frac{(q/3)}{OA} + \frac{(q/3)}{OB} + \frac{(-2q/3)}{OC}\right]$$

$$\Rightarrow \quad V = K\left[\frac{q/3}{R} + \frac{(q/3)}{R} + \frac{(-2q/3)}{R}\right] = 0$$

$$\Rightarrow \quad V = 0$$

Hence option (D) is NOT correct.   **Ans. (C)**

Sol. 6 Figure below shows the charge distribution on inner and outer surfaces of the shells based on net electric field inside metal bodies of shells must be zero.

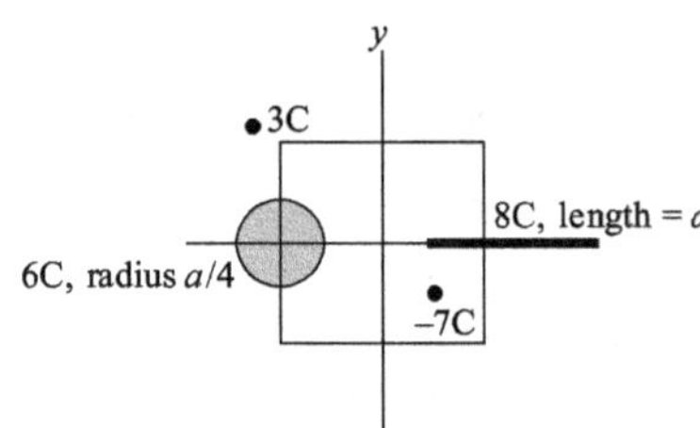

It is given that outer charge densities of the three shells are equal, so we use

$$\frac{Q_1}{4\pi R^2} = \frac{Q_1 + Q_2}{4\pi(2R)^2} = \frac{Q_1 + Q_2 + Q_3}{4\pi(3R)^2}$$

$$\Rightarrow \quad \frac{Q_1}{1} = \frac{Q_1 + Q_2}{4} = \frac{Q_1 + Q_2 + Q_3}{9}$$

$$\Rightarrow \quad \frac{Q_1}{1} = \frac{Q_2}{3} = \frac{Q_3}{5}$$

Thus option (B) is correct.   **Ans. (B)**

Sol. 7 Figure below shows the situation given in question

As half disc is inside cube so we use enclosed charge inside the cube is given as

$$q_1 = \frac{6C}{2} = 3C$$

As $\frac{1}{4}$ th of the rod is inside cube so its charge which is enclosed inside the cube is given as

$$q_2 = \frac{8}{4} = 2C$$

Enclosed net charge is used to calculate the flux, which is given as

$$\phi = \frac{-7 + 3 + 2}{\varepsilon_0} = \frac{-2C}{\varepsilon_0}$$

Hence option (A) is correct.   **Ans. (A)**

Sol. 8 Spherical oil drop is in equilibrium so net force on it is zero, for which we have

$$qE = mg$$

$$\Rightarrow \quad q\left[\frac{81\pi}{7}\times 10^5\right] = 900\times \frac{4}{3}\pi r^3 \times 9.8$$

$$\Rightarrow \quad q = \frac{900\times 4 \times r^3 \times 9.8 \times 7}{3\times 81\times 10^5} \qquad \ldots(1)$$

$$\Rightarrow \quad v_T = 2\times 10^{-3}\,\text{m/s}$$

$$\Rightarrow \quad 2\times 10^{-3} = \frac{2}{9}\times \frac{r^2 \times 900 \times 9.8}{1.8\times 10^{-5}}$$

$$\Rightarrow \quad r^2 = \frac{18\times 1.8\times 10^{-5}\times 10^{-3}}{2\times 900\times 9.8}$$

$$\Rightarrow \quad r^2 = 0.1836\times 10^{-10} = 18.36\times 10^{-12}$$

$$\Rightarrow \quad r = 4.284\times 10^{-6}\,\text{m}$$

$$\Rightarrow \quad q = \frac{3600\times 9.8\times 7}{243\times 10^5}\times 78.62\times 10^{-18}$$

$$\Rightarrow \quad q = 0.799\times 10^{-18} \approx 8\times 10^{-19}\,\text{C} \qquad \textbf{Ans. (D)}$$

Sol. 9 As electric pressure on the surface of shell is given as

$$p_e = \frac{\sigma^2}{2\varepsilon_0}$$

Thus the force of repulsion acting on the cross section is given as

$$F = \frac{\sigma^2}{2\varepsilon_0}\times \pi R^2$$

Same amount of force is needed to held the two parts of shells together hence option (A) is correct. **Ans. (A)**

Sol. 10 Figure below shows the given situation and surface in a three dimensional coordinate system.

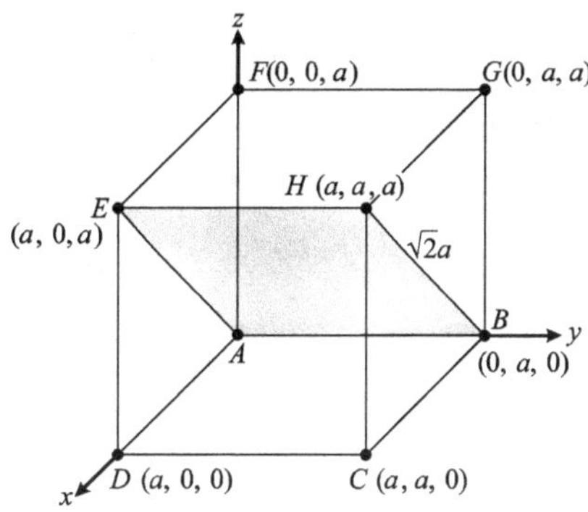

Flux through *EHBA* can be calculated as

$$\phi = \text{Electrical field} \times \text{projected area}$$

$$\Rightarrow \quad \phi = EA\cos 45°$$

$$\Rightarrow \quad \phi = E_0\,(\sqrt{2}a^2)\times \frac{1}{\sqrt{2}} = E_0 a^2 \qquad \textbf{Ans. (C)}$$

Sol. 11 Figure below shows the situation described in the question.

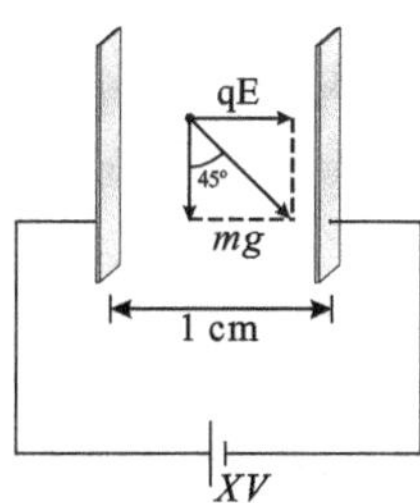

As the proton is moving at an angle 45° to the vertical that indicates force on it due to its weight is equal to the electric force on proton in horizontal direction, so we use

$$mg = qE$$

$$\Rightarrow \quad 1.67\times 10^{-27}\times 10 = 1.6\times 10^{-19}\times \frac{X}{0.01}$$

$$\Rightarrow \quad X = \frac{1.67}{1.6}\times 10^{-9}\,\text{V}$$

$$\Rightarrow \quad X = 1\times 10^{-9}\,\text{V} \qquad \textbf{Ans. (C)}$$

Sol. 12 For a charged spherical shell, electric field and potential plots are shown below

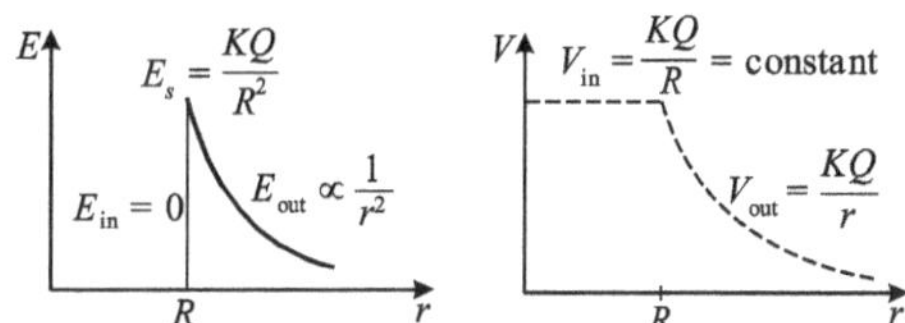

Hence option (D) is correct. **Ans. (D)**

Sol. 13 For the situation given in the question, electric fields E_1, E_2 and E_3 are given as

$$E_1 = \frac{Q}{4\pi \in_0 r^2}\,,\; E_2 = \frac{\lambda}{2\pi \in_0 r}\;\text{and}\; E_3 = \frac{\sigma}{2 \in_0}$$

At distance r_0, we use

$$\frac{Q}{4\pi \in_0 r_0^2} = \frac{\lambda}{2\pi \in_0 r_0} = \frac{\sigma}{2\in_0} \qquad \ldots(1)$$

$$\Rightarrow \quad \frac{Q}{4\pi \in_0 r_0^2} = \frac{\sigma}{2\in_0}$$

$$\Rightarrow \quad Q = 2\sigma\pi r_0^2$$

Hence option (A) is correct.

From equation (1), we also have

$$r_0 = \frac{\lambda}{\pi\sigma}$$

Hence option (B) is NOT correct.

At position $r_0/2$, we have

$$E_1\left(\frac{r_0}{2}\right) = \frac{Q}{4\pi \in_0 \dfrac{r_0^2}{4}} = \frac{Q}{\pi \in_0 r_0^2} \qquad \ldots(2)$$

and

$$2E_2\left(\frac{r_0}{2}\right) = \frac{2\lambda}{2\pi \in_0 \left(\dfrac{r_0}{2}\right)} = \frac{2\lambda}{\pi \in_0 r_0} \qquad \ldots(3)$$

Dividing equation (2) and (3) gives

$$\frac{E_1(r_0/2)}{2E_2\left(\dfrac{r_0}{2}\right)} = \frac{Q}{\pi \in_0 r_0^2} \cdot \frac{\pi \in_0 r_0}{2\lambda}$$

$$\Rightarrow \quad \frac{E_1(r_0/2)}{2E_2\left(\dfrac{r_0}{2}\right)} = \frac{Q}{2r_0\lambda} = 1$$

Hence option (C) is correct.

$$\frac{E_2\left(\dfrac{r_0}{2}\right)}{4E_3\left(\dfrac{r_0}{2}\right)} = \frac{\dfrac{\lambda}{2\pi \in_0 \dfrac{r_0}{2}}}{4\dfrac{\sigma}{2\in_0}} = \frac{\lambda}{\pi \in_0 r_0} \cdot \frac{\in_0}{2\sigma}$$

$$\Rightarrow \quad \frac{E_2\left(\dfrac{r_0}{2}\right)}{4E_3\left(\dfrac{r_0}{2}\right)} = \frac{\lambda}{2\pi r_0\sigma} = \frac{\lambda}{2\pi\sigma\dfrac{x}{\pi\sigma}} = \frac{1}{2}$$

Hence option (D) is NOT correct. **Ans. (C)**

Sol. 14 Figure below shows the situation described in the three uniformly charged spheres and position of point P.

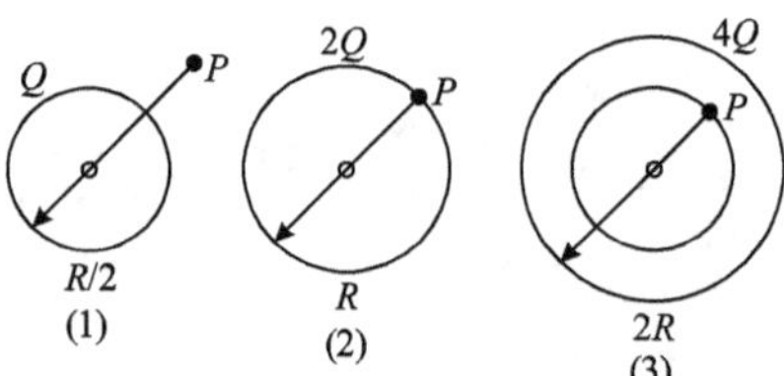

Electric field due to sphere 1 is given as

$$E_1 = \frac{KQ}{R^2}$$

Electric field due to sphere 2 is given as

$$E_2 = \frac{K.2Q}{R^2}$$

Electric field due to sphere 3 is given as

$$E_3 = \frac{K.(4Q)R}{(2R)^3} = \frac{KQ}{2k^2}$$

$$\Rightarrow \quad E_2 > E_1 > E_3 \qquad \textbf{Ans. (C)}$$

Sol. 15 If initial charge on the sphere is Q, its potential is taken as

$$V_0 = \frac{KQ}{R}$$

Charge removed from the shell is αQ due to hole made. Thus potential at the centre of shell becomes

$$V_C = \frac{KQ(1-\alpha)}{R}$$

Potential at a point $R/2$ distance from centre toward the hole is given as

$$V_P = \frac{KQ}{R} - \frac{2K\alpha Q}{R} = \frac{KQ}{R}(1-2\alpha)$$

$$\Rightarrow \quad \frac{V_C}{V_p} = \frac{1-\alpha}{1-2\alpha}$$

Hence option (A) is correct.

Initial electric field at centre was zero but after hole is made, electric field at centre will be due to the equal charge opposite to the hole, given as

$$(E_C)_{final} = \frac{K\alpha Q}{R^2} = \frac{\alpha V_0}{R}$$

Hence option (B) is NOT correct.

Initial electric field at a point located at a distance $2R$ from the centre along the line joining of hole and centre is given as

$$(E_P)_{initial} = \frac{KQ}{4R^2}$$

Final electric field at this point after hole is made is given as

$$(E_P)_{final} = \frac{KQ}{4R^2} - \frac{K\alpha Q}{R^2}$$

Reduction in electric field is given as

$$\Delta E_P = \frac{KQ}{4R^2} - \frac{KQ}{4R^2} + \frac{K\alpha Q}{R^2} = \frac{K\alpha Q}{R^2} = \frac{V_0\alpha}{R}$$

Hence option (C) is NOT correct.

The reduction in potential at the centre of shell is given as

$$\Delta V = \frac{KQ}{R} - \frac{KQ(1-\alpha)}{R} = \frac{K\alpha Q}{R}(\alpha) = \alpha V_0$$

Hence option (D) is NOT correct. **Ans. (A)**

Sol. 16 Figure below shows the initial dipole configuration as given in question.

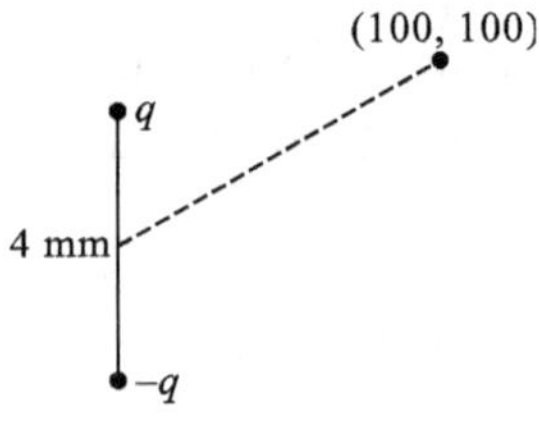

Dipole moment of the given dipole is written as

$$\vec{P}_1 = (4q)\hat{j}$$

Position vector of the given point is written as

$$\vec{r} = 100(\hat{i} + \hat{j}) \text{ mm}$$

Potential at given point is calculated as

$$V_0 = \frac{K\vec{P}_1 \cdot \vec{r}}{r^3} = \frac{K(100P_1)}{(100\sqrt{2})^3}$$

Now the below figure shows the new configuration of dipole charges at which new dipole moment is given as

$$\vec{P}_2 = P_2[-\cos\theta\,\hat{i} + \sin\theta\,\hat{j}]$$

Where $\tan\theta = 2$

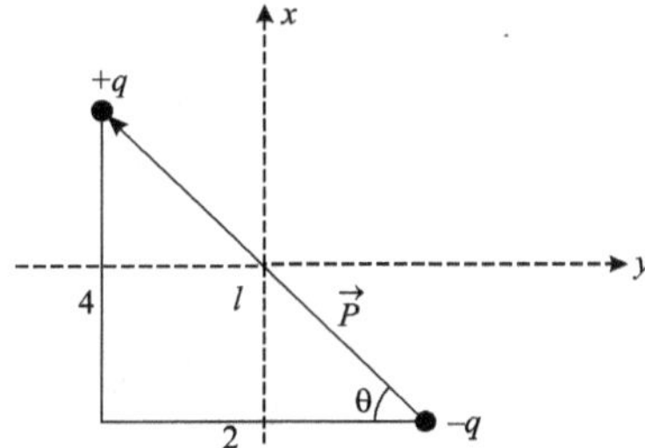

At $\vec{r} = 100(\hat{i} + \hat{j})$ mm, the potential is now calculated as

$$V = \frac{K\vec{P}_2 \cdot \vec{r}}{r^3}$$

$$\Rightarrow \quad V = \frac{K(100P_2)(-\cos\theta + \sin\theta)}{(100\sqrt{2})^3}$$

$$\Rightarrow \quad V = \frac{V_0 P_2}{P_1}(-\cos\theta + \sin\theta)$$

$$\Rightarrow \quad V = V_0 \frac{ql}{4q}(-\cos\theta + \sin\theta)$$

$$\Rightarrow \quad V = \frac{V_0}{4}[-2 + 4] = \frac{V_0}{2} \qquad \textbf{Ans. (B)}$$

Sol. 17 Electrostatic force is passing through axis so angular momentum is conserved, so torque is zero and so angular momentum is conserved. Linear momentum is not conserved as velocity keep changing. As distance of object from axis is changing so angular velocity is changing and it is not conserved.
Ans. (A)

Sol. 18 As expressed in the figure given in question below, the number of field lines emitting from Q_1 are more than number of field lines reaching at Q_2 so we can use

$$|Q_1| > |Q_2|$$

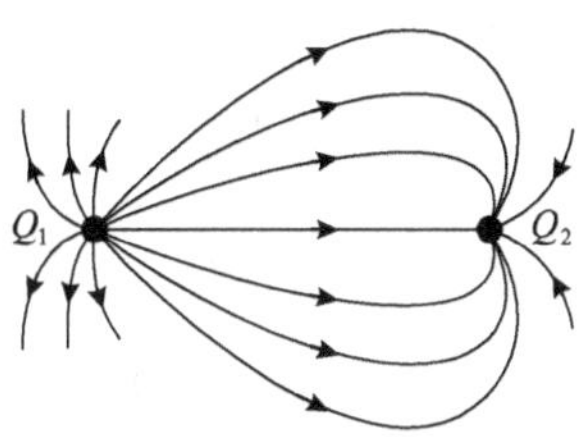

Thus electric field $\vec{E}$ at some point which is on the right side of Q_2 can be zero. **Ans. (A, D)**

Sol. 19 Inside metal shells electric field is always zero hence option (A) is correct. Figure below shows the situation described in the question.

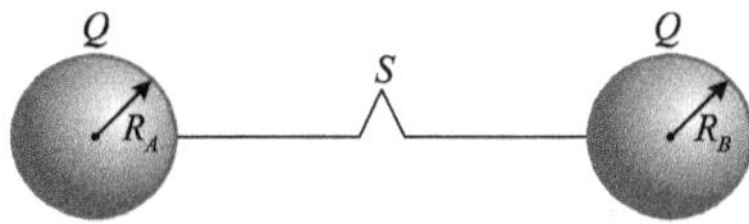

After the shells are connected, final potential of the two must be same so we use

$$\frac{kQ_A}{R_A} = \frac{kQ_B}{R_B}$$

$$\Rightarrow \quad \frac{Q_A}{Q_B} = \frac{R_A}{R_B}$$

As $R_A > R_B$ we have $Q_A > Q_B$. Hence option (B) is correct. Ratio of surface charge density of the two shells can be calculated as

$$\frac{\sigma_A}{\sigma_B} = \frac{\dfrac{Q_A}{4\pi R_A^2}}{\dfrac{Q_B}{4\pi R_B^2}} = \frac{\dfrac{R_A}{R_A^2}}{\dfrac{R_B}{R_B^2}} = \frac{R_B}{R_A}$$

Hence option (C) is correct.

As $R_A > R_B$ we have $\sigma_B > \sigma_A$ which gives $E_B > E_A$

Hence option (D) is correct. **Ans. (A, B, C, D)**

Sol. 20 When two same charges are placed near to each other then net force can be zero in between them. Hence option (C) is correct. Work done in moving a unit positive charge is given as

$$W = \Delta V = (V_B - V_A)$$

Hence option (D) is correct. For any given case Gauss law will

be valid only for $E \propto \dfrac{1}{r^2}$ hence option (A) is NOT correct.

Due to similar reason for an electric dipole Gauss law cannot be used to calculate electric field distribution hence option (B) is NOT correct. **Ans. (C, D)**

Sol. 21 Position of all the charges are symmetric about the planes $x = \dfrac{+a}{2}$ and $x = \dfrac{-a}{2}$. So net electric flux through these will be same. Similarly flux through $y = \dfrac{+a}{2}$ is equal to flux through $y = \dfrac{-a}{2}$ due to symmetrical placement of charges. Total flux passing through the cubical surface is given as

$$\phi = \dfrac{q_{encl}}{\varepsilon_0} = \dfrac{3q - q - q}{\varepsilon_0} = \dfrac{q}{\varepsilon_0}$$

By symmetry flux through $z = \dfrac{+a}{2}$ is equal to flux through the

plane $x = \dfrac{+a}{2}$ **Ans. (A, C, D)**

Sol. 22 Net electric field at O is along OD and calculated as

$$E_0 = \dfrac{1}{4\pi\varepsilon_0}\left(\dfrac{2q}{L^2} + \dfrac{2q}{L^2} + \dfrac{q}{L^2}\cos 60° \times 4\right) = \dfrac{1}{4\pi\varepsilon_0}\left(\dfrac{6q}{L^2}\right)$$

$$E_0 = 6K$$

Hence option (A) is correct.

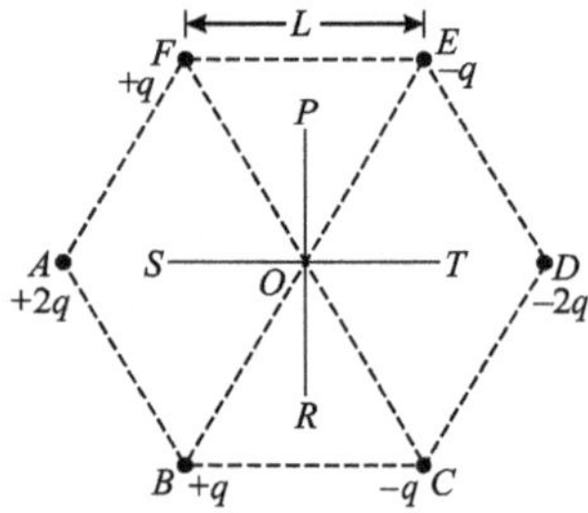

As sum of all charges is zero hence potential at point O is equal to zero as all charges are equidistant from O. Hence option (B) is correct.

Potential on line PR is also zero. As PR is perpendicular bisector of AD, BC and FE. Hence option (C) is correct.

For all points on line ST equal and opposite charges are not equidistant so potential at all points on this line cannot be same hence option (D) is NOT correct. **Ans. (A, B, C)**

Sol. 23 Figure below shows the situation, described in the question.

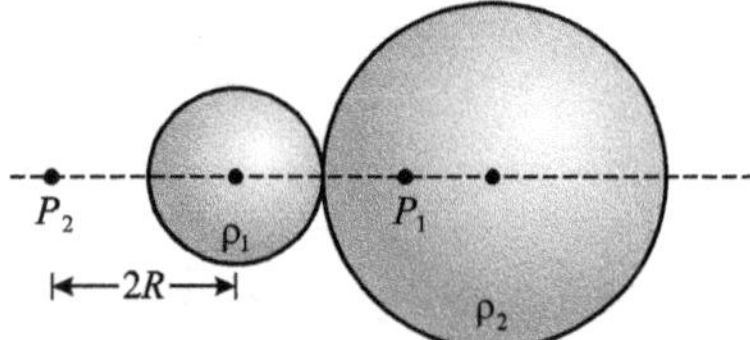

There can be two points P_1 and P_2 as shown in figure above where electric field can be zero as specified in the question. Considering electric field at point P_1 equal to zero gives

$$\dfrac{1}{4\pi\varepsilon_0}\dfrac{\rho_1(4/3)\pi R^3}{4R^2} = \dfrac{\rho_2 R}{3\varepsilon_0}$$

$$\Rightarrow \quad \dfrac{\rho_1 R}{12} = \dfrac{\rho_2 R}{3}$$

$$\Rightarrow \quad \dfrac{\rho_1}{\rho_2} = 4$$

Considering electric field at point P_2 equal to zero gives

$$\Rightarrow \quad \dfrac{\rho_1(4/3)\pi R^3}{(2R)^2} = \dfrac{\rho_2(4/3)\pi 8R^3}{(5R)^2}$$

$$\Rightarrow \quad \dfrac{\rho_1}{\rho_2} = \dfrac{32}{25} \qquad \textbf{Ans. (B, D)}$$

Sol. 24 Consider a point P in the overlapping region as shown in figure below.

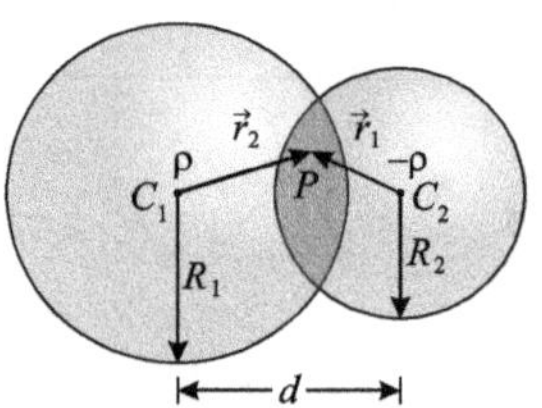

In triangle PC_1C_2, we have

$$\vec{r}_2 = \vec{d} + \vec{r}_1$$

Net electric field at point P is given as

$$\vec{E} = \dfrac{K\left(\rho\dfrac{4}{3}\pi R_1^3\right)\vec{r}_2}{R_1^3} + \dfrac{K\left(\rho\dfrac{4}{3}\pi R_2^3\right)(-\vec{r}_1)}{R_2^3}$$

$$\Rightarrow \quad \vec{E} = K\rho\dfrac{4}{3}\pi(\vec{r}_2 - \vec{r}_1)$$

$$\Rightarrow \quad \vec{E} = \dfrac{\rho}{3\varepsilon_0}\vec{d}$$

Hence option (A) and (B) are NOT correct. **Ans. (C, D)**

Sol. 25 Figure below shows the situation described in the question in which charge is displaced by a distance x.

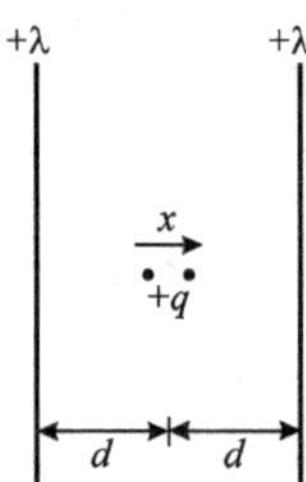

Net field at displaced position is given as

$$E = \dfrac{\lambda}{2\pi\varepsilon_0(d+x)} - \dfrac{\lambda}{2\pi\varepsilon_0(d-x)}$$

$$\Rightarrow \qquad E = \frac{\lambda}{2\pi\varepsilon_0}\left[\frac{(d-x)-(d+x)}{d^2-x^2}\right]$$

$$\Rightarrow \qquad E = \frac{-\lambda}{2\pi\varepsilon_0}\left[\frac{2x}{d^2-x^2}\right] \quad \text{For } x << d$$

$$\Rightarrow \qquad E = -\left(\frac{\lambda}{\pi\varepsilon_0 d^2}\right)x$$

At displaced position the net force is given as

$$F = \frac{-q\lambda}{\pi\varepsilon_0 d^2}\cdot x$$

$$\Rightarrow \qquad F \propto -x$$

This satisfies the condition of SHM for $+q$ as for $-q$ at the displaced position the net force will be towards right hence it will move in direction of displacement. **Ans. (C)**

Sol. 26 As already calculated in a previously asked question, the electric field inside cavity is given as $\dfrac{\rho\vec{a}}{3\varepsilon_0}$ and it is uniform and constant at every point inside the cavity. **Ans. (D)**

Sol. 27 As the distance of circumference of flat surface is same from charge so at every point electric potential will be same. As the charge is placed just outside the hemispherical surface, the flux entering in sphere is $\dfrac{Q}{2\varepsilon_0}$ but the flux coming out from flat surface is calculated by the flux through the flat surface, given as

$$\phi = \frac{\Omega}{4\pi}\cdot\frac{Q}{\varepsilon_0}$$

$$\Rightarrow \qquad \phi = \frac{2\pi(1-\cos\phi)}{4\pi}\frac{Q}{\varepsilon_0}$$

As $\theta = 45°$, we have

$$\phi = \frac{Q}{2\varepsilon_0}\left(1-\frac{1}{\sqrt{2}}\right)$$

This flux enters the curved surface and comes out from the flat surface thus net flux passing through the curved surface is given as

$$\phi_{\text{curved}} = -\phi$$

$$\Rightarrow \qquad \phi_{\text{curved}} = -\frac{Q}{2\varepsilon_0}\left(1-\frac{1}{\sqrt{2}}\right) \qquad \textbf{Ans. (A, B)}$$

Sol. 28 Figure below shows the situation described in the question using which we can calculate the net enclosed charge within the shell.

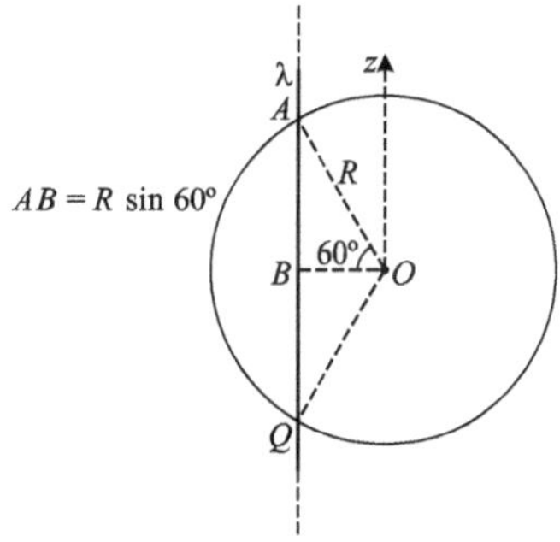

Net electric flux coming out of the shell is given as

$$\phi = \frac{1}{\epsilon_0}q_{\text{in}}$$

$$\Rightarrow \qquad \phi = \frac{1}{\epsilon_0}[\lambda \times 2R\sin 60°] = \frac{\sqrt{3}\lambda R}{\epsilon_0}$$

Further electric field is perpendicular to the wire therefore its z-component will be zero. **Ans. (A, B)**

Sol. 29 For option (A), cylinder encloses the shell, so this option is correct. For option (B), cylinder is fully enclosed by shell, thus $\phi = 0$, so this option is correct. For option (C), situation is shown in figure below.

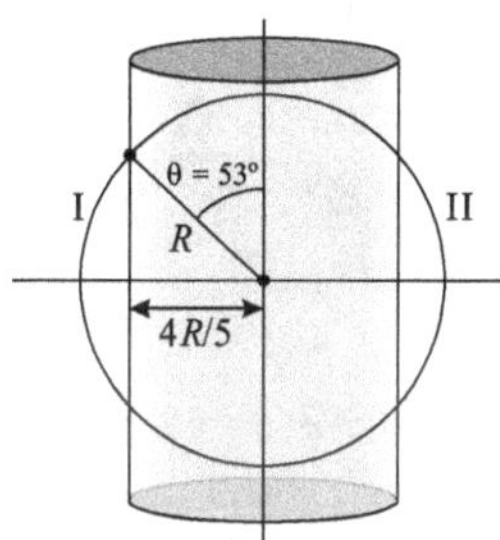

In this case flux can be calculated by the enclosed charge, given as

$$\phi = \frac{2\times Q}{2\epsilon_0}(1-\cos 53°) = \frac{2Q}{5\epsilon_0}$$

Hence option (C) is NOT correct. For option (D) also flux can be calculated in similar way, given as

$$\phi = \frac{2\times Q}{2\epsilon_0}(1-\cos 53°) = \frac{Q}{5\epsilon_0}$$

Hence option (D) is correct. **Ans. (A, B, D)**

Sol. 30 Dipole moment is given as

$$\vec{p} = \frac{p_0}{\sqrt{2}}(\hat{i}+\hat{j})$$

Electric field at point B along tangent should be zero since circle is equipotential so external electric field must be equal to the electric field of dipole at point B as shown in figure below, thus net electric field at point B is zero hence option (D) is correct and we have

$$E_0 = \frac{K\,|\,\vec{p}\,|}{R^3} \text{ as } E_B = 0$$

$$\Rightarrow \quad R^3 = \frac{Kp_0}{E_0} = \left(\frac{p_0}{4\pi \in_0 E_0}\right)$$

$$\Rightarrow \quad R = \left(\frac{p_0}{4\pi \in_0 E_0}\right)^{1/3}$$

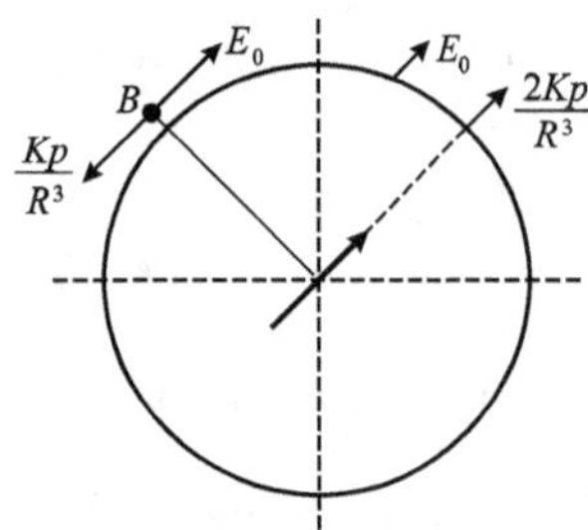

Hence option (A) is correct. Because E_0 is uniform & due to dipole electric field is different at different points, so magnitude of total electric field will also be different at different points.

Hence option (B) is NOT correct.

Total electric field at point A is given as vector sum of field due to dipole and external field which is given as

$$E_A = \frac{2Kp}{R^3} + \frac{Kp}{R^3} = \frac{3K}{R^3}\frac{p_0}{\sqrt{2}}(\hat{i} + \hat{j})$$

Hence option (C) is NOT correct. **Ans. (A, D)**

Sol. 31 Acceleration of particle in y direction is given as

$$a_y = -400\sqrt{3} \times 10^{10}\,\text{m/s}^2$$

Range of particle is given as

$$R = \frac{u^2 \sin 2\theta}{a_y} = 5 = \frac{40 \times 10^{12} \sin 2\theta}{400\sqrt{3} \times 10^{10}}$$

$$\Rightarrow \quad \sin 2\theta = \frac{\sqrt{3}}{2}$$

$$\Rightarrow \quad 2\theta = 60°, 120$$

$$\Rightarrow \quad \theta = 30°, 60°$$

At $\theta = 30°$, time of flight of particle is given as

$$T_1 = \frac{2 \times 2\sqrt{10} \times 10^6 \times \dfrac{1}{2}}{400\sqrt{3} \times 10^{10}} = \sqrt{\frac{5}{6}}\,\mu s$$

At $\theta = 60°$, time of flight of particle is given as

$$\text{Time of flight } T_2 = \frac{2 \times 2\sqrt{10} \times 10^6 \times \dfrac{\sqrt{3}}{2}}{400\sqrt{3} \times 10^{10}} = \sqrt{\frac{5}{2}}\,\mu s \;\textbf{Ans. (B, C)}$$

Sol. 32 We consider an elemental half ring as shown in figure below which is of radius x and width dx.

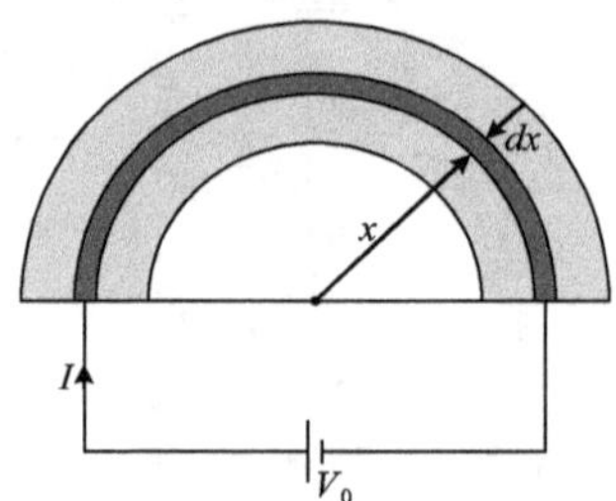

Resistance of this small elemental half ring is given as

$$dR = \frac{\rho l}{A} = \frac{\rho(\pi x)}{t \cdot dx}$$

As all such elements are in parallel, we use

$$\frac{1}{R} = \int \frac{1}{dR} = \int_{R_1}^{R_2} \frac{t\,dx}{\rho \pi x}$$

$$\Rightarrow \quad \frac{1}{R} = \frac{t}{\pi\rho} \ln\left(\frac{R_2}{R_1}\right)$$

$$\Rightarrow \quad R = \frac{\pi\rho}{t \ln\left(\dfrac{R_2}{R_1}\right)}$$

Current in the circuit is given as

$$I = \frac{V_0 t \ln\left(\dfrac{R_2}{R_1}\right)}{\pi\rho}$$

Hence option (A) is correct.

For flow of electrons along the length of all the elements, these electrons will experience an inward electric force $e\vec{E}$ in order to provide centripetal acceleration. Therefore electric field will be radially outward due to which outer surface will be at lower potential. Hence option (C) is correct.

If v_d is the drift speed of electrons then the induced electric field in radial direction developed can be calculated as

$$\frac{mv_d^2}{x} = qE$$

$$\Rightarrow \quad E = \frac{mv_d^2}{qx}$$

Potential difference developed across inner and outer surface will be directly proportional to the above electric field hence we can use

$$\Delta V \propto v_d^2$$

Drift speed of electrons is proportional to the current so we also have

$$\Delta V \propto I^2$$

Hence option (D) is correct. **Ans. (A, C, D)**

Sol. 33 The net electric force on any sphere is lesser but by

Coulomb law the force due to one sphere to another remain the same

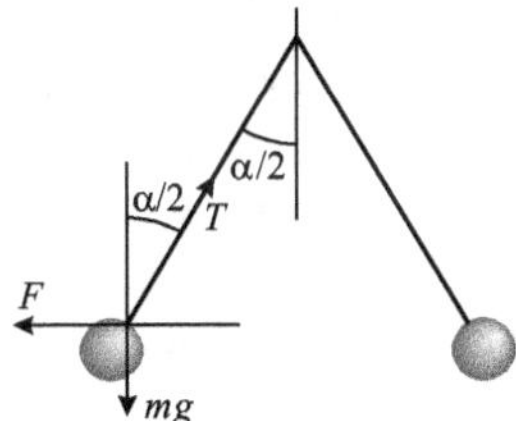

In equilibrium state of the sphere, we use

$$T\cos\frac{\alpha}{2} = mg$$

and $\quad T\sin\frac{\alpha}{2} = F$

After immersed in dielectric liquid as there is no change in angle α, for density of sphere d, we use

$$T\cos\frac{\alpha}{2} = mg\left(1-\frac{\rho}{d}\right)$$

and $\quad T\sin\frac{\alpha}{2} = \frac{F}{\epsilon_r}$

$$\Rightarrow \qquad \frac{mg}{F} = \frac{mg\left(1-\dfrac{\rho}{d}\right)}{\dfrac{F}{\epsilon_r}}$$

$$\Rightarrow \qquad \frac{1}{\epsilon_r} = 1-\frac{\rho}{d}$$

$$\frac{1}{21} = 1-\frac{800}{d}$$

$$\Rightarrow \qquad d = 840 \text{ kg/m}^3 \qquad\qquad \textbf{Ans. (A, C)}$$

Sol. 34 Due to symmetry of charges placed, if $x = q$ then at centre $\vec{E}_0 = 0$ hence option (A) is correct.

When $x = -q$, electric field at centre will be due to the charge x and other directly opposite to it which will be added up as by symmetry, electric field due to rest of the charges will become zero. This field is calculated as

$$E_0 = \frac{Kq}{(2d)^2}\times 2 = \frac{2q}{4\pi\varepsilon_0(\sqrt{3}a)^2} = \frac{q}{6\pi\varepsilon_0 a^2}$$

Hence option (B) is correct.

When $x = 2q$ the electric potential due to this $2q$ will be added up to the electric potential at centre due to other five charges. This is given as

$$V = \frac{K(7q)}{2d} = \frac{7q}{4\pi\varepsilon_0\cdot\sqrt{3}a} = \frac{7q}{4\sqrt{3}\pi\varepsilon_0 q}$$

Hence option (C) is correct.

Potential due to five existing charges and $-3q$ at centre is given as

$$V = \frac{K(2q)}{2d} = \frac{2q}{4\pi\varepsilon_0\cdot\sqrt{3}a} = \frac{q}{2\sqrt{3}\pi\varepsilon_0 q}$$

Hence option (D) is NOT correct. $\qquad$ **Ans. (A, B, C)**

Sol. 35 Charge within the inner sphere is calculated by considering an elemental shell of radius r and width dr is calculated as

$$q_1 = \int_0^1 kr\,4\pi r^2\,dr = \frac{4\pi k}{4} = \pi k$$

for the outer shell the charge within the region from radius 1 to r is calculated as

$$q_2 = \int_1^r \frac{2k}{r}\,4\pi r^2\,dr$$

$$\Rightarrow \qquad q_2 = 4\pi k\,[r^2-1] = 4\pi k r^2 - 4\pi k$$

Total charge is given as

$$q_{net} = q_1 + q_2 = 4\pi k r^2 - 3\pi k$$

$$\Rightarrow \qquad q_{net} = \pi k\,[4r^2-3]$$

For electric field to be zero everywhere outside B, net charge should be zero which gives

$$r = \frac{\sqrt{3}}{2}$$

Hence option (A) is NOT correct.

Electric potential just outside B is given as

$$V = \frac{Kq_{net}}{r} = \frac{1}{4\pi\varepsilon_0}\frac{\pi k(4r^2-3)}{r}$$

$$\Rightarrow \qquad V = \frac{k}{4\varepsilon_0}\left[4r-\frac{3}{r}\right]$$

$$\Rightarrow \qquad V = \frac{k}{4\varepsilon_0}\left[4\times\frac{3}{2}-\frac{3\times 2}{3}\right] = \frac{k}{\varepsilon_0}$$

Hence option (B) is correct.

Total charge of configuration for $r_B = 2$ is given as

$$q_{net} = \pi k\,[4(2)^2-3]$$

$$\Rightarrow \qquad q_{net} = 13\,\pi k$$

Hence option (C) is NOT correct.

Electric field just outside B is given as

$$E = \frac{Kq_{net}}{r^2}$$

$$\Rightarrow \qquad E = \frac{1}{4\pi\varepsilon_0}\frac{\pi k(4r^2-3)}{r^2}$$

At $r_B = \dfrac{5}{2}$ this electric field becomes

$$E = \frac{k}{4\varepsilon_0}\left[\frac{4\left(\dfrac{5}{2}\right)^2-3}{(5/2)^2}\right]$$

$$\Rightarrow \quad E = \frac{k}{25\varepsilon_0}[25-3] = \frac{22}{25}\frac{k}{\varepsilon_0}$$

Hence option (D) is NOT correct. **Ans. (B)**

Sol. 36 When particle starts from rest then in its motion from starting point to the origin, if the work done by the vertical force is more than or equal to the work done against the electric force by disk then particle will reach at origin. So these work can be calculated as

$$W_e = q(V_0 - V_{z0})$$

$$\Rightarrow \quad W_e = \frac{q\sigma}{2\epsilon_0}(R + z_0 - \sqrt{R^2 + z_0^2})$$

and $\qquad W_F = cz_0$

Condition to reach origin for particle is given as

$$cz_0 \geq \frac{q\sigma}{2\epsilon_0}(R + z_0 - \sqrt{R^2 + z_0^2})$$

$$\Rightarrow \quad R + z_0(1-\beta) \leq \sqrt{R^2 + z_0^2} \qquad \ldots(1)$$

For $\beta = \dfrac{1}{4}$ and $z_0 = \dfrac{25}{7}R$, in above equation (1) LHS and RHS will become

$$\text{LHS} = \frac{103}{28}R = \frac{25.75}{7}R$$

and $\qquad \text{RHS} = \dfrac{\sqrt{674}}{7}R = \dfrac{26}{7}R$

As RHS > LHS hence option (A) is correct.

For $\beta = \dfrac{1}{4}$ and $z_0 = \dfrac{3}{7}R$, in above equation (1) LHS and RHS will become

$$\text{LHS} = \frac{37}{28}R = \frac{9.25}{7}R$$

and $\qquad \text{RHS} = \dfrac{\sqrt{58}}{7}R$

As RHS < LHS hence option (B) is NOT correct.

For $\beta = \dfrac{1}{4}$ and $z_0 = \dfrac{R}{\sqrt{3}}$, in above equation-(1) LHS and RHS will become

$$\text{LHS} = \left(1 + \frac{\sqrt{3}}{4}\right)R$$

and $\qquad \text{RHS} = \dfrac{2}{\sqrt{3}}R$

As RHS < LHS so particle will not be able to reach origin and will return back to starting position hence options (C) & (D) are correct. **Ans. (A, C, D)**

Sol. 37 Both the statement are true, & statement-2 is not the correct explanation of statement-1 because, whatever be the value of potential it can be considered zero as a reference in different situational analysis. **Ans. (B)**

Sol. 38 (A) : When the charged capacitor is connected to ends of wire, it gets discharged so energy is dissipated as thermal energy. Hence option (q) is correctly related.

(B) : When a conductor is moved with constant velocity perpendicular to uniform magnetic field then voltage is developed across ends of conductor and induced charges appear at the ends of wire in motional electromotive force. Hence options (r) and (s) are correctly related.

(C) : Conductors have free electrons, when conductor is placed in static electric field charges are distributed till equilibrium occurs. As electric field is along length of wire, charges are accumulated at the ends of wire and due to the electric field. A constant potential difference is there due to electric field at the ends of wire but inside wire net electric field is zero so potential inside wire remain constant. Hence options (r) and (s) are correctly related.

(D) : A battery is constant emf source is there so constant current flows through wire due to which continuous power dissipation in form of heat will be there and a constant potential difference is there due to battery across the ends of wire. Hence options (p), (q) and (r) are correctly related.

Ans. [A (q); B (r, s); C (r, s); D (p, q, r)]

Sol. 39 In (q) and (t) at point M the electric field is not zero but electric potential is zero. When system is rotated about line PQ then equivalent current will be zero in case of (p), (q) and (t) hence in these cases $B = 0$ and $\mu = 0$. In (r) electric field at point M is zero but potential is not zero. In (s) at point M both field and potential are non zero.

Ans. [A (p, r, s); B (r, s); C (p, q, t); D (r, s)]

Sol. 40 In all cases below figures show the electric field configuration due to charges. Using these resulting direction of net force on q can be determined.

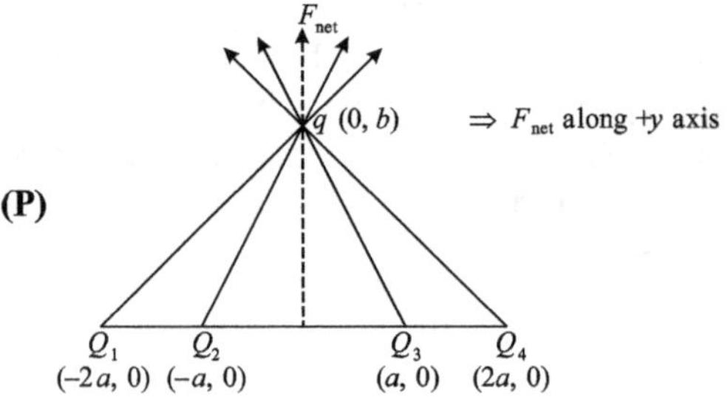

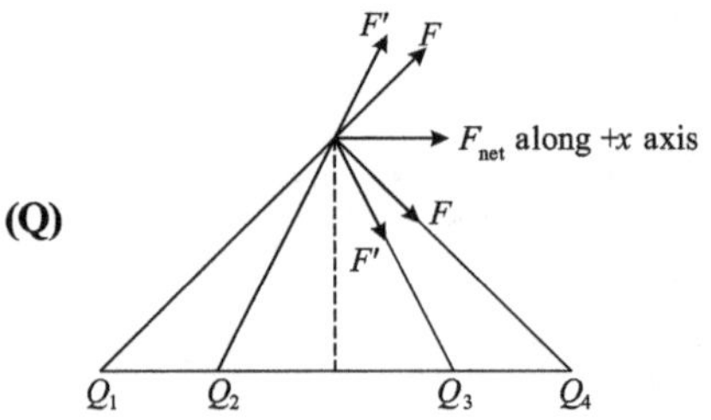

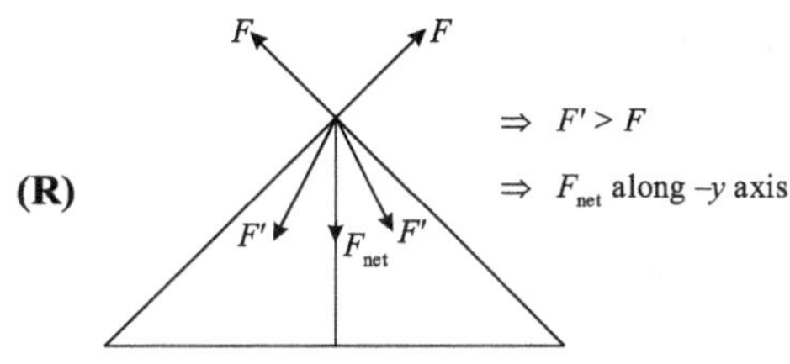

$\Rightarrow F' > F$

$\Rightarrow F_{net}$ along $-y$ axis

(R)

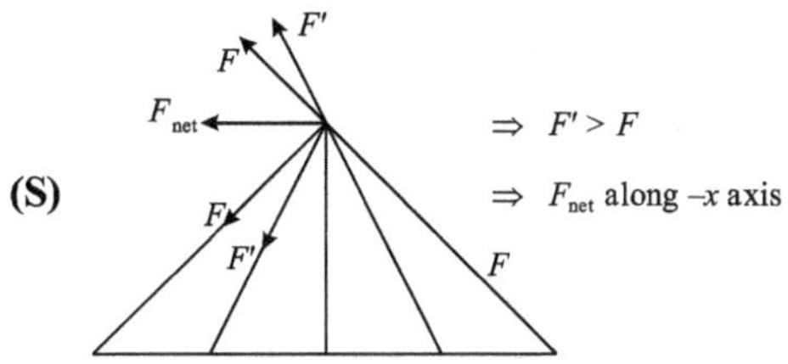

$\Rightarrow F' > F$

$\Rightarrow F_{net}$ along $-x$ axis

(S)

$\Rightarrow \quad P \to (3), R \to (4), Q \to (1), S \to (2)$ **Ans. (A)**

Sol. 41 For a point charge $E = \dfrac{KQ}{d^2}$ and for a dipole E is proportional to $\dfrac{Kp}{d^3}$. For an infinite long line charge $E = \dfrac{2K\lambda}{d}$ and for infinite plane charge $E = \dfrac{\sigma}{2\in_0}$ and for two infinite wires carrying uniform linear charge density, electric field is given as

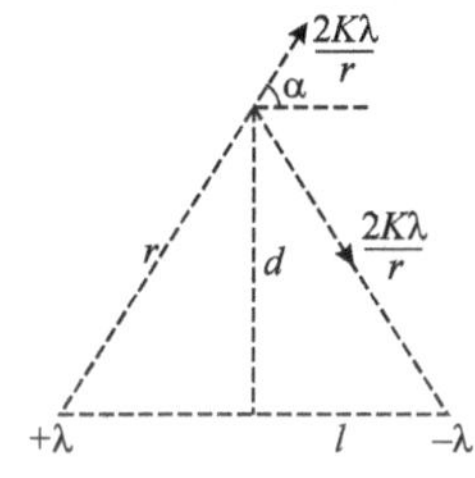

$$E = \frac{2K\lambda}{r}\cos\alpha = \frac{2K\lambda}{\sqrt{d^2+l^2}} \times \frac{l}{\sqrt{d^2+l^2}} = \frac{2K\lambda l}{d^2+l^2}$$

Ans. (B)

Sol. 42 At $r = R$, using Gauss law we have

$$E \cdot 4\pi R^2 = \frac{q_{encl}}{\in_0} = \frac{Ze}{\in_0}$$

$$\Rightarrow \qquad E = \frac{Ze}{4\pi \in_0 R^2}$$

Here E is independent of a. **Ans. (A)**

Sol. 43 For the given function for $r > a$ ($a = 0$ in this case), the density is given as

$$\rho(r) = d - \frac{dr}{R}$$

The charge inside the nucleus, is calculated as

$$Ze = \int_0^R \rho(r) \cdot 4\pi r^2 dr$$

$$\Rightarrow \qquad Ze = \int_0^R \left\{ \left(-\frac{d}{R}\cdot r + d\right)4\pi r^2 \right\} dr$$

$$\Rightarrow \qquad Ze = 4\pi\left[-\frac{d}{R}\cdot\frac{r^4}{r} + d\cdot\frac{r^3}{3} \right]_0^R$$

$$\Rightarrow \qquad Ze = 4\pi d\left[-\frac{R^3}{4} + \frac{R^3}{3} \right]$$

$$\Rightarrow \qquad Ze = \frac{\pi d R^3}{3}$$

$$\Rightarrow \qquad d = \frac{3Ze}{\pi R^3} \qquad\qquad \textbf{Ans. (B)}$$

Sol. 44 Electric field within the nucleus is linearly dependent on r is possible when the charge distribution is uniform which gives

$$a = R$$

$$\Rightarrow \qquad E\cdot 4\pi r^2 = \frac{q_{encl}}{\in_0} = \frac{d\cdot\frac{4}{3}\pi r^2}{\in_0}$$

$$\Rightarrow \qquad E = \left(\frac{1}{3t_0}d\right)r$$

$$\Rightarrow \qquad E \propto r \qquad\qquad \textbf{Ans. (C)}$$

Sol. 45 We use that dimensions of centripetal force is same as that of electrostatic force, so we have

$$[m\omega^2 l] = \left[\frac{e^2}{4\pi\varepsilon_0 l^2}\right]$$

$$\Rightarrow \qquad [\omega^2] = \left[\frac{e^2}{4\pi m\varepsilon_0 l^3}\right]$$

As dimensions of l^3 and $1/N$ are same, we use

$$[\omega^2] = \left[\frac{e^2 N}{4\pi m\varepsilon_0}\right]$$

As 4π is a dimensionless constant, value of ω is given as

$$\omega = \sqrt{\frac{Ne^2}{m\varepsilon_0}} \qquad\qquad \textbf{Ans. (C)}$$

Sol. 46 Wavelength and frequency are related as

$$c = \lambda f$$

$$\Rightarrow \qquad \omega_p = \omega = \frac{2\pi c}{\lambda} = \sqrt{\frac{Ne^2}{m\varepsilon_0}}$$

$$\Rightarrow \qquad \lambda = 2\pi c\sqrt{\frac{m\varepsilon_0}{Ne^2}} = \frac{2\pi c}{e}\sqrt{\frac{m\varepsilon_0}{N}}$$

$$\Rightarrow \qquad \lambda = \frac{2\times 3.14\times 3\times 10^8}{1.6\times 10^{-19}}\sqrt{\frac{(10^{-30})(10^{-11})}{4\times 10^{27}}}$$

$$\Rightarrow \qquad \lambda = 589\times 10^{-9}\,\text{m} \approx 600\,\text{nm} \qquad \textbf{Ans. (B)}$$

Sol. 47-48 Potential at a general point P as shown in figure below can be calculated and equated to zero as

$$V_P = V_- + V_+$$

$$\Rightarrow \qquad V_P = \frac{K(-Q)}{\sqrt{x^2 + y^2}} + \frac{K\left(\dfrac{Q}{\sqrt{3}}\right)}{\sqrt{(2-x)^2 + y^2}} = 0$$

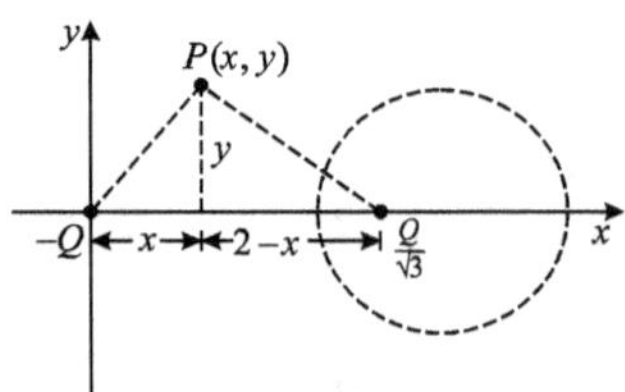

$$\Rightarrow \qquad \frac{KQ}{\sqrt{x^2 + y^2}} = \frac{KQ}{\sqrt{3}\sqrt{(2-x)^2 + y^2}}$$

$$\Rightarrow \qquad x^2 + y^2 = 3[(2-x)^2 + y^2]$$

$$\Rightarrow \qquad x^2 + y^2 = 3[4 - 4x + x^2 + y^2]$$

$$\Rightarrow \qquad x^2 + y^2 = 12 - 12x + 3x^2 + 3y^2$$

$$\Rightarrow \qquad 2x^2 + 2y^2 - 12x + 12 = 0$$

$$\Rightarrow \qquad x^2 + y^2 - 6x + 6 = 0$$

$$\Rightarrow \qquad (x^2 - 6x + 6) + y^2 = 0$$

$$\Rightarrow \qquad (x-3)^2 + y^2 - 3 = 0$$

$$\Rightarrow \qquad (x-3)^2 + y^2 = 3$$

$$\Rightarrow \qquad (x-3)^2 + y^2 = (\sqrt{3})^2$$

$$\Rightarrow \qquad R = \sqrt{3} = \mathbf{1.73}$$

Centre of this circle is located at

$$x = 3$$

$$\Rightarrow \qquad b = 3$$

Sol. 49 For the small elemental shell considered of width dr and radius r inside the sphere as shown in figure below, charge on the element is given as

$$dq = \rho dV$$

$$\Rightarrow \quad dq = kr^\alpha\, 4\pi r^2\, dr$$

$$\Rightarrow \quad q = \int dq = \int kr^\alpha\, 4\pi r^2\, dr$$

$$\Rightarrow \quad q = \frac{k 4\pi r^{\alpha+3}}{\alpha+3}$$

Electric field due to this charge at a distance r inside the sphere is given as

$$E_r = \left[\frac{K 4\pi r^{\alpha+3}}{\alpha+3}\right]\frac{1}{r^2}$$

$$\Rightarrow \quad E_R = \left[\frac{K 4\pi r^{\alpha+3}}{\alpha+3}\right]\frac{1}{R^2}$$

$$\Rightarrow \quad \frac{E_r}{E_R} = \frac{1}{8} = \frac{(R/2)^{\alpha+1}}{R^{\alpha+1}}$$

$$\Rightarrow \qquad \alpha = 2 \qquad\qquad \textbf{Ans. (2)}$$

Sol. 50 Figure below shows the situation described in the question.

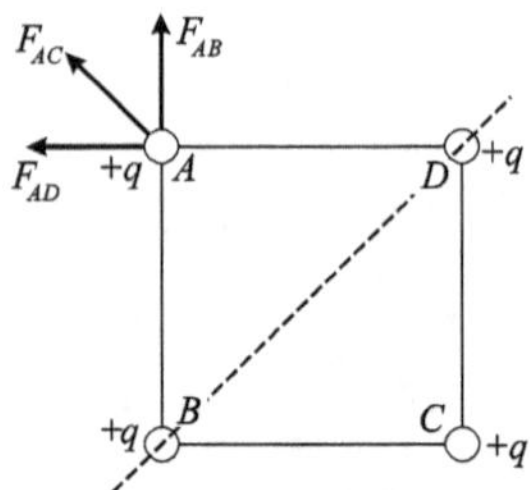

Electrostatic forces acting on any charge is as shown in above figure. These forces are given as

$$F_{AC} = \frac{q^2}{8\pi\varepsilon_0 a^2}$$

and $\qquad F_{AD} = F_{AB} = \dfrac{q^2}{4\pi\varepsilon_0 a^2}$

Resulting force on charge A which acts normal to the diagonal BD is given as

$$F_R = \frac{q^2}{4\pi\varepsilon_0 a^2}\left(2\cos 45^\circ + \frac{1}{2}\right)$$

This force should balance the net force on BD due to surface tension, given as

$$F_{ST} = \gamma(2BD) = \gamma(2\sqrt{2}\,a)$$

$$\Rightarrow \qquad a^3 = \frac{q^2\left(\sqrt{2} + \dfrac{1}{2}\right)}{8\sqrt{2}\pi\varepsilon_0\gamma}$$

$$\Rightarrow \qquad a = k\left(\frac{q^2}{\gamma}\right)^{1/3}$$

$$\Rightarrow \qquad N = 3$$

Where $\qquad k = \left(\dfrac{\sqrt{2} + \dfrac{1}{2}}{8\sqrt{2}\pi}\right)^{1/3} \qquad\qquad \textbf{Ans. (3)}$

Sol. 51 Electric field due to infinitely long cylinder at point P is given as

$$E_1 = \frac{\rho.R^2}{\varepsilon_0 \cdot 2R} = \frac{\rho R}{4\varepsilon_0}$$

Electric field due to spherical cavity is given as

$$E_2 = \frac{1}{4\pi\varepsilon_0} \cdot \frac{\rho \cdot \dfrac{4}{3}\pi \cdot \dfrac{R^3}{8}}{(2R)^2}$$

Net electric field at P is given as

$$E_1 - E_2 = \frac{\rho R}{4\varepsilon_0} - \frac{\rho \cdot R}{\varepsilon_0 \cdot 24 \times 4}$$

$$\Rightarrow \qquad E_1 - E_2 = \frac{\rho R}{4\varepsilon_0}\left[1 - \frac{1}{24}\right]$$

$$\Rightarrow \qquad E_1 - E_2 = \frac{23\rho R}{96\varepsilon_0} = \frac{23\rho R}{16k\varepsilon_0}$$

$$\Rightarrow \qquad k = 6 \qquad \textbf{Ans. (6)}$$

Sol. 52 The perpendicular from O to the line charge intersects the line charge at point P, such that

$$OP = \frac{\sqrt{3}a}{2}$$

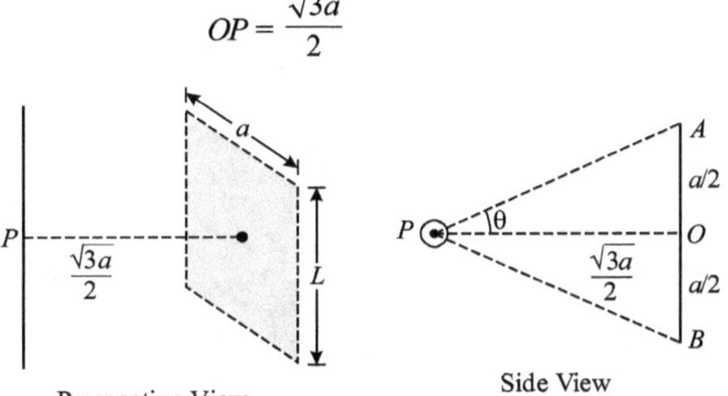

Perspective View

Side View

$$\Rightarrow \qquad \tan\theta = \frac{a/2}{\sqrt{3}a/2}$$

$$\Rightarrow \qquad \theta = \frac{\pi}{6}$$

Flux through surface $ABCD$ is given by Gauss's law as

$$\phi = \frac{\lambda L/\varepsilon_0}{2\pi} \times \frac{2\pi}{6} = \frac{\lambda L}{6\varepsilon_0} = \frac{\lambda L}{n\varepsilon_0}$$

$$\Rightarrow \qquad n = 6 \qquad \textbf{Ans. (6)}$$

Sol. 53 Given $\quad \vec{E} = \sin 10^3 t\,\hat{i}$

As only electric force is acting on the particle, we use

$$F = ma$$

$$\Rightarrow \qquad qE = m\frac{dv}{dt}$$

$$\Rightarrow \qquad dv = \frac{qEdt}{m} = \frac{q\sin 1000t\,\hat{i}}{m}dt$$

Maximum speed is attained when force becomes zero for the first time at $t = \pi/\omega$ thus we have

$$\int_0^v dv = \frac{q}{m}\int_0^{\pi/\omega}\sin 1000t\,dt$$

$$\Rightarrow \quad v = -\frac{q}{m}\left[\frac{\cos 1000t}{1000}\right]_0^{\pi/\omega} = -\frac{1}{10^{-3}} \times \frac{[\cos 1000t]_0^{\pi/\omega}}{1000}$$

$$\Rightarrow \quad v = -\left[\cos 1000 \times \frac{\pi}{1000} - \cos 0\right] = -[-1-1] = 2\text{ ms}^{-1}$$

$$\textbf{Ans. (2)}$$

Sol. 54 At equilibrium position of mass the electric force is balanced by spring force, so we use

$$kl = \frac{2kpq}{l^3} \qquad \qquad \ldots(1)$$

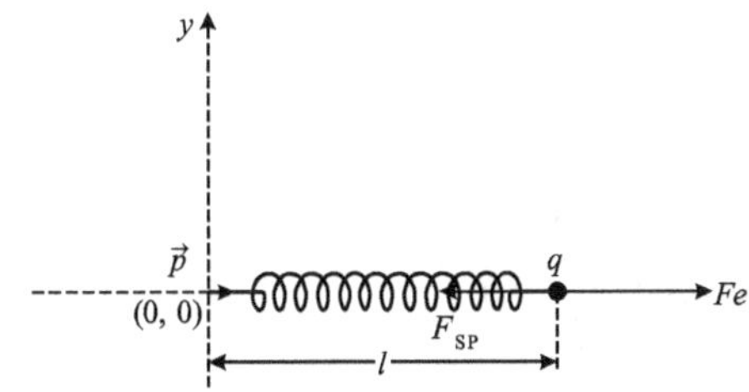

$$F_{\text{net}} = F_{\text{sp}} - F_e = k(l+x) - \frac{q(2kp)}{(l+x)^3}$$

$$\Rightarrow \qquad F_{\text{net}} = k(x+l) - \frac{q(2kp)}{l^3(1+x/l)^3}$$

$$\Rightarrow \qquad F_{\text{net}} = kx + kl - q\left(\frac{2kp}{l^3}\right)\left(1 - \frac{3x}{l}\right)$$

$$\Rightarrow \qquad F_{\text{net}} = kx + kl - q\left(\frac{2kp}{l^3}\right) + \frac{2kpq}{l^3}\cdot\frac{3x}{l}$$

$$\Rightarrow \qquad F_{\text{net}} = kx + kl\left(\frac{3x}{l}\right) = 4kx$$

Thus time period of oscillation can be given as

$$T = 2\pi\sqrt{\frac{m}{4k}} = \pi\sqrt{\frac{m}{k}}$$

$$\Rightarrow \qquad f = \frac{1}{\pi}\sqrt{\frac{k}{m}}$$

$$\Rightarrow \qquad \delta = \pi = 3.14 \qquad \textbf{Ans. (3.14)}$$

Sol. 55 Figure below shows the circular disc in which we consider an elemental ring of radius r and width dr.

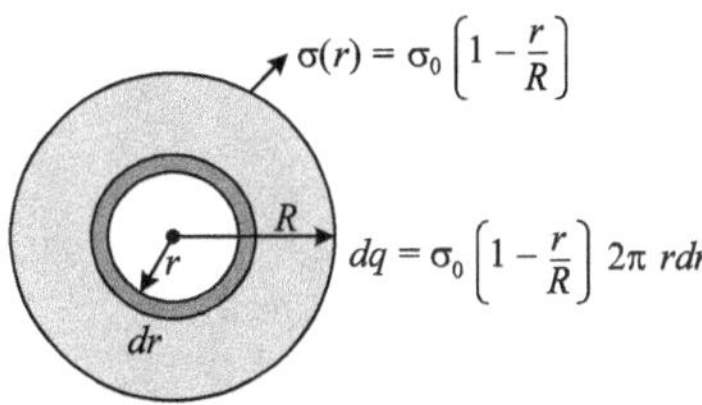

Charge on elemental ring is given as

$$dq = \sigma(2\pi r dr)$$

Total charge on disc is given as

$$q = \int dq = \int \sigma 2\pi r\, dr$$

Electric flux through large spherical surface can be given as

$$\phi_0 = \frac{\int dq}{\varepsilon_0} = \frac{\int_0^R \sigma_0\left(1 - \frac{r}{R}\right)2\pi r\, dr}{\varepsilon_0} \qquad \ldots(1)$$

Electric flux through sphere of radius $\frac{R}{4}$ is given as

$$\phi = \frac{\int dq}{\varepsilon_0} = \frac{\int_0^{R/4} \sigma_0\left(1 - \frac{r}{R}\right)2\pi r\, dr}{\varepsilon_0} \qquad \ldots(2)$$

Dividing (1) and (2) gives

$$\frac{\phi_0}{\phi} = \frac{\sigma_0 2\pi \int_0^R \left(r - \frac{r^2}{R}\right)dr}{\sigma_0 2\pi \int_0^{R/4} \left(r - \frac{r^2}{R}\right)dr}$$

$$\Rightarrow \quad \frac{\phi_0}{\phi} = \frac{\dfrac{R_2}{2} - \dfrac{R^2}{3}}{\dfrac{R^2}{32} - \dfrac{R^2}{3 \times 64}} = \frac{32}{5} = 6.40 \qquad \textbf{Ans. (6.40)}$$

Sol. 56 Figure below shows the situation described in the question and forces acting on the charge.

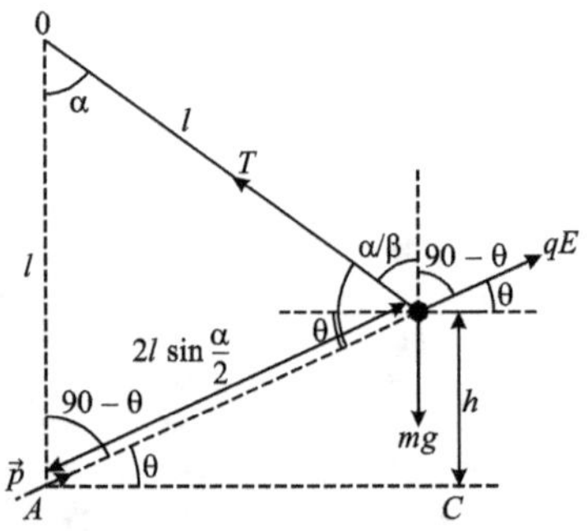

Interaction energy of dipole is given as

$$U = \frac{Kpq}{\left(2l \sin\dfrac{\alpha}{2}\right)^2} + mgh \qquad \ldots(1)$$

Now, from $\triangle OAB$, we have

$$\alpha + 90 - \theta + 90 - \theta = 180$$

$$\Rightarrow \qquad \alpha = 2\theta$$

From $\triangle ABC$, we have

$$h = 2l \sin\left(\frac{\alpha}{2}\right)\sin\theta$$

$$\Rightarrow \qquad h = 2l \sin\left(\frac{\alpha}{2}\right)\sin\left(\frac{\alpha}{2}\right)$$

$$\Rightarrow \qquad h = 2l \sin^2\left(\frac{\alpha}{2}\right)$$

Now charge is in equilibrium at point B. So using sine rule for the forces acting on charge, we have

$$\frac{mg}{\sin\left[90 + \dfrac{\alpha}{2}\right]} = \frac{qE}{\sin[180 - 2\theta]}$$

and

$$\frac{mg}{\cos\dfrac{\alpha}{2}} = \frac{qE}{\sin\alpha} = \frac{qE}{2\sin\dfrac{\alpha}{2}\cos\dfrac{\alpha}{2}}$$

$$\Rightarrow \qquad qE = 2mg \sin\left(\frac{\alpha}{2}\right)$$

$$\Rightarrow \qquad \frac{2Kpq}{\left[2l\sin\dfrac{\alpha}{2}\right]^3} = 2mg \sin\left(\frac{\alpha}{2}\right)$$

$$\Rightarrow \qquad \frac{Kpq}{\left[2l\sin\dfrac{\alpha}{2}\right]^2} = mg \sin\left(\frac{\alpha}{2}\right) \times \left(2l\sin\frac{\alpha}{2}\right)$$

$$\Rightarrow \qquad \frac{Kpq}{\left[2l\sin\dfrac{\alpha}{2}\right]^2} = mgh$$

From equation (1), now we have

$$U_f = mgh + \frac{Kpq}{\left[2l\sin\dfrac{\alpha}{2}\right]^2} = 2mgh$$

$$\Rightarrow \qquad W = \Delta U = Nmgh$$

$$\Rightarrow \qquad N = 2 \qquad \textbf{Ans. (2)}$$

Sol. 57 Electric field between plates is given as

$$E = \frac{V}{d} = \frac{200}{0.01} = 2 \times 10^4 \, \text{V/m}$$

When terminal velocity is achieved, net force on the drops will be zero, hence we use

$$qE = mg$$

$$\Rightarrow \quad n \times 1.6 \times 10^{-19} \times 2 \times 10^4 = \frac{4\pi}{3}(8 \times 10^{-7})^3 \times 900 \times 10$$

$$\Rightarrow \qquad n \approx 6 \qquad \textbf{Ans. (6)}$$

Sol. 58 Total flux coming out of complete closed surface is given as

$$\phi_{\text{hemisphere}} + \phi_{\text{cone}} = \frac{q}{\varepsilon_0} \qquad \ldots(1)$$

Through the hemisphere, half of flux originated by q will come out, given as

$$\phi_{hemisphere} = \frac{q}{2\varepsilon_0}$$

Thus equation-(1), flux coming out of conical surface is given as

$$\phi_{cone} = \frac{q}{2\varepsilon_0}$$

$$\Rightarrow \qquad \frac{nq}{6\varepsilon_0} = \frac{q}{2\varepsilon_0}$$

$$\Rightarrow \qquad n = 3 \qquad \text{**Ans. (3)**}$$

Ch-13 Capacitance

Sol. 1 When steady state is reached, the current I flowing through the battery is given as

$$9 = I(3+6)$$

$$\Rightarrow \qquad I = 1\,\text{A}$$

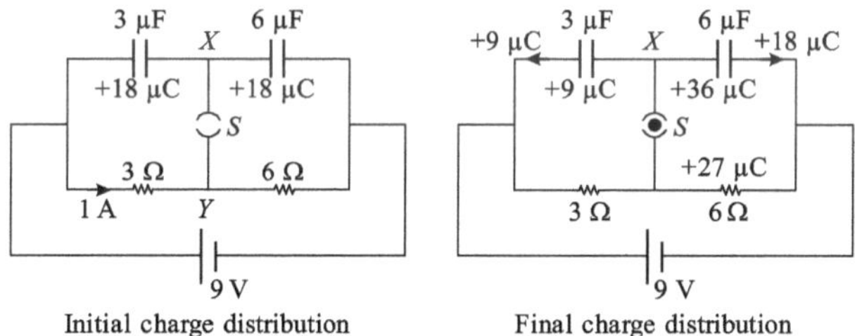

Initial charge distribution
(when switch S is open)

Final charge distribution
(when switch S is closed)

When switch is open the initial charges on the two capacitors are given as

$$q_1 = q_2 = 2 \times 9 = 18\,\mu\text{C}$$

After closing the switch, potential difference across $3\,\Omega$ resistance is 3 V and potential difference across $6\,\Omega$ resistance is 6 V thus final charges on $3\,\mu\text{F}$ and $6\,\mu\text{F}$ capacitor are calculated as

$$q_{1f} = 3 \times 3 = 9\,\mu\text{C}$$

and $\qquad q_{2f} = 6 \times 6 = 36\,\mu\text{C}$

Initial charge at node X is zero and after closing the switch at this node charge is given as $36 - 9 = 27\,\mu\text{C}$. This charge flows to X from Y. **Ans. (C)**

Sol. 2 The capacitance is given by

$$C = \frac{\varepsilon_0}{\left[d - \left(\dfrac{d}{3} - Vt \right) + \dfrac{1}{2}\left(\dfrac{d}{3} - Vt \right) \right]}$$

$$\Rightarrow \qquad C = \frac{6\varepsilon_0}{5d + 3Vt}$$

Time constant of circuit is given as

$$\tau = RC = \frac{6\varepsilon_0 R}{5d + 3Vt} \qquad \text{**Ans. (A)**}$$

Sol. 3 Initial stored energy in circuit is

$$U_i' = \frac{1}{2} \times 2 \times V^2 = V^2$$

After switch is turned to position 2, the two capacitors will be connected in parallel as shown below.

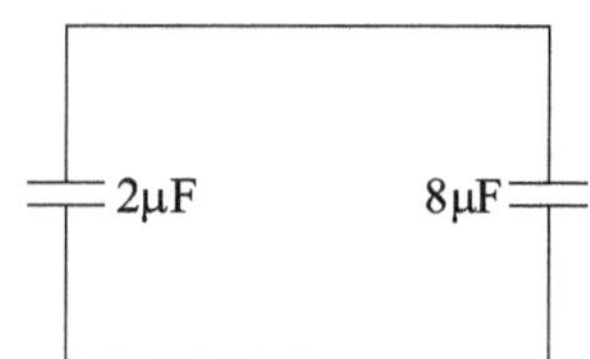

The final stored energy in circuit is given as

$$U_f = \frac{(2V)^2}{2(2+8)} = \frac{V^2}{5}$$

Change in stored energy is given as

$$\Delta U = V^2 - \frac{V^2}{5} = \frac{4V^2}{5}$$

Percentage energy dissipated is given as

$$\frac{\Delta U}{U_i} \times 100 = \frac{4}{5} \times 100 = 80\% \qquad \text{**Ans. (D)**}$$

Sol. 4 Total charge on plate is $80\,\mu\text{C}$. If q_B and q_C charges on plates B and C then

$$q_B + q_C = 80 \qquad \qquad \ldots(1)$$

As capacitor B and C are in parallel so potential across both are equal

$$\frac{q_B}{C_B} = \frac{q_C}{C_C}$$

$$\Rightarrow \qquad \frac{q_B}{2} = \frac{q_C}{3}$$

By equation-(1) we have

$$\Rightarrow \qquad \frac{80 - q_C}{2} = \frac{q_C}{3}$$

$\Rightarrow \quad 240 - 3q_C = 2q_C$

$\Rightarrow \qquad 5q_C = 240\,\mu C$

$\Rightarrow \qquad q_C = 48\,\mu C$

Charge on upper plate of 3 μF is +48 μC **Ans. (C)**

Sol. 5 For figure-(a) and (b) shows the two situations as described in question.

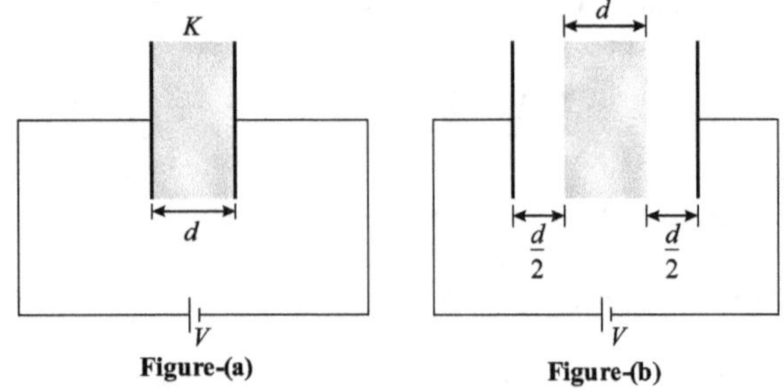

In figure-(a), electric field and capacitance are given as

$$E_0 = \frac{V}{d}$$

and $\qquad C = \dfrac{K\varepsilon_0 A}{d}$

In figure-(b) new capacitance becomes

$$C' = \frac{\varepsilon_0 A}{2d - d + d/k} = \frac{K\varepsilon_0 A}{(K+1)d} = \frac{C}{K+1}$$

Hence option (B) is correct.

As battery remains connected voltage between capacitor plates will remain same hence option (C) is NOT correct.

New potential difference across the dielectric slab can be calculated by considering two capacitors in series, one with dielectric and one with air in figure-(b) so it is given as

$$V' = \frac{V}{1+K}$$

Thus electric field in the dielectric is given as

$$E' = \frac{V'}{d} = \frac{E}{1+K}$$

Hence option (A) is NOT correct. **Ans. (B)**

Sol. 6 At $t = 10$ s the volume of liquid filled in container is given as

$$V = 2500\,\text{cc}$$

Height of liquid in container will be given as

$$h = \frac{2500}{50 \times 5} = 10\,\text{cm}$$

Capacitance of lower capacitor with dielectric is calculated as

$$C_d = \frac{A_d \varepsilon_0 k}{d}$$

$$\Rightarrow \quad C_d = \frac{50 \times 10^{-2} \times 10 \times 10^{-2}\,\varepsilon_0 \times 3}{5 \times 10^{-2}} = 3\varepsilon_0$$

Capacitance of air capacitor above the dielectric is calculated as

$$C_a = \frac{A_a \varepsilon_0}{d} = \frac{50 \times 10^{-2} \times 40 \times 10^{-2}\,\varepsilon_0}{5 \times 10^{-2}} = 4\varepsilon_0$$

As the two capacitors are in parallel combination, we have

$$C = C_a + C_d = 7\varepsilon_0$$

$$\Rightarrow \qquad C = 7 \times 9 \times 10^{-2} = 63\,Pf \qquad \textbf{Ans. (B)}$$

Sol. 7 After switch S_1 is closed, C_1 is charged with a charge $2CV_0$. Now S_1 is opened and switch S_2 is closed, so charge will distribute equally between C_1 and C_2 and they both have upper plate charge $+CV_0$ and lower plates $-CV_0$. When S_2 is opened and S_3 is closed, then upper plate of C_2 is charged with $-CV_0$ and lower plate by $+CV_0$. **Ans. (B, D)**

Sol. 8 Capacitance C_1 and C_2 are given as

$$C_1 = \frac{k\varepsilon_0 A/3}{d} = \frac{k\varepsilon_0 A}{3d}$$

and $\qquad C_2 = \dfrac{2\,\epsilon_0\,A}{3d}$

C_1 and C_2 are taken in parallel so total capacitance is given as

$$C = C_1 + C_2 = \frac{\varepsilon_0 A}{3d}(K+2)$$

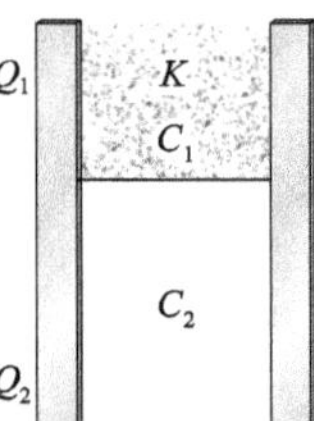

$$\Rightarrow \qquad \frac{C}{C_1} = \frac{K+2}{K}$$

Hence option (D) is correct.

As the potential difference across both capacitors will be same so the electric fields in these two will also be same so we have

$$\frac{E_1}{E_2} = 1$$

Hence option (A) is correct.

Ratio of charges on the two capacitors is given as

$$\frac{Q_1}{Q_2} = \frac{C_1 V}{C_2 V} = \frac{C_1}{C_2} = \frac{k}{2}$$

Hence option (C) is NOT correct. **Ans. (A, D)**

Sol. 9 Equivalent circuit of capacitance will be as follows

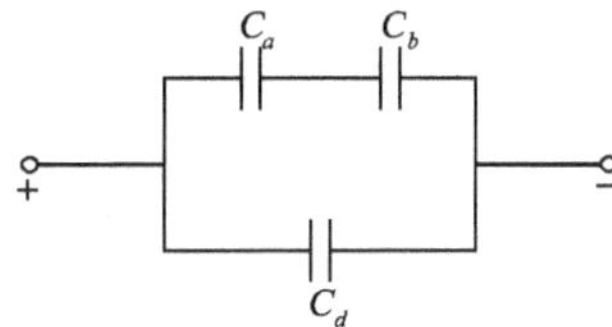

Initial capacitance in air is given as

$$C_1 = \frac{\varepsilon_0 S}{d}$$

When two dielectrics are introduced then capacitance of above three capacitors as shown in equivalent circuit can be calculated as

$$C_a = \frac{\varepsilon_0 \varepsilon_1 \left(\dfrac{S}{2}\right)}{\left(\dfrac{d}{2}\right)} = \frac{2\varepsilon_0 S}{d}$$

$$C_b = \frac{\varepsilon_0 \varepsilon_1 \left(\dfrac{S}{2}\right)}{\left(\dfrac{d}{2}\right)} = \frac{4\varepsilon_0 S}{d}$$

$$C_d = \frac{\varepsilon_0 \varepsilon_1 \left(\dfrac{S}{2}\right)}{d} = \frac{\varepsilon_0 S}{d}$$

Equivalent capacitance of system is now given as

$$C_2 = C_d + \frac{C_a C_b}{C_a + C_b}$$

$$\Rightarrow \quad C_2 = \frac{S\varepsilon_0}{d} + \frac{\dfrac{2S\varepsilon_0}{d} \times \dfrac{4S\varepsilon_0}{d}}{\dfrac{6S\varepsilon_0}{d}}$$

$$\Rightarrow \quad C_2 = \frac{S\varepsilon_0}{d} + \frac{4}{3}\frac{S\varepsilon_0}{d} = \frac{7}{3}\frac{S\varepsilon_0}{d} = \frac{7}{3}C_1$$

$$\Rightarrow \quad \frac{C_2}{C_1} = \frac{7}{3} \qquad\qquad \textbf{Ans. (D)}$$

Sol. 10 In figure below when S_1 is closed, just after closing the switch all capacitors will act like short circuit and current at this instant in circuit is given as

$$I = \frac{5}{200} = 25 \text{ mA}$$

Hence option (C) is correct. In steady state the three capacitors will be in series and charge on C_1 will be 40 μC and potential difference across it will be 4 V hence option (D) is correct. At this steady state potential difference across point P and Q will also be 4 V hence option (B) is NOT correct.

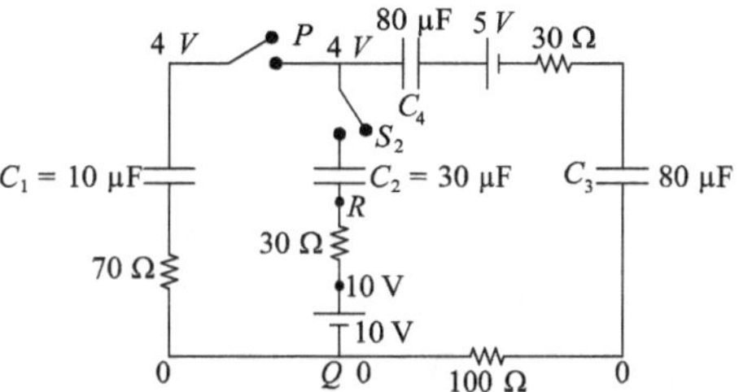

Just after closing the switch S_2, capacitor C_1 acts as a battery of 4 V, C_4 & C_3 act as a battery of 0.5 V each and C_2 act as short circuit. Just after closing S_2 the equivalent circuit shown in figure is given as

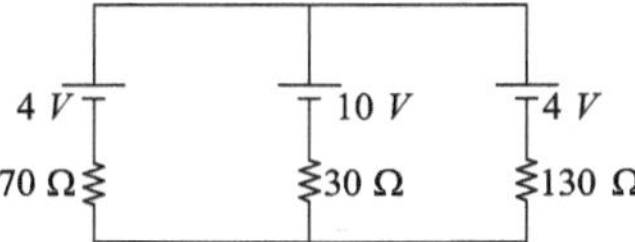

In above circuit considering the two 4 V batteries in parallel, further reduced circuit is drawn below.

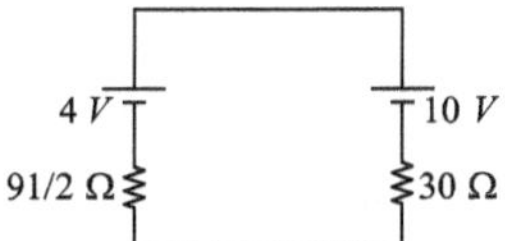

Current in circuit is given as

$$i = \frac{6}{30 + \dfrac{91}{2}} = 0.079 \text{ A}$$

Hence option (A) is NOT correct. **Ans. (C, D)**

Sol. 11 After connecting the switch to position P, circuit currents are shown in figure below.

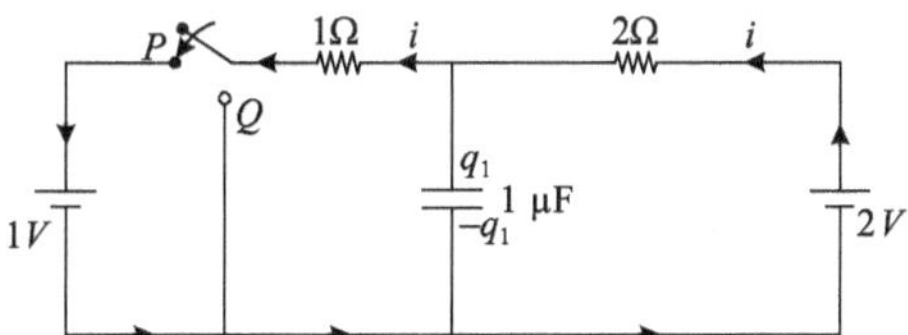

Using KVL equation in the largest loop gives

$$+2 - i \times 2 - i \times 1 - 1 = 0$$

$$\Rightarrow \qquad\qquad 1 = 3i$$

$$\Rightarrow \qquad\qquad i = \frac{1}{3} \text{ A}$$

Using KVL in loop including capacitor gives

$$2 - i \times 2 - \frac{q_1}{C} = 0$$

$$\Rightarrow \qquad 2 - \frac{2}{3} = \frac{q_1}{C}$$

$$\Rightarrow \qquad \frac{4}{3} = \frac{q}{C}$$

$$\Rightarrow \qquad q_1 = \frac{4}{3}C = \frac{4}{3} \times 1\,\mu C = 1.33\,\mu C$$

Ans. (1.33)

Sol. 12 After switch is shifted to position Q, circuit is shown in figure below. Now using KVL in outer loop gives

$$+2 - i_2 \times 2 - i_2 \times 1 = 0$$

$$\Rightarrow \qquad 2 = 3i_2$$

$$\Rightarrow \qquad i_2 = \frac{2}{3}\,A$$

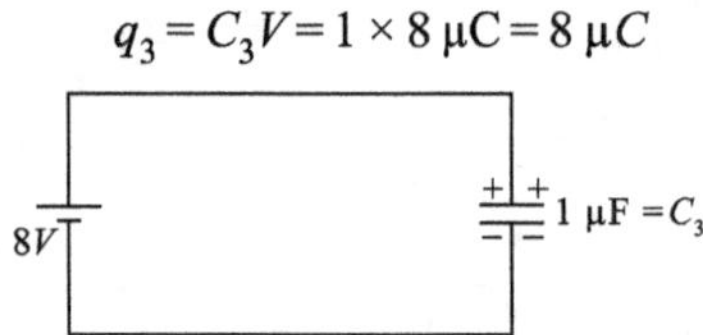

By KVL in loop with capacitor gives

$$+2 - i_2 \times 2 - \frac{q_2}{C} = 0$$

$$\Rightarrow \qquad 2 - \frac{2}{3} \times 2 = \frac{q_2}{C}$$

$$\Rightarrow \qquad \frac{2}{3} = \frac{q_2}{C}$$

$$\Rightarrow \qquad q_2 = \frac{2}{3}\,\mu C = 0.67\,\mu C$$

Ans. (0.67)

Sol. 13 For the equivalent circuit given below when battery is connected across, charging of capacitors as a function of time is given as

$$q = CV_0\left(1 - e^{-t/RC}\right)$$

Voltage across capacitors is given as

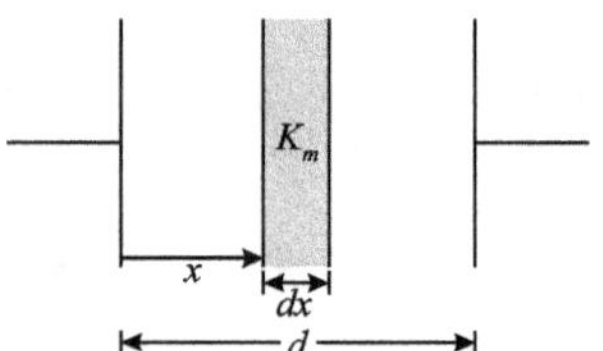

$$V = V_0\left(1 - e^{-t/RC}\right)$$

$$\Rightarrow \qquad 4 = 10\left(1 - e^{-t/4}\right)$$

$$\Rightarrow \qquad 3 = 5\,e^{-t/4}$$

Taking log both sides gives

$$\log 3 = \log 5 - \frac{t}{4}$$

$$\Rightarrow \quad 1.1 - 1.6 = -\frac{t}{4}$$

$$\Rightarrow \qquad t = 2\,s$$

Ans. (2)

Sol. 14 At initial condition when S_1 is closed, we have the charge on C_3 given as

$$q_3 = C_3 V = 1 \times 8\,\mu C = 8\,\mu C$$

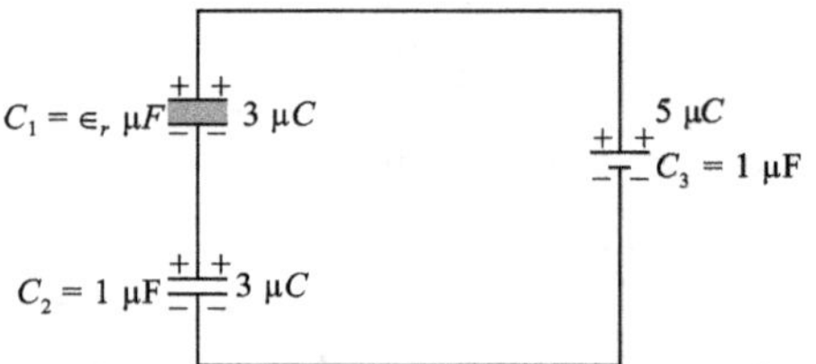

When switch S_1 is opened and S_2 is closed, as the charge on C_3 is found to be $5\,\mu C$ therefore charges on C_1 and C_2 are $3\,\mu C$ each as total charge must remain same. Final state is shown in circuit shown below.

Using Kirchhoff's law in this loop gives

$$\frac{5}{1} - \frac{3}{\epsilon_r} - \frac{3}{1} = 0$$

$$\Rightarrow \qquad 5 = 3\left[1 + \frac{1}{\epsilon_r}\right]$$

$$\Rightarrow \qquad \frac{1}{\epsilon_r} = \frac{5}{3} - 1 = \frac{2}{3}$$

$$\Rightarrow \qquad \epsilon_r = 1.5$$

Ans. (1.50)

Sol. 15 Considering a dielectric slab of thickness dx at a distance x from left end of plate as shown in figure

Here we consider for large value of N

$$\delta = dx = \frac{d}{N}$$

For the length x of dielectric slabs, we use

$$x = m\delta = m\left(\frac{d}{N}\right)$$

$$\Rightarrow \qquad \frac{m}{N} = \frac{x}{d}$$

$$\Rightarrow \qquad K_m = K\left(1 + \frac{m}{N}\right)$$

$$\Rightarrow \qquad K_m = K\left(1 + \frac{x}{d}\right)$$

Capacitance of elemental capacitor of width dx is given as

$$dC = \frac{K_m A \,\epsilon_0}{dx}$$

All such elemental capacitors are in series so equivalent capacitance is given as

$$\frac{1}{C_{eq}} = \int_0^d \frac{dx}{K_m A \,\epsilon_0} = \frac{1}{KA\,\epsilon_0}\int_0^d \frac{dx}{\left(1 + \dfrac{x}{d}\right)}$$

$$\Rightarrow \quad \frac{1}{C_{eq}} = \frac{d}{KA\,\epsilon_0}\left[\ln\left(1+\frac{x}{d}\right)\right]_0^d$$

$$\Rightarrow \quad \frac{1}{C_{eq}} = \frac{d}{KA\,\epsilon_0}\,[\ln 2 - \ln(1)]$$

$$\Rightarrow \quad C_{eq} = \frac{KA\,\epsilon_0}{d\ln 2}$$

$$\Rightarrow \quad \alpha = 1 \qquad\qquad \textbf{Ans. (1.00)}$$

Sol. 16 Energy stored by capacitors is given as

$$U = \frac{1}{2}\frac{C_1 C_2}{C_1 + C_2}V^2$$

For series combination, we use

$$\frac{1}{C_{eq} \pm \Delta C_{eq}} = \frac{1}{C_1 \pm \Delta C_1} + \frac{1}{C_2 \pm \Delta C_2}$$

$$\Rightarrow \quad C_{eq} \pm \Delta C_{eq} = \frac{C_1 C_2 + C_1 \Delta C_2 + C_2 \Delta C_1}{C_1 + C_2 + \Delta C_1 + \Delta C_2}$$

$$\Rightarrow \quad C_{eq} \pm \Delta C_{eq} = \frac{1200\left(1 \pm \dfrac{12}{1200}\right)}{\left(1 \pm \dfrac{25}{5000}\right)}$$

$$\Rightarrow \quad C_{eq} \pm \Delta C_{eq} = 1200\left[1 \pm \left(\frac{1}{100} - \frac{1}{200}\right)\right]$$

Error in energy stored is calculated as

$$\frac{\Delta U}{U} \times 100 = \frac{\Delta C_{eq}}{C_{eq}} \times 100 + \frac{2\Delta V}{V} \times 100$$

$$\Rightarrow \quad \frac{\Delta U}{U} \times 100 = \frac{1}{200} \times 100 + 2 \times \frac{0.02}{5} \times 100$$

$$\Rightarrow \quad \frac{\Delta U}{U} \times 100 = 1.3\% \qquad \textbf{Ans. (1.30)}$$

Sol. 17 Potential difference across the terminals of C_3 is 2 V hence charge on it is given as

$$Q_3 = CV = (4\,\mu)(2) = 8\,\mu C \qquad \textbf{Ans. (8)}$$

Ch-14 Current Electricity

Sol. 1 An unknown resistance of greater than 2 Ω is connected across gap as shown in figure below

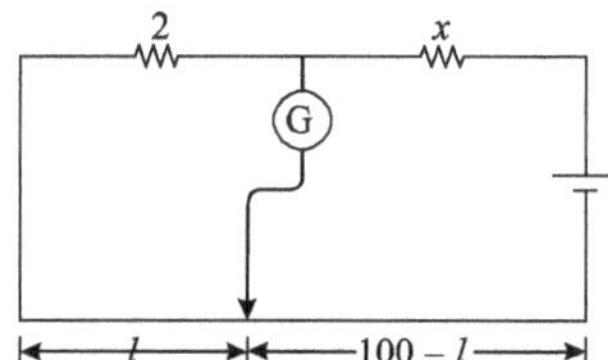

As $R > 2\,\Omega$ at balancing point we have $100 - l > l$
For balancing point, we use

$$\frac{2}{x} = \frac{l}{100 - l} \qquad\qquad \dots(1)$$

Now the resistances are interchanged so new balancing lengths will become $(l + 20)$ and $(80 - l)$ as shown in figure below

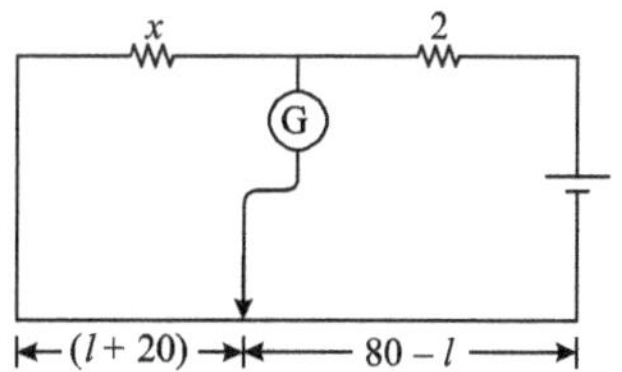

For balancing point, we use

$$\frac{x}{2} = \frac{l + 20}{80 - l} \qquad\qquad \dots(2)$$

Solving equations (1) and (2) gives

$$x = \frac{2(100 - l)}{l} = \frac{2(l + 20)}{80 - l}$$

$$\Rightarrow \quad x = 3\,\Omega \qquad\qquad \textbf{Ans. (A)}$$

Sol. 2 For the first configuration, it is a balanced Wheatstone bridge for which resistance R_1 is calculated from the equivalent circuit shown below

$$R_1 = 1\,\Omega$$

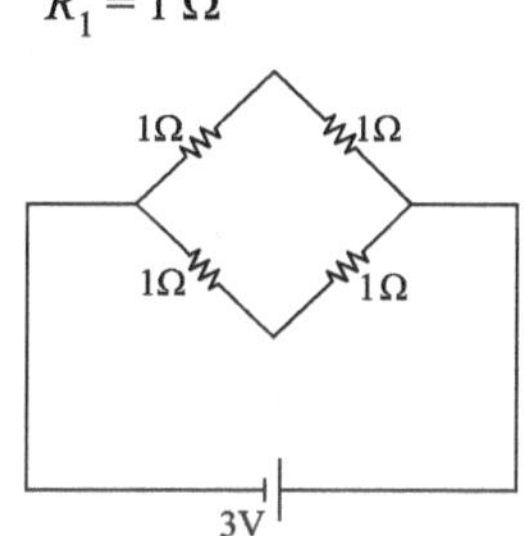

For the second configuration, equivalent resistance R_2 is given as

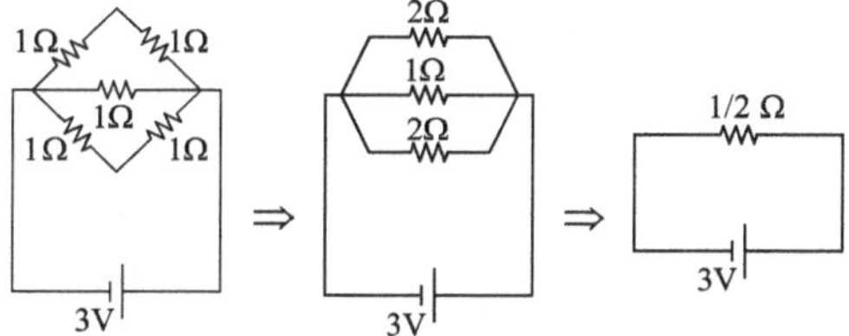

$$R_2 = \frac{1}{2}R$$

Similarly $\quad R_3 = 2\,\Omega$

Power dissipation across the resistance is given as

$$P = \frac{V^2}{R}$$

As V is same for all configuration, we use

$$\text{Power} \propto \frac{1}{R}$$

As $\quad R_2 < R_1 < R_3$

$$\Rightarrow \quad P_2 > P_1 > P_3 \qquad\qquad \textbf{Ans. (C)}$$

Sol. 3 Resistance of a conductor across the shaded areas is given as

$$R = \frac{\rho L}{A} = \frac{\rho L}{Lt}$$

$$\Rightarrow \qquad R = \frac{\rho}{t}$$

Thus R is independent of L. **Ans. (C)**

Sol. 4 Rated power for a bulb is given as

$$P = \frac{V^2}{R}$$

$$\Rightarrow \qquad R \propto \frac{1}{\text{Rated Power}}$$

As $P_1 > P_2 > P_3$ for the resistances, we have

$$\Rightarrow \qquad \frac{1}{R_1} > \frac{1}{R_2} > \frac{1}{R_3}$$

$$\Rightarrow \qquad \frac{1}{R_{100}} > \frac{1}{R_{60}} > \frac{1}{R_{40}} \qquad \textbf{Ans. (D)}$$

Sol. 5 For the galvanometer, it can be converted into ammeter and voltmeter as

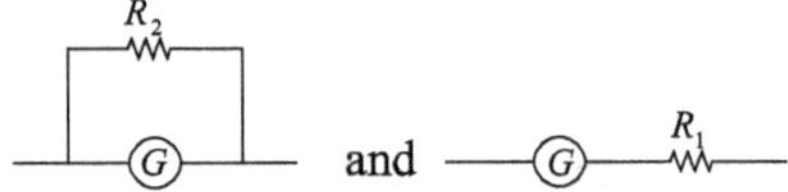

Voltmeter should be connected in parallel to R_T and ammeter should be connected in series with R_T. **Ans. (C)**

Sol. 6 Balancing condition of the meter bridge is given as

$$\frac{x}{10} = \frac{52+1}{48+2}$$

$$\Rightarrow \qquad x = \frac{53 \times 10}{50} = 10.6 \, \Omega \qquad \textbf{Ans. (B)}$$

Sol. 7 Electric lines of force for induced electric field are closed loop and magnetic lines of force are always closed loop hence option (C) can represent both fields. **Ans. (C)**

Sol. 8 Balancing condition of meter bridge is given as

$$\frac{R}{l} = \frac{90}{100-l}$$

$$\Rightarrow \qquad R = 90 \times \frac{l}{100-l}$$

$$\Rightarrow \qquad R = \frac{90 \times 40}{60} = 60 \, \Omega$$

Taking log on LHS and RHS gives

$$\ln R = \ln 90 + \ln l = \ln(100-l)$$

$$\Rightarrow \qquad \frac{\Delta R}{R} = \frac{\Delta l}{l} = \frac{\Delta l}{100-l}$$

$$\Rightarrow \qquad \frac{\Delta R}{60} = \frac{0.1}{40} + \frac{0.1}{60} = \frac{0.1}{20}\left(\frac{3+2}{6}\right)$$

$$\Rightarrow \qquad \Delta R = 0.1 \times \left(\frac{60}{24}\right) = 0.1 \times 2.5 = 0.25 \, \Omega$$

$$\Rightarrow \qquad R = 60 \pm 0.25 \, \Omega \qquad \textbf{Ans. (C)}$$

Sol. 9 Electric field at distance r is given as

$$E = \frac{2K\lambda}{r}$$

$$\Rightarrow \qquad E = \frac{\lambda}{2\pi \in_0 r}$$

Current density inside the material is given as

$$J = \frac{\sigma\lambda}{2\pi \in_0 r}$$

Current at any radial cross section in the material can be given as

$$\frac{dq}{dt} = J \, \text{A} = J(2\pi r l)$$

For line charge $\lambda = \dfrac{q}{l}$, we can write charge on line charge $q = \lambda l$ thus we have

$$\frac{d\lambda \cdot l}{dt} = -\frac{\sigma\lambda}{2\pi \in_0 r}(2\pi r l)$$

Here $-$ve sign indicates charge is decreasing with time and rearranging terms gives

$$\frac{d\lambda}{\lambda} = Cdt$$

Where C is representing all constants, integrating gives the linear charge density as a function of time given as

$$\lambda = \lambda_0 \, e^{-\sigma t/\varepsilon}$$

$$\Rightarrow \qquad J = J_0 \, e^{-\sigma t/\varepsilon}$$

Thus option (A) is correct. **Ans. (A)**

Sol. 10 Equivalent resistance of the circuit is given as

$$R_{eq} = \frac{6 \times 1.5}{7.5} + 2 = \frac{16}{5} \, k\Omega = 3.2 \, k\Omega$$

Current $I = \dfrac{24}{3.2} = 7.5$ mA & current through load resistance is given as

$$I_{L_0} = 6 \, \text{mA}$$

After interchanging R_1 with R_2, we have

$$R_{eq} = \frac{48}{7} \, \Omega$$

$$\Rightarrow \qquad I = 3.5 \, \text{mA}$$

Current through load resistance is calculated as

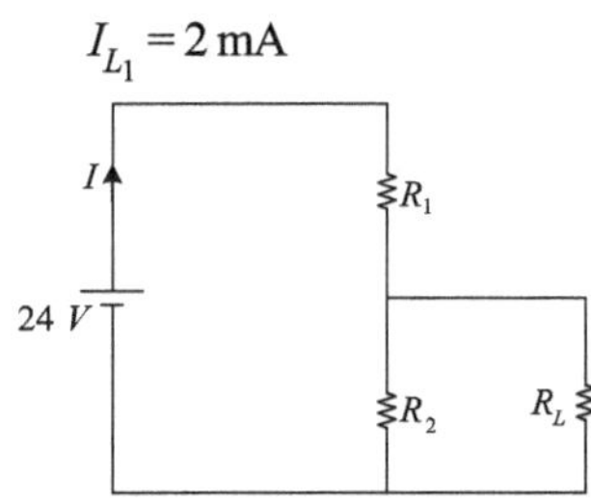

$$I_{L_1} = 2\,\text{mA}$$

$$\Rightarrow \qquad \frac{P_{L_0}}{P_{L_1}} = \frac{36}{4} = 9 \qquad\qquad \textbf{Ans. (A, D)}$$

Sol. 11 Due to input and output symmetry as shown in equivalent circuit below, points P and Q have same potentials and similarly points S and T also have same potential. Hence option (A) is correct. As current in circuit is flowing from left to right, potential of S will be less compared to Q hence option (C) is correct.

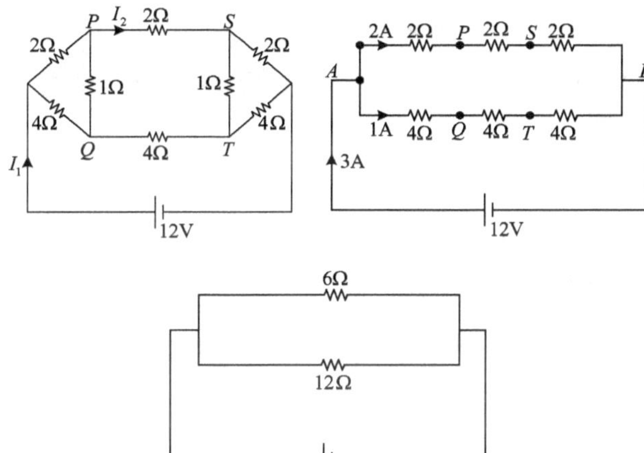

Equivalent resistance of the circuit across battery is given as

$$R_{\text{eq}} = \frac{6 \times 12}{18} = 4\,\Omega$$

Current supplied by the battery is given as

$$I_1 = \frac{12}{4} = 3\,\text{A}$$

Hence option (B) is correct. Current through $6\,\Omega$ resistance in the top branch is given as

$$I_2 = \frac{12}{6} = 2\,\text{A}$$

Hence option (D) is correct. \qquad **Ans. (A, B, C, D)**

Sol. 12 Resistance of wire in heater coil is taken as R then heat required to raise the temperature of water is given as

$$H = \frac{V^2}{R} \times 4$$

Resistance of new wires used in new heater have same length but diameter doubled so these will have cross sectional area four time higher so resistance of these wires are given as

$$R' = \frac{R}{4}$$

If these are connected in parallel, effective resistance becomes

$$R_P = \frac{R}{8}$$

For same amount of heat generation if time required is t_1 then we have

$$\frac{V^2}{R} \times 4 = \frac{V^2}{R} \times 8 \times t_1$$

$$\Rightarrow \qquad t_1 = 0.5\,\text{min}$$

When connected in series, effective resistance will be

$$R_S = \frac{R}{2}$$

For same amount of heat generation if time required is t_2 then we have

$$\frac{V^2}{R} \times 4 = \frac{V^2}{R} \times 2 \times t_2$$

$$\Rightarrow \qquad t_2 = 2\,\text{min} \qquad\qquad \textbf{Ans. (B, D)}$$

Sol. 13 As current in $R_2 = 0$, we can remove it for circuit analysis as shown in figure below. Current in loop now is given as

$$I = \frac{V_1 + V_2}{R_1 + R_3}$$

$$\Rightarrow \qquad I = \frac{2V}{R_1 + R_3}$$

As $V_{AB} = 0$, we have

$$\frac{V_1}{R_1} = \frac{V_2}{R_3}$$

$$\Rightarrow \qquad R_1 = R_3$$

Hence option (A) and (B) are correct as both are same and final state does not depend on R_2.

When $\qquad 2V_1 = V_2$

$$\Rightarrow \qquad 2R_1 = R_3$$

Hence option (D) is correct and option (C) is NOT correct.

\qquad **Ans. (A, B, D)**

Sol. 14 Equivalent electrical resistance between P and Q is calculated by parallel combination of Al & Fe bars, given as

$$R_0 = \frac{R_{\text{Al}}\,R_{\text{Fe}}}{R_{\text{Al}} + R_{\text{Fe}}}$$

Here
$$R_{Al} = \frac{\rho_{Al}\, l_{Al}}{A_{al}} = \frac{2.7 \times 10^{-8} \times 50 \times 10^{-3}}{45 \times 10^{-6}}$$

$$\Rightarrow \quad R_{Al} = 3 \times 10^{-5} = 30 \times 10^{-6}\ \Omega$$

and
$$R_{Fe} = \frac{\rho_{Fe}\, l_{fe}}{A_{Fe}} = \frac{1.0 \times 10^{-7} \times 50 \times 10^{-3}}{4 \times 10^{-6}}$$

$$R_{Fe} = \frac{50 \times 10^{-10}}{4 \times 10^{-6}} = 12.5 \times 10^{-4}\ \Omega$$

$$\Rightarrow \quad R_{Fe} = 1250 \times 10^{-6}\ \Omega$$

$$\Rightarrow \quad R_0 = \frac{(30 \times 10^{-6})(1250 \times 10^{-6})}{[30 \times 10^{-6} + 1250 \times 10^{-6}]}\ \Omega$$

$$\Rightarrow \quad R_0 = \frac{37500 \times 10^{-12}}{1280 \times 10^{-6}} = \frac{1875}{64} \times 10^{-6}\ \Omega$$

$$\Rightarrow \quad R_0 = \frac{1875}{64}\ \mu\Omega \qquad \textbf{Ans. (B)}$$

Sol. 15 Temperature is non uniform indicates variable power dissipation happens across length of conductor due to non uniform cross section hence option (A) is NOT correct.

As evaporation takes place means cross section of filament decreases differently at different sections of the filament. As cross section decreases means resistance of these sections will increase hence option (B) is NOT correct.

As temperature of filament increases, according to Wein's law, the wavelength of emitted light at peak intensities will be lesser which are corresponding to higher frequencies hence option (C) is correct.

As resistance increases due to evaporation the power consumption of filament decreases as power consumption varies inversely proportional to resistance hence option (D) is correct.   **Ans. (C, D)**

Sol. 16 For maximum voltage
$$V_{max} = I(R_g + S)$$

When all components are in series for maximum current S will be in parallel combination of two shunt and one galvanometer as maximum current.   **Ans. (A, C)**

Sol. 17 Just after key is pressed, capacitors behave as short circuit so initially voltmeter will display -5 V and after a long time in steady state capacitors behave as open circuit so voltmeter will display $+5$ V. Hence option (A) is correct. After a long time as no current flows through battery as voltmeter is considered ideal, ammeter reading becomes zero hence option (D) is correct.

In the circuit shown in figure both capacitors starts charging with time and charging current is given as

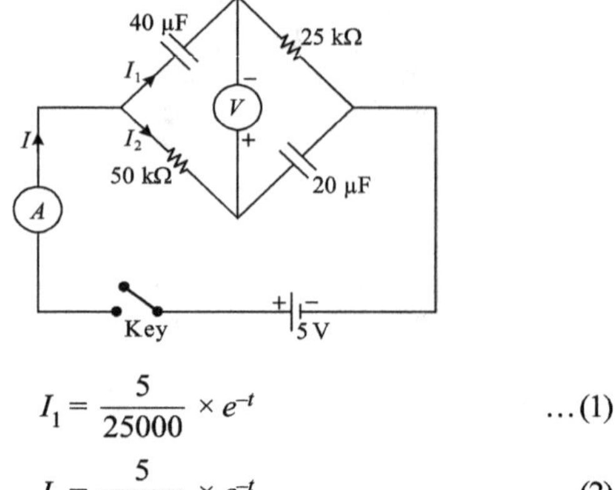

$$I_1 = \frac{5}{25000} \times e^{-t} \qquad \ldots(1)$$

$$I_2 = \frac{5}{50000} \times e^{-t} \qquad \ldots(2)$$

At $t = 0$ currents are given as 1/5 mA and 1/10 mA thus ammeter reading initially will be 3/10 mA

Charges on capacitors as a function of time t are given as

$$q_1 = (40)(5)(1 - e^{-t})\ \mu C$$

$$q_2 = (20)(5)(1 - e^{-t})\ \mu C$$

Value of current at $t = 1$ s is calculated by adding equations (1) and (2) which gives

$$I_{t=1} = \left(\frac{3}{10}\right) \times \left(\frac{1}{e}\right)$$

Hence option (C) is correct.

Potential difference across 25 $k\Omega$ resistance is given as

$$V_1 = \left(\frac{5}{25000} \times e^{-t}\right)(25000) = 5e^{-t}\, V$$

Potential difference across 20 μF capacitor is given as

$$V_2 = (5)(1 - e^{-t})\, V$$

Voltmeter reading is zero when $V_1 = V_2$ which gives

$$t = \ln 2$$

Hence option (B) is correct.   **Ans. (A, B, C, D)**

Sol. 18 For conversion into a voltmeter, we use a high resistance in series, calculated as

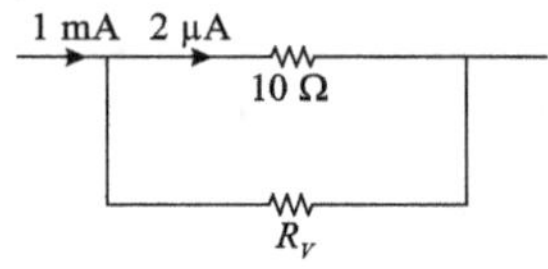

$$0.1 = 2 \times 10^{-6}(10 + R_V)$$

$$\Rightarrow \quad R_V = 49990\ \Omega$$

For conversion into an ammeter, we use a shunt resistance, calculated as

$$2 \times 10^{-6} \times 10 = 10^{-3}\, R_A$$

$\Rightarrow \qquad\qquad R_A = 0.02\,\Omega$

Hence option (C) is correct.

When these are used in Ohm's law experiment, circuit drawn is as shown below.

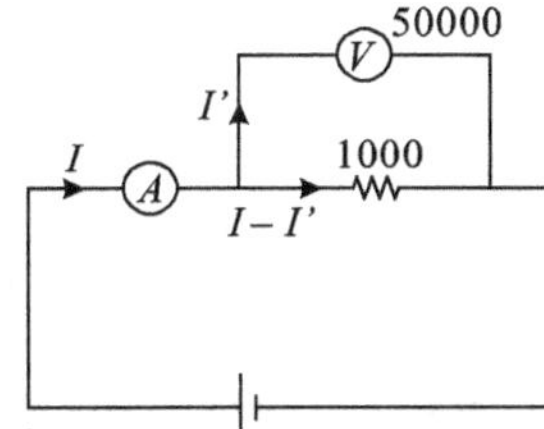

For the current distribution as shown above, we use

$$I'(50000) = (I - I')\,1000$$

$\Rightarrow \qquad\qquad 51\,I' = I$

If V_R and I_R are the voltmeter and ammeter readings than measured value of resistance is given as

$$R_{\text{Meas}} = \frac{V_R}{I_R} = \frac{I'(50000)}{I} = 980.4\,\Omega$$

Hence option (A) is correct.   **Ans. (A, C)**

Sol. 19 In below figure the given circuit in question is reduced by folding the lower part of circuit on upper half as top and bottom vertex are at same potential. Also re-arranging positions of 6 V battery and 1 Ω resistance in branch for optimising circuit for application of KCL.

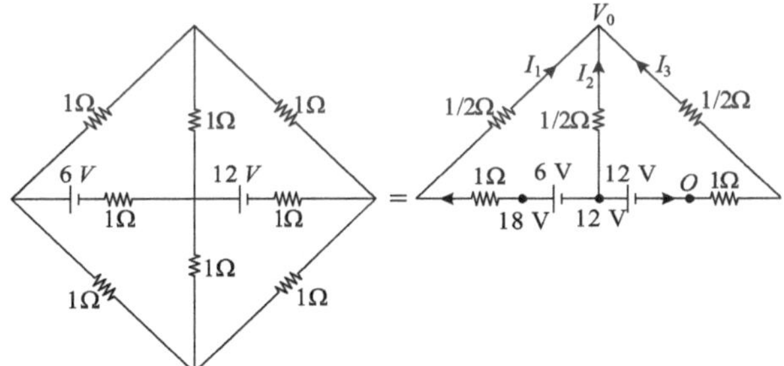

Distributing the currents as shown in the circuit with potential at the top vertex considering V_0 with respect to zero potential considered at point O. Now using KCL we have

$$i_1 + i_2 + i_3 = 0$$

$\Rightarrow \qquad \dfrac{18 - V_0}{3/2} + \dfrac{12 - V_0}{1/2} + \dfrac{0 - V_0}{3/2} = 0$

$\Rightarrow \qquad 18 - V_0 + 36 - 3V_0 - V_0 = 0$

$\Rightarrow \qquad\qquad 54 = 5V_0$

$\Rightarrow \qquad\qquad V_0 = \dfrac{54}{5}\,\text{V}$

Considering potential V' at left vertex, using KCL for this vertex, we have

$$\frac{2\left(\dfrac{54}{5} - V'\right)}{1} + \frac{18 - V'}{1} = 0$$

$\Rightarrow \qquad\qquad \dfrac{108}{5} + 18 = 3V'$

$\Rightarrow \qquad\qquad V' = \dfrac{198}{5 \times 3} = \dfrac{66}{5}\,\text{V}$

Now currents in all required resistances can be calculated as

$$I_{R_1} = \frac{54/5}{3/2} = \frac{36}{5} = 7.2\,\text{A}$$

$$I_{R_2} = \frac{12 - 54/5}{1} = \frac{6}{5} = 1.2\,\text{A}$$

$$I_{R_3} = \frac{18 - 66/5}{1} = \frac{24}{5} = 4.8\,\text{A}$$

$$I_{R_5} = \frac{66/5 - 54/5}{1} = \frac{12}{5} = 2.4\,\text{A}$$

NOTE : This question is also solved by Ashish Arora Sir using KVL in the Speed Solutions for JEE Advanced 2022. That method is very important to understand about how fast this question can be solved using KVL. Search for **"#SpeedSolutions JEE Advanced 2022 Physics"** on Youtube.   **Ans. (A, B, C, D)**

Sol. 20 Case (I) When both switches are open equivalent resistance in circuit 1 and 2 are given as

$$R_{C_1} = \frac{16}{11}\,\Omega$$

and $\qquad\qquad R_{C_2} = \dfrac{6}{11}\,\Omega$

For voltage source applied across A and B, power dissipation is given as

$$P = \frac{V^2}{R}$$

$\Rightarrow \qquad\qquad P \propto \dfrac{1}{R}$

As $R_{C_1} > R_{C_2}$, we have $P_2 > P_1$

Hence option (A) is correct.

For constant current source, circuit current remain constant so power dissipation is given as

$$P = i^2 R$$

$\Rightarrow \qquad\qquad P \propto R$

$\Rightarrow \qquad\qquad P_1 > P_2$

Hence option (B) is correct.

Case-II : When switches are closed, equivalent resistances in the two circuits are given as

$$R'_{C_1} = \frac{5}{11}\,\Omega$$

and
$$R'_{C_2} = \frac{1}{2}\,\Omega$$
$$\Rightarrow \quad R'_{C_1} < R'_{C_2}$$

For constant voltage source applied across circuit, we use

$$P \propto \frac{1}{R}$$
$$\Rightarrow \quad Q_1 > P_1$$

Hence option (C) is correct.

For current source applied across circuits, we use

$$P \propto R$$
$$\Rightarrow \quad Q_2 > Q_1$$

Hence option (D) is NOT correct. **Ans. (A, B, C)**

Sol. 21 When key is open then the circuit is shown below in which the potential V is calculated by writing voltage drop across 1 Ω

$$0 + 5 + 1 \times 1 = V$$
$$\Rightarrow \quad V = 6\,\text{V}$$

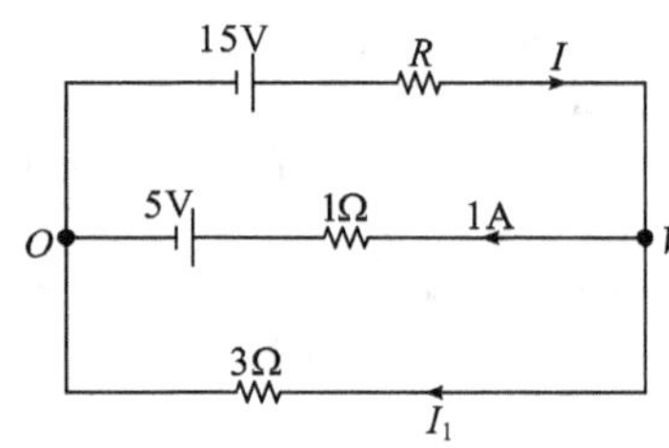

Similarly across resistance R we have

$$0 + 15 - I \times R = 6$$
$$\Rightarrow \quad IR = 9\,\text{V} \qquad \qquad \dots(1)$$

Across 3 Ω resistance, we have

$$6 - 3I_1 = 0$$
$$\Rightarrow \quad I_1 = 2\,\text{A}$$

Hence option (B) is correct. The current in resistance R is calculated as

$$I = 1 + 2 = 3\,\text{A}$$

Using equation-(1), we have

$$IR = 9$$
$$\Rightarrow \quad R = 3\,\Omega$$

Hence option (A) is correct. When key is closed the branch of capacitor is considered to be connected across three cells in parallel combination of EMFs 15 V, 5 V and 0 V with internal resistances 3 Ω, 1 Ω and 3 Ω respectively. For this combination equivalent emf and equivalent internal resistance is calculated as

$$\varepsilon = \frac{\dfrac{15}{3} + \dfrac{5}{1} + \dfrac{0}{3}}{\dfrac{1}{3} + \dfrac{1}{1} + \dfrac{1}{3}} = 10 \times \frac{3}{5} = 6\,\text{V}$$

and
$$r = 3\,\Omega \,\|\, 3\,\Omega \,\|\, 1\,\Omega = 0.6\,\Omega$$

The circuit below shows the modified situation after key is closed.

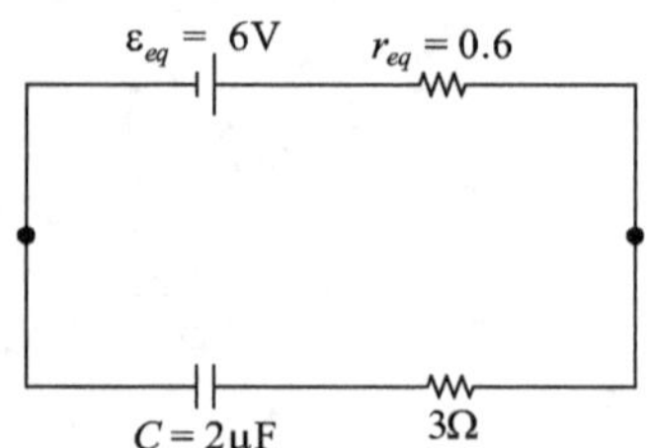

In steady state the charge on capacitor is calculated as

$$q_{\max} = 2 \times 6 = 12\,\mu\text{C}$$

Hence option (D) is correct. After closing the key the current through capacitor branch is calculated as

$$i = \frac{V}{R} e^{-\frac{t}{RC}} = \frac{6}{3.6} e^{-\frac{7.2}{7.2}}$$
$$\Rightarrow \quad i = \frac{5}{3} e^{-1}$$
$$\Rightarrow \quad i \approx 0.6\,\text{A}$$

Hence option (C) is correct. **Ans. (A, B, C, D)**

Sol. 22 Figure below shows the situation of meter bridge experiment as described in statements

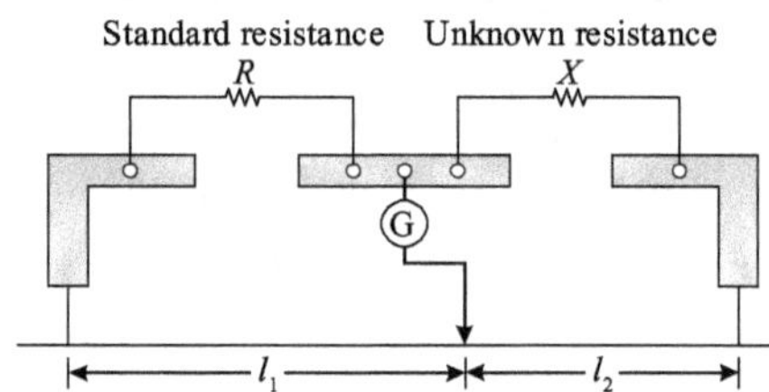

At balancing condition, we have value of unknown resistance given as

$$X = R \frac{l_1}{l_2}$$

As temperature increase x will increase to get same Null point i.e. same value of $\dfrac{l_1}{l_2}$, value of standard Resistance R should increase. Resistance of metal increases with increase in temperature. Assertion is false, However Reason statement is true. **Ans. (D)**

Sol. 23 (A) Bimetallic strip : Thermal expansion of both the strips occurs at different values so, strip bends. This application is used in switches electric heaters.

(B) Steam engine : It converts thermal energy to mechanical energy.

(C) In candescent lamp : It emits EM waves when it heat up.

(D) Electric fuse : It has low melting point so large current passes through it. By heating effect it melts and disconnect the circuit.   **Ans. [A (S); B (Q); C (P); D (R)]**

Sol. 24 For direct transmission, power dissipation is given as

$$P = i^2 R = (150)^2 (0.4 \times 20) = 1.8 \times 10^5 \, W$$

Percentage of power dissipation is given as

$$P_d = \frac{1.8 \times 10^5}{6 \times 10^5} \times 100 = 30\% \qquad \textbf{Ans. (B)}$$

Sol. 25 For step up transformer, we use

$$\frac{4000}{x} = \frac{1}{10} \qquad \qquad \ldots(1)$$

For step down transformer, we use

$$\frac{x}{200} = N \qquad \qquad \ldots(2)$$

Where x is the step up voltage. From equations-(1) and (2), we have

$$\frac{4000}{x} \times \frac{x}{200} = \frac{N}{10}$$

$$\Rightarrow \qquad N = 200$$

$$\Rightarrow \qquad \text{Ratio} = 200 : 1 \qquad \textbf{Ans. (A)}$$

Sol. 26 Balls will move up and stick with top plate and get negatively clayed and now top plate will repel and will move to the bottom plate.   **Ans. (A)**

Sol. 27 Current due to positive charge and negative charges will add up.   **Ans. (B)**

Sol. 28 Figure below shows the two situations of the two batteries connected in series and in parallel. Current through circuit when batteries are in series is

$$i_1 = \frac{2E}{R+2}$$

Rate of heat produced in resistor is given as

$$J_1 = \left(\frac{2E}{R+2}\right)^2 R$$

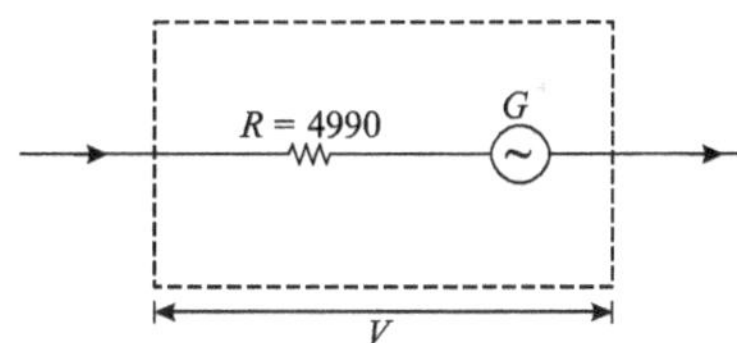

Current through circuit when batteries are connected in parallel is given as

$$i_2 = \frac{E}{R+0.5}$$

Rate of heat produced in resistor is given as

$$J_2 = \left(\frac{E}{R+0.5}\right)^2 R$$

It is given that $J_1 = 2.25 J_2$

$$\Rightarrow \qquad \left(\frac{2E}{R+2}\right)^2 R = 2.25 \left(\frac{E}{R+0.5}\right)^2 R$$

$$\Rightarrow \qquad \frac{2}{R+2} = \frac{1.5}{R+0.5}$$

$$\Rightarrow \qquad 2R+1 = 1.5R+3$$

$$\Rightarrow \qquad 0.5R = 2$$

$$\Rightarrow \qquad R = \frac{2}{0.5} = 4\,\Omega \qquad \textbf{Ans. (4)}$$

Sol. 29 Potential difference between terminals A and B is given as

$$V_A - V_B = \frac{\dfrac{E_1}{r_1} + \dfrac{E_2}{r_2}}{\dfrac{1}{r_1} + \dfrac{1}{r_2}}$$

$$\Rightarrow \qquad V_A - V_B = \frac{\dfrac{6}{1} + \dfrac{3}{2}}{\dfrac{1}{1} + \dfrac{1}{2}} = \frac{6+1.5}{1.5} = \frac{7.5}{1.5} = 5V$$

Or equivalent voltage in the circuit

$$E_{eq} = \frac{E_1 r_2 + E_2 r_1}{r_1 + r_2}$$

$$\Rightarrow \qquad E_{eq} = \frac{(6 \times 2) + (3 \times 1)}{1+2} = 5 \, V \qquad \textbf{Ans. (5)}$$

Sol. 30 For voltmeter conversion, high resistance is connected as shown in figure below and full deflection current is given as

$$I_g = 0.006 \, A$$

For full deflection at voltage range V, we use

$$\frac{V}{I_g} = G + R$$

$$\Rightarrow \qquad G = \frac{V}{I_g} - R$$

$$\Rightarrow \qquad G = \frac{30000}{0.006} - 4990 = 10 \, \Omega$$

For ammeter conversion, shunt is connected in parallel as shown in figure below, for which we use

$$GI_g = R(I - Ig)$$

$$\Rightarrow \quad R = \frac{GIg}{I - Ig} = \frac{10 \times 0.006}{1.5 - 0.006}\,\Omega$$

$$\Rightarrow \quad R = \frac{10 \times 0.0060}{1.4886} = \frac{6 \times 100}{14886}\,\Omega$$

$$\Rightarrow \quad R = \frac{10}{249} = \frac{5 \times 2}{249}\,\Omega$$

$$\Rightarrow \quad x = 5 \qquad \text{Ans. (5)}$$

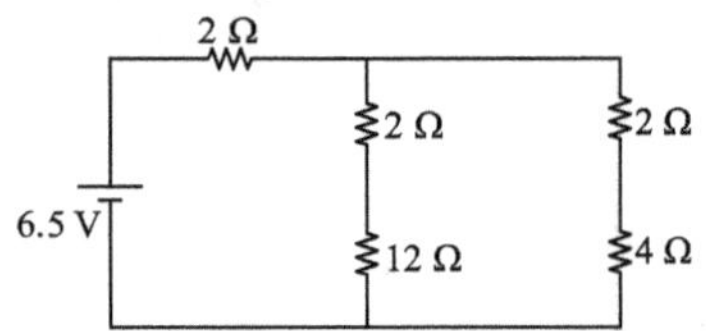

Sol. 31 With the balancing condition of Wheatstone bridge equivalent circuit is as shown in figure below

Equivalent resistance across the battery is given as

$$R_{eq} = \frac{6 \times 18}{24} + 2$$

$$\Rightarrow \quad R_{eq} = \frac{9}{2} + 2 = 6.5\,\Omega$$

Current I through the battery is given as

$$I = \frac{6.5}{6.5} = 1A \qquad \text{Ans. (1)}$$

Sol. 32 Current in moving coil galvanometer is given as

$$I_g = \frac{C\theta}{NBA} = \frac{10^{-4} \times 0.2}{50 \times 2 \times 10^{-4} \times 0.02} = 0.1\,A$$

For galvanometer conversion into ammeter if S is the shunt resistance used then we have

$$I_g R_g = (I - I_g)S$$

$$\Rightarrow \quad S = \frac{I_g R_g}{I - I_g} = \frac{0.1 \times 50}{1 - 0.1} = \frac{50}{9}\,\Omega \qquad \text{Ans. (5.55)}$$

Sol. 33 New resistance after rise in temperature is given as

$$R_3' = 300\,(1 + \alpha\Delta T)$$

$$\Rightarrow \quad R_3' = 312\,\Omega$$

For the circuit shown below, currents are given as

$$I_1 = \frac{50}{312}\,A \text{ and } I_2 = \frac{50}{600}\,A$$

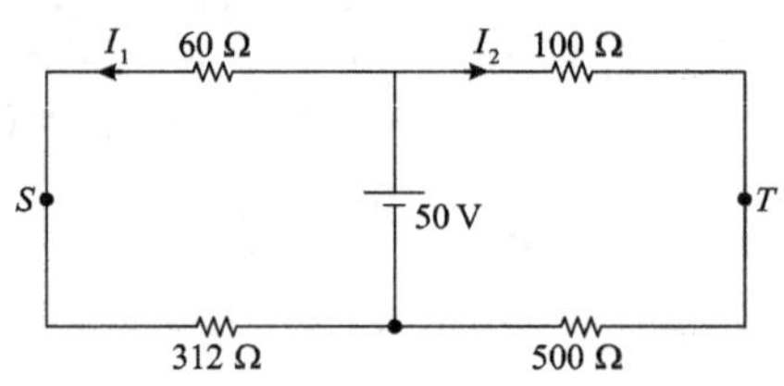

New potential difference across S and T is given as

$$V_S - V_T = 312\,I_1 - 500\,I_2$$

$$\Rightarrow \quad V_S - V_T = 41.94 - 41.67$$

$$\Rightarrow \quad V_S - V_T = 0.27\,V \qquad \text{Ans. (0.26 to 0.27)}$$

Sol. 34 The equivalent circuit of the given bridge is shown in figure below for which resistances on wire are in ratio of length of wire, given as

$$\frac{R_1}{R_2} = \frac{l_1}{l_2} = \frac{18}{7} \qquad \ldots(1)$$

$$\Rightarrow \quad R_1 = 36\,\Omega \text{ and } R_2 = 14\,\Omega$$

Current I in circuit at null deflection is given as

$$I = \frac{E}{r_1 + 36 + 14 + 25} = \frac{E}{75 + r_1} \qquad \ldots(2)$$

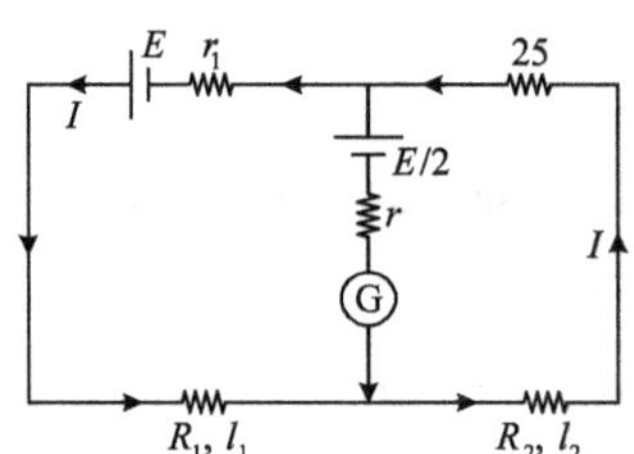

Using KVL in right side loop gives

$$\frac{E}{2} = \frac{E}{75 + r_1} \times (25 + 14)$$

$$\Rightarrow \quad r_1 = 3\,\Omega \qquad \text{Ans. (3)}$$

Sol. 35 If in the given circuit, resistance of left and right part of wire is taken as R_3 and R_4 then for the balanced Wheatstone bridge, the condition used is

$$\frac{R_1}{R_2} = \frac{R_3}{R_4} \qquad \ldots(1)$$

For a wire with radius linearly varying from one end to another from radius a to b then its resistance is given as

$$R = \frac{\rho l}{\pi ab}$$

$$\Rightarrow \quad \frac{X}{1} = \frac{1}{0.2}$$

$$\Rightarrow \quad X = 5\,\Omega \qquad \text{Ans. (5)}$$

Ch-15 Moving Charges and Magnetism

Sol. 1 Force on charged particle $\vec{F} = q\,(\vec{v} \times \vec{B})$ from a to $2a$ is given as

$$\vec{B} = B_0\,\hat{j}\,,\ \vec{v} = v_0\,\hat{i}$$

$$\Rightarrow \qquad \vec{F} = q\,(\vec{v}_0 \times \vec{B}_0) = qV_0 B_0\,\hat{k}$$

Thus particle gets deflected towards z-axis. Force on particle from $2a$ to $3a$ is given as

$$\vec{B} = B_0\,\hat{j}\,,\ \vec{v} = v_0\,\hat{i}$$

$$\Rightarrow \qquad \vec{F} = q\,(\vec{v} \times \vec{B}) = -qv_0 B_0\,\hat{k}$$

Thus particle gets deflected towards $-z$ axis.

As particle enters at $x = a$, particle will have z-coordinate zero hence according to the force directions obtained, resulting path of particle is as shown in figure below.

Ans. (A)

Sol. 2 Since the field is increasing, the flux in the region is increasing so the induced current should flow in an anticlockwise sense as shown in figure below.

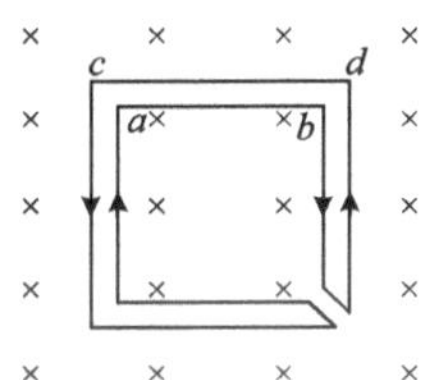

Hence option (D) is correct. **Ans. (D)**

Sol. 3 If T is the tension in loop then for every small segment of loop, the magnetic force will be equal to the inward components of tension at that segment. Below figure shows the forces acting on a small segment which subtend an angle $d\theta$ at the centre.

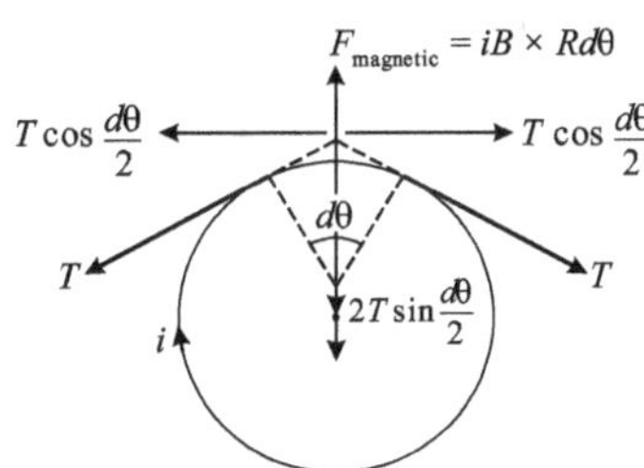

For equilibrium of the elemental segment, we use

$$2T\sin\left(\frac{d\theta}{2}\right) = I\,dl\,B$$

$$\Rightarrow \qquad IB \times R\,d\theta = 2T\sin\frac{d\theta}{2}$$

$$\Rightarrow \qquad T = BIR$$

As $2\pi R = L$, we use

$$\Rightarrow \qquad T = \frac{IBL}{2\pi} \qquad\qquad \textbf{Ans. (C)}$$

Sol. 4 No. of turns per unit radial distance of the spiral is given as

$$n = \frac{N}{b-a}$$

As shown in figure below, we consider an elemental circular strip of width dr and radius r. The number of turns in this elemental strip are given as

$$dN = \frac{N}{b-a}\,dr$$

Magnetic field at centre due to current in this element is given as

$$dB = \frac{\mu_0 (dN)I}{2r}$$

$$\Rightarrow \qquad dB = \frac{\mu_0 I}{2r}\left(\frac{N}{b-a}\right)dr$$

Total magnetic field at centre of spiral is given as

$$B = \frac{\mu_0 IN}{2(b-a)} \int_{a}^{b}\frac{dr}{r}$$

$$\Rightarrow \qquad B = \frac{\mu_0 IN}{2(b-a)} \ln\left(\frac{b}{a}\right) \qquad \textbf{Ans. (A)}$$

Sol. 5 Figure below shows the cross section of the hollow conducting cylinder as described in the question.

For $x < \dfrac{R}{2}$, $|B| = 0$

For $\dfrac{R}{2} \leq x < R$, by Ampere's law, we use

$$\int \vec{B}\cdot\vec{dl} = \mu_0 I$$

$$\Rightarrow \qquad |B|\,2\pi x = \mu_0\left[\pi x^2 - \pi\left(\frac{R}{2}\right)^2\right] J$$

$$\Rightarrow \qquad |B| = \frac{\mu_0 J}{2x}\left(x^2 - \frac{R^2}{4}\right)$$

For $x \geq R$, $|B| = \dfrac{\mu_0 I}{2\pi x}$

Hence option (D) is the most appropriate answer. **Ans. (D)**

Sol. 6 Total area enclosed by the current in given loop is calculated as

$$A = a^2 + 4 \times \frac{\pi\left(\dfrac{a}{2}\right)^2}{2}$$

$$\Rightarrow \qquad A = a^2 + \frac{\pi a^2}{2}$$

$$\Rightarrow \qquad A = \left(1 + \frac{\pi}{2}\right) a^2 c$$

Magnetic moment of loop is given as

$$\mu = IA\,\hat{k} = I\left(a^2 + \frac{\pi a^2}{2}\right)\hat{k} \qquad \textbf{Ans. (B)}$$

Sol. 7 The total magnetic field due to all the straight segments of the star is 12 times that of one segment as with respect to centre of loop all segments are identical. Figure below shows the angles subtended by segment ends A and B at centre.

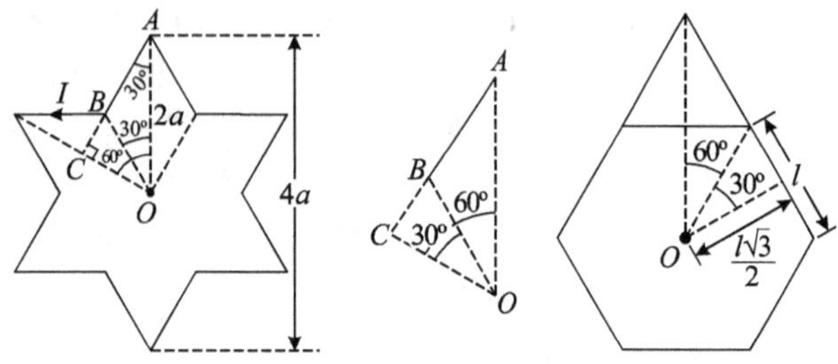

The magnetic field at O due to AB is given as

$$B = \frac{\mu_0}{4\pi}\frac{I}{a}\,[\sin 60° - \sin 30°]$$

$$\Rightarrow \qquad B = \frac{\mu_0}{4\pi}\frac{I}{a}\left[\frac{\sqrt{3}}{2} - \frac{1}{2}\right] = \frac{\mu_0 I}{4\pi a} \times \frac{1}{2}\,(\sqrt{3}-1)$$

Net magnetic field at O due to complete loop is given as

$$B = \frac{12\mu_0 I}{4\pi a}\left(\frac{\sqrt{3}}{2} - \frac{1}{2}\right)$$

$$\Rightarrow \qquad B = \frac{6\mu_0 I}{4\pi a}(\sqrt{3}-1) \qquad \textbf{Ans. (B)}$$

Sol. 8 Torque experienced by circular loop due to sudden flow of charge is given as

$$\tau = \overrightarrow{M} \times \overrightarrow{B}$$

At $\theta = 90°$ for the situation shown in figure, we have

$$\tau = i\pi R^2 N B_0$$

As charge flow is in a very short time ($Q = i\delta t$), the gain in angular momentum is calculated as

$$\vec{\tau}\delta t = d\vec{L} = i\pi R^2 N B_0 \delta t = Q\pi R^2 N B_0 \qquad \textbf{Ans. (B)}$$

Sol. 9 Magnetic field induction due to different wire segments in the given conductor is calculated as

$$\overrightarrow{B} = \frac{\mu_0 I}{4\pi L}\sin 45°\,(-\hat{k}) + \frac{\mu_0 I \pi}{4\pi \frac{L}{2}}\,(-\hat{k}) + \frac{\mu_0 I}{4\pi \frac{L}{4}} \times \frac{\pi}{2}\,(-\hat{k})$$

$$\overrightarrow{B} = \frac{\mu_0 I}{L}\left(\frac{1}{4\sqrt{2}\pi} + 1\right)(-\hat{k}) \qquad \textbf{Ans. (C)}$$

Sol. 10 When particle enters in magnetic field in normal direction, its path will be circular as shown in figure below. If radius of circle is more than l then particle will enter in region III. Radius of circular path of particle is given as

$$R = \frac{mv}{qB}$$

To enter in region III, we use

$$\frac{mv}{qB} > l$$

$$\Rightarrow \qquad v > \frac{qlB}{m}$$

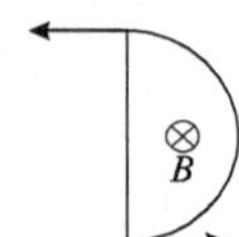

Hence option (A) is correct and option (B) is NOT correct.

When v is $\dfrac{qBl}{m}$ then particle will take semicircular path as shown above hence option (C) is correct.

For semicircular path time spent by particle in region II is given as half of its time period, given as

$$T = \left(\frac{2\pi m}{qB}\right)\frac{1}{2}$$

This time in region II is independent of velocity hence option (D) is correct. $\qquad$ **Ans. (A, C, D)**

Sol. 11 For electron and proton, as they enter in magnetic field in normal direction, they follow circular path as shown in the diagram below for which we can write

$$evB = \frac{m_e v^2}{R_e} \quad \text{and} \quad evB = \frac{m_p v^2}{R_p}$$

$$\Rightarrow \qquad R_e = \frac{m_e V}{eB} \quad \text{and} \quad R_p = \frac{m_p v}{eB}$$

$$\Rightarrow \qquad R_p > R_e$$

Time spent by the particles inside the magnetic field is given as

$$T = \frac{\pi R}{v} = \frac{\pi m}{eB}$$

$$\Rightarrow \qquad T_p > T_e$$

Here we consider that the two particles enter in the magnetic field at the same time they will come out at different times hence option (D) is correct. **Ans. (B, D)**

The most appropriate answer to this equation is (B, D), but because of ambiguity in language as it is not specified that the two particles have entered together or at the same time, answer can be given as [(B, C) or (B, D) or (B, C, D)].

Sol. 12 Figure below shows the situation described in the question

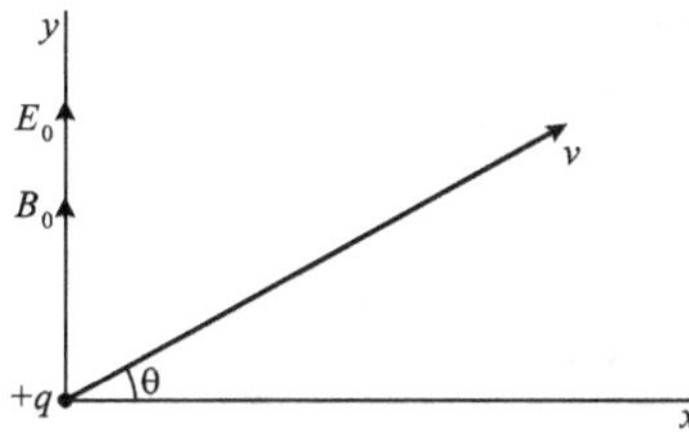

If $\theta = 0°$ then due to magnetic force path is circular but due to force qE_0 ($\uparrow$) q will have acceleration motion along y-axis. So combined path of q will be a helical path with variable pitch hence options (A) and (B) are NOT correct. If $\theta = 10°$ then due to $v\cos\theta$, path is circular and due to qE_0 and $v\sin\theta$, q has accelerated motion along y-axis so combined path is a helical path with variable pitch hence option (C) is correct. If $\theta = 90°$ then $F_B = 0$ and due to qE_0 motion is accelerated along y-axis hence option (D) is correct. **Ans. (C, D)**

Sol. 13 With the direction of emerging velocity it can be stated that the magnetic field is along – ve z-direction as shown in figure below. The time spent by particle in the magnetic field is calculated as

$$t = \frac{\pi M}{6QB}$$

$$\Rightarrow \quad B = \frac{\pi M}{60 \times 10^{-3} Q} = \frac{1000\pi M}{60Q}$$

$$\Rightarrow \quad B = \frac{50\pi M}{3Q} \qquad \text{**Ans. (A, C)**}$$

Sol. 14 The magnetic field of solenoid is non zero in region from $0 < r < R$ hence option (A) is correct. In the region between

the surface of cylinder and solenoid magnetic field is resultant of the field of solenoid and that due to the hollow cylinder hence it cannot be along the axis hence option (B) is NOT correct and with the same reason option (C) is also NOT correct. In outer region $r > 2R$ magnetic field exist due to current in conductor hence option (D) is correct. **Ans. (A, D)**

Sol. 15 For the given conductor the magnetic force can be calculated by considering it as a straight wire of length $2(L + R)$ carrying same current I. If magnetic field is along z direction magnetic force on the conductor is be given as

$$F_m = BI(2L + 2R)$$

Hence option (A) is correct and option (D) is NOT correct.

If $\vec{B}$ is along x-direction then net force on conductor is zero as current element length is along magnetic field direction hence option (B) is correct. When $\vec{B}$ is along y direction, magnetic force on the conductor is given as

$$F_m = BI(2L + 2R)$$

Hence option (C) is correct. **Ans. (A, B, C)**

Sol. 16 For $B = \dfrac{8}{13}\dfrac{p}{QR}$, radius of circular path of particle is given as

$$r = \frac{mv}{QB} = \frac{p}{Q}\left(\frac{13QR}{8p}\right)$$

$$\Rightarrow \quad r = \frac{13}{8}R$$

Thus for this circular path, center will be located at $(0, 5R/8)$ so equation of circle can be written as

$$x^2 + \left(y - \frac{5R}{8}\right)^2 = \left(\frac{13}{8}R\right)^2$$

The co-ordinate of point $P_2\left(\dfrac{3R}{2}, 0\right)$ will lie on this circle. Hence option (A) is correct.

For $B = \dfrac{2p}{3QR}$, radius of circular path of particle is given as

$$r = \frac{p}{Q}\left(\frac{3QR}{2p}\right) = \frac{3}{2}R$$

If $B > \dfrac{2p}{3QR}$ then $r < \dfrac{3R}{2}$ hence option (B) is correct. With the analysis of path of motion of charge in magnetic field options (C) and (D) are NOT correct. **Ans. (A, B)**

Sol. 17 Figure below shows the situation described in the question. If $I_1 = I_2$, then the magnetic fields due to I_1 and I_2 at origin O will cancel out each other. But the magnetic field at O due to the circular loop will be present hence option (A) is correct.

If $I_1 > 0$ and $I_2 < 0$, then the magnetic field due to both current will be in $+Z$ direction and will be added-up. The magnetic field due to current I will be in $-Z$ direction and if its magnitude is equal to the combined magnitudes of I_1 and I_2, then magnetic field can be zero at the origin. Hence option (B) is correct.

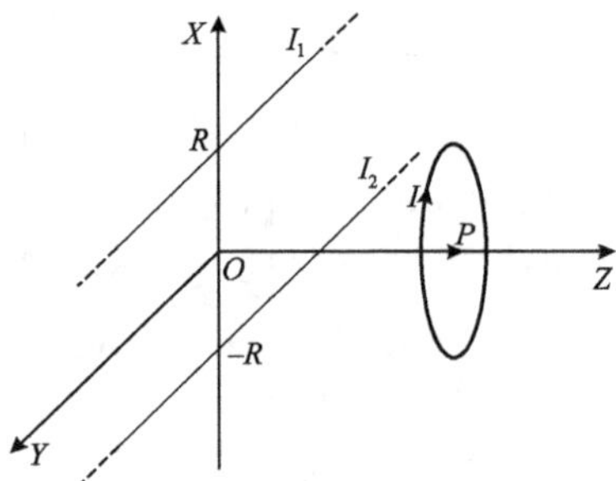

If $I_1 < 0$ and $I_2 > 0$ then their resulting magnetic field at origin will be in $-Z$ direction and the magnetic field due to I at origin will also be in $-Z$ direction. Thus magnetic field at origin cannot be zero. Hence option (C) is NOT correct.

If $I_1 = I_2$ then the resultant of the magnetic field at the centre of the circular loop at point P is along $+X$ direction as shown in figure below. Thus the magnetic field at P is only due to the current I which is in $-Z$ direction and is given as

$$\vec{B} = \frac{\mu_0 I}{2R}(-\hat{k})$$

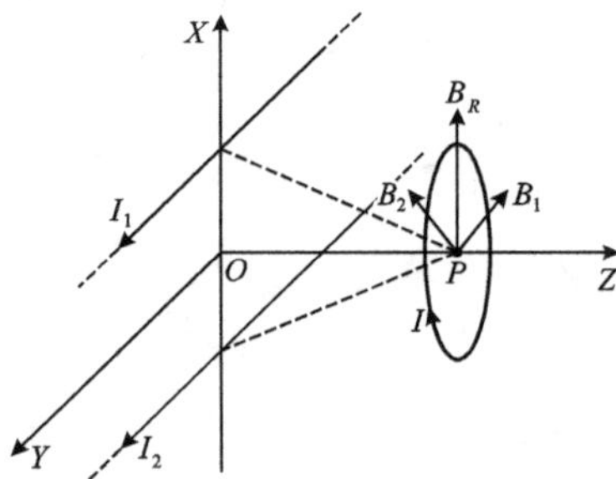

Hence option (D) is correct. **Ans. (A, B, D)**

Sol. 18 If the given wire is replaced by a straight wire with same height along y direction then induced emf remain same hence option (A) is correct. Given equation of parabolic wire is $y = x^2$ and magnetic field is given as

$$\vec{B} = B_0\left[1+\left(\frac{y}{L}\right)^\beta\right]\hat{k}$$

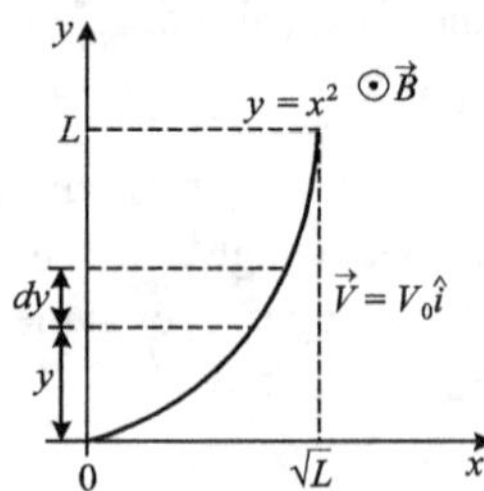

Motional emf induced in wire can be evaluated by considering an element in the wire of vertical height dy as shown in figure below and it is calculated as

$$|\Delta\phi| = \int d\phi = \int_0^L V_0 B_0\left(1+\frac{y^\beta}{L^\beta}\right)\cdot dy$$

$$\Rightarrow \quad |\Delta\phi| = V_0 B_0\left[L+\frac{L^{\beta+1}}{(\beta+1)L^\beta}\right]$$

$$\Rightarrow \quad |\Delta\phi| = V_0 B_0\left[L+\frac{L}{\beta+1}\right] \quad\quad \dots(1)$$

$$\Rightarrow \quad |\Delta\phi| = B_0 V_0\left(1+\frac{1}{\beta+1}\right)\cdot L$$

$$\Rightarrow \quad |\Delta\phi| \propto L$$

Hence option (B) is correct

For $\beta = 0$, from equation (1), we have

$$\Delta\phi = V_0 B_0[L+L]$$
$$\Delta\phi = 2V_0 B_0 L$$

Hence option (C) is NOT correct.

For $\beta = 2$, from equation (1), we have

$$\Delta\phi = V_0 B_0\left[L+\frac{L}{3}\right]$$

$$\Rightarrow \quad \Delta\phi = \frac{4}{3}V_0 B_0 L$$

Hence option (D) is correct. **Ans. (A, B, D)**

Sol. 19 EMF induced across semicircular conducting rod is calculated by considering an element of width dx at a distance x from the straight wire as

$$e = \frac{v\mu_0 I}{2\pi}\int_{1\,cm}^{4\,cm}\frac{dx}{x} = \frac{4\pi\times10^{-7}\times3\times2}{2\pi}\ln 4$$

$$\Rightarrow \quad e = 16.8\times10^{-7}\,V$$

Maximum current through resistor R can be given as

$$I_{max} = \frac{16.8\times10^{-7}}{1.4} = 12\times10^{-7}\,A = 1.2\times10^{-6}\,A$$

Maximum charge on capacitor C_0 is given as

$$q_{max} = 5\times10^{-6}\times16.8\times10^{-7} = 8.4\times10^{-12}\,C \quad \textbf{Ans. (A, C)}$$

Sol. 20 Magnetic field due to both loops is perpendicular to the $x - y$ plane hence their resultant will also be along this direction only hence option (A) is correct.

As the two loops are symmetric with respect to origin, the magnitude of magnetic field will only depend upon the radial distance from origin hence option (B) is correct.

For the given condition of current, at center field is inward and as we move radially out then close to $r = R_1$ field becomes outward so at some point it will be zero also hence option (C) is NOT correct.

From the directions of currents given magnetic field between the region of the two loops magnetic field is in inward direction. Hence option (D) is NOT correct.   **Ans. (A, B)**

Sol. 21 Sensitivity of a galvanometer depends upon the ratio of output to input. By placing a suitable magnetic material inside the coil, the magnetic moment of the coil will increase so, torque will increase and that increases sensitivity hence statement-1 is true. Highly permeable magnetic material can be easily magnetised & easily demagnetised hence statement-2 is false.
Ans. (C)

Sol. 22 (A) Due to current carrying wire 1 and 2, directions of magnetic field at point P can be obtained by right hand thumb rule due to the two wires it is in opposite direction. Thus magnetic field at midway point P will be zero.
Hence options (q) and (r) are correctly related.

(B) By right hand thumb rule magnetic field at point P due to both coils are in same direction. As currents are in same direction, they will attract each other. Hence option (p) is correctly related.

(C) By right hand thumb rule magnetic field at point P due to both the wires is in opposite direction and P is midway point so the fields are equal and opposite and thus net field is zero. Direction of force on each loop is towards each other so they attract each other, hence options (q) and (r) are correctly related.

(D) By right hand thumb rule magnetic field at P due to both wires are in opposite direction and as radius are different, so resultant field is non zero. Hence option (q) is correctly related.
Ans. [A (q, r); B (p); C (q, r); D (q)]

Sol. 23 Force on the electron due to electric field will cancel out with the force due to magnetic field. So velocity will remains constant. This can be mathematically proven as

$$\vec{F}_E = -e\,\vec{E} = -(-E_0\,\hat{x}) = eE_0\,\hat{x}$$

$$\Rightarrow \qquad \vec{F}_B = (v \times \vec{B}) = -e\left[\frac{E_0}{B_0}\,\hat{y} \times B_0\hat{z}\right]$$

$$\Rightarrow \qquad \vec{F}_B = -eE_0\,\hat{x} \qquad\qquad \textbf{Ans. (A)}$$

Sol. 24 For helical path electric field should be along axis of the helix. Hence option (C) is correct.   **Ans. (C)**

Sol. 25 This will happen when magnetic force will be zero and only electric force will accelerate the particle along $-y$ direction.
Ans. (D)

Sol. 26 It is given that $B_2 > B_1$ thus for critical temperature, we have

$$T_C(B_2) < T_C(B_1)$$

Resistance $\propto$ Temperature above critical hence option (A) is correct.   **Ans. (A)**

Sol. 27 At $B = 7.5$ T, $T_C = 75$ K

Thus at $B = 5$ T, $T_C(B) > 75$ K but less than 100 K hence option (B) is correct.   **Ans. (B)**

Sol. 28 For induced electric field, we use

$$\int E \cdot dr = A \cdot \frac{dB}{dt}$$

$$\Rightarrow \qquad E(2\pi R) = \pi R^2 \frac{dB}{dt}$$

$$\Rightarrow \qquad E = \frac{RB}{2} \qquad\qquad \textbf{Ans. (B)}$$

Sol. 29 Total change in angular momentum is given as

$$\Delta L = \int \tau dt$$

$$\Rightarrow \qquad \Delta L = Q\left(\frac{RB}{2}\right)R$$

$$\Rightarrow \qquad \Delta L = \frac{QR^2 B}{2}$$

Change in magnetic dipole moment is given as

$$\Delta\mu = -\gamma\Delta L = -\gamma\frac{QR^2 B}{2}$$

In above expression negative sign is considered due to induced current in opposite direction.   **Ans. (B)**

Sol. 30 Figure below shows the same situation as given in question.

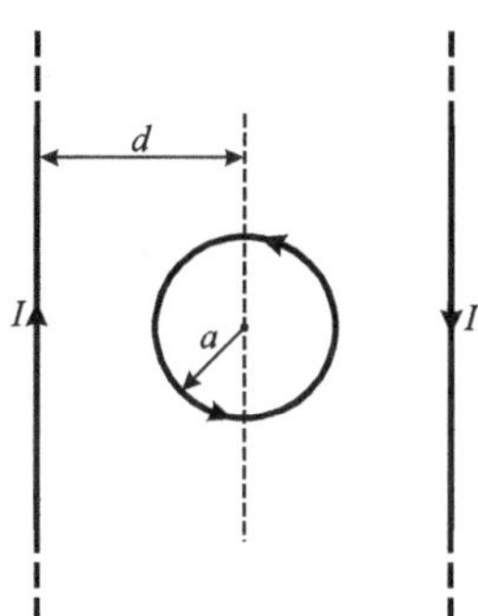

Net magnetic field at the given point will be zero if

$$|\vec{B}_{\text{wires}}| = |\vec{B}_{\text{loop}}|$$

At a height x above the loop, we use

$$B_{\text{loop}} = 2B_{\text{wires}} \cos\theta$$

$$\Rightarrow \quad \frac{\mu_0 I a^2}{2(a^2 + x^2)^{3/2}} = 2\frac{\mu_0 I}{2\pi(\sqrt{a^2 + x^2})(\sqrt{a^2 + x^2})}$$

$$\Rightarrow \quad \frac{a}{2(a^2 + x^2)^{1/2}} = \frac{1}{\pi}$$

$$\Rightarrow \quad (\pi a)^2 = 4(a^2 + x^2)$$

$$\Rightarrow \quad \pi^2 a^2 - 4a^2 = 4x^2$$

$$\Rightarrow \quad 4x^2 = 6a^2$$

$$\Rightarrow \quad x = \sqrt{\frac{3}{2}}a = 1.2a \qquad \textbf{Ans. (C)}$$

Sol. 31 Magnetic field at the centre of loop is given as

$$B_C = \frac{\mu_0 I}{\pi d}$$

Torque on the loop can be given as

$$\vec{\tau} = \vec{M} \times \vec{B}$$

$$\Rightarrow \quad |\vec{\tau}| = MB\sin\theta$$

$$\Rightarrow \quad |\vec{\tau}| = \pi a^2 \frac{\mu_0 I}{\pi d} \sin 30° = \frac{\mu_0 I a^2}{2d} \qquad \textbf{Ans. (B)}$$

Sol. 32 Magnetic force and electric force on charge careers in the strip is considered as

$$qv_d B = \frac{qV}{w}$$

$$\Rightarrow \quad q\left(\frac{i}{nqA}\right)B = \frac{qV}{w}$$

$$\Rightarrow \quad \left(\frac{i}{nwd}\right)B = \frac{qV}{w}$$

$$\Rightarrow \quad V \propto \frac{1}{d}$$

There is no dependence on w hence options (A) and (D) are correct.   **Ans. (A, D)**

Sol. 33 Similarly to previous question, we have

$$\frac{i}{nqwd}B = \frac{V}{w}$$

$$\Rightarrow \quad \frac{B}{n} \propto V$$

Hence options (A) and (C) are correct.   **Ans. (A, C)**

Sol. 34 Below figure shows the situation described in question

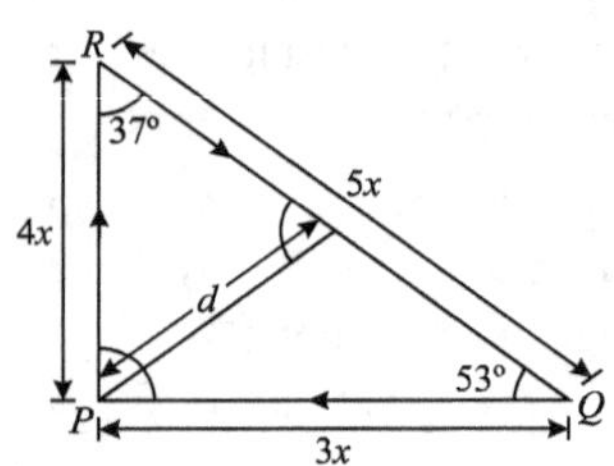

Here $d = 4x \cos 37° = 4x \times \dfrac{3}{5}$

Magnitude of magnetic field at P is given as

$$B_p = \frac{\mu_0 I}{4\pi d}\,[\sin 37° + \sin 53°]$$

$$\Rightarrow \quad B_p = \frac{\mu_0 I}{4\pi\dfrac{12x}{5}}\left[\frac{7}{5}\right] = \frac{7}{48}\frac{\mu_0 I}{\pi x}$$

$$\Rightarrow \quad B_p = 7\left(\frac{\mu_0 I}{48\pi x}\right)$$

$$\Rightarrow \quad K = 7 \qquad \textbf{Ans. (7)}$$

Sol. 35 Magnetic field due to current in tube is given as

$$B = \frac{\mu_0 I}{L}$$

$$\Rightarrow \quad B = \frac{\mu_0 I_0 \cos 300t}{10}$$

Magnetic flux through the loop is given as

$$\phi = BA$$

$$\Rightarrow \quad \phi = \frac{\mu_0 I_0}{10} \times 3.14 \times 0.01 \cos 300t$$

$$\Rightarrow \quad \phi = 3.14 \times \mu_0 I_0 \cos 300t \times 10^{-3}$$

Induced emf in loop is given as

$$e = -\frac{d\phi}{dt} = 3.14 \times 300\,\mu_0 I_0 \sin 300t \times 10^{-3}$$

Induced current in loop is given as

$$i = \frac{e}{R} = \frac{3.14 \times 300\mu_0 I_0 \sin 300t \times 10^{-3}}{0.005}$$

$$\Rightarrow \quad i = 3.14 \times 10\,\mu_0 I_0 \sin 300t$$

Magnetic moment of the loop due to induced current is given as

$$\mu = 3.14 \times 60 \times 3.14 \times \frac{0.01}{100} \times \mu_0 I_0 \sin 300t$$

$$\Rightarrow \quad \mu = 5.9\,\mu_0 I_0 \sin 300t$$

$$\Rightarrow \quad \mu = 6\,\mu_0 I_0 \sin 300t$$

$$\Rightarrow \quad N = 6 \qquad \textbf{Ans. (6)}$$

Sol. 36 Magnetic field for infinitely long cylinder at a distance r is given as

$$B_{\text{in}} = \frac{\mu_0 J r}{2}$$

$$B_{\text{out}} = \frac{\mu_0 J a^2}{2r}$$

Assuming bigger cylinder to carry a positive current density and smaller cylinder has a negative current density of magnitude of J then magnetic field at point P is given as

$$B_P = B_1 + B_2$$

Where $\quad B_1 = \dfrac{\mu_0 J a}{2}$

and $\quad B_2 = -\dfrac{\mu_0 J \left(\dfrac{a}{2}\right)^2}{2 \cdot \dfrac{3a}{2}} = -\dfrac{\mu_0 J a}{12}$

$$\Rightarrow \quad B_P = \frac{5}{12}\,\mu_0 J a$$

$$\Rightarrow \quad N = 5 \qquad\qquad\qquad \textbf{Ans. (5)}$$

Sol. 37 Magnetic field on the axis of circular loop due to a current i considered in the loop is given as

$$B = \frac{\mu_0 i R^2}{2(R^2 + X^2)^{3/2}}$$

$$\Rightarrow \quad B = \frac{\mu_0 i R^2}{2(R^2 + 3R^2)^{3/2}} = \frac{\mu_0 i R^2}{2(4R^2)^{3/2}}$$

$$\Rightarrow \quad B = \frac{\mu_0 i}{16R}$$

Magnetic flux through the square loop is given as

$$\phi = NBA \cos 45^\circ$$

$$\Rightarrow \quad \phi = 2\,\frac{\mu_0 i}{16R}\,a^2\,\frac{1}{\sqrt{2}}$$

$$\Rightarrow \quad \phi = \frac{\mu_0 i a^2}{8\sqrt{2}\,R}$$

Mutual inductance between the circular loop and square loop is given as

$$M = \frac{\phi}{i}$$

$$\Rightarrow \quad M = \frac{\mu_0 a^2}{2^{7/2} R}$$

$$\Rightarrow \quad p = 7 \qquad\qquad\qquad \textbf{Ans. (7)}$$

Sol. 38 Normal force on the charge in magnetic field of wires is calculated as

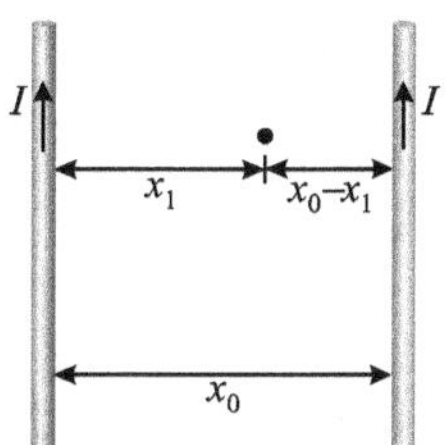

Magnetic field on the charge due to both wires

$$B = \frac{\mu_0}{2x}\left[\frac{I}{x_1} - \frac{I}{(x_0 - x_1)}\right]$$

In this magnetic field radius of curvature of charged particle is given as

$$R_1 = \frac{mv}{qB}$$

$$\Rightarrow \quad qR_1\left[\frac{\mu_0}{2\pi}\frac{I}{x_1} - \frac{\mu_0 I}{2\pi(x_0 - x_1)}\right] = mv$$

$$\Rightarrow \quad qR_1\left[\frac{I}{x_1} - \frac{I}{x_0 - x_1}\right]\frac{\mu_0 I}{2\pi} = mv \qquad \dots(1)$$

$$\Rightarrow \quad qR_2\left[\frac{x_0 - x_1 - x_1}{x_0\,(x_0 - x_1)}\right]\frac{\mu_0 I}{4\pi} = mv$$

Similarly for the second case when currents are in opposite directions magnetic fields due to these wires are in same direction, given as

$$qR_2\left[\frac{x_0 - x_1 + x_1}{x_0\,(x_0 - x_1)}\right]\frac{\mu_0 I}{4\pi} = mv \qquad \dots(2)$$

Dividing equation-(1) by (2) gives

$$\frac{qR_1}{R_2}\frac{[x_0 - 2x_1]}{x_0} = \frac{1}{2}$$

$$\Rightarrow \quad \frac{R_1}{R_2} = \left[\frac{x_0}{x_0 - 2x_1}\right] = \left[\frac{1}{1 - \dfrac{2x_1}{x_0}}\right]$$

$$\Rightarrow \quad \frac{R_1}{R_2} = \left[\frac{x_0}{x_0 - 2x_1}\right] = \left[\frac{1}{1 - \dfrac{2x_1}{x_0}}\right]$$

$$\Rightarrow \quad \frac{R_1}{R_2} = \left[\frac{1}{1 - \dfrac{2}{3}}\right] = \left[\frac{1}{\dfrac{1}{3}}\right] = 3 \qquad \textbf{Ans. (3)}$$

Sol. 39 Average speed along x-axis when particle crosses it second time is given as

$$v_{\text{avg}} = \frac{D_1 + D_2}{t_1 + t_2} = \frac{2(R_1 + R_2)}{t_1 + t_2}$$

$$\Rightarrow \quad v_{\text{avg}} = 2\left[\frac{\dfrac{mv_0}{qB_1} + \dfrac{mv_0}{q(4B_1)}}{\dfrac{\pi m}{qB_1} + \dfrac{\pi m}{q(4B_1)}}\right]$$

Using $v_0 = \pi$ m/s, we have

$$v_{\text{avg}} = 2\left[\frac{\dfrac{m\pi}{qB_1} + \dfrac{m\pi}{q(4B_1)}}{\dfrac{\pi m}{qB_1} + \dfrac{\pi m}{q(4B_1)}}\right]$$

$$\Rightarrow \quad v_{\text{avg}} = 2 \text{ m/s} \qquad \textbf{Ans. (2.00)}$$

Sol. 40 After accelerating by a potential difference V, the kinetic energy gained by the α-particles is given as

$$\frac{1}{2}mv^2 = qV$$

In uniform magnetic field the radius of particles is given as

$$r = \frac{mV}{qB}$$

$$\Rightarrow \quad r = \frac{\sqrt{2mqV}}{qB}$$

$$\Rightarrow \quad r \, \alpha \sqrt{\frac{m}{q}}$$

$$\Rightarrow \quad \frac{r_s}{r_\alpha} = \sqrt{\frac{32}{4} \times \frac{2}{1}} = 4 \qquad \textbf{Ans. (4)}$$

Ch-16 Electromagnetic Induction

Sol. 1 When the magnet is moved, it creates a state where the plate moves through the magnetic flux, due to which an emf is induced in the plate and eddy currents are induced in the plate body. These currents are such that these will oppose the relative motion and due to this disc will rotate in the direction of rotation of magnet. **Ans. (B)**

Sol. 2 When current is switched on in the coils, a sudden magnetic flux change occurs in the flux passing through the metal rings. Due to this induced emf in the rings is given as

$$E = -\frac{d\phi}{dt}$$

Depending upon the resistance of rings the charge flow in the rings is given as

$$q = \frac{\Delta\phi}{R} \propto \frac{1}{\rho} \qquad \ldots(1)$$

As the length of rings (circumference) is same for the two, the magnetic force on rings in upward directions can be given as

$$F \propto IB$$

$$C \int IBdt = mv$$

$$\Rightarrow \quad CBq = mv$$

$$\Rightarrow \quad v \propto \frac{q}{m} \qquad \ldots(2)$$

From equation (1), we use

$$v \propto \frac{1}{m\rho}$$

Height to which rings will jump can be written as

$$h \propto v^2 \qquad \ldots(3)$$

$$\Rightarrow \quad (m\rho)_A < (m\rho)_B$$

Thus options (B) and (D) are correct. **Ans. (B, D)**

Sol. 3 Figure below shows the situation described in the question.

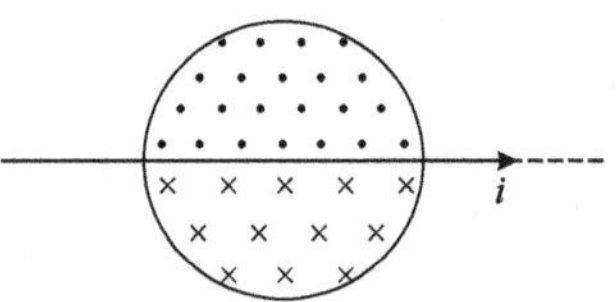

Magnetic flux through the loop is always zero in this situation because upper and lower half carry same amount of flux. So induced emf in all conditions will be zero. **Ans. (A, C)**

Sol. 4 Direction of induced current in long wire is same as that of current direction in hypotenuse as these two should repeal each other to oppose the flux changes hence current directions must be same. If a current i flows in the long wire, to calculate the mutual induction we first calculate the magnetic flux through the triangular loop which is calculated by considering an elemental strip of width dx at a distance x from the wire as shown in figure below. This gives

$$\phi = \int_0^\phi d\phi = \int_0^{0.1} \frac{\mu_0 i}{2\pi x}(2x\,dx)$$

$$\Rightarrow \quad \phi = \frac{\mu_0 i}{\pi}(0.1) = Mi$$

$$\Rightarrow \quad M = \frac{\mu_0}{10\pi}$$

EMF induced in straight wire due to change in current in triangular loop is given as

$$e = \frac{Mdi}{dt} = \frac{\mu_0}{10\pi}(10) = \frac{\mu_0}{\pi} \qquad \textbf{Ans. (B, D)}$$

Sol. 5 Induced current in loop is given as

$$i = \frac{Blv}{R}$$

Magnetic force on loop is given as

$$F = ma = -Bil$$

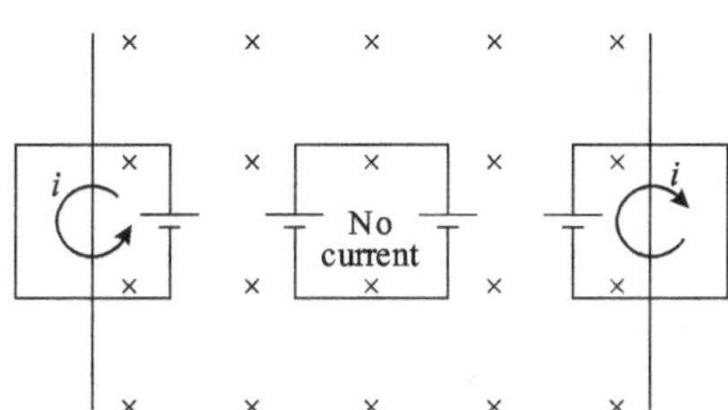

$$\Rightarrow \qquad m\frac{v\,dv}{dx} = -B\left[\frac{Blv}{R}\right]l$$

While entering into the field velocity of loop is given as

$$\int_{v_0}^{v} dv = -\frac{B^2 l^2}{mR}\int_{0}^{x} dx$$

$$\Rightarrow \qquad v - v_0 = -\frac{B^2 l^2}{mR}\,x$$

$$\Rightarrow \qquad v = v_0 - \frac{B^2 l^2}{mR}\,x$$

Hence force is given as

$$F = mv\frac{dv}{dx} = m\left(v_0 - \frac{B^2 l^2}{mR}\,x\right)\left(-\frac{B^2 l^2}{mR}\right)$$

As velocity is a linearly decreasing function with x, options (B), (C) and (D) are correct. **Ans. (B, C, D)**

Sol. 6 Total change in flux through the loop as a function of time is given as

$$\phi = \phi_{2A} - \phi_A$$

$$\Rightarrow \qquad \phi = B\,2A\cos\omega t - BA\cos\omega t = BA\cos\omega t$$

Induced emf in loop due to rotation is given as

$$e = -\frac{d\phi}{dt}$$

$$\Rightarrow \qquad e = BA\,\omega\sin\omega t \qquad\qquad \textbf{Ans. (A, D)}$$

Sol. 7 By Lenz's law current is induced in the ring and it opposes the change in flux of coil, so it induces a current in the direction opposite to coil. As current is in opposite direction, the ring will experience force in upward direction which can balance the weight of ring and it can float. Thus Statement-1 and Statement-2 are correct and statement-2 is correct explanation. **Ans. (A)**

Sol. 8 (A) : The energy of a capacitor is increased when connected to a battery hence option (p) is correctly related. By compressing a gas adiabatically, the internal energy increases hence option (q) is correctly related. By placing a loop of wire in a time varying magnetic field perpendicular to its plane due to which an emf is induced which causes an induced current and magnetic field. This increases the energy of the loop.

(B) : Mechanical energy of pushing the piston, does work on a gas, increasing its energy by increasing the velocity of random motion, hence option (q) is correctly related.

(C) : Internal energy of the system is converted into mechanical energy. Energy internal to system, is converted to energy of motion, temperature and photons in nuclear fission (natural radioactivity) of heavy fragments hence option (s) is correctly related.

(D) : The increase in the energy of the products of fission or radioactivity comes from a decrease in the initial mass hence option (s) is correctly related.

$$\textbf{Ans. [A }(p, q, t);\textbf{ B }(q);\textbf{ C }(s);\textbf{ D }(s)]$$

[When current will pass through loop its temperature will increase]

Sol. 9 As cylinder current is along the surface, by right hand thumb rule the magnetic field due to this current will be along the unit vector $\hat{n}$ which is rotating as given in column-I. The torque acting on circular loop can be calculated as

$$\vec{\tau} = \vec{M}\times\vec{B}$$

For all the rows given in column-I, we can assess the direction of torque by analysing through above equation where direction of magnetic moment of circular loop is calculated by Lenz's law.

(I) : $\qquad \vec{B} = \frac{\mu_0 mI}{\sqrt{2}}(\sin\omega t\,\hat{j} + \cos\omega t\,\hat{k})$

Due to above magnetic field the upward flux through loop is decreasing so induced current is such that its magnetic moment will be induced in $+\hat{k}$ direction hence direction of torque is along $-\hat{i}$ direction hence options (Q) or (T) can be correct. Here we will eliminate option (T) in explanation of point (III) of first column.

(II) : $\qquad \vec{B} = \frac{\mu_0 mI}{\sqrt{2}}(\sin\omega t\,\hat{i} + \cos\omega t\,\hat{j})$

Due to above magnetic field flux through the circular loop remain zero hence no current is induced and hence torque will be zero hence option (P) is correctly related here.

(III) : $\qquad \vec{B} = \frac{\mu_0 mI}{\sqrt{2}}(\sin\omega t\,\hat{i} + \cos\omega t\,\hat{k})$

Due to above magnetic field the upward flux through loop is decreasing so induced current is such that its magnetic moment will be induced in $+\hat{k}$ direction hence direction of torque is along $+\hat{j}$ direction hence options (S) is correctly related here.

In point (I) of first column the situation is exactly same like this point hence magnitude of torque in (I) must be exactly same like this hence option (T) cannot be the related option for point (I). Alternatively torque can also be mathematically calculated as explained below :

The magnetic flux through the circular loop is given as

$$\phi = \vec{B} \cdot \vec{A} = \frac{\mu_0 mI}{\sqrt{2}} \cos(\omega t) \cdot A$$

Induced emf in the circular loop is calculated as

$$\varepsilon = -\frac{d\phi}{dt} = \frac{\mu_0 mI\omega A}{\sqrt{2}} \sin(\omega t)$$

Induced current in the circular loop is calculated as

$$i = \frac{\varepsilon}{R} = \frac{\mu_0 mI\omega A}{\sqrt{2}R} \sin(\omega t)$$

Thus magnetic moment of the circular loop is given as

$$\overrightarrow{M} = i\vec{A} = iA(\hat{k}) = \frac{\mu_0 mI\omega A^2}{\sqrt{2}R} \sin(\omega t)(\hat{k})$$

The torque on loop can be written as

$$\vec{\tau} = \overrightarrow{M} \times \vec{B} = \frac{\mu_0 m^2 I^2 \omega A^2}{\sqrt{2}R} \sin^2(\omega t)(+\hat{j})$$

$$\Rightarrow \qquad \vec{\tau} = \frac{\alpha}{4}\hat{j}$$

In the same manner exact value of torque can also be calculated in point (I) of column-I.

(IV) : $\qquad \vec{B} = \frac{\mu_0 mI}{\sqrt{2}}(\cos \omega t\, \hat{j} + \sin \omega t\, \hat{k})$

Due to above magnetic field the upward flux through loop is increasing so induced current is such that its magnetic moment will be induced in $-\hat{k}$ direction hence direction of torque is along $+\hat{i}$ direction hence options (S) can only be correctly related here.

Alternatively torque can also be mathematically calculated as explained below :

The magnetic flux through the circular loop is given as

$$\phi = \vec{B} \cdot \vec{A} = \frac{\mu_0 mI}{\sqrt{2}} \sin(\omega t) \cdot A$$

Induced emf in the circular loop is calculated as

$$\varepsilon = -\frac{d\phi}{dt} = \frac{\mu_0 mI\omega A}{\sqrt{2}} \cos(\omega t)$$

Induced current in the circular loop is calculated as

$$i = \frac{\varepsilon}{R} = \frac{\mu_0 mI\omega A}{\sqrt{2}R} \cos(\omega t)$$

Thus magnetic moment of the circular loop is given as

$$\overrightarrow{M} = i\vec{A} = iA(\hat{k}) = -\frac{\mu_0 mI\omega A^2}{\sqrt{2}R} \cos(\omega t)(\hat{k})$$

The torque on loop can be written as

$$\vec{\tau} = \overrightarrow{M} \times \vec{B} = \frac{\mu_0 m^2 I^2 \omega A^2}{\sqrt{2}R} \cos^2(\omega t)(\hat{i})$$

$$\Rightarrow \qquad \vec{\tau} = \alpha \cdot \cos^2\left(\frac{\pi}{6}\right)\hat{i}$$

$$\Rightarrow \qquad \vec{\tau} = \frac{3\alpha}{4}\hat{i} \qquad\qquad \textbf{Ans. (C)}$$

Sol. 10 During fall a motional emf is induced in rod ($e = Bvl$) due to which a current flows in upper circuit and the direction of current in rod will be such that it experiences an upward magnetic force ($F = Bil$). During its fall the equation of motion of falling rod can be written as

$$mg - Bil = ma = \frac{mdv}{dt}$$

$$\Rightarrow \qquad mg - B\left(\frac{Bvl}{R}\right)l = \frac{mdv}{dt}$$

$$\Rightarrow \qquad \frac{mgR}{B^2l^2} - v = \frac{mR}{B^2l^2}\frac{dv}{dt}$$

$$\Rightarrow \qquad \frac{B^2l^2}{mR}\int_{t=0}^{t} dt = \int_{0}^{v} \frac{dv}{\left(\frac{mgR}{B^2l^2} - v\right)}$$

$$\Rightarrow \qquad \frac{B^2l^2 t}{mR} = -\ln\left(\frac{\frac{mgR}{B^2l^2} - v}{\frac{mgR}{B^2l^2}}\right) \qquad \ldots(1)$$

Numerical calculations of terms in above equation gives

$$\frac{mgR}{B^2l^2} = \frac{20 \times 10^{-3} \times 10 \times 10}{16 \times \frac{1}{16}} = 2$$

And $\qquad \dfrac{B^2l^2}{mR} = \dfrac{16 \times \frac{1}{16}}{20 \times 10^{-3} \times 10} = \dfrac{1}{0.2} = 5$

Thus from equation-(1), we have

$$-5t = \ln\left[\frac{2-v}{v}\right]$$

$$\Rightarrow \qquad v = 2(1 - e^{-5t}) \qquad \ldots(2)$$

At $t = 0.2$ s, we have

$$v = 2(1 - e^{-5 \times 0.2})$$

$$\Rightarrow \qquad v = 2(1 - 0.4) = 1.2 \text{ m/s}$$

(P) Now at $t = 0.2$ s

The magnitude of the induced emf is calculated as

$$e = Bvl = 4 \times 1.2 \times \frac{1}{4} = 1.2 \text{ V}$$

Hence option (3) is correct.

(Q) At $t = 0.2$ s, the magnitude of magnetic force on rod is calculated as

$$F = Bil = B\left(\frac{Blv}{R}\right)l = \frac{B^2l^2 v}{R}$$

$$\Rightarrow \qquad F = \frac{4 \times 4 \times \frac{1}{4} \times 1.3 \times \frac{1}{4}}{10} = 0.12\,\text{N}$$

Hence option (4) is correct.

(R) At $t = 0.2$ s, the power dissipated as heat is calculated as

$$P = i^2 R = \frac{e^2}{R} = \frac{1.2 \times 1.2}{10} = 0.144\,\text{W}$$

Hence option (2) is correct.

(S) Terminal velocity is attained by rod when its weight is balanced by the magnetic force and its acceleration becomes zero. This is calculated as

$$mg = Bil$$

$$\Rightarrow \qquad mg = \frac{B^2 l^2 v_T}{R}$$

$$\Rightarrow \qquad v_T = \frac{mgR}{B^2 l^2} = \frac{20 \times 10^{-3} \times 10 \times 10}{16 \times \frac{1}{16}}$$

$$v_T = 2\,\text{m/s}$$

This can also be alternatively calculated by equation-(2) by using $t \to \infty$ in it. Hence option (5) is correct. **Ans. (D)**

Sol. 11 Let I be the current passing through the loop then magnetic field $B = \dfrac{\mu_0 I}{2a}$ passes through the loop due to current I.

Net flux through the loop ϕ is zero

$$\left(\frac{\mu_0 I}{2a} \right) \times pa^2 - \left(\frac{\mu_0 m}{2\pi r^3} \right) \times \pi a^2 = 0$$

$$I = \frac{ma}{\pi r^3} \qquad \dots (1)$$

$$\Rightarrow \qquad I \propto \frac{m}{r^3} \qquad \textbf{Ans. (A)}$$

Sol. 12 $\qquad W_{ext} = \displaystyle\int \vec{F}_{ext} \cdot \vec{dr} = \int_{\infty}^{r} -\frac{km_1 m_2}{r^4}\, dr = \frac{km_1 m_2}{3r^3}$

Magnetic moment of loop is given as

$$m_1 = I\pi a^2 = \frac{ma^3}{r^3}$$

Magnetic moment of loop is taken as $m_2 = m$

$$\Rightarrow \qquad W_{ext} = \frac{km^2 a^3}{3r^6} \propto \frac{m^2}{r^6} \qquad \textbf{Ans. (C)}$$

Sol. 13 As velocity of wire PQ is constant so emf developed across it will also remains constant. If length of wire is l then emf induced is given as

$$\varepsilon = Blv$$

Induced current at any time t is given as

$$i = \frac{\varepsilon}{R}\left(1 - e^{-\frac{Rt}{L}} \right)$$

$$\Rightarrow \qquad i = \frac{Blv}{R}\left(1 - e^{-\frac{Rt}{L}} \right)$$

$$\Rightarrow \qquad i = 1 \times \left(\frac{10}{100} \right) \times \left(\frac{1}{100} \right) \times \frac{1}{1}\left(1 - e^{\frac{-1 \times 10^{-3}}{1 \times 10^{-3}}} \right)\text{A}$$

$$\Rightarrow \qquad i = \frac{1}{1000} \times (1 - e^{-1})\,\text{A}$$

$$\Rightarrow \qquad i = \frac{1}{1000} \times (1 - 0.37)\,\text{A}$$

$$\Rightarrow \qquad i = 0.63 \times 10^{-3}\,\text{A}$$

$$\Rightarrow \qquad x = 0.63 \qquad \textbf{Ans. (0.63)}$$

Sol. 14 In this case, due to mutual inductance the flux is produced in same direction as self inductance. The energy stored in system is given as

$$U = \frac{1}{2}L_1 I_1^2 + \frac{1}{2}L_2 I_2^2 + M I_1 I_2$$

$$\Rightarrow \qquad U = \frac{1}{2} \times (10 \times 10^{-3})\,1^2 + \frac{1}{2} \times (20 \times 10^{-3}) \times 2^2$$

$$+ (5 \times 10^{-3}) \times 1 \times 2$$

$$\Rightarrow \qquad U = 55\,\text{mJ} \qquad \textbf{Ans. (55)}$$

Sol. 15 EMF induced in circuit is given as

$$e = \left| \frac{AdB}{dt} \right| = \beta = 0.04\,\text{V}$$

Maximum current in circuit will flow when potential difference across inductor will be zero and it happens when capacitor charge will be at its mean position of oscillations which is $C\beta$ in this case because it is oscillating between 0 to 2 $C\beta$. Thus at this instant using energy conservation in the given circuit, we have

$$(C\beta)\beta = \frac{1}{2}C\beta^2 + \frac{1}{2}L I_m^2$$

$$\Rightarrow \qquad \frac{1}{2}L I_m^2 = \frac{1}{2}C\beta^2$$

$$\Rightarrow \qquad 0.1 \times I_m^2 = 0.001 \times (0.4)^2$$

$$\Rightarrow \qquad I_0 = \sqrt{\frac{10^{-3}}{0.1}} \times 0.04 = 0.004 = 4\,\text{mA} \quad \textbf{Ans. (4)}$$

Sol. 16 Considering magnetic induction due to wire at upper and lower end of the loop as B_2 and B_1 respectively, the induced emf in the loop for the figure shown below is given as

$$e = (B_1 - B_2)bv_y$$

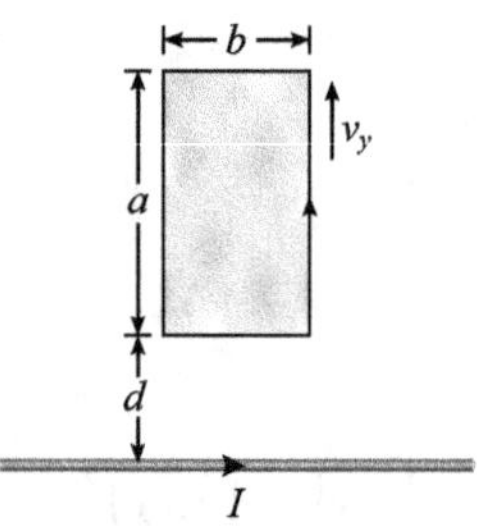

This is because the velocity component along the wire does not cause any emf induction in the loop. The induced current in loop is given as

$$i = \frac{e}{R} = \frac{\mu_0 I}{2\pi R}\left(\frac{1}{d} - \frac{1}{d+a}\right) b v_y$$

$$\Rightarrow \quad 10^{-5} = \frac{2\times 10^{-7} \times 10}{0.1}\left[\frac{1}{4} - \frac{1}{8}\right] \times 2.v_y$$

$$\Rightarrow \quad v_y = 2 \text{ m/s}$$

For the net velocity angle θ of the loop, we use

$$\tan\theta = \frac{v_y}{v_x} = \frac{1}{\sqrt{3}}$$

$$\Rightarrow \quad v_x = 2\sqrt{3} \text{ m/s}$$

Thus net velocity of the loop is given as

$$v = \sqrt{v_x^2 + v_y^2} = 4 \text{ m/s} \qquad \textbf{Ans. (4)}$$

Ch-17 Alternating Current

Sol. 1 Figure below shows the circuit described in the question.

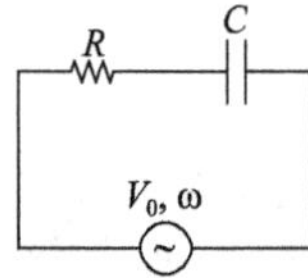

Impedance of series RC circuit is given as

$$Z = \sqrt{R^2 + \left(\frac{1}{\omega C}\right)^2}$$

As ω is increased Z is decreased due to which current in circuit increases so bulb will glow brighter. **Ans. (B)**

Sol. 2 As the phasor resultant of all three SHMs is zero, below figure shows the phasor diagram of the three SHMs.

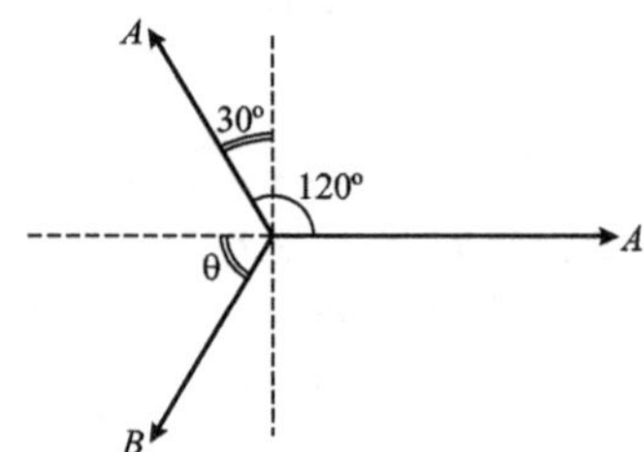

Here $\phi = \pi + \theta$ and for zero resultant, we use

$$B \sin\theta = A\cos 30^\circ = \frac{\sqrt{3}A}{2} \qquad \dots(1)$$

and $\quad A\sin 30^\circ + B\cos\theta = A$

$$\Rightarrow \quad B\cos\theta = \frac{A}{2} \qquad \dots(2)$$

Solving equations-(1) and (2) gives

$$B = A \quad \text{and} \quad \theta = 60^\circ = \frac{\pi}{3}$$

$$\Rightarrow \quad \phi = 240^\circ = \frac{4\pi}{3} \qquad \textbf{Ans. (B)}$$

Sol. 3 Impedance in cases (A) and (B) are given as

$$Z_1 = \sqrt{R^2 + \left(\frac{1}{\omega C}\right)^2}$$

and

$$Z_2 = \sqrt{R^2 + \left(\frac{1}{4\omega C}\right)^2}$$

As $Z_1 > Z_2 \quad \Rightarrow \quad I_R^A < I_R^B$

Hence option (B) is correct.

Circuit current is given as

$$I = \frac{V}{Z} = \frac{V_C}{\left(\frac{1}{\omega C}\right)}$$

$$\Rightarrow \quad V_C^A = \frac{I_K^A}{\omega C}$$

and

$$V_C^B = \frac{I_K^B}{4\omega C}$$

$$\Rightarrow \quad V_C^B < V_C^A$$

Hence option (C) is correct. **Ans. (B, C)**

Sol. 4 In above circuit, Capacitive reactance is given as

$$X_C = \frac{1}{\omega C} = \frac{1}{(100)(100\times 10^{-6})} \frac{1}{\omega C} = \frac{1}{(100)(100\times 10^{-6})} 100 \,\Omega$$

Inductive reactance is given as

$$X_L = \omega L = (100)(.5) = 50 \,\Omega$$

Impedance of the two branches of circuit is calculated as

$$Z_1 = \sqrt{X_C^2 + 100^2} = 100\sqrt{2}\,\Omega$$

$$Z_2 = \sqrt{X_L^2 + 50^2} = \sqrt{50^2 + 50^2} = 50\sqrt{2}\,\Omega$$

The time function of applied emf is given as

$$\varepsilon = 20\sqrt{2}\sin\omega t$$

Current in the two branches of circuit is given as

$$i_1 = \frac{20\sqrt{2}}{100\sqrt{2}} \sin(\omega t + \pi/4) = \frac{1}{5}\sin(\omega t + \pi/4)$$

$$i_2 = \frac{20\sqrt{2}}{50\sqrt{2}} \sin(\omega t - \pi/4) = \frac{2}{5}\sin(\omega t - \pi/4)$$

Total peak current through emf is calculated from the phasor diagram shown below

$$i = \sqrt{(.2)^2 + (.4)^2}$$

$$\Rightarrow \qquad i = (.2)\sqrt{1+4}$$

$$\Rightarrow \qquad i = \frac{1}{5}\sqrt{5} = \frac{1}{\sqrt{5}}\,A$$

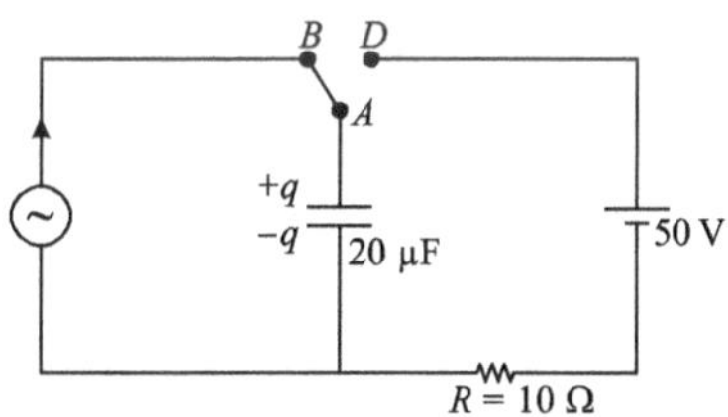

$$\Rightarrow \qquad i_{rms} = \frac{1}{\sqrt{2}\sqrt{5}} = \frac{1}{\sqrt{10}} = \frac{\sqrt{10}}{10} \approx 0.3\,A$$

$$\Rightarrow \qquad V_{100\Omega} = i_{1rms} \times 100$$

$$\Rightarrow \qquad V_{100\Omega} = \left(\frac{0.2}{\sqrt{2}}\right) \times 100 = \frac{20}{\sqrt{2}} = 10\sqrt{2}\,V$$

$$V_{50\Omega} = \left(\frac{0.4}{\sqrt{2}}\right) \times 50 = \frac{20}{\sqrt{2}} = 10\sqrt{2}\,V \qquad \textbf{Ans. (A, C)}$$

Sol. 5 Alternating current through circuit is given as

$$I = I_0 \cos \omega t$$

$$\Rightarrow \qquad I = \frac{dq}{dt} = I_0 \cos \omega t$$

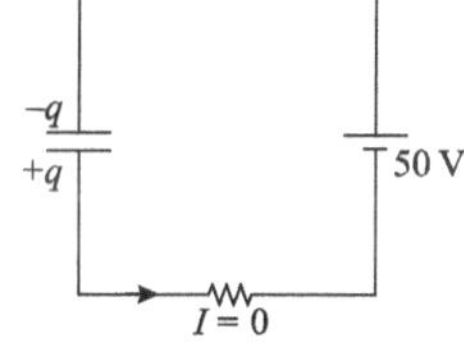

Charge on capacitor at time t is given as

$$\int_0^q dq = I_0 \int_0^t \cos \omega t\, dt$$

$$\Rightarrow \qquad q = \frac{I_0}{\omega} \sin \omega t$$

$$\Rightarrow \qquad q_{max} = \frac{I_0}{\omega} = \frac{1}{500} = 2 \times 10^{-3}\,C$$

Hence option (A) is NOT correct.

At $t = \dfrac{7\pi}{6\omega}$, charge is calculated as

$$\Rightarrow \qquad q = \frac{I_0}{\omega}\sin\left(\frac{7\pi}{6\omega} \cdot \omega\right)$$

$$\Rightarrow \qquad q = \frac{1}{500}\sin\left[\pi + \frac{\pi}{6}\right] = -\frac{1}{1000} = -10^{-3}$$

$$\Rightarrow \qquad q = -10^{-3}\,C$$

Thus upper plate of capacitor at this instant carries a negative charge

At $t = \dfrac{7\pi}{6\omega}$, current is given as

$$I = I_0 \cos\left(\frac{7\pi}{6\omega} \cdot \omega\right) = \cos\left(\pi + \frac{\pi}{6}\right) = -\frac{\sqrt{3}}{2}\,A$$

Negative sign indicates that current is anticlockwise. Hence option (B) is NOT correct.

Just after switch is shifted, current in circuit is given by KVL equation as

$$50 + \frac{10^{-3}}{20 \times 10^{-6}} - 10I = 0$$

$$\Rightarrow \qquad 50 + \frac{10^3}{20} = 10I$$

$$\Rightarrow \qquad 10I = 50 + 50 = 100$$

$$\Rightarrow \qquad I = 10\,A$$

Hence option (C) is correct.

Final charge on capacitor in steady state is given as

$$q = 20 \times 50 \times 10^{-6}$$

$$\Rightarrow \qquad q = 10^{-3}\,C$$

Now in steady state upper plate of capacitor carries a positive charge. Hence charge flown through battery is given as

$$\Delta q = 2 \times 10^{-3}\,C \qquad \textbf{Ans. (C, D)}$$

Sol. 6 For i and v in same phase, we have

$$iX_C = iX_L$$

$$\Rightarrow \qquad i \times \frac{1}{\omega C} = i\omega L$$

$$\Rightarrow \qquad \omega = \frac{1}{\sqrt{LC}} = 10^6\,\text{rad/s}$$

Hence option (A) is correct and option (D) is NOT correct.

At $\omega = 0$, capacitive reactance becomes $X_C = \dfrac{1}{\omega C} = \infty$ thus circuit current becomes zero hence option (B) is correct. At $\omega > \omega_0$ circuit impedance will become inductive hence option (C) is NOT correct. \qquad \textbf{Ans. (A, B)}

Sol. 7 For the given circuit as inductors are in parallel, we use

$$L_1 I_1 = L_2 I_2$$

$$\Rightarrow \quad \frac{I_1}{I_2} = \frac{L_2}{L_1}$$

Hence option (A) is correct.

Equivalent inductance of the two inductors in parallel is taken as

$$L_{eq} = \frac{L_1 L_2}{L_1 + L_2}$$

Current flowing through R-L circuit during growth is written as

$$I = \frac{V}{R}\left(1 - e^{-\frac{tR}{L_{eq}}}\right)$$

At $t = 0$ inductors behave like open circuits hence initial current in circuit is zero hence option (D) is NOT correct.

After a long time when $t \to \infty$ circuit current is given as

$$I = \frac{V}{R}$$

Circuit current can be written as sum of the current through two inductors, given as

$$I = I_1 + I_2$$

$$\Rightarrow \quad I = \left(1 + \frac{L_1}{L_2}\right) I_1$$

$$\Rightarrow \quad I_1 = \frac{L_2 I}{L_1 + L_2} = \frac{V}{R}\frac{L_2}{L_1 + L_2}$$

and $\quad I_2 = \frac{I_1 L_1}{L_2} = \frac{V}{R}\frac{L_2}{L_1 + L_2} \times \frac{L_1}{L_2}$

$$\Rightarrow \quad I_2 = \frac{V}{R}\frac{L_1}{L_1 + L_2} \qquad \textbf{Ans. (A, B, C)}$$

Sol. 8 Given voltages are drawn in phasor diagram as shown below

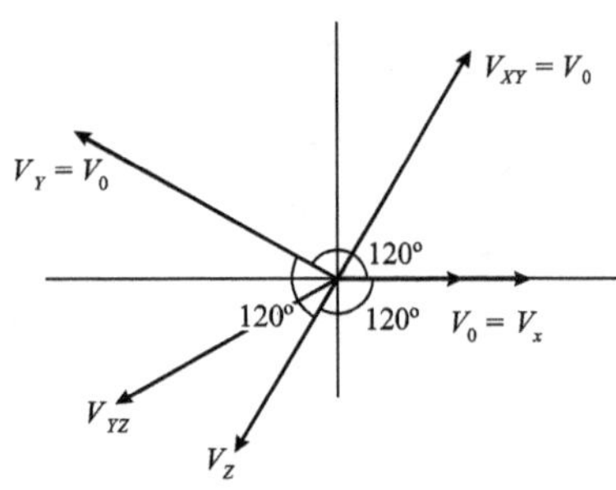

Potential difference between X and Y is calculated as

$$V_{XY} = V_X - V_Y = V_0 \sin \omega t - V_0 \sin\left(\omega t + \frac{2\pi}{3}\right)$$

$$V_{XY} = V_0 \left[2 \cos\left(\omega t + \frac{2\pi}{3}\right) \sin\left(-\frac{\pi}{3}\right)\right]$$

$$V_{XY} = \sqrt{3}\, V_0 \cos\left(\omega t + \frac{\pi}{3}\right)$$

$$V_{XY}^{\text{rms}} = \sqrt{3}\,\frac{V_0}{\sqrt{2}} = V_0 \sqrt{\frac{3}{2}}$$

Hence option (D) is correct. As all the voltages have same peak values and phasors are at $120°$ angle difference of potential between any two terminals will remain same hence option (C) is correct. Hence options (A) and (B) are NOT correct.

$$\textbf{Ans. (C, D)}$$

Sol. 9 Here currents in the two parts of circuits are taken as shown in figure below.

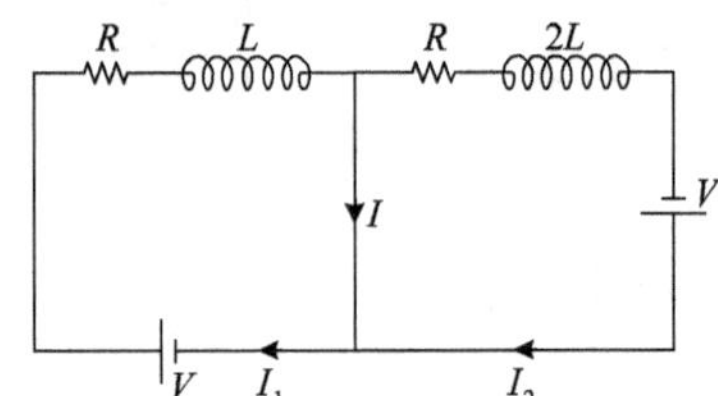

By KCL, we have

$$I = I_1 - I_2$$

$$\Rightarrow \quad I = \frac{V}{R}\left[1 - e^{\frac{-Rt}{2L}}\right] - \frac{V}{R}\left[1 - e^{\frac{-Rt}{L}}\right]$$

$$\Rightarrow \quad I = \frac{V}{R}\left[e^{\frac{-Rt}{L}} - e^{\frac{-Rt}{2L}}\right]$$

For I to be maximum, we use $\frac{dI}{dt} = 0$

$$\Rightarrow \quad \frac{V}{R}\left[\frac{-R}{L}e^{\frac{-Rt}{L}} - \left(\frac{-R}{2L}\right)e^{\frac{-Rt}{2L}}\right] = 0$$

$$\Rightarrow \quad e^{\frac{-Rt}{2L}} = \frac{1}{2}$$

$$\Rightarrow \quad \left(\frac{-R}{2L}\right) t = \ln 2$$

$$\Rightarrow \quad t = \frac{2L}{R} \ln 2$$

Hence option (D) is correct. This is the time when I is maximum thus maximum current is calculated as

$$I_{\text{max}} = \frac{V}{R}\left[e^{\frac{-R}{R}\left(\frac{2L}{R}\ln 2\right)} - e^{\frac{-R}{2L}\left(\frac{2L}{R}\ln 2\right)}\right]$$

$$\Rightarrow \quad I_{\text{max}} = \frac{V}{R}\left[\frac{1}{4} - \frac{1}{2}\right]$$

$$\Rightarrow \quad I_{\text{max}} = \frac{V}{4R}$$

Hence option (B) is correct. $\qquad \textbf{Ans. (B, D)}$

Sol. 10 For (p) in steady state when current becomes constant, we have

$$V_1 = 0 \text{ and } V_2 = V$$

Hence option (C) is correctly related.

For (q) in steady state when current becomes constant, we have

$$V_1 = 0 \text{ and } V_2 = V$$

Hence option (C) is correctly related and V_2 is proportional to I, options (B) and (D) are correctly related

For (r) inductive reactance is given as

$$X_L = \omega L = (100\,\pi)\,6 \times 10^{-3} = 1.88\,\Omega$$

$$R = 2\,\Omega$$

$$\Rightarrow \qquad V_2 > V_1$$

Hence options (A), (B) and (D) are correctly related

For (s) inductive reactance is same as calculated above and capacitive reactance is calculated as

$$X_C = \frac{1}{\omega C} = 1061\,\Omega$$

Here we have $V_1 \propto I$; $V_2 \propto I, I \neq 0$ and $V_2 > V_1$

Hence options (A), (B) and (D) are correctly related

For (t) capacitive reactance is same as calculated above and resistance value is $R = 1000\,\Omega$

$$\Rightarrow \qquad V_2 > V_1$$

Also we have $V_1, V_2 \propto I$ and $I \neq 0$

Hence options (A), (B) and (D) are correctly related

$$\textbf{Ans. [A}\,(r, s, t,);\,\textbf{B}\,(q, r, s, t);\,\textbf{C}\,(p, q);\,\textbf{D}\,(q, r, s, t)]$$

Sol. 11 For the given LCR circuit, the resonant frequency is given as

$$\omega_0 = 10^5 \text{ rad/s} = \frac{1}{\sqrt{LC}}$$

$$\Rightarrow \qquad C = \frac{1}{L\omega_0^2} = \frac{1}{5 \times 10^{-2} \times 10^{10}} = 2 \times 10^{-9}\,\text{F}$$

Current amplitude in circuit at resonance is given as

$$I_0 = \frac{45}{R}$$

At angular frequency $\omega = 8 \times 10^4$ rad/s $= 0.8\,\omega_0$ current amplitude changes to

$$I = 0.05\,I_0 = \frac{I_0}{20}$$

Thus $Z = 20R$ at this ω so inductive reactance at this frequency is calculated as

$$X_L = 8 \times 10^4 \times 5 \times 10^{-2}\,\Omega = 4\,\text{k}\Omega$$

Capacitive reactance at this angular frequency is calculated as

$$X_C = \frac{1}{8 \times 10^4 \times 2 \times 10^{-9}} = \frac{1}{16} \times 10^5\,\Omega = \frac{25}{4}\,\text{k}\Omega$$

Circuit impedance at this frequency is calculated as

$$Z^2 = R^2 + (X_C - X_L)^2$$

$$\Rightarrow \qquad 400\,R^2 = R^2 + \left(\frac{9}{4}\,\text{k}\Omega\right)^2$$

$$\Rightarrow \qquad R = \frac{\frac{9}{4}\,\text{k}\Omega}{\sqrt{399}} \approx \frac{9}{80}\,\text{k}\Omega = \frac{900}{8}\,\Omega$$

Maximum current amplitude is calculated as

$$I_0 = \frac{V_0}{R} = \frac{45 \times 8}{900} = \frac{8}{20}\,\text{A} \approx 0.4\,\text{A} = 400\,\text{mA}$$

Hence for (P), option (C) is correct.
Quality factor of circuit is calculated as

$$Q = \frac{1}{R}\sqrt{\frac{L}{C}} = \frac{8}{900}\sqrt{\frac{5 \times 10^{-2}}{2 \times 10^{-9}}}$$

$$\Rightarrow \qquad Q = \frac{8}{900}\sqrt{25 \times 10^6} = \frac{8}{900} \times 5000 = 44.4$$

Hence for (Q), option (A) is correct.
Quality factor of circuit in terms of bandwidth is written as

$$Q = \frac{\omega_0}{\Delta\omega}$$

$$\Rightarrow \qquad \Delta\omega = \frac{\omega_0}{Q} = \frac{10^5}{44.4} = 2250 \text{ rad/s}$$

Hence for (R), option (D) is correct.
Peak power dissipated in circuit is calculated as

$$P_{\text{max}} = I_0^2 R = \frac{45^2}{R^2} \times R = \frac{45^2}{R}$$

$$\Rightarrow \qquad P_{\text{max}} = \frac{45^2}{900} \times 8 = 18.4\,\text{W}$$

Hence for (S), option (B) is correct. **Ans. (B)**

Sol. 12 In process 1, energy stored in the capacitor and heat dissipated can be given as

$$E_C = \frac{1}{2}CV_0^2$$

$$E_D = \frac{1}{2}CV_0^2 \qquad\qquad \textbf{Ans. (A)}$$

Sol. 13 Energy stored in capacitor is given as

$$E_C = \frac{1}{2}CV_0^2$$

Work done by battery in charging the capacitor is given as

$$W_{\text{by battery}} = \frac{CV_0}{3}\frac{V_0}{3} + \frac{CV_0}{3}\frac{2V_0}{3} + \frac{CV_0V_0}{3}$$

$$\Rightarrow \quad W_{\text{by battery}} = \frac{CV_0^2}{9}[1+2+3]$$

$$\Rightarrow \quad W_{\text{by battery}} = \frac{2}{3}CV_0^2$$

In process 2 energy dissipated across resistance is calculated as

$$H = \frac{2}{3}CV_0^2 - \frac{1}{2}CV_0^2 = \frac{1}{6}CV_0^2$$

$$\Rightarrow \quad H = \frac{1}{3}\left(\frac{1}{2}CV_0^2\right) \qquad \text{Ans. (A)}$$

Sol. 14 Figure below shows the circuit as described in question.

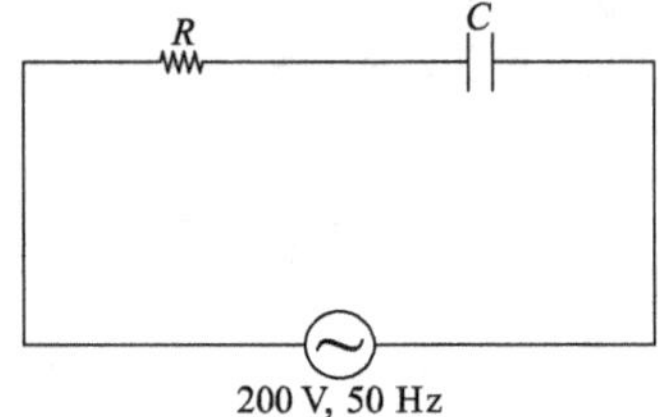

If circuit impedance is z, power consumed by lamp is given as

$$\left(\frac{200}{z}\right)^2 R = 500 \qquad \dots(1)$$

As the voltage drop across lamp is 100 V, we use

$$\left(\frac{200}{z}\right)R = 100 \qquad \dots(2)$$

$$\Rightarrow \quad \left(\frac{200}{z}\right)100 = 500$$

$$\Rightarrow \quad z = 40 \text{ and } R = 20$$

$$\Rightarrow \quad R^2 + X_C^2 = 1600$$

$$\Rightarrow \quad X_C = \sqrt{1200} = 20\sqrt{3}$$

$$\Rightarrow \quad \frac{1}{100\pi C} = 20\sqrt{3}$$

$$\Rightarrow \quad C = \frac{1}{2(\pi\sqrt{3})\times 1000} = 100 \ \mu\text{F} \qquad \text{Ans. (100)}$$

Sol. 15 Phase angle is given as

$$\tan\phi = \frac{X_C}{R} = \frac{20\sqrt{3}}{20} = \sqrt{3}$$

$$\Rightarrow \quad \phi = \frac{\pi}{3} = 60° \qquad \text{Ans. (60)}$$

Sol. 16 Impedance of circuit and time constant are given as

$$R^2 + \left(\frac{1}{500C}\right)^2 = Z^2$$

$$\Rightarrow \quad R^2 + \left(\frac{1}{500C}\right)^2 = R^2 \times 1.25$$

$$\Rightarrow \quad \left(\frac{1}{500C}\right)^2 = 0.25\,R^2$$

$$\Rightarrow \quad \frac{1}{500C} = 0.5R$$

$$\Rightarrow \quad \frac{1}{2500} = RC$$

$$\Rightarrow \quad \frac{1}{250} = RC$$

$$\Rightarrow \quad RC = 0.004\,\text{s} = 4\,\text{ms} \qquad \text{Ans. (4)}$$

Sol. 17 Circuit below shows the situation described in question. In steady state equivalent resistance of the circuit is given as

$$\frac{1}{R_{\text{eq}}} = \frac{1}{3} + \frac{1}{4} + \frac{1}{12} = \frac{4+3+1}{12}$$

$$R_{\text{eq}} = \frac{12}{8} = \frac{3}{2}\,\Omega$$

Maximum current through battery in steady state of circuit is given as

$$I_{\text{max}} = \frac{5\times 2}{3} = \frac{10}{3}\,\text{A}$$

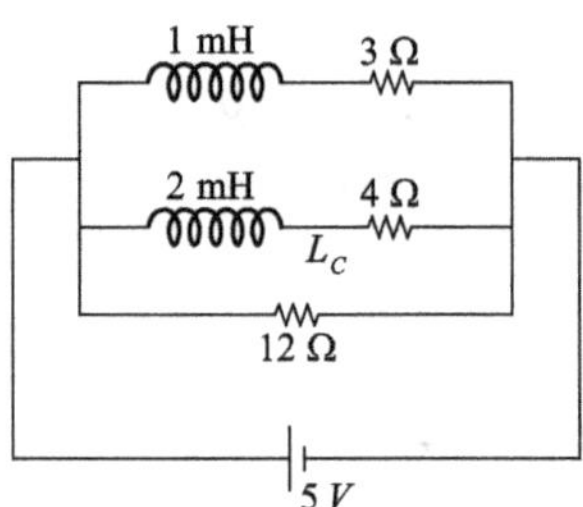

Minimum current in circuit will be at $t = 0$ when inductors behave as open circuit and it is given as

$$I_{\text{min}} = \frac{5}{12}\,\text{A}$$

$$\Rightarrow \quad \frac{I_{\text{max}}}{I_{\text{min}}} = \frac{10}{3} \times \frac{12}{5} = 8 \qquad \text{Ans. (8)}$$

Ch-18 Ray Optics and Optical Instruments

Sol. 1 Figure below shows the situation described in question.

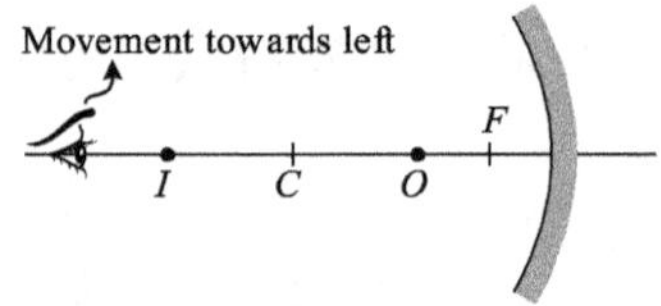

As shown in the figure, when the object O is placed between F and C, the image I is formed beyond C. It is in this condition that when the student shifts his eyes towards left, the image appears to the right of the object pin. **Ans. (B)**

Sol. 2 Figure below shows the situation described in question.

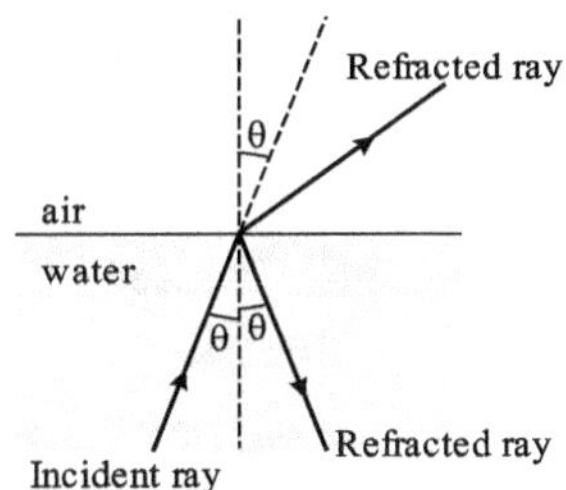

As $\theta < \theta_C$, both reflection and refraction will take place from figure angle between reflected and refracted ray will be $180° - 2\theta$.

Ans. (C)

Sol. 3 Figure below shows the situation described in question.

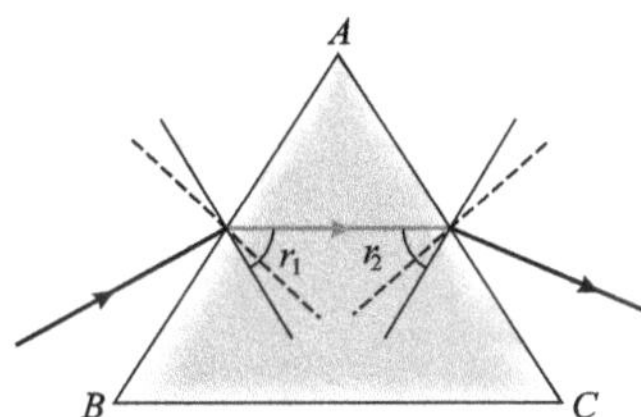

The angle of prism is given as
$$\angle A = 60°$$

For minimum deviation, for both colours we use
$$A = 2r$$

$$\Rightarrow \qquad r_1 = r_2 = \frac{A}{2} = 30°$$

Thus option (A) is correct. **Ans. (A)**

Sol. 4 If the angle of incidence between Region III and IV ϕ, then it should be at least critical angle of this interface, so we use

$$\frac{n_0}{6} \sin \phi = \frac{n_0}{8} \sin 90°$$

$$\Rightarrow \qquad \sin \phi = \frac{3}{4}$$

If the angle of incidence between Region II and III be α. Then by Snell's law we use

$$\frac{n_0}{2} \sin \alpha = \frac{n_0}{6} \sin \phi$$

$$\Rightarrow \qquad \sin \alpha = \frac{\sin \phi}{3}$$

As we have $n_0 \sin \theta = \dfrac{n_0}{2} \sin \alpha$

$$\Rightarrow \qquad \sin \theta = \frac{\sin \alpha}{2} = \frac{\sin \phi}{6} = \frac{1}{8}$$

$$\Rightarrow \qquad \theta = \sin^{-1}\left(\frac{1}{8}\right) \qquad \textbf{Ans. (B)}$$

Sol. 5 Figure below shows the situation described in question.

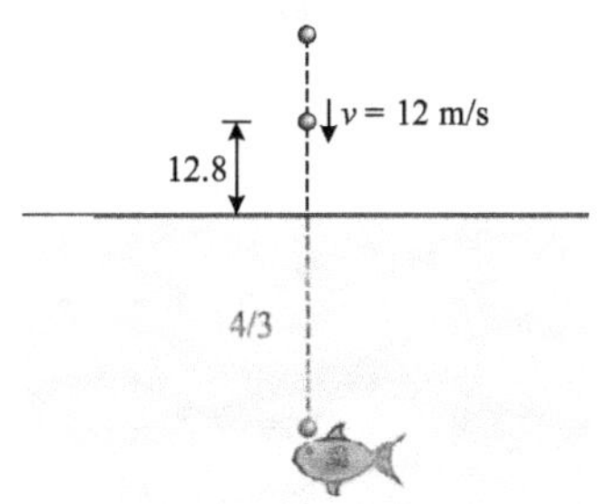

Velocity of ball when it is 12.8 above water surface is given as
$$v = \sqrt{2 \times 10 \times (20 - 12.8)} = 12 \text{ m/s}$$

Due to refraction at the water surface, we use
$$\frac{v}{\mu_2} = \frac{u}{\mu_1}$$

$$\Rightarrow \qquad \frac{dv}{dt} = \frac{\mu_2}{\mu_1} \cdot \frac{dv}{dt}$$

$$\Rightarrow \qquad \left|\frac{dv}{dt}\right| = \frac{4}{3} \times 12 = 16 \text{ m/s}$$

Thus option (C) is correct. **Ans. (C)**

Sol. 6 Figure below shows the situation described in question.

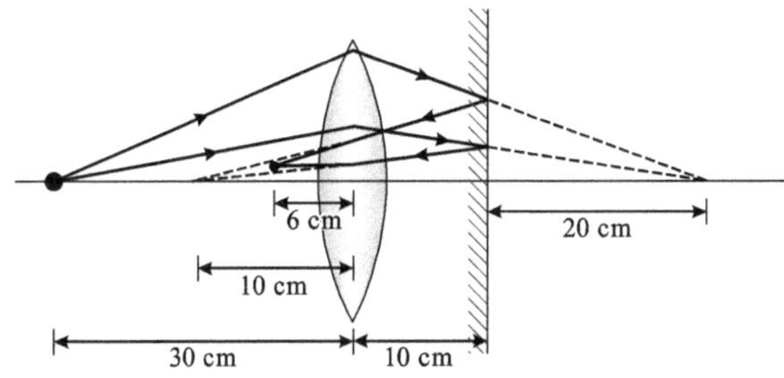

Here for refraction of reflected light by lens, we use
$$f = +15 \text{ cm}$$
$$u = +10 \text{ cm}$$

By lens formula, we get
$$\frac{1}{v} - \frac{1}{u} = \frac{1}{f}$$

$$\Rightarrow \quad \frac{1}{v} - \frac{1}{10} = \frac{1}{15}$$

$$\Rightarrow \quad v = +6\,cm$$

As refracted rays are converging thus final image is real.

Ans. (B)

Sol. 7 When $\theta > \theta_C$, no ray will transmit through medium, so for this case, we use

$$T = 0 \quad \text{and} \quad R = 100\%$$

and for $\theta < \theta_C$, $T + R = 100\%$ hence option (C) is correct.

Ans. (C)

Sol. 8 By lens maker formula for first lens, we have

$$\frac{1}{f_1} = (\mu - 1)\left[\frac{1}{R_1} - \frac{1}{R_2}\right]$$

$$\Rightarrow \quad \frac{1}{f_1} = (1.5 - 1)\left[\frac{1}{14} - \frac{1}{\infty}\right]$$

$$\frac{1}{f_1} = \frac{0.5}{14}$$

By lens maker formula for second lens, we have

$$\frac{1}{f_2} = (1.2 - 1)\left[\frac{1}{\infty} - \frac{1}{-14}\right]$$

$$\frac{1}{f_2} = \frac{0.2}{14}$$

Power of lens combination is given as

$$P = P_1 + P_2$$

$$\Rightarrow \quad \frac{1}{f} = \frac{1}{f_1} + \frac{1}{f_2}$$

$$\Rightarrow \quad \frac{1}{f} = \frac{0.5}{14} + \frac{0.2}{14}$$

$$\Rightarrow \quad \frac{1}{f} = \frac{0.7}{14}$$

Using lens formula.0 for combined lens, we have

$$\frac{1}{v} = \frac{7}{140} - \frac{1}{40}$$

$$\Rightarrow \quad \frac{1}{v} = \frac{1}{20} - \frac{1}{40} = \frac{1}{v} = \frac{2-1}{40}$$

$$\Rightarrow \quad v = 40\,cm$$

Ans. (B)

Sol. 9 Let angle between the directions of incident ray and reflected ray by θ, we use

$$\cos\theta = \frac{\vec{a} \cdot \vec{b}}{|\vec{a}||\vec{b}|}$$

$$\Rightarrow \quad \cos\theta = \frac{\frac{1}{2}(\hat{i} + \sqrt{3}\hat{j}) \cdot \frac{1}{2}(\hat{i} - \sqrt{3}\hat{j})}{1}$$

$$\Rightarrow \quad \cos\theta = -\frac{1}{2}$$

$$\Rightarrow \quad \theta = 120°$$

So angle of incidence

$$i = \frac{180 - 120}{2} = 30°$$

Ans. (A)

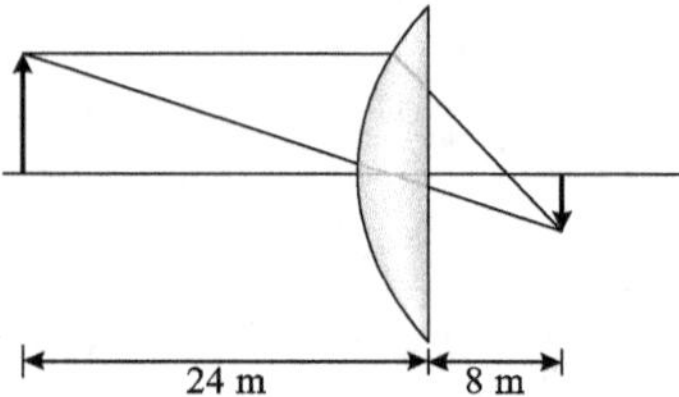

Sol. 10 Refractive index of lens is given as

$$\mu = \frac{\lambda_a}{\lambda_m} = \frac{3}{2}$$

Figure below shows the situation described in the question

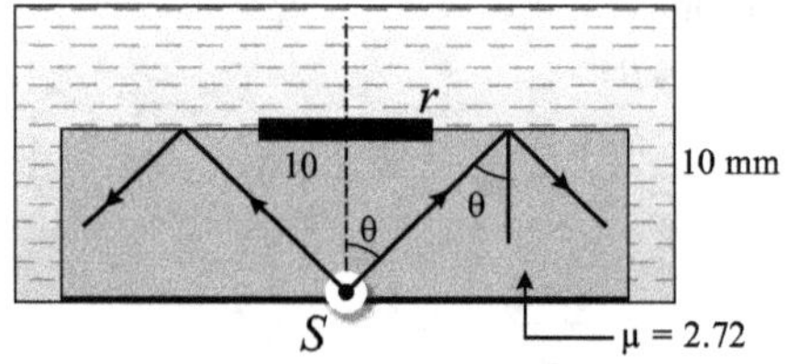

By lens maker formula for this lens, we have

$$\frac{1}{f} = \frac{1}{v} - \frac{1}{u} = (\mu - 1)\left[\frac{1}{R_1} - \frac{1}{R_2}\right]$$

As $R_1 = R$ and $R_2 = \infty$

$$\Rightarrow \quad \frac{1}{f} = \frac{\mu - 1}{R} = \frac{1}{2R}$$

By lens formula, we have

$$\frac{1}{f} = \frac{1}{v} - \frac{1}{u}$$

using $v = 8$ m, $u = -24$ m, we have

$$\Rightarrow \quad \frac{1}{8} - \frac{1}{-24} = \frac{1}{2R}$$

$$\Rightarrow \quad \frac{3+1}{24} = \frac{1}{2R}$$

$$\Rightarrow \quad R = 3\,m$$

Ans. (C)

Sol. 11 At the edges of spot and outside of it the light will be totally internally reflected as shown in figure below, so for total internal reflection if critical angle is θ_c, we use

$$\sin\theta_c = \frac{r}{\sqrt{r^2 + 10^2}}$$

Using $r = 5.77$, we have

$$\sin\theta_c = \frac{1}{2}$$

Using Snell's law we have

$$\sin\theta_c = \frac{\mu_1}{\mu_2} = \left(\frac{\mu_1}{2.72}\right) = \frac{1}{2}$$

$$\Rightarrow \qquad \sin\theta_c = \frac{\mu_1}{2.72}$$

$$\Rightarrow \qquad \mu_1 = \frac{2.72}{2} = 1.36 \qquad \textbf{Ans. (C)}$$

Sol. 12 By Snell's law at point A, as shown in figure below, we have

$$\sin\alpha = \sqrt{2}\sin r_1$$

At $\alpha = 45°$, $r_1 = 30°$, we have

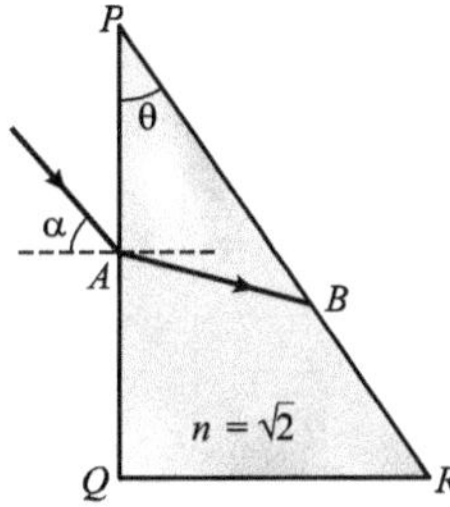

By shell's law of point B, we use

$$\Rightarrow \qquad \sqrt{2}\sin r_2 = 1\sin 90°$$

$$\Rightarrow \qquad r_2 = 45° = \theta + r_1$$

$$\Rightarrow \qquad \theta = 15° \qquad \textbf{Ans. (A)}$$

Sol. 13 If final image is formed at a distance x from the lens to its right as shown in figure below and it is between the lens and mirror then for lens formula, we use

$$u = -50 \text{ cm and } f = +30 \text{ cm}$$

By lens formula, we have

$$\frac{1}{f} = \frac{1}{v} - \frac{1}{u}$$

$$\Rightarrow \qquad v = \frac{fu}{f+u}$$

$$\Rightarrow \qquad v = \frac{(30)(-50)}{-50+30} = +75 \text{ cm}$$

This image will act as an object for mirror so the image must lie

on reflected ray from pole. Thus for mirror formula we use

$$u = -25 \text{ cm and } f = +50 \text{ cm}$$

By mirror formula, we have

$$\frac{1}{f} = \frac{1}{v} + \frac{1}{u}$$

$$\Rightarrow \qquad \frac{1}{50} = \frac{1}{v} - \frac{1}{25}$$

$$\Rightarrow \qquad v = -50 \text{ cm}$$

Thus distance of I_2 from pole of mirror is 50 cm. Hence coordinates of the image are given as

$$x = 50 - 50\cos 60° = 25 \text{ cm}$$

$$y = 50\sin 60° = 25\sqrt{3} \text{ cm}$$

Hence option (A) is correct. $\qquad \textbf{Ans. (A)}$

Sol. 14 For first lens L_1, using lens makers formula, we have

$$\frac{1}{f_1} = (\mu - 1)\left(\frac{1}{R_1} - \frac{1}{R_2}\right) = \left(\frac{3}{2}-1\right)\left(\frac{1}{20}+\frac{1}{20}\right) = \frac{1}{20}$$

For second lens L_2, using lens makers formula, we have

$$\frac{1}{f_2} = \left(\frac{3}{2}-1\right)\left(-\frac{1}{20}-\frac{1}{20}\right) = -\frac{1}{20}$$

Using lens formula for first lens, we have

$$\frac{1}{v_1} - \frac{1}{u_1} = \frac{1}{f_1}$$

$$\Rightarrow \qquad \frac{1}{v_1} + \frac{1}{10} = \frac{1}{20}$$

$$v_1 = -20 \text{ cm}$$

$$m_1 = \left(\frac{v_1}{u_1}\right) = \left(\frac{-20}{-10}\right) = 2$$

Using lens formula for second lens, we have

$$\frac{1}{v_2} - \frac{1}{u_2} = \frac{1}{f_2}$$

$$\Rightarrow \qquad \frac{1}{v_2} + \frac{1}{30} = -\frac{1}{20}$$

$$\Rightarrow \qquad \frac{1}{v_2} = -\frac{1}{30} - \frac{1}{20}$$

$$\Rightarrow \qquad \frac{1}{v_2} = -\frac{5}{60} = -\frac{1}{12}$$

$$m_2 = \left(\frac{v_2}{u_2}\right) = \frac{-12}{-30} = \frac{2}{5}$$

Total magnification of lens system is given as

$$m = m_1 \times m_2$$

$$\Rightarrow \qquad m = 2 \times \frac{2}{5} = 0.8 \qquad \textbf{Ans. (B)}$$

Sol. 15 By mirror formula, we have

$$\frac{1}{v}+\frac{1}{u}=\frac{1}{f}$$

The data set (66, 33) and (78, 39) does not satisfy the mirror formula. Hence options (C) and (D) are correct.   **Ans. (C, D)**

Sol. 16 Using Snell's law for refraction at first surface AB gives

$$\frac{\sin 60^\circ}{\sin r}=\frac{\sqrt{3}}{1}$$

$$\Rightarrow \qquad r=30^\circ$$

It hits at E on the face CD as shown in figure below and by geometry angles r_1 and r_2 are given as

$$r_1=45^\circ$$

and $\qquad r_2=45^\circ$

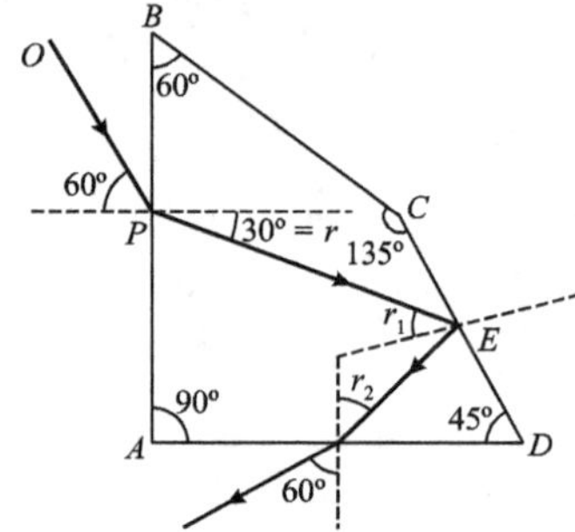

The critical angle for the interface is given as

$$\sin\theta_C=\frac{1}{\sqrt{3}}$$

Thus here $45^\circ > \sin^{-1}\dfrac{1}{\sqrt{3}}$ so total internal reflection occurs and light will incident on face AD at 30° as shown in figure. By Snell's law here we can state that light comes out making an angle 60° with the normal at AD.   **Ans. (A, B, C)**

Sol. 17 Here we will discuss the two cases, one for light incident from air to glass and other from glass to air.

Case - I : Air to Glass

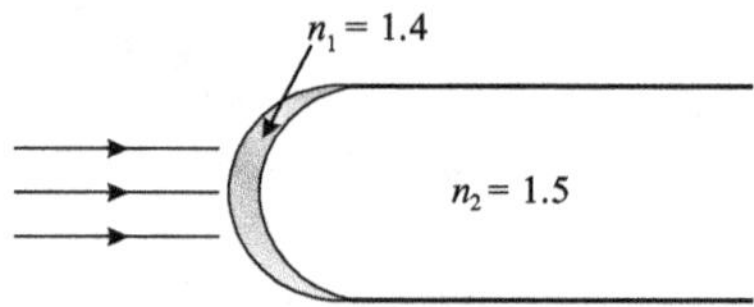

In this case for first refraction at curved surface, we use

$$\frac{\mu_2}{v}-\frac{\mu_1}{u}=\frac{\mu_2-\mu_1}{R}$$

$$\Rightarrow \quad \frac{1.4}{v}-\frac{1}{\infty}=\frac{1.4-1}{R}$$

$$\Rightarrow \qquad \frac{1.4}{v}=\frac{0.4}{R}$$

$$\Rightarrow \qquad v=\frac{14}{4}R=\frac{7}{2}R$$

For second refraction at curved surface, we use

$$\frac{1.5}{v}-\frac{1.4}{\dfrac{7R}{2}}=\frac{1.5-1.4}{R}$$

$$\Rightarrow \quad \frac{1.5}{v}-\frac{2.8}{7R}=\frac{0.1}{R}$$

$$\Rightarrow \qquad \frac{1.5}{v}=\frac{3.5}{7R}$$

$$\Rightarrow \qquad v=\frac{7\times1.5R}{3.5}=3R$$

$$\Rightarrow \qquad |f_1|=3R$$

Case-II : Glass to Air

In this case for first refraction at curved surface, we use

$$\frac{1.4}{v}-\frac{1.5}{\infty}=\frac{1.4-1.5}{R}$$

$$\Rightarrow \qquad \frac{1.4}{v}=\frac{-0.1}{R}$$

$$\Rightarrow \qquad v=-14R$$

For second refraction at curved surface, we use

$$\frac{1}{v}-\frac{1.4}{(-14R)}=\frac{1.14}{R}$$

$$\Rightarrow \qquad \frac{1}{v}=\frac{0.4}{R}-\frac{1.4}{14R}$$

$$\Rightarrow \qquad \frac{1}{v}=\frac{-0.4}{R}-\frac{1}{10R}$$

$$\Rightarrow \qquad \frac{1}{v}=\frac{-5}{10R}$$

$$\Rightarrow \qquad v=-2R$$

$$\Rightarrow \qquad |f_2|=2R \qquad\qquad\qquad \textbf{Ans. (A, C)}$$

Sol. 18 For refraction at curved surface of rod S_1, we use refraction formula as

$$\frac{\mu_2}{v}-\frac{\mu_1}{u}=\frac{\mu_2-\mu_1}{R}$$

$$\Rightarrow \quad \frac{1}{v}-\frac{3/2}{-50}=\frac{1-3/2}{-10}=\frac{1}{20}$$

$$\Rightarrow \qquad v=50\,\text{cm}$$

For refraction at curved surface of rod S_2, as light rays will become parallel to axis, we consider image is obtained at infinity.

$$\Rightarrow \quad \frac{3/2}{\infty}+\frac{1}{d-50}=\frac{3/2-1}{10}$$

$$\Rightarrow \qquad d=70\,\text{cm} \qquad\qquad\qquad \textbf{Ans. (B)}$$

Sol. 19 l is independent of n_2 because it depends on n_1 and $n(z)$. If emerging angle of light is θ_f then by Snell's law, we use

$$n_1 \sin \theta_i = n_2 \sin \theta_f$$

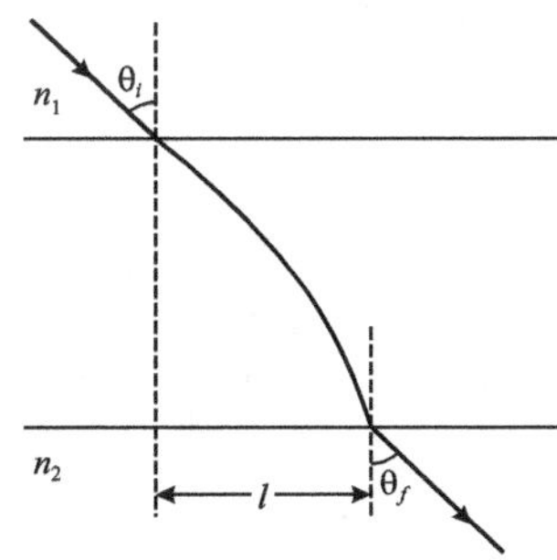

Ans. (A, B, D)

Sol. 20 Due to reflection from convex surface of lens, we use mirror formula as

$$\frac{1}{10} + \frac{1}{-30} = \frac{1}{R/2}$$

$$\Rightarrow \qquad R = 30 \text{ cm}$$

Due to refraction from lens, using magnification $m = 2$, we use lens formula as

$$\frac{1}{60} - \frac{1}{-30} = \frac{1}{f}$$

$$\Rightarrow \qquad f = 20 \text{ cm}$$

By lens maker formula, we have

$$\Rightarrow \qquad \frac{1}{f} = (n-1)\left(\frac{1}{30}\right)$$

$$\Rightarrow \qquad n = \frac{5}{2} \qquad\qquad \textbf{Ans. (A, D)}$$

Sol. 21 Minimum deviation occurs when

$$\angle i = \angle e$$

Minimum deviation angle is given as

$$\delta_{\min} = i + e - A$$

$$\Rightarrow \qquad \delta_{\min} = 2i - A$$

$$\Rightarrow \qquad i_1 = A$$

and $\qquad\qquad r_1 + r_2 = A$

$$\Rightarrow \qquad r_1 = \frac{A}{2} = \frac{i_1}{2}$$

By snell's law in the situation shown in figure below, we have

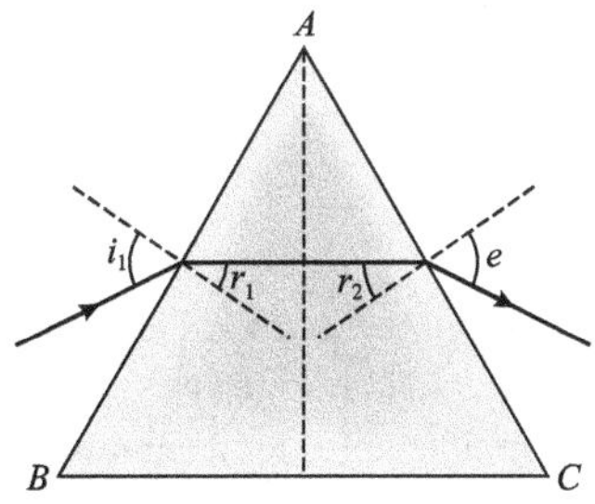

$$\sin i_1 = \mu \sin r_1$$

$$\Rightarrow \qquad \sin i_1 = \mu \sin \frac{A}{2}$$

$$\Rightarrow \qquad \sin A = \mu \sin \frac{A}{2}$$

$$\Rightarrow \qquad 2\sin \frac{A}{2} \cos \frac{A}{2} = \mu \sin \frac{A}{2}$$

$$\Rightarrow \qquad \cos \frac{A}{2} = \frac{\mu}{2}$$

$$\Rightarrow \qquad \frac{A}{2} = \cos^{-1}\left(\frac{\mu}{2}\right)$$

$$\Rightarrow \qquad A = 2\cos^{-1}\left(\frac{\mu}{2}\right) \qquad \textbf{Ans. (A, C, D)}$$

Sol. 22 The image of AB will be $A'B'$ as shown in the ray diagram below. Further the light ray along the inclined line after refection becomes parallel to the principal axis (Assuming paraxial rays reflection here) so the image of inclined wire will be horizontal of very large length hence option (D) is most appropriate.

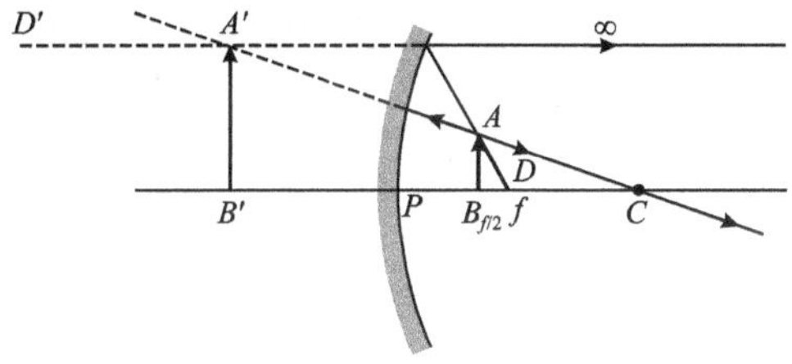

Ans. (D)

Sol. 23 When $n_1 = n_2 = n$ by lens maker formula, we use

$$\frac{1}{f} = (n-1) \times \frac{2}{R}$$

$$\Rightarrow \qquad f = \frac{R}{2(n-1)} \qquad\qquad \dots(1)$$

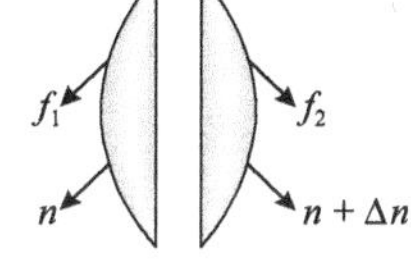

When refractive indices are n and $n + \Delta n$ the focal lengths of the two lenses are given as

$$\frac{1}{f_1} = \frac{n-1}{R}$$

and $\qquad \dfrac{1}{f_2} = \dfrac{(n+\Delta n)-1}{R}$

Focal length of the lens combination is given as

$$\frac{1}{f_{eq}} = \frac{1}{f + \Delta f} = \left(\frac{n-1}{R}\right) + \frac{(n+\Delta n)-1}{R} = \frac{2(n-1)+\Delta n}{R}$$

$$\Rightarrow \qquad \Delta f = \left(\frac{R}{2(n-1)+\Delta n}\right) - \left(\frac{R}{2(n-1)}\right)$$

$$\Rightarrow \qquad \Delta f = \frac{R}{2}\left[\frac{(n-1)-(n-1+\Delta n)}{(n-1+\Delta n)(n-1)}\right] = \frac{-\Delta n}{(n-1)^2} \times \frac{R}{2}$$

$$\Rightarrow \quad \frac{\Delta f}{f} = -\frac{\Delta n}{2(n-1)} \qquad \ldots(2)$$

Relation between $\dfrac{\Delta f}{f}$ and $\dfrac{\Delta n}{n}$ is independent of R hence option (A) is correct.

From above relation, we can see that

$$\frac{\Delta f}{f} > \left|\frac{\Delta n}{n}\right|$$

Hence option (B) is NOT correct.

From equation (2), we have

$$|\Delta f| = \frac{f\,\Delta n}{2(n-1)} = \frac{(20\times 10^{-3})}{2(1.5-1)} = 20\times 10^{-3} = 0.02$$

Hence option (C) is correct.

From equation (2), if $\dfrac{\Delta n}{n} < 0$ then $\dfrac{\Delta f}{f} > 0$ hence option (D) is

correct.   **Ans. (A, C, D)**

Sol. 24 Apparent depth in first case will be given as

$$H_1 = \frac{H}{n} = \frac{H}{(3/2)} = \frac{2H}{3} = \frac{2}{3}\times\frac{3}{10} = \frac{1}{5}\ \text{m}$$

For second case we use refraction at spherical surface which gives

$$\frac{n_2}{v} - \frac{n_1}{u} = \frac{n_2 - n_1}{R}$$

$$\Rightarrow \quad -\frac{1.5}{30} + \frac{1}{v} = \frac{1-1.5}{300}$$

$$\Rightarrow \quad \frac{1}{v} + \frac{3}{2H} = \frac{-1}{2(-3)}$$

$$\Rightarrow \quad \frac{1}{v} = \frac{1}{6} - \frac{10}{2} = \frac{1}{6} - \frac{30}{6} = \frac{-29}{6}$$

$$\Rightarrow \quad H_2 = \frac{6}{29}\ \text{m} > H_1$$

For third case we use refraction at spherical surface which gives

$$\frac{n_2}{v} - \frac{n_1}{u} = \frac{n_2 - n_1}{R}$$

$$\Rightarrow \quad \frac{-1.5}{-30} + \frac{1}{v} = \frac{1-1.5}{300}$$

$$\Rightarrow \quad \frac{1}{v} + \frac{3}{2H} = \frac{-1}{2(3)}$$

$$\Rightarrow \quad \frac{1}{v} = \frac{-1}{6} - 5 = \frac{-31}{6}$$

$$\Rightarrow \quad H_3 = \frac{6}{31}$$

$$\Rightarrow \quad H_3 < H_1 < H_2$$

$$(H_2 - H_1) = \frac{6}{29} - \frac{6}{31} = 0.68\ \text{cm} \qquad \textbf{Ans. (C, D)}$$

Sol. 25 Figure below shows the situation described in question.

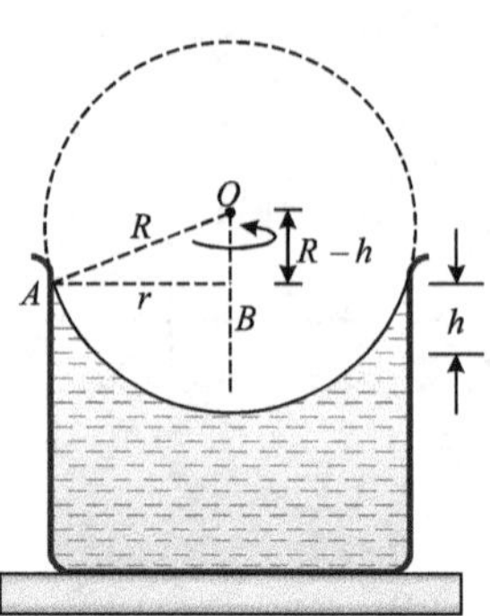

In ΔOAB, we have

$$R^2 = (R-h)^2 + r^2$$
$$R^2 = R^2 - 2hR + h^2 + r^2$$
$$\Rightarrow \quad 2hR = h^2 + r^2$$
$$\Rightarrow \quad R = \frac{h^2 + r^2}{2h}$$

Hence option (A) is correct.

Now considering equation of surface

$$y = y_0 + \frac{\omega^2 r^2}{2g}$$

$$\Rightarrow \quad h = \frac{\omega^2 r^2}{2g}$$

By refraction formula, we have

$$\frac{\mu_2}{v} - \frac{\mu_1}{u} = \frac{\mu_2 - \mu_1}{R}$$

$$\Rightarrow \quad \frac{1}{v} + \frac{4}{3(H-h)} = \frac{1-4/3}{-R}$$

$$\Rightarrow \quad \frac{1}{v} = \frac{1}{3R} - \frac{4}{3H}$$

$$\Rightarrow \quad \frac{1}{v} = \frac{2h}{3r^2} - \frac{4}{3H}$$

$$\Rightarrow \quad \frac{1}{v} = -\frac{4}{3H}\left[1 - \frac{\omega^2 H}{4g}\right]$$

$$\Rightarrow \quad v = \frac{3H}{4}\left[1 + \frac{\omega^2 H}{4g}\right]^{-1} \qquad \textbf{Ans. (A, D)}$$

Sol. 26 In this situation as $n_1\sin\theta > 1$ this means the angle of incidence of light ray at the interface of second media and air is more than angle of incidence so light cannot come out in air for any value of n_2 and it is reflected back into the medium of refractive index n_1. **Ans. (B, C, D)**

Sol. 27 By Snell's law at first surface, we have

$$\sin i_1 = \frac{3}{2}\sin 30°$$

$$\Rightarrow \quad \sin i_1 = \frac{3}{4}$$

$$\Rightarrow \quad \cos i_1 = \frac{\sqrt{7}}{4} = \cos i_2$$

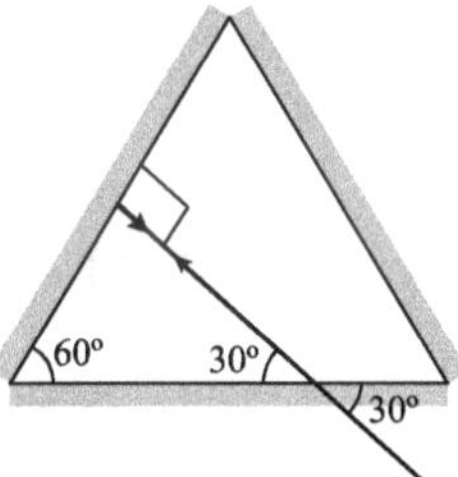

By Snell's law at second surface, we have

$$n_2 \sin r = 1\sin i_2$$

$$\Delta n \sin r = 1\,(\cos i_2)\,\Delta i_2$$

$$\Rightarrow \quad \Delta n\left(\frac{1}{2}\right) = \cos i_2\,\Delta i_2$$

$$\Rightarrow \quad \cos i_2 = \frac{1}{2}\frac{\Delta n}{\Delta i_2}$$

$$\Rightarrow \quad \Delta e \text{ or } \Delta i_2 = \frac{\Delta n\,4}{2\sqrt{7}} = \frac{2}{\sqrt{7}}\Delta n \qquad \textbf{Ans. (B, C)}$$

Sol. 28 Ray will come out after one reflection for $\theta = 30°$ & any value of l with $0 < l < L$ as shown in figure below as in this case light ray will normally incident on the mirror and retraces the path of incident ray.

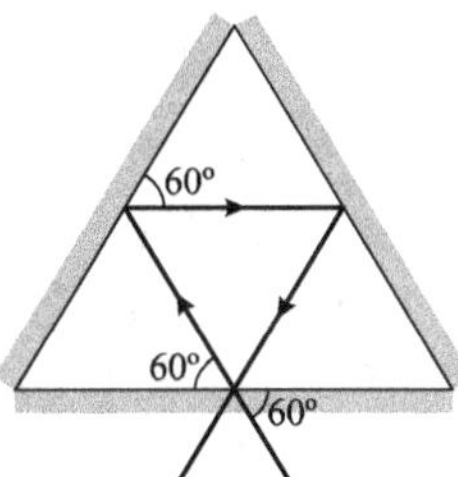

Hence option (A) is correct.

Light ray will come out after two reflections when $\theta = 60°$ & $l = \dfrac{L}{2}$ as shown in the ray diagram in figure below.

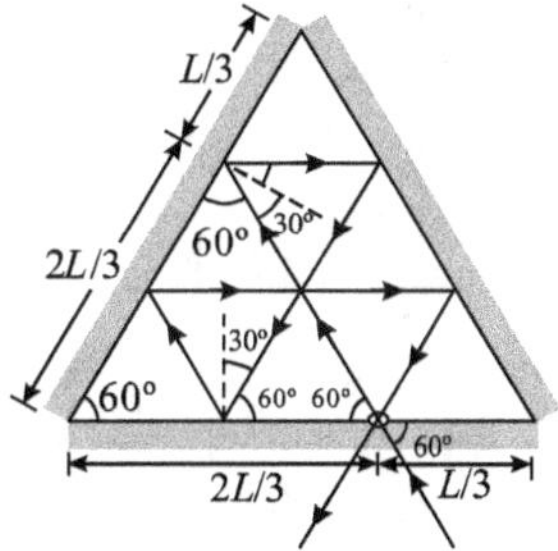

Hence option (B) is correct.

As shown in ray diagram in figure below, we can see that for value of $l = \dfrac{L}{3}$ & $\theta = 60°$ ray will come out after five reflections.

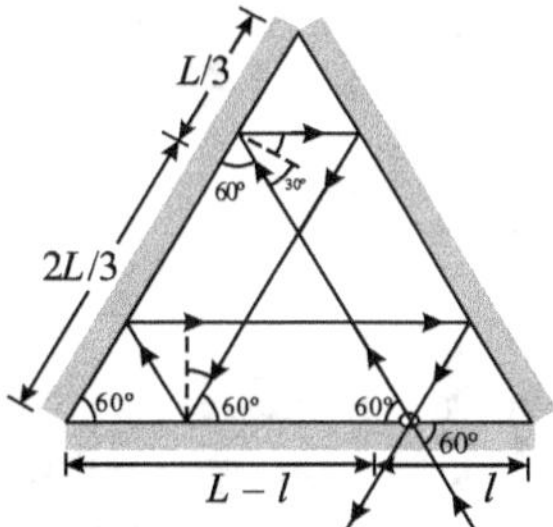

Hence option (C) is NOT correct.

As shown in ray diagram in figure below, we can see that for value of $\theta = 60°$ & $0 < l < \dfrac{L}{2}$, ray will come out after five reflections.

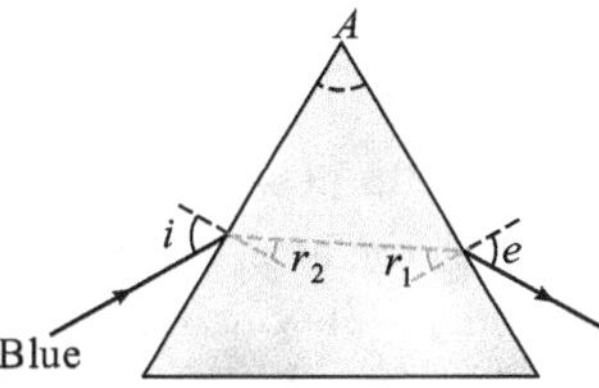

Hence option (D) is NOT correct. **Ans. (A, B)**

Sol. 29 For the given case it is specified that incident light is polarised and no reflection is taking place from the first surface of prism. This will happen only when the incident light is polarized in the plane of incidence and it is incident at Brewster's angle so no component is left to be reflected as at Brewster's angle. Hence option (A) is correct.

Figure below shows the incidence blue light getting refracted into the glass at refraction angle r_1.

For the polarised light to have no reflection from the surface it should incident at Brewster's angle so the angle of incidence of light is given as

$$\tan i = \mu_B = \sqrt{3}$$

$$\Rightarrow \quad i = 60°$$

Using Snell's law at this surface, we have

$$1\sin 60° = \sqrt{3}\sin r_1$$

$$\Rightarrow \quad r_1 = 30°$$

For the light refraction through a prism, we use

$$r_1 + r_2 = A$$

Angle of deviation is given as

$$\delta = (i + e) - A$$
$$\Rightarrow \qquad 60° = 60° + e - A$$
$$\Rightarrow \qquad e = A$$

Using Snell's law at the second surface, we have

$$\sqrt{3} \sin r_2 = 1 \sin e$$
$$\Rightarrow \qquad \sqrt{3} \sin (A - 30) = \sin A$$

Solving this equation gives

$$A = 60°$$
$$\Rightarrow \qquad e = 60°$$

Hence option (B) is NOT correct and option (D) is correct. For minimum deviation for red light, we use

$$\mu = \frac{\sin\left(\dfrac{A + \delta_{min}}{2}\right)}{\sin\dfrac{A}{2}}$$

$$\Rightarrow \qquad \mu = \sqrt{2}$$

Hence option (C) is correct.   **Ans. (A, C, D)**

Sol. 30 When light wave is incident on the glass slab, at the top where refractive index is n_2 speed of light is slow and at bottom where refractive index is less at n_1, the speed of light is higher means at bottom the light wave will cross the slab earlier compared to the light wave at the top. When the light wave at top crosses the slab by that time light wave at bottom would have travelled in air by some distance as shown in figure below. Thus the new wavefront of light wave when it completely comes out in air is shown here by the dotted line.

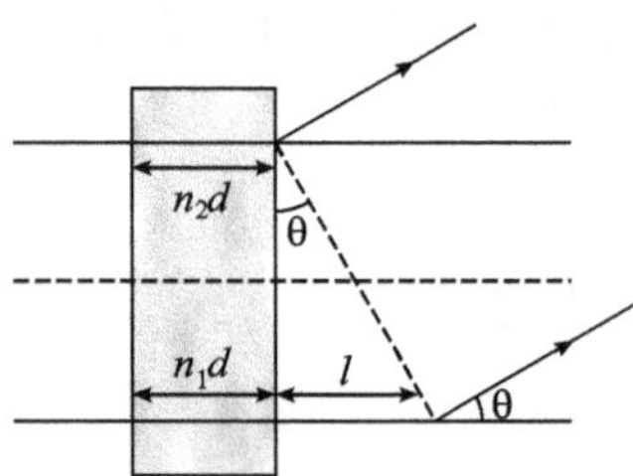

Light ray after coming out in air will be travelling normal to the plane of wavefront as shown at an angle θ. Actually light will continuously be bending while coming out from slab and this will be the final direction in which light will be travelling as complete wave has come out in air.

The optical path of upper and lower part of light will be same in same time duration until complete wave comes out in air, so we have

$$n_1 d + l = n_2 d$$

Angle θ is calculated as

$$\tan \theta = \frac{l}{h} = \frac{(n_2 - n_1)d}{h}$$

Alternative Solution:
We consider the bottom most light ray of the beam which incident

at a point on slab where refractive index is n_1. Here we consider this is incident in a grazing manner on an elemental slab at $y = 0$ as shown in figure below. In case of grazing incidence light bends toward the side of higher refractive index so before coming out of slab light continuously bend in upward direction as shown in figure below.

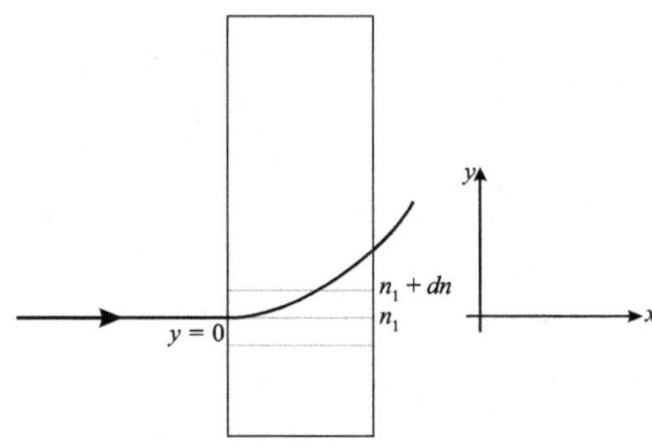

For the mathematical analysis for angle of deviation here we consider width of slab to be very small as well as angle of deviation also to be small. (This assumption is not given in question but to simplify mathematical analysis this is being taken here)

The refractive index is n_1 at $y = 0$ and it is n_2 at $y = h$. As the refractive index varies linearly from $y = 0$ to $y = h$ the refractive index at $y = y$ is given as

$$n = n_1 + \frac{(n_2 - n_1)}{h} y = n_1 (1 + \alpha y) \qquad \ldots (1)$$

Where

$$\alpha = \frac{n_2 - n_1}{n_1 h}$$

Let is consider two points in the path of light ray shown in figure below P at (x, y) and Q at (d, y_0)

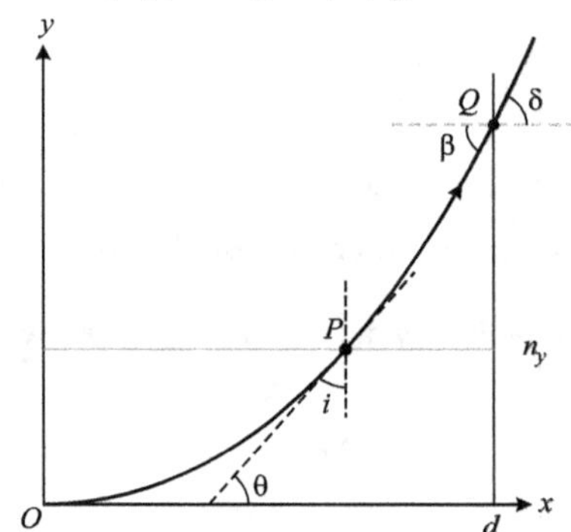

Let us calculate the trajectory equation of the light ray entering the slab at the point O $(0, 0)$. The angle of incidence at point O is 90° (grazing incidence) and at point P (x, y) is considered i. Using Snell's law at O and P gives

$$n \sin i = n_1$$

The slope of light trajectory at P is calculated as

$$\frac{dy}{dx} = \tan \theta = \cot i = \frac{\sqrt{1 - \sin^2 i}}{\sin i}$$

$$\frac{dy}{dx} = \sqrt{\left(\frac{n}{n_1}\right)^2 - 1} = \sqrt{(1+\alpha y)^2 - 1} \qquad \ldots(2)$$

Substituting $t = 1 + \alpha y$ gives

$$\frac{dt}{\sqrt{t^2 - 1}} = \alpha\, dx$$

Integrating in limits from $x = 0, y = 0$ to x, y gives

$$\left[\ln\left(t + \sqrt{t^2 - 1}\right)\right]_{y=0}^{y=y} = \left[\alpha x\right]_{x=0}^{x=x}$$

$$\Rightarrow \quad \ln\left(1 + \alpha y + \sqrt{(1+\alpha y)^2 - 1}\right) = \alpha x$$

$$\Rightarrow \qquad\qquad \sin h^{-1}(1 + \alpha y) = \alpha x \qquad \ldots(3)$$

This equation gives the trajectory of light ray through the slab in coordinate system shown in above figure. The ray exits the slab at Q so we use $x = d$ in equation-(2) with expansion of $\sinh(\alpha x)$ to calculate the y-coordinate of point Q, given as

$$1 + \alpha y_Q = \frac{e^{\alpha d} + e^{-\alpha d}}{2}$$

From equation-(2), at point Q, we use

$$\left.\frac{dy}{dx}\right|_{y_q} = \sqrt{(1+\alpha y)^2 - 1} = \frac{e^{\alpha d} - e^{-\alpha d}}{2}$$

At point Q using Snell's law for exit ray at horizontal normal gives

$$n_Q \sin \beta = \sin \delta$$

$$n_1(1 + \alpha y_Q) \sin \beta = \sin \delta \qquad \ldots(4)$$

Using Snell's law at point O and Q, we have

$$n_1 = n_1(1 + \alpha y_Q) \sin(90° - \beta)$$

$$\Rightarrow \qquad\qquad \cos \beta = \frac{1}{1 + \alpha y_Q} \qquad \ldots(5)$$

From equations-(4) and (5), we have

$$\left.\frac{dy}{dx}\right|_{y_q} = \tan \beta = \frac{\sin \delta}{n_1}$$

$$\Rightarrow \qquad \frac{e^{\alpha d} - e^{-\alpha d}}{2} = \frac{\sin \delta}{n_1}$$

Considering δ to be very small for small thickness of slab, we can use

$$\sin \delta \approx \tan \delta = n_1\left(\frac{e^{\alpha d} - e^{-\alpha d}}{2}\right)$$

$$\Rightarrow \qquad \tan \delta \approx n_1(\alpha d) = n_1\left(\frac{(n_2 - n_1)d}{n_1 h}\right)$$

$$\Rightarrow \qquad \delta = \tan^{-1}\left(\frac{(n_2 - n_1)d}{h}\right) \qquad \textbf{Ans. (B, D)}$$

Sol. 31 Assertion is correct as mirror formula is valid for paraxial rays. Thus Assertion is correct but Reason is false because laws of reflection is valid for all type of reflecting surfaces.

Ans. (C)

Sol. 32 Concave mirror and convex lenses can form real, as well as virtual images. When object at focus, image is produced at infinity and when object is placed between F and $2F$ image is produced is magnified. Thus for options (A), (C) and (D) all choices of column-II (p), (q), (r) and (s) are correctly relating. Convex mirror always forms virtual and diminished image for a real object hence only choice (q) is correctly related.

Ans. [A (p, q, r, s); B (q); C (p, q, r, s); D (p, q, r, s)]

Sol. 33 For case given in choice (p), $\mu_2 > \mu_1$ as light rays bend towards normal at first refraction and $\mu_2 = \mu_3$ as no refraction occurs at second surface hence it is correctly relating with option (A) and (C).

For case given in choice (q), $\mu_2 < \mu_1$ as light rays bend away from normal at first refraction and $\mu_3 < \mu_2$ as light bends away from normal at second surface hence it is correctly relating with option (B) and (D).

For case given in (r) $\mu_2 > \mu_1$ as light rays bend towards the normal at first refraction and $\mu_2 = \mu_3$ as no refraction occurs at second surface hence option (A) and (C) are correctly relating.

For case given in (s), $\mu_2 > \mu_1$ as light rays bend away from normal at first refraction and $\mu_3 < \mu_2$ as light rays bend away from normal at second surface hence options (B) and (D) are correctly matching.

For case given in (t), $\mu_2 > \mu_1$ as light rays bend away from normal at first refraction and $\mu_2 = \mu_3$ as no refraction occurs at second surface hence options (B) and (C) are correctly relating.

Ans. [A (p, r); B (q, s, t); C (p, r, t); D (q, s)]

Sol. 34 For light ray going from e to f $\mu_2 > \mu_1$ as light bends toward normal and $\mu_2 > \mu_3$ as at second refraction light bends away from normal hence option (2) is correctly related here.

For light ray going from e to g as light is not deviated, refractive index $\mu_1 = \mu_2$ hence option (3) is correctly related here.

For light ray going from e to h at first surface as light bends away from normal here $\mu_2 < \mu_1$ and at second surface light bends away from normal so $\mu_2 > \mu_3$ hence option (4) is correctly related here. Here as light is coming out from prism to block, we use by Snell's law

$$\mu_1 \times \frac{1}{\sqrt{2}} = \mu_2 \sin r$$

$$\Rightarrow \qquad \sin r = \frac{\mu_1}{\sqrt{2}\mu_2}$$

As $\sin r < 1 \Rightarrow \mu_1 < \sqrt{2}\mu_2$

For light ray going from e to i, it has to suffer total internal reflection at the inner surface of prism so $45°$ incidence angle has to be more than critical angle of prism. So by Snell's law, we use

$$\frac{1}{\sqrt{2}} > \frac{\mu_2}{\mu_1}$$

$$\Rightarrow \qquad \mu_1 > \sqrt{2}\,\mu_2$$

Hence option (1) is correctly related. **Ans. (D)**

Sol. 35 (P) : By lens maker formula, we have

$$\frac{1}{f} = (1.5 - 1)\left(\frac{1}{r} - \frac{1}{-r}\right)$$

$$\Rightarrow \qquad \frac{1}{f} = 0.5\left(\frac{2}{r}\right) = \frac{1}{r}$$

Combined focal length (f_{net}) for the two lenses is given as

$$\frac{1}{f_{net}} = \frac{1}{f} + \frac{1}{f} = \frac{2}{f} = \frac{2}{r}$$

$$f_{net} = \frac{r}{2}$$

(Q) : By lens maker formula, we have

$$\frac{1}{f} = (1.5 - 1)\left(\frac{1}{\infty} - \frac{1}{-R}\right)$$

$$\Rightarrow \qquad \frac{1}{f} = \frac{0.5}{R} = \frac{1}{2R}$$

For the combination of the two lenses, we use

$$\frac{1}{f_{net}} = \frac{1}{f} + \frac{1}{f} = \frac{2}{f} = \frac{1}{r}$$

$$f_{net} = r$$

(R) : By lens maker formula, we use

$$\frac{1}{f} = (1.5 - 1)\left(\frac{1}{\infty} - \frac{1}{r}\right) = \frac{-0.5}{r}$$

For the combination of the two lenses, we use

$$\Rightarrow \qquad \frac{1}{f_{net}} = \frac{1}{f} + \frac{1}{f} = \frac{2}{f} = \frac{-1}{r}$$

$$\Rightarrow \qquad f_{net} = -r$$

(S) : For the two given lenses, focal lengths are given as

$$\frac{1}{f_1} = \frac{1}{r}$$

$$\frac{1}{f_2} = \frac{-0.5}{r}$$

For the combination, we use

$$\frac{1}{f_{net}} = \frac{1}{f_1} + \frac{1}{f_2}$$

$$\Rightarrow \qquad \frac{1}{f_{net}} = \frac{1}{r} - \frac{0.5}{r} = \frac{1}{r}(0.5)$$

$$\Rightarrow \qquad f_{net} = \frac{r}{0.5} = 2r$$

Ans. (B)

Sol. 36 (I) : For convex lens as object is placed at $2F$, image will also be formed at $2F$ and this will act as a virtual object for plano convex lens with

$$u = +15\,cm$$

So by lens formula, image location is given as

$$v_2 = \frac{(15)(15)}{(15)+(15)} = +7.5\,cm$$

Hence option (P) is correctly related here.

(II) : In this case also we use lens formula for concave lens with

$$u = +15\,cm$$

$$\Rightarrow \qquad v_2 = \frac{(15)(-10)}{(15)+(-10)} = -30\,cm$$

Hence option (R) is correctly related here. At this point students can mark (A) as correct answer as in no other answer this combination exist.

(III) : In this case also we use lens formula for plano concave lens with

$$u = +15\,cm$$

$$\Rightarrow \qquad v_2 = \frac{(15)(-20)}{(15)+(-20)} = +60\,cm$$

Hence option (Q) is correctly related here.

(IV) : In this case for concave lens image is produced as

$$v_1 = \frac{(20)(-20)}{(-20)+(-20)} = -10\,cm$$

So for convex lens above image will act as a real object located at a distance 15 cm to the left of it for which we use

$$u_2 = -15\,cm$$

By lens formula for this convex lens we have

$$v_2 = \frac{(-15)(10)}{(-15)+(-10)} = +30\,cm$$

Hence option (T) is correctly related here. **Ans. (A)**

Sol. 37 (C) Meta material has a negative refractive index so by Snell's law we get

$$\Rightarrow \qquad \sin\theta_2 = \frac{n_1}{n_2}\sin\theta_1$$

$\Rightarrow$ Here n_2 is negative so we will have θ_2 negative **Ans. (C)**

Sol. 38 Refractive index is given as

$$n = \frac{c}{v}$$

For meta materials, we use

$$v = \frac{c}{|n|}$$

Ans. (B)

Sol. 39 (A) : S_1 S_2

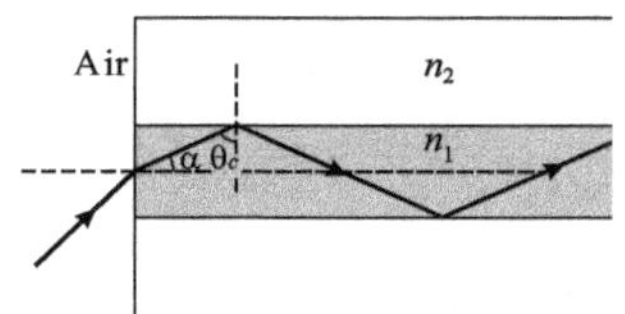

$$n_1 = \frac{\sqrt{45}}{4} \qquad n_1 = \frac{8}{5}$$

$$n_2 = \frac{3}{2} \qquad n_2 = \frac{7}{5}$$

$$\theta_c = \sin^{-1}\left(\frac{n_2}{n_1}\right)$$

For S_1 in mater θ_c is given as

$$\theta_c = \sin^{-1}\left(\frac{3 \times 4^2}{2\sqrt{45}}\right)$$

$$\Rightarrow \qquad \theta_c = \sin^{-1}\left(\frac{6}{\sqrt{45}}\right)$$

$$\Rightarrow \qquad \sin\theta = \frac{2}{\sqrt{5}}$$

$$\Rightarrow \qquad \theta_c = \sin^{-1}\left(\frac{2}{\sqrt{5}}\right)$$

By Snell's law, we use

$$\frac{\sqrt{45}}{4} \cdot \frac{1}{\sqrt{5}} = \frac{4}{3} \cdot \sin i_m$$

$$\Rightarrow \qquad \sin i_m = \frac{9}{16}$$

For S_2 we have

$$\theta_c = \sin^{-1}\left(\frac{7}{8}\right)$$

$$\Rightarrow \qquad \sin\alpha = \frac{\sqrt{15}}{8}$$

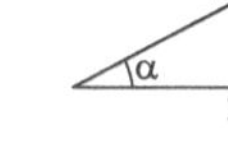

By Snell's law

$$\frac{16}{3\sqrt{15}} \cdot \sin i_m = \frac{8}{5} \times \sin\alpha$$

$$\Rightarrow \qquad \sin i_m = \frac{8}{5} \cdot \frac{8}{5} \times \frac{3\sqrt{15}}{16} = \frac{9}{16}$$

Hence option (A) is correct.

(B) : For S_1 in $\dfrac{6}{\sqrt{15}}$ For S_2 in water

$$\theta_c = \sin^{-1}\left(\frac{2}{\sqrt{5}}\right) \qquad \frac{4}{3} \times \sin i_m = \frac{\sqrt{15}}{8} \times \frac{8}{5}$$

$$\sin\alpha = \frac{1}{\sqrt{5}}, \qquad \sin i_m = \sqrt{\frac{3}{5}} \times \frac{3}{4} = \frac{3\sqrt{3}}{4\sqrt{5}}$$

$$\sin i_m = \frac{\sqrt{15}}{8}$$

Hence option (B) is NOT correct.

(C) : For S_1 in air and for S_2 in $\dfrac{4}{\sqrt{15}}$

By Snell's law, we use

$$1 \times \sin i_m = \frac{\sqrt{45}}{4} \cdot \frac{1}{\sqrt{5}}$$

$$\Rightarrow \qquad \sin i_m = \frac{3}{4}$$

For S_2 we have by Snell's law

$$\frac{4}{\sqrt{15}} \times \sin i_m = \frac{\sqrt{15}}{8} \times \frac{8}{5}$$

$$\Rightarrow \qquad \sin i_m = \frac{3}{4}$$

Hence option (C) is correct.

(D) : For S_1 placed in air, we use

$$1 \times \sin i_m = \frac{\sqrt{45}}{4} \times \frac{1}{\sqrt{5}}$$

$$\Rightarrow \qquad \sin i_m = \frac{3}{4}$$

For S_2 placed in water, we use

$$\frac{4}{3} \times \sin i_m = \frac{\sqrt{15}}{8} \times \frac{8}{5}$$

$$\Rightarrow \qquad \sin i_m = \frac{\sqrt{3} \times 3}{4\sqrt{5}}$$

Hence option (D) is NOT correct.   **Ans. (A, C)**

Sol. 40 Ray should enter according to smaller i_m in the material so as it is given that $NA_2 < NA_1$ we have $i_{m_2} < i_{m_1}$. If combination is placed in any order, total internal reflection if satisfied for lower i_m, it will satisfy for any lower angles as well.

So NA_2 will be numerical aperture of combined structure.

Ans. (D)

Sol. 41 Magnification of lens is given as

$$m = \frac{f}{f+u}$$

$$\Rightarrow \qquad m_{25} = \frac{20}{20-25} = -4;$$

and $$m_{50} = \frac{20}{20-50} = -\frac{2}{3}$$

$$\Rightarrow \quad \frac{m_{25}}{m_{50}} = 6 \qquad \textbf{Ans. (6)}$$

Sol. 42 When light is incident at critical angle, it goes parallel to surface after refraction at the edges of the circular area as shown in figure below.

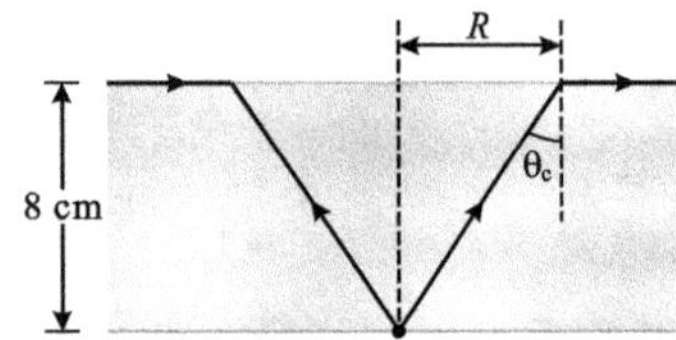

Here critical angle is given as

$$\sin \theta_c = \frac{3}{5}$$

$$\Rightarrow \quad \tan \theta_c = \frac{3}{4}$$

$$\Rightarrow \quad R = 8 \tan \theta_c$$

$$\Rightarrow \quad R = 8 \times \frac{3}{4} = 6 \text{ cm} \qquad \textbf{Ans. (6)}$$

Sol. 43 For position of object initially when image was at $\dfrac{25}{3}$ m is calculated from mirror formula as

$$-\frac{1}{10} = -\frac{3}{25} + \frac{1}{u}$$

$$\Rightarrow \quad \frac{3}{25} - \frac{1}{10} = \frac{1}{u}$$

$$\Rightarrow \quad \frac{12-10}{100} = \frac{1}{u}$$

$$\Rightarrow \quad u_1 = 50 \text{ cm}$$

For position of object when image is at $\dfrac{50}{7}$ m is calculated as

$$-\frac{1}{10} = -\frac{7}{50} + \frac{1}{u}$$

$$\Rightarrow \quad \frac{7}{50} - \frac{1}{10} = \frac{1}{u}$$

$$\Rightarrow \quad u_2 = 25 \text{ cm}$$

Speed of object can be given as

$$V_{object} = \frac{50-25}{30} = \frac{25}{30} \text{ m/s}$$

$$\Rightarrow \quad V_{object} = \frac{25}{30} \times \frac{3600}{1000} = 3 \text{ km/hr} \qquad \textbf{Ans. (3)}$$

Sol. 44 For refraction from a spherical surface, we use

$$\frac{\mu_3}{v} - \frac{\mu_1}{u} = \frac{\mu_2 - \mu_1}{R_1} + \frac{\mu_3 - \mu_2}{R_2}$$

$$\Rightarrow \quad \frac{4}{3v} - \frac{1}{-24} = \frac{\frac{7}{4}-1}{6} + \frac{\frac{4}{3}-\frac{7}{4}}{\infty}$$

$$\Rightarrow \quad \frac{4}{3v} + \frac{1}{24} = \frac{1}{8}$$

$$\Rightarrow \quad \frac{4}{3v} = \frac{1}{12}$$

$$\Rightarrow \quad v = 16 \text{ cm}$$

$$\Rightarrow \quad x = (18 - 16) \text{ cm} = 2 \text{ cm} \qquad \textbf{Ans. (2)}$$

Sol. 45 For the given system we consider first reflection at mirror and second refraction at lens for this optical combination. Now by mirror formula, we have

$$\frac{1}{v} + \frac{1}{u} = \frac{1}{f}$$

$$\Rightarrow \quad \frac{1}{v} - \frac{1}{15} = \frac{1}{-10} \quad \Rightarrow \quad \frac{1}{5}\left[\frac{1}{3} - \frac{1}{2}\right] = -\frac{1}{30}$$

$$v = -30 \text{ cm}$$

Thus magnification due to mirror is calculated as

$$|m_1| = \frac{30}{15} = 2$$

Now using lens formula, we have

$$\frac{1}{v} - \frac{1}{u} = \frac{1}{f}$$

$$\Rightarrow \quad \frac{1}{v} + \frac{1}{20} = \frac{1}{10}$$

$$\Rightarrow \quad v = 20 \text{ cm}$$

Magnification by lens here is 1 so total magnification of system is given as

$$M_1 = m_1 \times 1 \qquad \qquad \ldots(1)$$

When system is submerged in a medium, the new focal length of lens becomes

$$f = \frac{R}{2\left(\dfrac{\mu_2}{\mu_1}-1\right)} = \frac{10}{2\left(\dfrac{(3/2)}{(7/6)}-1\right)} = \frac{70}{4} = \frac{35}{2} \text{ cm}$$

Magnification due to lens is given as

$$\frac{f}{f+u} = -7$$

Total magnification of system after submerging in liquid is given as

$$M_2 = m_1 \times \frac{f}{f+u}$$

$$\Rightarrow \qquad \left| \frac{M_2}{M_1} \right| = 7 \qquad\qquad \textbf{Ans. (7)}$$

Sol. 46 By Snell's law, we have

$$\sin\theta = n \sin r_2$$

Differentiating the equation gives

$$\cos\theta \times \frac{d\theta}{dn} = n \cos r_2 \frac{dr_2}{dn} + \sin r_2 \qquad \ldots (1)$$

At $\theta = 60°$, $r_2 = 30°$ so we have

$$\Rightarrow \qquad \frac{1}{2} \frac{d\theta}{dn} = \sqrt{3} \, \frac{\sqrt{3}}{2} \frac{dr_2}{dn} + \frac{1}{2}$$

$$\Rightarrow \qquad \frac{d\theta}{dn} = 3 \frac{dr_2}{dn} + 1 \qquad \ldots (2)$$

For refraction at first face, we have

$$n \sin r_1 = \sin 60°$$

$$\Rightarrow \qquad n \sin r_1 = \frac{\sqrt{3}}{2}$$

$$\Rightarrow \qquad n \sin (A - r_2) = \frac{\sqrt{3}}{2}$$

$$n \cos (A - r_2) \left(-\frac{dr_2}{dn} \right) + \sin (A - r_2) = 0$$

$$\Rightarrow \quad \sqrt{3} \, \frac{\sqrt{3}}{2} \left(-\frac{dr_2}{dn} \right) + \frac{1}{2} = 0$$

$$\Rightarrow \qquad -\frac{dr_2}{dn} = -\frac{1}{3}$$

$$\Rightarrow \qquad \frac{dr_2}{dn} = \frac{1}{3}$$

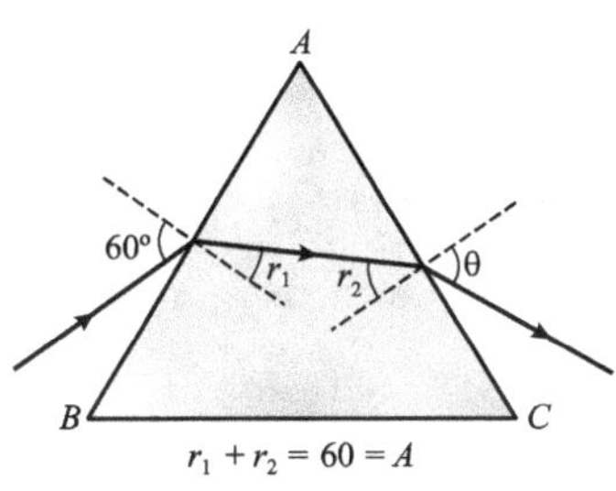

From equation (2), we have

$$\frac{d\theta}{dn} = 3 \times \frac{1}{3} + 1 = 2 \qquad\qquad \textbf{Ans. (2)}$$

Sol. 47 Here we use by Snell's law

$$n \sin 30° = (n - m\Delta n)\sin 90°$$

Here $\Delta n = 0.1$

$$n \times \frac{1}{2} = n - m\,\Delta n$$

$$\Rightarrow \qquad m\Delta n = \frac{n}{2}$$

$$\Rightarrow \qquad m = 8 \qquad\qquad \textbf{Ans. (8)}$$

Sol. 48 For maximum time the ray of light must undergo TIR at all surfaces at minimum angle i.e. θ_C

For total internal reflection $n_1 \sin\theta_C = n_2$

$$\Rightarrow \qquad \sin\theta_C = \frac{1.44}{1.5}$$

Figure below shows the path of light ray passing through the optical media

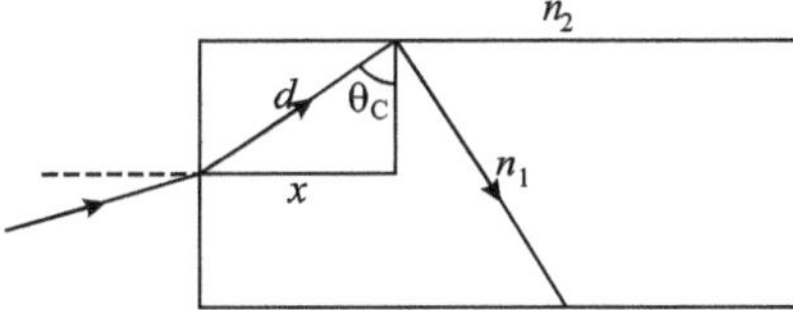

In above triangle, we have

$$\sin\theta_C = \frac{x}{d}$$

$$\Rightarrow \qquad d = \frac{x}{\sin\theta_C}$$

Similarly $\quad D = \dfrac{L}{\sin\theta_C}$

Where L is the length of tube and D is the length of path of light so time taken by light can be calculated as

$$\Rightarrow \qquad t = \frac{D}{C} = \frac{L/\sin\theta_C}{2\times 10^8} = 50 \times 10^{-9}\,\text{s} \quad \textbf{Ans. (50.00)}$$

Sol. 49 At $\theta = 60°$ ray incidents at critical angle at second surface. By Snell's law at first surface, we have

$$\sin\theta = \sqrt{3} \sin r_1$$

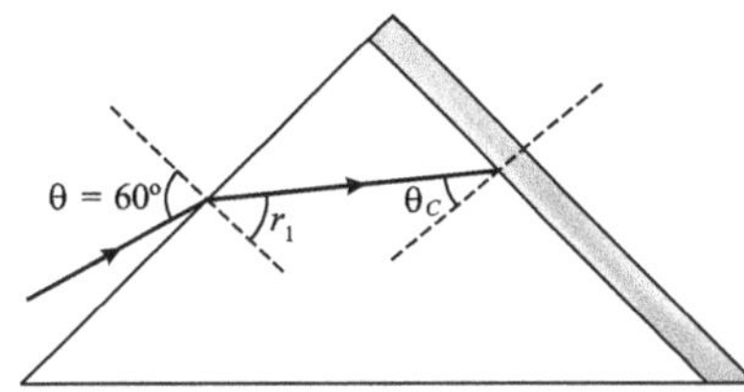

$$\Rightarrow \qquad \frac{\sqrt{3}}{2} = \sqrt{3} \sin r_1$$

$$\Rightarrow \qquad r_1 = 30°$$

$$\Rightarrow \qquad r_2 = 45° = \theta_C$$

By Snell's law at second surface we have

$$\sqrt{3}\sin 45° = n\sin 90°$$

$$\Rightarrow \quad n = \sqrt{\frac{3}{2}} \Rightarrow n^2 = \frac{3}{2} \qquad \textbf{Ans. (1.50)}$$

Sol. 50 For the given lens using lens formula gives

$$\frac{1}{f} = \frac{1}{v} - \frac{1}{u}$$

$$\Rightarrow \quad f = 20 \text{ cm}$$

Differentiation of lens formula gives

$$\frac{df}{f^2} = \frac{dv}{v^2} + \frac{du}{u^2}$$

$$\Rightarrow \quad \frac{df}{f} = f\left[\frac{dv}{v^2} + \frac{du}{u^2}\right]$$

$$\Rightarrow \quad \frac{df}{f} \times 100 = f\left[\frac{dv}{v^2} + \frac{du}{u^2}\right] \times 100\%$$

Using $f = 20$ cm, $du = dv = \dfrac{1}{4}$ cm as there are 4 divisions in 1 cm

on scale, error in measurement of u and v is 1/4 cm. Thus percentage error in measurement of f is given as

$$\frac{df}{f} \times 100 = 20\left[\frac{1/4}{(60)^2} + \frac{1/4}{(30)^2}\right] \times 100\%$$

$$\Rightarrow \quad \frac{df}{f} \times 100 = 5\left[\frac{1}{3600} + \frac{1}{900}\right] \times 100\%$$

$$\Rightarrow \quad \frac{df}{f} \times 100 = 5\left[\frac{5}{36}\right]\% = \frac{25}{36}\% \approx 0.69\% \qquad \textbf{Ans. (0.69)}$$

Sol. 51 There are multiple ways to solve this question but logically the images seen by an observer located far away along the line joining the source and edge of block, will be corresponding to the light rays which comes out parallel to this line as shown in figure below

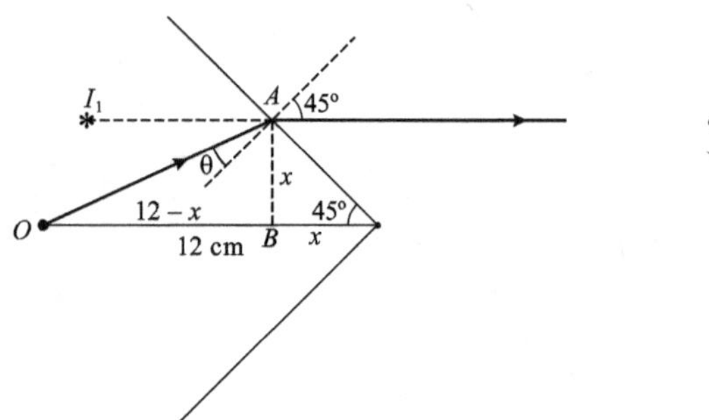

Using Snell's law for this light ray, we use

$$\frac{4}{3}\sin\theta = 1\sin 45°$$

$$\Rightarrow \quad \sin\theta = \frac{3}{4\sqrt{2}}$$

$$\Rightarrow \quad \tan\theta = \frac{3}{\sqrt{23}}$$

In ΔOAB, we have

$$\tan(45° + \theta) = \frac{12 - x}{x}$$

$$\Rightarrow \quad \frac{1 + \tan\theta}{1 - \tan\theta} = \frac{12 - x}{x}$$

$$\Rightarrow \quad \frac{\sqrt{23} + 3}{\sqrt{23} - 3} = \frac{12 - x}{x}$$

$$\Rightarrow \quad \frac{7.8}{1.8} = \frac{12 - x}{x}$$

$$\Rightarrow \quad 5.33\,x = 12$$

$$\Rightarrow \quad x = 2.25$$

Separation between images

$$d = 2x \approx 4.5 \text{ cm}$$

$$\Rightarrow \quad 4 < d < 5 \qquad \textbf{Ans. (4 or 5)}$$

Sol. 52 Below figure shows the image formed and the respective distances from the position of lens which are calculated by lens formula as given below.

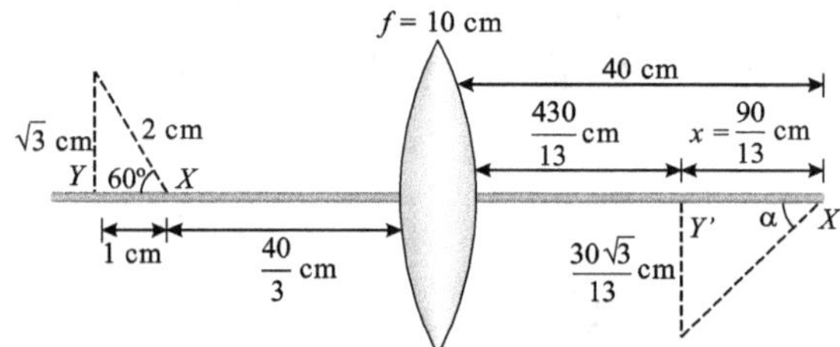

For position X of object, to obtain its image we use

$$\frac{1}{v} - \frac{1}{u} = \frac{1}{f}$$

$$\Rightarrow \quad \frac{1}{v} = \frac{1}{10} - \frac{3}{40}$$

$$\Rightarrow \quad v = 40 \text{ cm} \quad \text{(This is } OX' \text{ in figure)}$$

For position Y of object, to obtain its image we use

$$\frac{1}{v} - \frac{1}{u} = \frac{1}{f}$$

$$\Rightarrow \quad \frac{1}{v} + \frac{3}{43} = \frac{1}{10}$$

$$\Rightarrow \quad v = \frac{430}{13} \text{ cm}$$

Distance $X'Y'$ as shown in figure is calculated as

$$X'Y' = 40 - \frac{430}{13} = \frac{90}{13} \text{ cm}$$

Angle α can be given as

$$\tan \alpha = \frac{\dfrac{30\sqrt{3}}{13}}{\dfrac{90}{13}} = \frac{1}{\sqrt{3}}$$

$$\Rightarrow \qquad \alpha = \frac{\pi}{6}$$

$$\Rightarrow \qquad n = 6 \qquad\qquad \textbf{Ans. (6)}$$

Sol. 53 In the given situation described in question, we can calculate the displacement of the ray due to one unit is shown in figure below.

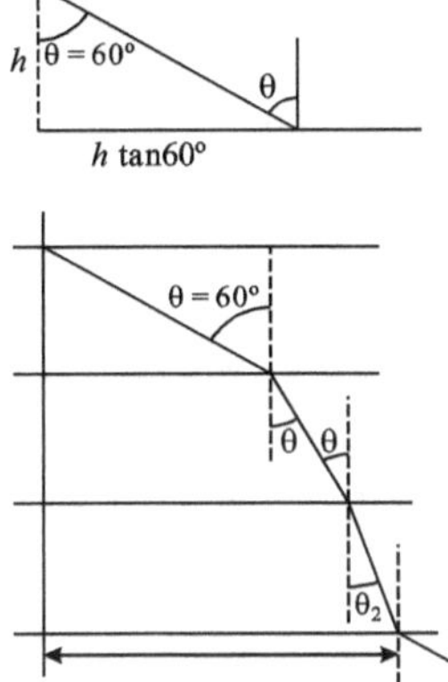

Using Snell's law at first surface, we have

$$1 \sin 60^\circ = \sqrt{\frac{3}{2}} \sin \theta$$

$$\Rightarrow \qquad \theta_1 = 45^\circ$$

At second surface using Snell's law gives

$$\sqrt{\frac{3}{2}} \sin 45^\circ = \sqrt{3} \sin\theta_2$$

$$\Rightarrow \qquad \sqrt{\frac{3}{2}} \, \frac{1}{\sqrt{2}} = \sqrt{3} \sin\theta_2$$

$$\Rightarrow \qquad \theta_2 = 30^\circ$$

Thus displacement of light ray due to one unit is given as

$$x = h \tan 60^\circ + d \tan 45^\circ + d \tan 30^\circ$$

$$\Rightarrow \qquad x = \frac{1}{3}\sqrt{3} + \left(\frac{\sqrt{3}-1}{2}\right) + \left(\frac{\sqrt{3}-1}{2}\right)\frac{1}{\sqrt{3}}$$

$$\Rightarrow \qquad x = \frac{2\sqrt{3} + 3\sqrt{3} - 3 + 3 - \sqrt{3}}{6}$$

$$\Rightarrow \qquad x = \frac{4\sqrt{3}}{6} = \frac{2}{\sqrt{3}} \text{ cm}$$

For n units, we use

$$n\left(\frac{2}{\sqrt{3}}\right) = \frac{8}{\sqrt{3}}$$

$$\Rightarrow \qquad n = 4 \qquad\qquad \textbf{Ans. (4)}$$

Sol. 54 As shown in figure below, we consider mirror velocity to be on the right side

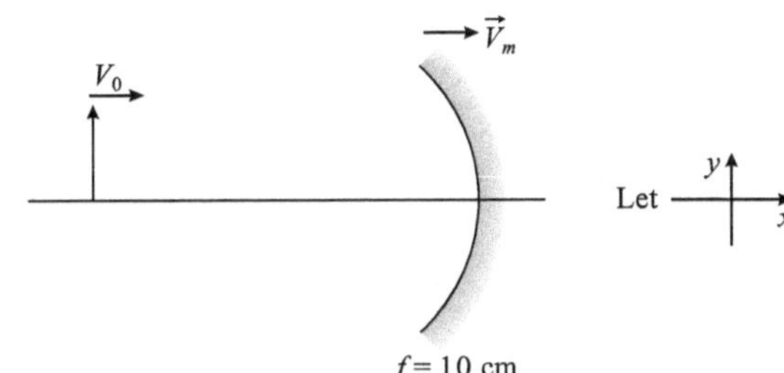

Using mirror formula, position of image is obtained as

$$u = -30 \text{ cm}$$

$$f = -10 \text{ cm}$$

$$\Rightarrow \qquad v = \frac{f_0}{u - f} = -15 \text{ cm}$$

Magnification of object is given as

$$m = \frac{1}{2}$$

Relative velocity of image with respect to mirror is given as

$$V_{IM} = m^2 V_{OM} = \frac{1}{4} V_{OM}$$

As image is at instantaneous rest, we use $V_I = 0$

$$V_M = \frac{1}{4}(V_0 - V_M)$$

$$\Rightarrow \qquad V_M = \frac{1}{5} V_0 = 3 \text{ cm/s} \qquad \textbf{Ans. (3)}$$

Sol. 55 There can be multiple cases of successive reflections and refractions after which image can be produced at S.

Case-1: Considering 1st refraction on lens

As S is located at focus of lens light rays will become parallel and incident on mirror M_1. As light rays are incident parallel on M_1 it will form the image at its focus i.e. at 10 cm from pole of M_1. Now for second refraction at lens we use

$$u = -(d - 10) \text{ cm}$$

$$f = 10 \text{ cm}$$

Using lens formula, we have

$$\frac{1}{v} - \frac{1}{u} = \frac{1}{f}$$

$$\Rightarrow \qquad \frac{1}{v} + \frac{1}{d - 10} = \frac{1}{10}$$

$$\Rightarrow \qquad \frac{1}{v} = \frac{1}{10} - \frac{1}{(d-10)} \qquad \qquad \dots(1)$$

This v is the position of image formed by lens and it will be the object for mirror M_2, and to coincides the image with S, it should be formed at 10 cm from pole of M_2. Thus for mirror M_2 we use

$$u = -(20-v)\,\text{cm}$$

and $\qquad\qquad f = -12\,\text{cm}$

Using mirror formula we have

$$\frac{1}{u} + \frac{1}{v_1} = \frac{1}{f}$$

$$\Rightarrow \qquad -\frac{1}{(20-v)} - \frac{1}{10} = -\frac{1}{12}$$

$$\Rightarrow \qquad \frac{1}{12} - \frac{1}{10} = \frac{1}{20-v}$$

$$\Rightarrow \qquad -\frac{2}{120} = \frac{1}{20-v}$$

$$\Rightarrow \qquad 20 - v = -60$$

$$\Rightarrow \qquad v = 80\,\text{cm}$$

From equation-(1)

$$\frac{1}{80} = \frac{1}{10} - \frac{1}{d-10}$$

$$\Rightarrow \qquad \frac{1}{d-10} = \frac{1}{10} - \frac{1}{80}$$

$$\Rightarrow \qquad \frac{1}{d-10} = \frac{80-10}{800} = \frac{70}{800}$$

$$\Rightarrow \qquad d - 10 = \frac{80}{7}$$

$$\Rightarrow \qquad d = 10 + \frac{80}{7} = \frac{150}{7}\,\text{cm}$$

$$\Rightarrow \qquad n = 150$$

Case-2: Considering 1st reflection on mirror M_2

We take

$$u = -10\,\text{cm}$$

and $\qquad\qquad f = -12\,\text{cm}$

Now using mirror formula we have

$$\frac{1}{v_1} + \frac{1}{-10} = \frac{1}{-12}$$

$$v_1 = +60\,\text{cm}$$

Thus diverging light rays are reflected from mirror M_2 such that for lens these rays appear to be coming from an object located at a distance 80 cm from the lens. So for lens reflection, we use

$$u_2 = -80\,\text{cm}$$

and $\qquad\qquad f = +10\,\text{cm}$

Using lens formula, we have

$$\frac{1}{v_2} - \frac{1}{-80} = \frac{1}{10}$$

$$\Rightarrow \qquad v_2 = +\frac{80}{7}\,\text{cm}$$

Now for reflection on M_2 if light rays fall normally on mirror, these will back trace and produce image at source location, so we use

$$d - \frac{80}{7} = 20$$

$$\Rightarrow \qquad d = \frac{220}{7}\,\text{cm}$$

$$\Rightarrow \qquad n = 220$$

If all light rays fall on pole of mirror M_2 then also these will be reflected such that image is produced on source, so we use

$$d = \frac{80}{7}\,\text{cm}$$

$$\Rightarrow \qquad n = 80 \qquad \textbf{Ans. (80 or 150 or 220)}$$

Ch-19 Wave Optics & Electromagnetic Wave

Sol. 1 Fringe width in YDSE is given as

$$\beta = \frac{\lambda D}{d}$$

In visible spectrum from violet to red colour wavelength λ increase so for $\lambda_R > \lambda_G > \lambda_B$ we have $\beta_R > \beta_G > \beta_B$ $\qquad$ **Ans. (D)**

Sol. 2 Intensity at a point where phase difference is ϕ, is given as

$$I = I_{\max} \cos^2 \frac{\phi}{2}$$

At a point half the peak intensity, we use

$$\frac{I_{\max}}{2} = I_{\text{m}} \cos^2\left(\frac{\phi}{2}\right)$$

$$\Rightarrow \qquad \cos\left(\frac{\phi}{2}\right) = \frac{1}{\sqrt{2}}$$

$$\Rightarrow \qquad \frac{\phi}{2} = \frac{\pi}{4}\,(2n+1)$$

$$\Rightarrow \qquad \phi = \frac{\pi}{2}\,(2n+1)$$

Phase difference is related to path difference as

$$\phi = \frac{2\pi}{\lambda} \cdot \Delta x$$

$$\Rightarrow \Delta x = \frac{\lambda}{2\pi}\phi = \frac{\lambda}{2\pi} \times \frac{\pi}{2}\,(2n+1) = \frac{\lambda}{4}\,(2n+1) \qquad \textbf{Ans. (B)}$$

Sol. 3 Fringe pattern obtained on screen will be circular because at a circle with centre at O, path difference due to the two sources will be same as shown in figure below. In this case only semicircles will be visible due to upper half of screen.

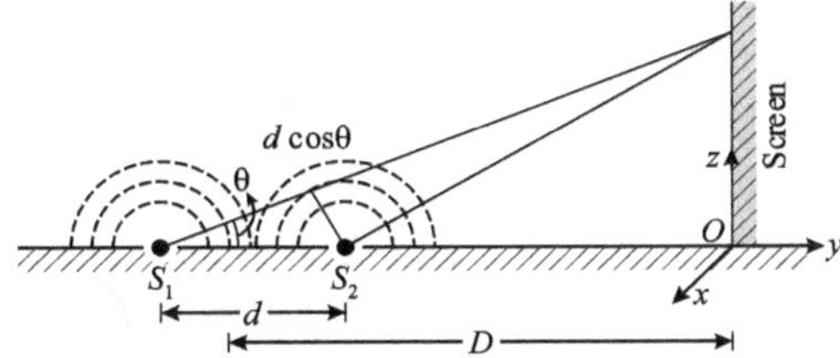

To calculate z-value (as explained in Physics Galaxy Vol. 4) at point O, we have

$$z = \frac{d}{\lambda} = \frac{0.6003 \times 10^{-3}}{600 \times 10^{-9}} = \frac{6003}{6} = 1000.5$$

$$\Rightarrow \qquad d = (1000.5)\lambda$$

Hence interference at O will be destructive so dark region is obtained near O. **Ans. (B, C)**

Sol. 4 Due to the convex lens wave front emerging out from the lens is concave because of converging light rays and from a concave lens wave front emerging out from the lens is convex because of diverging light rays hence option (A) is correct.
Ans. (A)

Sol. 5 Path difference between the lights from S_1 and S_2 reaching the point P, is given as

$$\Delta x = d \sin \theta$$

For maxima $d \sin \theta = n\lambda$. Now when $d = \lambda$, at ∞, $\Delta x = \lambda$ on side above the screen center and $\Delta x = -\lambda$ at ∞ on below the screen center. Thus there will be three maxima, one at centre and two are at infinite however screen can't be of infinite size hence option (A) is correct.

For $\lambda < d < 2\lambda$ due to the explanation above, three maxima are possible, one at centre, one above and one below the screen center.

Initial intensities of dark fringes is given as

$$I_D = (\sqrt{4I} - \sqrt{I})^2 = I$$

When intensity of both slit becomes equal then intensity of dark fringe will become zero Hence options (C) and (D) are NOT correct. **Ans. (A, B)**

Sol. 6 Fringe width in YDSE is given as

$$\beta = \frac{D\lambda}{d}$$

$$\Rightarrow \qquad \beta \propto \lambda$$

$$\Rightarrow \qquad \beta_2 > \beta_1$$

Hence option (A) is correct.

Number of fringes in a given distance y on screen are calculated as

$$m = \frac{y}{\beta} = \frac{y \cdot d}{D\lambda}$$

$$\Rightarrow \qquad m_1 > m_1$$

Hence option (B) is correct.

Distance of 3rd maxima in case of λ_2 is located at

$$y_2 = \frac{n\lambda D}{d} = 3 \times \frac{D \times 600}{d}$$

5th minima in case of λ_1 is located at

$$y_1 = \frac{(2n-1)\lambda D}{2d} = \frac{4.5 \times D \times 400}{d}$$

$$\Rightarrow \qquad y_1 = y_2 \qquad \textbf{Ans. (A, B, C)}$$

Sol. 7 Path difference at angle θ is given as

$$\Delta x = d\cos\theta = n\lambda$$

$$\Rightarrow \qquad \cos\theta = \left(\frac{n\lambda}{d}\right)$$

At point P_2 $\theta = 0°$, so we have

$$n\lambda = d$$

$$\Rightarrow \qquad n = \frac{d}{\lambda} = \left[\frac{1.8 \times 10^{-3}}{600 \times 10^{-9}}\right]$$

$$\Rightarrow \quad n = \frac{1.8 \times 10^6}{600} = \frac{1800 \times 10^3}{600} = 3000 \qquad \textbf{Ans. (C, D)}$$

Sol. 8 Path difference at point P is given (for small α) as

$$\Delta x = d\sin\alpha = d\alpha$$

$$\Rightarrow \qquad \alpha = \frac{.36}{180} = 2 \times 10^{-3}\,\text{rad}$$

$$\Rightarrow \qquad \frac{\Delta x}{\lambda} = \frac{(3 \times 10^{-4})\,(2 \times 10^{-3})}{6 \times 10^{-7}} = 1$$

Thus constructive interference will occur and hence option (A) is NOT correct.

As fringe width is given as

$$\beta = \frac{D\lambda}{d}$$

It does not depend upon α hence option (B) is NOT correct. At point P, the path difference is given as

$$\Delta x_p = d\alpha + \frac{dy}{D}$$

$$\Rightarrow \qquad \Delta x_p = 3 \times 10^{-4}\,(2 \times 10^{-3} + 11 \times 10^{-3})$$

$$\Rightarrow \qquad \Delta x_p = 39 \times 10^{-7}\,\text{m}$$

$$\Rightarrow \qquad \frac{\Delta x_p}{\lambda} = \frac{39 \times 10^{-7}}{6 \times 10^{-7}} = 6.5$$

Thus destructive interference will occur at P hence option (C) is correct.

For $\alpha = 0°$, path difference at P is given as

$$\Delta x_P = \frac{dy}{D} = (3 \times 10^{-4})\, 11 \times 10^{-3} = 33 \times 10^{-7}\,\text{m}$$

$$\Rightarrow \qquad \frac{\Delta x_p}{\lambda} = \frac{39 \times 10^{-7}}{6 \times 10^{-7}} = 5.5$$

Thus destructive interference will occur at P hence option (D) is NOT correct. **Ans. (C)**

Sol. 9 By Snell's law for refraction of light at the interface of the two media, we have

$$n_1 \sin\alpha = n_2 \sin\theta$$

Figure below shows the path of light rays refracting through the two media.

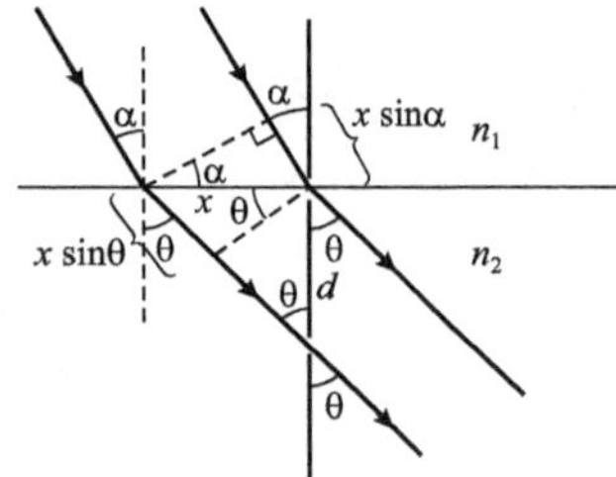

Optical path difference between the two rays is given as

$$\Delta x = n_1 x \sin\alpha - n_2 x \sin\theta = 0$$
$$\Rightarrow \qquad \Delta\phi = 0$$

Hence options (A) & (B) are correct. **Ans. (A, B)**

Sol. 10 From the given equation we can see that wave is travelling along positive z direction hence the direction of magnetic field vector is along the direction perpendicular to both electric field vector and propagation direction as shown in figure below.

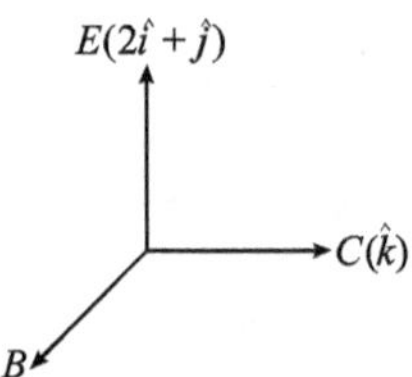

Speed of electromagnetic wave in medium is given as

$$c_m = \frac{\omega}{k} = \frac{5 \times 10^{14}}{10^7/3} = 1.5 \times 10^8\,\text{m/s}$$

$$\Rightarrow \qquad \mu = \frac{c}{c_m} = 2$$

Hence option (D) is correct.

For the electromagnetic wave, we have

$$c_m = \frac{E}{B}$$

$$\Rightarrow \qquad B = \frac{E}{c_m} = \frac{30\sqrt{5}}{1.5 \times 10^8} = 2\sqrt{5} \times 10^{-7}\,\text{T}$$

Unit vector along the direction of magnetic field is given as

$$\vec{B}_{\text{dir}} = \frac{\hat{k} \times (2\hat{i}+\hat{j})}{\sqrt{5}} \equiv \frac{2\hat{j}-\hat{i}}{\sqrt{5}}$$

Thus field vector of magnetic field is given as

$$\vec{B} = 2 \times 10^{-7} \times (-\hat{i}+2\hat{j})\, \sin\left[2\pi\left(5 \times 10^{17}\,t - \frac{10^7}{3}z\right)\right]$$

Hence option (A) is correct and option (B) is NOT correct. Polarization plane of electromagnetic wave is the plane containing electric field vector which is along $(2\hat{i}+\hat{j})$ as shown in figure below.

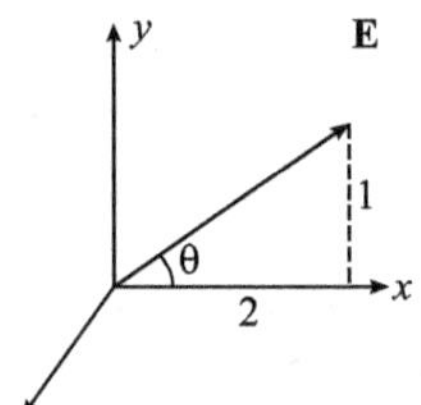

The direction of electric field vector or the plane of polarization is at an angle θ to x axis which is given as

$$\tan\theta = \frac{1}{2}$$

Hence option (C) is NOT correct. **Ans. (A, D)**

Sol. 11 (A) : Phase difference at points P_1 and P_2 are given as

$$\phi_1 = \frac{2\pi}{\lambda} \times \frac{\lambda}{4} = \frac{\pi}{2}$$

and

$$\phi_2 = \frac{2\pi}{\lambda} \times \frac{\lambda}{3} = \frac{2\pi}{3}$$

Intensity at these points is given by $I = I_{\max}\cos^2(\phi/2)$ which results

$$I(P_1) = I_{\max}\cos^2\frac{\pi}{4} = I_{\max}/2$$

$$I(P_2) = I_{\max}\cos^2\frac{\pi}{3} = I_{\max}/4$$

Phase difference at P_0 is zero and intensity here is maximum hence options (p) and (s) are correctly related.

(B) : Path difference at P_1 is same as that introduced by the film hence this will be the new position of central maxima hence option (q) is correctly related.

(C): The path difference at P_0 now is for destructive interference so this is minima now in this case and at P_2 and P_1 new path difference now is given as

$$\Delta x_{P1} = \frac{\lambda}{2} - \frac{\lambda}{4} = \frac{\lambda}{4}$$

and
$$\Delta x_{P2} = \frac{\lambda}{2} - \frac{\lambda}{3} = \frac{\lambda}{6}$$

Hence option (t) is correctly related.

(D): At P_0 path difference is $\Delta x = \dfrac{3\lambda}{4}$ so phase difference is given as

$$\phi_0 = \frac{3\pi}{2}$$

At P_1 path difference is $\Delta x = \dfrac{3\lambda}{4} - \dfrac{\lambda}{4} = \dfrac{\lambda}{2}$ thus destructive interference occurs at P_1 so $I(P_1) = 0$ and at P_2 path difference is $\Delta x = \dfrac{3\lambda}{4} - \dfrac{\lambda}{3} = \dfrac{5\lambda}{12}$ so phase difference here is given as

$$\phi_2 = \frac{2\pi}{\lambda} \times \frac{5\lambda}{12} = \frac{5\pi}{6}$$

Hence options (r), (s) and (t) are correctly related.

Ans. [A (p, s); B (q); C (t); D (r, s, t)]

Sol. 12 Light travels as a parallel beam in each medium because path difference between two wavefronts is equal. **Ans. (A)**

Sol. 13 All points in a given wavefront are in same phase so we use

$$\phi_d = \phi_c \text{ and } \phi_f = \phi_c$$
$$\Rightarrow \qquad \phi_d - \phi_f = \phi_c - \phi_c \qquad \textbf{Ans. (C)}$$

Sol. 14 In medium 2 angle of refraction r is less than angle of incidence i so medium 2 is denser thus speed of light decreases.
Ans. (B)

Sol. 15 Positions of maxima on surface of water is given by

$$x^2 = p^2 m^2 \lambda^2 - d^2$$
$$\mu = 4/3$$

Given $x_1 = \sqrt{x^2 + d^2}$ and $x_2 = \mu \sqrt{x^2 + d^2} = \dfrac{4}{3}\sqrt{x^2 + d^2}$

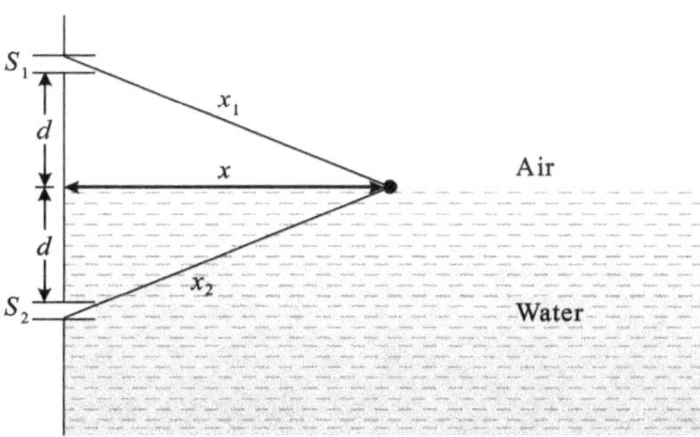

Path difference between the two waves is given as

$$\Delta x = \left[\frac{4}{3}\sqrt{x^2 + d^2} - \sqrt{x^2 + d^2}\right] = m\lambda$$

$$\Rightarrow \qquad \frac{\sqrt{x^2 + d^2}}{3} = m\lambda$$

$$\Rightarrow \qquad \frac{x^2 + d^2}{9} = m^2\lambda^2$$

$$x^2 = 9m^2\lambda^2 - d^2$$

$$\Rightarrow \qquad p = 3 \qquad \textbf{Ans. (3)}$$

Sol. 16 Figure below shows the situation described in question. In this $\triangle AFB$ and $\triangle CFD$ are similar, so we use

$$\frac{d}{D} = \frac{2}{20} = \frac{1}{10}$$

$$\Rightarrow \quad \text{Ratio of area} = \frac{d^2}{D^2} = \frac{1}{100}$$

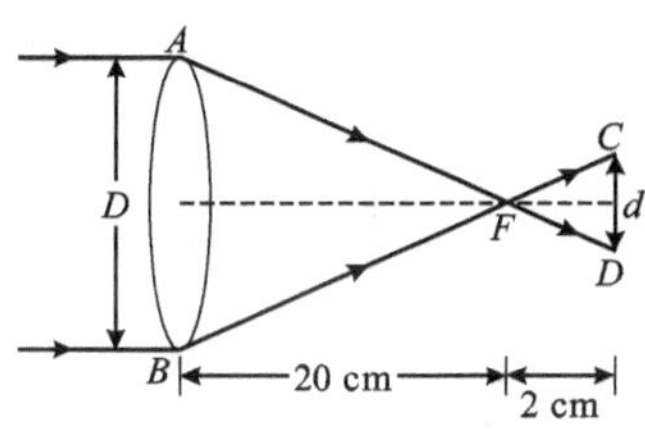

As there is no energy loss, we use average intensity of light at a distance 22 cm is given as

$$I = \frac{1.3 \times \pi D^2 / 4}{\pi d^2 / 4} = 1.3 \times 100 = 130.00\,\text{kWm}^{-2} \quad \textbf{Ans. (130)}$$

Ch-20 Dual Nature of Radiation, Matter & X-Rays

Sol. 1 De-Broglie wavelength of electrons with kinetic energy E is given as

$$\lambda = \frac{h}{\sqrt{2mE}} \qquad \ldots (1)$$

If λ_0 is the cut off wavelength of X-Rays, we use

$$E = \frac{hc}{\lambda_0} \qquad \ldots (2)$$

From equation-(1) and (2) we have

$$E = \frac{h^2}{2m\lambda^2}$$

$$\Rightarrow \qquad \lambda_0 = \frac{2mc\lambda^2}{h} \qquad \textbf{Ans. (A)}$$

Sol. 2 Cut off wavelength of continuous X-rays is given as

$$\lambda_c = \frac{hc}{\text{K.E.}} = \frac{hc}{eV}$$

Hence λ_c does not depend on atomic number of target but depends on potential difference between cathode and target.

Ans. (B)

Sol. 3 The work function for P is smallest so the kinetic energy of ejected electrons from P will be largest hence its stopping potential will also be largest and not all wavelength will be able to eject photoelectron from all three hence the saturation current will be different for the three metals. Hence option (A) is correct.

Ans. (A)

Sol. 4 Momentum of the object due to absorption of light is given as

$$p = \frac{Pt}{C} = \frac{30\times10^{-3}\times100\times10^{-9}}{3\times10^8} = 1.0 \times 10^{-17}\,\text{kg ms}^{-1}$$

Ans. (B)

Sol. 5 Relation between wavelength and atomic number is given by Moseley's law, given as

$$\sqrt{\frac{\lambda_{Cu}}{\lambda_{Mo}}} = \left(\frac{Z_{Cu}-1}{Z_{Mo}-1}\right)^{-1}$$

$$\Rightarrow \qquad \frac{\lambda_{Cu}}{\lambda_{Mo}} = \left(\frac{29-1}{42-1}\right)^{-2} = \left(\frac{28}{41}\right)^{-2} = \left(\frac{41}{28}\right)^{2}$$

$$\Rightarrow \qquad \frac{\lambda_{Cu}}{\lambda_{Mo}} = 2.14 \qquad\qquad \textbf{Ans. (B)}$$

Sol. 6 By photoelectric equation for the two metals, we use

$$K_{max} = h\nu - W_0$$

$$K_{max} = \frac{1}{2}mu_1^2$$

$$\Rightarrow \qquad \frac{1}{2}mu_1^2 = \frac{hc}{\lambda_1} - W_0 \qquad\qquad \ldots(1)$$

$$\text{and} \qquad \frac{1}{2}mu_2^2 = \frac{hc}{\lambda_2} - W_0 \qquad\qquad \ldots(2)$$

Dividing equation-(1) by (2) gives

$$\Rightarrow \qquad \frac{u_1^2}{u_2^2} = \frac{\dfrac{1240}{248} - W_0}{\dfrac{1240}{310} - W_0}$$

$$\Rightarrow \qquad \frac{u_2}{u_2^2} = \frac{4}{1} = \frac{5-W_0}{4-W_0}$$

$$\Rightarrow \qquad 16 - 4W_0 = 5 - W_0$$

$$\Rightarrow \qquad 11 = 3W_0$$

$$\Rightarrow \qquad W_0 = 3.7\,\text{eV} \qquad\qquad \textbf{Ans. (A)}$$

Sol. 7 From photoelectric equation, we use

$$V_0 = \frac{1}{e}\left(\frac{hc}{\lambda} - \phi\right)$$

$$\Rightarrow \qquad V_0 + \frac{\phi}{e} = \frac{hc}{e\lambda}$$

For different wavelengths of incident light, we have

$$2 + \frac{\phi}{e} = \frac{hc}{e(0.3\times10^{-6})} \qquad\qquad \ldots(1)$$

$$1 + \frac{\phi}{e} = \frac{hc}{e(0.4\times10^{-6})} \qquad\qquad \ldots(2)$$

$$0.4 + \frac{\phi}{e} = \frac{hc}{e(0.5\times10^{-6})} \qquad\qquad \ldots(3)$$

From equations (1), (2) and (3), we get

$$h = 6.4 \times 10^{-34} \qquad\qquad \textbf{Ans. (B)}$$

Sol. 8 By photoelectric equation, we have

$$\frac{hc}{\lambda} - \phi = \frac{1}{2}mv^2 = \frac{P^2}{2m}$$

Where momentum P is given as

$$P = \frac{h}{\lambda_d}$$

$$\Rightarrow \qquad \frac{hc}{\lambda} - \phi = \frac{h^2}{2m\lambda_d^2}$$

Differentiating the above equation gives

$$-hc\frac{\Delta\lambda}{\lambda^2} = \frac{h^2}{2m}\frac{(-2)}{\lambda_d^3}\frac{\Delta\lambda_d}{\Delta\lambda}$$

$$\Rightarrow \qquad -\frac{hc\,2m}{h^2(-2)} = \frac{\lambda_d^3}{\lambda^2} = \frac{\Delta\lambda_d}{\Delta\lambda} \qquad\qquad \textbf{Ans. (A)}$$

Sol. 9 When stopping potential is 6 V then by photoelectric effect equation, we have

$$\frac{hc}{\lambda} = \phi + 6 \qquad\qquad \ldots(1)$$

When stopping potential drops to 0.6 V then we use

$$\frac{hc}{4\lambda} = \phi + 0.6 \qquad\qquad \ldots(2)$$

Solving above equations, we get

$$\phi = 1.2\,\text{eV}$$

$$\text{and} \qquad \frac{3hc}{4\lambda} = 5.4\,\text{eV}$$

$$\Rightarrow \qquad \frac{3}{4}\times\frac{6.63\times10^{-24}\times3\times10^8}{5.4\times1.6\times10^{-19}} = \lambda = 1.72 \times 10^{-7}\,\text{m} \qquad \textbf{Ans. (A)}$$

Sol. 10 For the given orbit, we use

$$4.5\,a_0 = a_0 \frac{n^2}{Z} \qquad \ldots(1)$$

From Bohr's second postulate, we use

$$\frac{nh}{2\pi} = \frac{3h}{2\pi} \qquad \ldots(2)$$

From above equations, we get
$$n = 3 \ \text{and} \ Z = 2$$
Thus possible wavelength are

$$\frac{1}{\lambda_1} = RZ^2 \left[\frac{1}{1^2} - \frac{1}{3^2} \right]$$

$$\Rightarrow \qquad \lambda_1 = \frac{9}{32R}$$

and

$$\frac{1}{\lambda_2} = RZ^2 \left[\frac{1}{1^2} - \frac{1}{2^2} \right]$$

$$\Rightarrow \qquad \lambda_2 = \frac{1}{3R}$$

and

$$\frac{1}{\lambda_3} = RZ^2 \left[\frac{1}{2^2} - \frac{1}{3^2} \right]$$

$$\Rightarrow \qquad \lambda_3 = \frac{9}{5R} \qquad \textbf{Ans. (A, C)}$$

Sol. 11 From photoelectric equation, we have

$$\frac{hc}{\lambda} = \phi + ev_0$$

$$\Rightarrow \qquad v_0 = \frac{hc}{e}\left(\frac{1}{\lambda}\right) - \frac{\phi}{e} \qquad \textbf{Ans. (A, C)}$$

Sol. 12 Kinetic energy of electrons passing through anode is given as

$$K_e = \frac{hc}{\lambda_{ph}} - \phi + eV = \frac{p^2}{2m}$$

Momentum of electron passing through the anode is given as

$$p = \frac{h}{\lambda_e}$$

$$\Rightarrow \qquad \frac{hc}{e\lambda_{ph}} - \frac{\phi}{e} + V = \frac{h^2}{2me\lambda_e^2} \qquad \ldots(1)$$

For very large value of V, we use

$$V = \frac{h^2}{2me\lambda_e^2}$$

Here if V is made four times then λ_e can be considered to be reduced to approximately half. Hence option (A) is correct.

From equation (1) it can be seen that options (B), (C) and (D) are NOT correct. **Ans. (A)**

Sol. 13 Cut-off wavelength of X-rays is calculated as

$$\lambda_{\min} = \frac{hc}{eV}$$

$$\Rightarrow \qquad \lambda_{\min} \ \alpha \ \frac{1}{V}$$

As potential difference across the tube in increased to $2V$, the new cut-off wavelength becomes

$$(\lambda_{\min})_{\text{new}} = \frac{\lambda_2}{2}$$

Wavelength of characteristic X-rays depend only upon the material of target anode so these will remain same hence option (A) is correct.

As filament current is decreased, number of electrons producing X-rays will decrease hence X-rays intensity will decrease. Hence option (C) is correct. **Ans. (A, C)**

Sol. 14 Wavelength of characteristic X-ray depends on atomic number of target element and is independent of accelerating potential in X-ray tube.
Statement-2 is also true but it is not correct explanation as when electron beam strikes the target in an X-ray tube, part of kinetic energy is converted into X-ray energy. So option B is correct.
Ans. (B)

Sol. 15 After acceleration through V_0, kinetic energy of a particle becomes qV_0. Thus kinetic energy of alpha particle and proton will be

$$K_\alpha = 200\,\text{eV}$$

and $$K_p = 100\,\text{eV}$$

deBroglie wavelength of a moving particle with kinetic energy K is given as

$$\lambda = \frac{h}{\sqrt{2mK}}$$

$$\Rightarrow \qquad \frac{\lambda_p}{\lambda_\alpha} = \sqrt{\frac{m_\alpha K_\alpha}{m_p K_p}} = \sqrt{\frac{4 \times 200}{1 \times 100}} = 2\sqrt{2}$$

$$\Rightarrow \qquad \frac{\lambda_p}{\lambda_\alpha} = 2 \times 1.414 \cong 3 \qquad \textbf{Ans. (3)}$$

Sol. 16 Energy of incident photon is given as

$$E \approx \frac{1240}{200}\,\text{eV} = 6.2\,\text{eV}$$

Maximum KE of a electron is given as

$$K_{\max} = 6.2\,\text{eV} - 4.7\,\text{eV}$$

When potential on surface of sphere becomes equal to 1.5 V, we use

$$\frac{q}{4\pi \in_0 r} = 1.5\,\text{V}$$

$$\Rightarrow \qquad q = 1.5 \times 4\pi \varepsilon_0 \times r$$

No. of photoelectron emitted can be calculated as

$$n = \frac{1.5 \times (4\pi\varepsilon_0) r}{1.6 \times 10^{-19}} = 1.04 \times 10^7 \qquad \textbf{Ans. (7)}$$

Sol. 17 At closest approach electrostatic potential energy is equal to kinetic energy

$$\frac{Kq_1 q_2}{r} = \frac{p^2}{2m}$$

$$\Rightarrow \quad \frac{(9 \times 10^9)(120e)(e)}{10 \times 10^{-15}} = \frac{p^2}{2m} \qquad \ldots(1)$$

de-Broglie wavelength of proton at start is given as

$$\lambda = \frac{h}{p}$$

$$\Rightarrow \quad p^2 = \frac{h^2}{\lambda^2}$$

From equation (1), we have

$$2\left(\frac{5}{3} \times 10^{-27}\right) 10^{15} (9 \times 10^9) (12) e^2 = \frac{h^2}{2m\lambda^2}$$

$$\Rightarrow \quad (120)(3) 10^{-27+15+9} \lambda^2 = (4.2)^2 \times 10^{-30}$$

$$\Rightarrow \quad \lambda^2 = \frac{4.2 \times 4.2 \times 10^{-30}}{360 \times 10^{-3}} = \frac{42 \times 42}{360} \times 10^{-29}$$

$$\Rightarrow \quad \lambda^2 = 7^2 \times 10^{-30}$$

$$\Rightarrow \quad \lambda = 7 \times 10^{-15}\,\mathrm{m}$$

$$\Rightarrow \quad \lambda = 7\,\mathrm{fm} \qquad \textbf{Ans. (7)}$$

Sol. 18 Slop of graph is h/e which is a constant hence the ratio will be 1. **Ans. (1)**

Sol. 19 If the kinetic energy of ejected electron is K, we use

$$\frac{hc}{\lambda} = \text{Ionization energy} + K$$

$$\frac{hc}{\lambda} = \frac{13.6}{n^2} + 10.4$$

$$\Rightarrow \quad \frac{1242}{90} = 10.4 + \frac{13.6}{n^2}$$

$$\Rightarrow \quad 13.8 - 10.4 = \frac{13.6}{n^2}$$

$$\Rightarrow \quad 3.4 = \frac{13.6}{n^2}$$

$$\Rightarrow \quad n^2 = \frac{13.6}{3.4} = 4$$

$$\Rightarrow \quad n = 2 \qquad \textbf{Ans. (2)}$$

Sol. 20 Angular momentum of electron is given as

$$mvr = \frac{3h}{2\pi} = \frac{nh}{2\pi}$$

$$\Rightarrow \quad n = 3$$

The de-Broglie wavelength of the electron is given as

$$\lambda = \frac{h}{p} = \frac{hr}{mvr} = \frac{hr}{\dfrac{3h}{2\pi}} = \frac{2\pi r}{3}$$

radius of nth orbit of electron in terms of Bohr radius is given as

$$r = a_0 \frac{n^2}{Z}$$

$$\Rightarrow \quad \lambda = \frac{2\pi}{3} a_0 \frac{n^2}{Z}$$

$$\Rightarrow \quad 3\lambda = 2\pi \left(\frac{3^2}{3}\right) a_0$$

$$\Rightarrow \quad \lambda = 2\pi a_0 = \rho \pi a_0$$

$$\Rightarrow \quad p = 2 \qquad \textbf{Ans. (2)}$$

Sol. 21 Number of electrons emitted per second from the source are given as

$$N = \frac{200}{6.25 \times 1.6 \times 10^{-19} J}$$

Force due to radiation pressure is equal to the rate of change of linear momentum of electrons, given as

$$F = N\sqrt{2mK}$$

$$\Rightarrow \quad F = \frac{200}{6.25 \times 1.6 \times 10^{-19}} \times \sqrt{2 \times 9 \times 10^{-31} \times 1.6 \times 10^{-19} \times 500}$$

$$\Rightarrow \quad F = 24 \times 10^{-4}\,\mathrm{N} \qquad \textbf{Ans. (24)}$$

Sol. 22 If momentum of one photon is p and after reflection velocity gained by the mirror is v, by conservation of linear momentum we have

$$Np\hat{i} = -Np\hat{i} + mv\hat{i}$$

$$\Rightarrow \quad mv\hat{i} = 2pN\hat{i}$$

$$\Rightarrow \quad mv = 2Np \qquad \ldots(1)$$

Since v is velocity of mirror attached to spring at mean position, it can be given as

$$v = A\Omega$$

Where A is oscillation amplitude or maximum deflection of mirror from mean position and Ω is angular frequency of mirror spring system. Momentum of one incident photon is given as

$$p = \frac{h}{\lambda}$$

$$\Rightarrow \quad mv = 2Np \qquad \ldots(2)$$

$$\Rightarrow \qquad mA\Omega = 2N\frac{h}{\lambda}$$

$$\Rightarrow \qquad N = \frac{m\Omega}{h} \times \frac{\lambda A}{2}$$

Given values are $\dfrac{m\Omega}{h} = \dfrac{10^{24}}{4\pi}$ m^{-2} and $\lambda = 8\pi \times 10^{-6}$ m, so we have

$$N = \frac{10^{24}}{4\pi} \times \frac{8\pi \times 10^{-6} \times 10^{-6}}{2}$$

$$\Rightarrow \qquad N = 10^{12} = x \times 10^{12}$$

$$\Rightarrow \qquad x = 1 \qquad\qquad \textbf{Ans. (1.00)}$$

Sol. 23 Rate of cooling of an object due to radiation loss is given as

$$- MS\frac{dT}{dt} = \sigma e A T^4$$

$$\Rightarrow \qquad - MS\frac{dT}{dt} = \sigma A T^4$$

$$\Rightarrow \qquad \frac{\sigma A}{MS} \int\limits_{t_i}^{t_f} dt = - \int\limits_{t_i}^{t_f} \frac{dT}{T^4}$$

$$\Rightarrow \qquad \frac{t_1}{t_2} = \frac{\dfrac{1}{(100)^3} - \dfrac{1}{(200)^3}}{\dfrac{1}{(50)^3} - \dfrac{1}{(200)^3}} = \frac{1}{9}$$

$$\Rightarrow \qquad \frac{t_2}{t_1} = 9 \qquad\qquad \textbf{Ans. (9)}$$

Sol. 24 For Metal P, we have

$$E_P = \frac{hc}{\lambda_1} - 4 \qquad\qquad \ldots(1)$$

For Metal Q, we have

$$E_Q = \frac{E_P}{2} = \frac{hc}{\lambda_1} - 4.5 \qquad\qquad \ldots(2)$$

From equations-(1) and (2), we have

$$E_P = 1\,\text{eV}$$

For Metal R, we have

$$E_R = \frac{E_P}{2} = \frac{hc}{\lambda_2} - 5.5 \qquad\qquad \ldots(3)$$

$$\Rightarrow \qquad \frac{hc}{\lambda_2} = 6\,\text{eV} \qquad\qquad \textbf{Ans. (6)}$$

Ch-21 Atoms

Sol. 1 Largest wavelength in the ultraviolet region of the hydrogen spectrum corresponds to the transition from $n = 2$ to $n = 1$,

$$\frac{1}{\lambda} = R Z^2 \left(\frac{1}{n_1^2} - \frac{1}{n_2^2} \right)$$

$$\Rightarrow \qquad \frac{1}{122} = R \left(\frac{1}{1^2} - \frac{1}{2^2} \right) = R\left(1 - \frac{1}{4} \right) \qquad \ldots(1)$$

$$\Rightarrow \qquad R = \frac{1}{122} \times \frac{4}{3}$$

Transition from $n = \infty$ to $n = 3$ will produce the smallest wavelength in infrared region of hydrogen spectrum so

$$\frac{1}{\lambda} = R \left(\frac{1}{3^2} - \frac{1}{\infty} \right) \qquad\qquad \ldots(2)$$

$$\Rightarrow \qquad \frac{1}{\lambda} = \frac{1}{122} \times \frac{4}{3} \times \frac{1}{9}$$

$$\Rightarrow \qquad \lambda = \frac{122 \times 3 \times 9}{4} = 823.5\,\text{nm} \qquad \textbf{Ans. (B)}$$

Sol. 2 Energy of first spectral line of Balmer series is given as

$$E = \frac{hc}{\lambda} = 13.6\,Z^2 \left(\frac{1}{n_1^2} - \frac{1}{n_2^2} \right)$$

$$\Rightarrow \qquad \frac{hc}{6561} = 13.6 \left[\frac{1}{2^2} - \frac{1}{3^2} \right]$$

$$\Rightarrow \qquad \frac{hc}{6561} = 13.6 \times \frac{5}{36} \qquad\qquad \ldots(1)$$

Energy of second spectral line of wavelength λ is given as

$$\frac{hc}{\lambda} = 13.6 \times 4 \left[\frac{1}{2^2} - \frac{1}{4^2} \right]$$

$$\Rightarrow \qquad \frac{hc}{\lambda} = 13.6 \times 4 \times \frac{3}{16} \qquad\qquad \ldots(2)$$

Dividing equation-(1) by (2) gives

$$\frac{\lambda}{6561} = \frac{5}{36} \times \frac{4}{3}$$

$$\Rightarrow \qquad \lambda = \frac{6561 \times 5}{27} = 243 \times 5 = 1215\,\text{Å} \qquad \textbf{Ans. (A)}$$

Sol. 3 Radius of nth orbit is given as

$$r = a_0 \frac{n^2}{Z}$$

By differentiating this expression, we get

$$\frac{dR}{dn} = 2a_0 \frac{n}{Z}$$

$$\Rightarrow \qquad dR = 2a_0 \frac{n}{Z}\, dn$$

For two consecutive orbitals, we use $dn = 1$ so we have

$$dR = 2a_0 \frac{n}{Z} \times 1$$

$$\Rightarrow \qquad \frac{dR}{R} = \frac{2a_0 \dfrac{n}{Z}}{n^2 / Z} = \frac{1}{n}$$

Hence options (A) and (B) are correct.

Energy of electron in n^{th} orbit is given as

$$E = -13.6 \frac{Z^2}{n^2} \text{ eV}$$

Differentiating above expression gives

$$dE = +13.6 \frac{Z^2}{n^3} \, dn = \frac{13.6 Z^2}{n^3} \text{ eV}$$

$$\Rightarrow \qquad \frac{dE}{E} = \frac{1}{n}$$

Hence option (C) is NOT correct.

Angular momentum of electron in n^{th} orbital is given as

$$L = \frac{nh}{2\pi}$$

$$\Rightarrow \qquad \frac{dL}{dn} = \frac{K}{2\pi}$$

$$\Rightarrow \qquad dL = \frac{h}{2\pi}$$

$$\Rightarrow \qquad \frac{dL}{L} = \frac{1}{n}$$

Hence option (D) is correct.   **Ans. (A, B, D)**

Sol. 4 Energy absorbed by electron in transition from $n = 1$ to $n = 4$ is given as

$$\frac{hc}{\lambda_a} = 13.6 \left[\frac{1}{1} - \frac{1}{4^2} \right] \qquad \ldots (1)$$

Energy released by electron in transition from $n = 4$ to $n = m$ is given as

$$\frac{hc}{\lambda_e} = 13.6 \left[\frac{1}{m^2} - \frac{1}{4^2} \right] \qquad \ldots (2)$$

Dividing equation (2) by (1) gives

$$\frac{\lambda_a}{\lambda_e} = \frac{\left[\dfrac{1}{m^2} - \dfrac{1}{16} \right]}{\left[1 - \dfrac{1}{16} \right]} = \frac{1}{5}$$

$$\Rightarrow \qquad \frac{1}{m^2} - \frac{1}{16} = \frac{15}{16} \times \frac{1}{5}$$

$$\Rightarrow \qquad \frac{1}{m^2} - \frac{1}{16} = \frac{3}{16}$$

$$\Rightarrow \qquad \frac{1}{m^2} = \frac{3}{16} + \frac{1}{16}$$

$$\Rightarrow \qquad m = 2$$

Hence option (C) is correct.

From equation (2), we have

$$\frac{hc}{\lambda_e} = 13.6 \left[\frac{1}{2^2} - \frac{1}{4^2} \right] = 13.6 \times \frac{3}{16} \text{ eV}$$

$$\Rightarrow \qquad \lambda_e = \frac{12400 \times 16}{13.6 \times 3} \text{ Å}$$

$$\Rightarrow \qquad \lambda_e \approx 4862 \text{ Å}$$

Hence option (A) is NOT correct.

For kinetic energy of electron in n^{th} orbit, we use

$$\text{KE}_n \propto \frac{Z^2}{n^2}$$

$$\Rightarrow \qquad \frac{KE_2}{KE_1} = \frac{1}{4}$$

Hence option (B) is correct.

Momentum of photon is given as

$$\Delta P_a = \frac{h}{\lambda_a}$$

and $\qquad \Delta P_e = \dfrac{h}{\lambda_e}$

$$\Rightarrow \qquad \frac{\Delta P_a}{\Delta P_e} = \frac{\lambda_e}{\lambda_a}$$

Hence option (D) is NOT correct.   **Ans. (B, C)**

Sol. 5 In the potential energy field, force on particle is given as

$$F = \left| \frac{dU}{dr} \right|$$

This force provides the centripetal force for circular motion of particle in a circle of radius R so we use

$$F = \frac{mv^2}{R} \qquad \ldots (1)$$

Using Bohr's model, the angular momentum of particle is given as

$$mvR = \frac{nh}{2\pi} \qquad \ldots (2)$$

$$\Rightarrow \qquad F = \frac{m}{R} \times \frac{n^2 h^2}{4\pi^2} \times \frac{1}{m^2 R^2}$$

$$\Rightarrow \qquad R = \left(\frac{n^2 h^2}{4\pi^2 mF} \right)^{1/3} \qquad \ldots (3)$$

Hence option (A) is NOT correct.

$$v = \frac{nh}{2\pi m R}$$

$$\Rightarrow \qquad v = \frac{nh}{2\pi m} \left(\frac{4\pi^2 mF}{n^2 h^2} \right)^{1/3}$$

$$\Rightarrow \qquad v = \frac{n^{1/3} h^{1/3} F^{1/3}}{2^{1/3} \pi^{1/3} m^{2/3}} \qquad \qquad \ldots(4)$$

Hence option (B) is correct.

Total energy of particle in orbital motion is given as

$$E = \frac{1}{2} mv^2 + U = \frac{1}{2} mv^2 + FR$$

$$\Rightarrow \qquad E = \frac{1}{2} m \left(\frac{n^{2/3} h^{2/3} F^{2/3}}{2^{2/3} \pi^{2/3} m^{4/3}} \right) + F \times \left(\frac{n^2 h^2}{4\pi^2 mF} \right)^{1/3}$$

$$\Rightarrow \qquad E = \left(\frac{n^2 h^2 F^2}{4\pi^2 m} \right)^{1/3} \left[\frac{1}{2} + 1 \right]$$

$$\Rightarrow \qquad E = \frac{3}{2} \left(\frac{n^2 h^2 F^2}{4\pi^2 m} \right)^{1/3}$$

Hence option (C) is correct. **Ans. (B, C)**

Sol. 6 (A) When transition is from any level to $n = 2$, then it belongs to Balmer series for which longest wavelength is corresponding to least energy difference i.e. for transition from $n = 3$ to $n = 2$ and shortest wavelength is corresponding to maximum energy difference i.e. for transition $n = \infty$ to $n = 2$. The wavelengths can be calculated by Rydberg's formula given as

$$\frac{1}{\lambda} = RZ^2 \left[\frac{1}{n_1^2} - \frac{1}{n_2^2} \right]$$

$$\Rightarrow \qquad \frac{\lambda_{\text{longest}}}{\lambda_{\text{shortest}}} = \frac{\left[\frac{1}{2^2} - \frac{1}{\infty} \right]}{\left[\frac{1}{2^2} - \frac{1}{3^2} \right]} = \frac{9}{5}$$

Hence option (A) is correct.

The longest wavelength of Balmer series is given as

$$\lambda_{\text{longest}} = \frac{36}{5R}$$

The shortest wavelength of Paschen series is given as

$$\lambda_{\text{shortest}} = \frac{9}{R}$$

These do not overlap hence option (B) is NOT correct.

Wavelength of Lyman series from m^{th} orbit is given as

$$\frac{1}{\lambda} = R \left[\frac{1}{1^2} - \frac{1}{m^2} \right]$$

Shortest wavelength of Lyman series is corresponding to the transition from $n = \infty$ to $n = 1$ which is given as

$$\frac{1}{\lambda_0} = R$$

$$\Rightarrow \qquad \frac{1}{\lambda} = \frac{1}{\lambda_0} \left[1 - \frac{1}{m^2} \right]$$

$$\Rightarrow \qquad \lambda = \frac{\lambda_0}{1 - \frac{1}{m^2}}$$

Hence option (C) is NOT correct.

The longest wavelength of Lyman series is given as

$$\lambda_{\text{longest}} = \frac{4}{3R}$$

The shortest wavelength of Balmer series is given as

$$\lambda_{\text{shortest}} = \frac{4}{R}$$

These wavelength do not overlap hence option (D) is correct.

Ans. (A, D)

Sol. 7 (A) : The X-ray contains K_α and K_β and these are transition between two atomic level. Also in hydrogen spectrum lines are plotted corresponding to the energy emitted dur to transition of electron between two atomic levels. Hence option (p) and (r) are correctly related here.

(B) : Electron emission happens in photoelectric effect as well as in beta decay hence options (q) and (s) are correctly related.

(C) : Moseley's law gives the emission frequency of photons of the characteristic X-ray hence option (p) is correctly related.

(D) : In photoelectric effect photon is absorbed and with the use of photon energy, electron is ejected with some kinetic energy hence option (q) is correctly related.

Ans. [A (q, r); B (q, s); C (p); D (q)]

Sol. 8 When hydrogen atom transfers its total excitation energy (which is 10.2eV) to He$^+$ ion in first excited state then He$^+$ ion are excited to $n = 4$ level. **Ans. (C)**

Sol. 9 The wavelength of light emitted in the visible region by He$^+$ ions in final excited state is :

$$\lambda = \frac{hc}{\Delta E_{4\to3}}$$

Energy of photons emitted for this transition is given as

$$\Delta E_{4\to3} = (6.04 - 3.4)\, \text{eV} = 2.64 \text{ eV}$$

$$\Rightarrow \qquad \lambda = \frac{hc}{2.64 eV}$$

$$\Rightarrow \qquad \lambda = \frac{12.4 \times 10^{-7}}{2.64} \text{ m}$$

$$\Rightarrow \qquad \lambda = 4.8 \times 10^{-7} \text{ m} \qquad \textbf{Ans. (C)}$$

Sol. 10 Kinetic energy of electron in n^{th} orbit is given as

$$K \propto \frac{Z^2}{n^2}$$

$$\Rightarrow \quad \frac{K_{\text{H}}}{K_{\text{He}^+}} = \frac{Z_{\text{H}}^2}{Z_{\text{He}^+}^2} = \frac{(1)}{(2)^2} = \frac{1}{4} \qquad \textbf{Ans. (A)}$$

Sol. 11 There are n loops in standing wave so we use

$$a = n\left(\frac{\lambda}{2}\right)$$

$$\Rightarrow \quad \lambda = \frac{2a}{n}$$

Momentum of particles is given as

$$p = \frac{h}{\lambda} = \frac{nh}{2a}$$

$$\Rightarrow \quad E = \frac{n^2 h^2}{4a^2 2m} = \frac{n^2 h^2}{8ma^2}$$

$$\Rightarrow \quad E \propto a^{-2} \qquad \textbf{Ans. (A)}$$

Sol. 12 In ground state $n = 1$ is given as

$$E = \frac{h^2}{8ma^2} = \frac{(6.6 \times 10^{-34})^2}{8 \times 10^{-30} \times (6.6 \times 10^{-9})^2} \, \text{J}$$

$$\Rightarrow \quad E = \frac{1}{8} \times \frac{10^{-68}}{10^{-48} \times 1.6 \times 10^{-19}} = \frac{10^{-1}}{8 \times 1.6} \, \text{eV}$$

$$\Rightarrow \quad E = \frac{100}{8 \times 1.6} \, \text{meV} = 8 \, \text{meV} \qquad \textbf{Ans. (B)}$$

Sol. 13 Speed of particle will depend on energy in n^{th} orbit so we have

$$\Rightarrow \quad \frac{1}{2} mv^2 = \frac{n^2 h^2}{8ma^2}$$

$$\Rightarrow \quad v \propto n \qquad \textbf{Ans. (D)}$$

Sol. 14 By Bohr quantization principle, angular momentum of electron is given as

$$L = \frac{nh}{2\pi} = I\omega$$

$$\Rightarrow \quad \omega = \frac{nh}{2\pi I}$$

Rotational kinetic energy of electron is given as

$$K_{\text{rot}} = \frac{1}{2} I\omega^2 = \frac{1}{2} I \left(\frac{nh}{2\pi I}\right)^2 = \frac{n^2 h^2}{8\pi^2 I} \qquad \textbf{Ans. (D)}$$

Sol. 15 Change in kinetic energy from $n = 2$ to $n = 1$, we have

$$\Delta E = E_2 - E_i$$

$$\Rightarrow \quad \Delta E = \frac{2^2 h^2}{8\pi^2 I} - \frac{1^2 h^2}{8\pi^2 I} = \frac{3h^2}{8\pi^2 I} = h\nu$$

Using $\nu = \dfrac{4}{\pi} \times 10^{11}$ Hz and solving for moment of inertia gives

$$I = 1.87 \times 10^{-46} \, \text{kg-m}^2 \qquad \textbf{Ans. (B)}$$

Sol. 16 The moment of inertia of the molecule about its centre of mass (as shown in figure below) is given as

$$I = m_1 r_1^2 + m_2 r_2^2$$

For centre of mass we have

$$m_1 r_1 = m_2 r_2$$

$$r_1 + r_2 = r$$

Solving we get

$$I = \frac{m_1 m_2}{m_1 + m_2} r^2 = \left(\frac{48}{7} a.m.u.\right) r^2 = (11.43 \times 10^{-27} \, \text{kg}) r^2$$

$$\Rightarrow \quad r = \sqrt{\frac{1.87 \times 10^{-46}}{11.43 \times 10^{-27}}} = 1.28 \times 10^{-10} \, \text{m} \qquad \textbf{Ans. (C)}$$

Sol. 17 Energy gained by electron in ground state through the incident light is given as

$$E = \frac{hc}{\lambda} = \frac{1.237 \times 10^{-6}}{970 \times 10^{-10}} \approx 12.75 \, \text{eV}$$

$$E = 13.6 \, Z^2 \left(\frac{1}{n_1^2} - \frac{1}{n_2^2}\right)$$

$$\Rightarrow \quad 12.75 \, \text{eV} = 13.6 \left[1 - \frac{1}{n^2}\right]$$

$$\Rightarrow \quad n = 4$$

Thus number of spectrum lines emitted are given as

$$N = {}^4C_2 = \frac{4(4-1)}{2} = 6 \qquad \textbf{Ans. (6)}$$

Sol. 18 Ratio of potential energies is given as

$$\frac{V_i}{V_f} = 6.25$$

Potential energy of electron in n^{th} orbit is given as

$$V \propto \frac{1}{n^2}$$

$$\Rightarrow \quad \frac{V_i}{V_f} = \frac{n_f^2}{n_i^2} = 6.25$$

$$\Rightarrow \quad \frac{n_f}{n_i} = \frac{5}{2}$$

Thus minimum values can be taken as $n_f = 5$ when $n_i = 2$.

$$\textbf{Ans. (5)}$$

Sol. 19 As described in question, we have

$$\Delta E_{2-1} = 74.8 + \Delta E_{3-2}$$

Transition energy can be calculated as

$$\Delta E = 13.6\, Z^2 \left(\frac{1}{n_1^2} - \frac{1}{n_2^2}\right) eV$$

$$\Rightarrow \quad 13.6\, Z^2 \left[1 - \frac{1}{4}\right] = 74.8 + 13.6\, Z^2 \left[\frac{1}{4} - \frac{1}{9}\right]$$

$$\Rightarrow \qquad Z = 3 \qquad\qquad \textbf{Ans. (3)}$$

Sol. 20 The energies of electron in $n = 4$ and $n = 3$ are given as

$$E_3 = -1.51\, Z^2\, eV$$
$$E_4 = -0.85\, Z^2\, eV$$

Energy of photons emitted in transition between these orbits is calculated as

$$\Delta E = E_4 - E_3 = 0.66\, Z^2\, eV$$

Maximum kinetic energy of ejected photoelectrons from metal surface is calculated as

$$K_{max} = E - W$$

$$1.95 = 0.66\, Z^2 - \frac{1240}{310}$$

$$0.66 Z^2 = 1.95 + 4$$

$$\Rightarrow \qquad Z = 3 \qquad\qquad \textbf{Ans. (3)}$$

Ch-22 Nuclei

Sol. 1 Rest mass energy of U will be greater than the rest mass energy of the nucleus in which it breaks because after breaking the fragments always have some kinetic energies and Iodine and Yttrium are medium sized nuclei and therefore, have more binding energy per nucleon as compared to Uranium which has a big nuclei and less B.E./nucleon. **Ans. (A)**

Sol. 2 The activity of a radioactive sample is given as

$$R = \lambda N$$

Half life of a radioactive sample is given as

$$T = \frac{0.693}{\lambda}$$

For sample S_1, we have

$$T_1 = \frac{0.693 N_1}{5}$$

For sample S_2, we have

$$T_2 = \frac{0.693 N_2}{10}$$

$$\Rightarrow \qquad \frac{T_1}{T_2} = \frac{4}{1} \qquad\qquad \textbf{Ans. (A)}$$

Sol. 3 By radioactive decay law, we have

$$N = N_0 (2)^{-t/T}$$

$$\Rightarrow \qquad \frac{1}{64} = (2)^{-t/T}$$

$$\Rightarrow \qquad 2^6 = (2)^{t/18}$$

$$\Rightarrow \qquad t = 108\ \text{days} \qquad\qquad \textbf{Ans. (C)}$$

Sol. 4 Binding energy of $^{15}_8 O$ and $^{15}_7 N$ are given as

$$B_O = (8m_p + 7m_n - M_O)c^2$$
$$\text{and} \qquad B_N = (7m_p + 8m_n - M_N)c^2$$

Difference in binding energies of $^{15}_7 N$ and $^{15}_8 O$ is given as

$$\Delta E = (m_n + M_O - M_N - m_p)c^2$$

$$\Delta E = (1.008665 + 15.003065 - 15.000109 - 1.007825) \times 931.5\ \text{MeV}$$
$$\Delta E = 3.535974\ \text{MeV}$$

$$\Rightarrow \quad \frac{3}{5} \times \frac{8 \times 7 \times 1.44}{R} - \frac{3}{5} \times \frac{7 \times 6 \times 1.44}{R} = 3.535974$$

$$\Rightarrow \quad R = 3.42\ \text{fm} \qquad\qquad \textbf{Ans. (C)}$$

Sol. 5 For simultaneous decay of elements, we use

$$\lambda = \lambda_1 + \lambda_2 = 5 \times 10^{-10}\ \text{per year}$$

By radioactive decay law, we have

$$N = N_0 e^{-\lambda t}$$

In a given time t, number of decayed nuclei are given as

$$N_{decayed} = N_0 - N$$

Ratio of all decayed to the radioactive nuclei is given as

$$\frac{N_0 - N}{N} = 99$$

$$\Rightarrow \qquad \frac{N_0}{N} = 100$$

$$\Rightarrow \qquad \frac{N}{N_0} = e^{-\lambda t} = \frac{1}{100}$$

$$\Rightarrow \qquad \lambda t = 2 \ln 10$$

$$\Rightarrow \qquad \lambda t = 4.6$$

$$\Rightarrow \qquad t = 9.2 \times 10^9\ \text{years} \qquad\qquad \textbf{Ans. (A)}$$

Sol. 6 Total number of decays in one hour are given as

$$N_d = \left[1 - \left(\frac{1}{2}\right)^{t/T}\right] \times N_0$$

$$\Rightarrow \quad N_d = \left[1 - \left(\frac{1}{2}\right)^3\right] \times 1000 = \frac{7}{8} \times 1000 = 875$$

Thus number of α-decays are given as

$$N_\alpha = 875 \times 60\% = 525 \qquad\qquad \textbf{Ans. (D)}$$

Sol. 7 Energy is released when binding energy per nucleon increases in fusion of two nuclei of lower masses in range from 1 to 50 hence option (A) is correct. Mass numbers in range 51 to 100 are more stable as these have higher binding energy per nucleon hence option (B) is NOT correct. Nuclei of mass number 102 to 200 have binding energy per nucleon greater than those in range from 200 to 260 so those are more stable hence option (D) is correct. **Ans. (A, D)**

Sol. 8 By using mass and charge conservation for the given equation, we can find that for x and y their sum of charges is 0 and sum of masses is 2 hence options (B) and (C) are NOT correct.

In above fission reaction as initially $^{236}_{92}U$ was at rest, after fission momentum will remain conserved and kinetic energy of the released fragment is related to its momentum as

$$K = \frac{p^2}{2m}$$

As x and y are very small particles and will not carry very high momentum so energy of the smaller fragment has to be larger by conservation of momentum hence option (A) is correct.

Ans. (A)

Sol. 9 In the given reaction of decay process, number of α-particles can be calculated by mass conservation, given as

$$N_\alpha = \frac{232 - 212}{4} = \frac{20}{4} = 5$$

Thus reaction can be written as

$$^{232}_{90}Th \; \rightarrow \; ^{212}_{82}Pb + 5\,^4_2He + 2\,^{\;0}_{-1}\beta \qquad \textbf{Ans. (A, C)}$$

Sol. 10 In the given fission reaction $N \rightarrow P + Q$ as initially N was at rest then after decay we can use conservation of momentum which gives

$$M_P v_P = M_Q v_Q \qquad \ldots (1)$$

$$\Rightarrow \qquad M_P E_P = M_Q E_Q$$

Hence option (C) is correct.

The kinetic energy in fragments will come from the released energy in the reaction which is given as

$$(\delta)c^2 = E_P + E_Q \qquad \ldots (2)$$

Hence option (A) is correct.

From equations (1) and (2), we have

$$E_P \left[1 + \frac{M_P}{M_Q} \right] = \delta C^2$$

$$\Rightarrow \qquad E_P = \frac{M_Q \delta C^2}{M_P + M_Q}$$

Hence option (B) is NOT correct. If p_P is the momentum of P then we have

$$\frac{p_P^2}{2M_P} = \frac{M_Q \delta C^2}{M_P + M_Q}$$

$$\Rightarrow \qquad p_P = \sqrt{2\mu\delta C^2}$$

where $$\mu = \frac{M_P M_Q}{M_P + M_Q}$$

Hence option (D) is correct. **Ans. (A, C, D)**

Sol. 11 Binding energy of proton and neutron due to nuclear force is same so difference in binding energy is only due to electrostatic potential energy which is there only in case of protons which is positive so we have

$$E_0^p - E_0^n = \text{Electrostatic } PE$$

$$\Rightarrow \qquad E_0^p - E_0^n = Z \times PE \text{ of one proton due to all remaining}$$

$$\Rightarrow \qquad E_0^p - E_0^n = Z \times \frac{1}{4\pi\varepsilon_0} \frac{(Z-1)e^2}{R}$$

Hence option (A) is correct.

The separation between particles of nucleus is proportional to the nuclear radii as nuclear density always remain approximately constant so we can write

$$R \propto A^{1/3}$$

Hence option (B) is correct.

As potential energy of protons is positive hence $E_0^p - E_0^n$ will be a negative value hence option (C) is NOT correct.

When nucleus undergoes a beta decay then a positive charge inside nucleus increase due to which overall repulsion on each proton increases which decreases the binding energy of protons hence option (D) is NOT correct. **Ans. (A, B, D)**

Sol. 12 The given reactions in column-II are completely written below as

$$^{15}_{8}O \rightarrow ^{15}_{7}N + ^{\;0}_{1}\beta \quad \text{(Beta decay)}$$

$$^{238}_{92}U \rightarrow ^{234}_{90}Th + ^4_2He \quad \text{(Alpha decay)}$$

$$^{185}_{83}Bi \rightarrow ^{184}_{82}Pb + ^1_1H \quad \text{(Proton emission)}$$

$$^{239}_{94}Ph \rightarrow ^{140}_{57}La + ^{99}_{37}Rb \quad \text{(fission)}$$

Hence option (C) is correct. **Ans. (C)**

Sol. 13 (A): Source of energy of sun and stars is nuclear fusion hence options (r) and (t) are correctly related.

(B): In fission $_{92}U^{235}$ absorbs neutrons. Heavy nucleus divides into lighter nuclei and to control fission it involves heavy water as moderator. The fragments produced in fission reaction undergoes beta decay and also produces neutrinos hence options (p), (q), (s) and (t) are correctly related.

(C): β-decay occur in fusion reactions and it also involves with neutrino emission. Co-60 is a beta emitter here hence options (q), (r) and (t) are correctly related.

(D): γ-ray emission is involved in fission, fusion and radioactive alpha and beta decays hence options (p), (q) and (r) are correctly related.   **Ans. [(A) r, t; (B) p, q, s, t; (C) q, r, t; (D) p, q, r]**

Sol. 14 For a radioactive decay chain, number of alpha, beta + and beta – particles can be calculated by conservation of charge and mass number (nucleons) in equation. Consider the below given equation

$$_{Z_1}X^{A_1} \rightarrow _{Z_2}Y^{A_2} + a\,_2\text{He}^4 + b\,_1e^0 + c\,_{-1}e^0$$

Conservation of charge gives

$$Z_1 = Z_2 + 2a + b - c \qquad \ldots(1)$$

Conservation of nucleons gives

$$A_1 = A_2 + 4a$$

$$\Rightarrow \qquad a = \frac{A_1 - A_2}{4} \qquad \ldots(2)$$

From equations-(1) and (2) we have

$$b - c = Z_1 - Z_2 - \left(\frac{A_1 - A_2}{4}\right)$$

(P) $_{92}\text{U}^{238} \rightarrow _{91}\text{Pa}^{234}$

$$a = \frac{238 - 234}{4} = 1 \rightarrow 1\alpha$$

and $\qquad b - c = (92 - 91) - \left(\dfrac{4}{2}\right) = -1 \rightarrow \beta^-$

(Q) $_{82}\text{Pb}^{214} \rightarrow _{82}\text{Pb}^{210}$

$$a = \frac{214 - 210}{4} = 1 \rightarrow 1\alpha$$

$$b - c = (82 - 82) - \left(\frac{4}{2}\right) = -2 \rightarrow 2\beta^-$$

(R) $_{81}\text{T}l^{210} \rightarrow _{82}\text{Pb}^{206}$

$$a = \frac{210 - 206}{4} = 1 \rightarrow 1\alpha$$

$$b - c = (81 - 83) - \frac{4}{3} = -3 \rightarrow 3\beta^-$$

(S) $_{91}\text{Pa}^{228} \rightarrow _{88}\text{Ra}^{224}$

$$a = \frac{228 - 224}{4} = 1 \rightarrow 1\alpha$$

$$b - c = (91 - 88) - \frac{4}{2} = +1 \rightarrow 1\beta^+ \qquad \textbf{Ans. (A)}$$

Sol. 15 Plasma state is achieved at high temperatures.

Ans. (D)

Sol. 16 By conservation of mechanical energy, we use

$$U_i + K_i = U_f + K_f$$

$$\Rightarrow \qquad 0 + 2\,(1.5\,\text{kT}) = \frac{1}{4\pi\varepsilon_0}\frac{e^2}{d} + 0$$

$$\Rightarrow \qquad 3kT = \frac{e^2}{4\pi\varepsilon_0 d}$$

$$\Rightarrow \quad T = \frac{e^2}{3 \times 4\pi\varepsilon_0 kd} = \frac{1.44 \times 10^{-9}}{3 \times 8.6 \times 10^{-5} \times 4 \times 10^{-15}}$$

$$\Rightarrow \quad T = \frac{120}{86} \times 10^9 \approx 1.4 \times 10^9\,\text{K} \qquad \textbf{Ans. (A)}$$

Sol. 17 For Lawson criterion to be promising, we have

$$nt_0 > 8 \times 10^{14}\,\text{s cm}^{-3}$$

Out of given option nt_0 is highest for option (B) out of the given options in question.   **Ans. (B)**

Sol. 18 In beta emission the Q-value of nuclear reaction is distributed between beta particle and anti-neutrino as mass of proton is very high, its kinetic energy can be neglected so we have

$$E_{\beta^-} + E_{\bar{v}} = Q$$

Kinetic energy of emitted beta particle is maximum when energy of anti-neutrino is negligible and vice versa so we have

$$Q = 0.8 \times 10^6\,\text{eV}$$

Energy of anti-neutrino is maximum when kinetic energy of beta particle is negligible hence it is given as

$$E_{\bar{v}}(\text{max}) \cong Q \qquad \textbf{Ans. (C)}$$

Sol. 19 As antineutrino is considered with some mass, a small quantity of energy it will always carry so e^- can not have maximum kinetic energy as Q-value of reaction hence option (D) is correct.   **Ans. (D)**

Sol. 20 For option (A) the nuclear reaction can be written as

$$_3^6\text{Li} \rightarrow _2^4\text{He} + _1^2\text{H}$$

Mass defect of this reaction is given as

$$\Delta m = 6.015123 - 4.002603 - 2.014102$$

$$\Delta m = -0.001582\,u$$

As this is negative so α-decay is not possible hence option (A) is NOT correct.

For option (B) the nuclear reaction can be written as

$$_{84}^{210}\text{P}_0 \rightarrow _1^1\text{H} + _{83}^{209}\text{Bi}$$

Mass defect of this reaction is given as

$$\Delta m = 209.9828766 - 1.007825 - 208.980388$$

$$\Delta m = -0.005337\,u$$

As this is negative so this reaction is not possible hence option (B) is NOT correct.

For option (C) the nuclear reaction can be written as

$$^{2}_{1}H + {}^{4}_{2}He \rightarrow {}^{6}_{3}Li$$

Mass defect of this reaction is given as

$$\Delta m = 2.014102 + 4.002603 - 6.015123$$

$$\Delta m = 0.001582\,u$$

As this is positive so this reaction is possible hence option (C) is correct.

For option (D) the nuclear reaction can be written as

$$^{70}_{30}Zn + {}^{82}_{34}Se \rightarrow {}^{152}_{64}Gd$$

Mass defect of this reaction is given as

$$\Delta m = 69.925325 + 81.916709 - 151.919803$$

$$\Delta m = -0.077769\,u$$

As this is negative so this reaction is not possible hence option (D) is NOT correct. **Ans. (C)**

Sol. 21 The nuclear reaction of α-decay is written as

$$^{210}_{84}Po \rightarrow {}^{4}_{2}He + {}^{206}_{82}Pb$$

Q-value of this reaction can be calculated as

$$Q = (209.982876 - 4.002603 - 205.97455)\,c^2$$

$$\Rightarrow \quad Q = (209.982876 - 4.002603 - 205.97455) \times 932\,\text{MeV}$$

$$\Rightarrow \quad Q = 5.422\,\text{MeV}$$

By conservation of momentum we have

$$\sqrt{2K_{\alpha}(4)} = \sqrt{2K_{Pb}(206)}$$

$$\Rightarrow \quad 4K_{\alpha} = 206 K_{Pb}$$

$$\Rightarrow \quad K_{\alpha} = \frac{103}{2} K_{Pb}$$

$$K_{\alpha} + K_{Pb} = 5.422$$

$$K_{\alpha} + \frac{2}{103} K_{Pb} = 5.422$$

$$\Rightarrow \quad \frac{105}{103} K_{\alpha} = 5.422$$

$$\Rightarrow \quad K_{\alpha} = 5.319\,\text{MeV} = 5319\,\text{keV} \qquad \textbf{Ans. (A)}$$

Sol. 22 From the given graph slope of line is given as

$$m = \frac{1}{2} = 0.5\,\text{year}^{-1}$$

From radioactive decay law, we have

$$\frac{dN}{dt} = \lambda N e^{-\lambda t}$$

Taking natural log on both sides, we get

$$\ln\left(\frac{dN}{dt}\right) = \ln(N) - \lambda t$$

The slope of this graph is $\lambda = 0.5\,\text{year}^{-1}$ so half life of element is given as

$$t_{1/2} = \frac{0.693}{0.5}\,\text{years}$$

In the given time $t = 4.16$ years, number of half lives are

$$n = \frac{4.16}{0.693} \times 0.5 = 3$$

Thus the number of nuclei will reduce by a factor of $2^3 = 8$ so we have $p = 8$. **Ans. (8)**

Sol. 23 Activity of radioactive sample is given as

$$A = \lambda N$$

$$\Rightarrow \quad 10^{10} = \frac{1}{10^9} \times N$$

$$\Rightarrow \quad N = 10^{19}$$

Mass of sample $= 10^{19} \times 10^{-25} \times 1 \times 10^6 = 1\,\text{mg}$ **Ans. (1)**

Sol. 24 Decay constant of element is given as

$$\lambda = \frac{\ln 2}{1386} = 5 \times 10^{-4}\,\text{s}^{-1}$$

At $t = 0$, $\lambda N_0 = 1000$ dps so we use

$$\frac{N(t)}{N_0} = e^{(-\lambda t)} = e^{(-0.04)} = 0.96$$

Thus decayed amount will be $1 - 0.96 = 0.04 = 4\%$ **Ans. (4)**

Sol. 25 Plant will be able to supply the power needs of village till its power becomes 12.5% of initial power. Power production of the plant at any instant will be directly proportional to the number of undecayed nuclei present at that instant. If after time t the power generated becomes equal to the exact requirement, then by radioactive decay law, we have

$$N = N_0 e^{-\lambda t}$$

$$\Rightarrow \quad \frac{12.5}{100} \times N_0 = N_0 e^{-\lambda t}$$

$$\Rightarrow \quad 0.125 = 2^{-t/T}$$

$$\Rightarrow \quad 2^{-3} = 2^{-t/T}$$

$$\Rightarrow \quad t = 3T$$

$$\Rightarrow \quad n = 3 \qquad \textbf{Ans. (3)}$$

Sol. 26 Activity of radioactive substance is given as

$$A = A_0 e^{-\lambda t}$$

Rate of change of activity with time is given as

$$R = -\frac{dA}{dt} = \lambda A_0 e^{-\lambda t}$$

$$\Rightarrow \qquad \frac{R_P}{R_Q} = \frac{\lambda_P A_0\, e^{-\lambda_P t}}{\lambda_Q A_0\, e^{-\lambda_Q t}}$$

$$\Rightarrow \qquad \frac{R_P}{R_Q} = 2\, e^{(\lambda_Q - \lambda_P)t}$$

$$\Rightarrow \qquad \frac{R_P}{R_Q} = 2\, e^{\left[\frac{1}{2\tau} - \frac{1}{\tau}\right]\cdot 2\tau}$$

$$\Rightarrow \qquad \frac{R_P}{R_Q} = 2e^{-1} = \frac{2}{e}$$

$$\Rightarrow \qquad n = 2 \qquad\qquad \textbf{Ans. (2)}$$

Sol. 27 Q-value of nuclear reaction which is released in this reaction is given as

$$Q = (12.014u - 12u) \times 931.5 \, \text{MeV}$$

$$Q = 13.041 \, \text{MeV}$$

As $_6^{12}C^*$ is the excited state with energy 4.014 MeV, the maximum energy available for beta particle as kinetic energy is given as

$$K_\beta(\text{max}) = 9 \, \text{MeV} \qquad\qquad \textbf{Ans. (9)}$$

Sol. 28 Activity of sample after time t is given as

$$A = A_0 e^{-\lambda t}$$

Per unit volume activity can be used in above expression and for total volume of blood V, we have

$$\frac{115}{2.5} = \frac{A_0}{V} e^{-\lambda t}$$

$$\Rightarrow \qquad \frac{115}{2.5} = \frac{2.4 \times 10^5 e^{-\frac{\ln 2}{8 \times 24} \times 12}}{V}$$

$$\Rightarrow \qquad V = \frac{2.4 \times 10^2 \times 2.5 \times e^{-\frac{\ln 2}{16}}}{115}$$

$$\Rightarrow \qquad V = \frac{600}{115}\left(1 - \frac{\ln 2}{16}\right)$$

$$\Rightarrow \qquad V = \frac{600}{115} \times \left(1 - \frac{0.7}{16}\right)$$

$$\Rightarrow \qquad V = \frac{600 \times 15.3}{16 \times 115} = 4.989 \, \text{litre} \qquad \textbf{Ans. (5)}$$

Sol. 29 The nuclear reaction for the given situation described in question is written as

$$\text{Ra}^{226} \longrightarrow \text{Rn}^{222} + \alpha$$

Q-value released in the above reaction is calculated as

$$Q = (226.005 - 222 - 4)\, 931 \, \text{MeV}$$

$$\Rightarrow \qquad Q = 4.655 \, \text{MeV}$$

Kinetic energy of emitted α-particle is given as

$$K_\alpha = \frac{A-4}{A}\,(Q - E_\gamma)$$

$$\Rightarrow \qquad 4.44 \, \text{MeV} = \frac{222}{226}\,(Q - E_\gamma)$$

$$\Rightarrow \qquad Q - E_\gamma = (4.44)\left(\frac{226}{222}\right)\text{MeV}$$

$$\Rightarrow \qquad E_\gamma = 4.655 - 4.520 = 0.135 \, \text{MeV} = 135 \, \text{keV}$$

$$\textbf{Ans. (135)}$$

Sol. 30 The given nuclear reaction is

$$_7^{16}\text{N} + _2^4\text{He} \rightarrow _1^1\text{H} + _8^{19}\text{O}$$

As minimum kinetic energy is needed for incident alpha particle, we consider energy loss in collision to be maximum to provide the energy required for the reaction to occur. For this case we consider $_7^{16}$N and $_2^4$He will move together as the case of inelastic collision. If incident speed of $_2^4$He is u then after collision with N, final speed v_1 will become

$$4mv_0 + 0 = (4 + 16)\, mv_1$$

$$v_1 = \frac{u}{5}$$

Energy required to initiate the reaction is given as

$$E = (1.008 + 19.003 - 16.006 - 4.003) \times 930 = 1.86 \, \text{MeV}$$

This energy is provided by the loss of kinetic energy in collision which is given as

$$\frac{1}{2}(4m)\,u^2 - \frac{1}{2}(20m)\left(\frac{u}{5}\right)^2 = 1.86$$

$$\frac{8}{5}\, mu^2 = 1.86$$

$$mu^2 = \frac{1.86 \times 5}{8}$$

Kinetic energy of alpha particle is

$$K_\alpha = \frac{1}{2}(4m)u^2 = \frac{18.6 \times 5}{4}$$

$$K_\alpha = 2.325 \, \text{MeV} \qquad \textbf{Ans. (2.32 to 2.33)}$$

Sol. 31 The given reaction is accomplished with n alpha and m beta particles then it is written as

$$\text{Th}_{90}^{230} \rightarrow \text{Po}_{84}^{214} + n\alpha_2^4 + m\beta_{-1}^0$$

By conservation of mass, we have

$$230 = 214 + 4n$$

$$n = \frac{16}{4} = 4$$

By conservation of charge, we have

$$90 = 84 + n \times 2 - m \times 1$$

$$\Rightarrow \quad 90 = 84 + 4 \times 2 - m \times 1$$

$$\Rightarrow \quad m = 92 - 90 = 2$$

$$\Rightarrow \quad \frac{n}{m} = \frac{4}{2} = 2 \qquad \text{Ans. (2)}$$

Sol. 32 Initially both the sources have same activity A_0 and if after time $3T_1$ and $7T_2$ the activities become A_1 and A_2 then we have

$$\frac{A_1}{A_2} = \frac{A_0(2)^{-t/T_1}}{A_0(2)^{-t/T_2}}$$

$$\Rightarrow \quad \frac{A_1}{A_2} = \frac{(2)^7}{(2)^3} = 2^4 = 16 \qquad \text{Ans. (16)}$$

Ch-23 Errors and Experiments

Sol. 1 Young's modulus of wire is given as

$$Y = \frac{\text{stress}}{\text{strain}} = \frac{(F/A)}{(\Delta l / l)}$$

$$\Rightarrow \quad Y = \frac{Fl}{\pi \Delta l} = \frac{Fl}{\pi r^2 \Delta l} = \frac{4F \cdot l}{\pi D^2 \cdot \Delta l}$$

$$\Rightarrow \quad Y = \frac{4Fl}{\pi D^2 \Delta l}$$

Uncertainty factor in measurement of Young's modulus is given as

$$\frac{\Delta Y}{Y} = \frac{2\Delta D}{D} + \frac{\Delta(L)}{\Delta L} = 0.1125$$

$$\Rightarrow \quad \frac{\Delta Y}{Y} = -0.1125$$

$$\Rightarrow \quad Y = \frac{F \cdot l}{4 \Delta l} = \frac{9.8 \times 2}{\pi \times (0.2)^2 \times 0.8} \cong 2 \times 10^{11}$$

$$\Rightarrow \quad \Delta Y = -Y\left(\frac{2\Delta r}{r} + \frac{\Delta l}{l}\right)$$

$$\Rightarrow \quad \Delta Y = 0.225 \times 10^{11}$$

$$\Rightarrow \quad Y = (2 \pm 0.2) \, 10^{11} \qquad \text{Ans. (B)}$$

Sol. 2 Measurement of g by simple pendulum is done using the formula

$$g = \frac{4\pi^2 l}{T^2}$$

Percentage error in measurement of g using a simple pendulum is given as

$$\frac{\Delta g}{g} \times 100 = \frac{\Delta l}{l} \times 100 + \frac{2\Delta T}{T} \times 100$$

Using this relation for the three students percentage error in experimental measurement of g can be calculated. For measurement of time period of different number of oscillations, the error in time measurement per oscillation will be least count divided by number of oscillations so this can be calculated as

For Student I

$$\frac{0.1}{64} \times 100 + \frac{2 \times (0.1/8)}{16} \times 100 = 0.3125\,\%$$

For Student II

$$\frac{0.1}{64} \times 100 + \frac{2 \times (0.1/4)}{16} \times 100 = 0.4688\,\%$$

For Student III

$$\frac{0.1}{20} \times 100 + \frac{2 \times (0.1/4)}{9} \times 100 = 1.056\%$$

Hence option (B) is correct.   **Ans. (B)**

Sol. 3 Least count of a vernier calipers is given as

$$LC = 1\,\text{MSD} - 1\,\text{VSD}$$

Given that 20 divisions of vernier scale are matching with 16 divisions of main scale so we have

$$20\,\text{VSD} = 16\,\text{MSD} = 16\,\text{mm}$$

$$1\,\text{VSD} = \frac{16}{20}\,\text{mm}$$

$$\text{Least Count} = 1 - \frac{16}{20} = \left(1 - \frac{16}{20}\right)\text{mm} = 0.2\,\text{mm} \quad \text{Ans. (D)}$$

Sol. 4 Least count of screw gauge can be given as

$$LC = \frac{0.5}{50} = 0.01\,\text{mm}$$

Main scale, reading = 2.5 mm

Circular scale reading = 20

Measured diameter of the ball is given as

$$D = 2.5\,\text{mm} + (20 \times 0.01)\,\text{mm}$$

$$D = 2.5\,\text{mm} + 0.2\,\text{mm} = 2.7\,\text{mm}$$

Density of the ball can be given as

$$\rho = \frac{m}{\dfrac{4\pi}{3}\left[\dfrac{D}{2}\right]^3}$$

Fractional error in density is given as

$$\frac{\Delta \rho}{\rho} = \frac{\Delta m}{m} + 3\frac{\Delta D}{D}$$

Percentage error in density is given as

$$\frac{\Delta \rho}{\rho} \times 100 = 2\% + 3\left(\frac{0.01}{2.7}\right) \times 100 = 3.1 \qquad \text{Ans. (C)}$$

Sol. 5 Least count on scale is given as

$$\Delta l = \frac{0.5}{100}\,\text{mm}$$

Young's modulus of wire is given as

$$Y = \frac{4MLg}{\pi l d^2}$$

$$\Rightarrow \quad \left(\frac{\Delta Y}{Y}\right)_{max} = \frac{\Delta l}{l} + 2\frac{\Delta d}{d}$$

Error due to measurement of l is calculated as

$$\frac{\Delta l}{l} = \frac{0.5/100\,\text{mm}}{0.25\,\text{mm}}$$

Error due to measurement of d is calculated as

$$2\frac{\Delta d}{d} = \frac{2\times\dfrac{0.5}{100}}{0.5\,\text{mm}} = \frac{0.5/100}{0.25}$$

So error in Y due to l measurement = error in Y due to d measurement. **Ans. (A)**

Sol. 6 Main scale division $(s) = 0.05$ cm

Vernier scale division $(v) = \dfrac{49}{100} = .049$

Least count $= .05 - .049 = .001$ cm

Diameter $= 5.10 + 24 \times .001$

$$= 5.124\,\text{cm} \qquad\qquad \textbf{Ans. (B)}$$

Sol. 7 From the given expression, we have

$$2d\sin\theta = \lambda$$

$$\Rightarrow \quad d = \frac{\lambda}{2\sin\theta}$$

Taking natural log on both sides gives

$$\ln d = \ln\left(\frac{\lambda}{2}\right) - \ln\sin\theta$$

Differentiating the expression gives

$$\frac{\Delta d}{d} = 0 - \frac{\cos\theta\,\Delta\theta}{\sin\theta}$$

Maximum fractional error in value of d is given as

$$\left(\frac{\Delta d}{d}\right)_{max} = \pm\cot\theta\,\Delta\theta$$

As θ increases, in above expression $\cot\theta$ decreases hence option (D) is correct.

Absolute error in d is given as

$$(\Delta d)_{max} = d\cot\theta\,\Delta\theta$$

$$\Rightarrow \quad (\Delta d)_{max} = \frac{\lambda}{2\sin\theta}\cot\theta\,\Delta\theta = \frac{\lambda}{2}\frac{\cos\theta}{\sin^2\theta}\,\Delta\theta$$

As θ increases $\dfrac{\cos\theta}{\sin^2\theta}$ also decreases but above value of absolute error in d also depends upon the value of λ so we cannot comment on variation in absolute error in measurement of d. **Ans. (D)**

Sol. 8 Least count of

$$C_1 = 1\,\text{MSD} - 1\,\text{VSD} = 0.1\,\text{mm}$$

Here seventh division of vernier scale is coinciding so we use

Reading of $\quad C_1 = 2.8 + 0.01 \times 7 = 2.87$

and for C_2 least count

$$= 1\,\text{MSD} - 1\,\text{VSD} = -0.1\,\text{mm}$$

As least count is negative reading will be measured from far end. So in this case third division of vernier scale is coinciding, we use

Reading of $\quad C_1 = 2.8 + 0.01 \times 3 = 2.83$ **Ans. (C)**

Sol. 9 Total time taken by sound is calculated as

$$t = \sqrt{\frac{2h}{g}} + \frac{h}{300}$$

$$\Rightarrow \quad \Delta t = \Delta\left(\frac{h}{5}\right)^{1/2} + \frac{1}{300}\Delta h$$

$$\Rightarrow \quad \Delta T = \frac{1}{\sqrt{5}}\frac{1}{2\sqrt{h}}\Delta h + \frac{1}{300}\Delta h$$

$$\Rightarrow \quad \Delta T = \Delta h\left[\frac{1}{300} + \frac{1}{2\sqrt{5h}}\right]$$

$$\Rightarrow \quad 0.01 = \Delta h\left[\frac{1}{300} + \frac{1}{2\times10}\right]$$

$$\Rightarrow \quad \frac{\Delta h}{10}\left[\frac{1}{30} + \frac{1}{2}\right] = 0.01$$

$$\Rightarrow \quad \frac{\Delta h}{10}\left[\frac{1+15}{30}\right] = 0.01$$

$$\Rightarrow \quad \frac{0.01}{100} = \frac{\Delta h}{10}\times\frac{16}{30}$$

$$\Rightarrow \quad \frac{\Delta h}{L} = \frac{3\times100}{16\times200} = 1\% \qquad \textbf{Ans. (D)}$$

Sol. 10 Length of one division on vernier scale is given as

$$\text{VSD} = \frac{0.1\times9}{10} = 0.09$$

Given that MSD $= 0.1$ cm hence least count is given as

$$\text{LC} = 0.1 - 0.09 = 0.01\,\text{cm}$$

In first case we can calculate zero error which is calculated as

$$z = 0.5 - 6 \times 0.09 = 0.5 - 0.54 = -0.04 \text{ cm}$$

In second case reading is taken as

$$R = 3.1 + 1 \times LC$$

$$\Rightarrow \qquad R = 3.1 + 1 \times 0.01 = 3.11 \text{ cm}$$

Thus diameter of sphere is given as

$$D = 3.11 - (-0.04) = 3.15 \text{ cm} \qquad \textbf{Ans. (C)}$$

Sol. 11 Least count of screw gauge is given as

$$LC = \frac{0.1}{100} = 0.001 \text{ mm}$$

From the first data set, we can calculate the zero error in the instrument, given as

$$z = 4 \times 0.001 = 0.004 \text{ mm}$$

Reading 1 is calculated as

$$R_1 = 0.5 \times 4 + 20 \times 0.001 - 0.004 = 2.16 \text{ mm}$$

Reading 2 is calculated as

$$R_2 = 0.5 \times 4 + 16 \times 0.001 - 0.004 = 2.12 \text{ mm}$$

Mean value of the two readings is given as

$$R_{\text{meam}} = 2.14 \text{ mm}$$

Mean error value can be calculated as

$$e = \frac{0.02 + 0.02}{2} = 0.02$$

So diameter of the wire can be given as

$$d = 2.14 \pm 0.02 \text{ mm}$$

Cross sectional area of wire can be calculated using $\frac{\pi}{4} d^2$. Out of given options only (C) can be correct. **Ans. (C)**

Sol. 12 Time period is calculated as

$$T = \frac{\text{Total time } (t)}{\text{number of oscillations}} = \frac{40}{20} = 2 \text{ s}$$

For measurement of 40 s error in time measurement is 1 s hence fractional error in measurement of time is given as

$$\frac{\Delta T}{T} = \frac{1}{40}$$

$$\Rightarrow \qquad \Delta T = \frac{1}{40} \times 2 = 0.05 \text{ sec}$$

For measurement of g, we use

$$g = \frac{4\pi^2 l}{T^2}$$

Fractional error in measurement of g is given as

$$\frac{\Delta g}{g} = \frac{\Delta l}{l} + 2 \frac{\Delta T}{T}$$

Here there is no error in measurement of l and $\Delta T = 0.05$ s with $T = 2$ s so we have

$$\frac{\Delta g}{g} = \frac{2 \times 0.05}{2} = 0.05$$

Thus percentage error in measurement of g is given as

$$\frac{\Delta g}{g} \times 100 = 5\% \qquad \textbf{Ans. (A, C)}$$

Sol. 13 Main scale division length is given as

$$1 \text{ MSD} = \frac{1}{8} \text{ cm}$$

As 5 vernier scale divisions coincides with 4 main scale divisions, so we have

$$5 \text{ VSD} = 4 \text{ MSD} = \frac{4}{8} \text{ cm}$$

$$\Rightarrow \qquad 1 \text{ VSD} = \frac{4}{40} \text{ cm}$$

Least count of vernier calipers is given as

$$LC = 1 \text{ MSD} - 1 \text{ VSD}$$

$$\Rightarrow \qquad LC = \frac{1}{8} - \frac{1}{10} = \frac{1}{40} \text{ cm}$$

Least count of screw gauge

$$= \frac{0.5}{100} \text{ mm} = 0.005 \text{ mm} \qquad \textbf{Ans. (B, C)}$$

Sol. 14 Percentage error in measurement of r is calculated as

$$\frac{dr}{r} \times 100 = \frac{1}{10} \times 100 = 10\%$$

Percentage error in measurement of t is calculated as

$$\frac{\Delta t \times 100}{t_{\text{avg}}} = \frac{0.01 \times 100}{\left(\dfrac{0.52 \text{ s} + 0.56 \text{ s} + 0.57 \text{ s} + 0.54 \text{ s} + 0.59 \text{ s}}{5} \right)}$$

$$= 1.8\% \approx 2\%$$

$$T^2 \propto \frac{7(R-r)}{g}$$

Error in measurement of g is given as

$$\frac{\Delta g}{g} = 2 \frac{\Delta T}{T} + \frac{\Delta(R-r)}{R-r}$$

$$\Rightarrow \qquad \frac{\Delta g}{g} = 2(2\%) + \frac{2}{50} \times 100 = 4 + 4 = 8\% \qquad \textbf{Ans. (A, C)}$$

Sol. 15 Differentiating the given ratio, we get

$$\frac{dr}{da} = \frac{(1+a)(-1) - (1-a)}{(1+a)^2} = \frac{-2}{(1+a)^2}$$

Error in r can be given as

$$\Rightarrow \qquad |\Delta r| = \frac{2\Delta a}{(1+a)^2} \qquad \textbf{Ans. (B)}$$

Sol. 16 By radioactive decay law, we have

$$N = N_0 e^{-\lambda t}$$

Taking natural log on both sides gives

$$\ln N = \ln N_0 - \lambda t$$

Differentiating above expression with respect to λ gives

$$\frac{1}{N}\frac{dN}{d\lambda} = 0 - t$$

$$\Rightarrow \qquad |d\lambda| = \frac{dN}{tN} = \frac{40}{1 \times 2000} = 0.02 \qquad \textbf{Ans. (C)}$$

Sol. 17 Change in length

$$\Delta l = l = 25 \times 1 \times 10^{-5}$$

Young's modulus

Also $\qquad Y = \dfrac{FL}{Al}$

$$\Rightarrow \qquad \frac{\Delta Y}{Y}\% = \frac{\Delta l}{l} \times 100\%$$

$$\Rightarrow \qquad = \frac{10^{-5}}{25 \times 1 \times 10^{-5}} \times 100\%$$

$$\Rightarrow \qquad = 4\% \qquad \textbf{Ans. (4)}$$

Sol. 18 Energy of system is given as

$$E(t) = A^2 e^{-\alpha t}$$

Taking natural log on both side gives

$$\ln E = \ln A^2 + \ln e^{-\alpha t}$$

$$\Rightarrow \qquad \ln E = 2\ln A - \alpha t$$

Percentage error in measurement of E is given as

$$\frac{\Delta E}{E} \times 100 = 2\frac{\Delta A}{A} \times 100 + \alpha\Delta t \times 100$$

$$\Rightarrow \quad \frac{\Delta E}{E} \times 100 = 2 \times 1.25 + \frac{2}{10} \times 1.5 \times 5$$

$$\Rightarrow \quad \frac{\Delta E}{E} \times 100 = 2.5 + 1.5 = 4\% \qquad \textbf{Ans. (4)}$$

Sol. 19 The object and image distances from the lens are given as

$$u = 10 \pm 0.1 \text{ cm},$$
$$v = 20 \pm 0.2 \text{ cm}$$

Using lens formula, we have

$$\frac{1}{v} - \frac{1}{u} = \frac{1}{f} \qquad \ldots(1)$$

Differentiating the above formula gives

$$\frac{1}{v^2}dv + \frac{1}{u^2}du = -\frac{1}{f^2}df \qquad \ldots(2)$$

From equation-(1), we have

$$\frac{1}{20} + \frac{1}{10} = \frac{1}{f}$$

$$\Rightarrow \qquad \frac{1}{f} = \frac{3}{20}$$

$$\Rightarrow \qquad f = \frac{20}{3} \text{ cm}$$

From equation-(2), we have

$$\frac{1}{(20)^2}(0.2) + \frac{1}{(10)^2}(0.1) = \frac{9}{400}df$$

$$\Rightarrow \quad df = \frac{1}{9}\left(\frac{400}{400} \times 0.2 + \frac{400}{100} \times 0.1\right)$$

$$\Rightarrow \quad df = \frac{1}{9}(0.2 + 0.4)$$

$$\Rightarrow \quad df = \frac{0.6}{9}$$

$$\Rightarrow \quad \frac{df}{f} = \frac{0.6}{9} \times \frac{3}{20} = \frac{1}{100} = 0.01$$

Percentage error is calculated as

$$\frac{df}{f} \times 100 = 1\% \qquad \textbf{Ans. (1)}$$

$$* \quad * \quad * \quad * \quad *$$

www.ingramcontent.com/pod-product-compliance
Lightning Source LLC
LaVergne TN
LVHW080020150726
843364LV00042B/1599